Estimated σ_E:

$$s_{\overline{X}-\overline{X}} = \sqrt{\frac{s^2_{pooled}}{n_1} + \frac{s^2_{pooled}}{n_2}}$$

$t_{obtained}$:

$$t_{obtained} = \frac{(\overline{X}_1 - \overline{X}_2)}{s_{\overline{X}-\overline{X}}}$$

Degrees of Freedom: $\quad df = (n_1 - 1) + (n_2 - 1)$

t-Test for Two Related Samples:

Estimated standard error: $\quad s_{\overline{D}} = \dfrac{s_D}{\sqrt{n}}$

$t_{obtained}$:

$$t = \frac{\overline{D}}{s_{\overline{D}}}$$

Degrees of Freedom: $\quad df = n - 1$

Analysis of Variance:

Sums of Squares

SS_{Total} (for all ANOVAs):

$$SS_{Total} = \Sigma\Sigma X^2 - \frac{(\Sigma\Sigma X)^2}{N}$$

SS_{BG} and $SS_{Treatment}$ and SS_{IV}:

$$SS = \Sigma \frac{(\Sigma X)^2}{n} - \frac{(\Sigma\Sigma X)^2}{N}$$

$SS_{A\times B}$: (BS-ANOVA): $\quad SS_{A\times B} = SS_{BG} - SS_A - SS_B$
(RM-ANOVA): $\quad SS_{A\times B} = SS_{Treatment} - SS_A - SS_B$

SS_{WG}
(for BS-ANOVA): $SS_{WG} = SS_{Total} - SS_{BG}$

$SS_{Subjects}$
(for RM-ANOVA):

$$SS_{Subjects} = \Sigma \frac{(Subject\ Total)^2}{k} - \frac{(\Sigma\Sigma X)^2}{N}$$

$SS_{Treatment \times Subjects}$ (for RM-ANOVA):
$SS_{Treatment \times Subjects} = SS_{Total} - SS_{Treatment} - SS_{Subjects}$

Degrees of Freedom:

$df_{Total} = N - 1$
$df_{BG} = k - 1$
$df_{Treatment} = k - 1$
$df_{Main\ Effect} = $ # of levels of IV $- 1$
$df_{A\times B} = df_A \times df_B$
$df_{WG} = N - k$
$df_{Subjects} = n - 1$
$df_{Treatment \times Subjects} = df_{Treatment} \times df_{Subjects}$

Mean Squares:

$$MS_{BG} = \frac{SS_{BG}}{df_{BG}}$$

$$MS_{WG} = \frac{SS_{WG}}{df_{WG}} = MS_{Error}$$

$$MS_{Treatment} = \frac{SS_{Treatment}}{df_{Treatment}}$$

$$MS_{Main\ Effect} = \frac{SS_{Main\ Effect}}{df_{Main\ Effect}}$$

$$MS_{A\times B} = \frac{SS_{A\times B}}{df_{A\times B}}$$

$$MS_{Treatment \times Subjects} = \frac{SS_{Treatment \times Subjects}}{df_{Treatment \times Subjects}} = MS_{Error}$$

F:

$$F = \frac{MS_{Effect}}{MS_{Error}}$$

Critical Range (CR) for the Dunn Multiple
Comparisons Post Hoc Test:

$$CR_{Dunn} = d\sqrt{2\,\frac{MS_{Error}}{n}}$$

Nonparametric Tests (Nominal and Ordinal Data):

Chi Square (χ^2) Goodness-of-Fit Test
(One-way Designs):

Expected Cell Frequencies: $\quad E = \dfrac{N}{k}$

Chi Square: $\quad \chi^2 = \dfrac{\Sigma(O - E)^2}{E}$

Degrees of Freedom: $\quad df = k - 1$

Chi Square (χ^2) Test for Contingency Tables
(Two-way Designs):

Expected Cell Frequencies:

$$E = \frac{(row\ total)(column\ total)}{N}$$

Chi Square: $\quad \chi^2 = \Sigma \dfrac{(O - E)^2}{E}$

Degrees of Freedom:

$$df = (\#\ of\ rows - 1)(\#\ of\ columns - 1)$$

Cochran's Q: $\quad Q = \dfrac{(k-1)[k(\Sigma C^2) - T^2]}{kT - \Sigma R^2}$

Degrees of Freedom for Q: $\quad df = k - 1$

Wilcoxon-Mann-Whitney T (Rank Sum Test):

when groups have equal n:
$\quad T_{obtained} = $ the smaller ΣR

when groups have unequal n:
$\quad T' = n_1(n_1 + n_2 + 1) - \Sigma R_{n1}$
$\quad T_{obtained} = $ the smaller of T' and ΣR_{n1}

Kruskal-Wallis H:

$$H = \left[\frac{12}{N(N+1)} \Sigma \frac{(\Sigma R)^2}{n}\right] - 3(N+1)$$

Degrees of Freedom for H: $\quad df = k - 1$

Wilcoxon W (Signed Ranks Test): $\quad W = $ smaller ΣR

Confidence Intervals:

Confidence Intervals for the Mean:

Standard Error: $\quad \sigma_E = \dfrac{\sigma}{\sqrt{n}} \quad$ or $\quad s_E = \dfrac{s}{\sqrt{n}}$

Maximum Error of
the Estimate: $\quad E_{max} = t_{critical}\,(s_E) \quad$ or
$\quad E_{max} = z_{critical}\,(\sigma_E)$

Confidence Interval: $\quad CI = \overline{X} \pm E_{max}$

Confidence Intervals for Proportions
(or Percentages):

Maximum Error of
the Estimate: $\quad E_{max} = z_{critical}\sqrt{\dfrac{p(1-p)}{n}}$

Confidence Interval: $\quad CI = p \pm E_{max}$

Confidence Intervals for Pearson r:

$$CI_z = z \pm z_{critical}\sqrt{\frac{1}{n-3}}$$

Research Methods
and Statistics
An Integrated Approach

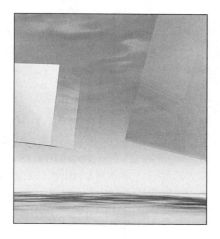

Research Methods
and Statistics

An Integrated Approach

Nancy E. Furlong | Eugene A. Lovelace | Kristin L. Lovelace

Alfred University   *Alfred University*   *University of California*
                                                              at Santa Barbara

HARCOURT COLLEGE PUBLISHERS

*Fort Worth   Philadelphia   San Diego   New York   Orlando   Austin   San Antonio
Toronto   Montreal   London   Sydney   Tokyo*

Publisher   Earl McPeek
Executive Editor   Carol Wada
Associate Acquisitions Editor   Lisa Hensley
Market Strategist   Kathleen Sharp
Project Editor   Michele Tomiak
Art Director   Carol Kincaid
Production Manager   Andrea Archer
Cover Image by Ryuichi Okano.

ISBN: 0-15-507162-9

Address for Domestic Orders: Harcourt College Publishers, 6277 Sea Harbor Drive, Orlando, FL 32887-6777
800-782-4479

Address for International Orders: International Customer Service, Harcourt College Publishers, 6277 Sea Harbor Drive, Orlando, FL 32887-6777
407-345-3800
(fax) 407-345-4060
(e-mail) hbintl@harcourtbrace.com

Address for Editorial Correspondence: Harcourt College Publishers, 301 Commerce Street, Suite 3700, Fort Worth, TX 76102

Web Site Address: http://www.harcourtcollege.com

Harcourt College Publishers will provide complimentary supplements or supplement packages to those adopters qualified under our adoption policy. Please contact your sales representative to learn how you qualify. If as an adopter or potential user you receive supplements you do not need, please return them to your sales representative or send them to: Attn: Returns Department, Troy Warehouse, 465 South Lincoln Drive, Troy, MO 63379.

Printed in the United States of America

9 0 1 2 3 4 5 6 7 8 039 9 8 7 6 5 4 3 2 1

Harcourt College Publishers

PREFACE

Research Methods and Statistics: An Integrated Approach was designed for the growing number of combined courses in research methods and statistics. It provides a unique combination of basic research methodology with the most common statistical procedures for analyzing data from correlational, experimental, and quasi-experimental designs.

We have organized *Research Methods and Statistics* so that it moves from introductory-level topics, such as measurement, descriptive statistics, and experimental versus nonexperimental design, to intermediate-level topics, such as one-way and factorial ANOVA. In addition, we have included coverage of topics that are not always available in introductory textbooks, such as chapters on single-subject designs and qualitative methods.

Our primary goal in writing *Research Methods and Statistics* was to produce a highly readable and easy-to-understand textbook. We chose to use a *conversational writing style* that minimizes the amount of dry, formal language that often discourages readers. The unavoidable technical material is supplemented with numerous examples and analogies, which should help students grasp concepts. Similarly, statistical procedures are presented in an easy-to-follow, step-by-step format, using a minimum number of symbols. We have tested this material over several years in our own courses, and our students consistently report that the material is easy to follow and understand.

In addition to a student-friendly writing style, we offer the students several pedagogical features designed to enhance the learning process. Each chapter begins with an *outline*, giving students a preview of upcoming topics. A truly unique pedagogical aid is a *prerequisites list*, or a list of key terms and concepts that students should understand *before* reading the upcoming chapter. These lists are referenced so that the student can easily find and review the material if needed. This feature should be especially useful in research methods/statistics courses because learning new concepts is so dependent upon a firm understanding of previous material. At the end of each chapter are *exercises* designed to test students' understanding of chapter content by having them *apply* the concepts to hypothetical research scenarios, rather than simply regurgitating definitions. The answers to odd-numbered exercises are provided in the appendix.

Not only is *Research Methods and Statistics* designed for ease of student use, but it is easy for instructors to use as well. Some combination texts attempt to integrate research methods and statistics within individual chapters. It has been our experience that this creates organizational and conceptual difficulties because quite simply, there is no perfect "match" of one research design with only one statistical procedure. This organization also limits the instructor's flexibility in organizing the course. By contrast, *Research Methods and Statistics* uses an *"interleaved" approach*, in which research design and statistics materials are covered in separate chapters, then organized in the order that seems most appropriate. However, instructors who prefer an alternate organization will find that the "modular" nature of the chapters offers instructors unlimited flexibility in customizing the course.

We have prepared two ancillaries to accompany *Research Methods and Statistics*. The *Student Workbook* encourages students to define the terms and identify the relationships among the concepts from the chapter, and presents additional exercises where students must apply the concepts to research scenarios. Students can test their knowledge of the material by taking practice tests that start with questions using a short-answer or fill-in format to assess recall, and then progress to multiple-choice format for students to assess their recognition memory of the material. Intermediate and advanced students are challenged with exercises focusing operational definitions, confounds, and the interpretation of data from factorial designs. Small data sets are provided for practice performing statistical analysis. The *Instructor's Solution Manual* includes the answers and solutions to all of the chapter exercises in the textbook, a *test bank* of multiple-choice questions for each chapter, and additional data sets for statistical analysis. To obtain copies of the *Student Workbook* and the *Instructor's Solution Manual*, please contact your local Harcourt sales representative.

We would like to thank Mark Fugate (Alfred University) for preparing the first draft of Chapter 15 (Single-Subjects Designs); Deborah Levine-Donnerstein (University of California at Santa Barbara) for reviewing early drafts of Chapter 16 (Qualitative Research Methods); Gordon Schaeffer for his editorial assistance on several chapters; and Kristin Perino for assisting us with the task of proofreading the statistical analyses. We are also very grateful to all the reviewers, whose comments and suggestions have greatly improved this text: Ray Bower, Olivet Nazarene University; Constance Jones, California State University–Fresno; Jerry Lee, Albright College; Leroy Metze, Western Kentucky University; Mark Nawrot, North Dakota State University; Richard Port, Slippery Rock University; and Ruth Sternberger, Loyola College–Maryland. Additionally, we would like to thank our book team at Harcourt: Lisa Hensley, Associate Acquisitions Editor; Laurie Runion, Developmental Editor; Michele Tomiak, Senior Project Editor; Carol Kincaid, Art Director; Andrea Archer, Production Manager; and Kathleen Sharp, Market Strategist.

Nancy E. Furlong, Ph.D.
Psychology Division
Alfred University
Alfred, New York 14802

e-mail: FFURLONG@alfred.edu

Nancy E. Furlong received her B.A. summa cum laude in psychology from the State University of New York at Fredonia, and her M.A. and Ph.D. in developmental psychology from the University of Dayton and the University of Pittsburgh, respectively. She joined the undergraduate faculty at Alfred University in January 1983, where her primary teaching responsibilities have included courses in research methods and statistics, cognitive, social, and life-span development, and introductory psychology. Since 1990, she has been an adjunct faculty member in Alfred University's graduate programs, where she teaches advanced developmental psychology and research design and statistical analysis. She was nominated to Who's Who Among America's Teachers in 1994 and 1998, and received an Honorable Mention for Excellence in Teaching in 1999. She has often served as a research consultant to colleagues and students, resulting in 10 research presentations in 10 years, and she has served on 17 dissertation committees in the six years since the inception of the Psy.D. in the School of Psychology program at Alfred University. She was granted a promotion to Professor of Psychology in 1999. In 1988, she joined the A. E. Crandall Hook and Ladder Company, the volunteer fire and ambulance service for Alfred, New York, and, in 1993, she became one of the first women in the state to be elected chief of a fire department, a position she still holds. In 1998 and 1999, she was honored by the students at Alfred University with an award for Outstanding Faculty Contribution to Campus Life.

Eugene A. Lovelace received his B.A. cum laude from SUNY–Binghamton (now Binghamton University), and his M.A. and Ph.D. degrees from the University of Iowa. After 21 years on the faculty at the University of Virginia, where he taught a research methods course, he joined the undergraduate faculty at Alfred University in 1985, where he regularly teaches an advanced research design course. His major areas of interest are perception, cognition, and adult development and aging. He held a NASA pre-doctoral fellowship at Iowa. While on the faculty of the University of Virginia, he was a visiting professor for one semester at the University of Colorado (Institute for Study of Intellectual Behavior), and spent a year at Duke University on a Senior Research Fellowship from the National Institute on Aging. He attended the 1980 White House Conference on Aging as a Governor's observer for the Commonwealth of Virginia. He is the author/editor of a book entitled *Cognition and Aging: Mental Processes, Self-Awareness, and Interventions,* and has published more than 40 articles in professional journals. For 16 years he served as a consulting editor for the Psychonomics Society's journal entitled *Memory and Cognition.* He has twice received an award given for outstanding teaching in the Liberal Arts and Sciences College of Alfred University. He enjoys woodworking, walking in the woods, and bird watching.

Kristin L. Lovelace is currently at the University of California at Santa Barbara (UCSB), where she is a candidate for a Ph.D. in cognitive psychology in the Department of Psychology, and an M.A. from the Department of Statistics and Probability. She holds an M.S. degree in design and environmental analysis from Cornell University, plus M.A. degrees in both human geography and cognitive psychology from UCSB, and serves as the Coordinator of Research for the University of California

Education Abroad Program, Universitywide Office. She has been involved in the development of statistics and research exercises for the interpretation of graphical data at UCSB. Elected to Phi Kappa Phi National Honor Society at Cornell University in 1992, she held a merit-based fellowship in UCSB's Department of Geography. In her spare time, she teaches rock climbing, goes for hikes, spoils her nieces, and makes pottery for friends and family.

BRIEF CONTENTS

CONTENTS

CONTENTS

CONTENTS

CONTENTS

CONTENTS

CONTENTS

CONTENTS

CONTENTS

CONTENTS

CONTENTS

CONTENTS

CHAPTER 1

AN INTRODUCTORY OVERVIEW

■ ■ ■ ■ ■ ■

In this chapter, you will find out why psychologists rely on the scientific method to gather data about human behavior. The key features of the scientific method are defined, and the steps researchers follow are outlined.

Look for These Important Terms and Concepts

empirical or scientific approach

description, prediction, explanation, and control

research methods

experimental, correlational, and quasi-experimental methods

reliability

validity

objective versus subjective measures

bias for positive instances (confirmatory bias)

working hypothesis

rival explanations

operational definition

replication and convergence of evidence

internal versus external validity

generality (generalizability)

Like it or not, science is an integral part of daily life, even for those who do not conduct scientific research. We are all "consumers" in a world of claims and counterclaims about everything from the effectiveness of one brand of deodorant over another to the impact of second-hand cigarette smoke on children's future health. Politicians, advertisers, doctors, psychologists, and educators are only a few of the groups who try to influence what we do or think by reporting the results of "research." But not all of the claims we hear are actually based on *scientific* research, so it is important to be able to recongnize good science and discard the bogus claims. Furthermore, different types of scientific data need to be interpreted in different ways, so each of us needs to know something about science in order to protect ourselves from misleading claims. In fact, we strongly believe that in today's world, being able to evaluate the quality of research is as important as knowing how to read and write, and so we have written this book with the hope that we can help prepare you to be an "educated consumer."

This textbook is an introduction to the central issues involved in conducting good research and interpreting its results, and we have tried to present the material clearly, using everyday language as much as possible. The book integrates the processes of data collection and data analysis, which are often covered in separate texts, in the hope that students will come to appreciate how the methods used to gather the data determine which types of analyses are appropriate. The relationship between the research methods and the interpretation of the results is emphasized because it is important to understand what the data actually mean as well as what they do not mean.

Knowing what we "know" and what we "don't know" is at the very heart of any science: We conduct studies to answer questions about what we don't already know. Psychologists, for instance, want to understand human behavior, both overt actions of individuals and their covert thoughts and feelings. In doing research, psychologists seek to discover the *facts* about behavior and how the various circumstances and conditions that surround humans relate to their behavior. The question is: *How* do we acquire these facts—or more precisely, how can we know that a "fact" is, in fact, a fact?

Ways of Knowing

People come to hold knowledge to be factual in a number of ways. Many of these ways provide no explicit means for testing the "truth" of the facts, but nearly all of us, research psychologists included, rely on them at least occasionally. One of these ways is by *intuition*. Suppose that you are driving a friend to find a used computer store in a nearby city. Neither of you has been on the road to that city. As you approach the city, the road you are driving on forks into two roads that appear equally traveled. Your friend immediately says, "Take the one on the left." You do so but then ask, "How do you know?" Your friend replies, "I'm quite sure; I just have a gut feeling that it must be this one." The act of saying "I'm quite sure" rather than simply "I'm sure" may reflect some level of understanding on the speaker's part that intuitions, while sometimes correct, are not a very reliable basis for believing a fact. This lack of reliability is a severe limitation of this "way of knowing," and psychologists typically place little credence in a "fact" that is based solely on intuition.

Another way of knowing facts might be called the _authority approach_—we rely on someone else who is knowledgeable to tell us the facts. Most of us get many facts this way every day. For example, we may learn from watching the evening news that a powerful member of the U.S. Senate will resign rather than face hearings on a sexual harassment charge brought by three women working in his office. Or we learn from a National Geographic special on television that when man traveled to the moon he brought back a variety of samples of lunar rocks. We learn much of what we know from teachers, our parents, newspapers, and "information" programs on television. We do not, of course, always believe everything we read or hear, depending on the *perceived expertise* of the source of information. If the information is about events involving nationally known politicians (such as the resignation of a U.S. senator), we will be more confident that the information is factual if we hear Peter Jennings say it on the "ABC Evening News" than if we hear it from the mechanic at our local service station. But if the information we encounter is that a certain kind of car frequently has trouble with the transmission, our relative confidence in the mechanic versus Peter Jennings might well be similar (or even reversed).

In general, it is not surprising to note that, on any topic of national news, television news anchors are generally considered highly credible sources. However, consider the Bible as a source of facts about creation and the New Testament as a source of facts about the death and resurrection of Jesus. The credibility of the Bible and the New Testament are, of course, highly controversial; many people accept these sources as authorities, and many people do not, simply on the basis of religious faith. Furthermore, Peter Jennings and other newscasters have at times had to retract earlier reports because the information was incorrect. (You may, for instance, recall the news reports that told us that Middle-East terrorists were responsible for the bombing of the Federal Building in Oklahoma City in April 1995. Most Americans who saw those reports were quite shocked when, within days, two American men were under arrest for the bombing.) Thus the authority approach to knowledge can be of questionable value to psychologists.

A third way to know a fact is the _rational-inductive_ approach. This approach is central to much of our reasoning and problem-solving activities. While driving home at noon on Tuesday you notice that one house has bottles for recycling along the curb beside an empty garbage can. You remember that, in your town, the garbage is picked up Tuesday morning and the recycled materials on Monday morning. You immediately entertain two hypotheses as to why those bottles are still there: (1) The bottles were put out too late on Monday, or (2) for some reason there was no pickup of recyclable items this Monday. An implication of the latter hypothesis is that many others might also have put out some materials to be recycled, and so there may be other recyclable material on the curb by other houses. On the remainder of your trip home, you see none and so conclude the fact is that the bottles were put out too late.

Consider this more complex case of the rational-inductive approach: John is sitting in an interior room of an apartment in a building on Park Avenue in Manhattan at 7 p.m. on a day near the end of March. Someone asks John whether he knows where the full moon is right now and asks him to point, as accurately as he can, to the position of the unseen full moon. John's first thought may well be, "How the heck should I know—I'm no astronomer"; but if he stops and reflects on it, he might be able to come to a well-reasoned (rational) decision before pointing. In late March (near the equinox), the night and day are of about equal length (12 hours). A full moon is "full" because the sun and moon are on opposite sides of the earth and so in opposite directions, thus just as the sun sets, the moon rises. At 7 p.m., the sun has been down for about an hour. In that hour, the moon will have traveled about 1/12 of the 180 degrees of our visible sky, so it is about 15 degrees above the horizon in the east. With all of this reasoned out, when asked to point to the east, John would then try to remember which direction the streets run in Manhattan. If he seems to recall that the avenues in Manhattan run north-south and that the building he entered was on the west side of the avenue, he can conclude that the front door of the building faces east. Keeping track of the number of turns he made going from the front door to the elevator and from the elevator to this apartment, he would reason that the door to this apartment, which is directly in front of him where he is sitting, faces west (so he's facing west, too, of course). Thus he would decide to point in a direction behind him and up at an angle of about 15 degrees. John thinks, by virtue of his reasoning, that the moon must be in about that location.

How accurate is John's pointing response? It would depend on the accuracy of his recall about equinoxes, full moons, Manhattan's streets, and turns inside this building. Because the avenues actually run from north-northeast to south-southwest, John will be pointing a bit too far south but will almost surely have come much closer than had he simply pointed somewhere without such reasoned thought. The rational-inductive approach results in "reasonable" answers to questions, but it depends largely on memory and logical reasoning skills, either or both of which may be faulty. Thus, this approach to acquiring facts is—like the intuition and authority approaches—of limited value to psychologists.

Instead of relying on these unreliable approaches to knowledge, psychologists who do research overwhelmingly rely on what is typically called the **scientific approach** because it allows us to obtain behavioral facts with the greatest rigor. The key feature of this approach is *systematic observation and recording* of events: Psychologists directly observe the behaviors they want to study and carefully record the circumstances and conditions under which the behaviors either occur or do not. This is also referred to as the **empirical approach** since the term *empirical* refers to the process of direct observation. These observations can take place in any context ranging from *real-life settings* (where the observations may be unstructured and performed under only loosely controlled conditions) to *laboratories* (where the observations are highly systematic and performed under carefully controlled conditions), and these different types of observational procedures tell us different things about behavior. That is, we can achieve different goals using different observational techniques.

The science of psychology, like other sciences, has the following basic goals: **description** (what, who, when, where, how), **prediction** (knowing the conditions under which an event is likely to occur), and **explanation** (knowing why an event occurs or identifying the causal factors of the event). Direct observation of behavior, whether it takes place in real-life settings or in controlled laboratory settings, allows us to determine what a behavior looks like, who engages in it, how often, and so forth. Once we have a thorough description of a behavior, we may then be able to make accurate predictions about when the behavior will occur next. Thus, most observational procedures help us meet the goals of description and prediction. The goal of explanation, however, can be met only if the observations are made under carefully controlled conditions, as in a laboratory experiment. Therefore, in this textbook, we discuss the various observational procedures (or *research methods*) and what they tell us about behavior.

In addition to description, prediction, and explanation, some psychologists would say that **control** of behavior is a goal of the science. For instance, if a behavior is socially unacceptable, then a goal might be to reduce or eliminate the behavior. If one knows the factors that cause a behavior, one can readily influence the behavior, at least to the extent that the causal factors can be controlled.[1] The relationship between the control of behavior and the broad discipline of psychology may be viewed as somewhat analogous to the relationship between mechanical engineering and the discipline of physics: just as mechanical engineering is a natural extension of physics, the control of behavior is a form of applied psychology.

Intuition and Reasoning Versus Empirical Observation: An Example

Imagine that you are in the studio audience of a television game show (like the old "Let's Make a Deal" program) and you find yourself facing what is called the *Monty Hall Dilemma*, which goes something like this:

> The game "host" explains that a fifty-dollar bill has been placed in one of three identical envelopes. You are asked to select one of the envelopes with the understanding that you can keep the money if you pick the correct one. After you make your selection, but before you open it, the "host" opens

---

[1] It is also possible to *control* events without full understanding of their causes. Sometimes knowing a lot about the who, what, when, and where of an event allows us to predict the next likely occurrence and possibly alter the conditions of future situations to reduce the event's likelihood. For instance, if I know that 8-year-old boys often exhibit aggressive behavior when they are in unsupervised groups, I may be able to prevent future aggression by providing supervision to groups of boys. This is possible even when I do not know what actually causes the aggression.

Furthermore, researchers have sometimes stumbled onto techniques for controlling behavior and find it difficult to understand why the technique works. For example, when it was first discovered—serendipitously—that stimulants such as Ritalin could be used to control hyperactive behavior, no one had any idea why it worked. Since then, research into the reasons for Ritalin's effectiveness has taught psychologists a lot about hyperactive behavior and neurological stimulants.

one of the remaining envelopes and shows that it is empty. You are then offered a chance to change your mind, and switch envelopes with the host. Should you switch or should you stay with your original choice?

If you are like the majority of people, you will either (1) decide that your odds of winning are highest if you stay with your original choice—that is, that "trusting your instincts" is the best strategy; or (2) you will reason that staying and switching are equally likely to result in a win because you now know that the money is in one of only two remaining envelopes, so the odds must be 50–50. The belief that staying is the best strategy provides an example of reliance on intuition because there is really no external reason to believe the money is more likely to be in the envelope you originally selected. The belief that staying and switching are equally likely to result in a win based on the idea of 50–50 odds of the money being in either of the two unopened envelopes is an example of the use of rational-inductive reasoning to reach a decision about the world of events. (In fact, problems like this are often used to assess the logical reasoning ability of adolescents and adults.) Thus, the intuitive and rational-inductive approaches lead to conflicting conclusions: Intuition says that staying is the best strategy, while logical reasoning says that there is no difference between the strategies. While most educated people will automatically favor the rational-inductive approach, are they necessarily correct? No, they are not, as we will see.

The scientific, empirical approach to answering the question about the best strategy would be to actually go through a large number of trials, systematically comparing the two strategies and keeping track of whether switching or staying produces a "win." This allows us to determine which of the two strategies results in the most number of wins. Thus, rather than simply accepting that logical reasoning necessarily leads to accurate conclusions, the scientific approach relies on direct observation of the phenomenon of interest. This is important because *logical reasoning alone can lead to erroneous conclusions*—as happens with the Monty Hall Dilemma. Kohn (1992) conducted 840 trials where students played the game (without the $50 prize, of course!) and found that participants won on 69% of the trials on which they *switched* compared with winning on *only 34%* of the trials on which they stayed with their original choice. Thus, Kohn empirically demonstrated that *switching is a better strategy* (because it leads to twice as many wins as staying), a finding that is both counter-intuitive and seemingly illogical.[2]

Kohn's (1992) work reveals a fault in the logical reasoning that leads most people—including many highly educated, highly intelligent people—to think that their

---

[2] The "Monty Hall dilemma"—named after the host of the 1960s television game show "Let's Make a Deal"—came to national attention when columnist Marilyn vos Savant printed it in her "Ask Marilyn" column in *Parade* magazine. She was asked whether one strategy was better than the other, and she said that switching was the better strategy. She was flooded with mail insisting that she was wrong, and it wasn't until people started to actually do the "empirical test" that they began to believe that she was correct. Ms. vos Savant describes the controversy in her book *The Power of Logical Thinking* (1996, St. Martin's Press).

| TABLE 1.1 | Systematically Testing the *Monty Hall Dilemma* |

In the following set of 60 trials, the player has selected envelope A, and the host holds envelopes B and C. The player elects to stay on the first 30 trials and to switch on the other 30. Each envelope (A, B, and C) is the actual winning envelope an equal number of times in each set of 30 trials (representing the fact that each envelope has an equal chance of being the winner). When A is the winning envelope (so the host holds two empty envelopes), B is shown to be empty on half of the trials and C on the other half. Of course, when the host holds the winning envelope, only the empty envelope can be opened.

Stays				*Switches*			
Actual Winning Envelope	Envelope Opened by Host	Player's Final Choice	Player's Outcome	Actual Winning Envelope	Envelope Opened by Host	Player's Final Choice	Player's Outcome
A	B	A	win	A	B	C	lose
A	C	A	win	A	C	B	lose
A	B	A	win	A	B	C	lose
A	C	A	win	A	C	B	lose
A	B	A	win	A	B	C	lose
A	C	A	win	A	C	B	lose
A	B	A	win	A	B	C	lose
A	C	A	win	A	C	B	lose
A	B	A	win	A	B	C	lose
A	C	A	win	A	C	B	lose
B	C	A	lose	B	C	B	win
B	C	A	lose	B	C	B	win
B	C	A	lose	B	C	B	win
B	C	A	lose	B	C	B	win
B	C	A	lose	B	C	B	win
B	C	A	lose	B	C	B	win
B	C	A	lose	B	C	B	win
B	C	A	lose	B	C	B	win
B	C	A	lose	B	C	B	win
B	C	A	lose	B	C	B	win
C	B	A	lose	C	B	C	win
C	B	A	lose	C	B	C	win
C	B	A	lose	C	B	C	win
C	B	A	lose	C	B	C	win
C	B	A	lose	C	B	C	win
C	B	A	lose	C	B	C	win
C	B	A	lose	C	B	C	win
C	B	A	lose	C	B	C	win
C	B	A	lose	C	B	C	win
C	B	A	lose	C	B	C	win

Thus, staying with the original choice (A) resulted in 10 wins versus 20 losses, while switching envelopes resulted in 20 wins versus 10 losses. Switching wins twice as often as staying.

Staying with the original choice wins *only* on those trials when the correct envelope was selected in the first place (33% of the trials), while switching envelopes will win on *every* trial where the first choice was incorrect (66% of the trials).

odds of winning with their first choice changes from 33% (at the beginning) to 50% when one of the other envelopes is "eliminated" (so that staying with their first choice will win half of the time and switching will win half of the time). However, a systematic empirical test, like that illustrated in Table 1-1, demonstrates that this simply is not the case: The two strategies do *not* have equal odds of winning, so being shown that one of the remaining two envelopes is empty does *not* increase the odds of winning with their first choice from 33% to 50%. (The results also indicate that trusting your gut instincts and staying with your first choice is not the best strategy either.)

Therefore, because the scientific, empirical approach to "finding the facts" can reveal flaws in both the intuitive and rational-inductive approaches, it is considered to be the most powerful tool available to researchers.

The Scientific Method

As noted above, the defining feature of the scientific method is observation. For this reason it is often called the empirical approach; the "truth" of facts is dictated by the observed data. But all people observe others' behaviors, don't they? Yes, but not in the systematic fashion that a research psychologist does when conducting a study. While we may casually notice (and later may only vaguely recall) some of the things going on around us, researchers focus their attention on the behaviors being studied and measure and carefully *record* those behaviors so that they do not have to rely on their memories of the events.

What is chosen for observation is typically determined by some ideas, or *hypotheses*, the researcher has about the behavior in question. For instance, one hypothesis may be that girls are more polite than boys, but only when other people are present to serve as an "audience" for the courteous behavior. In this case, the researcher would choose to observe/record three things: courteous behavior by children, sex of the child, and the presence (or absence) of other people. Thus, researchers may need to keep records not only of the specific behaviors of interest (such as courtesy), but also of other characteristics of the individuals being studied (*"subject" variables*, such as sex or age) or characteristics of the social and physical surroundings (*environmental variables*, such as the number of other people present). The way(s) we gather our observations will determine how we can interpret the findings, and the conclusions we can draw from research depend heavily on the particular **research methods** employed.

In this book, we consider three research methods in some detail, and we examine their relative advantages and disadvantages for achieving the basic goals of psychology. For example, the **experimental method** allows researchers to determine what *causes* a behavior by recording events under carefully controlled conditions. In contrast, studies that use the **correlational method** (which are sometimes referred to as nonexperimental designs) can help researchers generate thorough *descriptions* of behavior, which, in turn, may allow reasonably accurate *predictions* of future behaviors; but they do *not* demonstrate cause-and-effect relationships. The third research method we consider, known as the **quasi-experimental method**, looks like the experimental method but actually cannot be used to determine causality. It is important that students learn to distinguish among these research methods because the conclusions that can legitimately be drawn from the studies are very different.

Characteristics of Scientific Observations

While good science depends on observation, it is clearly the case that some observations are better than others. In fact, we spend every moment of the waking day engaged in the observation of human behavior: our own if no one else's. But most of these everyday observations would best be described as casual rather than systematic and so would not be considered scientific. For example, there is a simple task that has been used to measure spatial skills where the person is shown a drawing of an empty soda bottle being held steady at a 45-degree angle on a tabletop and asked to draw a line to show what the bottle would look like if it had some soda in it. Tilted bottles are certainly familiar objects we have observed hundreds or thousands of times, yet a surprising number of adults give incorrect answers. That is, despite years of experience with bottles of liquids, they do *not* seem to have noticed that liquids in stationary containers are always parallel to the tabletop (or ground), regardless of the angle. This illustrates how our casual, everyday observations do not always provide us with accurate knowledge about the world around us. To find the "truth," we need to use systematic observational procedures that consistently and accurately record the events taking place. To be truly scientific, our observations need to be reliable, valid, and unbiased. Let's look at each of these issues.

Reliability and Validity   Scientific observations produce measures that are both reliable and valid. **Reliability** has to do with whether the same event would receive the same score when measured again (i.e., the *consistency* of the observation), whereas **validity** has to do with whether a score can be taken to actually be a measure of what it purports (or claims) to measure.

To explore these concepts, let us consider the case of measuring people's weights. Suppose that a scale has not been calibrated properly, and it reads a person's weight as less than it actually is—but in a completely consistent manner. For example, each time a person who is actually 140 pounds steps on the scale, it reads 126. We might say that the scale provides measurements that *are* reliable (because it consistently gives the same score to the same person), but these weights are *not* valid (the person's weight in pounds is not accurately specified by the scale). Now consider the bathroom scale one of the authors used to own. If you got on the scale four times in rapid succession, the scale would typically show four different weights, sometimes differing by 10 or even 15 pounds. (Of course, you might be tempted to keep trying until you got a weight you liked!) A scale like this is clearly not even reliable—the same event is measured, but it receives different scores on different occasions. Because this scale is not reliable, it *cannot* be valid; it cannot be giving a person's weight in pounds accurately if it does not even give the same weight on successive measures. But note, as in the prior example of a scale that consistently gives the wrong weight, a measurement procedure can be reliable without being valid.

Objective Versus Subjective Observations   Another dimension on which observations may vary is the extent to which they can be said to be objective as opposed to subjective. **Objective measures** are based on direct use of sensory information from the external world that is "publicly available" (so that everyone who looks sees the same thing). For instance, counting the number of words spelled correctly on a spelling test would be an objective measure of spelling performance because everyone who looks at the spelling test will see the same misspellings. *The hallmark of objective measurements is that different observers will experience the event in the same manner and therefore give the same measurement.* In contrast, **subjective measures** are based on the personal, internal reactions of the observer.[3] That is, when observers have to *interpret* what they see and decide for themselves what the event represented, they are being subjective. For example, how would people react if someone looked at them and exclaimed, "What a sweater!"? Some people would take it as a compliment, and others would take it as a criticism of their taste in clothes. The actual intention of the speaker is not directly available to observers, so judgments about the speaker's meaning would be a subjective measure.

Let's consider another example. A researcher may ask participants to rate the attractiveness of human faces, and because "beauty is in the eye of the beholder" (and is a subjective phenomenon), we would certainly expect different people to find different faces more or less attractive. The question here is how do we record or measure an individual's feeling of attraction to a particular face? If we ask the participant to pick a number on a scale from 1 to 10 to indicate the attractiveness of a face, our measurement procedure can be considered objective because any researcher would read the rating scale in the same way and assign the same score to the participant. However, if the researcher (or observer) must make a judgment about how attractive a face is by watching participants' facial expressions, then different observers may make different decisions about the same expression. For example, one participant

---

[3] This distinction between objective and subjective *measurement procedures* should not be confused with the difference between objective and subjective *phenomena*, which refer to behaviors or characteristics of the participants. Subjective phenomena refer to covert behaviors such as a participant's feelings, thoughts, likes or dislikes, and so on, which cannot be observed directly by someone else. In contrast, objective phenomena include the outwardly observable behaviors, habits, or physical features that *are* directly observable by others. When psychologists want to measure subjective phenomena, they will typically either ask the participants for a self-report (e.g., "How much do you like watching horror movies?"), or they will record the number of horror movies the participants view over some period of time, thus using an objective phenomenon to estimate the subjective phenomenon.

This latter measurement procedure assumes that movie viewing behavior is an outward indication of the internal preference. Unfortunately, social psychologists have demonstrated that the assumption that attitudes and behaviors are closely entwined is not always valid.

may half close his eyes when looking at a particular face, and one observer may think this is a sign of strong attraction while another observer may think it is irrelevant and ignore it. Measurements based on this kind of personal, internal judgment by the observer are considered subjective and are potentially unreliable (because there may be no agreement or consistency among observers).

Many human experiences studied by psychologists are subjective in nature (e.g., how much better one flavor of ice cream is than another or how embarrassed a 4-year-old child is after wetting his pants at preschool). But from a scientific point of view, research observations need to be as objective as possible—we need to be sure that different observers show a high degree of agreement in their recorded observations. Researchers devote much of their time designing research procedures that provide objective measurements of these inherently subjective human experiences. In this way we can at least be assured of high *inter-rater reliability* (or *inter-observer agreement*) for our measures; the validity of the measures (such as a 10-point rating scale) will have to be tested. To the extent that our measures are subjective, we must be particularly concerned with the need to demonstrate inter-observer agreement.

Bias for Positive Instances (Confirmatory Bias)   We need to be concerned about objectivity and inter-observer agreement, in part, because people's perceptions and interpretations of events are often *biased* by their preconceived beliefs and expectations. That is, people tend to see what they expect to see, and they tend to remember only those "facts" that fit those expectations. Expectations form as we go through life; what we see, do, hear, and read about all come together in a personal *world view:* our own personal theory about the world and how it works. We use this world view to try to anticipate what others will do and to help explain people's actions after the fact. Once we have formed a world view, it typically introduces systematic errors, or bias, into our perception of ongoing events such that the events that stand out for us—and are, therefore, more likely to be remembered—are those that allow us to say "I was right." This is called a **bias for positive instances** (or a **confirmatory bias**). A positive instance is an event that supports (or confirms) our preconceived notions or expectations about the world. We pay an inordinate amount of attention to positive instances, often ignoring, misperceiving, or forgetting any negative instances.[4]

For example, Darley and Gross (1983, as cited by Tesser, 1995) asked adults to evaluate the academic performance of a fourth-grade child. Half the adults were informed that the child came from a high socioeconomic status family, and the other

---

[4] This selectivity (in both perception and memory) is *not* conscious but may result from broader mental mechanisms that reduce our memory load by extracting general or familiar patterns and help us sustain a positive self-concept. A familiar example of the confirmatory bias is stereotyping, where we associate specific characteristics with social categories (such as men, women, the elderly, etc.), thereby reducing the complexity of our social world. By noticing only the things that others do that fit a stereotype and ignoring the things that do not fit, we can respond to people as if they are generic members of their group rather than unique individuals.

half were told she was from a low socioeconomic status family, thus setting up differ-ent expectations in the minds of the adults. All of the adults *viewed the same videotape* where the child got some easy items wrong and some difficult items correct. Adults who believed she was from a high socioeconomic status family attended to and showed better memory for the child's success on the difficult items, while adults who believed she was from a low socioeconomic status family attended to and showed better memory for her failure on easy items.

Researchers are human and are also subject to such biases and expectations, par-ticularly because they are likely to have a **working hypothesis,** which is a belief about what types of relationships they will find in their study. This hypothesis can create a bias for positive instances, so we need to maximize the objectivity of our ob-servations and carefully record *all* instances—both positive and negative—in order to reduce the likelihood that we will find support for our "hunch" (the working hypothesis) by seeing only what we expect to see.

Rival Explanations

The training of a good researcher is, in many respects, a process of creating a skeptic. Rather than believing something to be fact with little evidence (as occurs for facts based on intuition or authority), the researcher learns to demand rigorous evidence and to critically evaluate all evidence. Of course, this "show-me" attitude is com-patible with the empirical approach and its demand for data based on careful ob-servation and recording. For any given set of data, a good researcher always tries to generate **rival explanations** (or alternative hypotheses) that could give rise to the same pattern of data. If two or more hypotheses can explain the phenomenon equally well and allow us to predict future events with equal accuracy, a good researcher will admit that it is too soon to conclude that one hypothesis is the "correct" one and will search for empirical data that will discriminate between the rival explanations.

Defining the Terms

One reason that different researchers sometimes report differences in the facts of some behavior has to do with definition of terms. Three different researchers may be interested in the same research question: Does being hungrier make it harder for children to learn? Given an interest in this general question, one needs to *sharpen the question.* What do the key words refer to? What age does *children* refer to? What sort of *learning* are we talking about? What is meant by *hungrier?* Terms used by researchers need to be carefully defined. For terms like *hungry* and *learning*, one needs to have an **operational definition.** An operational definition is a precise description of the exact procedures—or operations—used to measure some behavior or to produce some phenomenon. A good operational definition basically tells us how to recognize a particular behavior when we see it. If the three researchers operationalize some key terms in different ways, they could easily reach different conclusions about the relationship between hunger and learning in children. For example, hunger could be operationally defined in a number of different ways, such as: (a) asking the children to rate how hungry they feel by choosing a number between 0 and 4; (b) asking parents to keep a record of the food their children eat before school; or (c) taking a small blood sample and measuring the children's blood sugar levels just before the learning task is administered. Similarly, the researchers need to define *learning* by selecting a specific task, and because each task will be at least slightly different from other tasks, the results may not be exactly the same for each operational defintion. Essentially, every operational definition of *hunger* or *learning* may be measuring slightly different things, and these variations in definition may lead to different patterns of results. Therefore, it is necessary for researchers to identify their operational definitions as clearly as possible.

However, a precise operational definition does not assure that you are measuring a concept well. Suppose someone is using the term *intelligence* and you ask her how she would operationalize what she means by intelligence. She replies that it is the person's weight in pounds when nude divided by the circumference of that person's left wrist measured in millimeters. She has precisely operationalized the term, but you are probably inclined to suggest that although you now know exactly what she is referring to, she should call it something other than intelligence. From the terms introduced earlier in this chapter you may realize that while this measure of intelligence is likely to be quite consistent or reliable, it does not measure what it purports to measure and so is not a *valid* index of intelligence.

Replication

A good researcher should be somewhat skeptical of even his own empirical findings from any single study. As will be developed later in the book, it is nearly accurate to say "no single study ever *proved* anything." There is almost always at least one other possible explanation (rival hypotheses) for the pattern in your observed data, if nothing other than that it happened by chance (i.e., accidentally or coincidentally). For this reason, one of the most critical criteria for believing something to be a fact is that the observations can be repeated or **replicated.** When the study is performed again, preferably by several researchers who are very skeptical of this outcome, and the results remain the same, these replications strengthen the empirical evidence for the relationship. This **convergence of evidence** justifies believing in the relationship as a "fact" about behavior.

Internal and External Validity

Every research project has a stated purpose or goal, typically, to test a particular hypothesis about the relationship between two or more variables. When the study has been properly designed and conducted so that it allows us to answer the research question, the study is said to have high **internal validity.** Obviously, the internal validity of a research project is a top priority for us. Another concern is often the extent to which the results obtained in a given study, under a specific set of circumstances, would also be obtained for *different* participants and under slightly *different* circumstances. That is, we are often concerned with the **generalizability** (or **generality**) of the findings. If the results are broadly generalizable, the study is said to have good **external validity:** What we learned about the individuals who participated in the study can be applied to other people as well. As we shall see later on, certain research methods provide good internal validity, while others provide better external validity, and there is often a *tradeoff* between the two in a researcher's choice of one research method rather than another. That is, the procedures employed to maximize the internal validity of a study often reduce the external validity of the study by making the conditions within the study less realistic.

For example, consider a study designed to test a new motor oil and find out how many miles the car will go before an oil change is necessary. If the engineers test the oil by running car engines continuously at 2,000 revolutions per minute (rpm) until they seize up, it *would* tell them how long the oil lasts, so the study would have internal validity. However, running the engines continuously at the same speed (rpm) is not realistic because very few drivers maintain the same speed for such long periods of time. Instead, real driving often involves stops and starts and changes in speed, as well as many periods of time when the engine is turned off. Therefore, the results of the study may *not* generalize to real driving conditions. That is, the study may not have external validity.

Conducting a Research Study

The research process follows a fairly predictable sequence of events. These steps (which are illustrated in the flowchart presented in Figure 1-1) take the researcher from an initial question of interest through the process of gathering data and drawing conclusions, which usually lead to new questions. The research enterprise is a series of connected projects that build on one another, creating what we call a *research literature* on the topic. Before conducting a study, most researchers will familiarize themselves with the literature on their topic in order to see what other studies have already discovered and which puzzles still remain unsolved.

As you see in Figure 1-1, a research project typically begins with the statement of a *question of interest*, along with a hunch about the answer one will obtain, the working hypothesis. (This working hypothesis should be based on a thorough review of the relevant literature.) Good, scientific hypotheses are *testable*. This means that all of the terms in the hypothesis must be *observable:* It must be possible to develop valid operational definitions for each element in the hypothesis. The hypothesis proposed earlier, that girls are more courteous than boys only when there is an audience present, is a good, testable hypothesis because it is possible to define and record each of the terms: sex, courteousness, and the presence of other people. In contrast, the hypothesis that your new boss is an absolute tyrant because his id is fixated at the anal stage of psychosexual development (due to unresolved conflicts with his mom during

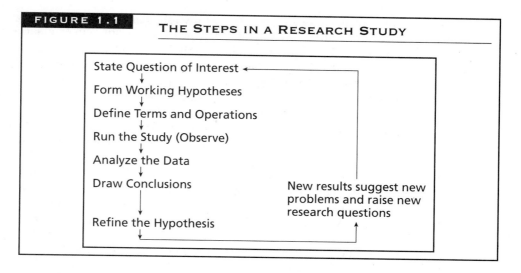

FIGURE 1.1

THE STEPS IN A RESEARCH STUDY

State Question of Interest
↓
Form Working Hypotheses
↓
Define Terms and Operations
↓
Run the Study (Observe)
↓
Analyze the Data
↓
Draw Conclusions

New results suggest new problems and raise new research questions

↓
Refine the Hypothesis
↓

his potty-training days) is *not* a testable hypothesis. While we could certainly operationally define *tyranny,* there is no independent operational definition of the id or for the id's anal fixation (and we probably have no records of your boss's potty-training days, either).

Many researchers also believe that a good, scientific hypothesis is *falsifiable.* Falsifiable hypotheses are ones that data could clearly *dis*prove because the hypothesis itself identifies events that *cannot* occur if the hypothesis is true. For example, medical researchers began to suspect that the reduction in estrogen that accompanies menopause causes an acceleration in the development of osteoporosis (the loss of bone calcium) in older women. It was then hypothesized that estrogen-replacement therapy would reduce the loss of calcium and preserve bone density. This hypothesis is falsifiable because it implicitly states that women who do not receive estrogen-replacement therapy will develop osteoporosis more rapidly than women who do receive estrogen. Therefore, if it is found that women who receive estrogen develop osteoporosis *at the same rate as* women who do not receive estrogen, the hypothesis has been disproved.

Because data can often be interpreted as support for two or more rival hypotheses, evidence consistent with a prediction from a particular theory may be said to "provide supporting evidence" for that theory, but one *cannot* say the data prove that theory correct. For example, some developmental psychologists hypothesized that human infants have an innate capacity to perceive human faces because the human face is so closely associated with the infant's survival. They predicted that young infants would spend more time looking at faces than other visual stimuli. Studies subsequently *supported* this hypothesis: Young infants do, indeed, show a preference for faces over other stimuli. The data, however, does not *prove* that infants have an instinctual ability to perceive faces due to their importance to survival. Other psychologists had proposed that infants' preferences are based on the physical features of the objects and that infants will prefer to look at objects that are curved rather than straight, symmetrical versus nonsymmetrical, and high instead of low in dark-to-light contrast. This hypothesis predicts that because human faces have all of these physical features, they would be more attractive to infants than other stimuli that have only some of these characteristics. Thus, the data indicating that young infants show a preference for faces also support *this* theory but cannot be said to prove it because the first (and *rival*) hypothesis may also explain the data.

However, when the data are clearly at odds with the implications of a theory, they can, if replicated, serve to disprove—or falsify—the theory. This asymmetry, when you think about it, fits well with the notion of researcher as skeptic: One knows the sort of data that will prove the hypothesis incorrect, while there is no set of data that *necessarily* means the hypothesis is correct.

When the question of interest and working hypothesis have been formulated, the next step in the research process is the careful definition of terms and operations. This process is accomplished through the development of the specifics of the *procedures* to be used in gathering the empirical data. The researcher uses these procedures to systematically make observations and record the data. (This phase is often referred to as "running" the study or as the "data-gathering" step.) With the data in hand, one begins the statistical analyses to determine what one can say about the observed performances. The statistical analyses one performs on the data are of two types: descriptive and inferential statistics.

Descriptive statistics are designed to help *summarize* the entire set of data. Most research involves observing a number of participants and recording their performance, so making sense of these data just by looking at all of the individual scores is very difficult. Descriptive statistics to help us understand how the "group" performed overall by telling us such things as what the average performance was like (e.g., the mean number of words spelled correctly on a spelling test) and how different individuals were from one another (e.g., the standard deviation for the group). *Inferential statistics* are intended to evaluate hypotheses and allow conclusions as to whether there is something very orderly or systematic about the data. In this book we introduce two of the many applications of inferential statistics: (1) measuring how closely the changes in one variable are related to changes in another variable, and (2) determining whether the average performance of one group of participants is the same as or different from the average performance of another group of participants.

In the final step of the research process, the researcher decides what to make of the statistical analyses. The sorts of *conclusions* one can reach depend on the research method used in the procedures/observation steps and on the particular statistical analyses performed. For example, as a general rule, correlational studies, such as naturalistic observations, allow us to reach conclusions as to whether certain events are systematically related and can be expected to co-occur. The presence of matic *covariation* is sufficient to allow prediction of one event from another, and inferential statistic reported is likely to be some sort of "correlation coefficient". the other hand, one may draw inferences about *causal* relationships among riables (i.e., provide an explanation for the behavior) *only if* the data are from a gorously controlled experiment. The logic of experimentation and the reasons the experimental method is our best technique to obtain facts about causation are developed in a later chapter.

rcises

1. Suppose you are asked to conduct a scientific study of helping behavior in teenagers. Identify three different ways that you could operationally define *helping* behavior for your study. Now suppose you are specifically interested in finding out how often teenagers "help" other teenagers *versus* how often they "help" adults. Are your operational definitions suitable for this specific research question? If not, identify two additional operational definitions for *helping* that *could* be used for this research purpose.

2. Generate an operational definition of *intelligence* that you find satisfactory. Can you generate a second operational definition that also sounds acceptable to you? How should we define "intelligence?"

Use the following scenario to answer questions 3–6:

For a long time, new parents were advised (by grandparents and others) to "let the baby cry himself out" because to respond to the crying baby simply teaches the baby that he can get what he wants by crying, and he becomes "spoiled." Dr. Joan Allsworthy designed a study to find out whether, in fact, babies cry more frequently (i.e., become spoiled) if their parents quickly pick them up each time they cry.

The first step in the project involved finding babies who *were* picked up quickly and babies who were *not* picked up quickly so that they could be compared on how spoiled they became. Dr. Allsworthy visited the homes of 100 families with newborn babies and installed a video camera to monitor the parents' responses to the babies' cries. On the basis of a month's observations, Dr. Allsworthy identified 30 families where the parents always responded to the crying infant within 2 minutes (this group was labeled "Responsive") and 30 families where the parents would let the baby cry until it fell asleep (the "Unresponsive" group). These classifications were based only on crying episodes that were not due to hunger or pain. (The other 40 families were not consistent in how they responded to the infant, so they were not included in the actual study of "spoiling.")

The hypothesis was then tested by returning to the homes (of the
when the babies were 12 months old. At that time, Dr. Allsworthy spe..,
with each family and measured how "spoiled" the baby was by record*(es)*
many times the infant started to cry and how long each crying episode last*s*

3. Does this research project meet the major criteria for being considered scientific? Explain your answer.

4. Is there any opportunity in this study (as it is described here) for the researcher's personal biases to interfere? If so, how could it be avoided?

5. How has Dr. Allsworthy operationally defined her two variables ("parental responsiveness" and "spoiled")?

6. Dr. Allsworthy selected only 60 families out of the original group of 100 families. What effect does leaving out 40 families have on the internal and external validity of the study?

Use the following scenario to answer questions 7–9:

Dr. John Smith is interested in the relationship between children's height and their muscle coordination. Dr. Smith believes that children who are either much too tall or much too short for their age will have poor muscle coordination. Therefore, Dr. Smith plans to conduct the following study.

Fifty 6-year-old children will be selected as participants from local schools. First, each child's height will be measured (in inches) using a standard tape-measure, and then each child will be asked to perform a series of muscle coordination tasks. These tasks will include tracing a drawing, throwing three darts at a dartboard from a distance of 7 feet, and playing a game of "catch" with the researcher using a tennis ball.

Dr. Smith will have three graduate students look at the children's tracings and rate them for smoothness and accuracy on a scale from 1 to 10 (where higher rating scores represent greater muscle coordination). For each dart, Dr. Smith will measure the distance between the dart and the center of the bull's-eye, and then he will compute the average distance, in inches, for the child's three throws. (A smaller average score would indicate greater muscle coordination.) During their game of "catch" with the tennis ball, which has a diameter of 2-3/8 inches, Dr. Smith will throw the ball to the child five times and have the child throw it back five times. Dr. Smith will mentally note how coordinated the child seems to be on the basis of his or her movements while throwing and catching the ball.

7. Is Dr. Smith's hypothesis testable and falsifiable? Explain your answers.

8. Identify potentially subjective measurement procedures in this study. Which measurement procedure(s) would be most objective? Explain your answers.

9. Which of Dr. Smith's variables is being measured with the most reliable procedure? Which procedure is likely to be the most unreliable? Explain your answers.

10. How many planets are there in our solar system? How do you know? (What "way of knowing" did you use in coming to believe this fact?) Can you separate your own "knowledge" into "facts" acquired through intuition, authority, rational-induction, or empirical observation? Give examples of each type of knowledge.

CHAPTER

2

ETHICS IN RESEARCH

■ ■ ■ ■ ■ ■

In this chapter, you will learn about the ethical principles that govern psychological research with human participants. The four primary rights of research participants are discussed, as are several other special issues that should be of concern to all researchers.

Look for These Important Terms and Concepts

Institutional Review Board
American Psychological Association's
   ethical principles
freedom from harm
informed consent

deception
reactivity
debriefing
privacy
anonymity versus confidentiality

All research exists within a world of values. Our implicit or explicit beliefs about what is proper give direction to our actions. This means that any decision to conduct research is based on our own views on issues such as: (1) what is right and wrong; (2) what questions are important and what information is important to know; and (3) what procedures for answering the research questions are acceptable. Research is an active process and *ethics is the study of proper action.* Issues of ethics in research with living organisms (human or animal) are among the hardest that a researcher faces. We must carefully weigh the importance of the questions we wish to ask against the well-being of the participants whom we must "use" to help us find the answers to the question of interest. Several sets of guidelines exist to help one decide on a proper course of action, but ultimately it rests upon the researcher to act in an ethical manner while conducting research.

For all sciences, ethical issues surround both the process and products of research. In designing, performing, reporting, and applying research, numerous ethical issues arise. Some of the most basic of these include reporting results accurately, carrying out research competently, managing resources honestly, considering the consequences to society of any research endeavor, and speaking out on societal concerns related to one's area of expertise (Shaughnessy & Zechmeister, 1994). These issues are relevant to scientists in every field. For psychologists, there is an additional concern over treatment of research participants.

Guidelines for Psychologists

The American Psychological Association (APA) has established a set of "Ethical Principles for Psychologists," which were most recently amended in 1992 (see Appendix A). These updated guidelines consist of six general principles (listed below) and 102 specific standards. In 1981, the APA also published a set of guidelines that focus on the care of animal subjects.[1] The overall emphasis of both sets of guidelines is the humane and sensitive treatment of participants (both human and animal) who may be placed at some degree of risk by the research process. These guidelines can help make researchers aware of potential problems when conducting research, but they are not rules. A researcher should follow some set of steps—such as those implied by these guidelines—while deciding on how to conduct the research, but ultimately, the responsibility of how to proceed and the consequences of that decision are borne solely by the researcher.

The steps that are followed may vary according to the nature of the research project under consideration. In the process of deciding how to use human participants in research, a researcher should utilize a number of sources, including

---

[1] Similar guidelines were published by the Institutional Animal Care and Use Committee (IACUC) in 1985.

reviewing guidelines of the APA,[2] looking at the types of procedures that have been acceptably and fruitfully used in similar research in the past, and conferring with colleagues and members of ethical review panels. Federal regulations require that organizations conducting research—including universities and colleges—establish an **institutional review board** (IRB; often called a "human research review committee"). Proposals for any research to be conducted with human participants must be submitted to the IRB and will be approved or rejected by them on the basis of ethical acceptability. Although IRB approval is not required for research using animal subjects, many institutions have voluntarily established ethical review committees for animal research.

As an example of why IRBs were established, consider a famous social psychology study conducted by Zimbardo and his students in 1973 (Haney, Banks, & Zimbardo, 1973). Normal, healthy students were offered $15 a day to be either prisoners or guards for a week in a mock prison, which was set up in the basement of a university building. The students were left alone to see how they would react in these roles. The experiment had to be stopped before the week was over, as several students assigned to be prisoners had breakdowns, and several students assigned to be guards had become excessively violent, verbally and physically abusing the "prisoners." This study violates several major ethical issues (discussed below), including privacy and freedom from harm.

The Basic Ethical Dilemma

Given that we are all entitled to "life, liberty, and the pursuit of happiness," what happens when the researcher and the participant have different goals? Two basic rights need to be balanced by any researcher deciding to conduct research with living beings. The first are the rights and welfare of the participant, who should not be harmed or changed in any negative way as a consequence of participation in a research project. The second is the right of the experimenter to ask questions and seek knowledge and understanding of human behavior. In the best possible situation, both happen: The researcher asks questions and gets answers, and a participant has an interesting, educational experience. It might be best to think of your research as a partnership and your participants as valued colleagues without whom you cannot conduct your research and who should, therefore, be treated with great care and respect. You may liken this to the Golden Rule: Treat others (including research participants) as you would wish to be treated yourself.

This ethical dilemma can be understood in terms of a "cost-benefit" ratio. All research involves tradeoffs, balancing a question of interest against possible ways to get an answer. One way to decide whether a piece of research should be performed is

---

[2] And/or similar guidelines published by other professional associations such as the American Sociological Association and the American Anthropological Association.

to do a cost-benefit comparison, weighing the potential costs of the research against its potential benefits. Deciding what the costs and benefits are is a very difficult task. Costs may come in the form of money or in terms of less tangible things such as human pain, stress, or other discomfort. Likewise, benefits may be tangible, such as a life-saving vaccine or monetary saving, or less tangible, such as the potential long-term effects of a new teaching method or a personal benefit to a participant from contributing to the advancement of science. Both costs and benefits may accrue to researchers, to participants, and/or to society as a whole.

Some studies clearly have too high a cost to be performed. Research with too high a monetary cost might include things such as space research or, more recently, the U.S. supercollider. These research programs have been canceled or scaled back because they did not seem to have reasonable costs for the potential outcome (benefits). Some research may have too high a human cost. For example, imagine if pharmaceutical companies or cosmetic companies were to test all of their potential new products on healthy children, risking immediate negative allergic reactions or long-range carcinogenic effects. We as a society are likely to say that the cost of such research would be too high. In retrospect, with perfect 20/20 hindsight, this is how many people now feel about much prior research, such as the nuclear weapons testing conducted in the southwestern United States in the 1940s.

Another kind of human cost relates to emotional rather than physical dangers. Some research may generate negative emotions in the participants such as anger, depression, anxiety, guilt, or low self-esteem. Research such as this can later leave a participant struggling with its effects.[3] A famous example is a study where people believed they were shocking another person with very high levels of electricity (Milgram, 1963). Milgram's study had an important purpose: He was trying to make sense of the "blind obedience" many Nazis exhibited during World War II, where men were willing to obey destructive and inhumane commands. Milgram wanted to know how far the average "man on the street" would go in hurting another human being simply because a person with authority told him to do so. In reality, the participants in Milgram's study were not actually hurting anyone, and this was explained to them immediately after the study. But even after being told that no one had been hurt by their actions, many of the participants later felt very uncomfortable with the fact that they had been *willing* to give electric shocks to another person.[4] Although it was not uncommon in the mid-1960s, this kind of research is generally considered unacceptable by today's ethical standards.

---

[3] One of these authors has done research on locations that provoked a fear of crime, which included a potential ethical issue. It is known that thinking about things that cause fear tends to make one even more afraid. Is it ethical to ask people to think about situations or places that frighten them, when that may, in turn, lead to more fear, and then to curtailed behaviors or uses of an area because of that fear?

[4] This study also demonstrates the power a researcher has over the participants. When participants wanted to stop administering shocks to the "target" who was no longer answering questions, the experimenter responded, "Treat no answer as incorrect and continue." Almost every participant proceeded to administer what they believed to be severe shocks, and 65% of them continued to the end, where the shocks were labeled as dangerous, simply because the researcher told them to do so.

Neither benefits nor costs are easily quantified. With such intangibles on both sides, it is difficult to make clear decisions, and setting hard and fast rules is nearly impossible. While performing a thorough cost-benefit analysis is a difficult task, the effort of doing so may lead to a more thorough investigation of ethical issues, as well as to a critical evaluation of the appropriateness of the proposed research methods. The general ethical principles set forth by the APA are intended to help psychologists make appropriate choices.

The Six General Ethical Principles

The following are the American Psychological Association's six general ethical principles (APA, 1992). As you will note, these principles are applicable to the professional activities of all psychologists, and, indeed, they are presented as part of a Code of Conduct. Here we have paraphrased and shortened them to relate specifically to experimental psychology, but the full text of these principles can be found in Appendix A.

A. *Competence* — Psychologists should use techniques for which they are qualified by education or training. Psychologists must exercise careful judgment and take precautions to protect those with whom they work.

B. *Integrity* — Psychologists should promote integrity in teaching and research. Psychologists are fair, honest, and respectful of others. They make no false, misleading, or deceptive statements about their research.

C. *Professional and Scientific Responsibility* — Psychologists clarify roles and obligations to the extent feasible. Psychologists' moral standards and conduct should not compromise or reduce the public trust in psychology and psychologists. Psychologists are concerned with their own and colleagues' ethical conduct.

D. *Respect for Peoples' Rights and Dignity* — Psychologists respect the fundamental rights, dignity, and worth of all people. They respect rights to privacy, confidentiality, self-determination, and autonomy. Psychologists do not knowingly participate in or condone discriminatory practices and try to eliminate the effect on their work of biases based on factors such as sex, race, religion, age, disability, language, national origin, and socioeconomic status.

E. *Concern for the Welfare of Others* — Psychologists weigh the welfare and rights of human and animal participants. When conflicts arise, they try to resolve them responsibly and avoid or minimize harm. Psychologists do not exploit or mislead others.

F. *Social Responsibility* — Psychologists are aware of scientific responsibility to the society in which they live and work. Psychologists strive to advance human welfare and the science of psychology and try to avoid misuse of their work.

Specific Ethical Issues in Research With Humans

Four major ethical issues are involved in psychological research with humans. These are: (1) risk and participants' right to be unharmed, (2) informed consent, (3) debriefing, and (4) privacy. Each of these is covered by one or more of the general principles and a number of the specific ethical standards of the APA guidelines, as noted below.

Risk or Freedom From Harm

See General Principles A, C, D, and E and Ethical Standards 1.11–1.14, 6.06–6.07, 6.17, and 6.20 (animals) in Appendix A.

Life itself is inherently risky. At any time, in any situation, there is a chance that we will come to harm, either physically or emotionally. Researchers, however, do not have the right to expose people to increased risk of harm. Participating in a research project may, in fact, pose a risk to the participant's well-being, so researchers must anticipate the risks that may occur in a given study and decide whether the level of risk is acceptable. Protecting participants from any harm (including physical or mental discomfort) that may result from the research procedures is a very important responsibility of the researcher. In most psychological research, the risk of physical harm is minimal, but the risk of negative social or psychological consequences (such as fear for your reputation with others or reduced self-esteem) may be quite high in some studies.[5]

At the very beginning of any study, all participants should be made aware of all possible risks. Research should not place any participant at risk unless the individual has given explicit permission *after* he or she has been fully informed of the risks involved. (This is known as getting "informed consent," which is discussed more fully in the next section.) It is the responsibility of the researcher to be aware of all potential risks before the study has begun and to make the participants aware of these risks so that they can make an informed decision to participate. To recognize risks, the researcher will have to very carefully review the research methods and try to imagine all of the possible reactions people may have to the procedures.

In addition, the researcher is responsible for recognizing the potential short- or long-term consequences of participation in the research. It is the researcher's responsibility to be prepared to provide either immediate or future support for participants if needed and/or to correct any such consequences to the best of their ability. (For example, in extreme cases, the researcher may need to have a clinical psychologist available for any participant who may experience emotional or psychological distress during or after the study.) It is important that participants know how

---

[5] Simply agreeing to participate in research can be anxiety producing for people. Therefore, *every* study must be considered potentially risky for participants, and the degree of risk must be weighed against all potential benefits.

to contact an investigator after a study has ended in case they begin to experience delayed effects.[6]

One example of research where the issue of **freedom from harm** was not carefully considered is the Milgram experiment mentioned earlier. The participants felt a high level of discomfort during the experiment because they believed they were seriously hurting another person. Another example is the research done by the United States military in the 1940s and 1950s where soldiers were exposed to varying levels of nuclear radiation. Because the participants were not informed of the true nature of the studies (a practice called "deception," discussed in the next section), they could not have known the risks they were accepting. It is highly unlikely that an IRB would give approval for such studies today, even if provisions for immediate debriefing (see next section) and counseling were made available.

Informed Consent

> See General Principles B, C, D, and E and Ethical Standards 1.07, 1.19, 3.03, 6.10–6.15, and 6.18 in Appendix A.

The issue of **informed consent** has three components. First, consent and participation should be voluntary. Second, volunteers should be informed of the general contents of the research in which they will be participating, and they should give formal consent only *after* being so informed. Third, participants must be free to withdraw at any time without penalty.

Voluntary participation means that no coercion should be used to get someone to participate in a study. This is particularly true when the researcher holds some position of authority over the participant. In addition, participants who are unable to make decisions for themselves (such as children or persons who are mentally disabled) require special care. Someone else—such as a parent or legal guardian—may make the decision for them to participate, but to whatever extent possible, the participants must understand what they are going to do, and they must be granted the right to refuse to participate. While permission must be obtained from a parent or guardian before they can participate, minors and the mentally disabled have *all the same rights* as adults. Once they have begun a study, they may withdraw at any time without the permission of the parent or guardian.

The core of informed consent is a statement presented to the potential participants before a study begins (usually in writing, but sometimes read aloud) that explains the research as thoroughly as possible. This statement also describes the responsibilities of both participant and investigator. (For example, the informed consent statement may specify that the participant's responsibility is to attend

---

[6] Participants should also know how to contact the chairperson of the Institutional Review Board (IRB) in case they have any concerns about the ethical practices of the researcher. For example, the name and phone number of the IRB chairperson can be included on the informed consent form that each participant fills out before the study begins, and each participant can be given a copy of the form to keep.

five sessions at the researcher's laboratory, and the researcher's responsibilities will include maintaining confidentiality and reporting the study's results in the form of group averages rather than individual performance records.) The volunteer examines the information in the informed consent statement, asks any questions, and makes a decision about whether to participate. After the investigator is sure that there are no questions, the volunteer gives consent by signing and dating the consent form.

Researchers must also explain that the participant may withdraw from the study at any time without penalty. The researcher *may* attempt to gently persuade the person to continue (for example, the researcher may make clear to the participant that there are easier or harder parts of the research task or that a long study is almost over), but the participant must not be pressured or coerced to continue. Again, it is important that this is made particularly clear when the investigator is in a position of authority over the participant outside the research setting, such as when students are recruited to participate in studies being conducted by their instructors.

There are two exceptions to the rule of informed consent. The first exception may be made when the research involves naturalistic observation in public places, such as street corners, shopping malls, or playgrounds. For instance, a researcher might be interested in determining which pieces of playground equipment are most popular, so she will want to observe children and measure the amount of time they spend on each apparatus. Informed consent would not be required in this case as long as the researcher can be certain that the *participants will remain anonymous* and that the behaviors recorded are: (1) *naturally occurring* ones that would have occurred even if the research were not being conducted and (2) *innocuous and neither revealing nor embarrassing.*

One example of a naturalistic observation experiment that involved behaviors for which a modern-day IRB would be *unlikely* to give permission was conducted by Middlemist, Knowles, and Matter (1976). Using a periscope, the experimenter hid in a bathroom stall and observed men at urinals. Confederates were either absent, standing at an adjacent urinal, or standing two urinals away from the person being observed. The length of time to onset of urination was recorded. Longer times were seen when the confederates were standing closer and Middlemist and his colleagues concluded this delay was because of the stress of having one's personal space invaded. Presumably, the men would have been embarrassed to know their urination behavior was being observed, so by today's standards, this study might be considered unethical.

A second exception to the informed consent rule deals with deception, one of the most confusing issues in research ethics. On occasion, it would be impossible to get participants to behave in a "normal" manner if they were aware of the purpose of the study, so researchers may find it necessary to use **deception** to avoid giving a complete description of the actual purpose of the research, at least until the experiment has been completed. For example, a social psychologist interested in studying racial prejudice in hiring practices would probably not want to tell potential participants (who may be asked to review applications and make recommendations about whom to hire for new positions) that the purpose of the study is to determine the effects of race on their recommendations. Most adults are aware that racial prejudice is considered to be unacceptable and, therefore, would want to avoid appearing prejudiced to the researcher. This phenomenon, where participants change their "real, normal" behavior because they know they are being observed, is called **reactivity.** In this example, the researcher would probably want to use less-than-full disclosure, possibly asking people whether they would be willing to participate in a study of decision-making without mentioning the fact that the true purpose is to study racial prejudice. In fact, a similar study was done by Newman and Krzystofiak (1979). In self-report measures, 86% of companies claimed that they would treat two racially different applicants identically. However, when given fake résumés for two applicants, similar except for race, less than half the companies treated the applicants identically.

In another example of deception (or less-than-full disclosure), Liebert and Baron (1972) studied children's aggressive behaviors after watching either violent or nonviolent television programs. If the children had known that the adults were interested in aggression, they might have changed their behaviors, particularly if they believed that the adults saw aggression as "bad." In that case, the researchers probably would not have recorded useful or valid data.

Deception, of course, violates the basic principles of informed consent because the participants do not know the true purpose of the experiment and perhaps not the true risks involved. To receive approval from an IRB to conduct research involving less-than-full disclosure, the researchers have to show that no alternative methods to deception are available and be extraordinarily protective of all of the participants' other rights. The risk of harm, for instance, must be minimized if the volunteer is not going to know what the risks actually are before consenting to participate. Deception should not be used without very good justification, and if it is used, the deception must be explained to the participants as soon as possible after the study is completed (during the debriefing session described below). Furthermore, deception should never be used solely for the purpose of convincing people to participate in research that they would refuse to volunteer for if they knew the actual purpose.[7] If at all possible, the ethical dilemma created by deception or less-than-fully-informed consent should be avoided by adopting a research design that makes deception unnecessary.

---

[7] Aside from the concerns for participants' rights, researchers who consider using deception may also consider the effects it has on the pool of potential participants available for other research projects. It has been discovered that frequent use of deception by researchers at a particular university leads to an expectation by the students at that institution—that is, the people who will be recruited by any faculty members doing any of a variety of studies—that *all* researchers use deception. For example, one of the authors had the experience of having a participant finish the memory task and announce, "I figured out what you were really trying to do!"—when the study was a memory study, plain and simple. Had that participant been really concentrating on the memory task, or had he been distracted by his belief that there was some hidden purpose? The internal validity of the memory study may have been endangered by the fact that other researchers at that institution had been using deception quite frequently.

If it can be argued that researchers at an institution have the "right" to have access to participants who are not automatically assuming that an experimenter is deceiving them, then the IRB's decision to allow deception in any particular study may need to take into consideration the number of such deceptive studies that have been done at the institution.

Debriefing

See General Principles B and E and Ethical Standards 1.07, 2.09, and 6.11 in Appendix A.

A **debriefing** session should be included at the end of any participants' participation. This is a time for participants to express any concerns and ask any questions about the study. It is the time for the researcher to clear up any misconceptions a participant may have and explain any deception used (as well as the reason why deception was necessary). In some cases, the debriefing session may resemble a brief counseling session, particularly if the research task may have made some participants feel uncomfortable about themselves or their performance.

It is very important to be sure that participants know how to reach the investigator with any future questions or concerns. For instance, should the participants find themselves, some days later, worrying about their performance in the study, they should know that they can contact the researcher to discuss their concerns or feelings. The researcher must be prepared to provide counseling (or a referral to a professional counselor) to any participants who experience delayed distress related to their participation in research. During the debriefing, the researcher should also remind the participants that they have the right to contact the chairperson of the Institutional Review Board (IRB) to discuss any concerns they have about the treatment they experienced as a research participant. While a debriefing should always be done at the end of a study, it is particularly crucial to devote sufficient time to this phase of the research in two kinds of cases: those where the participants' consent was obtained with anything less than full disclosure about the purposes of the research and those where there is a potential for the participant to feel current or future discomfort because of the methods used or subject matter of the experiment.

Privacy

See General Principles A and D and Ethical Standards 1.22, 1.24, 5.01–5.05, 5.07–5.09, and 6.10–6.11 in Appendix A.

Participants have the right to expect that their performance on the research tasks will not be made public and that only members of the research team will have access to their records. **Privacy** can be provided by either of two means: confidentiality or anonymity. **Anonymity** means that not even the researcher knows the identity of the participants; no personal information is gathered that would allow such identification to take place. For example, the participants may fill out a survey in a large room with 50 other people present. As long as the surveys are distributed randomly, without identifying marks, and as long as the participants are not asked questions that would give away their identities, this procedure guarantees anonymity to them.

In contrast, whenever the participants' performances are being observed individually and the researchers know how each individual responded, they must keep the information **confidential** (i.e., guarantee that they will not use the participants' names nor allow anyone else to see the records of the participants' performance). In most cases, data will be stored using an identification (ID) number, and researchers access the individual names only in cases where additional data need to be added to the appropriate file. For example, longitudinal research requires that the researcher keep a record of the ID numbers assigned to each participant so that subsequent observations can be recorded in the file.

In all cases, any identifying information should be made available only to the research team. Unless a participant agrees in advance, data should never be able to be connected to any individual; no public or published materials should make it possible to identify any specific person. These issues are very important in getting participants to respond honestly or naturally, rather than being worried that anything they say or do might later be made public. Therefore, the letter of consent provided to potential participants often includes a statement about how the participants' privacy will be protected.

At rare times it is necessary to violate a participant's right to privacy. If, for example, participants reveal that they are seriously planning suicide or a violent crime (and therefore pose an imminent threat to themselves or another person), the researcher may be ethically required to report it to the proper authorities. Although clinical psychologists and counselors may be faced with this dilemma once in a while, the situation is unlikely to arise in experimental settings.

Ethical Treatment of Animals as Research Subjects

In some cases, an investigator may choose to study animal behavior rather than human behavior. This may be because it improves understanding of some basic principles of behavior and/or because such studies can help us understand and improve conditions for humans. When choosing to work with animals as subjects, the researcher is ultimately responsible for the humane treatment and welfare of each and every animal. In 1981, the APA published principles for research work with animals, and nine important concerns were included in the 1992 Code of Conduct (see Ethical Standards 6.20a–6.20i).

You will notice that of the four major ethical issues listed earlier for humans, only the issue of risk is relevant for animals, as they cannot: (1) give consent, (2) understand privacy, or (3) need debriefing. Clearly, then, the issue of risk is of paramount importance for researchers working with animals. There is no chance that any harm done can be corrected after the fact with a debriefing or explanation, nor is there any way for an animal to ask to withdraw from the study. A thorough investigation of potential risk and alternate research methods must be made before research begins to assure that the animals will receive the most ethical treatment possible throughout all phases of research. Again, a tradeoff arises between the scientist's "need to know" and the well-being of the animals, and the investigator must ultimately take responsibility for the appropriateness of any decision regarding the research methods.

Special Issues About the Ethics of Research

Who Decides What Is "Right?"

An issue that should be of central concern but that is often taken for granted is the question "What criteria should we use when developing our ethical standards?" In a research world increasingly aware of multiculturalism and in research programs increasingly interested in multicultural questions, the question of "whose ethics?" is becoming a much larger concern. As this trend continues, psychologists may do well to look at the guidelines of organizations such as the American Anthropological Association (AAA), which have traditionally had to address such questions in conducting research in other cultures. Becoming aware of (and sensitive to) the cross-cultural aspects of research ethics may be especially important for the community of researchers, who may be operating within a culture of pragmatism that suggests that "the ends justify the means." The behaviors that researchers justify on this basis may, in fact, be viewed very differently by others, and it is important that researchers not alienate the groups being studied or create resentment or cause harm that may make future research attentions unwelcome or impossible.

Ethics of Funding

Another potential area of ethical conflict is between a researcher and the sponsor or funding agency for the research. These issues are relevant to nearly all research, because without funding, the majority of research projects would never be undertaken. Issues may arise in two areas: initial funding decisions and the dissemination of specific results. If the funding comes from a source to whom the answer to the question being researched is important (e.g., economically or politically), there is always the potential for subtle pressures on the scientist to investigate certain questions or to find certain answers. There may even be pressure on researchers to cover up undesirable results or, conversely, to widely disseminate preliminary, unconfirmed findings.[8]

---

[8] For example, the tobacco industry funded several studies comparing active smokers to "deprived" smokers on relatively simple cognitive skills (such as noticing a "new" letter in a string of 20 identical letters). The studies found that smoking increases alertness and decreases reaction time, and the tobacco industry advertised this conclusion widely. However, these studies failed to include nonsmokers as a *control group*, so they failed to report that all nonsmokers are significantly better on the tasks than are active smokers, which strongly suggests that smoking leads to a performance *deficit* and that smokers in a state of nicotine withdrawal suffer *further deficits* in performance. Did the scientists receiving funding from the tobacco industry knowingly omit the crucial control group? Were they under pressure to do so?

Even "neutral" funding sources are likely to have certain agendas that may become controversial.

One viewpoint is that no regulation or censorship should be applied to the topics of science because it is arrogant for any group or individuals to think that they can regulate or decide what is important to study. This viewpoint says that only the individual scientist can decide what is of most importance or interest to study. In this case, funding decisions would be made on the basis of the researcher's prior performance, proposed research methods, and skills, rather than on the subject matter being studied. Unfortunately, this is *not* the viewpoint adopted by most funding sources. Censorship of topic areas is quite common, with funding agencies often steering away from controversial research topics.

Ethics and Statistics

Because we are also concerned with statistics in this book, a few words may be said about the ethics of statistical evaluation. There are a few ways in which statistical methods may be used unethically (see also Ethical Standards 1.23 and 1.24). Most obviously, researchers should never fabricate data (what is often referred to as "dry-labbing" an experiment.) Another issue concerns dropping participants from the data. For example, statisticians have legitimate concerns over extreme scores called "outliers," and they often suggest omitting outliers from the analyses. Ethical concerns are raised when the researcher begins to use the concept of outliers as a pretext for dropping selected participants. Criteria for removing participants from analyses should be clearly defined *before* beginning the analyses and should be applied similarly across all participants.[9] Because the researchers may not even realize that they are showing a bias when they begin to drop participants, it may be a better practice to either (1) use statistical tests that are "tolerant" of outliers or (2) to perform the analyses twice, once *with* and once *without* the outliers, and to report *both* sets of results.

Another obvious unethical practice is to report only those results that are consistent with the researchers' hypotheses[10] or to deliberately mislead others about the strength of findings. For example, graphical presentations must be designed so that they provide an accurate sense of the data. It is quite easy to make insignificant or borderline results look better than they actually are by manipulating the graph that displays them. Several examples are presented in the classic book *How to Lie With Statistics* by Darrell Huff (1954). For instance, Huff describes a case in which a publication in Washington, D.C., was trying to encourage retailers and other firms to purchase advertising space by graphing data from the U.S. government's payroll.

---

[9] Some statisticians argue that dropping participants from the analyses should never be based on performance or scores on any of the measures, but only on considerations such as incomplete sets of data or experimenter error during the test. These statisticians do not feel that "outliers" should be dropped simply because they have extreme scores.

[10] For instance, did the scientists conducting research on the effects of smoking actually *include* nonsmokers but not report that they outperformed the smokers?

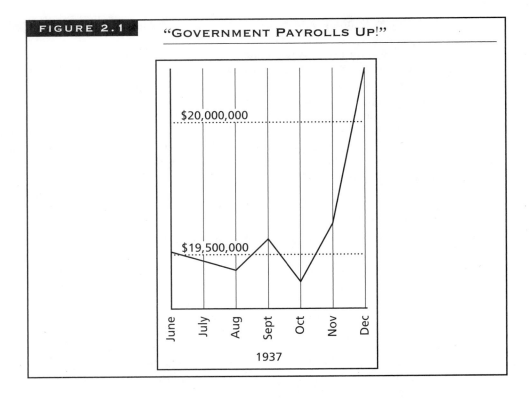

FIGURE 2.1 "GOVERNMENT PAYROLLS UP!"

$20,000,000

$19,500,000

June July Aug Sept Oct Nov Dec

1937

The graph (see Figure 2-1) was accompanied by the headline: "GOVERNMENT PAYROLLS UP!", and the intended message was that Washingtonians now had a lot more money to spend. The graph accurately reports that the payroll in December 1937 was $20.2 million, while from June through October the average had been $19.5 million. However, the visual representation of these numbers is very misleading—as you can see by comparing it with the graph in Figure 2-2 (which appears to deserve the headline: "GOVERNMENT PAYROLLS STABLE!"). In Figure 2-2, the vertical axis begins at 0, so the small increase in payroll (3.58%) looks small—exactly as it should.

What Becomes of What You Find?

Finally, scientists must struggle with questions about the applications of their findings. As a researcher, you have an obligation to do research that will improve the quality of life of people in the world, rather than provide ways to harm people. However, innovation inevitably leads to change, and any discovery may have either favorable or unfavorable consequences, depending on how it is used. It is not always possible to tell what uses may be devised for new knowledge. Still, it is the responsibility

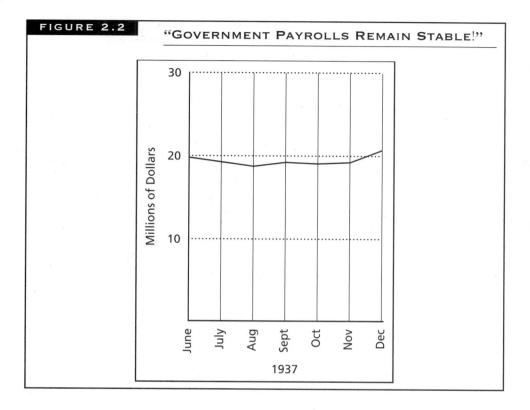

FIGURE 2.2   "GOVERNMENT PAYROLLS REMAIN STABLE!"

of the investigator to take precautions to see that the positive benefits of the discoveries clearly outweigh the potential negative applications of any research proposed.

Some people believe that decisions about the use of scientific results are the responsibility of all people. If this were the case, perhaps in an ideal world, there would be no need to limit inquiry into areas of research that have potentially harmful applications; rather, the applications themselves would be limited. (For instance, research on splitting atoms would still be funded, nuclear power plants would still be built, but nuclear weapons would not be developed.) At this point in history, unfortunately, that does not seem like a realistic or possible scenario, and some research programs are ended or denied funding because of potential negative applications of findings, regardless of the potential benefits.

Research that may have broad social consequences also raises special ethical concerns. For example, research on racial, ethnic, or class differences may have the effect of increasing tensions among racial, ethnic, or class groups, which could, in turn, have a number of negative consequences, such as increased prejudice, reduced self-esteem for individuals from minority groups, or even violence among groups.

A recent example of research that clearly has social consequences and raises questions about the dissemination of research results is the book *The Bell Curve*

(Herrnstein & Murray, 1994). The researchers reported that their data show a genetic component to intelligence and, further, that African-Americans have a lower average intelligence than whites because of their genetic heritage. This book has had a tremendous emotional impact on the American population, with some people dismissing it as scientifically flawed or overtly racist, and others embracing it as absolute truth and using it as evidence to support cutting educational programs, repealing affirmative action legislation, and so forth. The issue here is that the potential negative social consequences of such research should be weighed against the potential positive benefits to society. Many might argue that from an ethical standpoint, the book should not have been published. It is a serious dilemma whether such research should be conducted and provides an additional dilemma in the area of funding. Often such research is not funded because of its controversial subject matter. Is such a biased decision a threat to freedom of inquiry? Or should receipt of funding be tied to ethical issues?

A Final Note for New Researchers

Ethical decisions in research planning, performance, and application are of vital importance to psychologists. The ethical behavior of every individual scientist reflects on the field and on our society as a whole. For new researchers in psychology, many questions about ethical practice may arise. They should be sure to become familiar with the guidelines provided by the American Psychological Association, consult with their experienced colleagues, and think very seriously about alternative research methods whenever an ethical conflict arises. It will always be the ultimate responsibility of the researchers to see that their participants are treated well in research they design.

Exercises

1. Write a brief description of research you would like to see conducted with human participants on the potential harmful effects of crowding in grade-school classrooms. What ethical issues may arise in such a study?

2. What ethical dilemmas are involved in research on (a) domestic violence, (b) the suitability of homosexuals as adoptive parents, (c) the effects of a new psychoactive drug on rats, and (d) racial differences in intelligence?

3. In 1963, Stanley Milgram published his classic study on blind obedience, where participants thought they were administering electric shocks to another person (Milgram, 1963). Based on your understanding of that study, which ethical principle do you think would be of most concern to a modern IRB?

4. How could we study blind obedience (in which Milgram was interested) in a more ethically responsible way?

5. Some research poses dilemmas for a scientist who may not know how the research findings will be applied. Imagine that you are researching how people lie convincingly. Write a few paragraphs about the ethical issues involved in such research. After you have thought about it, would you continue to study this issue? Why or why not? Provide arguments related to the ethical issues raised in this chapter.

6. The following classic studies, described in every introductory psychology textbook, were all conducted before the APA's Ethical Principles for Research with Human Participants were established. Based on this chapter and your knowledge of these experiments, which ethical principles would be central if an IRB were considering a proposal for the study today?
   a. Zimbardo's study on the power of social roles where college men played the roles of prisoners and guards in a simulated prison (Haney, Banks, & Zimbardo, 1973).
   b. Rosenhan's study where normal people got themselves admitted to mental wards (Rosenhan, 1973).
   c. Asch's studies of conformity where participants heard several other people give an obviously wrong answer before they had to answer the question (Asch, 1955).

7. Suppose that you are the campaign manager for a presidential campaign and you want to use the following unemployment figures to make your candidate look good to the public:

	At Time of Last Election	Current
Population of Employable Adults	240,000,000	280,000,000
Unemployment Rate (%)	7.0	6.2
Number of Unemployed Adults	16,800,000	17,360,000

Suppose your candidate is the incumbent president who wants to win a second term in office. Could you present the unemployment data in a speech or in a graph that would make voters believe your candidate has been an effective president and deserves re-election? Now suppose that you are managing the campaign of the challenger. Could you present the unemployment data in a speech or in a graph that would make voters believe the current president has been bad for the economy? What ethical principles are at issue here?

CHAPTER

3

VARIABLES

■ ■ ■ ■ ■

In Chapter 1, you learned why psychologists adopted
approach for discovering the facts about human behavior.
the goals of psychology each involve understanding the var
learn the difference between variables and constants and h
another. Of particular importance are the criteria for establ
its effect.

Look for These Important Terms and Concepts

variable
constant
value (or score)
experimental control (holding variables
    constant)
quantitative versus qualitative variables
continuous versus discrete variables
correlation
spurious relationship

causal r
moderat
associati
    dering
    rationa
necessary
cause
confound

exactly alike, physically, psychologically, or behaviorally.
...sted in understanding the psychological and behavioral dif-
No two ind... ...w physical differences relate to psychological and behavioral
Psycholo... ...understand a behavior—such as aggression or altruism—psy-
feren... ...over why one individual is more aggressive or altruistic than
fu... ...and why an individual is more aggressive or altruistic in one
...her.

...want to: (1) be able to accurately *describe* the variation within and
...ls; (2) be able to *predict* variation in an individual's performance as a
...nges in other factors; (3) *control* an individual's performance (i.e., in-
..., acceptable behaviors and minimize negative, harmful behaviors) by
...changing the conditions that lead to negative behavior patterns, thus
...variation in performance; and (4) *explain* the variation within or among
...by identifying the causal mechanisms that underlie the behavior.

...rsus Constants: Definitions and Examples

...tired do you feel right now? How tall are you? (How tall were you on your 13th
...day?) How shy are you? How many brothers and sisters do you have? How
...ch money did you earn last year? What was your grade point average (GPA) last
...mester? How many bull's-eyes will you make if you throw 10 darts at a board from
...) feet away? Different people will, of course, give different answers to these ques-
...ions. In fact, for some of these questions, a person may give different answers at different times. Fatigue levels, height, shyness, number of siblings, annual income,
GPA, and dart-throwing prowess are all characteristics of people or behaviors that
can have *different values*, and, therefore, they are examples of **variables.** Other variables include situational or environmental conditions such as room temperature,
level of crowding, noise levels, and the amount of physical violence depicted in a
television program. The definition of a variable, then, is *any attribute or characteristic
of people, places, or events that takes on different values.* The opposite of a variable is a
constant: when each person, situation, or event has the *same value*, the attribute is
constant.

The **value** of an attribute refers to an individual's "**score**" on the characteristic.
(The terms *value* and *score* can be used interchangeably.) If you are 5 feet, 8 inches
tall and your roommate is 5 feet, 9 inches tall, then height is a variable, and 5'8" is
your *value* and 5'9" is your roommate's *value* on the variable height. If you have three
brothers and two sisters and your roommate only has one sister, then the number of
siblings is a variable, and your score is 5 while your roommate's score is 1. Your *value*
on the attribute of sex is either "male" or "female," and your score on the variable of
race is "Caucasian," "African-American," "Hispanic," "Asian," and so forth.

Some attributes will be *variable across individuals* yet will remain *constant within an
individual across time.* For example, sex and eye color vary across individuals because
one person may be male with blue eyes while other individuals may be female or
have brown eyes, but they do *not* vary across time within an individual: Males remain

male, and blue-eyed people remain blue-eyed. Likewise, childhood experiences d[i]from one adult to another, but because the past cannot be changed, individu[a]childhood experiences will remain constant across the rest of their lives. For exam[ple,]whether or not individuals attended daycare, the quality of the program, and how old they were when they began daycare are all examples of attributes that are *variable across* individuals but *constant within* individuals over time. In contrast, attributes of the environment may be constant across individuals yet be variable across time. For example, if the outside temperature reaches 95°F, then everyone who is outside is exposed to the same air temperature, but the temperature changes across time (falling at night, for example).

Other attributes will vary *both* across individuals *and* across time within an individual. For example, fatigue or motivational levels will differ from person to person as well as varying within the same person across time. That is, on some days you may feel bright-eyed and bushy-tailed and ready to tackle that term paper even if it is not due for another three weeks, but on other days you may be so tired that you do not want to get out of bed, much less lift a pencil. And some attributes are more variable at some points in time than at others. For example, during childhood, height changes over periods of months and years, but once the individual reaches adulthood, height remains the same until late adulthood (when conditions such as osteoporosis may result in a loss of bone mass so that the elderly adult is shorter than before).

As we have pointed out, the goals of the science of psychology are to describe, predict, control, and explain human behavior, which boil down to understanding the variation in behavior. For example, we would like to be able to answer questions such as: "Is shyness a stable trait across the lifespan?" or "What effect does repeated questioning have on preschool children's recall of events they have witnessed?" or "Do joint custody arrangements have negative effects on children's behavior?" Psychologists study the relationships among variables in an effort to identify patterns that may help us understand variability in human behavior, and in order to explore the relationships among particular variables, researchers may need to control other variables by holding them constant during the course of the research.

For example, let's imagine that there is evidence that children engage in more physical aggression on weekends than they do during the week. When trying to understand this relationship between aggression and time of the week, a researcher may generate a number of possible factors that may account for a difference between weekday and weekend aggression. For example, during the weekend, children may spend more time at home with their siblings while during the week, they spend more time at school with their peers, so perhaps children are more aggressive toward siblings than peers and the weekday/weekend difference is just an "accident." The only way to find out is to compare weekdays with weekends while the target of the aggression is being held constant, that is, to study aggression directed at *either* siblings *or* peers. Another possible factor is the fact that many children are from divorced families and spend weekends with one parent and weekdays with the other parent, so perhaps the increased aggression on weekends is related to changes in living arrangements for these children. The only way to find out is to compare the amount of aggression on weekends and weekdays when the children from divorced families are *with the same parent*. If more aggression still occurs on weekends than on weekdays, we can conclude that the difference is not due to changes in living arrangements.

Thus, research often involves *holding variables constant* during the study. This is referred to as exerting **experimental control** over relevant variables, and it is an important element of the scientific approach, which requires that we use systematic observation procedures. Systematic observations, by definition, are made under the *same* conditions using the *same* measurement procedures; otherwise, the reliability and validity of the observations are questionable. Therefore, good science inevitably involves holding potential variables constant, such as who is observed, where and when the observations are made, what is said to the participants, and how their responses are recorded. At the very least, a scientific study will hold the observation procedure constant; at most, studies will apply experimental control from beginning to end by limiting the selection of participants to specific subgroups (such as only "6-year-old boys who have two younger siblings and who come from divorced families with joint custody agreements"), giving them identical instructions, observing them in the same location (such as the researcher's laboratory), and then recording their performance on identical tasks.[1]

The extent to which relevant variables are held constant by the researcher is one of the major distinctions among the research methods we will discuss in this text, and it determines the conclusions that can be drawn from a study. As we will see in Chapter 7, the experimental method allows researchers to determine the *cause* of behavioral changes because—in principle, when the experiments are properly designed and conducted—*all* relevant variables are held constant. Quasi-experiments and correlational studies do *not* exert experimental control over every relevant variable and, hence, do not allow us to determine the cause of a change in behavior.

How to Identify Variables Versus Constants

Whether or not a particular characteristic is a variable or a constant depends on whether there are multiple values of the characteristic present in the data set. Suppose there is a group of 10 children in a classroom. Is their biological sex a variable or a constant within the group? Sex is a characteristic that can take on one of two values (or more if you consider some of the genetic abnormalities that have been identified, such as the XXY syndrome). If all of the children in the room are boys, then sex is a constant. If there are some boys and some girls in the room, then sex is a variable for the group. (Sex, obviously, is a constant across the lifetime of most individuals.)

---

[1] Note that as the degree of experimental control exerted over potential variables increases, the internal validity of the study also increases. However, this increase in internal validity often comes with a price: a *loss* of external validity (or generalizability). If the study were indeed limited to "6-year-old boys who have two younger siblings and who come from divorced families with joint custody agreements," then the findings of the study could not be generalized to girls or to boys of other ages or from other family constellations.

What other variables and constants can be presumed to exist in the group of 10 children? If they are all in the room at the same time, we might expect the room temperature and the amount of light to be constants. (Each child is experiencing the same temperature and degree of lighting).[2] The level of crowding, defined as the number of people in the room, would be another constant for the group. If all of the children are first-graders, then grade level is a constant. We would expect, however, that height and weight would be *variables* in the group, as would personality, intelligence, family size, parental income, and so forth: The children are probably not all alike on these dimensions.

For characteristics such as height, weight, and intelligence to be constants in a group of children, we would have to search very carefully to find a group of 10 children who have the same scores on these measures. We would have to reject many children because they would not have the values we were seeking. The process of selecting research participants on the basis of particular values or scores is very common (as another form of experimental control), as we will later see, because it helps keep us focused on the relevant factors in the relationships we study.

Types of Variables

There are two general categories of variables: quantitative and qualitative variables. A **quantitative variable** is characterized by *differences in amount*. That is, different values on a quantitative variable indicate a difference in amount of the underlying attribute. For instance, height is a quantitative variable because some people have *more* of it than others and because a score of 5'10" represents more height than a score of 5'7". Place-of-finish in a race is a quantitative variable because a score of 1 (first place) represents *less* time to complete the race (or faster pace) than a score of 2 (second place). The values of a quantitative variable will allow us to put the participants in order from most to least (or largest to smallest, and so forth). In contrast, **qualitative variables** are characterized by *differences in kind or category:* Different values represent different sorts or types rather than differences in amount. Religion is a qualitative variable because being Catholic is simply different from being Jewish, but Catholics do not have more or less religion than Jews. Nationality, race, sex, and political affiliation are other examples of qualitative variables. Being American is not more or less national than being Canadian or German; being Caucasian is not more or less racial than being African-American or Hispanic; being male is not more or less sexual than being female; and being Democratic is not more or less political than being Republican. In each case, the groups are simply different in kind from each other. Basically, qualitative variables are categorical in nature: We sort things into groups based on *what kind of* thing they are rather than how much of the attribute they have.

---

[2] This is based on the assumption that light and temperature are uniform throughout the room—which may not be the case if there is a wall of windows. Children seated near the windows may be exposed to greater amounts of natural light and possibly different temperatures, such as when the windows are drafty.

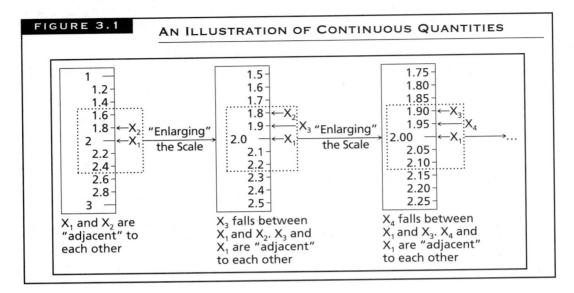

FIGURE 3.1 — AN ILLUSTRATION OF CONTINUOUS QUANTITIES

Quantitative variables come in two varieties: continuous and discrete variables. A **continuous variable** is one where it is theoretically possible to have a value that falls *anywhere* along the score scale—that is, any numerical value is possible. Figure 3-1 illustrates the point that continuous variables have an infinite number of possible values by showing that no matter how close together two objects may be in value, it is theoretically possible to have another value that falls between them as long as you have a measuring instrument with enough precision. Liquid amounts, length, time, and weight are all clear examples of continuous variables. Psychological and behavioral examples may include intelligence, aptitude, reasoning ability, attitudes toward social policies, maturity, aggressiveness, creativity, and so forth. For continuous variables, it is theoretically possible to find someone who is "a little more than" Johnny but "a little less than" Billy—no matter how close Johnny and Billy are to each other. Continuous variables should seem to flow from one value to another, as if we are pouring milk into a glass in slow motion: The exact amount of milk in the glass changes by infinitesimal amounts in each passing moment.

In contrast, **discrete variables** are made up of units or "chunks" that are detached and distinct from one another, and changes in value occur in whole units at a time. Therefore, discrete scales have a limited number of possible values, and every case will have one of these values. It is not possible to have a case that lies between two values on a discrete scale. For instance, how many pennies are you carrying right now? Your score on this variable will be a whole number (0, 1, 2, 3, etc.) because each penny is a separate, discrete item, and it is not possible for someone to have a fraction of a penny. (Therefore, if Johnny has two pennies and Billy has three pennies, we will *not* find someone who has a score somewhere between Johnny and Billy.) If we imagine pouring pennies into a jar, instead of a smooth, flowing change in quantity, we'll hear a distinct "clink" every time a penny lands in the jar: The number of pennies in the jar increases by whole numbers, not by tiny fractions. Other examples of discrete variables would include family size or number of children in a household, the number of spelling errors in a term paper, the number of words a speaker mispronounces during a presentation, and the number of turkeys donated to a food bank for Thanksgiving. In each of these examples, the attribute or behavior being recorded consists of distinctly separate (i.e., discrete) units or events that can be counted.

Qualitative variables that have a limited number of categories into which all individuals will fall (so no one lies between two of the categories) are also said to form discrete scales. For example, suppose marital status is measured by classifying people as "married," "divorced," "separated," "widowed," or "never married." Every person can be classified into one of these five categories, and, therefore, it forms a discrete scale. In contrast, if race is measured by classifying people as "Caucasian," "African-American," "Hispanic," "Asian-American," or "Native-American," people of mixed heritages would not easily fit into any of these categories. Therefore, race is a qualitative variable that may not form a discrete scale.

Types of Relationships

A limited number of possible relationships between two variables operating in nature have been identified.[3] Basically, two variables will either be unrelated or show a correlation.

No Relationship

The first possible relationship between two variables (X and Y) is that there is actually no relationship at all between them. When X and Y have no relationship, it means that we cannot learn anything about variable Y by looking at variable X. For example, if we told you that Chris has blue eyes, could you predict Chris's height with any reasonable degree of accuracy? Although you may get it right, you would be using pure guesswork. Suppose we listed 20 of our friends and gave you their eye colors—how often would you guess their heights correctly? Not very often because eye color is unrelated to height, and knowing a person's eye color provides no useful information about the individual's height.

Correlation

The second type of relationship is that X and Y are *systematically related* in such a way that as X changes, Y changes in a predictable manner. In other words, X and Y *covary*. This kind of systematic covariation is often called a **correlation** (and this relationship is measured by computing a *correlation coefficient*, which is described in

---

[3] By convention, variables are generically labeled with letters such as X, Y, and Z.

Chapter 8). When X and Y covary, it becomes possible to use our knowledge about X to make reasonably accurate predictions about Y. For example, suppose X is the amount of rainfall during the last week in June and Y is the number of lawnmowers in operation on the first sunny day in July. If you know X, could you reasonably predict Y? Yes, certainly to the point of predicting that if X = .01 inches, fewer lawnmowers would be at work than if X = 2.5 inches.

Correlations between two variables can result from three very different types of relationships, and the simple existence of a correlation between two variables can *never* tell us which type of relationship is present. The possibilities are spurious, causal, and moderator relationships.

Spurious Relationships   Variables X and Y are said to have a **spurious relationship** when the correlation between them is due to their separate, independent relationships with some third variable (Z). For instance, there is a correlation between the number of ice cream sales at a concession stand and the number of drownings at public beaches. The more ice cream sold, the more people drown. It is also the case that the more firefighters to respond to a fire, the more damage left behind when they return to the firehouse. These correlations allow us to make reasonably accurate predictions, but they do *not* indicate that buying ice cream *causes* people to drown and that firefighters *cause* damage.

Instead, these correlations exist because, in each example, there is a *third variable* that independently—but simultaneously—causes X and Y. Summer heat (Z) causes an increase in ice cream sales *and* an increase in swimming (which, in turn, increases the number of drownings), and the size or extent of a fire (Z) determines how many firefighters will be called to the scene: Larger fires cause more damage *and* cause fire chiefs to send for more firefighters.

Causal Relationships   Variables X and Y have a **causal relationship** if changes in X *produce* changes in Y (or vice versa). For example, eating large quantities of fatty foods can produce—that is, *cause*—a gain in weight, while reducing the intake of fatty foods can produce a weight loss. Such a causal relationship produces a correlation that allows us to predict Y from X: Someone who eats a lot of fatty foods can be expected to gain more weight than a person who eats few fatty foods.

Thus, correlations may be the result of either causal or spurious relationships. Unfortunately, the correlation coefficient itself does *not* tell us which type of relationship is at work. No matter how tempting it is to assume that a correlation provides evidence of causality, this conclusion is *never* warranted on the basis of a correlation alone. Consider, for example, the fact that there is a correlation between race and Intelligence (IQ), where African-Americans are lower in intelligence than Caucasians and Asian-Americans. Based on this fact alone, it is *not* legitimate to conclude that IQ is determined (i.e., caused) by race. An alternative—and equally legitimate—explanation for the correlation is that socioeconomic status (SES) is a third variable that creates a spurious relationship. For example, because African-Americans tend to be lower is SES, they tend to live in poorer school districts, so their education is of lower quality than the education available to middle- and upper-class Caucasians, which, in turn, may result in lower IQ scores for African-Americans. This alternative explanation sounds very reasonable and may easily convince you that the correlation between race and IQ is not necessarily due to a causal relationship between them. *But even if we could not think of a reasonable alternative explanation like this, we still could not interpret the correlation between race and IQ as proof of causality!* The most important thing to remember is that correlation does *not* imply causation; *any* correlation may be the result of an unidentified third variable Z that links X to Y in a spurious relationship.

Because the issue of causality is central to the research enterprise and our goal of explaining human behavior, we will return to it shortly.

Moderator Relationships   Another type of relationship that results in a correlation between X and Y is a **moderator relationship.** Moderator relationships are similar to spurious relationships in that Y is actually caused by a third variable, Z, but they differ from spurious relationships in that Z is *not* the cause of X. Instead, X moderates the relationship between Z and Y by suppressing or by strengthening Z's ability to cause Y. For example, despite a popular theory from the 1940s and 1950s, frustration (X) does not appear to be a direct cause of aggression (Y), yet they *are* correlated. In contrast, we know that observing a model behaving aggressively (Z) *does* cause imitative aggression (Y). What happens if the individual is experiencing frustration while observing the aggressive model? The imitative aggression may be *more intense* than if the individual were not frustrated. Thus, frustration (X) serves to moderate the effect of the aggressive model (Z) on imitative aggression (Y), and this may account for the correlation between X and Y. That is, because people in our society are constantly exposed to aggressive models, there will be a steady degree of imitative aggression. If frustration levels are then increased, the amount of aggression will also tend to increase in intensity. Thus, knowing the level of frustration helps us predict the amount of aggression, even though the frustration is not the actual causal mechanism.

As another example, consider the effect of a teacher's presence on a child who has just observed an aggressive model. Presumably, the teacher's presence would moderate the effect of the model by *suppressing* or minimizing the child's imitative aggression. Again, this moderator relationship would create a correlation between the presence of a teacher (X) and aggression (Y) while the direct cause of the child's aggression was the observation of the aggressive model (Z). The possibility that X is correlated with Y because it moderates the effect of Z on Y is yet another reason why correlations cannot be automatically interpreted as evidence for a causal relationship between two variables.

Causality

The ultimate goal of science is to be able to explain the phenomena of interest: Chemists try to explain chemical actions and reactions, physicists try to explain physical events, and psychologists try to explain human behaviors. Explanation requires identifying the *causes* of events and the mechanisms by which the causal event produces the effect. For scientists to conclude that X causes Y, we must meet the following criteria:

1. There must be a systematic covariation (a correlation or **association**) between X and Y such that changes in X are predictably associated with changes in Y. (Certainly, if X causes Y, then a change in X will systematically result in changes in Y.)

2. There must be a **"time priority"** or **temporal ordering** of X and Y such that the cause (X) precedes the effect (Y). For example, if air temperatures of 32°F or below cause water to freeze, then the air temperature should fall to 32°F *before* freezing begins. If we noticed water freezing before the air temperature dropped to 32°, we would conclude that the air temperature is not the cause of the freezing.

3. The relationship between X and Y must be **nonspurious** (such that the covariation between them is *not* due to a third variable that is simultaneously but independently causing both X and Y). To establish that a relationship is nonspurious, a researcher must conduct an *experiment*. The experimental method is the *only* research method that controls all possible third variables and prevents them from creating a spurious relationship between X and Y. (The common research methods—and the conclusions we can draw from them—are discussed in detail in later chapters.)

Additionally, it is desirable to be able to provide some **rationale** for the causal relationship: Is there a theoretical justification for the relationship? Can we postulate an underlying mechanism that makes sense in the context of our current knowledge? In the absence of a rationale that makes sense, we will often remain skeptical of claims that X has been proven to cause Y. For example, the conclusion that smoking causes lung cancer has become widely accepted despite the fact that true experiments have been conducted only with animals such as rats and dogs, not with humans. This is, in part, because the physiological mechanisms known to result in malignant cells are consistent with smoking, and cell physiology is similar across most species of mammals (including rats and humans).

In contrast, when Francine Shapiro (1995) claimed that having patients rapidly moving their eyes back and forth causes a reduction in post-traumatic stress disorder (PTSD) symptoms, her claim was met with great skepticism because she could not convincingly describe a mechanism—either neurological or psychological—that could explain why rapid eye movements would have any effect on PTSD symptoms. Many psychologists will remain doubtful until a reasonable mechanism is identified and tested experimentally.

Necessary, Sufficient, and Contributory Causes

Three types of causal relationships may exist between variables. The first of these is called a **necessary cause** because X (the causal condition) *must be present* for Y (the effect) to occur. Clouds (X), for example, are necessary for rain (Y) to fall; if there are no clouds, rain simply cannot happen.

Although necessary for rain, clouds are not enough to ensure that rain will fall. Other conditions must also be present in order to cause rain. Clouds, therefore, do *not* fit into the second category of causes, known as **sufficient causes.** A sufficient cause is one that, by itself, is enough to produce Y. For example, a dose of aspirin (X) is sufficient to reduce pain; no other remedies have to be used in conjunction with aspirin to produce the pain relief (Y).[4]

The third type of causal relationship—known as **contributory cause**—is where X is neither necessary nor sufficient to produce Y, but it makes Y *more likely to occur.* Familiar examples of contributory causal relationships include smoking (X_1) and lung cancer (Y_1) and drunk driving (X_2) and car accidents (Y_2). Almost everyone knows a heavy smoker who lived cancer-free to some ripe old age. Everyone also knows someone who arrived home safely after driving while intoxicated. Smoking, therefore, is apparently *not sufficient* to cause lung cancer, and driving while intoxicated is *not sufficient* to cause an accident.

Furthermore, smoking is *not necessary* for lung cancer, either, as evidenced by the existence of lung cancer victims who never smoked a day in their lives. And intoxication is *not necessary* for accidents, either. But people who smoke are at much higher risk of lung cancer than are nonsmokers, and drunk drivers are at a much higher risk of an accident than sober drivers because smoking and drunk driving are contributory causes.

Simple Versus Multiple Causation

In simple causation, whenever the causal event (X) occurs, the effect (Y) always follows. Furthermore, Y never occurs unless X is present. In other words, a simple causal relationship exists when X is the *one and only* cause of Y. In such a relationship, X is said to be necessary *and* sufficient to cause Y: "necessary" because nothing else will cause Y; "sufficient" because X does not need any help in causing Y. For instance, sexual reproduction is caused by the fertilization of an egg cell by a sperm cell. Reproduction cannot occur without fertilization, so the sperm cell is necessary, and one sperm cell uniting with the egg is sufficient for reproduction.

Such simple causal relationships are quite uncommon in the behavioral and social sciences. Instead, human behavior, both individually and collectively, most often has *multiple causes:* Any number of different causes may be sufficient to produce a particular effect. For example, a low grade on a test may be the result of any number of factors, including not attending lectures, not studying, illness, misreading the problems, unfair test questions, or inaccurate scoring. None of these alone is necessary for a low grade, but any of them (alone or in combination) is sufficient to cause a low test grade.

---

[4] Because Tylenol and Advil can *also* produce pain relief, aspirin is not a necessary cause; aspirin, Tylenol, and Advil are each sufficient, but none of them is necessary to reduce pain.

Researchers interested in identifying the causes of a particular multiply determined phenomenon will find it helpful to study the separate possible causes in isolation or only a few at a time. To determine whether lack of attendance is a cause of low test grades, the researcher will need to conduct an experiment where all other possible causes of low grades are experimentally controlled (or held constant). If Francine Shapiro, for instance, wants to test the hypothesis that rapid eye movements can produce a reduction in PTSD symptoms, she will need to compare people who use rapid eye movements with those who do not, and she will have to ensure that these two groups of people are equal on all other possible causes of reduced PTSD symptoms (such as the nature of the traumatic event, the amounts and types of other therapies being received, the severity of the symptoms at the start, and the length of time since the trauma).

Failing to control for the other causal factors by holding them constant (and thus allowing two or more possible causal factors to operate at the same time) creates what is called a **confound.** By definition, a study is confounded whenever there are two or more possible explanations for the observed behaviors. That is, whenever there are two or more potential causal mechanisms operating in the same study, there is a confound. Confounded studies cannot be interpreted because there are at least three possible outcomes, but there is no way to know which one has actually occurred. The three possibilities are: (1) A causal relationship is correctly identified; (2) a spurious relationship between X and Y is mistaken for a causal relationship because the actual causal variable (Z) was not controlled; and (3) a causal relationship between X and Y is overlooked because the effect of X was canceled out by another, uncontrolled causal mechanism (Z) that had the opposite effect on Y (thus *masking* X's effect on Y). Let's consider some examples.

As an example of the second potential outcome, let's return to the example of the relationship between race and IQ. A comparison between average Caucasians and average African-Americans will indicate that Caucasians have higher IQs than African-Americans. However, these results do not prove that the difference in IQ is caused by the difference in race because the relationship may be spurious: The difference in IQ scores may actually be caused by the fact that Caucasians tend to come from higher socioeconomic environments than African-Americans, and the difference in socioeconomic status (SES) may cause the difference in IQ scores. Thus, the difference in SES between the two racial groups is a potential confound: It provides an alternative explanation for the difference in IQ. Before we can determine whether race has a causal relationship with IQ, this potential confound must be eliminated by *holding SES constant through experimental control* and comparing Caucasians and African-Americans who come from the *same SES* background. (It is important to note that SES is not the only potential confound in a comparison between the races, so even if we control SES, we would still be faced with a potentially spurious relationship. Before we can draw causal conclusions, we need to be able to control *all possible* confounding factors, and only the experimental method can do so. These issues are discussed in detail in Chapter 7.)

To illustrate the possible *masking effects* of confounding variables (the third potential outcome), consider a case where a teacher wanted to see whether extra study time improved test performance, so she compared the grades of students who took the test on schedule with those of students who took a make-up exam the following day. (Luckily, the make-up exam was identical to the original test—otherwise, there would be another confound in the study.) The teacher found that the grades for the two groups of students were just about the same. It appeared that extra time to prepare had no beneficial effects on performance, but the teacher did not take into account that the students taking the make-up exam did so because they were ill, and ill students may not study as effectively as healthy students. That is, extra time to prepare may, in fact, cause an improvement in performance, but illness may cause a decrease in performance, and the two factors would have canceled each other out in this study because they were operating simultaneously. Thus, the illness of the students in the make-up group constitutes a confound that may have masked the effect of extra study time on performance. The study needs to be repeated where all of the students are equally healthy. We discuss confounds—and how to handle them—in greater detail later in the book.

Exercises

1. A sports medicine researcher is interested in the effectiveness of a new exercise machine that claims to be better at reducing some types of back pain than traditional flexibility exercises. The researcher recruited participants suffering from either arthritis in the back or ruptured discs in the spine and assigned them at random to either the new machine or a flexibility exercise regime. After four weeks, the participants were asked to indicate the level of pain they were still experiencing on a 20-point scale (where 1 = no pain at all and 20 = constant, excruciating pain). This study involved three separate variables: type of back pain (arthritis versus ruptured disc), type of exercise (machine versus flexibility exercises), and amount of pain. Are these variables qualitative or quantitative? Are they continuous or discrete? Explain your answers.

2. Suppose the researcher described above found that the arthritic participants who used the new exercise machine for four weeks were experiencing very little pain while the arthritic participants who had been doing flexibility exercises for four weeks were still experiencing a lot of intense pain. Do you think it would be reasonable to conclude that the new exercise machine had *caused* a decrease in arthritic pain? If so, which type of causal relationship do you think it would be (necessary, sufficient, or contributory)? Explain your reasoning.

3. An economist was interested in the correlation between the yearly average price of tea in China (measured in U.S. currency to the nearest penny) and

the annual amount of rainfall in Liechtenstein (measured to the 1/100th of an inch). The economist collected data on these two variables for the past 30 years and found that when there was a lot of rainfall in Liechtenstein, the price of tea in China was very low, but when there was little rain in Liechtenstein, the price of tea in China was high. What kind of relationship do you think this economist has identified (spurious versus causal versus moderator)? Explain your reasoning.

For each of the research scenarios below: (a) Identify the *variables* of interest to the researcher; (b) make up *values* (or *scores*) for two hypothetical research participants (call them "Chris" and "Pat"); and (c) identify any *constants* (or experimentally controlled variables) that are specified in the scenario.

4. A department chairperson measured the relationship between a teacher's effectiveness and his/her teaching experience. Effectiveness was measured using the median score the professor received on the evaluation forms completed by students, where 1 = very low effectiveness and 7 = very high effectiveness. Experience was measured as the number of semesters the professor had been teaching college-level courses.

5. A sociologist is studying drug abuse among teenagers. In one study, she asked high school juniors to indicate their willingness to try crack cocaine using a 4-point rating scale. The researcher then asked the students' parents to report their annual income as they had reported to the IRS the previous April.

6. After three weeks of basic training, Marine recruits were asked to estimate the height (in feet and inches) of several officers on base. The researcher wanted to see whether the officers' rank (e.g., captain, major, general, etc.) correlated with the recruits' estimates of the officers' heights.

7. Four-year-old children were asked to predict how many items in an array they would be able to remember after the items were removed from sight. Then their memory for the array of items was actually tested, and the number of items they correctly recalled was recorded and compared with their predictions.

8. A researcher wants to test the hypothesis that training in Freudian psychoanalytic dream analysis correlates with an art therapist's tendency to find sexual symbols in a client's drawings. A sample of art therapists was asked to indicate the number of courses they took on Freud's theory of dreams. Then they were given a case study and a series of drawings, and they were asked to prepare an interpretation of the artwork. The researcher then counted the number of sexual symbols identified by each art therapist.

9. Based on interviews with parents, a researcher identified a group of preschool children who frequently watched "Mr. Rogers" on television and a group who never watched that program. The researcher then asked the

preschool teacher to rank the children on their helpfulness toward others. The researcher wanted to find out whether children who watch "Mr. Rogers" frequently are more helpful than children who do not watch the program.

CHAPTER

4

MEASURING VARIABLES

■ ■ ■ ■ ■ ■

In this chapter, you will learn about five techniques for gathering data about human behavior and the central elements of the measurement process. Procedures for assessing the reliability and validity of the measurements are discussed, and four different scales (or levels) of measurement are defined.

Look for These Important Terms and Concepts

data set
reactivity
multimethod approach
measurement
operational definitions and
    operationalizing concepts
test-retest reliability
alternate forms reliability
internal consistency
split-half reliability
inter-rater reliablity (or agreement)

construct validity
face validity
content validity
criterion validity
concurrent validity and predictive
    validity
levels (or scales) of measurement
nominal scales
ordinal scales
interval scales
ratio scales

Before Reading This Chapter, You May Wish to Review

Chapter 1:
- systematic observations
- reliability and validity
- operational definitions
- internal and external validity
- the basic steps in the research process

Chapter 3:
- variables
- values (or scores)
- quantitative versus qualitative variables

To scientifically establish the existence of a systematic relationship between two (or more) variables, researchers must conduct systematic observations and create a permanent record of the variations in the values of X and Y at different points of time or across different individuals or settings. In other words, the researcher must be able to *observe and measure* X and Y and record those measurements. The permanent record of the measurements is called the **data set,** so the observational step in the research process is often referred to as gathering the data.

Data-Gathering Techniques

There are several different data-gathering techniques, each with its own advantages and limitations. The specific conditions under which data are gathered are very important because the conditions determine whether or not causal relationships can be drawn. This issue will be discussed in more detail in Chapter 7, but for now, let's briefly consider the data-gathering strategies most frequently employed by psychologists.

Behavioral Observations

As the name implies, behavioral observation techniques involve watching people and recording their behavior. For example, as part of a diagnostic screening for attention deficit disorder, a school psychologist may visit a classroom and measure how much time a child spends on- and off-task. Alternatively, a video camera could be installed in the classroom to record the child's behavior and the school psychologist could view the tape later in the day and measure the time spent on- and off-task. In both cases, the child's behavior is being *directly* recorded *as it happens*. A substantial proportion of psychological research uses direct observation, and the issues involved are discussed in more depth throughout this text. At this point, however, you should appreciate that the primary advantage of such direct behavioral observations is that there can be little doubt that the behavior actually took place. The major limitation, however, is that many behaviors are difficult or impossible to observe directly, either because they are behaviors performed in private (so that the presence of the researcher suppresses them, such as criminal or socially taboo behaviors) or because they are subjective, mental events (such as thoughts or feelings). Similarly, behaviors that tend to be very infrequent are difficult for researchers to record directly because the researchers may not be able to prolong the observations over long periods of time.

Self-Reports

As an alternative to direct observation, where the researchers personally witness and record the behaviors of interest, they may ask the participants to describe their own behavior. These self-reports may be obtained during face-to-face *interviews,* or the participants may complete a paper-and-pencil *questionnaire* or *survey.* The researcher typically poses a number of questions about behavior that ask for either *after-the-fact* reports about the participants' past or *before-the-fact* reports of what they believe they would do in some hypothetical future situation. The self-report technique is particularly useful in studying behaviors that are difficult to observe directly because they are either subjective in nature (such as attitudes, perceptions, beliefs, and feelings) or too personal or private (e.g., a person's sexual activity).

A major problem with self-report procedures, of course, is the slippage between the reported behavior and the actual behavior. Responses will be inaccurate, for instance, if the person lacks the necessary self-awareness to answer the questions accurately (e.g., "During the past 5 minutes of conversation, how many times did you interrupt your own sentence and start a new one?"). Responses will also be inaccurate if the person misinterprets the question or simply lies to the researcher. Suppose, for example, that a husband and wife were asked to report the frequency of their intimate sexual contacts during the past year: Would their responses be similar? Not necessarily. Substantial differences between the couple's responses could arise in several ways, such as: (a) one of them may include extramarital sexual activity, or (b) they may have different interpretations of the meaning of "intimate sexual contact" (different operational definitions). However, if we are to set aside those possibilities and assume we have a faithful monogamous married couple who have the same activities in mind, it would still not be uncommon to find a difference in their answers. The same event can have different meaning for (or impact on) different individuals, which may alter their reports about that event. For example, sexual activities between the married couple may be more meaningful and, therefore, more memorable for one spouse than the other. This could lead to a discrepancy in the couple's reports about the frequency of sexual contact. Another possibility is that some people may feel uncomfortable recalling or discussing behaviors they feel are socially undesirable or socially unacceptable, and if the husband and wife have different views about what is socially acceptable and what is not, it could turn out that one spouse does not report all of the sexual activities that took place.

Social desirability can lead to outright lies on self-report instruments, as has been seen in recent political polls. A number of voter polls have resulted in an overestimation of the number of votes cast for African-American or other minority candidates. Both in pre-election polls, where the participants are reporting what they will do when they vote at some time in the future, and in exit polls, where voters are asked as they leave the voting area who they just voted for, the proportion of voters indicating they will (or did) vote for the minority candidates is much higher than the actual proportion of votes the minority candidate receives. Apparently, some voters will say they are voting for the minority candidate to keep from appearing to be prejudiced. They give what they think may be the more socially acceptable answer, even though it is not an accurate reflection of their actual behavior. This is an example of **reactivity,** which is a change in behavior caused by the knowledge that someone is watching. Unfortunately, in most self-report situations, the researcher is not in a position to know the magnitude of the discrepancy between self-reports and actual behavior (unlike the election situation, where actual voting proportions become a matter of public record). And even if the amount of this slippage in reporting can be determined, one would rarely be in a position to know *which* individuals were giving accurate self-reports and which were giving inaccurate reports.

Behavioral Ratings

Another technique for gathering data about a person's behavior is to ask people who spend a lot of time with the individual—such as parents, teachers, and peers—to complete a rating scale or behavioral checklist that focuses on specific behaviors or characteristics. For instance, researchers may ask Jimmy's classmates to indicate how much they like him in order to measure Jimmy's popularity, or the researcher may ask Jimmy's teacher to complete the *Devereux Behavior Rating Scale* (Naglieri, LeBuffe, & Pfeiffer, 1993) in order to find out how often Jimmy engages in inappropriate behaviors or displays inappropriate feelings (such as annoying others, being disruptive in class, appearing anxious around others, and so forth).[1] The primary advantage of these behavioral rating techniques is their efficiency: The researchers can gather a tremendous amount of information in a very short period of time. The major limitations, like those of self-report surveys, include the possibility that the researchers and the respondents do not have the same definitions in mind (for example, the researcher who asks a teacher how often a child engages in "helping behavior" may be interested only in helping behavior directed toward other children, while a teacher may include helpfulness directed toward herself). And even if the respondents understand the terms properly, the researcher cannot be certain that the ratings are accurate. For example, Michael's reputation, based on his past behavior, might lead people to describe him in ways that are more congruent with his reputation than with his more recent behavior patterns. Thus, Michael, the "bully," might be rated as highly aggressive even when he has not engaged in any aggressive actions in months. As is the case with self-reports, researchers who use behavior ratings are usually unable to determine exactly which ratings are accurate and which are not.

Archival Records

Another technique for gathering data is to examine the archives or the written historical record. Data have been collected by government agencies, schools, and research organizations (both public and private), and many of these data sets are available to researchers. For example, your birth certificate contains information about your birthweight, your elementary school has your report cards on file, the Motor Vehicle Bureau has a record of your traffic citations, and so forth. The National Education Longitudinal Study (NELS) collected data from a national sample of 24,599 eighth-graders and their families and then gathered follow-up data

---

[1] The Devereux Behavior Rating Scale is only one example of many behavior rating scales that have been published. Standardized rating scales have been developed that assess a wide variety of behaviors for a wide range of ages. Researchers can look at these instruments and select the one that is most suitable to the purposes of the study, or they can design their own rating scale that asks about the behaviors of particular interest to them.

from those same families when the children were in 10th and 12th grades. This massive data set is available to researchers who are interested in studying academic achievement. Thus, from archival records such as these, a researcher could find out whether people who weighed more than 8 pounds at birth receive more speeding tickets in their first year of driving than people who were under 8 pounds, or whether eighth-graders whose parents say they want their children to go to college do better academically during 12th grade than eighth-graders whose parents do not say they want their children to go to college.

Research projects that take advantage of archival data sets are relatively quick to complete because they do not require any contact between the researcher and the individuals under study; the researcher needs only to retrieve the data for individuals by using whatever identifying label was used in each of the archives (such as a social security number, a full name and birth date, or the I.D. number assigned by the researcher). Thus, these studies involve a *nonreactive* measurement. There are, however, important limitations to the archival approach. Among the disadvantages is the fact that these data sets were typically gathered for purposes other than those the researcher has in mind. As a result, it may be that the instrument used to create this data set asked a slightly different question than the one the researcher would ask if she were doing the study "from scratch." For example, the researcher may be interested in the parents' annual income as an indicator of family social status, but the existing data set may not contain this information. In such a case, the researcher may need to alter the operational definition of the concept (e.g., use the occupations of the parents as a rough index of social status) or alter the question of interest to conform to measures taken in the existing data. Another disadvantage is that the researcher often cannot be certain of the extent to which any sampling biases occurred. For example, in using police records to compare rates of various crimes as a function of climate and region of the country, there is no way to assure that crimes were defined the same way across locations, nor that the intensity of the investigations of certain criminal activities was the same. What looks like regional variation in the commission of certain crimes might actually be regional variation in the choice by the police departments to pursue such convictions.

Physical Trace Approach

The last data-gathering technique that we will introduce is called physical trace research. This approach involves recording the physical evidence that behavior leaves behind. For example, drinking soda leaves bottles, cans, or cups; smoking cigarettes leaves cigarette butts; and pro-recycling attitudes result in less recyclable material in the trash can. Like archival research, physical trace research is *nonreactive* because it takes place after the person has left. Some physical traces are in the form of accumulating material (such as the amount of litter or the number of noseprints on the glass cage at a zoo, which may indicate the popularity of particular locations or animal exhibits). These are referred to as *accretion measures*. Other physical traces are found in the wear-and-tear on materials in the environment (such as creases in the binding of a book or the wear on a lawn, which may indicate how often the book is used and how much foot traffic has occurred along a particular route). These are known as *erosion measures.* While both accretion and erosion are the by-products of behavior, a third type of physical trace evidence is the purposeful creation or *product* of the behavior (such as the number of letters an advice columnist receives or the doodles drawn on placemats). Other physical traces do not easily fit into any of these categories. For example, the setting on a clock or watch is a physical trace that is neither a product nor the result of accretion or erosion, yet it can be informative. Levine, West, and Reis (1980) used the settings of public clocks and personal watches as a way to assess attitudes about punctuality and found that Brazilian clocks and watches tended to be less accurate than American timepieces. The hypothesis that Brazilians are less concerned about punctuality than Americans was further supported by the finding that Brazilians reported being late to appointments more often (and expressed less regret at their tardiness) than Americans.

The major limitation of physical trace research is that not all trace materials are equally durable, so comparisons between traces may not be valid. For example, an examination of the carpeting may lead us to believe that a museum exhibit on expressionism is more popular than the exhibit on impressionism, but it is possible that the impressionism room had a higher-quality carpet than the other room and, therefore, showed less wear and tear. Researchers who use the physical trace approach should also try to gather other types of evidence to confirm their findings—that is, it is recommended that they adopt a **multimethod approach.** Direct observations, for example, could confirm that more people visit the expressionism exhibit than the impressionism exhibit. Or, as Levine and colleagues (1980) found, self-report measures of attitudes about punctuality were consistent with the differences in clock setting.

Measurement

These data-gathering techniques allow us to observe (directly or indirectly) the behaviors of interest to the study, and these observations need to be recorded in a systematic manner. **Measurement** is defined as *the use of rules (or standardized procedures) to assign values to the properties or characteristics of individuals, objects, or events.* The values assigned during the measurement process may be numerical or symbolic, and they are usually referred to as *scores.* Numerical scores are typically used when we are measuring quantitative variables such as intelligence, income, or aggressiveness. Symbolic scores serve as labels or category names for values on qualitative variables, such as "M" for male and "F" for female. (Numbers may also be used with qualitative variables—such as "1" is male and "2" is female—but they do not have any numerical properties; they serve only as symbols for the category.) Ideally, a measurement procedure will consistently (or reliably) assign the same score to everyone with the same value on the variable. For example, if two 10-year-old children weigh exactly the same amount, the measurement device needs to give them the same weight score.

What about individuals with very similar but not exactly equal weights, such as one 10-year-old child weighing only half an ounce more than another child?

Different measurement devices will have different levels of precision, so some devices *will* assign different scores to these children (e.g., 80 pounds, 13 ounces versus 80 pounds, 13.5 ounces), while other devices will "ignore" such a small difference and assign the children the same score. (In fact, the electronic, digital scales commonly used today would round the scores to the nearest pound and give both of these children weight scores of 81 pounds.)

Before measurement can begin, researchers must determine exactly what it is they want to record. Then they must choose a measurement device or procedure that measures the X and Y of interest. This process of *defining the variables* is crucial because the results of a study can tell us only about the relationship between the variables actually measured in the study. Common sense should tell you that if we fail to measure the right things or if we fail to measure them the right way, we will be unable to answer the right questions.

Obviously, if a researcher is studying exercise and weight loss, she needs to measure weight in such a way that changes in weight over time can be recorded. One obvious measurement device is a scale that measures weight in pounds. But there are alternative ways of measuring (and defining) weight, including measuring waist size (in inches or clothes sizes) or body fat concentrations. These three concepts of weight are not identical, so the relationship between exercise and these different measures of weight might be quite different, at least at the start. For example, it is quite common for a person to gain weight (in pounds) after beginning a new exercise regimen because muscle tissue is heavier than fat tissue, but simultaneously, the waist size and body fat may be decreasing.

If the simple concept of body weight can be defined in at least three different ways, what about the complex, hard-to-define concepts involved in human psychological and behavioral functioning, such as aggression, intelligence, and emotion? In cases like these, researchers must **operationalize** the concept or variable in such a way that it can be measured or identified (Vogt, 1993) and select an appropriate measurement procedure or device. Then, in what may seem like an odd twist of logic, the measurement device itself provides (even *becomes*) the definition of the variable for that study. This is known as an **operational definition**. Formally, the term *operational definition* has two related meanings. First, an operational definition is a description of the way researchers will observe and measure a variable, and second, an operational definition establishes criteria for identifying or creating the research conditions (Vogt, 1993).

Operational Definitions: Measuring Variables

Let's start with an example. Human intelligence is often operationally defined as the standard score an individual achieves on a particular IQ test. What about intelligence in rats? If a researcher wants to study rat intelligence, he first needs to operationalize the concept and develop a measurement procedure. The researcher must ask: "What would seem to be a reasonably direct indicator of intelligence in a rat?" One answer may be, for example, speed of learning; it may make sense to say that smart rats can learn faster than stupid rats. Now the researcher must ask: "How can I measure speed of learning?" and, even before that, "What is being learned?" The researcher may choose to use maze-learning as the task, where a food reward is found at the end of the maze, and speed of learning may then be operationally defined as *the number of trials it takes the rat to run the maze twice in a row without making any turning errors.* The rats that take only a few trials to master the maze will be considered more intelligent than the rats who take a lot of trials to learn the maze, but we must always remember how the researcher operationally defined intelligence and that this definition was actually quite limited in scope.

How will the researcher know when learning has occurred in the rats? The operational definition in the example above establishes the criterion of two consecutive error-free runs of the maze as the indicator that the learning process is complete. Thus, this definition of intelligence in rats performs two functions of operational definitions: It specifies how the researcher is to measure learning (by counting trials on a maze-learning task), and it provides the criterion for knowing when the learning has occurred (two consecutive error-free trials).

Another researcher studying intelligence in rats may have also selected speed of learning as a direct indicator of intelligence but may have chosen a different task, such as the number of trials required before a rat avoids drinking a sweet-tasting fluid that causes nausea. This study utilizes a different operational definition of speed of learning and, hence, uses a different definition of intelligence. Yet another researcher may not choose to use speed of learning at all as an indicator of intelligence but may instead look at the amount of time rats spend exploring a novel environment (expecting that smart rats will spend more time exploring).

Would these three different measures of intelligence give the same results if they were all used with the same group of rats? Would the rat that learns the maze fastest also learn to avoid the nauseating drink soonest and spend the most time exploring in a novel environment? Quite possibly, no. Each of these measurement procedures uses a different definition of intelligence, and, therefore, they are probably measuring at least slightly different things. Because a change in a measurement procedure means a change in the operational definition of the variable, researchers must be extraordinarily concerned with selecting operational definitions and measurement procedures that actually measure what they intend to study. When a measurement device does, in fact, measure what it is intended to measure, the device is considered valid, and because valid measurements are necessary for both the internal and external validity of the study, appropriate operational definitions are also essential. (You may recall from Chapter 1 that internal validity is the extent to which a study adequately addresses its research question, and external validity is the extent to which the findings of a study can be generalized to other people, places, and times.)

Operational Definitions: Establishing Research Conditions

Suppose a team of neuropsychologists has hypothesized that environmental stimulation causes increased growth in the brain, which results in higher intelligence. To test this hypothesis, the researchers would need to compare the intelligence of rats who have been raised in unstimulating, dull environments with the intelligence of rats who have been raised in highly stimulating, enriched environments. Not only does the team need to operationally define intelligence and develop a procedure to measure it, the team needs to create the experimental conditions it wishes to compare. What is an "unstimulating, dull" environment? What constitutes a "highly stimulating, enriched" environment? The team of researchers must generate precise definitions of these conditions and then raise some rats in each of the two conditions.

For example, the researchers may operationally define a "dull" environment as a $16'' \times 24''$ cage that contains only a food tray and a water dispenser and is kept in a room with dim lighting and "white noise" played constantly at 30 decibels (dB). They may further specify that rats in the "unstimulating" condition are not to be handled or talked to by their human caretakers. Thus, they have limited the visual, auditory, tactile, and motor stimulation available to the rats in the "dull" environment condition. The research team may then operationally define an "enriched" environment as one where the cage is a spacious $48'' \times 60''$ and contains a "jungle gym" (for climbing and jumping) and a maze. Mobiles are suspended over the cage to provide visual stimulation, and a different one is hung every six hours. The light level in the room ranges from dim to bright and changes every 45 minutes. Music and tapes of various environmental sounds are played throughout the day at decibel levels ranging from 25dB to 50dB, and the rats are handled and talked to by their caretakers for 10 minutes every six hours.

From this example you should see that operationally defining the experimental conditions of a study requires the researcher to make very detailed decisions about the research procedures. For example, the researcher needs to ask questions such as: "Just how loud should the white noise be in the 'dull' environment condition?," "How often should the rats in the 'stimulating' environment be handled?," and "How complex should the maze in the 'stimulating' cage be?" Once these decisions are made and put into practice in a study, *they determine what the study is really about.* Imagine, for example, that our "very stimulating, enriched" environment was actually overstimulating for rats, which resulted in a withdrawal response. The results of the study may indicate no difference in intelligence between the two groups of rats, but these results *may not be relevant* to the original hypothesis, which stated that increased stimulation will lead to increased brain growth. Increased stimulation is not the same thing as overstimulation, so if our "enriched" environment is actually overstimulating, the experiment would have failed to test its own hypothesis. That is, the study would lack internal validity.

In this example, the researchers needed to decide how they would raise the rats in order to compare two different conditions. This is an example of an *experimental manipulation* of the conditions. Some research, however, does not involve experimental manipulations but instead makes comparisons between different types of participants, such as introverts versus extraverts, or conservatives versus liberals, or depressed versus nondepressed patients. In these studies, the researchers must operationally define the categories to be compared. That is, they must precisely specify how they will determine which individuals belong in which groups. In some cases, standardized tests can be used to categorize participants. For example, to conduct a study comparing the parenting styles of parents whose intelligence is below average,

average, and above average, we could administer the Wechsler Adult Intelligence Scale (WAIS). The WAIS is designed so that individuals with average intelligence receive an IQ score of 100. Therefore, for the purposes of our study on parenting styles, we could define "below-average intelligence" to be IQ scores of 85 or less and "above-average intelligence" to be IQ scores of 115 or above. "Average" intelligence would then be defined as IQ scores from 86 to 114. As an operational definition, this is quite straightforward, and because it is based on a widely accepted standardized test, we will not need to convince others that it is a valid definition.

In contrast, suppose we wanted to compare the parenting styles of adults who had secure attachments to their own parents during their infancy with adults who had insecure attachments with their parents. No standard test is available that measures an adult's attachment history, so we would need to generate our own operational definition based on our expert knowledge about the topic and our theories of development. First we would need to decide what differences there *should be* (theoretically) between adults who were securely attached to their parents and adults who were insecurely attached, and then we would need to develop a test to measure those differences so that we could categorize our participants into the two research groups.[2] Then we could do our study comparing their parenting styles. We would need to be extremely cautious in interpreting the results of the study, however, until the validity of our operational definitions could be adequately assessed.

Reliability and Validity

As discussed in Chapter 1, the scientific method relies on observations that are both reliable and valid. Because measurement is the process by which our observations are converted into numeric form, measurements must also be reliable and valid.

Reliability

If a measurement device or procedure *consistently assigns the same score to individuals or objects with equal values,* the device is considered reliable. Unreliable measurement devices pose serious problems for researchers: If two different scores are assigned to the same object (when there has been no change in value), which score is the "correct" one, or are they both wrong? Researchers must establish the reliability of their measurement devices in order to be certain that they are obtaining a systematic and consistent record of the variation in X and Y; otherwise, the relationship between X and Y cannot be determined.

---

[2] For instance, our theory may predict that securely attached children will grow up into adults who are able to maintain stable, positive relationships with lots of different people while insecurely attached children will grow up into adults whose relationships with others are stormy and short-lived, so that they tend to have few close friends. Therefore, we could operationally define adults with "secure attachment" histories to be those adults who "have at least six close friends with whom they have remained close for at least five years," and so forth. Whether or not this is a valid operational definition depends upon both the accuracy of the theory's prediction of differences in close relationships *and* on our operational definition of "lots of stable friendships."

One common procedure used to assess reliability involves using the measurement device to measure the exact same individual or object on two separate occasions. This is called **test-retest reliability.** For example, the reliability of a bathroom scale can be tested by placing an object on the scale, recording the weight, removing the object and letting the scale reset to zero, and then replacing that same object on the scale. If the resultant weight is not the same, the scale is not reliable (and should not be used for the purposes of research). A test-retest reliability procedure is most suitable for tests that are intended to measure relatively stable attributes. Common sense should tell you that there may be little consistency in scores over time if the trait is undergoing real change and that this lack of consistency would not necessarily mean the test is unreliable.

Additionally, test-retest reliability procedures may not be very useful when participants may be able to recall their previous responses and simply repeat them upon retesting. This would result in an inflated degree of consistency but would not demonstrate that the test will reliably measure the attribute. In cases where readministering the exact same test will not necessarily be a good test of reliability, we may use **alternate forms reliability.** As the name implies, two or more versions of the test are constructed that are equivalent in content and level of difficulty. For example, if one version of the third-grade arithmetic aptitude test asked children to calculate 3 + 6, the alternate version may ask them to compute 2 + 7. They are both addition problems with single-digit numbers. The alternate version test would not change the problem to a subtraction problem or use two-digit numbers because that would alter the content and difficulty of the second version. If the two versions of the test have been matched closely, item by item, then if the same individuals take both versions, their scores on the two forms should be very similar. This is alternate form reliability.[3]

When it is impractical or inadvisable to administer two tests to the same participants, it is possible to assess the reliability of some measurement procedures by examining their **internal consistency.** This type of reliability assessment is useful with tests that contain a series of items intended to measure the same attribute. For example, to test your ability to do long division problems without a calculator, we would probably want to give you a set of division problems to solve—a single problem would certainly not be considered adequate. So we might construct a 60-problem test where each problem uses different numbers to test your ability to do long division. Internal consistency refers to the degree to which the 60 separate items on the test measure the same trait or ability—that is, long-division skill.

One approach used to assess the internal consistency of a test is known as **split-half reliability,** which compares the scores for one half of the test to the scores for the other half of the test. The split-half reliability of my long-division test would be assessed by administering the 60-item test once and then splitting the test in half and scoring the two halves separately. Generally, the test should not be split in half based on the original order of the items. That is, the first 30 items should not be compared

---

[3] Some texts discuss parallel form reliability, too, which is a variant of alternate forms where the two versions must have the same mean and standard deviation and the same degree of correlation with other measures.

with the last 30 items because many tests are constructed so that the easier items come first (so the two halves are not equally difficult). Furthermore, during the test, people may become tired or lose interest, so their performance levels may decline. This would decrease the consistency between the two halves of the test. Instead, it is more common to split the test in half by putting the odd-numbered items together and comparing them with the even-numbered items. If the 60 division problems chosen for the test *are* consistently measuring the same long-division ability, then the score for the odd-numbered items should be about the same as the score for the even-numbered items.[4]

The internal consistency of the individual items of a test can also be assessed using either Cronbach's Alpha or the Kuder-Richardson 20.[5] These procedures compare the participants' response on each item (such as correct versus incorrect) with their responses on the other items on the test. If the items on the test are *homogeneous* and measure a single attribute, these measures of inter-item consistency will be high.

Another form of reliability assessment, known as **inter-rater reliability** or **inter-rater agreement,** is needed when the observers must use their own judgment to interpret the events they are observing (including live or videotaped behaviors and written answers to open-ended interview questions). That is, whenever the study involves *subjective observations*, the inter-rater reliability of the measurements must be established.

For example, to measure spontaneous courtesy among strangers, a researcher must watch strangers interacting and record any instance of courteous behavior. But just what *is* courteous behavior? It may take on a variety of forms, and different observers may judge the strangers' gestures differently. Is it ever possible to confuse a deliberate act of courtesy with an unthinking, even selfish act? Yes, it is. For example, it is generally considered courteous to hold a door open for another person, but it often may be the case that a person opens a door so widely that a second person has the chance to go through, too. Was the first person being courteous? It depends on whether the person deliberately threw the door wide open for the purpose of helping the next person. A researcher who observes an event like this will have to make a decision about the event: Should it be scored as an act of courtesy or not?

To establish the reliability of this kind of subjective measurement procedure, we need at least two observers who watch the same events (or read the same written responses, and so forth) and make independent decisions about how to score the events/answers. These judgments are then compared, and the degree of agreement

---

[4] This example may be a case where administering the same test twice is not a good idea because, while the reliability of this division test *could* be measured using a test-retest procedure (as long as the participants were willing to do each problem a second time), it is possible that taking the test the first time would make the participants a little better in division (through practice). Therefore, at the time of the second test, they no longer have the same value on the variable of long-division skill, and a different score on the retest could *not* be taken to mean the test was unreliable.

[5] The formulas and computational procedures for Cronbach's Alpha and the Kuder-Richardson 20 can be found in most psychological testing and measurement textbooks, such as Cohen, Montague, Nathanson, and Swerdlik (1988) or Gregory (1992).

is assessed. If the two (or more) observers consistently agree with each other's interpretation of the events they have observed, the observation procedure (that is, the measurements) are considered to be reliable.

You should realize that researchers do not leave the reliability of their measurement procedures to chance. In order to maximize the inter-rater reliability of subjective observations, the researcher will establish operational definitions that are as explicit and concrete as possible and then *thoroughly train* the research assistants in the application of those operational definitions before conducting the actual study. For example, the researcher may decide that throwing a door wide open is only to be scored as a courteous gesture if the person looked back at the person behind them just before or while they were opening the door. A person who throws the door wide open without looking back would not be given credit for being courteous. (Note, of course, that observers may not be certain whether a person "looked at the person behind them," so there is still an element of subjectivity in this measurement procedure.)

As pointed out earlier, an unreliable device means we do not have interpretable scores. For example, emergency medical technicians (EMTs) are trained to take a patient's blood pressure (BP) and to select a treatment plan according to the BP reading. If the sphygmomanometer (fondly known to EMTs as the "BP cuff") is malfunctioning, it may give a reading that suggests that the patient is stable when, in fact, the patient is going into shock—a potentially fatal condition that must be aggressively treated by the EMTs. The EMTs rely on the blood pressure cuff to give accurate readings; an unreliable cuff can be deadly. While research psychologists rarely face such dramatic consequences if they use unreliable measurement devices, they may reach incorrect or misleading conclusions from their data, which may then be taken as factual by others.

Validity

Clearly, reliability is a necessary element for scientific measurement devices. However, reliability is not sufficient: Our measurements must not only be consistent, they must also be valid. A measurement device is *valid if it measures what it is supposed to measure.* In the above example of research on intelligence in rats, one researcher elected to measure intelligence by measuring the amount of time a rat spent exploring a novel environment. Does time spent exploring *really* reveal intelligence? If it does, then the measurement procedure is valid; but if time spent exploring is *not* directly determined by intelligence, then the measurement procedure—as well as the entire operational definition—is not valid. Studies using invalid measures are, minimally, a waste of time, energy, and resources, and at worst, they are likely to yield misleading answers to the research questions.

A number of different forms of validity are relevant to a course on research methodology, and the term is used in various forms throughout texts such as this one. But in each case, the term *validity* refers to whether the definitions, the measurements, or the studies themselves do what they are supposed to do.

Construct Validity Many research studies in psychology are designed to examine relationships between variables such as intelligence and personality, and the researchers must select appropriate measurement procedures for the variables of interest. Variables such as intelligence and personality, however, are unlike characteristics such as height or weight: Intelligence and personality cannot be directly observed, and so, in fact, their very existence is *hypothetical*. We believe in the existence of intelligence, for instance, because we have found that the people who perform very well on memory tasks also tend to do well on problem-solving tasks, logical reasoning problems, reading comprehension tasks, and mathematics. That is, generally, some individuals do well in all academic and day-to-day problem solving, and others do not do so well, and we believe that these different patterns of performance are due to an underlying attribute we call intelligence. Actually, memory, reading, logic, and problem-solving tasks all require distinctly *different* actual behaviors for successful completion, but most psychologists feel that they share an underlying similarity in that they all require abstract processing of information, and we have labeled this intangible, higher-order cognitive ability "intelligence."

Thus, intelligence is considered to be a hypothetical construct. The term *hypothetical construct* refers, then, to something that exists in theory but cannot be directly observed, so measuring the underlying construct requires some inferential leaps that may prove to be more or less correct (or valid). We may have defined intelligence to be higher-level abstract thought processes as opposed to simpler sensory or perceptual processes, and this may sound quite convincing, but we need to verify (or validate) our definition (or even our theory) of intelligence by demonstrating that the patterns of behavior the theory says should exist, in fact, can be observed in people. In other words, we need to establish the **construct validity** of intelligence by showing that scores on tests that theoretically require intelligence do, indeed, predict performance on other tasks that require intelligence. That is, memory performance, problem solving, logical reasoning, reading comprehension, and all other tasks that theoretically require the abstract processing called "intelligence" should be related to one another. Obviously, construct validation is a lengthy process, and no single procedure is sufficient to validate a construct. The basic approach involves testing theory-derived predictions. Let's look at a brief example using the construct of "altruism."

Personality traits such as "altruism" are hypothetical constructs because they are internal, intangible qualities that influence a variety of behaviors that may be superficially quite different but that are, theoretically, linked by some underlying motivational force. To test the construct validity of the concept of "altruism," we would first make a list of overt behaviors we believe to be external manifestations of altruism, and then we would measure each of these behaviors to see whether, indeed, they are correlated as the construct says they should be. For example, if our theory of altruism defines it as a willingness to help others even if there is some price to be paid for helping, we might predict that altruism leads to donation behavior, which involves giving away personal property. This theory of altruism would also say that stopping to help a stranded driver is altruistic because the helper is giving up personal time.

If this concept of altruism is valid, we should see that people who stop to help stranded motorists are also the people who donate to charities, while those who do not stop also do not donate.

Remember the example we used earlier in this chapter, concerning the intelligence of rats, to illustrate the issues involved in creating operational definitions? We suggested that researchers could use either speed of learning or exploration behaviors as possible operational definitions for intelligence in rats. At this point, it is appropriate to ask: Is the time a rat spends exploring a novel environment *really* a reflection of the rat's underlying intelligence? If we find that a rat's exploratory behavior does not predict performance on other theoretically relevant intelligence tasks, such as those measuring the speed of learning, then we would conclude that this measurement procedure—regardless of how consistently and accurately it measures exploratory behaviors—does not have construct validity and would not be an appropriate measure for our study of rat intelligence.

Face Validity **Face validity** is determined by looking at a measurement procedure to see whether it appears, on the face of it, to be measuring the variable of interest. In the earlier example of intelligence in rats, you may have intuitively agreed with choosing speed of learning as an operational definition of intelligence, but you may have wondered whether exploring a novel environment made sense as a measure of intelligence. The speed of learning measure may, on the face of it, seem to be more valid than the exploration measure. Face validity is often assessed by having experts in the field judge a measurement as making sense or not, but the face validity may be most important from a public relations standpoint: If the participants doubt the validity of the test you have given them, their performance motivation may suffer, and their scores may not be relevant to the purposes of the testing.

Students should be aware that the measurement procedures used in published research reports—especially those procedures that are used by a number of different researchers—are typically granted face validity status, and many researchers will not try to create a brand new measurement device but will instead borrow one from the published literature. To adopt another researcher's research methods is *not* considered unethical.

Content Validity A measure has **content validity** when the items of the test accurately represent the concept being measured (Vogt, 1993). For example, a test to measure your knowledge of arithmetic should *not* be limited to addition problems, nor should it include questions about 18th-century French literature. Instead, the test should include problems from the entire range of possible arithmetic problems (such as subtraction, multiplication and division, and these problems should include 1-, 2-, and 3-digit numbers, and so forth), but the test should *not* include problems that belong in other categories such as algebra, geometry, or calculus. Like face validity, content validity is determined by experts who can judge the representativeness of the items on a test.

Both face and content validity may be of limited value to researchers studying hypothetical constructs because these validity tests may fail in either of two directions: (1) a measure may *look* valid when it does not, in fact, measure the underlying construct (for instance, measuring the speed of maze-learning by counting the number of trials to criterion may *sound like* a valid indicator of intelligence, but it may not have construct validity); or (2) a measure that does *not* appear to be a useful, valid test may actually be an excellent indicator of the underlying construct.

Criterion Validity   A powerful indicator of the validity of a measure is its *ability to accurately predict performance on other, independent outcome measures* (referred to as criterion measures). For example, if the California Achievement Test (CAT) is a truly valid measure of academic achievement, then performance on the CAT should predict school performance in children. The extent to which children's CAT scores correlate with school grades is an indication of the CAT's **criterion validity.** There are two approaches to criterion validity: **concurrent validity** and **predictive validity.** In concurrent validity, the test scores and the criterion measures are obtained at roughly the same time. For example, if the CAT scores are compared with the children's most recent school grades, we would be assessing the concurrent validity of the CAT scores. In predictive validity, the test scores are kept on record and compared with a criterion measure obtained sometime in the future. For instance, in 1984, Dr. Stephen Bavolek developed the Adult-Adolescent Parenting Inventory (AAPI) to measure attitudes toward parenting and child rearing. It has been suggested that adolescents' scores on this survey could predict abusive behavior when they became parents. To assess the criterion validity of this instrument as a *predictor* of abusiveness, we would want to administer the AAPI to a wide variety of adolescents and then wait until they became parents and measure their abusiveness. If abusive parents had systematically lower scores on the AAPI than nonabusive parents, we would have demonstrated the predictive validity of the AAPI.

Levels (or Scales) of Measurement

Remember that measurement is a process whereby values (i.e., scores) are assigned to properties or characteristics of people, places, things, or events. For example, you might ask people to rate their preferences for a number of perfumes by choosing a first, second, and third favorite, or you might count the number of times people report feeling depressed within a year. You may want to collect information on the marital status or sex of a person. *These different measures all have different properties, which, in turn, lead to different sorts of appropriate statistical tests.* The **level** (or **scale**) **of measurement** refers to the amount of information the measurement procedure (or scores) can convey about the actual quantity of the variable present and about the actual differences among individuals with different scores. There are four levels of measurement, which are classified by the degree to which numerical measurements (or "scores") match up with the properties of the real number system. The four properties of the real number system are: (1) identity, where each number serves as a label for a different numerical value; (2) order (or ranking), where the numbers can be placed in order based on amount or magnitude; (3) equal intervals, where an equal difference in the numbers always represents an equal amount of change in magnitude; and (4) a true zero point, where the number zero always means zero amount (or a complete absence of quantity). A measurement procedure (which assigns a number to the values of the variable) may provide numbers that have all or only some of these four properties. Therefore, there are four levels (or scales) of measurement: nominal, ordinal, interval, and ratio. As each level of measurement is explained, you will see how it satisfies these properties.

The **nominal scale** of measurement is the most basic. It seeks to name things, to categorize or classify them. Nominal scales satisfy only the property of identity (that is, each value represents a unique case). Some examples are sex (male or female), religion (Buddhist, Hindu, Christian, Jewish, Muslim, etc.), or job title (cook, professor, dietician, taxi driver, etc.). These are all qualitative properties, rather than quantitative properties. If we assign numbers to represent each category, the numbers are completely arbitrary and have no true numerical value. For example, we may assign a "1" to males and a "2" to females, but this does not mean that a female is twice a male or somehow greater or better. We could just as easily assign the numbers in the opposite order. Nominal scales do not satisfy the properties of ranking, equal intervals, or a true zero.

The **ordinal scale** of measurement deals with order or ranking. In our example of rating perfumes, the order in which scents were rated would produce an ordinal scale from most-favored to least-favored scent. Other common examples are grades of A, B, C, D, and F, "top 20" ratings for sports teams, or "top 40" ratings for music. These scales produce a relative ordering of the members. Unlike a nominal scale, the numbers assigned to sports teams *do* have a quantitative meaning; they reflect the performance of each team by indicating the order in which the teams fall. However, while an ordinal scale allows us to know which category is larger, higher, or better, it does not allow us to say anything about the interval between the rankings—or *how much* larger, higher, or better one team is than the next. We know that the first-place team is better than the second-place team, but we do not know how big that difference is. Nor can we expect that the difference between the first- and second-place teams is the same as the difference between the 14th-place team and the 15th-place team.

The **interval scale** of measurement tells us about the rank order *and* about the intervals between the numbers. On an interval scale, a difference of 1 point always means the same thing: the difference between a person with a score of 1 and a person with a score of 2 is *exactly equal to* the difference between a person with a score of 10 and a person with a score of 11. This property of interval scales is referred to as equal intervals between numbers.

For example, temperatures measured with either the Celsius or Fahrenheit scales provide scores on an interval scale. One degree is always equal to the same amount of heat ("a degree is a degree is a degree"). When we measure temperature, we know that a larger number means that there is more heat and that the equal differences between temperature scores means that there has been an equal change in the amount of heat (e.g., the difference between 40° Celsius and 45° Celsius is the same as the difference between 75° and 80° Celsius). However, these thermometers do not have true zero points: a temperature of 0° Fahrenheit or 0° Celsius does *not* indicate the absence of heat (which is why temperatures can be *below* zero—just ask residents of Barrow, Alaska, who may spend weeks each winter with temperatures that never climb above −5°F). Because there is no true zero point on the thermometer, we cannot say that 80° Celsius is twice as hot as 40° Celsius.

The "highest" level of measurement, the **ratio scale,** has all of the properties of the real number system. In addition to identity, order, and equal intervals, ratio scales have a true or **absolute zero point.** Our standard measures of time, distance, volume, height, and weight all use ratio scales. For example, we measure time by counting the number of minutes between one event and another, and a minute is always equal to the same amount of time ("a minute is a minute is a minute"), and should the two events occur simultaneously, we would assign a score of 0 minutes. On a ratio scale, *a value of 0 means that none of this thing has been measured*, and taking a ratio (one value divided by another) has meaning. For example, 1 minute is half as long as 2 minutes, and 4 feet is twice as tall as 2 feet. If we stacked two 2-inch blocks, the stack would be the same height as one 4-inch block.

Because ratio scales match the properties of the real number system, we can perform all mathematical operations with these numbers (addition, subtraction, division, and multiplication) and get meaningful results. Interval scales allow only addition and subtraction, and nominal and ordinal scales do not allow any meaningful arithmetical operations.

When conducting psychology experiments, measurements of variables may be on any of these scales. Depending on which scale is used, different descriptive and inferential statistics should be used. A summary of the levels of measurement and their properties is given in Table 4-1.

TABLE 4-1	**Summary of Levels of Measurement and Their Characteristics**			
	Nominal	**Ordinal**	**Interval**	**Ratio**
Examples	Sex Religion Ethnicity	Top 40 hits SES Preferences	Temperature (°C or °F)	Age Height Reaction time
Mathematical Properties	Identity	Identity Magnitude	Identity Magnitude Equal interval	Identity Magnitude Equal interval True zero
Mathematical Operations	None	Ranking	Addition Subtraction	Addition Subtraction Multiplication Division

tivity of Measurements

ther important point to make about the process of measurement is that the cedure needs to be sensitive enough to detect small, yet meaningful changes or ferences that occur in the attribute under study. For example, a scale that rounds the nearest pound will not be able to detect changes or differences of an ounce or wo, but these small changes may be very important theoretically. Likewise, asking teachers to rate a child's noncompliant behavior using a rating scale with only three points (such as "Not At All Compliant," "Average," and "Consistently Compliant") may not be sensitive to small, gradual, incremental changes in the child's behavior. If the purpose of the study is to test the effectiveness of a treatment program for noncompliance, the measurement may be unable to detect systematic—but small— improvements in behavior due to the treatment. The issue of measurement sensitivity will be revisited in Chapter 15 when we discuss single-subject designs.

Exercises

1. In the following scenario, the "success" of different styles of counseling is being tested. Generate an alternate measurement procedure for the variable "success" (i.e., generate a new operational definition). Which operational definition seems to be more valid? How could you go about assessing the validity of these measurement procedures?

A researcher was interested in the effects of a counselor's "style" on the success of the therapy for severely depressed people. In order to vary "style," a counselor (Dr. Smith) was trained to use three types of comments: (1) "self-disclosing comments" (i.e., telling clients about personal past experiences similar to the clients': "I flunked stats the first time I took it, too"); (2) "client-focused comments" (i.e., comments about how the client's behaviors make the counselor feel: "I feel very good that you were able to stand up to your roommate about having overnight guests during finals week"); and (3) "neutral comments" (similar to the "reflection and restatement" techniques used by Rogerian therapists: "So you are saying that you were annoyed at your roommate.").

One-third of the counselor's depressed clients were assigned to each of these experimental conditions. After six counseling sessions, each client was given a 4-point rating scale (where 0 = not at all and 3 = extremely) and asked "How helpful has seeing Dr. Smith been?" These rating scores were used as a measurement of the success of the counseling style.

For each of the following scenarios, (a) identify the level of measurement for each of the variables of interest and (b) identify an appropriate procedure for assessing

the reliability of the measurement procedure for each variable and ~~e~~
you think that reliability test is suitable for the variable. ~~why~~

2. A teacher assessed the relationship between students' amount of sleep
   an important scholarship exam and their performance on the qualifying
   exam. The teacher asked the students to write down the number of hour~~s~~
   they had slept the night before and then analyzed the data to determine
   whether the students who passed the exam (and qualified for the scholarship
   had gotten more sleep than those who failed to qualify for the scholarship.

3. A researcher was interested in the relationship between a child's popularity
   with classmates and the *teacher's perception* of the child's popularity. To measure peer popularity, all the children in the class were asked to name the
   "three nicest kids in class." Then the researcher counted the number of
   times the child was identified by a classmate as one of the "nicest kids." To
   measure the teacher's perception of the children, the teacher was asked to
   evaluate each child on a scale from 0 ("Seems Very Unpopular") to 7
   ("Seems Very Popular").

4. The professors and coaches at a small university were interested in the academic achievement of football players versus that of basketball players.
   (There were no students who played on both teams.) The registrar provided
   the players' GPAs for analysis.

5. A department chairperson measured the relationship between a teacher's
   effectiveness and his/her teaching experience. Effectiveness was measured
   using the median score the professor received on the evaluation forms
   completed by students, where 1 = very low effectiveness and 7 = very high
   effectiveness. Experience was measured as the number of semesters the
   professor had been teaching college-level courses.

6. An economist was interested in the correlation between the yearly average
   price of tea in China (measured in U.S. currency to the nearest penny) and
   the annual amount of rainfall in Liechtenstein (measured to the 1/100th of
   an inch). The economist collected data on these two variables for the past 30
   years.

7. A school psychologist was screening first-graders for hyperactivity. Of 80
   boys, 30 showed signs of hyperactivity, and 50 did not. Of 70 girls, 10
   showed signs of hyperactivity, and 60 did not.

8. A researcher wanted to assess the relationship between family income and
   the level of education attained by the oldest child. Income was measured as
   the amount of money earned by the parents per month, and the level of
   education of the oldest child was measured by counting the number of
   college credit hours he/she completed (including graduate credits).

9. To test the hypothesis that infants who form strong, positive relationships with their mothers feel more secure with other people, too, a developmental psychologist videotaped the interactions between mothers and infants in a strange playroom and then counted the number of times the infant *initiated* a positive interaction exchange. Then the researcher rated the infants' degree of "stranger anxiety" (on a scale from 0 to 6) by observing the infants when a stranger approached them and tried to pick them up.

CHAPTER

5

DESCRIPTIVE STATISTICS

■ ■ ■ ■ ■ ■

In this chapter, you will learn how to summarize a set of data by reporting frequencies, averages, and measures of variability. The basic concepts of probability are introduced, and simple data transformations are discussed.

Look for These Important Terms and Concepts

descriptive and inferential statistics
populations versus samples
frequency and frequency tables
bar chart
histogram
frequency polygon
stem-and-leaf plot
probability
proportion and percentage
sample statistics versus population
   parameters
joint probability
normal curve (or distribution)
skewed distribution

central tendency
mode
median
mean
outliers
variability (or disperson)
deviation scores $(X - \overline{X})$
variance and standard deviation
median absolute deviation
range
variation ratio
z-scores
z-to-X conversion formula

Before Reading This Chapter, You May Wish to Review

Chapter 3:
- variables
- values (or scores)
- quantitative versus qualitative variables
- discrete versus continuous variables

Chapter 4:
- nominal scales (or levels)
- ordinal scales (or levels)
- interval scales (or levels)
- ratio scales (or levels)

Statistics is the branch of applied mathematics concerned with collection, summary, and analysis of numerical data (Vogt, 1993). By definition, a statistic is a number that summarizes some feature of a body of information. There are two broad categories of statistics: descriptive and inferential. **Descriptive statistics,** as their name implies, are most commonly used to "describe" the characteristics of the set of raw scores on a variable, such as how often particular values occurred or what the average score was. This is in contrast to **inferential statistics** (to be dealt with later in this book), which summarize the *patterns* among scores for two or more variables and use sample data to draw inferences about the relationship among variables in the population. The process of describing data is usually the first step in statistical analysis; in addition to providing useful information about the sample, it is often used to be sure there are no obvious irregularities with the measures taken before inferential statistics are used to try to understand and explain any patterns found in the data.

Populations and Samples

When we are interested in answering a research question, we would like the answers generated by our study to be relevant to the entire group of interest, or at least to be as widely applicable as possible. The *large group of interest* is called a **population.** All of the white rats in the world form a population, as do all teenagers, as do all people with weights over 200 pounds. Populations can be relatively small, too, such as the population of sophomores at Belmore College in 1999. That is, populations are defined by the purposes of the research as the group being investigated. While smaller, specialized populations may be accessible to researchers (such as the entire sophomore class being asked to complete a survey), in most basic psychological research, it is unlikely that we will be able to study all members of a population in one study; it may even be impossible to *find* all members of the population of interest. For this reason, we need to choose some subset of the larger population for testing. A subset of a population is referred to as a **sample,** and the purpose of inferential statistics is to *generalize from the sample to the population.* This generalization is possible when the sample that has been selected is *representative* of the population. The process of choosing a sample of members to represent the whole population is discussed in Chapter 6. For now, it is necessary to understand only that once we have our group of participants (sometimes the group consists of an entire population, but much more often it is only a sample from a population), we measure the variables of interest for each member of the group. (This is called collecting the data.) Descriptive statistics summarize the characteristics of the data collected from the group.

About the Computations in This Text

To minimize the impact of rounding error in our computations for this text, we have chosen to carry the values out to the last decimal place on a hand calculator *until the final step of the computation.* We have found that rounding at every step of a computation can result in values that appear substantially different than they should, and this can be confusing for students who are still mastering the computational procedures. By taking the time to use every decimal point until the computation is complete, the answers are more accurate. However, this does *not* mean that the statistics are reported with six or seven decimal places. Once the "final" value of the statistic has been computed, we use the standard rounding procedure, where we select an appropriate number of decimal places and round up if the *next* decimal place equals 5 or higher, down if it equals 4 or less. Generally, descriptive statistics are reported to one *significant digit*, which means that if the raw scores were whole numbers, the statistic is reported with *one* decimal place, or if the raw scores had one decimal place, the statistic is reported with *two* decimal places, and so forth. (By convention, various inferential statistics, which are covered in later chapters, are reported with two decimal places, regardless of the number of decimal places in the raw data.)

Frequency

The most basic descriptive statistic is **frequency.** This simply refers to how often something occurs. For example, let's suppose that we surveyed a class of 28 students and asked them to tell us how old they are. Table 5-1 presents an example of a **frequency table** for the age data. The table has several columns, which we will look at one by one.

TABLE 5.1	Frequency Table			
Age (X)	Frequency (f)	Percentage	Cumulative Frequency	Cumulative Percentage
31	1	3.6%	28	100.0%
30	0	0.0%	27	96.4%
29	0	0.0%	27	96.4%
28	0	0.0%	27	96.4%
27	0	0.0%	27	96.4%
26	1	3.6%	27	96.4%
25	0	0.0%	26	92.9%
24	0	0.0%	26	92.9%
23	0	0.0%	26	92.9%
22	2	7.1%	26	92.9%
21	4	14.3%	24	85.7%
20	7	25.0%	20	71.4%
19	8	28.6%	13	46.4%
18	4	14.3%	5	17.9%
17	1	3.6%	1	3.6%
	N = 28	100.1%		

NOTE: The percentages do not sum to exactly 100% because of rounding error.

The first column in the table contains all the different values of the raw data (referred to as the values of "X"); in our example, X is the variable *Age*, and the first column lists all the ages of the students (or the participants), starting from the highest value. The second column contains the frequency (f_X), or number of participants of each age. For instance, one participant is 17 years old, four participants are 18 years old (i.e., $f_{x=17} = 1$ and $f_{x=18} = 4$). The third column in the frequency table contains the percentage of participants at each age, which is computed by dividing the number of participants of a given age (f) by the total number of participants (N) and then multiplying by 100. For example, seven of the 28 students were 20 years old, so the percentage is equal to

$$\text{percentage of group} \atop \text{who are 20 years old} = \frac{7}{28} \times 100 = .25 \times 100 = 25\%.$$

Therefore, 25% of the students in this class are 20 years of age.

The fourth column gives a cumulative frequency. This shows the total number of participants who fall at the given age *or below*. In this chart, we can see that 13 participants are 19 years old or younger and that 26 participants are 22 or younger. We can also use this cumulative frequency to create a cumulative percentage by taking the percentage of participants that fall at each age or below. Here, we see from the cumulative frequency column that thirteen students are 19 years old or younger:

$$\text{cumulative percentage} \atop \text{for X = 19 or younger} = \frac{13}{28} \times 100 = .4642857 \times 100 = 46.4\%.$$

Therefore, 46.4% of the students are age 19 or below. (You should not be surprised to see that 100% of the students are age 31 or below because 31 was the highest age score in the group.)

Graphing Frequencies

Another way to look at frequencies is graphically. If the variable is qualitative or if the data are on a nominal scale, the most appropriate way to graph the data is to use a **bar chart.** If the variable is quantitative, with data on ordinal, interval, or ratio scales, we can use a **histogram.** These two graphs both use bars to indicate the frequencies for each value of X (which are placed along the horizontal X-axis). The height of the bars indicate the frequencies (which are on the vertical Y-axis). The difference between bar charts and histograms is that the bars are separated by a space on a bar chart, but they are contiguous on a histogram. The space between the bars on the bar chart is a visual representation of the qualitative differences among the categories, while the fact that the bars run together in a histogram is a visual reminder of the increasing quantity of the variable. The space between the bars on the bar chart also reminds us that the order of the values of X along the X-axis are arbitrary: We can arrange the bars in any order (such as placing them in ascending or descending order). The bars on the histogram, however, have an inherent order that

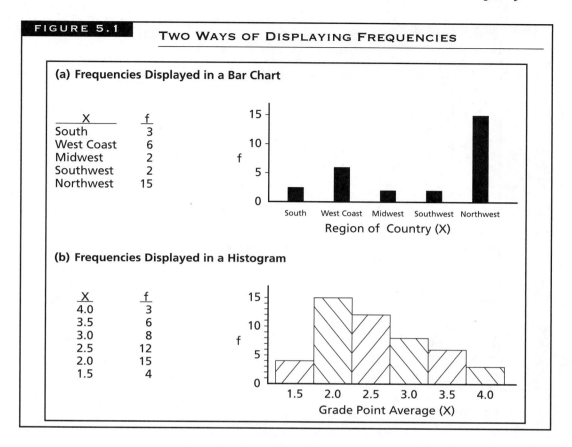

FIGURE 5.1   TWO WAYS OF DISPLAYING FREQUENCIES

(a) Frequencies Displayed in a Bar Chart

X	f
South	3
West Coast	6
Midwest	2
Southwest	2
Northwest	15

(b) Frequencies Displayed in a Histogram

X	f
4.0	3
3.5	6
3.0	8
2.5	12
2.0	15
1.5	4

cannot be rearranged on a whim. The following examples should illustrate this distinction.

Figure 5-1a presents an example of a bar chart where we look at the number of students in a class who are from various regions of the United States. The region of the country is a qualitative variable, so a bar chart is appropriate. Note that we could list the regions in any order along the X-axis. Figure 5-1b presents an example of a histogram for frequencies of student grade point averages (GPAs). These bars cannot be reordered because GPAs of 2.0 lie between GPAs of 1.5 and 2.5.

Another type of graph that is appropriate for quantitative data is a **frequency polygon.** Figure 5-2 presents an example of a frequency polygon that plots the age data from Table 5-1. Here the ages are plotted on the X-axis, and the frequency is on the Y-axis. The points come from plotting the frequency at each age; these points are then connected together with a line, producing a polygon enclosed below the line. Frequency polygons are especially useful for continuous data (such as age, height, or reaction time, where it is theoretically possible to have a value that falls *anywhere* along the score scale); histograms may be more appropriate when the data are

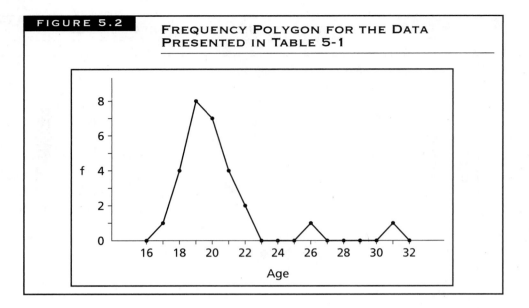

FIGURE 5.2

FREQUENCY POLYGON FOR THE DATA
PRESENTED IN TABLE 5-1

discrete (such as number of siblings or number of traffic tickets received, which are measured in whole units so that it is not possible to have a case that lies between two adjacent values).

Grouped Frequencies

Sometimes you may want to look at grouped data rather than raw data. For example, if we wanted to look at the weights of our group of 28 students, we might find we have 28 different weights, all with a frequency of one. In this case, we might choose to group the data into categories or classes. Many issues must be considered when deciding how to choose the number and size (range) of these classes. In general, we would like to have between 5 and 20 classes. For weight scores for adults, for example, we might group the weights into categories in 10-pound intervals.[1] Table 5-2 presents a grouped frequency table.

If we were to look at this grouped data graphically, we could use a frequency polygon like the one in Figure 5-2, using the weight categories on the X-axis. (To create a frequency polygon using grouped data, the midpoint of the class is used as the location on the X-axis for all members of that class. Therefore, for the grouped weight data in Table 5-2, the first frequency point would be above the score of 104.5, which is the midpoint for the 100 to 109 class, the next frequency point would be above 114.5,

---

[1] If we were measuring the weights of newborn infants, however, our grouped frequencies would probably be based on *ounces* rather than pounds!

TABLE 5.2	Grouped Frequency Table			
Weight (X)	Frequency (f)	Percentage (%)	Cumulative Frequency	Cumulative Percentage
190–199	1	3.6%	28	100.0%
180–189	2	7.1%	27	96.4%
170–179	0	0.0%	25	89.3%
160–169	4	14.3%	25	89.3%
150–159	4	14.3%	21	75.0%
140–149	3	10.7%	17	60.7%
130–139	6	21.4%	14	50.0%
120–129	5	17.9%	8	28.6%
110–119	1	3.6%	3	10.7%
100–109	2	7.1%	2	7.1%
	N = 28	100.0%		

which is the midpoint of the 110 to 119 class, and so forth.) Alternately, we could use a figure known as a **stem-and-leaf plot,** which allows us to look at the general distribution of the data in groups while still maintaining all the information contained in the raw data. This plot is called a stem-and-leaf plot because it takes the "stem" of the scores, or the underlying consistent part (i.e., the tens, hundreds, etc.) of the scores, and attaches the "leaf" to it. The leaf is the variable part (the units) of the data.

Figure 5-3 presents the grouped-weight data from Table 5-2 in a stem-and-leaf plot. For example, we know from Table 5-2 that two participants weighed between 100 and 109. Let's suppose the first of these participants weighed 100 pounds and the other participant weighted 105 pounds. On the stem-and-leaf plot presented in Figure 5-3, the 100–109 category is found on the first row, and the two individuals in that group are represented by the final digit of their actual weights: 0 and 5. (Note

FIGURE 5.3	STEM-AND-LEAF PLOT

Weight Scores	
Stem (first two digits)	Leaf (last digit)
100	0, 5
110	4
120	0, 2, 5, 5, 8
130	0, 0, 4, 5, 5, 6
140	0, 5, 9
150	0, 2, 3, 7
160	0, 5, 5, 7
170	
180	5, 8
190	0

that the last digit in a weight score tells us how much we need to add to the base value of 100 to find the actual score). From the stem-and-leaf plot, we can see that five people had weight scores between 120 and 129, and by looking at the "leaf" scores (0, 2, 5, 5, 8), we can determine that those weights were 120, 122, 125, 125, and 128. The advantage of a stem-and-leaf plot over a grouped frequency table is that every individual score can be determined from the plot. From the grouped frequency table in Table 5-2 (or from a frequency polygon if we drew one from Table 5-2), we cannot know the actual weights of the two individuals in the 100–109 category, but the stem-and-leaf plot tells us that their weights were 100 and 105.[2]

Another advantage of this graphing method is that it allows us to visually examine patterns in the raw data. In this example of weights, we do see an unusual pattern that might give us cause to think about whether these self-reports of weight provide accurate measures. Look again at the data reported in the stem-and-leaf plot. Seventeen of the 28 students—more than 60% of them—reported weights ending in 0 or 5 (such as 105, 130, and 165), and *none* of them reported a weight ending in 1. Because there is no reason to expect that a distribution of weight scores would not include weights ending *equally often* in every number of pounds (that is, weights ending with values from 0 to 9), we would have expected to see about 10% of the students reporting weights ending in 0, another 10% reporting weights ending in 1, and so forth. Therefore, we would have expected that only about 20% (only five or six out of 28) of the weights scores would end in 0 or 5. Yet we found that over 60% of the reported weights ended in 0 or 5, and this pattern suggests that people have a tendency to round up or down to the nearest 5 pounds rather than reporting a more precise weight. If the weight data had been presented in a standard grouped frequency table, rather than a stem-and-leaf plot, we would have missed this phenomenon.

Probability

Whenever we seek to test a hypothesis, the conclusions that we make cannot be asserted with certainty. Some degree of doubt is always associated with the outcome. The concept of **probability** allows us to determine the degree of certainty with which we can assert support of a hypothesis.

Probability is, in essence, a measure of the likelihood that a particular event will occur. We might look at the probability of rolling a six with a die, or of tossing a coin and getting a head. For each example, there is a set of possible outcomes on each trial, which has an associated probability. For the coin toss, if we use a normal coin, there is a 50% chance that it will land with the head facing upward. For the die,

---

[2] Notice that if you turn the stem-and-leaf plot on its side, you will see a diagram very much like the frequency polygon we used with the age data in Figure 5-2: For each member of a category, a "leaf" number is added to the list, so that categories with higher frequencies have longer "lists" of numbers and, therefore, visually resemble the peaks on a sideways polygon. (The same is true for the height of the bars of a histogram.)

there are six possible outcomes, with the probability of each being 1/6 (or .1667 or 16.67%). As long as we are dealing with a subject like dice, cards, or coins, we can be fairly sure that there is an equally likely chance that any outcome may occur. While not all problems clearly fit this model, for the most part, it is a useful way to examine many naturally occurring events.

Another way to think about probability is in terms of the relative frequency, or how often the event has occurred in the past. The relative frequency of event X is simply the observed frequency of event X (f_X) divided by the number of trials or observations made (i.e., relative frequency = f_X/N; this gives us the **proportion** of all events that were X). Probability is a property of a population, and the relative frequency of the event within some samples provides an *estimate* of that probability. That is, given a sufficiently large number of observations, we would expect the ratio or percentage of times an event was observed in our sample to approach the probability (*p*) of the event happening in the population. (Note that the statistics we compute from the sample data are referred to as **sample statistics,** while the characteristics of a population of data are referred to as **population parameters.** Therefore, in this case, we want to use the relative frequency in the sample *as an estimate of* the population probability.)

As an example, suppose that we want to predict the percentage of female children being born in the population. We might look at a set of birth records to see how many girls have been born compared with boys. For instance, we may look at last week's 10 births at the local hospital and find that four of those babies were girls. Thus, 40% of the babies born last week were female, and we might conclude that 40% of all babies will be girls. This conclusion, however, is based directly on the single sample of 10 births last week. If we looked at larger samples (maybe 100 births, or 1,000, or even more), we may find that the percentage of female births is not exactly 40%, and we would place more faith in the results of these larger samples because, generally, we have found that as *sample size (N) increases, sample statistics become more accurate estimates of the population parameters.*

Since larger samples give us more accurate estimates of the distribution of events in the population, our predictions about the probabilities of those events are more accurate if they are based on larger samples. Table 5-3 presents some hypothetical data about the percentage of female births from five samples with different sample sizes (N). Here we see that the relative frequency appears to be converging on a value of about 48%. This is, then, an estimate of the hypothetical value *p*, and we would conclude that the probability that the next baby to be born will be female is .48 (or 48%).

TABLE 5.3	Hypothetical Data Concerning Percentages of Female Births				
Number of Births (N)	10	100	1,000	10,000	100,000
Frequency of Female Births	4	52	479	4,836	48,013
Relative Frequency of Female Births	40%	52%	47.9%	48.36%	48.01%

Finally, there are often times when we may wish to look at an event and determine the probability that the event has particular values on two or more separate, unrelated variables at the same time. For instance, what is the probability that a child will be born female *and* have blue eyes? The **joint probability** of being female and having blue eyes is determined by the probabilities for each variable separately: If the probability of being female is .48 and the probability of having blue eyes is .25, then the probability that a particular child will be both female and blue-eyed is equal to the product of the separate probabilities (.48 × .25 = .12, or 12%). This is known as the multiplication rule of probability, and it assumes that sex and eye color are independent of each other (Roscoe, 1975). Joint probability is the probability of an event falling into two classes simultaneously.

As another example, we may be interested in the sex of babies and the age of the mothers, so we might look at the percentage of male or female children born and the percentage of women of different ages becoming mothers. Let us imagine that we have divided mothers into three age categories (under 25, 25–35, and over 35) and that the relative percentages of mothers belonging to these three age categories are 36%, 44%, and 20%. If we can assume that a woman's age is independent of (and, therefore, has no influence upon) her child's sex, then we can compute the joint probabilities by using the multiplication rule. If we place the information about babies' sex and mothers' age into a table, we might get something like Table 5-4.

The information in the margins of Table 5-4 (that is, the last column and last row) are the proportions of male (52%) and female (48%) births and the proportions of new mothers who are under 25 (36%), between 25 and 35 (44%), and over 35 (20%). The values within the cells of the table are the joint probabilities of any child being *both* of a given sex and born to a mother of a certain age. For example, there is a 23% chance that a child will be *both:* (a) born to a mother 25–35 years and (b) male.[3] We will return to the concept of joint probabilities when we discuss the inferential statistics used with categorical data in Chapter 13.

TABLE 5.4	**Hypothetical Data Illustrating Joint Probabilities (Assuming Independence of the Variables)**			
Sex of Baby	Mother Under 25 Years	Mother Between 25 and 35 Years	Mother Over 35 Years	All Mothers
Male	.187	.229	.104	.52
Female	.173	.211	.096	.48
Both	.36	.44	.20	1.00

[3] The assumption that maternal age and sex of the baby are independent is, of course, an empirical question. It is possible that maternal aging *does* affect the sex of a baby. For instance, biochemical changes in the mother's womb may favor one sex more than the other, or older men may produce more sperm of one type than the other. In order to determine whether or not the two variables are independent, we can perform a chi square (χ^2) test of independence (Roscoe, 1975), which compares an obtained sample of data to the joint probabilities that would be expected if the variables are independent (such as those in Table 5-4). This inferential procedure is covered later in the book.

Frequency data and probabilities can be very informative, but in order to provide thorough descriptions of their data, most statisticians will compute measures of *average* (which indicate where the typical scores tend to fall) and *variability* (which indicate how spread out the scores tend to be). There are several measures of average (or central tendency) and variability, and the appropriate measure to use for a particular data set depends upon the level (or scale) of measurement. Let's begin by discussing statistics for identifying the average score in a data set.

Central Tendency

Measures of **central tendency** are intended to describe the most "average" or typical value in the data set, and generally, the typical score will be located somewhere near the center of the distribution (hence the term *central tendency*). The three most common measures of "average" are the mean, the median, and the mode.

Mode

The **mode** is the easiest measure to understand; it simply reports the most frequently occurring value of the variable. On a frequency polygon, the mode is the score at the peak of the distribution. Looking back at the examples earlier in this chapter, we can determine the modal age of our 28 participants in Table 5-1 (p. 81) by looking at the second column (*f*) and finding the largest value of *f*. The age that has the largest value of *f* is the mode. As you can see, the largest value of *f* is 8, and, therefore, the *modal age* for the group is *19 years of age*. As a second example, look at the bar chart and histogram in Figure 5-1 (p. 83). The tallest bar indicates the mode, so we can see that more students come from the Northwest than from any other region; so *Northwest* is the mode of the distribution in Figure 5-1a, and the mode of the grade point averages in Figure 5-1b is *2.0*.

Although it is also relevant for all scales of measurement, the mode is mainly used with nominal data. (In fact, the mode is the *only* measure of central tendency that is appropriate for categorical, nominal data.) Sometimes there may be two modes; in this case, the distribution is said to be *bimodal*. The mode is very easy to compute but not very stable, as changes in the frequencies of one or two values can change the mode. In addition, for ordinal, interval, or ratio scales, the mode will be near the "center" only in relatively symmetrical distributions, which peak near the middle of the distribution and taper off at high and low values. In asymmetrical distributions, the mode will not be in the "center."

Median

The **median** finds the value in the *middle* of the distribution where an equal number (50%) of scores fall above and below that point. All scores are arranged in numerical order to find a median, making this statistic useful for ordinal data. (Although the median can also be used with interval and ratio data, it is not usually the preferred measure of average for these scales.) With a small data set and an odd number of scores, the middle score (after the scores have been placed in order of magnitude) will be the median. For an even number of scores, the median will be the average of the two middle scores (i.e., halfway between them).

Finding the Median of a Set of Scores   The first step is always to *reorganize the data* so that the scores are in numerical order (either from high to low or low to high). Then you must find the score in the middle of the ordered list of scores. *If N is an odd number,* one of the scores in the list will be identified as the median, and we can identify the ordinal position of the median by dividing N in half and then adding 0.5. *If N is an even number,* the median will fall *between* the two scores in the middle of the ordered data set. We can identify the ordinal position of these middle scores by dividing N in half. Let's work through some examples where we find the median weight for groups of adults. In the first two examples, we have an even number of adults, and in the third example, we have an odd number of weight scores in the data set. (Example 2 illustrates what we do when there are duplicated scores in the middle of the distribution.)

EXAMPLE 1: AN EVEN NUMBER OF PARTICIPANTS (N)

Suppose we weighed six adults and found their weights to be:

Data (X)	
Juan	203
Bill	182
Jim	134
Jamal	201
Pete	157
Dave	166

Step 1: Put Xs in order:

X
134
157
166
182
201
203

Step 2: Divide N in half:

$$N = 6, \text{ therefore,}$$

$$\frac{6}{2} = 3$$

(continued)

EXAMPLE 1: *(continued)*

Thus, there are three scores above and three scores below the median on the ordered list.

Step 3: Find the median:

$$\underline{X}$$

134
157
<u>166</u> the median lies halfway
182 between 166 and 182
201
203

To find the midpoint between two numbers, add them together and divide by 2:

$$Mdn = \frac{166 + 182}{2} = \frac{348}{2} = 174$$

The median weight of the sample is 174.
(Half the sample weighs less than 174, and half weighs more than 174.)

EXAMPLE 2: AN EVEN NUMBER OF PARTICIPANTS (N) WITH DUPLICATED SCORES

Suppose we weighed eight adults and found their weights to be:

Data (X)	
Juan	203
Bill	182
Jim	134
Jamal	201
Pete	157
Gary	182
Dan	166
Tyler	193

Step 1: Put Xs in order:

X
134
157
166
182
182
193
201
203

(continued)

EXAMPLE 2: *(continued)*

Step 2: Divide N in half:

$$N = 8, \text{ therefore,}$$

$$\frac{8}{2} = 4$$

Thus, there are four scores above and four scores below the median on the ordered list.

Step 3: Find the median:

X
134
157
166
182
182
193
201
203

the median lies halfway between 182 and 182, so Mdn = 182

(Half the adults weigh 182 or less, and the other half weigh 182 or more.)

EXAMPLE 3: AN ODD NUMBER OF PARTICIPANTS (N)

Suppose we weighed five adults and found their weights to be:

Data (X)	
Juan	203
Bill	182
Jim	134
Jamal	201
Pete	157

Step 1: Put Xs in order:

X
134
157
182
201
203

(continued)

EXAMPLE 3: *(continued)*

Step 2: Divide N in half and add .5 to find the midpoint:

$$N = 5, \text{ therefore,}$$

$$\frac{5}{2} = 2.5 + .5 = 3$$

Thus, the third score in the ordered list is the median.

Step 3: Find the median:

$$\underline{X}$$

134
157
182 = Median
201
203

The median weight is 182.
(Half the adults weigh less than 182, and the other half weigh more than 182.)

To summarize, the median falls in the middle of an ordered set of scores from an ordinal, interval, or ratio scale. If the number of scores in the set is odd, then the middle score itself is the median. If the number of scores in the set is even, the median will fall between the two middle scores, and we can find the midpoint between two scores by adding the two scores together and dividing by 2. In cases where the two middle scores are equal in value, we let the median equal that value as well (see Example 2).[4]

Mean

The most common measure of central tendency for interval or ratio data is the **mean.** This is the *arithmetic average* of all scores. All the values are added together and then divided by the number of values, as shown in the formula below:

$$\overline{X} = \frac{\Sigma X}{N}$$

---

[4] Some textbooks emphasize the fact that scores on a *continuous variable* always involve some rounding error (for example, in measuring weight to the nearest ounce, a score of 3 ounces may mean the object weighed as little as 2.5 ounces or as much as 3.4 ounces), and they present a more precise procedure for finding the median in cases of duplicated scores known as interpolation. Students who are interested in this level of precision can find discussions of *real limits* and interpolation in texts such as Gravetter and Wallnau's *Essentials of Statistics for the Behavioral Sciences* (1991).

The $\overline{X}$ (pronounced "X bar") is the symbol for the mean. The Greek letter *sigma* (Σ) is known as the *summation sign*, and it is an algebraic instruction telling us to find the sum of the variable that is named immediately after Σ. In the case of the mean, we are instructed to get the sum of the X scores, where X denotes each individual score. N denotes the number of scores or values being added together.

Computing the Mean   Let's use the weight data from the six adults to illustrate the computation of the mean.

EXAMPLE: COMPUTING THE MEAN

We have measured the weight of six adults, and their scores (X) are:

X
203
182
134
201
157
166
$\Sigma X = 1043$

Step 1: Find the sum of the Xs (i.e., ΣX).
Step 2: Divide the sum of the Xs by N:

$$\overline{X} = \frac{1043}{6}$$
$$= 173.83333$$
$$\approx 173.8$$

The mean weight of the six adults is 173.8 pounds.

Means Versus Medians: The Case of Outliers

The mean is an appropriate measure of central tendency for interval and ratio scales because these data can be meaningfully added (and divided). That is, the sum of a set of interval or ratio scores is a meaningful quantity. For example, suppose we had measured the number of jelly beans each child has received, and we add Emma's two jellybeans to Jesse's three jellybeans. We end up with a total of five jellybeans. In contrast, addition is not appropriate for ordinal or nominal scales because the sum is *not* a meaningful quantity. For example, suppose we had asked the teacher to rank order the children on the basis of their reading ability, and Emma's rank score was 2 and Jesse's rank score was 3. If we add Emma's reading ability (rank score = 2) to Jesse's reading ability (rank score = 3), the addition may give us a sum of 5, but we do *not* end up with a *total reading ability* that would be given a rank score equal to 5.

Therefore, the mean is mathematically appropriate for interval and ratio data, but it is not appropriate for ordinal or nominal data. (As you will recall, the mode is the only appropriate measure of central tendency for nominal data, and the median can be used with ordinal data.)

However, despite the fact that it is mathematically appropriate to compute the mean for interval and ratio data, there are times when the median may be a more *descriptive* measure of central tendency for interval and ratio data because highly irregular values (called **outliers**) in the data set may affect the value of the mean (*especially in small sets of scores*), but they have *no* effect on the value of the median. For example, suppose we weighed the starting players for two basketball teams and reported to you that the mean weight of Team A is 161 pounds and the mean weight for Team B is 185 pounds. Based only on these means, you might expect to find that members of Team B are, on average, about 24 pounds heavier than players on Team A. However, let's look at the actual weight scores:

Team A	Team B
139	134
145	152
165	157
174	178
182	304

We see that Team B has one extremely heavy player (an outlier), and if we calculate the *median* weights for each team, they turn out to be 165 for Team A and 157 for Team B. If you had originally been told that the "average" weight of Team A was 165 and the "average" weight of Team B was 157, you would have expected to see players who were pretty close in size. And with only one major exception, this expectation would be closer to reality than the 24-pound difference you would expect to see if you knew only the *mean* weights of the teams. Outliers "pull" the mean in their direction so that large scores increase the value of the mean while very small scores decrease the value of the mean, and this effect is most evident in small samples. The resulting distortion of the mean reduces its value as a descriptive statistic. Therefore, when outliers are present in *small* sets of interval or ratio data, researchers will often choose to report the median as the descriptive measure of central tendency. Alternatively, the researchers may choose to report *both* the mean and the median, which has the advantage of allowing readers to see the impact of the outlier on the mean as the measure of average for the data set.

Distributions of Scores

Once we know the value of the typical or average score in a distribution, we usually turn our attention to the other scores in the data set, and we may ask how they are distributed around the group average and how spread out they are from the center. For quantitative variables, the pattern of scores in the distribution can be determined by visually examining the frequency polygon. Essentially, in large data sets, if there is a pattern at all, it generally fits one of three possible patterns: multimodal, symmetrical, or skewed. Multimodal distributions, by definition, have two or more scores with equally large frequencies (i.e., modes), and their frequency polygons have peaks at each of these modes. For example, as we mentioned earlier, a bimodal distribution has two modes, so its frequency polygon has two peaks. In contrast, symmetrical and skewed distributions are unimodal, so they have a single peak. The difference between them is the location of the mode: In symmetrical distributions, the mode is in the center of the distribution, while in skewed distributions, the mode lies to one side of the center. Let's look at a symmetrical distribution that plays a crucial role in research and data analysis: the normal curve.

The Normal Distribution

For some continuous, quantitative attributes, the frequency distribution for the population forms a symmetrical, bell-shaped polygon called the **normal curve** (or **distribution**), which is illustrated in Figure 5-4. Many biological, physical, and psychological characteristics that are influenced by a large number of natural factors have been found to be normally distributed in the population. In a normal distribution, the mean, the median, and the mode are all *equal to the same value:* The mean is in the middle of the distribution, and it is the most frequently occurring score. Thus, the normal curve peaks at the mean of the distribution and tapers off to infinity at both ends without touching the X axis, indicating that there are an equal number of scores above and below the mean and that the scores closest to the mean are more frequent than values farther from the mean. For example, the most common IQ

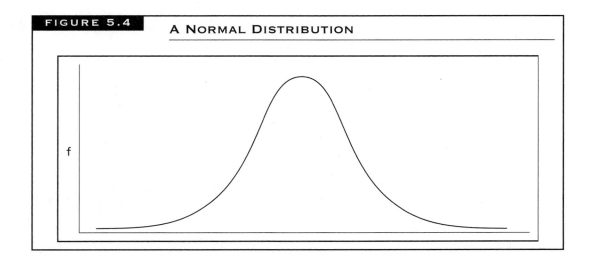

FIGURE 5.4   **A NORMAL DISTRIBUTION**

f

score is 100, which is the mean, and for every individual with an IQ score below 100, there is an individual with an IQ score an equal distance above 100. (That is, for every IQ score of 95, there is an IQ score of 105.) The frequency of particular IQ scores decreases as they get farther from the mean, so that, for example, an IQ of 90 is more common than an IQ of 80. Because the probability of an event depends upon its frequency, the normal distribution of IQ scores tells us that the probability that a person selected at random will have a very high IQ score (such as 140) is very, very low, while the probability of selecting a person with an average score (such as 100) is relatively high. Furthermore, it is common to refer to "segments" of the normal distribution, such as the "tails" of the curve. For example, the normal distribution of IQ scores may be summarized by saying: "Most people have IQ scores between 85 and 115, and only a very few have IQ scores above 130 or below 70."

Skewed Distributions

An important characteristic of the normal curve is its symmetry. Unimodal variables that do *not* distribute themselves normally in the population form *asymmetrical* curves, which are referred to as **skewed distributions.** For example, if we recorded a woman's age at the time she gave birth to her first child and drew a frequency polygon for the population of first-time mothers, we would find that most of the women were in their twenties, some were in their teens or their thirties, a small number were in their forties or older, while none were under the age of about 12 (since giving birth is physiologically impossible until after puberty). Therefore, the distribution of age scores for first-time mothers is not symmetrical but instead has a "tail" on the high end of the age range but ends rather abruptly on the low end of the age range. If there is a concentration of scores at low values and fewer scores or events at high values, the distribution is *positively skewed*. Conversely, if there is a concentration of scores at high values, the distribution is *negatively skewed*. The age of first-time mothers data would form a positive skew. Positive and negative skews are illustrated in Figure 5-5.

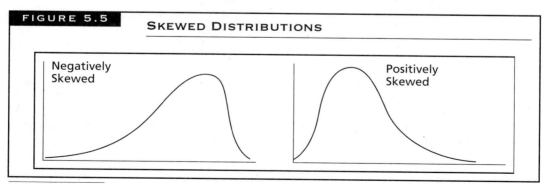

FIGURE 5.5 — SKEWED DISTRIBUTIONS

Negatively Skewed

Positively Skewed

Note: If the tail "points" in the direction of the higher values of X, it is a positive skew. If the tail "points" at the smaller values of X, then it is a negative skew.

Variability

Measures of central tendency tell us something about the center of a distribution, and the shape of the distribution gives us some sense of the pattern among the scores. Another important piece of information is the variability of the measurements. **Variability** measures the **dispersion** among the scores (or how spread out the data are) around the central measure. Two sets of scores can be symmetrical and have the exact same mean but widely differing amounts of variance. If we measure the hours of sleep per night of average adults versus the hours of sleep per night of patients in a mental institution, we might find a similar mean (probably about 7.5 or 8 hours). However, we might suspect that there would be a much greater variability among the hospital patients, due to factors such as medications (affecting sleep patterns or ability to sleep), agitation, or lethargy. To find out whether this is the case, we need to look at a measure of variability.

Variance and Standard Deviation

Measures of variability used with interval and ratio scales take advantage of all scores in the distribution, and, basically, they measure the distance between each score and the group average (which is called a *deviation* from the mean: $X - \overline{X}$) and then calculate the "average" of these **deviation scores.** This "average" deviation tells us about how far from the mean the individual scores tend to lie. Two measures of variability are derived in this manner: the **variance,** which is an inferential statistic, and the **standard deviation,** which is a descriptive statistic. The formulas for the variance and the standard deviation presented first are appropriate for a *sample* of scores; the difference between sample and population formulas is briefly highlighted at the end of this section.

The **variance** calculates the *average squared deviation of each individual score from the mean.* That is, the deviations from the mean are squared (so that they are all positive numbers; if we do not square the deviation scores, the sum always equals 0), and these deviations are then added together (to produce the *sum of squares,* or sum of the squared deviations from the mean). The sum of squares is then divided by $N - 1$, which produces a mean or an average of the squared deviations. The formula for the variance of a sample of scores, called "s-squared," is given below:

$$\text{Variance for a sample of scores} = s^2 = \frac{\Sigma(X - \overline{X})^2}{N - 1}$$

This formula is called the definitional formula because it *shows* how the deviations of each score (X) from the mean ($\overline{X}$) are squared and then summed, and then divided by the degrees of freedom, which are equal to the number of scores minus one. Calculating the variance by hand, however, is easier if you use a different version of the formula, which is referred to as the computational formula:

$$s^2 = \frac{\Sigma X^2 - \frac{(\Sigma X)^2}{N}}{N - 1}$$

As you will notice in the examples below, this formula does *not* require us to compute a deviation score for each score. Instead, we square each score (X^2) and then get the sum of the squared Xs (ΣX^2) and enter it into the formula along with the sum of the original X scores (ΣX) and the sample size (N). Although this version of the formula looks more complicated than the definitional formula, it is easier to work with the X^2s than the $(X - \overline{X})$s.

The variance itself is not a useful *descriptive statistic* because we had to square each deviation score before computing the average. To get a good description of the average variability of scores from the mean, we need to get the variance back into the same units as the original data. Specifically, we need to *undo the squaring* that was done to the deviation scores during the computation of the variance. Taking the square root of the variance produces the descriptive statistic called the **standard deviation** (symbolized as **s**, the square root of s^2). The definitional and computational formulas for the standard deviation are the same as the formulas for the variance except that the last step is to take the square root of the variance:

Definitional formula:

$$\text{Standard deviation for a sample of scores} = s = \sqrt{\frac{\Sigma(X - \overline{X})^2}{N - 1}}$$

Computational formula:

$$\text{Standard deviation for a sample of scores} = s = \sqrt{\frac{\Sigma X^2 - \dfrac{(\Sigma X)^2}{N}}{N - 1}}$$

Computing the Variance and Standard Deviation   To compute the variance (s^2) and then the standard deviation (s) using the computational versions of the formula, we must know N, and we must compute two sums: ΣX is the sum of the X scores (which we will then square), and ΣX^2 is the sum of the squared X scores. The easiest way to begin is to create a second column of numbers where each of the original X scores has been squared and then get the total for each of the two columns of numbers:

X	X^2	
203	41209	
182	33124	
134	17956	N = 6
201	40401	
157	24649	
166	27556	
$\Sigma X = 1043$	$\Sigma X^2 = 184895$	

These sums are entered into the standard deviation formula:

$$s = \sqrt{\frac{184895 - \dfrac{1043^2}{6}}{6 - 1}}$$

Now we solve the formula:

$$s = \sqrt{\frac{184895 - \dfrac{1087849}{6}}{5}}$$

$$s = \sqrt{\frac{184895 - 181308.17}{5}}$$

$$s = \sqrt{\frac{3586.8333}{5}}$$

$s = \sqrt{717.36667}$ **Note: The variance (s^2) equals 717.36667.**

$s = 26.7837$

$s \approx 26.8$

The standard deviation tells us the "average" difference between individual scores and the group mean. Therefore, on average, the scores in our data set were 26.8 points away from the mean: Certainly, some scores were closer to the mean than that, while some were more than 26 pounds away from the mean, but generally, we can interpret the standard deviation as indicating that many of the scores were "within one standard deviation from the mean." That is, in our example, because the adults in the study had a mean weight of 173.8 pounds and a standard deviation of 26.8 pounds, we can conclude that many of them weighed between approximately 147 and 200.6 pounds (the mean ± standard deviation: 173.8 ± 26.8).[5]

The standard deviation is measured in the same units as the mean, so it is readily interpretable, but the variance is on a "squared score scale" and is not easily understood. That is why the standard deviation is used as the descriptive measure of variability for interval and ratio data. Researchers typically report *both the mean and*

---

[5] Because there were only six scores in this data set, you may wonder why we are going to all this trouble—a quick glance tells us what the scores actually were. Imagine, however, a *large data set* that includes the weights from 100 adults. A "quick glance" will no longer give you a good idea about the data set, while simply by knowing the mean is 173.8 and the standard deviation is 26.8 tells you a great deal about the scores. You could, for instance, presume that many of the weight scores fell between 147 and 200.6.

standard deviation of their data, and together these measures of central tendency and variability give a good summary of the data set. For example, if it is reported that the mean SAT-Verbal score for the freshman class at a large university is 600 and the standard deviation is 50, we would know that the majority of freshmen had SAT-Verbal scores within 50 points of 600; (i.e., most of them had scores between 550 and 650; relatively few freshmen would have scored below 550, and a few would have scored above 650).[6] Thus, we have a pretty good understanding of the verbal abilities (as measured by the SATs) of an entire group of freshmen based on only two statistics: central tendency and variability (in this case, the mean and the standard deviation).

Population Formulas   When researchers have data from an entire population, they should compute the variance and standard deviation using the formulas below. The symbol for the population variance (that is, the population *parameter*) is σ^2, and the symbol for the standard deviation of a population is σ (which is the lowercase Greek letter *sigma*). The only difference between the sample statistics and the population parameters is that the demoninator for the parameter is N rather than N − 1. The definitional formulas are as follows (and the computational formulas would be the same as above, except with the change in the denominator):

$$\text{Variance for a population of scores} = \sigma^2 = \frac{\Sigma(X - \overline{X})^2}{N}$$

$$\text{Standard deviation for a population of scores} = \sigma = \sqrt{\frac{\Sigma(X - \overline{X})^2}{N}}$$

The change in the denominator from N (for the population parameter) to N − 1 (for the sample statistic) makes our sample statistic a better estimate of the population parameter because samples tend to be less variable than the population as a whole. Dividing by N − 1 instead of the actual number of participants (N) corrects for the slight decrease in sample variability by giving us a slightly larger value, so s and s^2 are closer to the values of σ and σ^2.

Median Absolute Deviation

For ordinal scales, where the arithmetic operations involved in calculating the mean and standard deviation are not appropriate, we can measure the *average deviations of scores from the center* by using the median instead of the mean. The **median absolute**

---

[6] Here we are assuming that the SAT scores for this class are normally distributed because SAT scores are known to follow the normal curve in the population. Recall that a normal curve (frequency polygon) peaks in the middle, which means that the scores in the middle of the range are more common than scores in the "tails." Therefore, more students score between 450 and 500 than between 400 and 450, and so forth.

deviation (MAD) is logically equivalent to the standard deviation, yet it uses the median as the measure of average. The first step is to calculate the deviation scores where the median is subtracted from each X score. The *absolute values* of these deviations are used in this procedure, so all negative signs are dropped. Then the median of these *absolute deviation scores* is found, following the rules for finding the median for any set of X scores. The result, then, is a measure of the average[7] difference between X scores and the median of the X scores.

Finding the Median Absolute Deviation   As an example, let's find the MAD for the same sample of weight scores.

EXAMPLE: CALCULATING THE MAD

Data	
Juan	203
Bill	182
Jim	134
Jamal	201
Pete	157
Dave	166

Step 1: Put the Xs in order:

X
134
157
166
182
201
203

Step 2: Find the median:

X in Order

134
157
166   The median lies halfway
182   between 166 and 182
201
203

(continued)

---

[7] Do not forget that the term *average* can refer to any of the measures of central tendency.

EXAMPLE: (*continued*)

$$Mdn = \frac{166 + 182}{2}$$

$$Mdn = \frac{348}{2}$$

$$Mdn = 174$$

Step 3: Get the absolute deviations:

$|X - Mdn|$
$|134 - 174| = 40$
$|157 - 174| = 17$
$|166 - 174| = 8$
$|182 - 174| = 8$
$|201 - 174| = 27$
$|203 - 174| = 29$

Step 4: Put the deviations in order and find the median:

$|X - Mdn|$ in Order

8
8
17   The median of these absolute
27   deviation scores lies halfway
29   between 17 and 27
40

$$MAD = \frac{17 + 27}{2}$$

$$MAD = \frac{44}{2}$$

$$MAD = 22$$

Thus, the median absolute deviation for the set of weight scores is equal to 22. Since the MAD itself is a median, it tells us that *half of the deviation scores* are equal to 22 or less and the other half of the deviation scores are equal to 22 or more. (That is, half of scores are within 22 points of the group median.) This indicates that half of the scores lie between 152 and 196 (which is the Mdn ± MAD; that is, 174 ± 22).

As we pointed out earlier, a data set can be summarized quite thoroughly by reporting a measure of central tendency and a measure of variability. For ordinal data,

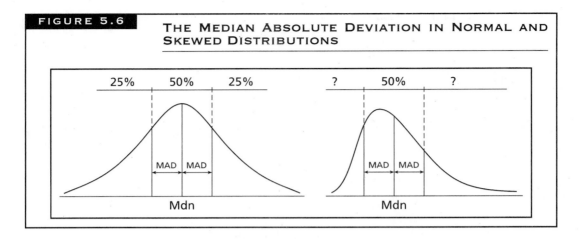

FIGURE 5.6 THE MEDIAN ABSOLUTE DEVIATION IN NORMAL AND SKEWED DISTRIBUTIONS

the combination of the median and the median absolute deviation provides an informative description of the data. For example, suppose the university's registrar reports that the incoming freshman class has a median high-school class rank of 15 and a median absolute deviation of 5. The median tells us that half of the incoming students placed in the top 15 of their class, and the median absolute deviation tells us that half of the students were within 5 points of the median. Therefore, from these two statistics, we know that 50% of the incoming students placed between 10th and 20th in their high-school class (i.e., Mdn ± MAD). If the distribution of class ranks for this group of incoming students is *normal* (and, hence, symmetrical), we would also be able to say that 25% of the students placed in the top 10 of their class while 25% had class ranks above 20. However, if the distribution of class ranks is *skewed* (which is quite likely), we would *not* know exactly what proportion of students ranked in the top 10 or below 20—we could only be certain that altogether, the students above 10 and below 20 make up that half of the incoming students with class ranks more than 5 points from the group median. Figure 5-6 illustrates the MAD for normal and skewed distributions.

Standard Deviations Versus the Median Absolute Deviation: The Case of Outliers

The MAD was designed to be used with ordinal data, but it is also appropriate for interval or ratio scales when *outliers* (extremely high or extremely low scores) cause a distortion in the standard deviation. Consider our earlier example of the weight scores for two basketball teams (see page 95). We saw that the presence of an outlier affected the value of the mean so that it no longer gave a realistic picture of the average basketball player. A similar distortion occurs when we measure the variability among the players on Team B. The standard deviation for Team B is equal to 68.34 pounds.

Is it really accurate to say that the *average difference between the players on the team is over 68 pounds?* Is this a reasonable description of the players on Team B? Of course not. Leave out the heavy player, and you see that the other four players are all *within* 44 pounds of one another—not even close to an *average* difference of 68 pounds. That one extremely heavy player (the outlier) has had a strong impact on the value of the standard deviation. Therefore, when an outlier is present in a data set of interval or ratio scores, the standard deviation may provide a distorted estimate of the variability among the typical scores in the sample—especially when the sample size is small. Consequently, the MAD can be used as an alternative measure of variability. The MAD for Team B is 21 pounds—a much more reasonable description of the team as a whole.[8]

Range

The most basic measure of variability that can be used with ordinal, interval, or ratio scales is the range. The **range** is simply the smallest value subtracted from the largest value. In our example of basketball players' weights, if the heaviest player on Team A weighs 182 pounds and the lightest player weighs 139 pounds, the range would be 43 pounds (182 minus 139); if the heaviest player on Team B weighs 304 pounds and the lightest player weighs 134 pounds, the range would be 170 pounds (304 minus 134). The range is a useful statistic for getting a sense of the overall variability, but because it is so sensitive to outliers (as in the data for Team B), it is *not* a very good descriptive measure of the "average" variability. For instance, if the outlier is omitted, the range of scores for Team B becomes 44 pounds—178 minus 134—rather than 170.

Number of Categories/Values

For nominal data, we can measure variability simply by counting the number of separate categories or values of the attribute represented in the data. For example, if you surveyed a class of students and asked them to identify their religious affiliations, you could then report how many *different* religions are reported by the students. A group would be considered more variable if eight different religions are represented than if only four religions are represented.[9]

---

[8] The amount of distortion in the mean and standard deviation caused by an outlier depends heavily on the size of the sample: Even very extreme scores will have little impact on large samples. If you suspect that there is an outlier in the data set, you could compute the mean and standard deviation *twice:* first with the outlier, and then without it. If there is a substantial change in the value of $\overline{X}$ and s, the Mdn and MAD may provide a more accurate summary of the data.

[9] This statistic is highly dependent on the measurement procedure employed. If you surveyed the group using a questionnaire that listed only four different religious affiliations and asked the participants to check the appropriate category, you may get fewer different answers than if you simply asked the participants, "What is your religious affiliation?" Even if your list includes a category labeled "Other" with a blank space for them to name it, this procedure may limit the number of religions that appear in the data. Therefore, using this statistic to describe the variability of a group may require that you also report how many *choices* the participants had, and you can make comparisons only between samples that were given the same number of choices.

The Variation Ratio

Another statistic that can be used to measure the variability of categorical, nominal data is the **variation ratio (v)**, which is the proportion of cases that fall outside the modal category. For example, imagine that we observed 20 preschool children and recorded which crayon they selected first from a full box of eight different colors. Suppose we found that six children selected the red crayon, four children selected the green crayon, eight children selected the blue crayon, and two children selected the yellow crayon. The mode of this distribution is blue crayon, since that crayon was selected by more children than any other color. The variation ratio would be computed by counting the number of children who did *not* select the blue crayon and dividing by the total number of children:

$$v = \frac{f_{red} + f_{green} + f_{yellow}}{N} = \frac{6 + 4 + 2}{20} = \frac{12}{20} = 0.60 \text{ (or 60\%)}$$

Alternatively, we can compute the variation ratio by calculating the proportion of scores in the modal category and subtracting from 1.00:

$$v = 1.00 - \frac{f_{mode}}{N} = 1.00 - \frac{8}{20} = 1.00 - .40 = 0.60 \text{ (or 60\%)}$$

Therefore, the results of our observations on color choices could be summarized by saying that the modal color choice was blue and the variation ratio was 60% (indicating that 60% of the children did *not* choose the blue crayon while 40% of them did.) Additionally, if we also reported that only four colors were selected *at all* from the box of eight crayons (i.e., the number of categories present in the data), we would have done a thorough job of describing our nominal data set to others by presenting information about central tendency and variability.

Selecting Appropriate Descriptive Statistics

It should be apparent from the discussions above that the level of measurement of the data set is the primary factor that determines which statistical procedures are appropriate. While frequencies (including percentages) can be calculated for data on any scale, the measures of central tendency and variability may be limited to particular levels of measurement. The chart presented in Table 5-5 should help you select the descriptive statistics most suitable to the data and informative to your readers.

Simple Data Transformations

At some time or other, every student is likely to hear a professor announce that the exam grades have been "curved." This usually means that the professor has added points to everyone's exam score. What effect does this grading curve have on the

TABLE 5.5	The Appropriate Descriptive Statistics for Each Level of Measurement

	Level of Measurement		
	Nominal	**Ordinal**	**Interval/Ratio**
Central Tendency	MODE	MEDIAN (mode)	MEAN (median*) (mode)
Variability	NUMBER OF CATEGORIES or VARIATION RATIO	MAD (range) (number of categories) (variation ratio)	STANDARD DEVIATION (MAD*) (range) (number of categories) (variation ratio)

NOTE: The statistic that is presented in CAPITALS is the most appropriate or preferred statistic for each level of measurement. The statistics listed in parentheses ( ) can be computed, but they are not usually preferred. The asterisked (*) statistics may be preferred for interval or ratio data if an outlier is present that distorts the value of the mean and the standard deviation.

distribution of exam grades? If the professor has added the same number of points (that is, a *constant*) to every score, the mean will increase by that same constant value, but the standard deviation will remain unchanged because the difference between the individual scores and the group mean stays the same. For example, consider the following set of exam grades before and after a 5-point curve (where 5 points is added to each score):

Original Scores	
Adam	72
Bob	68
Catya	79
Damon	70
Ellen	67
Fran	73

$$\Sigma X = 429$$
$$N = 6$$

$$\overline{X} = \frac{429}{6} = \mathbf{71.5}$$

$$s = \sqrt{\frac{30767 - \frac{429^2}{6}}{6 - 1}}$$

$$= \sqrt{\frac{30767 - \dfrac{184041}{6}}{5}}$$

$$= \sqrt{\frac{30767 - 30673.5}{5}}$$

$$= \sqrt{\frac{93.5}{5}}$$

$$= \sqrt{18.7}$$

$$= 4.3243497$$

Curved Scores

Adam	77
Bob	73
Catya	84
Damon	75
Ellen	72
Fran	78

$$\Sigma X = 459$$
$$N = 6$$

$$\overline{X} = \frac{459}{6} = \mathbf{76.5}$$

$$s = \sqrt{\frac{35207 - \dfrac{459^2}{6}}{6 - 1}}$$

$$= \sqrt{\frac{35207 - \dfrac{210681}{6}}{5}}$$

$$= \sqrt{\frac{35207 - 35113.5}{5}}$$

$$= \sqrt{\frac{93.5}{5}}$$

$$= \sqrt{18.7}$$

$$= 4.3243497$$

$$\approx 4.3$$

As you can see, adding the constant (5 points) to every score increased the group mean from 71.5 to 76.5. Thus, when a constant (c) is added to each score, the group mean also increases by the value of the constant:

$$\overline{X}_{new} = \overline{X}_{original} + C$$
$$76.5 = 71.5 + 5$$

Unlike the mean, however, the standard deviation did *not* change when five points were added to each score. This makes sense if you look at the relationship between the individual scores and the means: You see that it does not change. For example, Adam's original exam score (X = 72) was only one-half point above the original mean ($\overline{X}$ = 71.5), and after the curve, his new score (X_{curved} = 77) was still only one-half point above the new group mean ($\overline{X}_{curved}$ = 76.5). Likewise, Catya's original exam score (X = 79) was 7.5 points above the mean and her curved score (X = 84) was 7.5 points above the curved mean. Thus, the deviation of scores from the mean—which is measured by the standard deviation—remains the same when a constant is added to every score.

Now consider a situation where every score is *multiplied* by a constant. For example, suppose you measured the amount of time, in minutes, runners took to run a mile and then gave runners training designed to increase their speed. Because training may yield systematic but *small* improvements in experienced runners, you may decide to change your data to seconds rather than minutes (in hopes of having a more sensitive measurement). To change the original times from minutes to seconds, you need to multiply each score by 60. What happens to the distribution of time scores when they are multiplied by a constant? Let's look at an example.

EXAMPLE: MULTIPLYING BY A CONSTANT

Minutes	
Adam	7.2
Bob	6.8
Catya	7.9
Damon	7.0
Ellen	6.7
Fran	7.3

$$\Sigma X = 42.9$$
$$N = 6$$

$$\overline{X} = \frac{42.9}{6} = 7.15$$

(continued)

EXAMPLE: *(continued)*

$$s = \sqrt{\frac{307.67 - \frac{42.9^2}{6}}{6 - 1}}$$

$$= \sqrt{\frac{307.67 - \frac{1840.41}{6}}{5}}$$

$$= \sqrt{\frac{307.67 - 306.735}{5}}$$

$$= \sqrt{\frac{0.935}{5}}$$

$$= \sqrt{0.187}$$

$$= 0.43243497$$

$$\approx 0.43$$

Seconds	
Adam	432
Bob	408
Catya	474
Damon	420
Ellen	402
Fran	438

$$\Sigma X = 2574$$
$$N = 6$$

$$\overline{X} = \frac{2574}{6} = 429$$

$$s = \sqrt{\frac{1107612 - \frac{2574^2}{6}}{6 - 1}}$$

$$= \sqrt{\frac{1107612 - \frac{6625476}{6}}{5}}$$

(continued)

EXAMPLE: *(continued)*

$$= \sqrt{\frac{1107612 - 1104246}{5}}$$

$$= \sqrt{\frac{3366}{5}}$$

$$= \sqrt{673.2}$$

$$= 25.946098$$

$$\approx 25.95$$

As you can see, if we multiply every minute score by the constant (60 seconds per minute), the mean is also multiplied by the value of the constant:

$$\overline{X}_{original} \times c = \overline{X}_{new}$$
$$7.15 \times 60 = 429$$

Furthermore, multiplying every score by the constant (60 seconds) increased the standard deviation 60-fold. That is, the standard deviation was also multiplied by the constant:

$$S_{original} \times c = S_{new}$$
$$0.43243497 \times 60 = 25.946098$$

Again, we can see the change in the standard deviation if we look at the difference between individual scores and the group mean. Adam's time of 7.2 minutes was only 0.05 minutes above the mean ($\overline{X}_{minutes} = 7.15$), but after the transformation of the scores into seconds, Adam's score of 432 seconds was 3.0 seconds above the mean ($\overline{X}_{seconds} = 429$): 0.05 times 60 equals 3.0. Thus, we see that multiplying the scores by 60 also multiplied the standard deviation by 60.[10]

---

[10] Transforming scores by *subtracting* a constant has the same *pattern* of effects on the distribution as the addition of a constant: The mean is reduced by the value of the constant, but the standard deviation does not change. (That is, $\overline{X}_{original} - c = \overline{X}_{new}$). Transforming scores by *dividing by* a constant has the same *pattern* of effects on the distribution as the multiplication by a constant: Both the mean and the standard deviation are divided by the value of the constant. That is, $\overline{X}_{original} \div c = \overline{X}_{new}$ and $s_{original} \div c = s_{new}$.

z-Scores

Transforming scores by adding (or subtracting) constants or by multiplying (or dividing) by constants can make the data easier to use or interpret. For example, multiplying probabilities or proportions by 100 converts them to percentages and removes the decimal points—making the scores easier to use. Another type of transformation that is very useful involves *standardizing* the score scale, which allows us to compare scores from different distributions to one another. For example, using a standardized score scale, we could compare students' SAT-Verbal scores (which are on a scale from 200 to 800) to their IQ scores (which have a possible range from 0 to approximately 200). If John Smith has an IQ score of 110 and an SAT-Verbal score of 650, we may want to ask how his SAT performance compared with his performance on the intelligence test: Was his performance on the SAT better (or worse) than his IQ test performance? Unfortunately, because they use different score scales (with different means and standard deviations), we cannot directly compare the raw SAT and IQ scores. We can, however, compute a *standardized score*, known as a **z-score,** which specifies the exact location of a raw score within its own distribution, and we can then compare any two z-scores (from distributions with similar shapes) to find out whether one score is relatively better or worse than another.

Specifically, a z-score measures the distance between a score (X) and the group mean ($\overline{X}$) by counting the number of standard deviations (s) between them. The z-score will also indicate whether the score is above or below the mean. For instance, John's IQ score of 110 is 10 points above the average IQ score of 100, so we know he is "above average" in intelligence. However, the standard deviation for IQ scores is 15 points, which tells us that the *average* difference between scores and the mean is 15 points, which, in turn, suggests that IQ scores can be substantially more than 15 points above or below the mean (i.e., 116 and higher or 84 and lower). In this context, John's "10-points-above-average" IQ score is not really very far above average: He is only about two-thirds of the *"average distance" from the mean*; that is, his score was only *two-thirds of one standard deviation above the mean.* Hence, on the standardized z-score scale, John's z-score for IQ would be equal to +0.67, where the positive sign indicates that his score was above average. In contrast, if the mean SAT-Verbal score is 500 and the standard deviation is 100, John's SAT-V score of 650 is considerably above average because the 150-point difference between his score and the mean is one-and-a-half times greater than the "average distance" between scores and the mean, indicating that his SAT score was one-and-a-half standard deviations above average. Therefore, his SAT score would have a standardized z-score equal to +1.50.

Raw scores from *any* distribution can be converted into z-scores because it is possible to specify the location of any score within its own distribution. The formula for z is:

$$z = \frac{X - \overline{X}}{s} \qquad \textbf{where } \overline{X} \textbf{ is the mean and}$$

s is the standard deviation

Raw scores that are equal to the group mean will have a z-score equal to 0.0, which reflects the fact that there was no "distance" or difference between the X and X̄. *Therefore, the distribution of z-scores always has a mean equal to 0.0 and the standard deviation of the z-distribution is always equal to 1.0.* (The shape of the z-distribution will be the same as the original distribution of X scores.) Converting raw scores into z-scores makes it possible to compare scores from different distributions (as long as they have similar shapes).

For example, imagine that a group of fourth-grade children recently took two tests, including a math test (which had a total of 18 problems) and a vocabulary test (which included 60 words). Columns 2 and 4 in Table 5-6 present the raw scores for each of the children on the two tests. One of the children (Andy) had 9 correct answers on the math test and correctly defined 43 words on the vocabulary test. Is Andy doing better in math or in vocabulary? To answer this question, we must convert his raw scores to z-scores.

As you can see in Table 5-6, the mean score on the math test was 12 correct answers, and the standard deviation was 2.0. The mean number of correct vocabulary words was 45, and the standard deviation was 5.0. Using this information, each child's z-scores were computed (and are presented in columns 3 and 5 of Table 5-6). We can see that Andy scored well below the mean on the math test, leading to a z-score of −1.5. He also scored below the mean on the vocabulary test, but this vocabulary z-score of −0.4 is closer to the mean, indicating that he is doing better in vocabulary than in math. In contrast, Dave has scored *above* average on both tests but is doing better in math than in vocabulary (as indicated by the fact that his z-score for math of +1.5 is farther above the mean than his z-score for vocabulary of +1.0).

TABLE 5.6   **Examples of z-Scores**

Participant	Math Raw X	Math z-Score	Vocabulary Raw X	Vocabulary z-Score
Andy	9	−1.5	43	−0.4
Bill	12	0.0	49	+0.8
Carl	13	+0.5	41	−0.8
Dave	15	+1.5	50	+1.0
Eddy	11	−0.5	38	−1.4
Fred	12	0.0	49	+0.8
ΣX	72		270	
N	6		6	
X̄	12		45	
s	2.0		5.0	

Computation Example: Andy's z-Score for Math

$$z = \frac{9 - 12}{2.0} = \frac{-3}{2.0} = -1.50$$

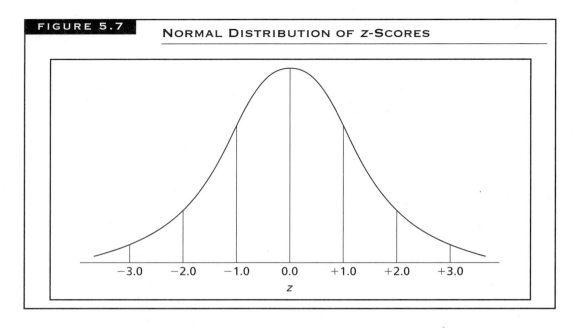

FIGURE 5.7 NORMAL DISTRIBUTION OF Z-SCORES

The locations of z-scores can be represented in a frequency polygon. In Figure 5-7, you can see where z scores of −3 to +3 would fall on the normal curve. By using the z-scores rather than raw scores, we can now look at performance on two tests that are not comparable in their original form.

z-Scores as Inferential Statistics: Areas Under the Normal Curve

Using z-scores to make comparisons between scores from separate distributions (such as IQ scores and SAT scores, or between GPA scores and GRE scores) is certainly an important descriptive statistical procedure. But for most researchers, z-scores (and similar standardized scales) are at the heart of an even more important process: the inferential decision-making process whereby we decide whether or not two variables are significantly related to each other. (This hypothesis-testing process is the topic of Chapter 6.)

The characteristic of z-scores that is central to the inferential decision-making process is the fact that, *in a normal distribution* of scores, the proportion (or percentage) of scores that have a particular value of z is always the same, regardless of the mean and standard deviation of the distribution. For example, consider IQ and SAT-Verbal scores. The distribution of IQ scores in the population is normal, with a mean of 100 and a standard deviation of 15, while the distribution of SAT-Verbal scores is also normal, but with a mean of 500 and a standard deviation of 100. As illustrated in Figure 5-8, an individual with an IQ of 130 will have a z-score equal to +2.0, as will an individual with an SAT-Verbal score of 700. How many people have an IQ score

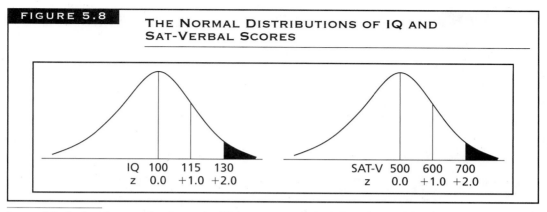

FIGURE 5.8

THE NORMAL DISTRIBUTIONS OF IQ AND SAT-VERBAL SCORES

| IQ | 100 | 115 | 130 |
| z | 0.0 | +1.0 | +2.0 |

| SAT-V | 500 | 600 | 700 |
| z | 0.0 | +1.0 | +2.0 |

In normal distributions, the proportion of scores that fall above a *z*-score of +2.0 is always the same. Therefore, the proportion of people with IQ scores of 130 or above is the same as the proportion of people with SAT-Verbal scores of 700 or higher.

of 130 or higher? How many will receive a score of 700 or higher on the SAT-Verbal test? Because these distributions are both normally distributed, and because an IQ of 130 has *the same z-score* as does an SAT-Verbal score of 700, we know that the same percentage of people will have these scores.

This percentage can be found using the table of "Areas Under the Normal Curve (*z*-Table)," which is Table B1 in Appendix B (at the back of this text). The *z*-Table consists of three columns: (1) the value of *z*; (2) the area (or *proportion of scores*) between *z* and the mean; and (3) the area beyond *z* (which gives the proportion of scores with values equal to or greater than *z*). (For every value of *z*, the proportions in the second and third columns add up to .50000, which indicates that 50% of the scores are either between the mean and *z*, or beyond the value of *z*. This makes sense when you remember that, in normal distributions, the mean is equal to the median, so by definition, half of the scores will fall above the mean and half will fall below it.) Figure 5-9 illustrates how the *z*-Table is laid out and how the information is interpreted.

Returning to the example, we want to know what percentage of the population has an IQ score of 130 or higher or an SAT-V score of 700 or higher. Because we know that an IQ score of 130 has a *z*-score of +2.0, we can look down the first column of Table B1 until we find 2.00. The second column tells us the proportion of scores that fall between the mean (in this case, an IQ of 100) and our *z* of 2.00 (an IQ of 130), while the third column tells us the proportion of scores that are equal to *z* or greater. The proportion beyond *z* for *z* = 2.00 is .02275, so the percentage is equal to 2.275%. Thus, about 2.3% of the population have IQ scores of 130 or higher. Similarly, because an SAT-Verbal score of 700 also has a *z*-score equal to 2.00, we also know that about 2.3% of the population have SAT-V scores of 700 or better. *Again, in a normal distribution, a particular value of z always has the same proportion of scores above it.*

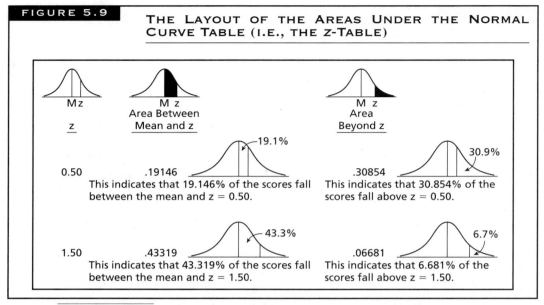

FIGURE 5.9

THE LAYOUT OF THE AREAS UNDER THE NORMAL CURVE TABLE (I.E., THE Z-TABLE)

Note: .19146 + .30854 = .50 and .43319 + .06681 = .50

Because normal curves are symmetrical, the mean is also equal to the median.

The fact that normal distributions always have the same proportions of scores with the same values of z allows researchers to answer a variety of questions about distributions. For instance, when new federal regulations required school districts to provide special education services to all children who have been diagnosed with mental retardation, it was possible to predict how many students would be eligible using the z-Table. (This example is illustrated in Figure 5-10a.)

1) In Pennsylvania, for example, mental retardation is defined as having an IQ score of 80 or below. To find out what proportion of the population fits this classification, we first compute the z-score for an IQ of 80:

2) $$Z_{IQ = 80} = \frac{80 - 100}{15} = \frac{-20}{15} = -1.33$$

3) Using Table B1, we find that the proportion of the population with a z-score of -1.33 or less[11] is .09175 (or 9.175%). Local school boards could now estimate how many students in their district would probably need special education services:

---

[11] Because normal distributions are symmetrical, the z-Table includes only the positive values of z, but the proportions that score at $-z$ or below are the same as the proportions that score at $+z$ or higher.

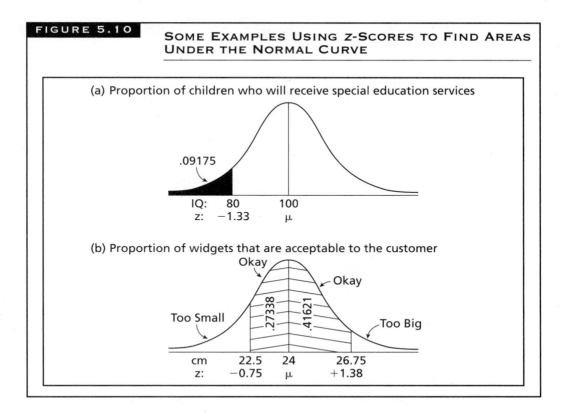

FIGURE 5.10 **SOME EXAMPLES USING z-SCORES TO FIND AREAS UNDER THE NORMAL CURVE**

(a) Proportion of children who will receive special education services

.09175

IQ: 80   100
z: −1.33   μ

(b) Proportion of widgets that are acceptable to the customer

Okay
Okay
Too Small
.27338
.41621
Too Big

cm   22.5   24   26.75
z: −0.75   μ   +1.38

4) If a school district serves 50,000 children, it will probably need to provide special education services to 4,588 children:

$$\text{number of children} = .09175 \times 50{,}000$$
$$= 4587.5$$

As a second example, illustrated in Figure 5-10b, imagine that a manufacturer who makes widgets knows that the widget-making process generates widgets that are an average of 24 cm. long but that they vary slightly in length. Imagine that this variation results in a normal distribution with a standard deviation of 2 cm. If a customer orders widgets from the manufacturer but can use only widgets that range in length from 22.50 cm. to 26.75 cm., the manufacturer can use the *z*-Table to determine what percentage of his widgets will satisfy the customer's requirements. The first step will be to determine what percentage of the "smaller-than-average" widgets will be okay, the second step will be to determine what percentage of the "bigger-than-average" widgets will be okay, and the final step will be to add those two percentages together:

Step 1 (a): Calculate the z-score for the smaller-than-average widgets that are acceptable:

$$z = \frac{22.50 - 24}{2}$$

$$= \frac{-1.5}{2}$$

$$= -.75$$

(b): Find the proportion of scores that fall between z and the mean (using the second column of the z-Table). For $z = \pm.75$:

Proportion between μ and $z = .27338$ (or 27.338%)

Step 2 (a): Calculate the z-score for the larger-than-average widgets that are acceptable:

$$z = \frac{26.75 - 24}{2}$$

$$= \frac{2.75}{2}$$

$$= 1.375 \text{ (rounded to 1.38)}$$

(b): Find the proportion of scores that fall between z and the mean (using the second column of the z-Table). For $z = \pm1.38$:

proportion between μ and $z = .41621$ (or 41.621%)

Step 3: Find the total proportion (percentage) of widgets that are acceptable to the customer:

$$.27338 + .41621 = .68959 \text{ (or 68.959\%)}$$

Thus, the manufacturer can estimate that only about 69% of his widgets will be suitable, so he'll need to make a greater number of widgets in order to fill the customer's order. That is, if the customer wants 100 widgets, the manufacturer will probably need to produce at least 146 widgets in order to have 100 widgets that fit the customer's needs. We determined this by dividing the desired number of widgets by the proportion of widgets that would be acceptable:

$$100 \div .68959 = 145.0137$$

In each of the examples thus far, we have started by computing a z-score and then looking up the proportion of scores either beyond z or between z and the mean. The z-Table can also be used for problems that ask for the value of z that cuts off a

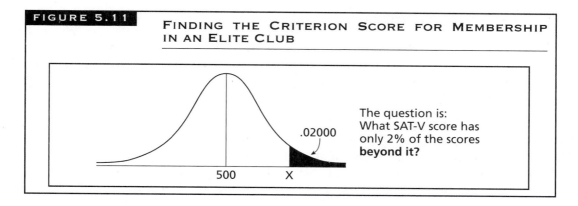

FIGURE 5.11

FINDING THE CRITERION SCORE FOR MEMBERSHIP IN AN ELITE CLUB

.02000

The question is:
What SAT-V score has
only 2% of the scores
beyond it?

500   X

given proportion (or percentage). For example, suppose you wanted to start a new elite club—a club where *only* 2% of the population would be eligible to join. You may decide that the eligibility requirement is that members must be in the top 2% of the SAT-Verbal test. What SAT-Verbal score, then, would be the criterion for membership? As you can see from the shaded region of the distribution in Figure 5-11, you need to find the z-score that has 2% of the scores *beyond* it.

The first step is to scan down the *third column* of the z-Table until you find the proportion closest to .02000 and then convert the critical value of z (which is found in column 1) into the SAT-Verbal score that "cuts off" the top 2% of all scores. Converting z into a value of X requires a variant of the z-score formula, which we refer to as the **z-to-X conversion formula**:

$$X = z(s) + \overline{X}$$

Step 1: Find the z with 2% (.02000) of the scores at or above it (using the second column of Table B1):

z = 2.05 (because its proportion of .02017 is closest to .02000)

Step 2: Convert z to X (in this case, an SAT-Verbal score) using the z-to-X conversion formula, using the SAT-V mean of 500 and standard deviation of 100:

$$
\begin{aligned}
X &= z(s) + \overline{X} \\
&= 2.05(100) + 500 \\
&= 205 + 500 \\
&= 705
\end{aligned}
$$

Thus, in order to be eligible to join your new club (by being in the top 2% of the population in SAT-Verbal scores), an individual needs to have received a score of 705 or higher.

Essentially, as discussed in detail in Chapter 6, researchers make decisions about whether or not two variables are related based on whether or not the research sample can be labeled as one of the "most rare" events. Typically, psychologists use the most rare 5% as the criterion used in inferential decision making, although it is not uncommon to use 1% as the criterion. Thus, researchers and statisticians need to be able to determine the cut-off score for these criteria. If we consider very low scores as well as very high scores, then the most rare 5% actually consists of the lowest 2.5% and the highest 2.5% of the scores, while the most rare 1% consists of the lowest 0.5% and highest 0.5% of the scores. By looking up the z-score that has 2.5% of the scores (a proportion of .02500) at or beyond it, using the third column of the z-Table, researchers can then convert that z into critical values (or cut-off points) for identifying the most rare 5%. (At the same time, of course, these cut-off points will identify the middle 95% of the scores.) Or they can look up the z with a proportion of .00500 beyond it in order to identify the cut-off points for the most rare 1% and the middle 99%. (And because the same value of z always cuts off the same proportion of scores in a normal distribution, we really need look up these z-scores only once!)

Most rare 5%: $z_{top\ 2.5\%} = +1.96$ and $z_{bottom\ 2.5\%} = -1.96$
Most rare 1%: $z_{top\ 0.5\%} = +2.58$ and $z_{bottom\ 0.5\%} = -2.58$

Exercises

The following problems are intended to give you practice computing various descriptive statistics.

1. Using the data in Table 5-2 on page 85, draw a grouped frequency polygon.

2. Assume the following scores are from a calculus quiz. Compute each of the descriptive statistics listed below.

X
8
11
15
7
16
17
10
9
10
12

   a. Mean
   b. Median
   c. Mode
   d. Standard deviation

   e. Median absolute deviation
   f. Range
   g. Number of categories
   h. Variation ratio

3. Assume the following scores are from a chemistry exam. Compute each of the descriptive statistics listed below.

X
40
50
40
30
50
20
10
30
40
20

   a. Mean
   b. Median
   c. Mode
   d. Standard deviation
   e. Median absolute deviation
   f. Range
   g. Number of categories
   h. Variation ratio

4. Using the means and standard deviations for the data in problems 2 and 3 above:

   a. calculate the z-score for an individual whose score on the chemistry exam (X) was 25.
   b. calculate the score on the calculus quiz (X) an individual would have to obtain in order to have a z-score of $+1.25$.

5. John is a student taking the classes in calculus and chemistry. He received a score of 30 on the chemistry exam (in problem 3) and a 12 on the calculus quiz (in problem 2). Based on these scores, is John's current class standing higher in chemistry or calculus?

Use the following information for problems 6–9:
   A psychologist wanted to examine the effects of diet on learning. Two groups of rats were selected with 12 rats in each group. One group was fed the regular diet of Purina Rat Chow while the other group had special vitamins and minerals added to the Rat Chow. After six months, each rat was tested on a discrimination problem. The psychologist recorded the number of errors each animal made before it solved the problem. The data for the experiment were as follows:

Regular Diet: 13, 11, 12, 13, 11, 9, 12, 10, 12, 14, 10, 12
Special Diet: 9, 8, 7, 8, 9, 10, 7, 8, 9, 6, 8, 10

6. Sketch a frequency polygon for the Regular Diet group, and then use a different color and sketch the distribution for the Special Diet group (using the same graph). From looking at your graph, would you say that the vitamins and mineral supplements in the special diet had any effect on learning? Explain your answer.

7. Compute the mean and standard deviation for each group of rats separately. Do you still think the difference in diets has (or has not) had an effect on performance?

8. Suppose you agreed to take one of the rats to keep as a pet. If a rat were selected for you at random from the Regular Diet group, what is the probability that you would get a rat that had made 12 or more errors on the discrimination task?

9. Again suppose that you agreed to take one of the rats as a pet. If your new pet rat were selected at random from the entire sample of rats, what is the probability you would end up with a rat that had made 12 or more errors?

Use the following information for problems 10–13:
In a psychology class of 60 students, there are 15 males and 45 females. Of the 45 women, 20 are freshmen while only five of the men are freshmen. If you were to randomly select one individual from the class (by drawing a name from a hat):

10. What is the probability of selecting a female?

11. What is the probability of selecting a freshman?

12. What is the probability of selecting a male freshman?

13. Determine whether sex and class are independent of each other in this sample.

14. Find the proportion of the normal distribution that lies in the tail beyond each of the following regions:

   a. above $z = +0.50$
   b. between $z = +0.25$ and $z = +2.50$
   c. above $z = +1.75$
   d. below $z = -1.34$
   e. between $z = -0.75$ and $z = +1.35$
   f. between $z = -2.40$ and $z = -1.70$

15. For a normal distribution with a mean of 80 and a standard deviation of 12, what is the probability of randomly selecting a person with a score *less than* 92?

16. For a normal distribution of SAT scores with a mean of 500 and a standard deviation of 100, what is the probability of randomly selecting a person with a score *between* 540 and 640?

17. It takes Jill an average of 26 minutes to ride her bike to the ice cream parlor. The distribution of biking times is nearly normal with a standard deviation of 3 minutes. If Jill leaves home at 8:38, what is the probability that she will be in time to get ice cream before the parlor closes at 9:00?

18. A developmental psychologist has developed a new test designed to measure sociability in children. The scores on this test form a normal distribution with a mean of 60 and a standard deviation of 9. Based on these test scores, the psychologist wants to classify the population into five categories of sociability:

    I: Inhibited children (the lowest 10%)
    II: Shy children (the next 20%)
    III: Average children (the middle 40%)
    IV: Friendly children (the next 20%)
    V: Extraverted children (the top 10%)

    What scores on the test form the boundaries (or cut-off points) for these categories?

19. The ACME Scholarship Foundation provides college scholarships to the top 3% of students who take the ACME Prep Test. The mean on the test is 78 and the standard deviation is 4, and the scores are normally distributed. If Joe received a score of 85 on the test, will he receive a scholarship?

20. For each scenario in problems 2–9 at the end of Chapter 4, identify the appropriate measures of central tendency and variability for the variable(s) of interest.

CHAPTER

6

HYPOTHESIS TESTING

■ ■ ■ ■ ■ ■

In this chapter, you will learn how statistical analysis of data from samples of participants can be used to answer research questions such as "Is acupuncture effective?" or "Is the popularity of children's first names related to their popularity with their peers?" The logic which underlies the hypothesis testing process is presented along with a discussion of some of the potential misunderstandings which may arise.

Look for These Important Terms and Concepts:

hypothesis testing

representativeness

sampling procedures

sample statistics and population
    parameters

random sampling

stratified random sampling

convenience sampling

null hypothesis

random sampling error (or chance
    fluctuations)

research (or alternate) hypothesis

sampling distributions

normal distribution (or curve)

rare and common events

standard error

rejecting the null hypothesis

significance level and alpha (α)

critical values (or cut-off points)

region of rejection

Type I error

Type II error

beta (β)

power

Before Reading This Chapter, You May Wish to Review:

Chapter 5
- samples versus populations
- frequency polygon

- probability
- normal distributions
- means and standard deviations

Typically, research is designed to answer questions about the relationship between two variables in the population: "Is X correlated with Y?" or "Does a change in X cause a change in Y?" These research questions are answered by using sample data to estimate the characteristics of a population in a process known as **hypothesis testing** (or statistical decision-making). Research questions such as "Does flouride toothpaste prevent cavities?" have only two possible answers (or hypotheses): Yes or no. We test these two hypotheses with inferential statistics, which use the relationship between the variables (X and Y) in a sample to determine which of the two hypotheses (or answers) is most likely true in the population. Samples are used as estimates of populations because researchers generally do not have access to the entire population of interest. For example, a psychologist studying schizophrenia is very unlikely to be able to study every person diagnosed with schizophrenia; instead the researcher studies a *sample* of patients in hopes of learning something that can be generalized to the population of schizophrenics.

To illustrate the process of statistical decision-making, let's use the following example. In recent years, there has been an increase in the use of "crack" (a form of cocaine) by teens and young adults. Public health officials are particularly concerned about the potential consequences of maternal crack use during pregnancy and the possibility that crack may cause birth defects. There is anecdotal evidence from hospital nurses that the infants born to crack users are unusually small for their gestational age, and a researcher may decide to perform a carefully designed study to determine whether, in fact, crack users give birth to significantly smaller babies than non-users. The researcher would select a sample of "crack babies" (i.e., babies born to women who used crack during pregnancy) and compare their average birthweight with that of normal, non-exposed infants. The researcher would then use the *sample* to draw some conclusions about the relationship between prenatal exposure to crack cocaine and neonatal birthweight in the *population*. Whether or not our research samples give us an accurate "picture" of the population depends on the **representativeness** of the samples, which, in turn, depends upon our **sampling procedures.**

To distinguish between the statistical characteristics of samples and populations, statisticians have adopted the convention of using English letters as symbols for sample characteristics (which are referred to as **sample statistics**) and Greek letters as symbols for population characteristics (which are referred to as **population parameters**). For instance, if we calculate the *mean* for a set of scores, we use the letter X with a bar over it ($\overline{X}$) if the set of scores comes from a sample of participants. If, however, we have scores for every member of the population and we calculate the mean, we would use the Greek letter *mu* (μ) instead of "X-bar." Similarly, the letter "s" is used as the symbol for the standard deviation of a sample, while the lower-case Greek letter *sigma* (σ) is the symbol for the standard deviation within the population.[1] In Chapter 8, we discuss correlation coefficients (which measure the relationship between two variables on a scale from 0.00 to ± 1.00), and the symbol used

---

[1]Remember from Chapter 5 that, while the formula for the mean is the same for both samples and populations ($\overline{X}$ and μ), there is a slight difference in formulas for the standard deviation for samples and the population:

(continued)

to represent the correlation between X and Y in a sample is the letter *r*, while the correlation between X and Y in the population is represented with the Greek letter *rho* (ρ). In essence, then, we use sample statistics ($\overline{X}$, *s*, and *r*) as estimates of population parameters (μ, σ, and ρ), and the accuracy of these estimates depends on the representativeness of the samples.

Representativeness and Sampling Procedures

A representative sample is one that is similar to the population in terms of the central tendency (or average), variability, and relative proportions (or frequencies) of X scores. For example, suppose the population mean (μ) is equal to 20. A sample with a mean ($\overline{X}$) of 18 would be considered more representative than a sample with a mean ($\overline{X}$) of 15 or a mean ($\overline{X}$) of 24 since 18 is closer to the population mean of 20. Furthermore, if a population is composed of 50% females and 50% males, a sample with 48% females and 52% males would be more representative than a sample with a 45–55% split, since 48–52% is more similar to the population's 50–50% split. Figure 6-1 illustrates the concept of a representative sample. When a sample is representative of its population, we can then *generalize* our conclusions from the sample to the population as a whole. This is, of course, what scientists want to do: Learn something about the population by studying a sample.

Usually, of course, we do not know the exact characteristics of the population, and, therefore, we cannot know whether our sample is a good representation of the population or not. Instead, we must use *sampling procedures* that maximize the chances that our sample is representative. The most effective sampling procedures include random sampling and stratified random sampling.

Random Sampling

By definition, an event is *random* when its characteristics or properties are unrelated to its occurrence, so, consequently, its occurrence is unpredictable (Vogt, 1993). **Random sampling** is a sampling procedure that allows every member of the population to have an *equal chance* of being selected for the sample, and it is impossible to predict who will be selected. (Imagine having a hat—or a computer database—with the name of every member of the population in it, and imagine being able to reach into the hat to draw a name: The probability that you will select Bill Jones is exactly the same as the probability that you will select Sally Smith, and there is no way to know in advance who will be selected.) When every member of the population has an

---

$$\sigma = \sqrt{\frac{\sum (X - \overline{X})^2}{N}} \qquad s = \sqrt{\frac{\sum (X - \overline{X})^2}{N - 1}}$$

This reduction in the denominator makes *s* a better estimate of σ because samples are consistently less variable than the population as a whole.

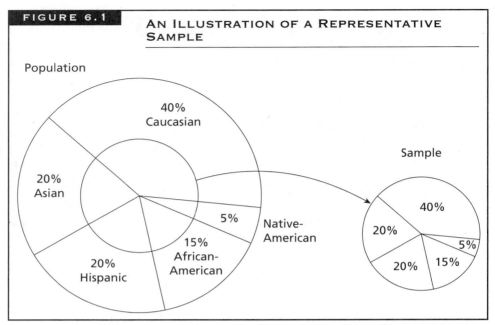

FIGURE 6.1

AN ILLUSTRATION OF A REPRESENTATIVE SAMPLE

Let's assume that the American population is 40% Caucasian, 15% African-American, 20% Asian, 20% Hispanic, and 5% Native American. A representative sample would have the same proportions.

equal chance of being selected for a sample, and if the selection of each participant is done at random (or "blindly"), then samples have a strong likelihood of having means, standard deviations, and relative proportions that are comparable to those in the population. This is especially true when the samples include larger numbers of participants; larger samples are generally more representative than smaller samples, and, therefore, they generally give us a more accurate estimate of the population.

The relationship between the representativeness of a sample and the sample's size (N) is very strong and very predictable. Samples that are very small (say, fewer than five participants) can almost never be representative of the entire population. For instance, suppose you wanted to know the proportion of males and females in the population and randomly selected five people. At best, you would find that there is a 60%–40% split (assuming your sample had three people of one sex and two of the opposite sex). At worst, you may select a sample of five people who are all male or all female—and this will happen very frequently if you select only five people. Because researchers often do not have access to large numbers of participants, it is important to know just how small our samples can be and still be sufficiently representative. Statisticians have determined that the chances of selecting representative samples are good if we have at least 20 participants in each experimental group or approximately 70 participants in a correlational study. (Larger samples, if available, are better, of course.)

Stratified Random Sampling

Stratified random sampling can be used when the researcher already knows something about the relative proportions within the population. For example, the U.S. Census data, which are available to researchers, tell us what percentage of the U.S. population lives in the northeast, the south, the midwest, etc. The census data also include information about age, sex, income level, occupation, religious affiliation, race, and ethnicity. Therefore, it is possible to find out what proportion of the population is Catholic, Jewish, or Protestant, or what proportion of the population in the midwest is African American, white, or Asian American. With this census data, a researcher can create a sample that matches the proportions within the population.

For instance, if we wanted to conduct a study on attitudes toward federal funding for abortion and we have reason to believe that religious affiliation influences attitudes toward abortion, we want to be sure that our sample of 100 people has the "right mix" of religious groups. If the census data indicates that 23% of the population is Catholic, 3% of the population is Jewish, and 60% is Protestant, then we would randomly select 23 Catholics, 3 Jews, and 60 Protestants to be in our study. This procedure gives us a stratified random sample, and we can be certain that it gives us a sample that is representative of the overall population in terms of religious affiliation. Large social research groups, such as the Gallup Polls and the Nielsen television ratings groups, use stratified random sampling. Most psychological research, however, does not have a population database available. There is no U.S. Census data concerning behaviors such as reaction time, memory span, or deductive reasoning, so most psychologists cannot expect to use a stratified sampling procedure. Instead, they generally rely on random sampling to create samples similar to the population in terms of relative proportions.

Available Samples and Convenience Sampling

While true random sampling is the ideal procedure for most psychological research studies, it is rarely feasible. Researchers almost never have access to the entire population, so it is not really true that "every member of the population has an equal chance of being selected." Instead, researchers conduct studies using participants who live nearby, and very frequently the participants are drawn from the local schools and colleges. These samples are sometimes referred to as available samples and the process involved in selecting them is referred to as **convenience sampling.** Because the representativeness of—and, therefore, the generalizability of the results from—these "convenient samples" can be questionable, researchers who must rely on convenience samples depend heavily on replication and convergence of evidence. If the results of a single study are confirmed with new samples and by different researchers in different places, it indicates that the convenient samples were, in fact, representative. Furthermore, the question of generalizability may be an empirical one: It can be scientifically tested.

For example, a study conducted in rural Western New York on the willingness of bystanders to stop and help another person may indicate that 60% of all adults are willing to help a stranger. Can we legitimately generalize these results to the population and claim that 60% of all adults in all areas of the country, including the inner cities of New York, Los Angeles, or Chicago, would be willing to help? While our intuition may tell us that the answer is "no, we cannot generalize from rural to urban settings," this is actually an empirically-testable hypothesis. Studies could be conducted to compare the helpfulness rates in rural and urban settings. If these studies found a difference between the settings, then later researchers (in both rural and urban settings) would need to limit their generalizations to only their regions. If, however, the rates of helping in rural settings were found to be equivalent to the rates of helping in urban settings, then subsequent research, conducted in either setting, could be legitimately generalized to the other setting. Psychologists doing research on basic processes (such as memory or conformity) with samples of college sophomores can be assured that their convenient, available samples are providing generalizable results because there is a substantial literature indicating that groups of college students tend to be representative of the population of young adults.

Statistical Hypotheses

Let's return to our example concerning the effect of crack cocaine on the birthweight of infants and assume that we have used random selection to create our samples. A comparison of the birthweights of the two randomly selected groups of babies will result in one of two outcomes (or conclusions): Either the crack babies will be different from normal babies, or they will *not* be different from normal babies. These two possibilities represent the two statistical hypotheses that are present in every research study: (1) the research (or alternate) hypothesis, which may also be referred to as the working hypothesis, which claims the crack babies *are* different from normal babies, and (2) the null hypothesis, which claims there is no difference between the groups. From a statistical point of view, the null hypothesis is the more "central" hypothesis in a study because it is the claim that can be directly tested.

The Null Hypothesis (H_0)

The **null hypothesis (H_0)** of a study always states that there is *no relationship* between the variables in the population, and that any patterns observed in the samples are due solely to random sampling error or chance fluctuations in the data. (Chance fluctuations result from individual differences among people, random measurement errors, or unsystematic experimenter errors during the collection of data.) In studies designed to look for correlations between two variables, the null hypothesis states that, if we were able to measure X and Y for every member of the entire population, we would find that the correlation between X and Y in the population is zero ($\rho = 0.00$). In studies designed to compare the average performance of two or more groups of participants (such as a quasi-experiment comparing males with females or an experiment comparing children who have received training with those who have not), the null hypothesis says that, if we measured *every* female and *every* male or *every* trained child and *every* nontrained child in the population, we would find no difference in average performance between the groups ($\mu_{female} - \mu_{male} = 0.0$ or $\mu_{trained} - \mu_{untrained} = 0.0$).[2]

According to the null hypothesis, if the correlation coefficient (r) for X and Y in your sample is not zero, it is only because your sample is not completely representative of the population due to random sampling error; your sample statistic (r) is really only a chance fluctuation from a population parameter (ρ) of 0.00. Likewise, if in an experiment or quasi-experiment you discover a difference between the means of your research samples, the null hypothesis says that observed difference is due solely to chance (or random sampling error) and that it is only a random fluctuation from the true population difference of zero.

Research or Alternate Hypothesis (H₁)

The **research** (or **alternate) hypothesis (H₁)**, as you might expect, is the exact opposite of the null hypothesis. H_1 states that, in the population, there *is* a significant relationship between the variables; either there is a significant correlation (and $\rho \neq 0.00$) or a significant difference between the groups in an experiment or quasi-experiment ($\mu_1 - \mu_2 \neq 0.0$ or $\mu_1 \neq \mu_2$).[3] According to the research hypothesis, if you find a sample correlation of $r = 0.32$, it is because the true population parameter (ρ) is also approximately 0.32, indicating that, in the population, X and Y have a significant correlation between them. If your experiment results in a 5-point difference in the means for your two groups, H_1 says it is because, in the population at large, the members of one group systematically score an average of 5 points higher. (For example, men may be an average of 5 inches taller than women; $\mu_{male} = 5'9''$ versus $\mu_{female} = 5'4''$.)

In our example of a study on the effects of prenatal exposure to crack on birthweight, the null hypothesis states that there is no difference in the average birthweight of normal infants and babies exposed to crack. (Another way of phrasing it is to say, "Exposure to crack during the mother's pregnancy has no effect on the birthweight of the baby.") According to the null hypothesis, crack babies and normal babies are from the same population, so they have the same distribution of birthweights: That is, they have the same mean, variability, and relative proportions of birthweights. Therefore, the null hypothesis says, any differences between the groups that a researcher may observe must be due to random differences among samples drawn from the population. For example, suppose the researcher used con-

---

[2]See Chapter 7 for a full discussion of correlational, experimental, and quasi-experimental research methods, and Chapter 8 for a discussion of correlation coefficients.

[3]Sometimes the research hypothesis will specifically predict the *direction* of the relationship, such as saying that group 1 will have *higher* scores than group 2 ($\mu_1 - \mu_2 > 0.0$). In the current example, for instance, it is predicted that "crack babies" will be smaller than normal babies. While such directional (or "one-tailed") hypotheses are common in psychological theory, we usually do not apply them to the statistical analysis of the data; instead we generally prefer to use nondirectional (or "two-tailed") statistical tests. Therefore, the hypothesis-testing process is illustrated here using the more preferred nondirectional test even though the research hypothesis for the example sounds directional. The underlying logic of the two procedures is the same, and the differences between them are detailed in Chapter 11.

venience sampling by asking doctors and nurses at the emergency room at a county hospital to identify newborns who had been exposed to crack before birth. Would this sampling procedure produce a representative sample? Not necessarily. Maybe small newborns are more likely to end up in an emergency room; perhaps average or above-average babies are healthier than small babies. Consequently, the convenient sample would be made up of mostly smaller "crack babies," so the average birth-weight of the sample would underestimate the mean for its population. Thus, the sample would be unrepresentative, thus making it look like "crack babies" are smaller than nonexposed babies when, in fact, there is no difference between them in the population. This would be an example of random sampling error.

The research (alternate) hypothesis (H_1) says that "crack babies" weigh signifi-cantly less than normal infants at birth or that "Exposure to crack during pregnancy is associated with a reduction in birthweight."[4] That is, the research hypothesis states that "crack babies" are systematically different from nonexposed babies so that "crack babies" and nonexposed babies form two distinctly *separate populations* that have dif-ferent means. According to the research hypothesis, the difference between samples of "crack babies" and normal infants reflects a true, systematic difference between the population means. (Systematic differences between populations are typically re-ferred to as "significant differences.")

Imagine, then, that our researcher obtains the birth records from all hospitals and finds that the average birthweight of all babies is 112 ounces. (Thus, $\mu = 112$). The researcher then selects a random sample of babies born to women who used crack during their pregnancy and calculates their average birthweight to be 100 ounces ($\overline{X} = 100$). The question the researcher faces is whether this 12-ounce differ-ence between the sample mean ($\overline{X} = 100$ ounces) and population parameter ($\mu = 112$ ounces) reflects: (a) a random sampling error where the 100 ounces is nothing more than a chance fluctuation from the true mean of 112 in the population of "crack babies," as the null hypothesis claims; or (b) a significant difference between normal babies and "crack babies," which the research hypothesis claims. If we decide that the difference between μ and $\overline{X}$ is due only to random sampling error, then we are concluding that there is *no evidence* that "crack babies" weigh less than normal ba-bies. In other words, "crack babies" and normal babies would seem to have the same distribution of birthweights and to be from the *same* population. If, however, we con-clude that there *is* a significant difference between normal and "crack babies," we are concluding that there are actually *two distinctly separate* populations of babies that have different mean birthweights and possibly different amounts of variability.

How will the researcher be able to decide which of these hypotheses is most likely true? The decision process will be based on the probability that a 12-ounce difference between the sample and the population parameter occurred as a result of

---

[4]The research hypothesis for this example does not claim that exposure to crack causes a reduction in birthweight be-cause the study used in this example is a quasi-experiment. Exposure to crack is a subject variable, rather than a true ex-perimental manipulation of randomized groups, and, therefore, causal conclusions cannot be drawn from this study, as explained in Chapter 7.

random sampling error. That is, we will measure the random differences among samples drawn from the same population to see how often a 12-ounce difference occurs solely by chance. If a 12-ounce difference is a common occurrence, we will conclude that our research outcome may reflect only random sampling error. If a 12-ounce difference is uncommon (or rare), we will conclude that our research outcome probably reflects a significant difference between separate populations. We measure random sampling error using sampling distributions.

Sampling Distributions

A **sampling distribution** is a frequency distribution (or set) of sample statistics (such as means or correlation coefficients) calculated for samples drawn at random from the same population and then treated alike so that the differences among the samples are the result of random differences. To illustrate, imagine selecting a random sample from a population and calculating the mean for the sample (or any other statistic), and then starting all over and selecting a new sample from that population and calculating the statistic for the new sample. (In each case, the samples are the same size and the individual members of the samples are treated exactly the same.) The two sample statistics are unlikely to be equal, even though the samples were both drawn from the same population and the individuals were measured under identical circumstances. This difference between the samples is due solely to chance and reflects **random sampling error** (or **chance fluctuations** among random samples).

If we then selected a third random sample, then a fourth sample, and so on, until every possible random sample (of a given size) had been drawn, we would be able to construct a frequency distribution of the sample statistics and draw a frequency polygon that visually summarizes the distribution of sample statistics.[5] From this distribution of statistics, we could determine the average difference between the population parameter and the statistics from the random samples. For instance, if we computed the mean for every random sample, we could measure the average amount of fluctuation between sample $\overline{X}$s and the population μ, and these differences would be due solely to chance. That is, the variability among the samples provides a measure of the *random sampling error*. In addition to a measure of the variability among the sample statistics, we could measure the average for the sample statistics, and we can use the frequencies of the sample statistics to determine the probability that a particular sample statistic would occur at random. Tables 6-1 and 6-2 present an

---

[5]Each sample size has a sampling distribution with a slightly different shape. It is also important to note that sampling distributions are really theoretical distributions based on the assumption that an infinite number of samples have been drawn from the population; mathematicians derived formulas for these frequency distributions rather than going through the actual exercise of drawing all possible samples from large populations.

TABLE 6.1		Hypothetical Birthweights From a Population of 36 Infants	
Population	*N = 36 Newborns*	*Frequency Table (for Population)*	
Newborn	Birthweight	Birthweight	f
a	112	134	1
b	110	126	2
c	90	122	3
d	112	118	4
e	102	114	5
f	114	112	6
g	122	110	5
h	118	106	4
i	134	102	3
j	106	98	2
k	112	90	1
l	110		N = 36
m	98		
n	114		
o	126		
p	112		
q	110		
r	106		
s	114		
t	118		
u	110		
v	106		
w	98		
x	114		
y	102		
z	112		
α	118		
β	106		
γ	122		
σ	122		
ϵ	118		
ξ	112		
η	126		
θ	110		
λ	102		
π	114		

Frequency Polygon (for Population)

population mean (μ) = 112
population s.d. (σ) = 8.6

TABLE 6.2			Constructing a Sampling Distribution by Drawing Random Samples	

Sampling Distribution (Table) of Means

Random Sample Number	Sample Members	Sample Mean	$\overline{X}$	f
1	f e m c	101.0	122.0	1
2	i s t b	119.0	119.0	1
3	a b o t	116.5	118.5	1
4	m c i γ	111.0	116.5	2
5	p ϵ λ x	111.5	115.5	1
6	g x l k	114.5	114.5	3
7	u v γ π	113.0	113.5	2
8	o i t b	122.0	113.0	1
9	i y f a	115.5	112.0	5
10	w y ξ β	104.5	111.5	2
11	a o h t	118.5	111.0	3
12	m c q λ	100.0	110.5	2
13	a b f k	112.0	109.5	1
14	e c α γ	108.0	108.5	1
15	π a b e	109.5	108.0	1
16	v p s σ	113.5	104.5	1
17	s n v p	111.5	101.0	1
18	p j ϵ z	112.0	100.0	1
19	α u r θ	111.0	k =	30
20	η d ϵ l	116.5		
21	f j z q	110.5		
22	e σ q x	112.0	(where k = the number of samples in the distribution)	
23	d h w x	110.5		
24	u ξ π g	114.5	*Sampling Distribution (frequency polygon)*	
25	j k r θ	108.5		
26	n z β σ	113.5		
27	λ η ϵ ξ	114.5		
28	g l q r	112.0		
29	b l p z	111.0		
30	π θ ξ d	112.0		

μ (Mean of the Sample Means) = 112.0

(This is not a normal distribution because only 30 — out of a possible 58,905 — samples have been drawn.)

illustration of a sampling distribution of $\overline{X}$s where 30 random samples (of four scores each) have been drawn from a population of 36 scores.

Because every individual in every sample is treated alike when we are creating the sampling distribution, all of the variation in the scores (between individual scores and between sample statistics) can be attributed to chance alone, and, therefore, this distribution of sample statistics represents a case where the null hypothesis is *true*. (Recall that the null hypothesis always states that there is no systematic relationship between the variables within the population and that chance fluctuations account for any apparent relationship observed within a sample.) When we construct a sampling distribution by drawing every random sample from the same population and treating them alike, we have met the criterion for the null hypothesis: Chance alone is operating. Thus, a sampling distribution provides a "picture" of the chance fluctuations among samples drawn from a population where there is *no* difference between the groups. The sampling distribution, which measures the frequencies of sample statistics, allows us to determine how many random samples drawn from a population with a mean (μ) of 112 will have a mean ($\overline{X}$) of 100. That is, the sampling distribution allows us to determine the *probability* that we will select a sample with a mean ($\overline{X}$) that is 12 points away from the population parameter (μ) just by chance.

The Shape of the Sampling Distribution

The samples drawn at random from a population are representative of the population (more or less, depending on the size of the samples), so the value of the sample statistic will provide an estimate of the population parameter. However, some of the sample statistics will overestimate the value of the population parameter, while others will underestimate it. That is, the sample statistics distribute themselves around the population parameter. Mathematicians have demonstrated that this distribution follows predictable patterns, so the frequency polygons for sampling distributions can be expressed with mathematical equations. Sampling distributions for some statistics, such as the mean, form a **normal distribution or curve.** That is, when random samples are drawn from the same population, the sample $\overline{X}$s form a bell-shaped, symmetrical curve where the mean, median, and mode are equal to one another. The exact shape of the "bell" depends upon the size of the samples drawn and the variability among scores in the population. When the scores in the population are similar (so σ is small), samples tend to be more alike, so the sampling distribution tends to be "tall and skinny." If there is a lot of variability in the population (σ is large), samples also tend to be more variable, so the sampling distribution is "wide and flat." (This is illustrated in Figure 6-2a.)

You should recall from Chapter 5 that we can convert any distribution—including distributions of sample statistics—to z-scores, which form a standardized scale. If the original statistics are normally distributed, the distribution of z-scores will also be normal. Consequently, we are able to use the "Areas Under the Normal Curve" table (the z-Table) to answer questions such as: "What is the probability that a random sample of babies will have a mean birthweight of 100 if the population mean is really 112?" Other statistics commonly used in psychological research, such as Pearson's *r*, chi square (χ^2), Student's *t*, and the analysis of variance *F*, do not fit the normal curve

FIGURE 6.2

DISTRIBUTIONS OF VARIOUS STATISTICS

(a) Normal Distributions of Means
(different values of σ)

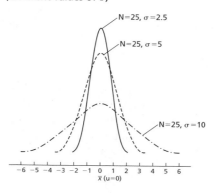

(b) Normal z-Distribution

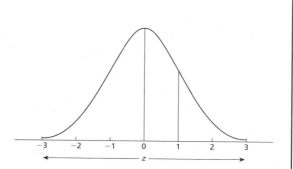

(c) Student's *t*-Distributions
(different sample sizes)

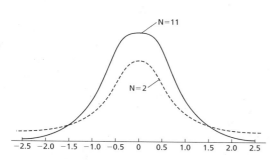

(d) χ² Distributions
(different numbers of groups)

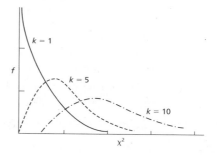

(e) *F* Distributions
(different sample sizes)

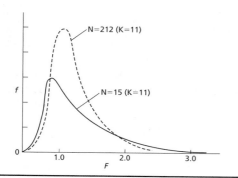

(see Figure 6-2), but their distributions have been mathematically defined, and they are standardized and predictable—which is the important thing for the hypothesis-testing process. Statisticians have been able to calculate the areas under these non-normal curves and thus determine the probabilities that particular sample statistics will occur by chance. The remainder of this chapter presents the hypothesis-testing process in the context of the normal distribution of means and z-scores, but the underlying logic applies to all of the statistical tests to be covered in this text.

The Average of the Sampling Distribution

Basically, in normal sampling distributions, for every sample statistic that overestimates the population parameter, there is a sample that underestimates it to the same degree. So, if one sample has a mean that is 20 points above the parameter, there is one sample with a mean that is 20 points below the parameter. Furthermore, more samples will have statistics close in value to the parameter, and fewer samples will have values far from the parameter. As a result, the mean of the sampling distribution of sample statistics is equal to the population parameter. This principle is illustrated in Table 6-2, where the mean of the 30 sample means is exactly equal to the population mean. (Of course, the distribution of samples in Table 6-2 does not form a normal curve, as the frequency polygon clearly illustrates. This is because only 30 of the 58,905 possible random samples of four scores have been drawn from the population of 36 scores.) When *all* random samples have been drawn, the distribution of $\overline{X}$s is normal, so the mean, median, and mode of the sampling distribution will all be equal to the population mean (μ). Thus, when a random sample is selected, the values of $\overline{X}$ that are most likely to occur are those that are equal to or very similar to the value of μ. Furthermore, half of the samples will have $\overline{X}$s that are less than μ, while the other half have $\overline{X}$s that are greater than μ.

Variability of Sampling Distributions

The variability among the sample statistics in the distribution could be computed, just as we can compute the variability for any set of individual scores. The measure of variability among the sample statistics in the sampling distribution is called the **standard error (σ_E),** and it represents the average difference between a random sample statistic and the population parameter. The amount of variability among the samples depends, in part, on the size of the samples (n) being drawn from the population. Larger samples tend to be more representative of their population and, therefore, tend to cluster closer together near the population parameter.

With small samples, however, there are many more samples that look quite different from the population, so the small samples are more "spread out." As a result, the standard error (σ_E) of a distribution of large samples is *less than* the standard error for small samples. The formula for estimating the standard error is:

$$\sigma_E = \frac{\sigma}{\sqrt{n}}$$

**where σ = the standard deviation of the population
and n = number of scores in the samples**

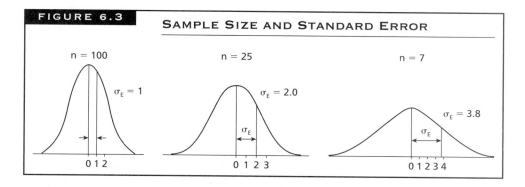

FIGURE 6.3   SAMPLE SIZE AND STANDARD ERROR

Figure 6-3 presents an illustration of the relationship between sample size and standard error. In the population, $\mu = 0$ and $\sigma = 10$.

Probabilities of Samples

Once we have a sampling distribution, it is possible to calculate the probability that particular sample statistics would be drawn at random from a population of samples where the null hypothesis is true. (Remember that we have treated each sample exactly alike, so the differences among them are due solely to random sampling error, and, therefore, the null hypothesis is known to be true in the sampling distribution.) As you will recall from Chapter 5, we can use the z-Table (Table B-1) to look up the areas under the normal curve for any value of z, and we can look up the value of z for any specified area under the normal curve. For example, according to the z-Table, the area between the mean of the distribution and a z-score of 1.00 is equal to .34134 (or 34.134%). Thus, the probability of randomly selecting a sample with a z-score between 0.0 and 1.00 is just over 34%. The area under the normal curve that lies in the tail *beyond* a z of 1.00 is equal to .15866, indicating that the probability that we will randomly select a sample with a z-score of 1.00 or higher is 15.866%. Because the normal distribution is symmetrical, areas under the curve are the same for +z and −z, therefore, the probability of selecting a sample with a z-score between 0.0 and −1.00 is also equal to 34.134%, and so forth.

From the z-Table, we know that in normal sampling distributions, only 2.5% of the samples have a z-score of +1.96 or higher, and another 2.5% of the samples have a z-score of −1.96 or lower. (That is, for z = ±1.96, the area in the tail *beyond* z is equal to 0.025, or 2.5%.) Together, the two "groups" of samples in the tails of the polygon constitute the most rare, or infrequent 5% of all sample statistics. These samples, which are so uncommon, and, therefore, have such a low probability of occurring, are called **rare events**. In contrast, 95% of the samples in the sampling, distribution have z-scores ranging from −1.95 to +1.95 (that is, they lie in the middle of the polygon), and these sample statistics are called **common events** because there are so many of them and they occur so frequently. Therefore, if a sample is randomly drawn from a distribution where the null hypothesis is true, there is a 95% chance that the sample will be one of the common events, and only a 5% chance that the sample will be one of the rare events (with a z-score of +1.96 or higher, or −1.96 or lower). In other words, the probability that we will draw a common sample is 95% and the probability of drawing a rare sample is only 5%.

Making the Decision

In our example about the effects of crack cocaine on the birthweight of infants, we found that a sample of crack-exposed infants had a mean weight of 100 ounces while the population parameter (for normal babies) is 112 ounces. There are two possibilities at work here: (1) the null hypothesis is false, and "crack babies" form a distinctly separate population from normal babies, so the mean for the population of "crack babies" is not equal to the mean for normal babies (and, instead, is closer to 100 ounces rather than 112 ounces); or (2) the null hypothesis is true, and the sample mean of 100 ounces for "crack babies" is simply a chance fluctuation from a true population mean of 112 ounces (so that "crack babies" and normal babies come from the same population with the same average birthweight). These two possibilities are illustrated in Figure 6-4.

We need to decide whether or not we can reject the null hypothesis. If we reject the null hypothesis, we are concluding that crack-exposed babies are *significantly smaller* at birth than normal babies and that there are actually two distinctly separate subpopulations of babies: Those who are exposed to crack and those who are not exposed to crack. If we cannot reject the null hypothesis, we must conclude that the 12-point difference in mean weights may have happened by chance alone, as the result of random sampling error. This decision is based on the probability that our sample statistic is the result of random sampling error. That is, we will reject the null hypothesis if the difference between the sample $\overline{X}$ and the population μ is so large—

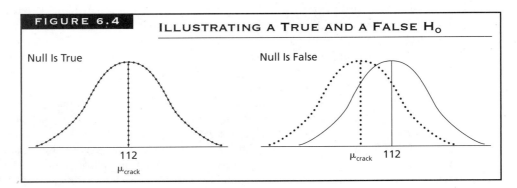

FIGURE 6.4 **ILLUSTRATING A TRUE AND A FALSE H_o**

Null Is True

Null Is False

112
μ_{crack}

μ_{crack} 112

Note: The solid line represents the sampling distribution, and the dotted line represents the hypothetical distribution of samples from the real population.

and, therefore, so infrequent and improbable—that it would be considered to be a rare event: An event that has a very low probability of occurring by chance alone. However, when the difference between the sample $\overline{X}$ and the population μ is a common event that occurs often simply as a result of random sampling error, we cannot reject the null hypothesis.

As we discussed above, the samples in the tails of the sampling distribution are the most uncommon of all sample statistics, and so they constitute the rare events. That is, they are random samples that occur infrequently when the null hypothesis is true and chance alone is operating. Thus, if the mean from a research sample falls into the tail of the sampling distribution, it will be considered a rare event, and we will reject the null hypothesis. By convention, psychologists and statisticians define rare events as those sample statistics that occur 5% of the time or less (just as we did in our discussion of sample probabilities above). That is, in normal distributions, rare events are those samples with z-scores equal to or greater than ±1.96. These rare events are the samples that are the most different from the population parameter and, hence, are the least representative of the population. In contrast, 95% of all random samples will have z-scores between +1.96 and −1.96, and they are known as the common events because they occur frequently when chance alone is operating. The value of these samples statistics is close enough to the value of the population parameter predicted by the null hypothesis that these samples are considered to be representative of a population where the null hypothesis is true.

Therefore, the logic of hypothesis testing goes something like this:

If the null hypothesis is really true in the population, 95% of all random samples will have a mean $(\overline{X})$ that is a common fluctuation from the population mean (μ). Therefore, when we select our research sample, there is a 95% chance that it will have one of these common values of $\overline{X}$; there is only a 5% chance that we will draw a sample with a rare value of $\overline{X}$. So if our research sample turns out to be one of those rare samples, which would be unrepresentative of a population in which the null is true, we would decide that our sample is actually representative of a population where the null hypothesis is false. That is, instead of believing that our sample is a rare event from a world where there is no difference between the groups, we would conclude that there are two distinctly separate populations with significantly different values of μ. This decision is called **rejecting the null hypothesis.**

If, however, our research sample turns out to be one of those common samples that would be representative of a population in which the null is true (because the difference between the sample and the population can be attributed to random sampling error), we do *not* reject the null hypothesis.

Let's apply this logic to our "crack baby" study. The null hypothesis says that prenatal exposure to crack has no effect on the birthweight of infants, so the average birthweight of "crack babies" is the same as the average birthweight of non-exposed, normal infants, which is 112 ounces. To test this hypothesis, we will construct a sampling distribution of random samples drawn from a population with a mean (μ) of 112. This distribution of means will fit the normal curve, which will allow us to determine how often various values of the mean ($\overline{X}$) occur simply due to random sampling error, and we can then decide which samples will be considered common and which will be considered rare.

If the mean of our sample of "crack babies" ($\overline{X} = 100$) has a value that is *rare* when the null hypothesis is true, we will *reject* the null hypothesis and conclude that there are actually two distinctly different populations and that "crack babies" are significantly smaller than normal babies (100 < 112). On the other hand, if the mean of our sample of "crack babies" ($\overline{X} = 100$) has a value that is *common* when the null is true (because it happens frequently due to random sampling error), we cannot reject the null hypothesis, but must admit that we do not have sufficient evidence to conclude that prenatal exposure to crack is related to the birthweight of the babies.

In effect, if we make the decision to reject the null hypothesis because our sample mean is a rare event when the null is true, we are taking a gamble by playing the odds. There is a 5% chance that our rare sample $\overline{X}$ really is the result of simple random sampling error and that the null is actually true. However, there is a 95% chance that a so-called rare sample is *not* the result of random sampling error but is, instead, a representative sample from a population where the null hypothesis is actually false. The 95% probability is the one we bet on!

Significance Levels (α)

How do we know which events are rare and which events are common when the null hypothesis is true? First we decide how to define "rare" by choosing a **significance level** (which is referred to as an alpha level, or α). In our example so far, we have been using an alpha level of .05: That is, we have defined "rare" to mean those events that occur only 5% of the time or less. This level of significance ($\alpha = .05$) is the accepted standard in the field of psychological research, and any event that has a probability of occurring that is *less than or equal to .05* (i.e., occurs 5% of the time or less just by chance) is considered rare and leads us to reject the null hypothesis. Some researchers will choose an alpha level that is even smaller than .05 (such as .02 or .01 or even .001), but we do not let alpha exceed .05.

Although, a researcher occasionally performs a "one-tailed" or directional test where the rare events are all located in one tail of the sampling distribution, the preferred procedure, which we will follow here, is to conduct a two-tailed, nondirectional test where half of the rare events are in each tail of the sampling distribution. (The difference between directional and nondirectional tests are discussed in detail in Chapter 11.) The rare events are typically illustrated in a sampling distribution polygon by shading in the rare events (which are always in the "tails" of the distribution because that is where the low-frequency events are found in a normal distribution; see Figure 6-5). This shaded region, representing the rare events, is sometimes called the "alpha region" but more often is nicknamed the **region of rejection** because we will reject the null hypothesis if our research sample's statistic falls in this region.

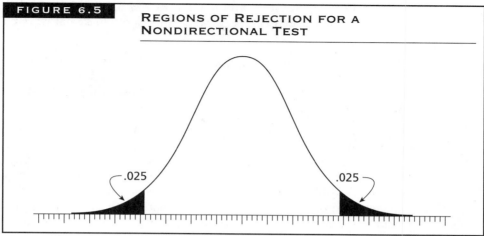

FIGURE 6.5

REGIONS OF REJECTION FOR A NONDIRECTIONAL TEST

.025   .025

Shaded regions = regions of rejection when α = .05 for a nondirectional test (each shaded portion represents 2.5% of the distribution).

Critical Values

Once we have set our significance level (α) and determined the size of the regions of rejection, we need to know exactly where the region of rejection starts. That is, we need to know the value of the cut-off point between the common region and the region of rejection. These cut-off points are officially called critical values. If alpha is set at .05, the cut-off points for a two-tailed (directional) test have z-scores of ±1.96, because the proportion of scores that fall beyond a z-score of ±1.96 is .02500 (or 2.5%), and when we add the two tails together, it equals our alpha level of .05 (or 5%). If alpha is set at .01, the critical values for the two-tailed (nondirectional) test have z-scores of ±2.58. (The area under the normal curve beyond a z of ±2.58 is equal to .00494, which is close to the desired value of .005 for a two-tailed test with alpha set at .01. The two tails together equal .00988, so the region of rejection contains 0.988%—almost 1%—of the scores.)

For sampling distributions that fit the normal curve, we could convert these critical z-scores into our sample statistic using a variant of the z-to-$\underline{X}$ conversion formula presented in Chapter 5. This one could be called a "z-to-$\overline{X}$ conversion" formula:

$$\overline{X}_{Critical} = z(\sigma_E) + \mu$$

[To find the critical value of $\overline{X}$, we multiply the z-score for the cut-off point by the standard error of the sampling distribution, and then we add the population mean.]

Once we have computed the critical value of the mean, we compare the mean ($\overline{X}_{obtained}$) from our research sample to $\overline{X}_{Critical}$ in order to make our research decision. The decision rule is:

> If the research sample statistic falls in the region of rejection, we reject the null hypothesis. That is, if the sample statistic is equal to or greater than the critical value (so that it lies in the tail of the sampling distribution), we reject the null hypothesis.

Let's return to our study on the effects of prenatal exposure to crack. The mean of the sampling distribution is $\mu = 112$ (since the null hypothesis claims that "crack babies" are the same as normal infants). Let's assume that the standard deviation (σ) among normal babies in the population is 8.6 and that we had a sample of four ($n = 4$) "crack babies." Using the formula presented on page 138, we would find that the standard error (σ_E) of the sampling distribution would be equal to 4.3, and we could now compute the critical values for the region of rejection. The critical value for the tail below μ is computed by substituting the appropriate values (including $z = -1.96$) into the "z-to-$\overline{X}$ conversion" formula presented above:

$$\overline{X}_{Critical} = z(\sigma_E) + \mu$$
$$\text{Lower Critical Value} = -1.96(4.3) + 112$$
$$= -8.428 + 112$$
$$= 103.572$$

The upper critical value would use $z = +1.96$ in the formula:

$$\overline{X}_{Critical} = z(\sigma_E) + \mu$$
$$\text{Upper Critical Value} = +1.96(4.3) + 112$$
$$= 8.428 + 112$$
$$= 120.428$$

From this we now know that, when random samples of 4 are drawn from a population with a mean of 112 and a standard deviation of 8.6, 95% of those samples have means ranging between 103.572 and 120.428. Only a rare 5% of the samples have means that are 103.572 or less or 120.428 or higher. Because our crack-exposed babies have a mean weight of only 100 ounces, and because a mean of 100 is less than the critical value of 103.572 (and is therefore a rare event), we would decide to reject the null hypothesis and conclude that newborn "crack babies" weigh significantly less than normal, non-exposed newborns.

Tables of Critical Values

In this example, we were able to calculate the relevant critical values for our statistical test because the sampling distribution of means is a normal curve and we could use the z-Table to find the cut-off points for the regions of rejection. We could not have done so without previous knowledge about the population of normal birth-weights. That is, we needed to know the mean weight (μ) for the population of babies as well as the standard deviation for the population (in order to estimate the standard error for the sampling distribution). The sample statistic we were working with in this example was the mean of one group (i.e., "crack babies"), and we have conducted what is commonly known as a *z-test*, which is covered in detail in Chapter 11.

Most research, however, does not compare a single sample to a known population. Instead, we usually have two (or more) separate samples that we compare with each other using various inferential tests. (Or in correlational research, we have a single sample, but we measure the correlation coefficient between two variables.) For each inferential statistical test, sampling distributions for different sample sizes have already been constructed by statisticians and the critical values (for different significance levels) have been published in tables. Therefore, researchers typically do not need to compute their own critical values (as we did in the above example). Instead, we need only look up the appropriate critical value in the appropriate table. If our research sample falls beyond the critical value (so that it lies within the region of rejection), we will reject the null hypothesis and conclude that there is a significant difference between the groups (or a significant correlation between X and Y). If our research sample falls within the "common region" of the sampling distribution, we will conclude that there is *no* significant difference between the groups (or *no* significant correlation between X and Y). In other words, we acknowledge that our research results may reflect nothing more than random sampling error and that the data from our sample do *not* provide sufficient evidence to conclude that a significant relationship exists within the population.

Have We Made the Correct Decision?

So we will either reject the null hypothesis or not, and either the null is really true or it is false within the population. Hence, there are four possible outcomes of the decision-making process, which are illustrated in Table 6-3:

TABLE 6.3	Four Possible Research Outcomes	
Research Decision:	We Reject H_0 (Research sample is rare event)	We Do Not Reject H_0 (Research sample is common event)
State of the Real Population:		
H_0 is **TRUE** in Population	Type I Error probability = α	Correct Decision probability = $1 - \alpha$
H_0 is **FALSE** in Population	Correct Decision probability = $1 - \beta$ (Power = $1 - \beta$)	Type II Error probability = β

When our research sample falls within the shaded region of rare events on the sampling distribution, we choose to play the odds and bet that the event was *not* simply due to random sampling error, and we reject the null (see the first column in the chart in Table 6-3). We make this decision because there is only a 5% chance (if our alpha level is .05) that the sample *does* represent sampling error. (If alpha is set at .01 and our research sample is still considered a rare event, there is only a 1% chance that our sample resulted from random sampling error.) By playing the odds in this fashion, we are minimizing the likelihood that our decision about the population is the wrong one, but we cannot be 100% certain that the decision is correct (since 5% of the samples drawn at random when the null is true *do* have values that fall in the tails just by chance and there is a 5% chance that we actually picked one of those samples).

If we reject the null hypothesis (because our sample was in the region of rejection) but, in fact, our sample was the result of random sampling error and the null is really true, we have made what is called a Type I error. The probability of a Type I error is equal to alpha because alpha determines how many random samples are labeled rare and how large the region of rejection is. (Don't forget that all of the events in the region of rejection actually *did* happen just by chance when the sampling distribution was being constructed, and, therefore, could happen again when you are conducting your study.)

If our research sample is a common event that occurs frequently just by chance when the null is true, and we cannot reject the null hypothesis (see the second column in Table 6-3), there is the possibility that we are making what is called a Type II error. The null hypothesis may actually be false, but our research sample may "resemble" a random sampling error, which requires us to conclude that our results do not provide sufficient evidence to reject the null hypothesis. Therefore, a Type II error occurs when we fail to reject a false null hypothesis. Type II errors are most likely to occur when the relationship between the variables (either the difference between treatment groups or the magnitude of the correlation between X and Y) is relatively small.

Let's consider a case where the correlation between two variables in the real population is relatively small. As we will discuss in detail in Chapter 8, correlations range in value from 0.0 (indicating that X and Y have no systematic relationship) to ± 1.00, (indicating that X and Y go together perfectly). The null hypothesis claims that X and Y are unrelated, and that ρ is equal to 0.0. Now suppose the true correlation between X and Y in the population (ρ) is equal to $+0.20$, and imagine drawing random samples from this population: It should be apparent that a great many samples will have sample correlations (ρ) that are less than $+0.20$. In fact, many of the random samples will have a correlation equal to 0.00, and X and Y will be completely unrelated to each other in these samples. Obviously, if we randomly select a sample and find that the sample correlation (r) is equal or very close to 0.00, we would *not* reject the null hypothesis, and thus we would be making a Type II error. Furthermore, even if we randomly selected a perfectly representative sample with a correlation equal to the population parameter ($+0.20$), we may be unable to reject the null hypothesis, because a sample correlation of $+0.20$ may also be a *common event* when the null hypothesis is actually true. That is, when ρ *is* equal to 0.0, many samples may, just by chance, have correlations of 0.20. Consequently, it may be difficult for us to successfully identify small correlations between variables, because random samples from populations with weak relationships tend to look like the random events that occur just by chance when there is no relationship at all. Thus, when the correlation between X and Y is small, there is a high probability that we will make a Type II error by failing to reject the null hypothesis.

In contrast, if the true correlation between X and Y is strong (for instance, if $\rho = 0.75$ or higher), very few random samples from that population would have correlations close to 0.0. Instead, most samples would fall into the region of rejection of the sampling distribution, and we would correctly reject the null hypothesis. When the true correlation is strong, the probability of a Type II error is quite low because we are unlikely to select a sample that looks like simple random sampling error.

When a true relationship exists in the population, but we end up making a Type II error because the sample statistic resembles a common event attributable to chance, we say that our statistical test did not have enough **power.** Power is the ability of a test to detect an effect when there is one; that is, to reject the null hypothesis when it is false. When the relationship between variables is small, the researcher will need a more powerful test in order to reach the correct decision. If the test is not powerful enough, the researcher will make a Type II error.

As another example, suppose that the effect of prenatal exposure to crack cocaine (in the population) is to reduce the fetal growth rate by 6% so that crack-exposed babies weigh an average of 105 ounces at birth. If it were possible to draw every possible random sample of "crack babies" and calculate the sample means, we would see that their distribution overlaps substantially with the distribution of samples of normal babies, who weigh an average of 112 ounces (see Figure 6-6a). In our earlier example, the sample of crack-exposed babies had a mean weight of 100 ounces, and we rejected the null hypothesis. But as Figure 6-6b illustrates, if "crack babies" weigh an average of 105 ounces, more than half of the samples of "crack babies" that we might select would actually lead us to make a Type II error because the sample means resemble common random fluctuations from a mean of 112 (that is, they fall *between* the upper and lower critical values of 120.4 and 103.6, so they would be classified as common events, and we would not reject the null hypothesis).

In contrast, let's suppose that prenatal exposure to crack has an even stronger impact, and it slows the growth rate by 10% (so that babies are born weighing an average of 100.8 ounces). The degree of overlap between the distributions for samples of normal and crack-exposed babies is greatly reduced (see Figure 6-6c), and the majority of samples of "crack babies" would now lead us to make the correct decision to reject the null (because they fall in the region of rejection of the sampling distribution of normal infants).

Type II errors are made whenever the null is actually false (and there are two distinctly separate populations with different means) but our research sample falls in the common region of the sampling distribution. The degree of overlap between the common region in the sampling distribution and the real population is called **beta (β),** and the samples in this region are the ones that will lead to Type II errors. That is, beta is the proportion of samples from the real population (where the null is actually false) that look like common random sampling errors, so we fail to reject the false null hypothesis. (β is represented by the striped area in Figures 6-6b and 6-6c.) The larger β, the

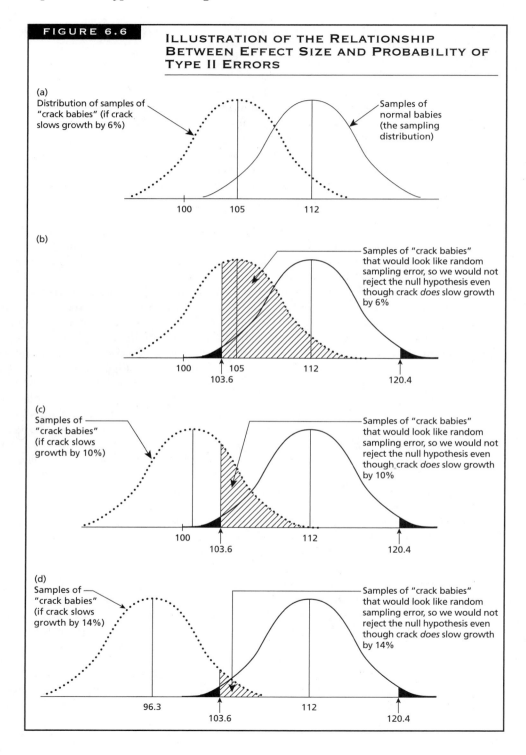

FIGURE 6.6

ILLUSTRATION OF THE RELATIONSHIP BETWEEN EFFECT SIZE AND PROBABILITY OF TYPE II ERRORS

(a) Distribution of samples of "crack babies" (if crack slows growth by 6%)

Samples of normal babies (the sampling distribution)

100   105   112

(b) Samples of "crack babies" that would look like random sampling error, so we would not reject the null hypothesis even though crack *does* slow growth by 6%

100   105   112
103.6   120.4

(c) Samples of "crack babies" (if crack slows growth by 10%)

Samples of "crack babies" that would look like random sampling error, so we would not reject the null hypothesis even though crack *does* slow growth by 10%

100   112
103.6   120.4

(d) Samples of "crack babies" (if crack slows growth by 14%)

Samples of "crack babies" that would look like random sampling error, so we would not reject the null hypothesis even though crack *does* slow growth by 14%

96.3   112
103.6   120.4

greater the probability of making a Type II error. The power of the test is represented by the proportion of the real population that overlaps with the region of rejection: These samples will lead to the correct decision to reject. This region is equal to $1 - \beta$, so as β increases, the power of the test decreases and vice versa.

While it is fairly easy to understand the principle that beta will decrease as the relationship between the variables gets stronger, we cannot determine the value of β because we do not know how strong the relationship is in the real population—if we knew, we would not need to do the research study! So we must always remember that whenever we fail to reject the null hypothesis, there is a possibility that we have made a Type II error because our test did not have enough power. The concept of power (and what researchers can do to maximize it) is discussed more fully in Appendix C.

Threats to the Validity of Hypothesis-Testing: Pitfalls to Avoid

The null-hypothesis-testing procedure we have presented is routinely employed by the vast majority of psychologists who conduct research. It is by no means a perfect procedure, if by "perfect" we mean that it ensures that researchers will reach accurate and valid conclusions about the relationships among variables. Indeed, a number of mistakes are so commonly made by researchers that, in 1996, a group of methodologists made a serious effort to convince the American Psychological Association (APA) to ban the use of null-hypothesis-tests in all APA journals (Shrout, 1997). While we see such a ban as an overreaction to the problems and very unlikely to go into effect, the controversy has served as an important wake-up call to researchers, reminding us that a tool is effective only when it is used properly. That is, null-hypothesis-tests are valid only if their results are interpreted properly. The major points that were raised by the "anti-null-hypothesis-tests" methodologists are outlined here in hopes that you may avoid the traps inherent in null-hypothesis-testing.

Statistical Versus Practical and Psychological Significance

According to the null-hypothesis testing procedure, when the value of a sample statistic (such as a difference between means or a correlation coefficient) is larger or smaller than would be expected by chance alone, we reject the null hypothesis, and conclude that there is a "significant" difference or relationship between the variables. It is a common mistake, however, to confuse this *statistical significance* with the importance or usefulness of the findings. That is, statistically significant results do not necessarily have any practical or theoretical value. For instance, studies with large sample sizes—and, consequently, lots of power—often find small, inconsequential relationships to be statistically significant. Consider the National Education Longitudinal Study (NELS), which collected data from a national sample of 24,599 eighth graders, their families, and their teachers. With a sample size of this magnitude, even very weak relationships will be statistically significant, but the findings may have no *practical significance* for society and little theoretical value for scientists.

For example, suppose lower student-teacher ratios at schools are associated with increased academic achievement, but the differences in achievement are no more than one percentage point (1%). With a sample that includes thousands of students, this relationship would reach statistical significance, but such small gains in achievement may not be worth the expense of hiring new teachers to improve the student-teacher ratios in all schools. Thus, the finding has little practical value. Furthermore, this weak relationship between student-teacher ratio and academic achievement would shed little light on our understanding of the individual differences among students.

Another mistake that is easy to make is to confuse statistical significance with *psychological significance*. The psychological significance of a study is the extent to which it contributes to our knowledge. There are three components to the psychological significance of a study: (1) the quality of the researcher's hypotheses or theoretical ideas, which, for example, need to be consistent with, or able to explain, existing data; (2) the adequacy of the study as a test of the hypotheses, including whether or not it was designed and implemented properly, and whether it used up-to-date, valid measurement instruments; and (3) the clarity of the results. A statistically significant result does *not* always contribute to our understanding of human behavior, yet there may be a tendency to concentrate on the statistical significance of the results, while overlooking weaknesses in the quality of the ideas, the study, and the meaningful interpretation of the data.

The Relevant Error Rate and Accepting the Null Hypothesis

Most researchers are comfortable with the idea that our significance level (α, which determines the critical values for deciding to reject the null hypothesis or not) gives us the probability of a Type I error, in which we mistake random chance fluctuation for a significant effect. Unfortunately, many researchers then come to think of α as the "error rate" for the study and believe that: "Since I set α to be equal to .05, there is only a 5% chance that I will make an error, and, therefore, I can be 95% confident that my conclusions are valid." This belief, in turn, generalizes to a belief that 95% of the research studies conducted reach accurate conclusions. However, John Hunter (1997) points out the fallacy in this reasoning by reminding us that Type I errors are relevant only in situations where the null hypothesis is actually *true*, so α is the "error rate" *only* in those studies that are looking for a *nonexistent* relationship; when the null hypothesis is actually false, α is irrelevant.

If the "error rate" for a study is defined as the probability of reaching the wrong conclusion, then the odds of making a mistake when the null hypothesis is false is equal to β, not α. This is a Type II error. Recall that the value of β is unknown and that it depends largely on the size of the effect or the strength of the relationship between the variables (see Figure 6-6). When the relationship is very weak, β is very large, and the chances of making an error (by *not* rejecting the null hypothesis) are very high. Even when the relationship is very strong, β is probably larger than .05, and, therefore, when there is a systematic relationship to be detected, the actual "error rate" will probably be higher than 5%. For instance, for our hypothetical example of "crack babies," crack needs to reduce the growth rate by about 14% in order to have an error rate (i.e., β) of .05 or less, as illustrated in Figue 6-6d. If the effect of crack is anything less than a 14% reduction in growth, the probability of making a Type II error will be greater than .05.

In the study of human behavior, effects of this magnitude are likely to be the exception and not the rule; so even when a systematic relationship exists, the value of β is likely to be higher than the error rate we might think we are selecting when we set α at .05. Unfortunately, because they are applying the wrong error rate, many psychologists automatically assume that nonsignificant findings indicate a 95% chance that the null hypothesis is true. In actuality, however, only studies where we reject the null have an error rate of 5%: When we reject the null hypothesis, we *can* be at least 95% confident that the null really is false (and there is only a 5% chance that we have made an error). But there is no single error rate for studies where we do *not* reject the null hypothesis because β varies from one study to another, and we simply cannot say how confident we are that the null hypothesis is really true.

This is why an increasing number of statisticians have argued that we should not use the traditional phrase "accepting the null hypothesis" when our statistic is nonsignificant. They feel that the term is too often misinterpreted to mean that "the null is true"—and when the wrong error rate is also being applied, it is too often misinterpreted to mean that "there is a 95% chance that the null is true!" In fact, whether the null hypothesis for a particular study is actually true or false is completely unrelated to the significance level (α) adopted in the statistical test, and nonsignificant results are quite likely to occur even when the null hypothesis is false because β can be substantial. Consequently, it is now common for researchers to say that they have "failed to reject" the null hypothesis when the statistic is nonsignificant. This phrase emphasizes the possibility that a systematic effect may exist but that the study was not powerful enough to detect it.

While this concern over the misuse of the term "accepting the null hypothesis" has merit, we believe it is important for researchers to realize that a time may come when it is appropriate to truly accept the null hypothesis. Specifically, when a sufficient number of well-designed studies have been conducted that all consistently fail to find evidence for some theoretical effect, it is incumbent upon us to admit that the theory may simply be wrong or that, for all practical purposes, the effect is so elusive as to offer little benefit to society. If we never allow ourselves to reach the conclusion that a null hypothesis is true, we will never be able to refute the false beliefs that arise through ignorance or charlatanism.

The Arbitrary Cut-off Point Between "Rare" and "Common" Events

Geoffrey Loftus (1996) argues that the validity of the null-hypothesis testing process is further threatened by the arbitrary nature of alpha (α), which is set at .05 or less simply by convention. When pressed, Loftus says, most people "will agree that there is no essential difference" (pp. 163–164) between a finding that occurs 50 times in 1,000 ($p = .050$) and one that occurs 51 times in 1,000 ($p = .051$). Yet when we set α at .05, the former finding will be statistically significant, and the latter will be nonsignificant. The problem arises when the researchers try to translate the statistical findings into an understanding about the relationship between variables. Significant findings are usually seen as proof that there is a real effect at work, while nonsignificant findings, as pointed out above, are often (mis)interpreted as proof that the effect does not exist. Thus, our knowledge about how the world works may depend on whether the statistical test yields a probability of .050 versus .051.

Loftus (1996) feels that too many researchers have lost sight of the fact that the dichotomy between "significant" and "nonsignificant" is artificial and based on arbitrary cut-off points. Loftus puts the problem this way:

> [T]he world of perceived reality tends to become divided into "real effects" ($p \leq .05$) and "non-effects" ($p > .05$). Statistical conclusions about such real effects and non-effects made in Results sections then somehow are sanctified and transmuted into conclusions that endure into Discussion sections and beyond, where they insidiously settle in and become part of our discipline's general knowledge structure. The mischief thereby stirred up is incalculable. For instance, when one experiment shows a significant effect ($p \leq .05$), and an attempted replication shows no significant effect ($p > .05$), a "failure to replicate" is proclaimed. Feverish activity ensues, as Method sections are scoured and new experiments are run, in an effort to understand the circumstances under which the effect does or does not show up—and all because of an arbitrary cutoff at the .05 α level. (p. 164)

Put simply, Loftus believes that similar results—such as $p = .050$ and $p = .051$— should lead to *similar* conclusions, and he argues for a ban of the null-hypothesis-testing process because it can lead to *opposite* conclusions for highly similar results.

Proposed Alternatives to the Null-Hypothesis-Testing Procedure

Geoffrey Loftus (1996) and John Hunter (1997) have proposed that the traditional null-hypothesis-testing procedure be replaced with statistical techniques that are less likely to lead to misinterpretations of the data. The most highly recomended alternative procedure calls for the computation of confidence intervals, which are used to estimate the value of population parameters by indentifying the most likely *range of values* for the parameter.[6] (Confidence intervals are covered in detail in Chapter 14.) Additionally, Loftus recommends that researchers use graphs, which plot the data (rather than tables of numbers), because the effects may be easier to interpret visually. Figure 6-7 illustrates this by presenting the same results in two formats. Imagine the data are from a study on the effects of bedtime stories on vocabulary development in boys and girls from 18 months to 48 months of age. These hypothetical results can be summarized like this: "The data indicate that bedtime reading significantly increases the vocabulary of preschool children, especially boys, aged 36 months and older." Loftus believes that most people will find the graphical presentation easier to interpret.

---

[6]For example, during the last week of August, 1998, *Newsweek* reported that between 59% and 65% of Americans approved of Bill Clinton's performance as president. This range, 62 ± 3%, is a confidence interval. See Chapter 14 for details about how to find confidence intervals for various parameters.

FIGURE 6.7

TWO FORMATS FOR PRESENTING THE FINDINGS OF A STUDY

Presenting the Data in a Table:

Mean Number of Vocabulary Words

Condition	Sex	Age (in months)					
		18	24	30	36	42	48
Bedtime Stories	Boys	20	25	36	60	75	100
	Girls	23	28	41	66	79	102
No Stories	Boys	21	24	37	51	64	82
	Girls	24	27	42	62	73	95

Presenting the Data in a Graph:

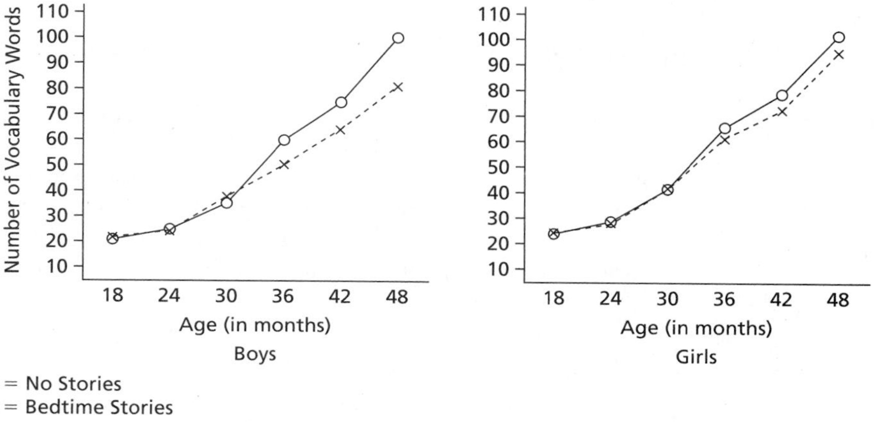

×--× = No Stories
o—o = Bedtime Stories

A Call for Compromise: Using a Combination of Approaches

In this chapter, we have presented the logic behind the hypothesis-testing procedure that is employed in the vast majority of psychological research. We also pointed out the limitations of this process that have led some methodologists to call for a ban on null-hypothesis-testing. While it is unlikely that such a ban will take effect, it is important for researchers to be aware of the common errors that are made and to try to avoid misinterpretations of their findings. One suggestion that we would make is that alternative procedures, such as confidence intervals and graphs, be used *in conjunction with* traditional hypothesis-testing. A combination of statistical procedures, coupled with a thorough understanding of the relevant error rates for each statistical outcome, may help us avoid misinterpretations and increase our chances of reaching valid conclusions from the data.

Exercises

For each pair of terms, define each concept and explain how the two relate to each other:

1. Random sample and representative sample

2. Sampling distribution and chance fluctuations

3. Null hypothesis and research hypothesis

4. Random sampling error and alpha

5. Beta and power

6. Rejecting H_0 and not rejecting (or failing to reject) H_0

7. Type I Error and Type II Error

For scenarios 8–10, verbalize the **Null Hypothesis** and the **Research Hypothesis:**

8. Based on interviews with parents, a researcher identified a group of preschool children who frequently watched *Mr Rogers* on television, and a group who never watched that program. The researcher then asked the preschool teacher to rank the children on their helpfulness toward others. The researcher wanted to find out if the children who watch *Mr Rogers* frequently are more helpful than children who do not watch the program.

9. A researcher was interested in the effects of crowding on test performance. A group of 20 students took a series of four similar exams (all based on the SATs) under four levels of crowding. Alone, one other person in the room; 10 other people in the room; and 30 other people in the room. All of the tests were given in the same 40′ by 40′ room. The number of errors on the exams was compared across the four levels of crowding.

10. A sociologist is studying drug abuse among teenagers. In one study, she asked high school students to indicate their willingness to try crack cocaine using a 4-point rating scale. The researcher then asked the students' parents to report their annual income as they had reported it to the IRS the previous April.

11. Draw diagrams of a sampling distribution and the "real population" (including regions of rejection and a research "outcome") that illustrate each of the following:

    (a) Correct Decision to Reject the Null

    (b) Correct Decision to Not Reject the Null

    (c) Type I Error

    (d) Type II Error

12. How does the size of the sample influence the hypothesis-testing process?

13. A researcher was interested in the impact of cocaine use on professional adults. From U.S. Census data, the researcher was able to determine that the sampling distribution for annual salaries for American engineers in 1992 had a mean of $100,000 and a standard error of $5,000. Therefore, using an alpha level of .05, the researcher calculated the critical values for salary to be $109,800 and $90,200. Suppose the researcher then randomly selected a group of engineers who admitted using cocaine at least three times per week between 1990 and 1992 and found that their mean 1992 salary was $88,700. What conclusion will the researcher reach and which error might have occurred?

14. Label the following diagrams by identifying the regions of rejection, the critical values, and β. Which of the four possible outcomes is represented in each figure?

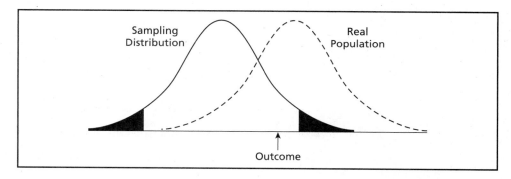

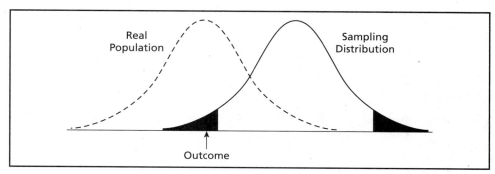

CHAPTER

7

GENERAL RESEARCH METHODS

■ ■ ■ ■ ■ ■

In this chapter, you will learn to distinguish among three major approaches to psychological research and to understand how the findings from each of these research methods should be interpreted.

Look for These Important Terms and Concepts

causal conclusions
experimental control
experimental manipulation
experiment
"all else equal"
independent variable
controlled variables
directly controlled variables
dependent variable
selection bias (or non-equivalence)
  confound
non-standardization confound
confound

subject variables
random assignment
probabilistically controlled variables
laboratory versus field experiments
quasi-experiment
non-equivalent groups designs
time-series designs
association (or correlation)
intervention versus nonintervention
correlation does not imply causation
naturalistic observation
unobtrusive (or nonreactive) observation

Before Reading This Chapter, You May Wish to Review

Chapter 1:
• scientific method
• systematic observation

Chapter 3:
• experimental control
• correlation versus causation
• criteria for causality
• confounds

Chapter 4:
• data-gathering techniques

Chapter 6:
• random sampling error

Most research in psychology can be said to fall into one of three broad categories: the experimental method, the quasi-experimental method, and the correlational method. The experimental and correlational approaches address different kinds of questions, employ different types of statistical analyses, and ultimately tell us different things about the relationships among the variables being studied. The experimental and quasi-experimental methods employ the same types of statistical procedures, but the conclusions that can be reached based on the findings are very different. As we mentioned in Chapter 3, the experimental method is the only research method that allows us to determine whether there is a *causal relationship* between two variables. The correlational method allows us to detect systematic *covariation (or correlation)* between two variables, but, as pointed out in Chapter 3 and reviewed below, it cannot distinguish among the three possible relationships that generate covariation (i.e., causality, a moderator relationship, or a spurious relationship resulting from a third variable). The quasi-experimental method allows us to detect *systematic differences* between different groups or conditions, but does not allow us to infer the cause of these differences. The purpose of this chapter is to help you understand why experiments allow us to draw **causal conclusions** and why correlational and quasi-experimental studies do not. As you will see, the answer rests, ultimately, with the amount of control the researcher has over the relevant aspects of the study.

The Experimental Method

Let's start the discussion of the experimental method by looking at a straightforward example. Suppose your physics professor asks you to determine whether changing the amount of weight suspended on a pendulum causes a change in how fast the pendulum swings. That is, you are asked to determine whether or not the oscillation rate (at least in part) is caused by the amount of weight on a pendulum. How would you go about testing the hypothesis that changing the weight causes a change in the oscillation rate?

To test the hypothesis, you would want to compare the oscillation rates for two pendulums that are identical except for the amount of weight on the string (or, more likely, you would observe the same pendulum with different amounts of weight). To be identical, the pendulums would need to have strings of the same length and the ball would need to be set in motion from the same height (or angle) and with the same amount of force. These variables need to be **experimentally controlled** (and held constant) at some value you choose.

For your assignment, then, you would start by operationally defining "oscillation rate" and selecting your measurement procedure. For example, you may decide to use a stop watch and measure the time it takes for the pendulum to complete two full swings. Then you would choose at least two different amounts of weight, such as 2 ounces and 6 ounces, and find objects that are the same shape and size, but that differ in weight. You would then "build" your pendulum (including hanging a string that will remain the same length after attaching the two different weights). The last steps in preparing to do your experiment would be to decide how high the weight will be and how much force will be applied to set it in motion. You need a way of making sure each weight starts from the same height with the same force. For example, you may decide to simply release the weight from a height of 12 inches, allowing gravity to provide the force.

Once these preparations were completed, you would attach the 2-ounce weight to the pendulum, raise it until it was 12 inches off the table, release it (allowing gravity to set it into its swinging motion), and start the stopwatch at the moment the weight was released. When the weight completed its second full swing (which was chosen as the operational definition of oscillation rate), you would stop the clock and record the time. Then you would replace the 2-ounce weight with the 6-ounce weight, release the pendulum from the same 12-inch height, and record the oscillation rate (again recording how long it takes to complete two full swings). Changing the weights to see what happens to the oscillation rate is an **experimental manipulation,** and you have conducted an **experiment.**

This experiment would allow you to test the hypothesis that weight is a causal factor in the oscillation rate of pendulums by comparing the two observations. If the pendulum swings at a different rate with the heavier (6-ounce) weight than with the lighter (2-ounce) weight, you could conclude that changing the amount of weight causes a change in oscillation rate. This conclusion is warranted as long as everything about the pendulums is the same *except for* the amount of weight. It is this **all else equal** principle (or the "rule of one variable") that allows us to draw causal conclusions.

From this example, you should see that the essence of experimentation is captured by the notion of concurrent *control* and *manipulation* of variables. In an experiment, the researcher systematically varies one thing, often some aspect of the environment (such as amount of weight), to see what impact this change has on a particular behavior of interest (such as oscillation). The factor that is believed to be causal is called the **independent variable (IV),** and this variable is systematically manipulated by the experimenter in order to see what happens when the independent variable is changed from one level to another. The term *independent variable* reflects the fact that the researcher is free to set its value (or level) at any time, independent of any other variables—just as you would be able to use a 2-ounce weight or a 6-ounce weight at any time.

At the same time that the researcher manipulates the levels of the IV, other potential causes should be controlled or held constant. In the pendulum experiment, the amount of weight was changed from 2 to 6 ounces, but other factors that might affect oscillation rate (including length of string, height of the drop, and amount of force used to set the pendulum in motion) were all held constant: They were the same for both 2- and 6-ounce weights. Therefore, we refer to these variables as **controlled variables (CVs).** More specifically, these particular variables were directly controlled by the experimenter, who actively ensured that these variables would not change over the course of the experiment, and hence they are examples of what can be called **directly controlled variables (DCVs).**

The behavior that we record after we have manipulated the IV is called the **dependent variable (DV).** The dependent variable is the phenomenon that we are trying to understand or explain; that is, we are trying to identify the causes of the dependent variable. The experimental hypothesis says that changing the IV will *cause* a change in the DV, so we can think about the IV as the "cause" and the DV as the "effect" that depends on the IV. In the pendulum experiment, the amount of weight was the IV, and the oscillation rate was the DV. The hypothesis was that the oscillation rate of the pendulum would depend on the amount of weight on the string.

The Logic of Experiments

To determine that the changes in behavior (DV) that we observe when the IV has been manipulated really have been caused by the changes in the IV, we must rule out the possibility that something else really brought about the change in the behavior. This is accomplished by carefully varying the IV while holding everything else constant and recording the DV under the different levels of the IV. Stated simply, the logic behind experiments is that *if the situations are identical to begin with, and if the researcher treats each participant exactly the same way except for the level of the IV (so that nothing else changes), then any differences in the DV* must *be due to the changes in the levels of the IV.*[1]

Thus, in a psychology experiment, in order to establish a causal relationship between the independent variable and the dependent variable, we need to expose *similar groups* of participants to different levels of the independent variable while treating them *alike* in all other ways. Consequently, there are two general types of confounds that can arise during an experiment. First, if the groups of participants are not similar before the manipulation begins, there is a **selection bias (or non-equivalence) confound:** Differences in behavior observed after the manipulation of the independent variable might be due to differences between the groups that existed *before* the study began. (We'll discuss this confound in more detail later in this chapter.) Second, if, during the manipulation of the independent variable, the groups of participants are not treated exactly alike in every other respect, there is a **non-standardization confound.** For example, suppose a researcher believes that students are more likely to learn new skills faster if they can interact with the tutor during the training process. To test this hypothesis, suppose the researcher decided to compare an interactive computer-based software package to a standard training manual for teaching typing and keyboarding skills. The researcher designed an experiment in which one group of students used the software package and another group used the manual, and both groups were instructed to follow all of the steps in the training programs. At the end of the training, the students who used the interactive software demonstrated more typing skills than the students who used the manual. Do these results support the hypothesis that interaction during training is more effective than non-interactive learning? That is, do the results indicate that *interactive* training causes an increase in

---

[1] This is based on the philosophical principle of determinism, which states that all behaviors have causes that can be discovered. If behaviors can be generated spontaneously and at random, then the logic of experimentation would not hold. This principle of determinism, of course, is the prevailing philosophical position in our modern-day world, and underlies the research in all sciences.

the rate of learning? The answer is: Only if the two training programs were identical in every respect other than the level of interaction. Of course, there are any number of possible differences between the programs that would explain the difference in outcome, and hence, there are any number of variables that could create a non-standardization confound. For example, suppose the computer program prevented students from moving ahead until they mastered a particular skill or until they passed a timed test. The students using this program would probably have to spend more time practicing than the students in the other group (who could move to more advanced exercises before mastering earlier skills). Thus, the improved performance of the students in the computer-based training group may have been due to an increased amount of practice time rather than to the interactive nature of the software program. In this case, then, the manipulation of the independent variable (interactive versus non-interactive training) systematically varied with the amount of practice time, such that the interactive training procedure required more practice time than the manual. Consequently, the two groups were not treated exactly alike, resulting in a non-standardization confound. Identifying potential confounds and controlling relevant extraneous variables by holding them constant during the experiment allow researchers to avoid non-standardization confounds.

While the logic of the ideal experiment is simple and compelling, psychologists find it difficult to conduct the ideal experiment because we cannot exercise control over all other variables while we are manipulating the IV. We cannot do this for two reasons: (a) We cannot specify the totality of other variables (that is, we cannot identify all of the variables that might impact the DV), and (b) some of those variables could not be controlled by the researcher in any case.

Consider an experiment on the effects of background sounds on learning and memory. The participants will be asked to read lengthy passages from a book while a radio is playing in the room. For some participants, the radio will be broadcasting an interview (i.e., spoken conversation between two people), and for the other participants, instrumental music will be playing. The experimenters will measure how well the participants remember the passages they read. In this study, the experimenters would be systematically varying what was coming from the radio, and this independent variable has two values (or levels): Spoken conversation and instrumental music. The behavior that may be affected by this manipulation of the IV is the amount that people remember of what they have read, so the DV must be some measure of memory for the content of what they were reading. The experimenters know that, ideally, while the radio broadcasts are systematically varied, they should hold "all else constant," but just what is "all else"? While they could not generate a complete, exhaustive list of "all else," the researchers would know that the list includes things like the lighting, temperature, atmospheric pressure, and any fluctuations in the earth's magnetic field. The experimenters may be able to influence the lighting and temperature in the room where the study will take place, but momentary fluctuations in the earth's magnetic field are beyond their control. But does it really matter? Do the experimenters really need to hold *all* else constant, even in the ideal experiment?

The answer is "No, they need to control only those variables that have some influence on the dependent or independent variables." If some variable (say, the magnetic field) has no effect on reading or memory, then it does not matter whether it varies during the manipulation of the IV. The logic of even the ideal experiment requires only that we hold all relevant variables constant, that is, those that can have some impact on the behavior of interest. While that must reduce the variables to be held constant to a small fraction of "all else," as researchers we are still in the bind that we cannot generate a list of all the relevant variables. We can make rational judgments, however. For instance, since, to our knowledge, people do not have any receptors that allow them to detect momentary fluctuations in the earth's magnetic field, this is probably an irrelevant variable, and we will spend no time worrying about how to hold it constant.

In contrast, it is easy to think of a number of things that *would* have an impact on how much people will remember from what they read. For example, memory is likely to be affected by how difficult the reading material is to comprehend, how many times the participants are allowed to read it, how much time passes before they are given the memory test, and what sort of test is used. Since these are factors that could reasonably be expected to influence the amount remembered, they are *relevant* variables, and as such we would want to make them controlled variables by holding them constant. For example, we would make sure that everyone reads the same short story. In fact, we would probably select a story that has never been published in order to be certain that none of the participants has prior knowledge about the story content. Next, we would arrange it so that participants are tested exactly two hours after they finish reading the material and that the same multiple-choice test is used with everyone. By exercising these controls we can assure that any differences in amount remembered under the conversation versus music conditions did not result from any of these sources—it could not be due to differences in the retention interval, for example, since that is two hours in all cases. Remember that controlling relevant variables allows us to rule them out as possible sources of any variation seen in the DV (performance on the memory test).

But what of those relevant variables that do not occur to the experimenter and so are not controlled during the study? For example, intelligence (or IQ) may be relevant to the ability of participants to remember what they have read. Since the researcher did not systematically control IQ or hold it constant, there will be differences among the participants. These individual differences in IQ will *not* be a particular problem as long as the differences are *distributed randomly across the IV groups* so that neither group has an advantage over the other. Thus, by this definition, a characteristic, such as IQ, would be distributed randomly across our treatment groups if the average IQ of the participants in the music group is comparable to the average IQ of the participants in the conversation group, *and* if the standard deviation in IQ in the music group is similar to the standard deviation in IQ in the conversation group.[2] If IQ is, indeed, distributed randomly, so that the IV groups

---

[2] To oversimplify this concept, we could say that IQ is distributed randomly if approximately half of the high-IQ participants are in the music group and the other half are in the conversation groups, and approximately half of the average-IQ participants are in the music group and half in the conversation group, and so forth. If this is true, then the average and standard deviations of the two groups will be similar.

contain the same "mixture" of IQ scores, then a significant difference between the groups in their memory performance would not be due to a selection bias confound where one group had systematically higher IQ scores—and, hence, better memory ability from the very outset—than the other group.

When the IV groups have the same mixture of individual differences, we say the groups are equivalent. We cannot say the groups are equal because no two people are identical, and so no two groups of individuals can be identical, either. But as long as each group has pretty much the same range of variation on a relevant variable that might affect our DV, we can eliminate that variable as an explanation for any differences in performance we observe between the IV groups. Specifically, groups are said to be equivalent when the inevitable differences between them are not systematically related to the experimental manipulations or the dependent variable but are instead due to random sampling error or chance fluctuations. The amount of random variation between two (or more) randomly selected groups will vary, and as we saw in Chapter 6, only large differences—the ones that occur less than 5% of the time by chance alone—are interpreted as evidence for a significant, systematic difference between the groups. Therefore, our hypothesis-testing procedure is designed to compensate for the inevitable differences between our experimental groups that occur by chance, and groups can be considered to be equivalent as long as the random difference between them does not have a probability of .05 or less of occurring by chance alone.

Let's return to our experiment on the effects of music versus conversation as background noise during a reading task. Imagine that the results of the study indicated that participants in the music conditions remembered significantly more of what they read than the participants who had conversation in the background while they were reading. Your first impulse would be to conclude that reading while other people are talking is less effective than reading with music in the background. But suppose it occurs to you only *after* conducting the experiment that the amount one remembers might be related to the time of day when they perform the task. If you had happened to carefully record the time at which each person participated in your study, you could go back and see whether the two levels of the IV differ in this respect.

In the best of all possible worlds, you would find that the two conditions are the same: For instance, 25% of each group were observed at 11 a.m., 50% at 4 p.m., and 25% at 7 p.m. Note that although time of day was not held constant at a single value (as would happen if people were allowed to participate only at 11 a.m.), the two conditions do have the same mixture of testing times (i.e., the distributions of testing times are identical for the two levels of the IV), so time of day is a controlled variable in your study and cannot account for the difference in memory performance between the IV groups. This even distribution could, of course, have been deliberately planned by the researcher rather than accidental, in which case we would say that time of testing has been directly controlled. Thus, there are two types of controlled variables: those which have been held constant across each individual in the study, and those which have a similar distribution of values across levels of the IV so that the groups can be considered equivalent on that variable.

Suppose, however, it turns out that the conversation condition was mostly administered in the evening while the music condition was given most often in the late morning and afternoon. In that case, your experiment has a serious flaw. The IV groups do not have a similar distribution of testing times, so the groups are not equivalent on a variable that could potentially affect memory performance. Therefore, you cannot conclude that the difference in memory performance was due to the difference in type of background noise; it may have been the result of the unintended but systematic differences between the groups in the time of day that the reading/memory task took place. For instance, participants may have been more tired during the evenings than during the day, and since most of the participants in the conversation group were tested in the evenings, their fatigue levels may explain why their recall performance was lower than that of the participants in the music group (most of whom were tested earlier in the day, when they were more alert).

In technical terms, then, if it can be shown that some other potentially relevant variable happened to co-vary with the IV, that other variable is said to be confounded with the IV, and confounds preclude any clear interpretation of the results of your experiment. Remember, by definition, a **confound** exists whenever there are two or more reasonable explanations for the observed differences in performance. If the memory scores were, on average, a good bit better for the music condition than the conversation condition, we cannot say that it was really due to music versus conversation, because it could have been due to performing the task in the daytime versus evening, or some combination of the two. The point is that because the IV (background noise) was confounded with time of day, it is not possible to say which produced the difference in memory performance. Specifically, this is an example of a *non-standardization confound:* The two groups were not treated exactly alike during the study.

Therefore, in order to be able to draw causal conclusions, an experimenter must avoid confounds: The only systematic difference between the IV groups must be the IV treatment itself and nothing else. All other relevant variables must be controlled in order to prevent confounding. This is accomplished using a combination of three forms of control: (1) holding relevant variables constant across individuals (so that each participant in the study has the same value of the variable); (2) holding relevant variables constant across treatment groups (so that the range of variation in each IV group is exactly the same; and (3) using random assignment to make the IV groups equivalent on all of the relevant situational or personal characteristics (which are generally referred to as **subject variables**) that we either do not think of or cannot directly control. **Random assignment** is a procedure that assigns individuals to IV treatment groups completely by chance so that each participant has an equal probability of being placed in any of the treatment groups. (Pulling names from a hat or flipping a coin are some simple techniques for randomly assigning individuals to treatments.) Statisticians have demonstrated that when large numbers of participants are assigned to groups at random, all of the individual differences among them are spread evenly across the groups. That is, when we randomly assign participants to our treatment conditions, all subject variables (such as intelligence and personality) will probably be randomly and evenly distributed across the treatments. (Recall that when characteristics are randomly distributed across treatments, they cannot explain systematic differences in performance, hence they are not confounded with the IV manipulation.)

For example, in our experiment on music versus conversation as background during reading, the process of random assignment would have made our groups equivalent on intelligence by randomly distributing IQ scores across the groups (e.g., by assigning about half of the above-average participants to the music group and half to the conversation group, and so forth). Simultaneously, then, random assignment would have made our groups equivalent on all other relevant subject variables, such as memory capacity, reading ability, vocabulary, visual acuity, academic achievement, distractibility, auditory acuity, motivation, and need for achievement. For each of these variables and all of the others we can't even think of, random assignment would distribute the values of the variable evenly across the groups so that the groups have equivalent mixtures of each of these potentially relevant variables.

Thus, random assignment is a powerful tool for researchers who want to conduct experiments to test the hypothesis that changing the IV causes a change in the DV. Random assignment controls variables we have not measured as well as variables we have not even thought about. However, random assignment does not work perfectly every time. It is subject to random sampling error (which we discussed in Chapter 6), where by chance alone, the values of a relevant variable are not distributed evenly across the IV groups. For example, suppose our sample of participants included four individuals with severe hearing loss (so that background noise does not interfere with their reading). Random assignment, ideally, would assign two of these people to each of our two groups, but by chance alone, there is a possibility that three or even all four of these people would be assigned to the same group, which might give that group an advantage over the other. For example, if all four of the hearing-impaired participants had been assigned to the music-as-background condition, the greater memory performance of that group overall may have been due to these four individuals being undistracted by the music rather than to a difference in the distraction posed by music versus conversation. In other words, the research groups were not equivalent in the auditory sensitivity of their members, so the study was confounded (there are two possible explanations for why the music group recalled more from the story). This would be an example of a selection bias confound.

How often will random assignment fail to create equivalent groups? That is, how often will the difference between the experimental groups be so large that we mistakenly conclude that there is a systematic effect due to the treatment? As we saw in Chapter 6, this will happen only 5% of the time or less. Therefore, if we use random assignment and then find a significant difference between the IV groups, we can be 95% certain that the difference in the DV was caused by the IV. There is only a 5% chance that the observed difference between randomly assigned groups is due to random sampling error and that the groups were, in fact, not equivalent from the outset of the experiment. Thus, when we use random assignment, we can say that we have probably controlled all of the personal characteristics and individual differences the participants bring with them to our laboratory. The term for this type of

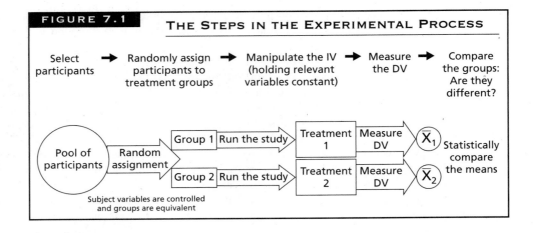

FIGURE 7.1   THE STEPS IN THE EXPERIMENTAL PROCESS

experimental control is *probabilistic control* (and the subject variables controlled in this way, such as auditory acuity, personality and intelligence, are called **probabilistically controlled variables,** or PCVs).

An Overview of the Experimental Method

To be able to draw the conclusion that the IV causes the DV, the researcher must conduct a true, unconfounded experiment. The steps of this process are presented in Figure 7-1.

After operationally defining the DV and selecting the levels of the IV needed to test the hypothesis, the researcher needs to identify relevant variables in the experimental setting that need to be held constant (either as directly controlled variables held constant across individuals or as probabilistically controlled variables randomly distributed across the treatment groups). Then a process for ensuring that these variables actually are controlled during the study itself must be developed. Next, the participants must be selected for the study and assigned to a treatment group in a way that will maximize the chances of having groups that are equivalent on all relevant subject variables. Then the study must be conducted where the IV is systematically manipulated and the DV is measured while all other situational factors are controlled, following the procedures developed for that purpose. If the groups of participants are equivalent at the start of the study, and if the groups are treated exactly alike except for the level of the IV they receive, then a difference in performance between the groups can be attributed to the manipulation of the IV: We can conclude that the IV caused the change in the DV.

Suppose we wanted to know whether taking the drug Redux can cause weight loss among obese adults. We would start by defining "weight loss" and determine what experimental conditions to include as levels of our IV. Let's suppose that we decide to use number of pounds lost over a six-month period as our measure of weight loss and to compare two groups of participants: (1) obese adults who are prescribed Redux and (2) obese adults who are not taking any weight-control drugs. Thus our IV has two levels (Redux versus no drug). Our next step would be to find a representative sample of obese adults[3] and assign them to our treatment groups. We could simply use random assignment, or we could decide to use direct control over a few very important variables such as age and sex and then use random assignment to probabilistically control all of the other possibly confounding individual differences among the participants.

For instance, we could directly control sex by taking all of the men in the sample and randomly assigning them to the treatment groups (so that half of the men get Redux and half do not). Similarly, we could randomly assign the women to the treatment groups (so that half of the women get Redux and half do not). Thus our Redux group is exactly equal to the no-drug group in terms of the number of men and women in the groups. The same procedure could be used to control for differences in age, degree of obesity, and so on. By randomly deciding which group a particular participant is in, we are probabilistically controlling for any subject variables not being directly controlled.

After assigning the participants to our treatment groups, we need to manipulate the IV while systematically controlling other potential confounds. The only difference between the groups is to be whether or not they take the drug Redux; therefore, we need to make sure that other things (such as amount and type of exercise) are either held constant for all participants or equivalent across the groups. We could control exercise by putting all participants on a prescribed exercise regimen where they engage in exactly the same activities for the same amount of time each day. For obvious reasons, we would probably decide to directly control time of year and make sure that if participants in the Redux group are being studied over the Thanksgiving-Christmas holiday season, participants in the no-drug group are also being tested during that time period.

Finally, we would measure the number of pounds lost after the specified six-month period of time. If we find that the Redux group has lost significantly more weight than the no-drug group, we can conclude that the Redux really works (and causes weight loss) because we have controlled all of the alternative, potentially confounding factors. By using a combination of both direct and probabilistic controls in this experiment, we have minimized the chances that our results are due to confounds in our procedures, and we can be at least 95% certain that the difference in weight loss was caused by the difference in treatment. However, because there *is* that nagging 5% chance of a Type I error, we should conduct replication studies and find a convergence of evidence before we are fully convinced that Redux works. As

---

[3] We would have to operationally define "obese" in order to determine who would be eligible to participate in the study. We might, for example, select individuals who are 20% or more over their "ideal weight" as determined by the American Medical Association's guide to body size and weight.

we saw in Chapter 6 when we discussed Type I and Type II errors, no single experiment can prove anything.[4]

When someone reports the methods and results of an experiment, others need to think critically about the study. Did some variable other than the IV differ systematically across the treatment groups? If so, there is a confound and behavioral differences are not readily interpretable. It is part of the training of scientific researchers to become skeptical consumers of research and to look for rival hypotheses or alternative explanations for the observed performance differences (including the possibility of confounds).

Well, if any single experiment might have been confounded just by chance, then when can we be confident that our research has demonstrated a real effect of the IV? Consider our example above, where time of day happened by chance to be out of balance so that music was mostly given in the daytime and conversation in the evening. Since that did not happen as a result of something being done systematically by the experimenter in the conduct of the study, is it likely that it would happen again if the study were conducted again? No, since the most probable outcome would be for the distribution of times of day to be very similar for the two groups. Thus, if the effect was not due to the IV but to some other variable that happened by chance to differ across the treatment groups, then this same effect is not likely to occur when the study is repeated. This is why, for most scientists, the most compelling evidence that an IV has had a true effect is converging evidence across a series of replication studies. If we get the same results when the study is repeated, we can be more confident (but not 100% certain) that the results of any one study were not due solely to chance.

Indeed, science, as a means of identifying natural laws, is a self-correcting procedure. If a result is published and someone else is skeptical about it, they are likely to attempt to repeat it. If they are unable to do so, they may then publish a "failure to replicate" note. Because no journal editor wants to publish work that will become the subject of a subsequent failure-to-replicate note, most journal editors now prefer to publish studies that include a replication of the results. That is, before having their work accepted for publication, researchers are now expected to conduct their studies more than once, either as a straight replication, or more commonly as a *variant replication* in which the same IV was examined under another set of similar circumstances. Furthermore, researchers' reputations may become tarnished if their published work cannot be replicated, and for that reason alone, replication of the results of individual experiments is always in order.

---

[4] It is also important to understand that no set of experiments can prove anything either. Even if 20 experiments have been conducted and each of them finds a significant effect of the IV, there is always a chance that all 20 experiments had made Type I errors and that the IV actually has no real effect. The odds of this happening, of course, are minuscule but they are not zero. Just as each single study may commit an error (either Type I or Type II), any group of studies may have consistently made the same error. Therefore, researchers very carefully avoid claiming that they have "proved" anything.

An Alternative to Random Assignment: Repeated Measures

In many cases, if researchers have the option of randomly assigning participants to the treatment conditions (in what is called a *random groups design*), they also have a second option: Exposing every participant to every one of the treatments (in what is called a *repeated measures design* or a *within-subjects design*). For example, in our experiment on music versus conversation as background during reading, we could have participants read a passage while a conversation is played on the radio, test their memory for the passage, have them read a second passage while music is played on the radio, and then test their memory for the second passage. In this design, the dependent variable is measured repeatedly for the same participants, once after each of the treatments. Obviously, the individual differences among the participants would remain constant across the treatments. For instance, if four of the participants suffer from severe hearing loss, their disability would impact both experimental conditions equally. Similarly, the intelligence, personality, vocabulary, distractibility, and visual acuity of the participants would not change during the study, so the conversation and music conditions would be equivalent (even equal) on all of these subject variables. Thus, repeated measures (or within-subjects) designs provide direct control over these subject variables. However, the fact that participants are given the same test on at least two occasions at different points in time raises the possibility that changes in performance are due to the passage of time rather than the independent variable. If the researcher is able to control the effects of time and repeated testing by spreading their effects evenly across the treatments, then the treatment conditions will be equivalent on all relevant variables, and the study is a true experiment. These designs and the techniques used to control "time-related effects" are discussed in detail in Chapter 10.

Research Settings for Experiments: Laboratory Versus Field Experiments

In the ideal experiment, as we have described it, the researcher has controlled each and every potential confound, either through direct, experimental control or through randomization and probabilistic control. Maximum control over extraneous variables can be achieved if the study is conducted in a *laboratory*. A laboratory can be any room or space controlled by the researcher so that everything that happens to the participant is planned in advance and where every participant can be exposed to the exact same sequence of events. For example, in a laboratory, the researcher can prevent any unexpected interruptions or distractions, place the objects in the room in particular positions, and determine exactly what the participants will see and hear. Some laboratories are located in permanent research facilities, but some can go on the road and be set up in places like empty classrooms in schools. The key feature of a laboratory is that the researcher has created the experimental situation and has a high degree of control over the entire environment.

Assuming that the operational definitions of the independent and dependent variables are valid, and the procedures are followed systematically, **laboratory**

experiments will have the highest level of internal validity. That is, a well-designed and well-executed laboratory experiment is the best procedure available to us for successfully addressing the research question "Does X cause Y?" because X and Y have been isolated from other factors that could potentially influence performance. (Remember that a study has internal validity if the design and conduct of the study allow us to answer the question it was intended to answer.)

There is, however, a price to be paid for the internal validity of laboratory experiments: We sacrifice generalizability because what happens when X and Y have been isolated in a lab may not be an accurate portrayal of what happens when they are operating within the complexity of the natural environment. In technical terms, then, laboratory experiments may have a high degree of internal validity but may have low external validity (i.e., the results may not generalize to the world outside the laboratory). In general, as the degree of experimental control increases in a laboratory, the internal validity of the experiment increases, but the external validity decreases (since the behaviors that occur in highly controlled environments may bear little resemblance to the behaviors that would occur under normal circumstances).

To increase the external validity or generalizability of an experiment, we can conduct the experimental manipulation in a natural setting rather than in a laboratory. In other words, we can conduct a **field experiment.** For example, in 1972, Isen and Levin published the results of a study they had conducted to test the hypothesis that people who are in a good mood are more likely to help others. The study took place in a shopping mall, and the participants were adults who had just finished using a public telephone. Isen and Levin had a female confederate "accidentally" drop a folder of papers just as the participant emerged from the phone booth, and they recorded whether or not the participant stopped to help pick up the papers. The experimental manipulation occurred in the phone booth: Half of the participants were put in a "good" mood by finding a dime in the coin return slot of the phone—placed there by the researchers—while the remaining participants did not find any money. Isen and Levin (1972) reported that 87.5% of the people who found money in the coin return stopped to help the stranger while only 4% of the people who did not find money stopped to help. This study is an example of a field experiment because an independent variable was systematically manipulated in a natural setting where the participants were engaged in their normal, everyday routine. (In most field studies, participants do not know their behavior is being observed, so the researchers must be certain that they stay within the ethical guidelines presented in Chapter 2.)

In field experiments, many potentially confounding factors are not controlled by the researcher but instead are allowed to vary naturally. This makes the field study more realistic than a laboratory study and increases the generalizability or external validity of the findings. However, at the same time, the lack of experimental control over relevant extraneous variables increases the likelihood that a confound will occur, which in turn decreases the internal validity of the study. For example, Isen and Levin had no control over the contents of the phone calls made by the participants, so the phones calls varied naturally. Consequently, some people may have received news that put them in a good mood and others may have received news that put them in a bad mood. This could certainly influence the effect of the independent variable manipulation, and would create a confound if more people in the money condition received good news over the phone while more people in the no-money condition received bad news over the phone. A confounded experiment does not answer its research question ("Does X cause Y?"). Consequently, if field experiments are more likely to be confounded than laboratory experiments, we must be more cautious about drawing causal conclusions from their results.

Quasi-Experimental Research Methods

The experimental method allows us to draw causal conclusions because, when an experiment is well designed and executed, it makes rival hypotheses that may account for the observed effects implausible. The two requirements of a true experiment are equivalent groups at the outset and standardized treatments that differ only in the value of the independent variable. If either of these elements is missing, the study will be confounded, and causal conclusions will be unwarranted. Ideal experiments, however, cannot always be conducted: For some hypotheses, and in some settings, the researcher will be unable to meet one or the other of these requirements. In the event that an ideal experiment cannot be performed, the researcher may elect to conduct a **quasi-experiment.** Quasi-experiments have the same structure of experiments (with independent variables and a dependent variable and possibly some controlled variables), and they are analyzed using the same statistical procedures that compare group averages, but causal conclusions cannot be drawn from quasi-experimental studies. Let's look at two types of quasi-experiments: **non-equivalent groups designs** (which have different participants at each level of the independent variable), and **time-series designs** (which use repeated measures on the same group of participants).[5]

Non-Equivalent Groups Designs

As the name implies, there are times when the researcher cannot presume that the IV treatment groups are equivalent at the outset of the study. Essentially, whenever the researcher cannot or does not use random assignment to the levels of the IV, the groups cannot be considered equivalent. The two most common applications of **non-equivalent groups designs** are (1) studies with subject variables as independent variables where random assignment is simply impossible due to the nature of subject variables and (2) situations where random assignment is not used because of ethical, political, or practical reasons.

Suppose a psychologist hypothesizes that males have better spatial skills than females, or that older adults have poorer perceptual memory than young adults. To test these hypotheses, the researcher would need to make comparisons between

---

[5] Other quasi-experimental designs have been described by Campbell and Stanley (1963).

different sexes and different age groups, but participants cannot be randomly assigned to these groups: Each individual is already male or female and already belongs to a particular age group. Sex and age are examples of subject variables—characteristics the participants bring with them into the research setting that are not under the control of the researcher. Therefore, it might be appropriate to think of the IV in this kind of quasi-experiment as being "manipulated by selection"—that is, participants are selected because they already have the values of the IV that we want to study. This is in contrast to the true experimental manipulation, where the researcher can decide (at random) who will be exposed to which treatment and the IV is then imposed upon the participants. Manipulation by selection does not provide probabilistic control over relevant extraneous variables that could account for the observed differences, and hence these quasi-experiments are confounded *from the outset* by a selection bias (or non-equivalence) confound.

For example, to test the hypothesis that males have better spatial skill than females, the researcher would administer a spatial-skills task to a representative group of men and a representative group of women and compare their average performance. If there is a significant difference between the two groups, the researcher could not say that the difference in spatial ability was *caused* by the biological sex difference between the groups. A group of males is different from a group of females in more than just biological sex, so biological sex is automatically confounded with other variables, such as sex-role stereotyping and pressure to engage in sex-typed activities. Boys and girls are raised very differently in our culture, and the different sex roles and sex-typed activities they are encouraged to adopt may result in different levels of performance in many arenas. For example, boys are more likely to be encouraged to play with erector sets and to build model cars, activities that could help develop stronger spatial ability.[6] Researchers need to keep in mind that *all* subject variables correlate with a number of other important factors, and, therefore, any time we sort people into groups based on a subject variable, we have to admit that the groups cannot be considered to be equivalent on every factor other than the IV. Consequently, while one may be able to demonstrate a strong relationship between some behavior and the subject variable, and while this may have a good predictive value, there would be any number of possible explanations for differences between the groups; therefore we cannot draw causal conclusions from this type of non-equivalent groups design.[7]

A second type of non-equivalent group design is characterized by an actual experimental manipulation where different participants receive different treatments,

---

[6] As another example, it is widely known that girls and boys have equal aptitudes in math and science until they reach high school, but girls start to avoid taking math and science classes (and guidance counselors do not push them to do so). This may lead to sex differences in performance in math and science classes during college that are not simply a function of biological sex differences.

[7] This type of design is sometimes referred to as an ex post facto design, and some textbooks classify it as a "non-experimental" or "correlational" design rather than as a quasi-experiment. The actual categorical label applied to the design is not as important as understanding that these studies with "subject variables as IVs" are confounded by the pre-existing differences between the groups, so no conclusion can be drawn about the specific causal mechanisms.

but the participants were not randomly assigned to the treatment conditions. For example, a school psychologist may believe that many children who are failing academically suffer from depression—not as a consequence of failure, but as its cause. That is, the psychologist may hypothesize that childhood depression interferes with cognitive functioning, which, in turn, leads to poor academic performance. If this hypothesis is correct, it may suggest that treating children with antidepressant medication could cause an improvement in their school work. To test this hypothesis, the psychologist would have some children take the drug and then compare their subsequent school performance to that of children who did not take the drug. However, for ethical reasons, the researcher cannot be the one to determine exactly which children receive the drug—this is serious stuff, and the parents must decide. Therefore, the researcher must settle for finding parents who volunteer to allow their children to be treated with the antidepressant medication. This is not random assignment. Families who are willing to volunteer for such a study may be dramatically and systematically different from families who do not volunteer (and who then become part of the "No-Drug Control Group"). For example, they may be more highly educated and more convinced that research is important, or they may be more deeply concerned about the problems their children face, and so forth. Parents who volunteer their children for this study may also be doing other things to help their children improve academically, such as helping children with their homework or limiting television viewing. Therefore, we cannot presume that the volunteers are equivalent to non-volunteers, and the study has a selection bias (non-equivalence) confound from the start, and consequently, we cannot draw causal conclusions from these designs.

Time-Series Designs

In a simple **time-series design,** there is one group of participants, and their performance on the dependent variable is measured several times before and at least once after the experimental manipulation is imposed. The premanipulation measurements provide a baseline against which changes in performance following the experimental manipulation can be assessed. For example, a school psychologist may want to find out whether play therapy reduces the aggressiveness of boys who have been diagnosed as conduct-disordered. In a time-series design, the psychologist would measure the children's aggressive behavior once a week for a month before the play therapy sessions begin, run the therapy sessions twice a week for a month, and then measure aggression once a week for a month. The aggression scores are then plotted on a graph to see whether there is any systematic change in the patterns from pretherapy to posttherapy. Figure 7-2 illustrates several possible patterns that may be found.

The graphs in Figures 7-2a and 7-2b suggest that the experimental manipulation—the play therapy—was followed by a systematic reduction in aggressiveness (at least temporarily), while Figures 7-2c and 7-2d do not show any evidence that play therapy, per se, had any impact on the children's aggressiveness. (Figure 7-2c indicates that the aggression scores were steadily declining even before the play

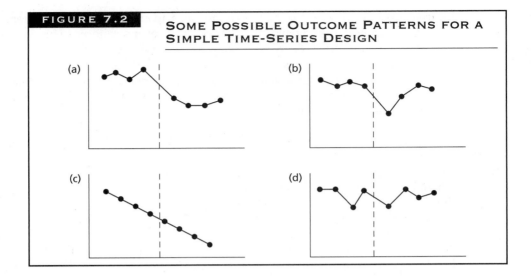

FIGURE 7.2

SOME POSSIBLE OUTCOME PATTERNS FOR A SIMPLE TIME-SERIES DESIGN

therapy began, so the continued decline may not be attributable to the therapy. Figure 7-2d shows no overall decline after the treatment.) However, even if the data resemble Figure 7-2a or 7-2b, the researcher must be very cautious about drawing causal conclusions because the change in aggressiveness may have actually been triggered by some other historical event that, by chance, coincided with the onset of play therapy. (For instance, perhaps the peer group became more assertive toward the conduct-disordered children simply as a function of time and familiarity, so the participants then began to behave less aggressively, but not because of the play therapy.) This type of confound, called a *history confound*, is described in more detail in Chapters 10 and 15.

Two Approaches to Analyzing the Results

It should be noted here that when data from a research study are being analyzed, it is not uncommon for the same data set to be analyzed in more than one way. Sometimes these include analyses that treat the study as if it is simply a correlational study while other analyses treat it as a quasi-experimental study. For example, suppose a researcher tested the hypothesis that people who are sensitive to criticism are less likely to express critical opinions about another person's work by asking participants to "both describe and evaluate" some art work produced by students in a school of art and design. The researcher computed the proportion of comments the participants made about the art work that were critical about the quality of the work. Following this, in another setting, the participants were given several paper-and-pencil tasks, including a test to measure their sensitivity to criticism. Thus, the researcher had two scores for each participant: The proportion of critical comments about the art work, and a measure of their sensitivity to criticism. One approach to analyzing these data would be to compute a coefficient that quantifies the degree of correlation between these two variables within the sample of participants. Another way to analyze the data would be to sort the participants on the basis of their sensitivity to criticism and select two sub-groups for comparison. For example, the researcher may decide to compare the people with the highest sensitivity scores with those with the lowest sensitivity scores. In this analysis, the sensitivity to criticism is the independent variable (or "grouping factor"), and the proportion of critical comments made about the art work would be the dependent variable. This quasi-experimental analysis would compare the mean proportion of critical comments made by members of these two groups to see whether those high in sensitivity tended to make fewer critical comments. (Discussion of the details of appropriate correlation coefficients are covered in Chapter 8, and analyses for experimental and quasi-experimental studies are covered in Chapters 11–13).

Summary of Quasi-Experimental Methods

Quasi-experiments closely resemble true experiments in terms of the basic structure of the study: The average performance of groups varying along an independent variable are compared in order to see whether there is a significant difference between them (non-equivalent groups designs), or the average score before a treatment is compared to the average score after the treatment to see whether a systematic difference can be detected (time-series designs). These studies can provide important information that helps us achieve the goals of describing and predicting behavior (that is, quasi-experiments help us to know the "who, what, when, and where" of human behavior). However, quasi-experiments are not true experiments and, consequently, do not allow us to draw causal conclusions—they cannot tell us "why" a behavior occurs. Non-equivalent groups designs are confounded by the fact that the groups do not start out equivalent, either because the independent variable is a subject variable or because the researcher was unable to use random assignment to the treatment conditions. Time-series designs are potentially confounded by a variety of time-related factors such as historical events that take place during the course of the study and change the participants' behavior. We discuss some other specific types of time-related confounds in Chapter 10, and we give an overview of how time-series designs can be used in studies with just one or a few participants in Chapter 15.

Correlational Methods

The correlational method of research is very different from experiments and quasi-experiments, both structurally and functionally. Structurally, both experiments and quasi-experiments consist of an independent variable (or a "grouping factor") and a dependent variable, and functionally, they both address the question "Is there a difference in performance between the groups?" In contrast, correlational studies do not involve the manipulation of an independent variable (participants are not sorted into separate groups but are all observed under the same conditions). Instead, correlational studies use measures of **association (or correlation)** to assess the relationship between two variables (X and Y) within a single group of participants whose responses have not been influenced by the researcher. Two variables are said to be associated, or correlated, when there is a systematic relationship between them such that as the value of X changes, the value of Y changes in a uniform, predictable fashion. Essentially, then, correlational studies ask the question "Do people with high (or low) scores on X also tend to have high (or low) scores on Y?"

One of the key distinctions between experiments and the correlational method is the extent to which the researcher actively *intervenes* in an effort to cause particular behaviors rather than simply recording naturally occurring behaviors. As we have seen, experiments use **intervention** (through the manipulation of the independent variable and control of potentially confounding variables), and quasi-experiments may or may not include direct intervention by the researcher, depending on the nature of the independent variables in the study. In contrast, the correlational method is typically characterized by a **nonintervention** approach.

Correlational studies can be conducted in a variety of settings using any of the data-gathering techniques discussed in Chapter 4, as illustrated in the examples on page 177. In each of these examples, two (or more) behaviors are measured for each participant, but the researcher makes no attempt to influence the participants' performance. Rather, the purpose is to record "natural, on-going" behaviors—behaviors that would have occurred, presumably, even if the study was not taking place. Furthermore, in correlational studies such as these, researchers generally do not attempt to measure, much less control, all of the relevant extraneous variables that may be influencing the participants' behavior. Consequently, as we discussed in Chapter 3, a correlation between the variables of interest (X and Y) may be a reflection of any of three very different types of relationships: spurious relationships (where the correlation between X and Y is due to a third variable, Z), causal relationships (where X causes Y), or moderator relationships (where X suppresses or strengthens Z's ability to cause Y). Because correlational research is characterized by nonintervention and limited experimental control of extraneous variables (so potential third variables, Zs, are not held constant), it is impossible to determine which type of relationship explains a correlation between X and Y. As we stressed in Chapter 3, the principle to remember is that **correlation does *not* imply causation.** Any correlation may be the result of a third variable which links X to Y in a spurious relationship—even if we cannot identify the variable Z. Take a few minutes to consider the examples of correlational research using different data-gathering techniques presented in the box on page 177.

Notice that example 5 includes a behavioral observation that takes place in a laboratory setting: the room with the wheelchair. It is important to note that the researcher was controlling the setting in order to give the participants the opportunity to display the behavior of interest (i.e., sitting in an empty wheelchair) and that this is not the same as experimentally manipulating an independent variable. (This study could become an experiment if half of the participants were left with a

EXAMPLE 1: PHYSICAL TRACES

A researcher interested in studying the relationship between alcohol consumption and safe-sex practices among teenagers could visit the local "Lover's Lane" and count the number of empty alcohol containers and used condoms that are found early on Saturday and Sunday mornings.

EXAMPLE 2: ARCHIVES

A university administrator interested in the impact of Internet access on academic performance could get the students' grade-point average from the registrar's office and ask the computer center to provide records of the number of hours each student was logged onto the campus ethernet.

EXAMPLE 3: SELF-REPORTS

A sociologist interested in attitudes concerning major ethical issues could construct a survey and mail it to a sample of respondents. A simple survey like the one presented in Table 7-1 measures five different variables, and the associations among all of these variables can be assessed.

TABLE 7.1	A Sample Survey

Instructions: Answer each of the questions below. Do not include your name or other identifying information so that your anonymity is assured.

1. What is your annual income? _____
2. How many years of college have you completed? _____

For the remaining items, indicate your opinion using the following scale:

    1 = very much against
    2 = somewhat against
    3 = somewhat in favor
    4 = very much in favor

3. How do you feel about imposing the death penalty on serial rapists? _____
4. How do you feel about legalizing physician-assisted suicide? _____
5. How do you feel about legalizing partial-birth abortion? _____

Thank you for your cooperation. Please use the enclosed self-addressed, stamped envelope to return this survey to Dr. John Smith, Sociology Department, Belmore College.

EXAMPLE 4: BEHAVIORAL RATINGS

A school psychologist interested in social withdrawal in young children may ask kindergarten teachers to rate each child's shyness and ask the parents to rate their child's emotional maturity at home.

EXAMPLE 5: BEHAVIORAL OBSERVATIONS

A psychologist interested in attitudes about physically handicapped people could arrange for participants to be left alone in a room where a motorized wheelchair is the only seat and measure how much time the participant spends sitting in the wheelchair. Later, on another day and in another place, the participants could be asked to make a contribution to a disabled veterans' fund, and the amount of money contributed could be recorded.

wheelchair that is a brand new display model and the other participants are left with an old, well-worn wheelchair that has someone's personal belongings in the side pockets. Then you might expect to find a difference between these two groups in how much time they spend sitting in the chair, and you may also see whether there is a difference in the amount of money they later donate to the disabled veterans' fund.)

Behavioral observations may, of course, also be conducted in the field, using a research procedure that is known as **naturalistic observation.** Let's look at naturalistic observation procedures in more detail to illustrate why correlational methods do not allow us to test causal hypotheses (such as "Drinking alcohol causes teenagers to engage in unprotected sex").

Naturalistic Observation

The purpose of naturalistic observation is to record behavior as it is occurring in its natural setting. (A general name for the study of ongoing behavior in the natural environment is the *ethological* approach.) The key feature of this approach is nonintervention: The researcher does not attempt to influence the events or cause particular behaviors to occur, but rather records naturally occurring events. By recording occurrences of some behavior of interest, along with a number of environmental variables and characteristics of the individual being observed, researchers may be able to discover some other variables to which the particular behavior of interest is related. Of course, we cannot readily observe or record all aspects of situations or even total behavior, so the data are typically about some selected subset of behaviors and environmental conditions. Since the researcher exercises no control over the situation, variables other than the subset observed and recorded may vary in unknown ways from one set of observations to another. Consequently, the researcher cannot rule out the possibility that some unobserved, unmeasured relevant variable is systematically influencing the variables of interest (X and Y), and creating a spurious relationship between them. A correlation between X and Y cannot be interpreted as evidence for a causal relationship.

Naturalistic observations are often used in the early phases of research as an exploratory exercise to try to discern what, if anything, may be systematically varying with the behaviors in question. For example, suppose that, during a trip to the ocean, we observe a bird running along the sand dunes with its breast down near the ground and its extended wings fluttering rapidly. If this strikes us as a peculiar behavior, we may want to find out more about it, such as what else may be happening at the same time that relates to it. To find out in an empirical manner, we would need to make systematic observations of the behavior of that species of birds over an extended period of time, recording both the behaviors of the birds and the conditions of the environment. If we start out with no idea of just what it is we are looking for, then this first naturalistic observation study is an exploratory "fishing expedition." We'd like to know everything that happens over time to see whether any particular events show covariation with the occurrences of this "breast-down-wings-fluttering" behavior. However, given the limitations on human processing capacities, we would be able to observe, keep, and record only a few aspects of the situation, not everything.

Traditionally, researchers making naturalistic observations prepare a checklist of specific events they believe are important and then, during the observations, carry a pad so that they can note which events on their checklist occur, when, and for how long. They may also attempt to record some of the circumstances surrounding the specific events of interest—such as what happened just before, during, or just after the bird went running down the beach flapping its wings. Modern technology, however, would allow us to overcome much of the limitations of our capacity for attention and processing; for example, we can videotape the birds and make oral comments about important details onto a tape. These videotapes allow us to observe the same event several times, each time focusing on and recording a different aspect of the situation. Of course, many aspects of the situations are still not recorded. The video camera cannot watch in all directions, and no record might be made of wind speed, air pressure, or other subtle aspects of the environment that might be related to the birds' behavior.

Nearly always the observations made are guided by some, at least implicit, hypotheses. If we record our observations about other birds in the vicinity, we typically do so because we are wondering about some specific potential connections. For example, we may suspect that the wing-fluttering behavior is part of a mating activity designed to attract opposite-sex members of the same species, or we may believe that it is an effort to attract attention to the birds themselves and keep members of other, predatory species from finding their nest and destroying their eggs or young.

Note that for the latter hypothesis we might need to be relating this bird's wing-fluttering behavior to the presence of certain other species of birds, perhaps in the air, well overhead. But will our recorded observations pick up all the relevant data? (Is there a video camera pointed skyward to record what is happening in the sky overhead?) One major issue for the method of naturalistic observation, then, is whether one can record enough of the relevant aspects of the situation to have the raw data that will allow discovery of systematic relationships. To appreciate this issue of behavioral complexity and adequacy of one's observations, imagine trying to watch a schoolyard full of about 150 children where the task you've set yourself is to observe conditions that are related to physical aggression of children at play.

In using naturalistic observation, a central methodological problem has to do with whether the actions of the researcher during the process of making the observations might alter the very behavior to be recorded. If we simply go out on the sand dune and stand there with our video and tape machines set up on tripods, our presence may clearly alter the behaviors of the target species we are interested in studying or behaviors of other species involved in conditions necessary for the wing-fluttering behavior. Whereas our intent was to record normally occurring, on-going behavior in the natural environment, the behavior of interest has been altered by our attempt to record it. In some way the individuals whose behavior we wished to observe are now showing behavior that is reactive to our recording procedures.

In the example regarding observation of physical aggression among children at play, if you go into the center of the playground with cameras, tapes, and note pads, you can expect the children's behavior to be altered; many will now "perform" for your camera. (And if they suspected that you were interested in videotaping aggression, that alone might assure that they gave you what you came for.) To succeed at naturalistic observation, then, researchers may need to use **unobtrusive (or nonreactive)** observation procedures. In ethological field work with animals, this may involve the construction of a blind to conceal the researcher and recording equipment, or the use of cameras with high-powered lenses that allow the researcher to record the animals' behaviors from a distance. Unobtrusive observations of human behavior often involves hidden cameras, one-way mirrors, or observers trying to look inconspicuous.

Another potential problem arises when the researcher focuses on the conditions under which the behavior of interest occurs but fails to keep equally good records of the conditions when the behavior is not occurring. Clearly, one must know about events both when the behavior does and does not occur in order to ascertain that a systematic relationship exists. Consider the researcher who sets out to make naturalistic observations to test the specific hypothesis that women "jay-walk" (here defined as crossing the street in urban business districts anywhere along the block other than at marked crosswalk areas) more than men. The researcher parks his car in the downtown business district mid-morning one weekday and for the next two hours records the sex of everyone he sees jay-walking. He records that the sex distribution of jaywalkers was 75 women, 15 men, and 5 individuals whose sex was "indeterminate." He reports this evidence as strong support for his hypothesis, and concludes that women jaywalk 4 or 5 times more often than men.

What is problematic about this conclusion? It rests upon the untested assumption that there was a 1-to-1 ratio of men to women on the street. Certainly, this assumption seems reasonable because in our society the two sexes exist in about equal numbers. But what if the researcher had also observed people crossing the street at the marked crosswalk and again found that women outnumbered men by a ratio of about 5 to 1? Rather than support a claim that women are more likely to jaywalk than men, this would suggest that, for some reason, on that street in that block of that city on that morning, women outnumbered men. (Perhaps this block has many stores that cater exclusively to women, for instance.) Thus, naturalistic observations may fail to record relevant data, and, consequently, the conclusions from these studies must be considered tentative.

Summary of the Correlational Method

It is important to remember that all correlational research methods have one thing in common: They do not allow us to draw causal conclusions about the variables under study. Because these research methods fail to establish experimental control (either direct or probabilistic) over possible confounding variables, the results can tell us only that the variables X and Y are (or are not) associated with each other, but the relationship might be spurious. As discussed in Chapter 3, to determine that the relationship between X and Y is causal, we must establish the fact that the relationship is not the result of some uncontrolled third variable that is confounded with X or Y. Only the experimental method, with its use of random assignment to establish probabilistic control over all relevant variables, allows us to conclude that the relationship between X and Y (the IV and DV) is nonspurious.

Exercises

For each of the following scenarios, which research method (experiment, quasi-experiment, or correlational) has been used?

For correlational studies, identify X and Y; for experiments and quasi-experimental studies, identify the IV(s), the DV, and any DCVs that are mentioned.

Note: Experiments and quasi-experiments often include more than one IV (or comparison factors). If any of the IVs in a study is a subject variable, then the study (as a whole) should be identified as a quasi-experiment. (Chapter 10 will discuss in detail how to interpret research designs with multiple IVs.)

1. To test the effectiveness of a public speaking class, debates were held between students who had taken the course and students who had not. Observers rated each debater's persuasiveness on a scale from 0 to 4.

2. A researcher presented young adults, middle-aged adults, and elderly adults with two lists of 24 words. After reading one list, the participants were asked to recall as many of the words as they could (recall task). After the other list, the participants were given a recognition task in which they were given five words and had to say which of them had been on the list. (This was repeated for each of the 24 words on the list.) The researcher recorded the number of words each participant remembered correctly.

3. In a study of our culture's changing sex-role stereotypes and the influence of the increasing number of mothers working outside the home on children's beliefs about appropriate occupations for males and females, a researcher asked 6-year-old boys and girls whose mothers either worked outside the home or not to name as many different jobs they could think of that would be "okay" for them to have. The researcher then computed a score for each child by counting the number of traditionally sex-inappropriate occupations they mentioned. (For example, if a boy said that he could be a nurse, it would be counted as a traditionally sex-inappropriate occupation.) The hypothesis of the study was that children of working mothers would have higher scores than the children of the more traditional mothers who do not work outside the home.

4. A sports medicine researcher was interested in the effectiveness of a new exercise machine that claims to be better at reducing some types of back pain than traditional flexibility exercises. The researcher recruited participants suffering from either arthritis in the back or ruptured discs in the spine and assigned them at random to either the new machine or a flexibility exercise regimen. After four weeks, the participants were asked to indicate the level of pain they experienced on a 20-point scale.

5. A teacher recorded the number of absences for each student and the number of correct answers each student had on the final exam.

6. Based on interviews with parents, a researcher identified a group of preschool children who frequently watched *Mr. Rogers' Neighborhood* on television and a group who never watched that program. The researcher then asked the preschool teacher to rank the children on their helpfulness toward others. The researcher wanted to find out if the children who watch *Mr. Rogers* frequently are more helpful than children who do not watch the program.

7. A researcher was interested in the effects of crowding on test performance. A group of 20 students took a series of four similar exams (all based on the SATs) under four levels of crowding: Alone; one other person in the room; 10 other people in the room; and 30 other people in the room. All of the tests were given in the same 20′ by 20′ room. The number of errors on the exams was compared across the four levels of crowding.

8. A researcher was interested in the relationship between a child's name and his/her popularity. Children with either a common name or an uncommon name were used as participants. Their popularity was measured using a sociometric rating scale where their classmates were asked to indicate how much they liked the participants on a scale from 1 to 5 ("dislike a lot" to "like a lot"). Each participant was given a popularity score equal to the average rating received from his/her classmates.

9. A department chairman measured the relationship between the popularity of each course and the number of *A*s given by the teachers. Popularity was measured using the average score the course received on the evaluation forms completed by the students (where 1 = very unfavorable evaluation and 7 = very favorable evaluation).

10. A researcher asked teachers to rate children on a 7-point scale (where 7 = very aggressive and 1 = very passive) and then observed the children's interactions with peers during free play periods. The total number of prosocial behaviors each child exhibited during free play over a period of five days was recorded.

11. A researcher conducted a study to test the effects of models on children's sharing behavior. Four boys and four girls were each exposed to three models (in counterbalanced order). The number of M&Ms the children donated to a needy child in the "selfish model" condition was compared with the number of M&Ms donated in the "neutral/generous model" and "happily generous model" conditions.

12. The dean of students conducted a longitudinal study where male and female students were asked, "Would you prefer to live on campus or off-campus?" when they were freshmen, sophomores, and then juniors.

13. In the Coronary Drug Project, middle-aged men with heart trouble were randomly assigned to receive either Clofibrate or a placebo (control). The participants were asked to take the same number of tablets each day for five years. The researcher recorded the number of incidents of chest pain the men experienced during the five-year study period. At the end of the study, the prescription refills were examined, and the participants in each group were classified as either "Adherers" (meaning they had taken at least 85% of the tablets they were supposed to take) or "Non-Adherers" (meaning they had taken less than 85% of the prescribed dosages). The researcher then wanted to see whether "Clofibrate/Adherers" had experienced less chest pain than the other three groups of participants.

14. To study the relationship between family circumstances and attitudes toward euthanasia, a researcher surveyed 60 families and asked two questions: "Do you currently have primary responsibility for an aging relative? Yes or no?" and "Do you believe euthanasia should be legalized in the U.S.? Yes or no?"

15. Male and female participants who were either young adults (20–29 years old) or elderly adults (65–80 years old) were asked to rate their opinion of a new, strict DWI law on a scale from 0 (totally against) to 10 (totally in favor). After making their rating, the participants were shown a film that graphically depicted the injuries people suffer in accidents. They then were asked to rate their opinion again.

CHAPTER

8

CORRELATION COEFFICIENTS

■ ■ ■ ■ ■ ■

In this chapter, you will learn how the relationship between two variables can be measured using a statistic known as a correlation coefficient. The formulas for calculating three correlation coefficients—which are suitable for different scales of measurement—are presented. You will also learn how to draw inferences about the relationship between two variables in the population based on the value of the sample correlation coefficient. A procedure for testing the difference between two correlations is also presented.

Look for These Important Terms and Concepts

correlation coefficient
magnitude (or strength)
zero correlation
perfect correlation
direction
positive correlation
negative correlation
scatterplot (or scattergram)

Pearson r
decision rule
Spearman r
rank scores
tied ranking procedure
Phi coefficient
r-to-z transformation
critical ratio

Before Reading This Chapter, You May Wish to Review

Chapter 3:
• quantitative versus qualitative variables

Chapter 4:
• levels (scales) of measurement

Chapter 5:
• frequencies

• variance and standard deviation
• z-scores and area under the normal curve

Chapter 6:
• sampling distributions
• critical values and rejecting the null hypothesis

In Chapter 5 we looked at descriptive statistics (such as central tendency and variability) for one variable at a time. Frequently, however, we are interested in how two variables are related to each other. What is the relationship between weight and height? Or between sunscreen use and skin cancer? Or between sunscreen use and height? To explore these relationships, we can calculate a statistic called the **correlation coefficient.** As you recall from Chapters 3 and 7, there is a **correlation** when changes in the value of X are accompanied by systematic, predictable changes in the value of Y. In this definition, the term "change" may refer to actual changes in an individual's score over time (such as a change in a child's height during childhood), or to the differences among individuals. For example, if John has an IQ score of 100 and has a grade point average (GPA) of 2.5, Bill has an IQ of 110 and a GPA of 3.0, and Sue has an IQ of 120 and a GPA of 3.5, we would describe this correlation by saying that as IQ *changes,* so does GPA, indicating that individuals with higher IQ scores tend to have higher GPAs as well.

By tradition, the term *correlation* has been limited to relationships where, as X increases, Y consistently goes in one direction—either up or down. These are known as *monotonic* relationships, and if the changes in Y are also uniformly *proportional* to the changes in X, the relationship is *linear.* In contrast, relationships where, as X increases, Y starts out in one direction and reverses and goes the other way are known as *curvilinear* relationships, and they are not typically called correlations even though they fit the general definition stated above. Analysis of curvilinear relationships is beyond the scope of this textbook, so the coefficients covered here are appropriate only for monotonic or linear correlations. Correlation coefficients provide us with two pieces of information about the relationship between the variables: magnitude and direction.

Magnitude

Essentially, the **magnitude (or strength)** of a correlation is determined by how consistently the values of Y change with changes in X. For instance, the strongest possible relationship is one where Y changes in a uniform fashion *every time* X changes, with no exceptions to the rule. This is known as a **perfect correlation,** and it means that every value of X is associated with a unique value of Y. There is a perfect correlation, for example, between the quantity of water in a container and the weight of the container: Every increase in the amount of water increases the weight, and the increases in weight are uniform because every gallon of water weighs 8.3 pounds. If identical containers hold the same quantity of water, they will always have the same weight, and different quantities of water (in these identical containers) will always have different weights. When the relationship between two variables is perfect, we can use the value of X to predict the value of Y with perfect accuracy.

The opposite of a perfect correlation is a **zero correlation,** where there is *no relationship* between X and Y, and where changes in X are not associated with systematic changes in Y. Zero correlations occur when each value of X is associated with every value of Y equally often, so that two people with the same value of X need not have the same (or even similar) values of Y. For example, there is a zero correlation between women's hair color and the length of their hair. As hair color changes, the length of the hair does not change in a systematic fashion: Blonde hair may be of any length, brunette hair may be of any length, and red hair may be of any length. When there is no relationship between two variables, knowing X cannot help us predict Y. For example, knowing that a woman has blonde hair will not help us accurately predict the length of her hair.

Between the two extremes of perfect and zero correlations lie all of the relationships where changes in X are sometimes, but *not always*, associated with uniform changes in Y. In other words, when there is a general tendency for X and Y to change together, but there are exceptions to the rule, the relationship will be greater than zero, but less than perfect. The fewer exceptions to the rule, the stronger the relationship. For example, let's consider the relationship between age and vocabulary size in children. In general, older children know more words than younger children, but there will be exceptions to the rule because some younger children have larger vocabularies than older children. If there are only a few such cases, the magnitude of the relationship will be very high, but if there are a great many children who do not fit the pattern, the relationship will be weak. Thus, the magnitude of a correlation is an indicator of how consistently the changes in X go with the changes in Y, and it decreases as the number of cases where X and Y do *not* change together increases. (That is, the more exceptions to the rule, the weaker the correlation.)

Correlation coefficients measure the magnitude of the relationship on a scale from 0.0 to ±1.0, where, unsurprisingly, a coefficient of 0.0 indicates a zero correlation, and a coefficient of +1.0 or −1.0 indicates a perfect correlation. Higher values on the scale indicate stronger relationships, while lower values indicate weak relationships. By convention, we usually refer to correlations with absolute values that range from about 0.01 to 0.29 as "low" (or "weak") correlations, while we refer to correlations from about 0.30 to 0.69 as "moderate" and those from 0.70 or above as "strong" correlations (Sheskin, 1997). For instance, if a textbook says that there was a "low-to-moderate relationship" between children's moral judgments and their helpful behavior, it would indicate that the correlation coefficient was probably somewhere between 0.25 and 0.35.

As another example, consider the relationship between adults' height and the number of charitable contributions declared on their income tax return. "What relationship?" you ask. Exactly. These two variables would seem to have no systematic relationship, because some people who are 5'4" declare few charitable deductions and some declare lots of charitable deductions, and the same is true for people who are 5'7", 5'11", 6'1", and 6'4". Knowing a person's height would not help at all in guessing how many charitable deductions they declared. These variables have a *zero correlation*.

In contrast, in a perfect world full of honest people, we would expect to find *a perfect relationship* between the number of charitable contributions declared on the tax return and the number of charitable contributions actually made. People who made 10 charitable contributions should declare 10 contributions, people who made no contributions should not declare any, and so forth. In this world of honest people, knowing how many charitable contributions a person declared on his tax return would allow you to precisely predict how many contributions the person actually made and vice versa.

This example may seem to be a poor one since it rests on an obviously incorrect assumption (i.e., that all people are honest when it comes to taxes), but realistic examples of perfect correlations in psychology are virtually impossible to find because human behavior is multidetermined and not perfectly predictable. Even your performance on an IQ test today would not perfectly predict your performance on the same IQ test tomorrow because performance is influenced by any number of conditions that could change overnight (such as your levels of fatigue or motivation). Hence, we would not find a perfect correlation between today's IQ score and tomorrow's IQ score. (As a consequence, when we are trying to determine the test-retest reliability of a measurement procedure, we cannot require that the measurement result in a perfect correlation between the two scores. Instead, we are generally satisfied with test-retest correlations of .65 or higher, depending on the behavior being measured and the type of measurement device we are looking at.)

Direction

Correlation coefficients also tells us the **direction** of the relationship. There are two possible directions: either the two variables are changing in the *same* direction or they are changing in *opposite* directions. We use the terms "positive" and "negative" to refer to these directions, respectively, and the sign of the coefficient indicates the direction of the correlation. Positive relationships will have correlation coefficients between 0.0 and +1.0 (which indicates a *perfect positive* correlation), and negative relationships will have correlation coefficients between 0.0 and −1.0 (which indicates a *perfect negative* correlation).

Intuitively, for example, we would expect there to be a **positive correlation** between weight and height: as height increases, weight is likely to increase as well (and if we are studying children we would expect the *magnitude* of this correlation to be higher than the correlation for adults).[1] This is a *positive* correlation because the changes in X and Y are in the same direction: They both increase or they both decrease. In contrast, we would probably predict a **negative correlation** between sunscreen use and skin cancer in adults: As sunscreen use increases, skin cancer incidence probably decreases (i.e., the scores change in *opposite directions*). In contrast, there is no compelling reason to suspect either a positive or a negative relationship between adults' sunscreen use and their height, so we might predict a zero (or at best, a very small) correlation between these variables.[2]

---

[1] Remember that correlations do not imply causality. That is, the correlation between height and weight does not suggest that increased height causes increased weight or vice versa. It simply gives a measure of how systematically the two variables change relative to each other.

[2] However, it may be reasonable to hypothesize that women are more likely to use sunscreen than men, and because women tend to be shorter than men, we could predict that there will be a low-to-moderate *negative* correlation between height and sunscreen use: As height increases (from women to men), sunscreen use decreases.

When we are interpreting correlations, it is extremely important to realize that the direction of a correlation may be determined by the specific operational definitions used in measuring the variables, and changing the operational definition may change the direction of the correlation. Therefore, the interpretation of a correlation coefficient must rely on knowledge about the measurement procedures. Consider, for example, the fact that academic performance in college is negatively correlated with acceptance into graduate programs. Yes, *negatively*. As the academic performance scores go up, acceptance into graduate programs goes down. Before you decide to let your grades slide in order to increase your chances of getting into graduate school, you should remind yourself that correlation does not imply causation, and then you should ask the crucial question: "How was academic performance being measured?" While you may have assumed that academic performance was operationally defined as grade point average (where larger numbers represent better performance), in fact, we operationally defined academic performance as class standing (where *smaller* numbers represent better performance because being first in the class, with a score of 1, is the best possible score). As class standing scores go down, acceptance into graduate programs goes up, and therefore, we find a *negative* correlation coefficient, but the nature of the underlying relationship between the variables is what we would expect: Students who do better academically are more likely to be accepted into graduate programs.

Thus, we cannot properly interpret correlation coefficients unless we know how X and Y were operationally defined. It may help to remember that many behaviors can be measured from opposite directions, and the direction selected by the researcher will determine whether increasing values of X represent improvements or declines in performance. Some common choices researchers may face include: (1) recording the number of correct answers versus the number of errors; (2) counting the number of classes missed versus the number of classes attended; (3) the amount of time spent looking at the target versus the amount of time looking away from the target; (4) the degree of independence displayed versus the degree of dependence; and (5) percent of time spent on-task versus the percent of time off-task. Another common choice researchers face is the labeling of a Likert rating scale: Does 1 mean "very much in favor" or "very much opposed"? In each of these examples, the exact same behavior is recorded, but one of the operational definitions will produce a positive correlation while the other will produce a negative correlation. These correlation coefficients will have the same *absolute value*, indicating that the strength of the relationship between the two variables is unaffected by the choice of measurement. That is, if the correlation between number of hours of sleep the night before an exam and the percentage of correct responses is $+0.45$, then the correlation between hours of sleep and the percentage of *errors* on that exam would be -0.45. In other words, the magnitude of a relationship is independent of the direction of the coefficient.

Graphing the Relationship Between Two Variables

One of the best ways to look at data to be correlated is to produce a **scatterplot** (or **scattergram**). A scatterplot places the values of one variable on the X axis and the

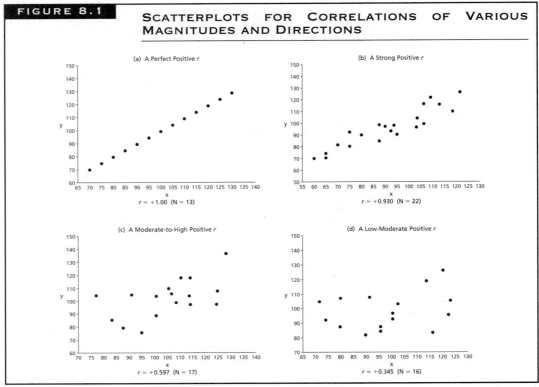

FIGURE 8.1 SCATTERPLOTS FOR CORRELATIONS OF VARIOUS MAGNITUDES AND DIRECTIONS

(*Continued*)

other on the Y axis. (A dot on the scatterplot represents a participant's scores on both X and Y.) In a perfect positive or negative correlation, the data will fall on a straight line (see Figures 8-1a and 8-1h). As the magnitude (or strength) of the relationship decreases (from 1.0 to 0.0), the points on the scattergram become more and more "scattered" and less linear. This is illustrated in Figures 8-1a to 8-1e.

Scatterplots also allow us to see the direction of the relationship. For example, compare Figure 8-1b to Figure 8-1g. They each depict very strong correlations, but the points on 8-1b generally move from the lower left corner to the upper right corner (indicating a *positive* correlation: as the value of X increases from left to right on its axis, the value of Y increases from the bottom to the top of its axis) while the points on Figure 8-1g generally move from the upper left corner to the lower right corner (indicating a *negative* correlation: as the value of X increases from left to right on its axis, the value of Y decreases from the top to the bottom of its axis).

FIGURE 8.1

(*Continued*)

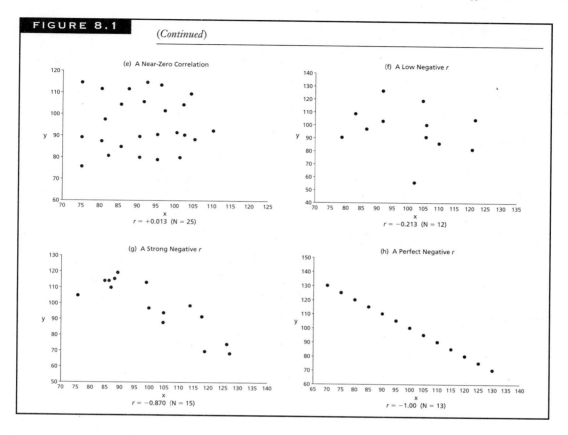

Selecting the Appropriate Correlation Coefficient

With different types of data, different correlation coefficients will be calculated. A chart that summarizes when to use which coefficient is presented in Table 8-1. Note that the chart includes coefficients that are not illustrated in this text, but references to other sources are included in the table.

For *quantitative data* (i.e., ordinal, interval, or ratio scales), correlation coefficients measure patterns of changes within the data. Do both scores always go up together? Does one decrease while the other increases? If the pattern of data is highly consistent, then we will find a large value (approaching ± 1.0) for the correlation coefficient. If the patterns are unrelated, we will find a small value (approaching 0.0).

When either X or Y (or both) are ordinal scales, an appropriate correlation coefficient is the *Spearman rank-order correlation coefficient* (r_s), which, as the name implies, examines the rank orders and measures the degree to which *ranks on X* are systematically related to *ranks on Y*. For example, suppose we measured the academic performance of high school students by recording their grade point average (GPA)

TABLE 8.1	**Appropriate Correlation Coefficients**			
	X Is Nominal (Dichotomous)	**X Is Nominal (Nondichotomous)**	**X Is Ordinal**	**X Is Interval or Ratio**
Y Is Nominal (Dichotomous)	Phi coefficient (ϕ) Tetrachoric r *	Cramér's ϕ Contingency C	Point-biserial r Biserial r *	Point-biserial r Biserial r *
Y Is Nominal (Nondichotomous)	Cramér's ϕ Contingency C	Cramér's ϕ Contingency C	—	Omega squared (ω^2) Eta squared (η^2)
Y Is Ordinal	Point-biserial r Biserial r *	—	Spearman r Kendall tau	Spearman r Kendall tau
Y Is Interval or Ratio	Point-biserial r Biserial r *	Omega squared (ω^2) Eta squared (η^2)	Spearman r Kendall tau	Pearson r

*The tetrachoric and biserial rs are used when a continuous variable has been dichotomized (such as test performance measured as pass/fail). The point-biserial r is appropriate for natural dichotomies (such as male/female). The phi coefficient is used with both types of dichotomies.
NOTE: This table was adapted from Roscoe (1975) and Sheskin (1997). Formulas for the coefficients not covered in this text can be found in Sheskin (1997) or in Yaremko, Harari, Harrison, and Lynn (1986).

and also measured their peer popularity by having classmates rate one another on a 7-point scale from "dislike very much" to "like very much." Both of these measurements are quantitative, and the peer rating variable is clearly an ordinal scale, so the Spearman rank-order correlation is the appropriate test. Essentially, the Spearman puts the students in order according to their GPA and then sees whether the students at the top of the list for GPA are also at the top of the list for peer popularity while the students at the bottom of the GPA list are also at the bottom of the popularity list. (This would result in a *positive* correlation between these variables. A negative correlation would result if the students with higher GPAs were disliked while the students with lower GPAs were well-liked.)

When *both X and Y* are quantitative variables with *interval or ratio scales*, the *Pearson product-moment correlation coefficient* (r) is the appropriate measure of correlation. The Pearson r measures the extent to which changes in the *amount of X* are related to changes in the *amount of Y*. For example, if we measured the length and weight of newborn infants, we could determine whether a difference of 1 inch in length is typically associated with an 8-ounce difference in weight. Recall that the primary characteristic of interval and ratio scales is that there are *equal intervals* between the points on the score scale, so a difference of one point in the scores is always equal to same amount of change in the variable (1 inch is always the same length and 1 ounce is always the same weight.) Because the Pearson r is based on the exact amount of change in X and Y scores, it requires that these changes be interpretable, and, therefore, both X and Y must have interval or ratio levels of measurement.

Coefficients that measure relationships among nominal (or categorical, qualitative) variables examine the *frequencies* of X and Y to see whether being in category X_1 is associated with being in category Y_1 more often than being in category Y_2. For example, do more Catholics vote Republican while more Methodists vote Democratic? If so, then there is a correlation between religion and political preference. To illustrate the correlation between categorical variables, we will present the *phi coefficient*, which is the appropriate measure of correlation when *both* X and Y are dichotomous variables (i.e., when there are only two possible categories).

Pearson Product-Moment Correlation Coefficient

The **Pearson product-moment correlation coefficient** is appropriate to use when both X and Y are interval or ratio scales. The *definitional formula* for the Pearson coefficient (denoted by an *r*) is as follows:

$$ r = \frac{\Sigma(X - \overline{X})(Y - \overline{Y})}{\sqrt{\Sigma(X - \overline{X})^2 \Sigma(Y - \overline{Y})^2}} $$

Looking at this formula, we can see that it has three separate elements, and the two in the denominator should be familiar: $\Sigma(X - \overline{X})^2$ is the sum of the squared deviations of X scores from the group mean, nicknamed the "sum of squares," and it is the numerator of the variance and standard deviation formulas presented in Chapter 5. Thus, this piece of the formula is a measure of the variability among the X scores (SS_X). Similarly, $\Sigma(Y - \overline{Y})^2$ is a sum of squares, this time it is measuring the variability among the Y scores (SS_Y). The Pearson *r* calls for us to multiply these two measures of variability together, and this product can be conceptualized as the "grand total" of all variation in the data (with X and Y combined).

The numerator of the formula for the Pearson *r* is the new, unfamiliar piece. It is known as the sum of the products (SP) because it tells us to compute a deviation from $\overline{X}$ and a deviation from $\overline{Y}$ for each participant and then multiply these deviation scores together, creating a cross-product. If X and Y are highly correlated, then large changes in X will be accompanied by large changes in Y, and, therefore, the cross-products of the deviations will also be large. If the correlation is weak, then many of the large changes in X will be accompanied by small changes in Y, so the cross-products will be relatively small. Thus, the sum of these cross-products provides a measure of how much X and Y are systematically changing together, that is, it measures the amount of variability that X and Y *share* (or have in common).

Using the concepts of sums of squares and the sum of the cross-products, the formula can be re-written like this:

$$ r = \frac{SP}{\sqrt{SS_x SS_y}} \qquad \begin{array}{l} \textbf{where } \textbf{SP} = \Sigma(\textbf{X} - \overline{\textbf{X}})(\textbf{Y} - \overline{\textbf{Y}}) \\ \textbf{and } \textbf{SS}_\textbf{X} = \Sigma(\textbf{X} - \overline{\textbf{X}})^2 \\ \textbf{and } \textbf{SS}_\textbf{Y} = \Sigma(\textbf{Y} - \overline{\textbf{Y}})^2 \end{array} $$

The measure of "shared" variability (SP) is then divided by the measure of "total" variability, and, thus, the Pearson r provides us with a measure of how much of the change in X is systematically linked to change in Y—which is exactly what a correlation coefficient is supposed to measure. (Beware that, despite appearances, the ratio in the Pearson r formula does *not* measure the *proportion* of total variation that is shared between X and Y. This conceptualization of the elements of the Pearson r is intended to help you understand the statistic and what it does, but you must be careful not to take the analogy too far. Researchers can determine the proportion of variation in Y that is systematically accompanied by variation in X by computing a statistic known as the *coefficient of determination*, which is discussed in Chapter 9.)

Just as we found the definitional formulas for variance and standard deviation to be cumbersome, the definitional formula for the Pearson r is not easy to use. Calculating deviation scores is always tedious, and tedium can lead to clerical errors. Therefore, we prefer to use a computational formula that does not require deviation scores. The formula presented here uses the same computational shortcuts that we used when we computed the variance and standard deviation in Chapter 5. Although it looks daunting, you should think of it as three separate pieces that can be computed one at a time.

Computational Formula for Pearson r

$$r = \frac{\Sigma XY - \dfrac{(\Sigma X)(\Sigma Y)}{N}}{\sqrt{\Sigma X^2 - \dfrac{(\Sigma X)^2}{N}}\sqrt{\Sigma Y^2 - \dfrac{(\Sigma Y)^2}{N}}}$$

To illustrate the computation of the Pearson r, let's imagine that we have scores for five participants on tests of visual acuity (X) and motion detection (Y). To prepare for the Pearson formula, we need to do several things:

1. Add the X scores to get ΣX.

2. Add the Y scores to get ΣY.

3. Compute the cross-products by multiplying X times Y for each participant and then add the cross-products to get ΣXY.

4. Square each X and then add the X^2s to get ΣX^2.

5. Square each Y and then add the Y^2s to get ΣY^2.

A Numerical Example   These steps are all shown on the opposite page, along with the data from our five participants:

Participant	Visual Acuity (X)	Motion Detection (Y)	X^2	Y^2	XY
a	3	3	9	9	9
b	2	4	4	16	8
c	3	5	9	25	15
d	2	1	4	1	2
e	4	3	16	9	12
	$\Sigma X = 14$	$\Sigma Y = 16$	$\Sigma X^2 = 42$	$\Sigma Y^2 = 60$	$\Sigma XY = 46$

Now, along with N (the number of participants), we are ready to plug the numbers into the formula and solve for *r*. (Although it is not apparent here in print, we computed the numerator first, then computed the sum of squares for X, and then computed the sum of squares for Y. Then we calculated the denominator and solved for *r*.)

$$r = \frac{46 - \dfrac{(14)(16)}{5}}{\sqrt{42 - \dfrac{(14)^2}{5}} \ \sqrt{60 - \dfrac{(16)^2}{5}}}$$

$$r = \frac{46 - \dfrac{224}{5}}{\sqrt{42 - \dfrac{196}{5}} \ \sqrt{60 - \dfrac{256}{5}}}$$

$$r = \frac{46 - 44.8}{\sqrt{42 - 39.2} \ \sqrt{60 - 51.2}}$$

$$r = \frac{1.2}{\sqrt{2.8} \ \sqrt{8.8}}$$

$$r = \frac{1.2}{(1.67332)(2.9664793)}$$

$$r = \frac{1.2}{4.9638691}$$

$$r = +0.2417469$$

We would round the value of *r* to two decimal places, and report that: "For the five participants in the study, the correlation between visual acuity and motion detection was equal to +0.24."

Recall that the values of r can range from $+1.00$ to -1.00. A value of $+1.00$ indicates a perfect positive correlation, where *every* increase in variable X leads to a proportionately equal increase in variable Y. Conversely, a value of -1.00 indicates a perfect negative correlation, where *every* increase in X leads to a proportionately equal decrease in Y. Any correlations (positive or negative) with absolute values near 0.0 represent very weak correlations. Here our correlation of 0.24 is a low positive correlation. This indicates that people with better visual acuity show a slight tendency to be better in detecting motion than people with poorer visual acuity. This would suggest that the physiological mechanisms involved in motion detection are not exactly the same as those involved in focusing images, which seems reasonable. However, this correlation was based on a sample of only five people. What conclusion could we draw from these data about the relationship between visual acuity and motion detection *in the population*? We need to do some hypothesis testing.

The Pearson r as an Inferential Statistic: Testing the Null Hypothesis

The null hypothesis for a correlational study states that X and Y have a zero correlation in the population (and that any non-zero correlation observed within a sample is due solely to sampling error or chance). To test this hypothesis we need to compare our *obtained value* of r (which is symbolized as $r_{obtained}$ or r_{obt}) to a *critical value* of r from a sampling distribution (which is symbolized as $r_{critical}$ or r_{crit}). Table B-3 (in Appendix B) presents the critical values for the Pearson product-moment correlation coefficient. This table provides critical values with four decimal places, and therefore, we test the null hypothesis using four-digit values of the Pearson r. For our example, then, we will compare $r = 0.2417$ to the critical value from the table. To use this table, we need to know our sample size (N, or the number of participants in the sample) and the value of *alpha* (α, or our level of significance, which is typically set at .05 or less). Note that the first column of the table is labeled "Number of pairs minus two," which indicates that we must go down that column until we get to N – 2 and then read across to the appropriate column (α). (Number of "pairs" is equal to the number of participants because "pairs" refers to the pairs of X and Y scores—and each participant has *one pair* of scores.) If the obtained value of r (computed from the data) is greater than or equal to the critical value (from the table), we reject the null hypothesis. The notation for this **decision rule** is:

> If $r_{obt} \geq r_{crit}$, reject the null hypothesis (H_0)

In our sample of N = 5, we obtained a correlation coefficient equal to $+0.2417$. Should we conclude that visual acuity is significantly (if only weakly) correlated to motion detection in the population? In other words, can we say that, in general, people with better visual acuity tend to be better at motion detection? If we look up r_{crit} on the Pearson table, for N = 5 and $\alpha = .05$, we find that $r_{crit} = \pm 0.8783$. This indicates that when the null hypothesis is true in the population (and the population correlation is equal to zero; $\rho = 0.0$), 95% of all samples of N = 5 will have sample rs between -0.8783 and $+0.8783$ *just by chance alone*. Sample correlations between

0.0 and ±0.8783 are common events by chance alone, and since our obtained *r* of 0.2417 is one of these common events, we *cannot reject* the null hypothesis, and we conclude that there is not enough evidence to support the claim that visual acuity and motion detection are correlated in the population. We cannot be certain that the variables have no relationship, because, as you should recall from Chapter 6, failure to reject the null hypothesis could mean the null is actually true, and a person's ability to focus on an object is *not* related to how well the person detects motion, or it could be the result of a Type II error. You may also recall from Chapter 6 that small samples have little power, and that they will only be able to detect large effects (or strong relationships). This is evident in our example when we look at the critical value ($r_{critical}$ = .8783): The correlation in a sample of five has to be very, very strong before we will reject the null hypothesis. Suppose, however, that our sample had included 72 participants rather than only five. When N = 72, the critical value (with alpha set at .05) would be $r_{critical}$ = .2319, indicating that 95% of random samples will have a correlation between 0.0 and ±.2319 when the null hypothesis is true. If the correlation in a large sample is *r* = +0.2417, we would reject the null hypothesis because our sampler *r* is greater than $r_{critical}$. Hence, the large sample is able to detect smaller (or weaker) relationships than the small sample.

Spearman Rank-Order Correlation Coefficient

The **Spearman rank-order correlation coefficient** (designated r_s) is appropriate to use when both variables are ordinal scales, or when one variable is ordinal and the other is either interval or ratio. (The Spearman correlation coefficient cannot be used with nominal or categorical data.) Recall that ordinal scales tell us about the order of the scores but not how different two scores are from each other. Therefore, the fact that one person got a score of 10 and another person got a score of 12 tells us only that the first person had a lower score than the second person, but the two-point difference between the scores does not tell us *how much better* the second person was than the first. Therefore, the Spearman starts by converting the raw values of X and Y (separately) into rank scores and then measures the degree of association between the rank scores. The formula for the Spearman rank-order correlation coefficient is as follows:

$$r_s = 1 - \frac{6\Sigma d^2}{N(N^2 - 1)}$$

In the formula for the Spearman r_s, the "d" refers to the difference between a participant's rank scores on the two measures.

A Numerical Example To illustrate the computation of the Spearman rank-order correlation coefficient, pretend that seven college students were participants in a study looking at attitudes toward good academic habits and academic performance. During their orientation week in their freshman year, the students were asked to complete a brief survey where they used a 10-point scale to answer one question: "Are you willing to attend every class and to spend at least six hours studying every day while you're in college?" (1 = "You are out of your ever-loving mind" and 10 = "Well, of course, absolutely, since my parents are spending their hard-earned money to give me this chance to become an educated person.") At the end of four years, the students' class standing (or class rank) was recorded. Both variables (attitude about studying and attending class and class standing) are ordinal scales; therefore, the Spearman is the appropriate correlation coefficient. The data are below:

Participant	Attitude	Class Standing
Anna	9	72
Brett	7	47
Carlos	2	13
Dashiel	5	60
Elias	8	93
Fatima	1	29
Gregory	10	51

The first step is to convert the raw scores to **rank scores**, which puts the participants in order based on their raw scores. (We rank the participants on X and Y *separately*.) It does not matter whether we put the participants in order from highest to lowest or vice versa, but we must be certain that we do it the same way for both X and Y. Our preference is to give the *smallest value* of X (and Y) a rank score of 1; therefore, Fatima gets a rank score of 1 for X, Carlos has the next smallest attitude score and gets a rank score of 2, Dashiel is next and gets a rank of 3, and so forth.

After ranking the participants on their attitude scores (X), we repeat the procedure for the class standings (Y). We see that Carlos has the smallest value of Y and is therefore assigned a rank of 1, Fatima has the next smallest value and is ranked 2, etc. After the ranks have been assigned for both X and Y, we need to calculate the difference (d) in rank scores for each participant by subtracting rank-on-Y (R_Y) from rank-on-X (R_X):

$$d = R_X - R_Y$$

Then, because the Spearman formula requires that we square each difference score, we also create a column of d^2s:

Ss	X	Y	Rank on X	Rank on Y	d	d^2
Anna	9	72	6	6	0	0
Brett	7	47	4	3	1	1
Carlos	2	13	2	1	1	1
Dashiel	5	60	3	5	−2	4
Elias	8	93	5	7	−2	4
Fatima	1	29	1	2	−1	1
Gregory	10	51	7	4	3	9
						$\Sigma d^2 = 20$

The sum of the d^2s is inserted into the numerator of the formula, N (the number of participants) is inserted into the denominator, and we get:

$$r_s = 1 - \frac{6(20)}{7(7^2 - 1)}$$

$$r_s = 1 - \frac{120}{7(49 - 1)}$$

$$r_s = 1 - \frac{120}{7(48)}$$

$$r_s = 1 - \frac{120}{336}$$

$$r_s = 1 - .3571428$$

$$r_s = +0.6428572$$

We would round the obtained value of r_s to two decimal places, and report that, for the seven students in the study, the correlation between attitude toward class attendance and class standing at graduation was equal to +0.64. This moderate-to-high positive correlation tells us that as the attitude scores increased (showing greater commitment to good academic habits), class standing scores also increased. Keeping in mind that a "high" class standing score indicates *poorer* academic performance (since the person with the best performance gets a class standing of 1—first in the class), our data indicate that the students who started out with a higher commitment to good academic habits tended to perform *worse* than students who, as freshmen, indicated that they were not planning on attending every class and studying a lot each day.

The Spearman r as an Inferential Statistic: Testing the Null Hypothesis

Before we get too excited by this counterintuitive result, however, we need to remind ourselves that these results are based on a sample of only seven college students. Before we generalize to the population, we need to compare our results to a sampling distribution of Spearman correlation coefficients. Table B-2 (in Appendix B) presents the table of critical values for the Spearman correlation coefficient. The critical values on this table are reported to three decimal places, so we will compare our obtained correlation of +0.643 to the critical value from the table.

To find the critical value for our sample of seven participants, we read down the first column of the table (Number of pairs) to our N of 7 and then read across to the desired level of significance (α). Thus, if we set alpha at .05, the critical value of r_s for a sample of seven participants is equal to ±0.786. This critical value tells us that when X and Y have a zero correlation within a population, 95% of samples drawn from that population that have only seven participants will have sample correlations from −.786 to +0.786. These values of r_s are common events just by chance alone and do not provide evidence for a systematic relationship between X and Y within the population. Like the Pearson r, if the obtained value of the Spearman r_s is greater than or equal to the critical value of r_s (from the table), we reject the null hypothesis. The notation for this **decision rule** is:

$$\text{If } r_{S\text{ obt}} \geq r_{S\text{ crit}}, \text{ reject the null hypothesis } (H_0)$$

Therefore, when we compare our sample correlation of $+0.643$ to the critical value of $+0.786$, we find that our sample statistic is a common event just by chance alone, and we cannot reject the null hypothesis. We must conclude that the sample data provide no evidence that freshman attitudes about attending class and studying regularly are systematically related to academic performance over four years at college. Keep in mind, of course, that the sample size was quite small, making it difficult to detect anything but strong relationships. We cannot conclude that the null hypothesis is actually true because we may have made a Type II error. (The relationship between sample size and Type II errors is discussed more fully in Appendix C, where we review the concept of power in some detail.)

Tied Ranking Procedure

In our sample data above, each of the seven participants chose a different point on the 10-point rating scale used to measure attitude about studying and attending class. With a larger sample (and certainly with 11 or more participants), we would encounter a situation where two or more participants have equal raw scores. When this occurs, we must use a **tied ranking procedure** when assigning rank scores to the participants in preparation for calculating the Spearman correlation coefficient. Participants who have the same raw score should receive equal rank scores, and a simple procedure for doing this is as follows:

1. List the raw scores in order (preferably from lowest to highest). Participants with tied raw scores will be in adjacent positions in the list. Be sure to keep track of which score belongs to which participant so that the rank scores for X and Y are properly paired up after the ranking procedures are complete.

2. Assign an *ordinal position number* to the scores by labeling them 1 to N. (That is, the first score in the list is in ordinal position 1, and the last score in the list is in ordinal position N.)

3. For participants with tied scores, compute the average (mean) of the ordinal positions they share by adding the ordinal positions and dividing by the number of tied scores. This *average ordinal position* is the tied rank score assigned to each of the tied scores. For participants who have unique (or untied) raw scores, their rank score is equal to their ordinal position number.

The first steps of this tied ranking procedure are illustrated in the following table. In this example, 15 college students responded to our single-question survey with our 10-point rating scale. The first step was to put the participants in order (from low to high) and assign ordinal position numbers to each score. Next, the tied scores and shared ordinal positions were identified. The final step will be to assign rank scores to each participant.

Original Scores:		*Steps in the Ranking Procedure:*		
Student	**X**	**X (in order)**	**Student (in order)**	**Ordinal Position**
Anna	4	1	Elias	1
Brett	5	2	Karl	2
Carlos	9	3 ⎤ tied	Gregory	3 ⎤ shared
Dashiel	4	3 ⎦ scores	Louise	4 ⎦ positions
Elias	1	4 ⎤	Anna	5 ⎤
Fatima	7	4 ⎥ tied scores	Dashiel	6 ⎥ shared positions
Gregory	3	4 ⎦	Hyun-Sun	7 ⎦
Hyun-Sun	4	5 ⎤ tied	Brett	8 ⎤ shared
Irena	7	5 ⎦ scores	Olivia	9 ⎦ positions
Juan	8	6	Marsha	10
Karl	2	7 ⎤ tied	Fatima	11 ⎤ shared
Louise	3	7 ⎦ scores	Irena	12 ⎦ positions
Marsha	6	8	Juan	13
Ngan	10	9	Carlos	14
Olivia	5	10	Ngan	15

As you can see, Gregory and Louise each had raw scores of 3, and they occupy ordinal positions 3 and 4. Because we have no good reason to say that Gregory ranked higher or lower than Louise we will assign each of them a rank score of 3.5, which is the *average* of their ordinal positions. This average is computed by adding 3 and 4 and dividing by 2 (because there are two scores being averaged).

Anna, Dashiel, and Hyun-Sun each had raw scores of 4, and they occupy rank positions 5, 6, and 7. If we average these rank positions, we find that these three participants should be assigned a rank score of 6 (i.e., 5 + 6 + 7 = 18, and 18/3 = 6). Following the same procedure, we find that Brett and Olivia get rank scores of 8.5 (the average of positions 8 and 9), and Fatima and Irena get rank scores of 11.5 (the average of positions 11 and 12). Therefore, the column of rank-on-X scores that we would use in computing r_s should look like this:

Ss	X	Rank$_X$
Anna	4	6
Brett	5	8.5
Carlos	9	14
Dashiel	4	6
Elias	1	1
Fatima	7	11.5
Gregory	3	3.5
Hyun-Sun	4	6
Irena	7	11.5
Juan	8	13

(*Continued*)

Ss	X	Rank$_X$
Karl	2	2
Louise	3	3.5
Marsha	6	10
Ngan	10	15
Olivia	5	8.5

We would follow the same ranking procedure for variable Y, then compute the difference between the two rank scores (d), and then finish the computation of the Spearman correlation coefficient as described above.

Correlating Nominal Data

To determine whether there is a relationship between qualitative, categorical variables, we look at the *frequencies:* the number of participants that fall into each of the categories. If, for example, we looked at the correlation between the presence or absence of Y-chromosomes and type of external genitalia, we would expect to find a (nearly) perfect correlation:

	Y-chromosome	
	Present	**Absent**
Penis/Testes	985	1
Clitoris/Vagina	15	999

From this (hypothetical) data, you see that just about every individual with a Y-chromosome has a penis and testes and just about every individual without a Y-chromosome has a clitoris and a vagina. In contrast, if we looked at Y-chromosomes and red hair, we would probably expect to find a zero correlation, where about half of the redheads have a Y-chromosome and half do not:

	Y-chromosome	
	Present	**Absent**
Red-headed	120	122
Not Red-headed	880	878

It is also possible to look for correlations between categorical and continuous variables, such as sex (male versus female) and spatial ability (measured as the number of correct answers on a 100-item test—a ratio scale). If sex is correlated with spatial ability, we will find that men tend to have systematically different scores than women on the spatial abilities test. The appropriate correlation coefficient depends on whether one or both variables are on nominal scales, whether the nominal scale is a *dichotomy* (where there are only two categories), and whether the dichotomy is a "true" dichotomy versus a dichotomy created by splitting a continuous variable into only two possible values. A "true" dichotomy, for example, would be sex: there are truly only two sexes: male and female. Test performance, however, is a continuous variable that at times is "dichotomized" into only two values: pass versus fail.

As mentioned earlier, the chart in Table 8-1 indicates which correlation coefficient is appropriate under the various circumstances, but we will illustrate only the computation of the phi coefficient, which is appropriate when both X and Y are dichotomies (of either type).

Phi Coefficient

The **phi coefficient** (ϕ) is appropriate for measuring the correlation between two dichotomous variables. Like the Pearson and Spearman coefficients, the phi coefficient can range from 0.00 to 1.00, and the larger the value of ϕ, the stronger the relationship between the variables. For example, if *every* individual with a penis and testes has a Y-chromosome and every individual with a clitoris and a vagina does *not* have a Y-chromosome, ϕ will equal 1.00, indicating a perfect correlation. If half of the individuals with red hair have a Y-chromosome and half do not, ϕ will equal 0.00. However, because nominal scales do not establish *ordering* among scores, the concept of direction in a relationship (where as X changes, Y either goes in the same direction or the opposite direction) is irrelevant. Therefore, *the positive or negative sign of ϕ has no meaning and can be ignored.*

Because both X and Y are dichotomous variables, they create four categories (as illustrated in the example of Y-chromosomes and types of external genitalia). The phi coefficient requires that we know how many participants fall in each of these categories, and these cell frequencies are labeled a, b, c, and d. We also need to know the totals for each level of variable X and each level of variable Y, which we get by calculating the *row and column totals* for the data set. (These row and column totals are labeled j, k, l, and m.) Thus, the data set is arranged to look like this:

		Variable X		
		X_1	X_2	**Row Totals**
Variable Y	Y_1	a	b	j
	Y_2	c	d	k
column totals		l	m	N = total number of participants

The formula for the phi coefficient is:

$$\phi = \frac{(b \times c) - (a \times d)}{\sqrt{j \times k \times l \times m}}$$

A Numerical Example To illustrate the computation of ϕ, let's assume that a university fundraiser is interested in the relationship between having pledged with a Greek fraternity during college and being a major donor to the university, which is defined as giving $1000 or more for at least 5 years in a row. Suppose the fundraiser randomly selected the college records of 60 major donors and 60 other alumni and categorized them as Greek vs. Not Greek, and found the following cell (or category) frequencies:

	Not Greek	Greek
Major Donor	21	39
Not a Major Donor	34	26

To compute ϕ, we need to compute the row and column totals and then plug them into the formula above.

	Not Greek	Greek	Row Totals
Major Donor	21	39	60
Not a Major Donor	34	26	60
column totals	55	65	N = 120

$$\phi = \frac{(39 \times 34) - (21 \times 26)}{\sqrt{60 \times 60 \times 55 \times 65}}$$

$$\phi = \frac{1326 - 546}{\sqrt{12870000}}$$

$$\phi = \frac{780}{3587.4782}$$

$$\phi = 0.2174229$$

As mentioned earlier, the sign of a phi coefficient is meaningless because different values of categorical variables represent changes in type or kind, not increases or decreases in quantity or amount. Consequently, there is no direction in a relationship between categorical variables. However, for any set of data, the numerical value of ϕ may have a negative sign. This negative sign can be *ignored* because it is the result of the completely arbitrary decision by the researcher to put the frequencies for one category in the first column instead of the second column. For example, in the problem above, we placed the frequencies for the Non-Greek alumni in the column labeled X_1. Suppose, instead, we had placed the frequencies for the Greek alumni in that column (X_1). The magnitude of the coefficient would remain the same, but ϕ would now have a negative sign ($\phi = -0.2174229$), simply because we reversed the columns in the data matrix. The same thing would happen if we reversed the *rows* in the data matrix. (If we reversed *both* the rows and columns, the sign would not change.) Perform these computations for yourself, and you should become convinced that the sign of ϕ is arbitrary and meaningless. Basically, ϕ measures the magnitude of the relationship between qualitative variables, but the relationship has no direction because categorical variables do not "increase" or "decrease" in quantity, so it makes no sense to say that X "increases" from being a Greek to not being a Greek, or from being Non-Greek to being a Greek.

The Phi Coefficient as an Inferential Statistic: Testing the Null Hypothesis With Chi-Square   Should the university's fundraiser conclude that this relationship can be generalized to all alumni and to other universities? We must, of course, compare the value of ϕ obtained from our sample to a critical value from a sampling distribution. Because the distribution of ϕ coefficients is identical to a distribution of a very popular statistic known as chi-square (χ^2), most textbooks include a table of critical values only for chi-square and require that the phi coefficient be transformed into chi-square in order to test the null hypothesis. The transformation formula is as follows:

$$\chi^2 = N(\phi^2)$$

Therefore, when we convert our ϕ of 0.2174229 into χ^2, we get:

$\chi^2 = 120\ (0.2174229^2)$
$\chi^2 = 120\ (0.0472727)$
$\chi^2 = 5.672724$
$\chi^2 \approx 5.673$ (rounded to three decimals for hypothesis testing)

To determine whether a value of chi-square equal to 5.673 is statistically significant (or just a common event by chance alone), we need to compare it to a critical value of χ^2 from Table B-5 (in Appendix B). The decision rule for chi-square (and thus for phi as well) is the same as the decision rules for the Pearson and Spearman correlation coefficients. If the obtained sample statistic is greater than or equal to the critical value from the table, reject the null hypothesis:

$$\text{If } \chi^2{}_{obt} \geq \chi^2{}_{crit}, \text{ reject the null}$$

The first column of the chi-square table refers to "degrees of freedom" (df). The degrees of freedom for chi-square are based on the number of categories (or cell frequencies) in the data set, and they are explained in detail in Chapter 13. For now, it is enough to know that, because the phi coefficient is limited to four categories, representing the combination of two dichotomous variables, all phi coefficients (and their associated values of chi-square) *have only one degree of freedom.* Therefore, looking at Table B-5, with one degree of freedom, and with alpha set at .05, we see that $\chi^2{}_{crit} = 3.841$. This indicates that values of χ^2 ranging from 0.00 to 3.840 are common by chance alone. Our obtained value of χ^2 is 5.673, which is greater than the critical value of 3.841, and therefore, we can reject the null hypothesis and conclude that, in the population, there is a significant (if low) correlation between having been a member of a fraternity and being a major donor to the university. That is, the major donors to the university tend to be Greek alumni, while non-major donors are slightly more likely to be non-Greek alumni. (Remember, this is a correlational study, so we can describe the relationship that is identified, but no causal conclusion can be drawn. That is, we cannot conclude that membership in a fraternity causes people to become major donors to their *alma mater*.)

Testing the Difference Between Two Correlations

Occasionally, a researcher will be interested in comparing two Pearson correlations to see whether the magnitude of the relationship between X and Y is the same for two different populations. For example, is the relationship between watching violence on television and behaving aggressively equally strong for girls and boys? Or is it possible that television violence has a stronger link to boys' aggressiveness than to girls'?

To answer this question, we would compute the Pearson correlations between television violence and aggressiveness for boys and girls separately (but using the same operational definitions and measurement procedures), and use the **r-to-z Transformation** table (Table B-4) to transform these correlation coefficients into z-scores (z^*_1 for the first value of r, and z^*_2 for the second value of r). Then we compute a statistic known as the **critical ratio (CR)** which is a measure of the difference between the two correlations:

$$CR = \frac{(z^*_1 - z^*_2) - 0.0}{\sqrt{\dfrac{1}{N_1 - 3} + \dfrac{1}{N_2 - 3}}}$$

where: 0.0 = the difference between the correlations predicted by the null hypothesis

N_1 = the sample size for the first correlation coefficient;

N_2 = the sample size for the second correlation coefficient

This CR is a z-score that is compared to the critical value of z that cuts off the rare values of z. If CR falls in the region of rejection, we reject the null hypothesis and conclude that the two correlations are significantly different. The critical values of z for a nondirectional (two-tailed) test, as we saw at the end of Chapter 5, are:

for $\alpha = .05$, $z_{critical} = \pm 1.96$ for $\alpha = .01$, $z_{critical} = \pm 2.58$

The **decision rule** for nondirectional (two-tailed) tests is:

If CR $\geq \pm z_{critical}$, reject the null.

Let's work through an example. Suppose the Pearson correlation between television violence and aggression for a sample of 50 boys is $+0.35$, and for a sample of 42 girls it is $+0.23$. First we go to the *r*-to-*z* transformation table (Table B-4) and look up z for the two correlations:

for boys, $r = .35$, so $z^*_1 = .3654$
for girls, $r = .23$, so $z^*_2 = .2342$

Next, we compute CR:

$$CR = \frac{(.3654 - .2342) - 0}{\sqrt{\dfrac{1}{50 - 3} + \dfrac{1}{42 - 3}}}$$

$$CR = \frac{.1312}{\sqrt{\dfrac{1}{47} + \dfrac{1}{39}}}$$

$$CR = \frac{.1312}{\sqrt{(.021276596) + (.025641026)}}$$

$$CR = \frac{.1312}{\sqrt{.046917621}}$$

$$CR = \frac{.1312}{.216604758}$$

$$CR = 0.605711532$$

CR ≈ 0.61

Finally, we use this CR as a z-score and compare it to the $z_{critical}$, which is equal to 1.96 (for a two-tailed test with $\alpha = .05$). A CR of 0.61 is *not* greater than or equal to 1.96, and therefore, we cannot reject the null hypothesis. We would conclude that the relationship between television violence and aggressiveness for boys is not significantly different in magnitude than the correlation for girls. That is, the difference between $r = +.35$ and $r = +.23$ can be attributed to chance alone, so there is no evidence that television violence is more closely related to aggressiveness in boys than in girls.

If a researcher decides that it is reasonable to conduct a *directional (one-tailed) test* because there is strong evidence to predict that one of the correlations is likely to be the higher of the two, there is only one region of rejection, and the appropriate values of $z_{critical}$ are:

for $\alpha = .05$, $z_{critical} = +1.64$ or -1.64

for $\alpha = .01$, $z_{critical} = +2.33$ or -2.33

The **decision rule** for a directional test is based on the specific prediction that is being tested. If research hypothesis (H_1) predicts that r_1 will be *greater than* r_2, the rule is:

If CR $\geq +z_{critical}$, reject the null

If, in contrast, the research hypothesis (H_1) predicts that r_1 will be *less than* r_2, the rule is:

If CR $\leq -z_{critical}$, reject the null

(In our example, CR is not significant using a one-tailed test.)

Exercises

1. A researcher asked teachers to rate children on a 7-point scale (where 7 = "very aggressive" and 1 = "very passive") and then observed the children's interactions with peers during free play periods. The total number of prosocial behaviors each child exhibited during free play over a period of five days was recorded. Calculate the appropriate correlation coefficient and test its significance with alpha set at .05. Verbally summarize (or interpret) the results.

Aggressiveness Ratings	Prosocial Behaviors
3	3
1	2
6	4
2	1
5	7
3	2
1	0
6	9
5	4
7	8

2. A teacher recorded the number of absences for each student and the number of correct answers each student had on the final exam. Calculate the appropriate correlation coefficient and test its significance with alpha set at .05. Verbally describe (or interpret) the results.

Absences	Exam Score
3	20
5	18
6	12
2	24
1	23
4	18
3	21
2	15
7	10
5	17

3. The dean of a small college suspects that performance in the freshman English composition course is a significant predictor of college success. To test this hypothesis, the dean collected the following data from the past four years:

		Graduated With B.A.	
		Yes	No
Passed Freshman Composition	Yes	64	21
	No	25	30

Calculate the appropriate correlation coefficient and test its significance with alpha set at .05. Verbally summarize (or interpret) the findings.

4. To study the relationship between family circumstances and attitudes toward euthanasia, a researcher surveyed 60 families and asked two questions: "Do you currently have primary responsibility for an aging relative? Yes or no?" and "Do you believe euthanasia should be legalized in the United States? Yes or no?" The data are below. Calculate the appropriate correlation coefficient and test the significance of this relationship. Verbally summarize the results.

		Caring for an Aging Relative	
		Yes	No
Legalize Euthanasia	Yes	25	15
	No	5	15

5. A kindergarten teacher counted the number of darts her students could get into a 5-inch circle on a dart board and wanted to know whether this skill was related to their ability to stand on one foot without losing their balance. So she also timed how long (in seconds) each child could keep one foot off the floor. The data are below. Calculate the appropriate correlation coefficient and test the significance of this relationship. Verbally summarize the results.

Darts	Time
2	5
6	22
0	9
3	12
8	16
4	16

6. Following the Olympics, an advertising executive studied the relationship between the medals athletes won and the amount of money they earned in product endorsements over the next six months (in thousands of dollars).

The data are below, where 0 = fourth place or worse; 1 = bronze medal; 2 = silver medal; and 3 = gold medal). Calculate the appropriate correlation coefficient and test its significance with alpha set at .05. Verbally summarize the results.

Medal	Money
0	4
3	45
2	23
0	1
1	12
1	29

7. A researcher has been studying the relationships among intelligence and various areas of academic performance in a sample of 100 college students. He has discovered that the correlation between IQ scores and overall G.P.A. is +0.53 but that the correlation between IQ and grades in math and sciences classes is +0.68. Is this a significant difference?

8. Design a study to test the hypothesis that sense of humor is correlated with overall health. Operationally define your measures and identify the appropriate correlation coefficient for your study.

For each of the following scenarios, identify the appropriate correlation coefficient based on the levels of measurement for X and Y.

9. A sociologist is studying drug abuse among teenagers. In one study, she asked high school students to indicate their willingness to try crack cocaine using a 4-point rating scale. The researcher then asked the students' parents to report their annual income, as they had reported to the IRS the previous April.

10. A researcher wants to test the hypothesis that training in Freudian psycho-analytic dream analysis correlates with an art therapist's tendency to "find" sexual symbols in a client's drawings. A sample of art therapists were asked to indicate the number of courses they took on Freudian theory of dreams. Then they were given a case study and a series of drawings, and they were asked to prepare an interpretation of the artwork. The researcher then counted the number of sexual symbols identified by the art therapist.

11. Four-year-old children were asked to predict how many items in an array they would be able to remember after the items were removed from sight. Then their memory for the array of items was actually tested and the number of items they correctly recalled was recorded.

12. To determine whether or not training in public speaking is associated with persuasiveness, a researcher organized debates between students who had

taken a college course on public speaking and students who had not. Observers rated each debater's persuasiveness on a scale from 0 to 4.

13. A researcher was interested in the relationship between a child's popularity with classmates and the teacher's perception of the child's popularity. To measure peer popularity, all of the children in the class were asked to name the "three nicest kids in class." Then the researcher counted the number of times the participant was identified by a classmate as one of the "nicest kids." To measure the teacher's perception of the participants, the teacher was asked to evaluate each participant on a scale from 0 ("Seems Very Unpopular") to 7 ("Seems Very Popular").

14. To test the hypothesis that 4-year-old children's height is correlated with their muscle coordination, a researcher spent a day at an amusement park observing children. He recorded whether they were tall enough to ride the "loop-de-loop" and whether or not they won a prize at the ball-toss.

15. In a study on the relationship between sex and reaction time, men and women played a video-arcade game involving a "dog fight" between jets. Players needed to react quickly to the sudden appearance of an enemy plane in a random location, so players with better reaction times would be expected to perform better. The game was programmed to declare the player a winner if (s)he hit three opponents before being shot down.

16. After six weeks of basic training, new Marines were asked to guess the height (in feet and inches) of the officers on base. The rank (e.g., captain, major, or general, etc.) of the officers is to be correlated with the perceived heights.

CHAPTER

9

INTRODUCTION TO REGRESSION ANALYSIS

■ ■ ■ ■ ■ ■

In this chapter, you will learn how to use the correlation between two variables to predict individuals' scores and to estimate the accuracy of those predictions. You will also be introduced to the basic concepts involved in using several different measures to predict performance on a criterion variable.

Look for These Important Terms and Concepts

slope and intercept
regression equation and Y'
subpopulation
predictor and criterion variables
regression line
method of least squares
least squares criterion
assumptions of independence, linearity,
   normality, and homoscedasticity
monotonic and nonmonotonic

curvilinear
standard error of the estimate
explained variance and error
   (unexplained) variance
coefficient of determination
coefficient of nondetermination
Venn diagrams
multiple regression
multicollinearity

Before Reading This Chapter, You May Wish to Review

Chapter 5:
- normal and skewed distributions
- mean and standard deviation
- z-scores
- the z-to-X conversion formula

Chapter 6:
- representativeness
- standard error

Chapter 7:
- correlational method

Chapter 8:
- magnitude
- scatterplot (or scattergram)
- Pearson r

Being able to make predictions about events or about an individual's abilities or characteristics is an important tool in many areas of life. For example, employers want to hire people who will do the job effectively, and graduate schools want to admit students who can successfully complete the degree requirements. Making predictions about other people is easier when we start with some *relevant* information about them. That is, if we know how they performed on measures that are *correlated* with the task of interest, we can make more accurate predictions. So if potential employers know how much previous experience a job candidate has had in similar jobs, they can more accurately predict how well the individual would do in the new position. The accuracy of our predictions will depend on the magnitude (or strength) of the correlation between the two variables: If previous experience is highly correlated to job performance, the employer's prediction will be more accurate than if previous experience is only weakly correlated to job performance. Likewise, graduate admissions committees can make more accurate predictions about the success of an applicant if they know how well the student did in an undergraduate program, and the higher the correlation between undergraduate performance and graduate school performance, the more accurate these predictions will be.

The Logic Behind Simple Regression Analysis

The process of predicting (or estimating) variable Y using variable X is called **regression.** In order to understand the logic of regression analysis, let's imagine that a kindergarten teacher would like to be able to predict how popular individual children (e.g., Margery, Sasha, and Jordan) will be by the end of the school year. Let's suppose that popularity is measured by asking each classmate "Is Margery nice or is Margery not nice?" and recording the percentage of children who label the target child as "nice." Let's further suppose that, for kindergarteners, the average popularity score ($\overline{Y}$) is 75%. In the absence of any relevant information about the children, the teacher's best guess would be to predict that Margery, Sasha, and Jordan are average children and that 75% of their classmates will consider them to be "nice." That is, when we have no evidence to the contrary, we assume that any given individual is a "typical member" of the population, since average scores are the most common (i.e., have the highest frequency) in normal distributions. Although this assumption will lead to many inaccurate predictions, there would be even more error in our predictions if we made the assumption that the children were not average.

Now, however, suppose the teacher knows that children's popularity (or percentage of classmates who label a child as "nice"—variable Y) is positively correlated with children's performance on a social-problem-solving task (SPST—variable X), which asks children to think of as many solutions as they can to a series of social dilemmas (such as getting another child to share a toy) and is scored by counting the number of positive or non-aggressive responses generated. Let's suppose that the average score on this task for children in this age group ($\overline{X}$) is 8.0 and that the Pearson correlation (r) between number of solutions and popularity is equal to +0.60. If the kindergarten teacher administered the SPST to the children and found that

Margery received a score of 8, Sasha received a score of 2, and Jordan received a score of 10, what would the teacher then predict about the popularity of each of these children?

Instead of expecting each of the children to be average and to have a popularity score of 75%, the teacher could use the difference in their SPST scores to predict differences in the percentage of classmates who think each child is "nice." The positive correlation between the two variables indicates that as the number of positive solutions to social dilemmas increases, so does popularity. That is, children who can generate many nonaggressive solutions to social problems tend to be liked the most, and children who generate few solutions to the dilemmas tend to be liked least. Children who generate an average number of positive solutions tend to be average in popularity. Therefore, the teacher could now predict that Margery will have a popularity score of 75% since her SPST score of 8 was equal to the average SPST score; Sasha will be considered nice by *fewer than* 75% of her classmates since her SPST score of 2 was below average; and Jordan's popularity score will be *higher than* 75% since his SPST score of 10 was higher than average.

Furthermore, since Sasha's SPST score of 2 is quite a bit below the average score of 8, while Jordan's SPST score of 10 is only a little bit above average, we would expect Sasha's popularity to be quite a bit below average and Jordan's popularity to be only a little bit above average. But can we be more specific about what Sasha's and Jordan's popularity scores will be? Yes, because regression analysis allows us to make precise predictions for each individual.

The predictions that result from regression analysis are based on the assumption that any given individual is a typical representative of the *subpopulation of people who receive the same score* on variable X. That is, if we think of children who receive a score of 1 on the SPST as a subpopulation, and if we know the average popularity for children in this sub-group, this subpopulation average becomes our best guess for any given child with an SPST score of 1. Similarly, the children who receive an SPST score of 6 are considered to be a separate subpopulation, and the average popularity score for this subpopulation is our best guess for any child with an SPST score of 6. Essentially, every unique SPST score represents a unique supopulation, and the mean popularity score for each subpopulation ($\overline{Y}_{Subpopulation}$) can be used as an estimate of the popularity of any individual in that subpopulation. This is illustrated in Figure 9-1.

Panel A in Figure 9-1 presents a scatterplot for the relationship (in the population) between children's SPST scores (X) and their popularity with their classmates (Y), where the population correlation (ρ) is approximately +0.60. Panels B and C show how it is possible to separate the children into subpopulations defined by their SPST scores and construct frequency polygons of the popularity scores for each separate SPST subpopulation. These frequency polygons visually indicate which values of Y are common and uncommon within the subpopulations. For example, panel C in Figure 9-1 indicates that popularity scores ranging from 50 to 60 are quite common among children with an SPST score of 2, but are quite rare among children with an SPST score of 10. Of course, in addition to visually examining the frequency polygons, we can compute the mean popularity score for each subpopulation and the

FIGURE 9.1

SCATTERPLOTS AND FREQUENCY POLYGONS FOR SUBPOPULATIONS

(a) Scatterplot for a hypothetical population where $\rho = 0.60$

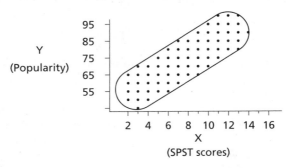

(b) Identifying subpopulations based on SPST scores

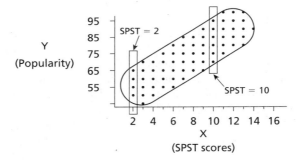

Note: The upper and lower "boundaries" of the scatterplot's oval indicate the maximum and minimum values of Y for individuals in the subpopulation.

(c) Frequency polygons and means for the separate subpopulations

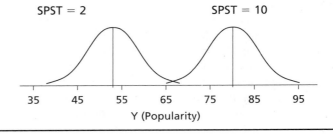

standard deviation of the popularity scores. The mean for a particular subpopulation ($\overline{Y}_{\text{Subpopulation}}$) can be used as our best estimate of Y for children who receive that particular score on X (the Social-Problem-Solving Task).

In summary, if the teacher wants to predict how popular Sasha and Jordan will be, she could compute the mean popularity score for all children who receive scores of 2 and 10, respectively, on the Social-Problem-Solving Task and then use these subgroup means as predictions about the popularity of these children. (Of course, this prediction is based on the assumption that Sasha and Jordan are typical members of their subpopulations such that their performance is "average" for those subgroups.)

At this point, the regression analysis process must sound long and tedious. Fortunately, however, as long as we meet a few basic assumptions (which are discussed later in this chapter), we can use the **regression equation** presented below to calculate a predicted-value of Y (Y′—which is pronounced "Y-prime") for *any value of* X. In other words, it is not actually necessary to calculate means for each separate subgroup ($\overline{Y}_{\text{Subpopulation}}$) in the data set because we can compute a value of Y′ using the regression equation, and Y′ is equal to $\overline{Y}_{\text{Subpopulation}}$ (except, possibly, for rounding error).

The Regression Equation

The regression equation is an equation for a straight line and follows the general form:

$$Y' = bX + a$$

where "a" stands for the intercept of the line (which is the value of Y when X equals zero) and "b" stands for the slope of the line (or how much Y changes when X changes by one unit). The formulas for the intercept and the slope are:

$$\text{Intercept} = a = \overline{Y} - r\frac{s_Y}{s_X}(\overline{X})$$

$$\text{Slope} = b = r\frac{s_Y}{s_X}$$

Thus, if we combine these two formulas, we find that the regression equation can be written as:

$$Y' = r\frac{s_Y}{s_X}(X) + \left[\overline{Y} - r\frac{s_Y}{s_X}(\overline{X})\right]$$

Before discussing this formula and its elements in more detail, let's finish our example by predicting the popularity scores of Margery, Sasha, and Jordan using their SPST scores. Recall that the mean SPST score is 8, the mean popularity score is

75%, and the correlation between these scores is +0.60. Let's further suppose that the standard deviation for the SPST scores (s_X) is 2.1 and that the standard deviation of popularity scores (s_Y) among this age group is 12.8. Thus, we have the following information and we can compute Y' for each of the three children:

$$r = +0.60 \qquad \overline{X} = 8 \qquad s_X = 2.1 \qquad \overline{Y} = 75 \qquad s_Y = 12.8$$

For Margery: $X = 8$; therefore, the regression equation is:

$$Y' = r\frac{s_Y}{s_X}(X) + \left[\overline{Y} - r\frac{s_Y}{s_X}(\overline{X})\right]$$

$$Y' = 0.6\frac{12.8}{2.1}(8) + \left[75 - .06\frac{12.8}{2.1}(8)\right]$$

$$= 0.6(6.095238)(8) + [75 - 0.6(6.095238)(8)]$$

$$= 3.6571428(8) + [75 - 3.6571428(8)]$$

$$= 29.257142 + (75 - 29.257142)$$

$$= 29.257142 + 45.742858$$

$$= 75$$

Thus, the subpopulation of children who receive a score of 8 on the Social-Problem-Solving Task are labeled "nice" by an average of 75% of their classmates. Therefore, since we assume that Margery is a typical member of her subpopulation, we predict that she will have a popularity score of 75%. (As we mentioned earlier, children with average SPST scores are expected to have average popularity scores.)

For Sasha, $X = 2$; therefore, the regression equation is:

$$Y' = r\frac{s_Y}{s_X}(X) + \left[\overline{Y} - r\frac{s_Y}{s_X}(\overline{X})\right]$$

$$Y' = 0.6\frac{12.8}{2.1}(2) + \left[75 - .06\frac{12.8}{2.1}(8)\right]$$

$$= 0.6(6.095238)(2) + [75 - 0.6(6.095238(8)]$$

$$= 3.6571428(2) + [75 - 3.6571428(8)]$$

$$= 7.3142856 + (75 - 29.257142)$$

$$= 7.3142856 + 45.742858$$

$$= 53.057143$$

$$\approx 53$$

Thus, the subpopulation of children who receive a score of 2 on the Social-Problem-Solving Task are labeled "nice" by only about 53% of their classmates.

Therefore, since we assume Sasha is a typical member of her subpopulation, we predict that she will have a popularity score of 53%.

You may have noticed that the first steps in the computation of Y' for Sasha was identical to the early calculations we did for Margery. These first steps involved the computation of the slope and the intercept, which remain constant for all values of X. In fact, the only difference between the regression equations for the children is the value of X. Therefore, after computing Y' for the first child, we can extract the slope and intercept and use them for all subsequent computations of Y'. As you can see from the computation for Margery (and Sasha), the slope of the relationship between popularity and SPST scores is equal to 3.6571428 and the intercept is equal to 45.742858. Therefore, we can quickly calculate Y' for Jordan.

For Jordan, X = 10; therefore, the regression equation is:

$$Y' = r \frac{s_Y}{s_X} (X) + \left[\overline{Y} - r \frac{s_Y}{s_X} (\overline{X}) \right]$$

or

$$Y' = \text{slope}(X) + \text{intercept}$$
$$Y' = 3.6571428(10) + 45.742858$$
$$= 36.571428 + 45.742858$$
$$= 82.314286$$
$$\approx 82$$

Thus, the subpopulation of children who receive a score of 10 on the Social-Problem-Solving Task are labeled "nice" by an average of 82% of their classmates. Therefore, since we assume Jordan is a typical member of his subpopulation, we predict that he will have a popularity score of 82%.

Thus, the regression equation gives us predicted values of Y' that reflect the positive correlation between the two variables: The child with an average score on the SPST is expected to be average in popularity, the child with the low SPST score is predicted to be below average in popularity, and the child with an above-average SPST score is expected to be above average in popularity.

About the Regression Equation

As indicated earlier, the regression equation is actually an equation for a straight line, and it follows the general form:

$$Y = \text{slope} (X) + \text{intercept}$$

The slope of a line indicates how much Y changes when X changes by one unit, and the intercept is the value of Y when X = 0.0 (or when the line crosses the Y-axis on a graph). Generally, the slope of the line that connects two points can be calculated by dividing the amount of change in Y (ΔY—read "delta Y" or "change in Y") by the amount of change in X (ΔX—"delta X"):

$$\text{slope} = \frac{\Delta Y}{\Delta X} = \frac{\text{change in Y}}{\text{change in X}}$$

For example, look at the lines in Figure 9-2. The intercept for each of the lines in Figure 9-2 is equal to 3, as indicated by the dashed line extending to the Y-axis, but they each have different slopes. Line 9-2a has a positive slope equal to 2 because an increase of 1 point on X is associated with an increase of 2 points on Y. Line 9-2b has a positive slope of 0.5 because a 4-point increase on X is associated with a 2-point increase on Y; and Line 9-2c has a *negative* slope of -0.5 because the 2-point increase in X is associated with a 1-point *decrease* on Y. From these slopes, we know that Figures 9-2a and 9-2b represent positive correlations and Figure 9-2c represents a negative correlation because positive correlations always result in positive slopes (where points on the scatterplot move from the lower left to the upper right) and negative correlations always result in negative slopes (where the points on the scatterplot move from the upper left to the lower right).

The formula for a line allows us to set the value of X and determine what the value of Y is for that point along the line. This, essentially, is what regression analysis is all about: Using the score for one variable (X) to predict the value of another variable (Y). The regression equation allows us to take any value of the **predictor variable (X)** and compute a predicted value of the **criterion variable (Y).** If every value of X is entered into the regression equation, the resulting set of Y' scores will form a straight line, which is called the **regression line.** This line is referred to as

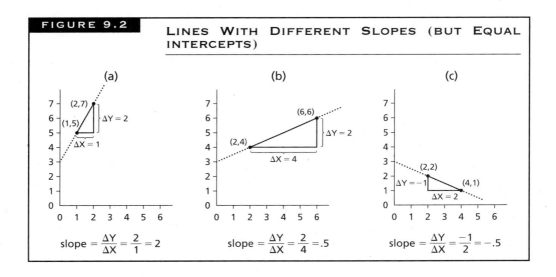

FIGURE 9.2   LINES WITH DIFFERENT SLOPES (BUT EQUAL INTERCEPTS)

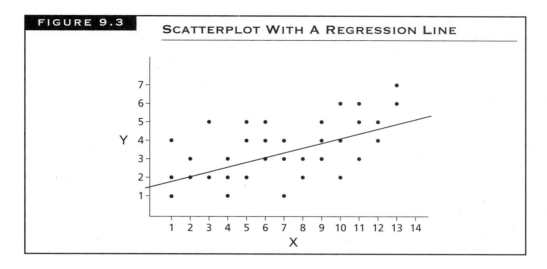

FIGURE 9.3

SCATTERPLOT WITH A REGRESSION LINE

the "best-fitting line" because, if it is superimposed onto the scatterplot of the data, as illustrated in Figure 9-3, it comes *closer than any other line* to passing through all of the data points on the scatterplot. That is, if we measure the distance from the regression line (Y′) to each point on the scatterplot (the actual values of Y), the total amount of this "prediction error" (Y − Y′) is less than it would be if any other line is drawn through the data. Because the difference between Y and Y′ is *squared*, and the regression line is the line that minimizes these squared differences, this analysis is sometimes called the **method of least squares,** and the regression equation defines the line that meets the **least-squares criterion.** If we wish to draw this regression line through the data points on a scatterplot, we need only calculate Y′ for two values of X and then draw the line that connects those two points.

In our example of predicting the popularity of kindergarten children by using their scores on a Social-Problem-Solving Task, we explained that the best estimate (or prediction) for a given child is equal to the average popularity score for the sub-population of children who have the same SPST score. The regression equation gives us the best predictions because the points along the regression line—that is, the values of Y′—correspond to the average scores (on Y) for each of the subpopulations defined by unique scores on X. In technical terms, for every value of X, the regression equation gives us a Y′ that is equal to $\overline{Y}_{Subpopulation}$. This is illustrated in Figure 9-4.

Assumptions and Limitations of the Least-Squares Method of Regression

Several important assumptions underlie the least-squares method of regression. If any of these conditions are violated, the accuracy of Y′ (as a predictor of Y) becomes

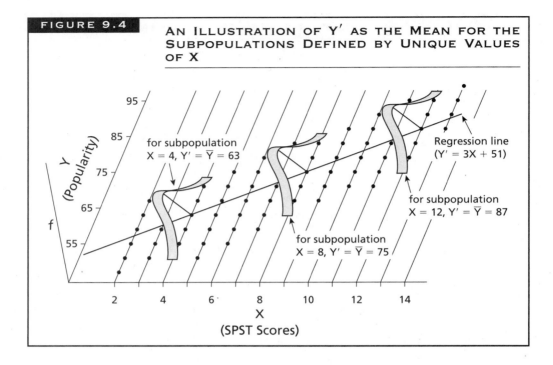

FIGURE 9.4

AN ILLUSTRATION OF Y′ AS THE MEAN FOR THE SUBPOPULATIONS DEFINED BY UNIQUE VALUES OF X

doubtful. One assumption—the **assumption of independence**—is that the score of one participant has no bearing on the score of another (i.e., the participants are independent). An example of a violation of this assumption of independence would be a situation where pairs of children are observed sharing a bag of M&Ms and we record the number of candies each child eats: If Marcus eats 80% of the M&Ms, then Brandon's score cannot exceed 20%—the two scores are linked. (This assumption is actually important to most statistical procedures covered in this text.) Three other important assumptions are described separately below.

Linearity

The least-squares method of regression, which is based on the Pearson correlation coefficient, presumes that the relationship between X and Y is **linear,** so that the regression line that comes closest to all of the points on the scatterplot is a *straight* line. In fact, the Pearson r was designed to measure the degree of linearity in the relationship between two variables, and it can greatly underestimate the magnitude of nonlinear relationships. Therefore, the Pearson r and least-squares regression analysis are not appropriate when the best-fitting regression line for the relationship between X and Y is not a straight line.

The defining feature of *linear* relationships (and straight lines, in general) is that whenever the value of X changes by a given amount, the *amount of change in Y is consistent.* In other words, in a linear relationship, the amount of change in Y is the same across all values of X, and, therefore, the slope of the line remains constant. For example, Figure 9-2a illustrates a linear relationship where *every time* the value of X increases by 1 point, the value of Y increases by 2 points (and therefore has a slope of +2.0). If this graph were expanded to include larger values of X and Y, the relationship would remain unchanged: A 1-point change in X from 99 to 100 would result in a 2-point change in Y from 201 to 203.

Technically, linear relationships are a special subclass of **monotonic** relationships, which are characterized by a pattern in which the changes in Y consistently go in the *same direction* across all values of X, so that in *positive relationships*, as X increases, Y always increases while in *negative relationships*, as X increases, Y always decreases. All linear relationships are monotonic. A monotonic but nonlinear relationship is one where the amount of change in Y is *not* consistent across all values of X. For example, an exponential relationship, such as $Y = X^2$, fits the definition of a positive monotonic relationship but fails to meet the criterion for linearity. That is, as the value of X increases (from 2 to 3 to 4), the value of Y always increases (from 4 to 9 to 16), but the amount of change in Y is *not* consistent across all values of X: The 1-point change in X from 2 to 3 is associated with a 5-point increase in Y, while the 1-point change in X from 3 to 4 is associated with a 7-point increase in Y. Hence, this exponential relationship is monotonic but nonlinear. If we graph this exponential relationship, we will see that there is a distinct "bend" or curve in the function, so the relationship is often called **curvilinear** (see Figure 9-5a). Because the regression equation generated through the least-squares method applies the linear rule (where a one-unit change in X always results in a given amount of change in Y), it will not produce the best-fitting function for such nonlinear relationships.

There are also curvilinear relationships that are *nonmonotonic* (and obviously, therefore, nonlinear). Consider the relationship between anxiety (or arousal) level and performance on an exam. Most students can appreciate the fact that high levels of anxiety are often associated with poor performance, but it is also true that very low levels of anxiety are associated with poor performance, as well. (Students who feel no anxiety about an upcoming test are less likely to study thoroughly, and if the exam is more difficult than expected, their grades may suffer.) The highest performance levels are typically associated with intermediate levels of anxiety. Hence, it is *not* accurate to describe the relationship between the variables by saying: "As anxiety increases, performance decreases." It is more accurate to say: "As anxiety increases from low to moderate, performance increases, but as anxiety increases from moderate to high, performance decreases." This relationship, which is illustrated in Figure 9-5b, is described as being **curvilinear but nonmonotonic:** As values of X increase, the values of Y start off in one direction and then change and go the other way.

In summary, the least-squares method of regression analysis is not appropriate for curvilinear relationships since the values of Y′ are based on a formula for a straight line rather than a curved function. Therefore, researchers should routinely examine a scatterplot of their data, and if the relationship appears to be non-linear, the researchers should not use the least-squares method of regression. Furthermore, they need to remember that the Pearson *r* will underestimate the magnitude of a

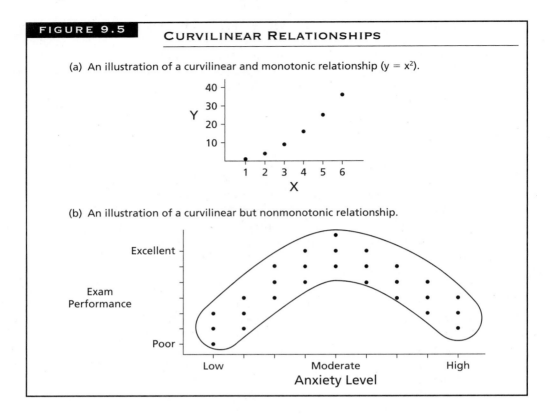

FIGURE 9.5   **CURVILINEAR RELATIONSHIPS**

(a) An illustration of a curvilinear and monotonic relationship ($y = x^2$).

(b) An illustration of a curvilinear but nonmonotonic relationship.

curvilinear relationship between X and Y, so they should be cautious in their interpretation of the correlation coefficient, or they should select a more appropriate statistic. For instance, if the curvilinear relationship is *monotonic*, the Spearman rank order correlation coefficient can be used to measure the magnitude of the relationship because it does not assume that X and Y have a linear relationship.

Normal Distributions and Homoscedasticity

Two other important assumptions that underlie the least-squares method of regression have to do with the subpopulations for each unique value of the predictor variable (X). First it is assumed that the scores on Y form a **normal distribution** for each separate value of X. This is important because, as we discussed earlier, the least-squares regression analysis uses the subpopulation mean as the best estimate (or prediction) for any particular individual because the squared differences between actual Y scores and Y' (i.e., $\overline{Y}_{Subpopulation}$) are thus minimized. However, the squared

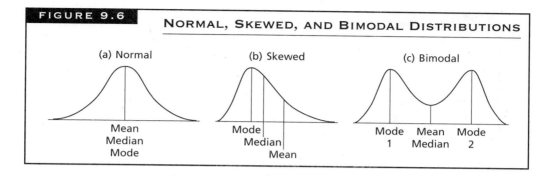

FIGURE 9.6   NORMAL, SKEWED, AND BIMODAL DISTRIBUTIONS

differences between actual scores and the group means are minimal only when the scores are normally distributed. Remember that normal distributions are symmetrical, so that the group mean falls in the middle of the distribution and the mean is the score with the highest frequency (see Figure 9-6a). Therefore, the deviations between actual scores and the mean $(Y - Y')$ will include many values of zero and a great many values that are quite small, and the total of the squared deviation scores will be smaller than if any other value of Y' was used.

If the Y-scores are skewed rather than normally distributed (as in Figure 9-6b) or if they are bimodal (as in Figure 9-6c), the mean is no longer in the center of the distribution, or it is not the most frequently occurring score. Hence, the deviation scores $(Y - Y')$ will tend to be larger since the mean is farther away from more of the actual scores in the group. Therefore, the regression equation that uses the subpopulation mean as its estimate for an individual's score will fail to meet the least-squares criterion: The regression line will not be the function that comes closest (in total) to the actual values of Y. Therefore, the accuracy of the least-squares method of regression depends on the shape of the distribution of the Y-scores for each subpopulation with a unique value of X: All of these subpopulations must have normal distributions of Y. (It is important to note that we are talking about the distribution of Y within *populations*, and not samples; it is unlikely that each subgroup with a unique value of X within a typical research sample will have a normal distribution of Y scores.)

Similarly, both the Pearson r and the least-squares method of regression assume that the standard deviation of the Y scores is *similar* for every subpopulation with a unique value of X. This is known as the assumption of **homoscedasticity.** (This term comes from *homo*, which means "same" or "equal" and *scedasticity*, which means "tendency to scatter." The opposite term would be *heteroscedasticity*, which would refer to situations where the standard deviations are *not* the same.) The assumption of homoscedasticity says that there should be just as much variability among individuals with an X score of 2 as there is among individuals with an X score of 20. If this is not the case, and the scatterplot shows heteroscedasticity, it means that different values of X will have different average deviation scores (that is, the difference between the predicted values of Y' and the actual values of Y will vary from one value of X

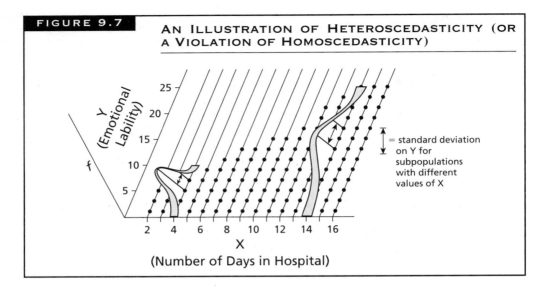

FIGURE 9.7

AN ILLUSTRATION OF HETEROSCEDASTICITY (OR A VIOLATION OF HOMOSCEDASTICITY)

to another). This, in turn, leads to a situation where our predictions will be more accurate for some values of X than for others, and therefore, the least-squares method of regression is not appropriate.

Figure 9-7 illustrates a violation of homoscedasticity (i.e., *heteroscedasticity*) in a hypothetical study of the correlation between the length of time patients are hospitalized for mental disturbances and their emotional lability over time. The scatterplot indicates that the patients who are briefly hospitalized tend to have low levels of emotional lability (i.e., their emotional state remains fairly consistent over time), and more importantly, they tend to be very similar to one another. For example, the patients with the shortest hospital stays have emotional lability scores ranging from 2 to 8. In contrast, patients who remain hospitalized for long periods of time tend to vary tremendously in their emotional lability. For example, the patients who were hospitalized for 14 days have lability scores ranging from 2 to 25 (the full range of the scale). Thus, the assumption of homoscedasticity has been violated and, in principle, the least-squares method of regression would not be appropriate for this set of data.

Having said this, however, we should point out that, in practice, statisticians have found that regression analysis can tolerate some degree of heteroscedasticity. While the accuracy of our predictions are compromised if the standard deviations of Y are grossly unequal across different values of X, small or moderate differences do not seem to be a great cause for alarm. (When a statistical procedure can provide valid results despite violations of its underlying assumptions, the statistical test is said to be *robust*. Thus, the least-squares method of regression analysis is robust concerning the assumption of homoscedasticity.)

Evaluating Y′: How Accurate Are Our Predictions?

Because the variables are correlated, using children's performance on a Social-Problem-Solving Task improves our ability to predict how popular children will become during kindergarten. That is, Y′ (the average score for the subpopulation) is generally a more accurate estimate of an individual child's score on Y than is the overall $\overline{Y}$ (which is the estimate we use in the absence of a predictor variable X). However, the predicted value of Y′ will often differ from the actual score on Y, so the question becomes: How accurate are the predictions made using the regression equation?[1]

The accuracy of the prediction for a single individual can be determined by finding the difference between the predicted value of Y′ (which is based on the predictor variable X) and the individual's actual score on Y. Obviously, if our regression equation is providing accurate estimates, then this difference score (Y − Y′) will be relatively small. These difference scores will not be the same for every score, so in order to evaluate the *overall accuracy* of the regression analysis, we need to find the *average difference* between actual Y scores and the predicted values of Y′, which we will call the **standard error of the estimate (s_{est}):**

Definitional formula:

$$\text{Standard error of the estimate} = s_{est} = \sqrt{\frac{\Sigma(Y - Y')^2}{N - 1}}$$

This formula is structurally equivalent to the definitional formula for the *standard deviation* of a sample of scores (see Chapter 5), which tells us that we are computing the "average difference" between Y and Y′. In fact, the standard error of the estimate is a measure of the variation among Y scores within the separate subpopulations defined by unique values of X. Let's look at some examples of regression analyses and assess the accuracy of the predicted values of Y′.

The first two columns in Table 9-1 present the data from a hypothetical study on the correlation between IQ scores for 30 pairs of same-sex fraternal twins. The correlation between the twins' IQ scores was +0.675, and the regression equation was found to be:

$$Y' = .6008X + 41.108$$

This equation was used to predict the IQ scores for each of the second twins, using the first twins' IQ as the predictor variable (X). The values of Y′ are presented in the

---

[1] The natural variability among the Y-scores is obviously important to the accuracy of our predictions. When there is very little variability, predictions will tend to be more accurate. For example, predictions of the number of chromosomes a person has in each body cell, are going to be very accurate since the number of chromosomes in humans is extremely consistent. Predictions of people's intelligence, however, are going to be less accurate due to the wide range of intelligence scores among individuals.

| TABLE 9.1 | | Example 1: Hypothetical IQ Scores for Pairs of Same-Sex Fraternal Twins | | |

X (Twin 1)	Y (Twin 2)	Y' (Twin 2)	(Y − Y')	(Y − Y')²
116	134	110.80	23.20	538.2400
93	96	96.98	−0.98	0.9604
121	105	113.80	−8.80	77.4400
102	99	102.39	−3.39	11.4921
101	77	101.79	−24.79	614.5441
106	102	104.79	−2.79	7.7841
95	107	98.18	8.82	77.7924
90	107	95.18	11.82	139.7124
89	95	94.58	0.42	0.1764
104	101	103.59	−2.59	6.7081
81	73	89.77	−16.77	281.2329
107	107	105.39	1.61	2.5921
89	88	94.58	−6.58	43.2964
121	118	113.80	4.20	17.6400
99	102	100.59	1.41	1.9881
73	98	84.97	13.03	169.7809
112	116	108.40	7.60	57.7600
86	91	92.78	−1.78	3.1684
85	98	92.18	5.82	33.8724
105	106	104.19	1.81	3.2761
78	83	87.97	−4.97	24.7009
117	122	111.40	10.60	112.3600
92	84	96.38	−12.38	153.2644
70	81	83.17	−2.17	4.7089
121	103	113.80	−10.80	116.6400
126	108	116.81	−8.81	77.6161
96	97	98.78	−1.78	3.1684
96	102	98.78	3.22	10.3684
91	104	95.78	8.22	67.5684
92	104	96.38	7.62	58.0644

$\overline{X} = 98.47$ $\overline{Y} = 100.27$ $\overline{Y'} = 100.27$ $\Sigma = 2717.9172$

$s_X = 14.74$ $s_Y = 13.12$ $s_{Y'} = 8.85$

$r = +.675$

$$\text{Regression equation } Y' = r\frac{s_Y}{s_X}(X) + \left[\overline{Y} - r\frac{s_Y}{s_X}(\overline{X})\right]$$

$$= .675\frac{13.12}{14.74}(X) + \left[100.27 - .675\frac{13.12}{14.74}(98.47)\right]$$

$$= .6008X + 41.108$$

third column of Table 9-1. Then, for each pair of twins, the difference between Y and Y' for each pair was computed and squared (see the fourth and fifth columns of the table). Now we can calculate the standard error of the estimate—an indicator of the overall accuracy of our predictions:

$$\text{Standard error of the estimate} = s_{est} = \sqrt{\frac{\Sigma(Y - Y')^2}{N - 1}}$$

$$s_{est} = \sqrt{\frac{2717.9172}{30 - 1}}$$

$$s_{est} = \sqrt{93.721283}$$

$$s_{est} = 9.6809753$$

$$s_{est} \approx 9.68$$

Therefore, we can conclude that our estimate of the IQ score for one twin based on the other twin's IQ score will be "off" by an *average* of 9.68 IQ points—in many cases, our prediction will be within 9.68 points of the actual score, while for other cases, we will be farther off the mark. Is this good? Let's compare it to what would happen if we predicted the children's IQ scores without using regression analysis. Remember that when we do not have a relevant predictor variable, our best guess is that any particular individual is a typical member of the population. Therefore, we would predict that any given child would have an IQ score of 100. Now consider the fact that standardized IQ scores have a standard deviation of 15 or 16 points, which indicates that the *average difference* between individual scores and the mean is 15 or 16 points. Therefore, our "predictions" would be off by an average of 15 or 16 points. From this perspective, then, our regression analysis which gave us predictions that were, on average, within 10 points of the actual IQ scores, is certainly an improvement. Hence, the regression analysis allows us to make more accurate predictions.

Let's explore the question of accuracy further by comparing our study on fraternal twins to two other examples. Again, the situations involve using the IQ score of one family member to predict the IQ score of another family member, but in example 2, we will use parents' IQ scores to predict their children's IQ scores, and in example 3, we will use children's IQ scores to predict the IQ scores of their same-age step-siblings who live with them but are genetically unrelated to them.

For example 2 (presented in Table 9-2), the correlation between the IQ scores for the parent-child pairs was +0.362, and the regression equation was found to be:

$$Y' = .3755X + 61.22$$

Each parent's IQ score was entered into the regression equation and a predicted value of IQ (Y') was computed for each of the children (see the third column of Table 9-2). Columns 4 and 5 of the table present the deviation scores (Y − Y') and

TABLE 9.2		Example 2: Hypothetical IQ Scores for Parent and Child Pairs		

X (Parent)	Y (Child)	Y' (Child)	(Y – Y')	(Y – Y')²
84	92	92.76	−0.76	0.5776
118	115	105.53	9.47	89.6809
99	100	98.40	1.60	2.5600
108	113	101.77	11.23	126.1129
88	91	94.26	−3.26	10.6276
90	118	95.02	22.98	528.0804
119	123	105.91	17.09	292.0681
108	92	101.77	−9.77	95.4529
93	95	96.14	−1.14	1.2996
80	89	91.26	−2.26	5.1076
82	102	92.01	9.99	99.8001
113	129	103.65	25.35	642.6225
104	89	100.27	−11.27	127.0129
79	91	90.89	0.11	0.0121
93	74	96.14	−22.14	490.1796
123	108	107.41	0.59	0.3481
94	96	96.52	−0.52	0.2704
88	77	94.26	−17.26	297.9076
102	111	99.52	11.48	131.7904
127	83	108.91	−25.91	671.3281
86	73	93.51	−20.51	420.6601
94	109	96.52	12.48	155.7504
110	93	102.53	−9.53	90.8209
104	108	100.27	7.73	59.7529
93	116	96.14	19.86	394.4196
101	94	99.15	−5.15	26.5225
97	95	97.64	−2.64	6.9696
117	102	105.15	−3.15	9.9225
101	92	99.15	−7.15	51.1225
118	98	105.53	−7.53	56.7009

$\overline{X} = 100.43$ $\overline{Y} = 98.93$ $\overline{Y'} = 98.93$ $\Sigma = 4885.4813$

$s_X = 13.42$ $s_Y = 13.92$ $s_{Y'} = 5.04$

$r = +.362$

$$\text{Regression equation } Y' = r\frac{s_Y}{s_X}(X) + \left[\overline{Y} - r\frac{s_Y}{s_X}(\overline{X})\right]$$

$$= .362\frac{13.92}{13.42}(X) + \left[98.93 - .362\frac{13.92}{13.42}(100.43)\right]$$

$$= .3755X + 61.22$$

the squared deviation scores, and we can now compute the standard error of the estimate as an indicator of the accuracy of our predictions:

$$\text{Standard error of the estimate (example 2)} = s_{est} = \sqrt{\frac{\Sigma(Y - Y')^2}{N - 1}}$$

$$s_{est} = \sqrt{\frac{4885.4813}{30 - 1}}$$

$$s_{est} = \sqrt{168.46487}$$

$$s_{est} = 12.979402$$

$$s_{est} \approx 12.98$$

Therefore, we can conclude that our estimate of the child's IQ score based on the parent's IQ score will be "off" by an average of almost 13 IQ points. Therefore, these predictions will be less accurate than the predictions made for twins since this standard error of the estimate is *larger* than in our first example, in which we could predict the twin's IQ to within approximately 10 points, on average.

Now let's consider the third example (presented in Table 9-3), where the correlation between the IQ scores for 30 pairs of step-siblings was +0.1532 and the regression equation was found to be:

$$Y' = .194X + 75.04$$

After using this formula to make a prediction for child 2 in each pair of step-siblings and then calculating the difference between these predicted scores and the children's actual IQ scores, the standard error of the estimate comes out to be:

$$\text{Standard error of the estimate (example 3)} = s_{est} = \sqrt{\frac{\Sigma(Y - Y')^2}{N - 1}}$$

$$s_{est} = \sqrt{\frac{9663.8728}{30 - 1}}$$

$$s_{est} = \sqrt{333.23699}$$

$$s_{est} = 18.25478$$

$$s_{est} \approx 18.25$$

Therefore, we can conclude that our estimate of a child's IQ score based on a step-sibling's IQ score will be "off" by an average of more than 18 IQ points. This standard error of the estimate is larger than both of the previous examples, and therefore, these estimates are the most inaccurate overall.

What accounts for the difference in the accuracy of these three regression analyses? The *magnitude of the correlation* between the pairs of IQ scores. In the first example, the correlation between the twins' IQ scores was +.675, which is higher in mag-

TABLE 9.3		Example 3: Hypothetical IQ Scores for Pairs of Step-Siblings		
X (Child 1)	Y (Child 2)	Y' (Child 3)	(Y − Y')	(Y − Y')²
99	114	94.25	19.75	390.0625
100	90	94.44	−4.44	19.7136
103	83	95.02	−12.02	144.4804
78	70	90.17	−20.17	406.8289
115	109	97.35	11.65	135.7225
107	110	95.80	14.20	201.6400
121	88	98.52	−10.52	110.6704
86	98	91.73	6.27	39.3129
120	79	98.32	−19.32	373.2624
108	107	95.99	11.01	121.2201
114	99	97.16	1.84	3.3856
93	104	93.08	10.92	119.2464
104	81	95.22	−14.22	202.2084
109	75	96.19	−21.19	449.0161
81	108	90.76	17.24	297.2176
128	96	99.88	−3.88	15.0544
130	147	100.26	46.74	2184.6276
113	80	96.96	−16.96	287.6416
112	94	96.77	−2.77	7.6729
85	91	91.53	−0.53	0.2809
116	107	97.55	9.45	89.3025
114	62	97.16	−35.16	1236.2256
89	72	92.31	−20.31	412.4961
97	72	93.86	−21.86	477.8596
114	97	97.16	−0.16	0.0256
114	100	97.16	2.84	8.0656
89	76	92.31	−16.31	266.0161
107	121	95.80	25.20	635.0400
77	119	89.98	29.02	842.1604
89	106	92.31	13.69	187.4161

$\overline{X} = 103.73$ $\overline{Y} = 95.17$ $\overline{Y'} = 95.17$ $\Sigma = 9663.8728$
$s_X = 14.586$ $s_Y = 18.473$ $s_{Y'} = 2.83$
$r = +.1532$

$$\text{Regression equation } Y' = r\frac{s_Y}{s_X}(X) + \left[\overline{Y} - r\frac{s_Y}{s_X}(\overline{X})\right]$$

$$= .1532\frac{18.473}{14.586}(X) + \left[95.17 - .1532\frac{18.473}{14.586}(103.73)\right]$$

$$= .194X + 75.04$$

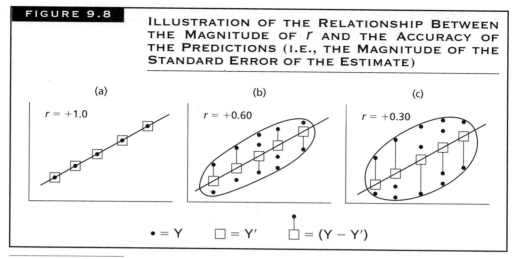

FIGURE 9.8

ILLUSTRATION OF THE RELATIONSHIP BETWEEN THE MAGNITUDE OF *r* AND THE ACCURACY OF THE PREDICTIONS (I.E., THE MAGNITUDE OF THE STANDARD ERROR OF THE ESTIMATE)

Note: As *r* decreases, the values of (Y − Y′) tend to increase.

nitude than the correlation of +.362 between the parents and children in the second example, and therefore, the predictions for the twins were more accurate, on average, than those based on parental IQ (s_{est} = 9.68 for the twins versus s_{est} = 12.98 for the parent-child pairs). The correlation between the step-siblings was the weakest of all three examples, at +.153, and the predictions we made were the most inaccurate, being more than 18 points off, on average (s_{est} = 18.25). Basically, the general rule of regression analysis is that *as the correlation between X and Y becomes stronger, the predictions will be more and more accurate.* That is, as the correlation coefficient increases in magnitude, the values of Y′ will get closer and closer to the actual value of Y (and, consequently, the standard error of the estimate will be decreased). When there is a *perfect linear correlation* between X and Y (so Pearson *r* = ±1.0), the predictions will be perfectly accurate: Y′ will be exactly equal to Y in every case and the standard error of the estimate will be equal to 0. The scatterplots in Figure 9-8 illustrate this principle.

In contrast to perfect correlations, when there is *no correlation* between X and Y (so Pearson *r* = 0.0), the regression formula for Y′ is reduced to:

$$Y' = r\frac{s_Y}{s_X}(X) + \left[\overline{Y} - r\frac{s_Y}{s_X}(\overline{X})\right]$$

$$Y' = 0.0\frac{s_Y}{s_X}(X) + \left[\overline{Y} - 0.0\frac{s_Y}{s_X}(\overline{X})\right]$$

$$Y' = 0.0(X) + [\overline{Y} - 0.0(\overline{X})]$$

$$Y' = 0.0 + (\overline{Y} - 0.0)$$

$$Y' = \overline{Y}$$

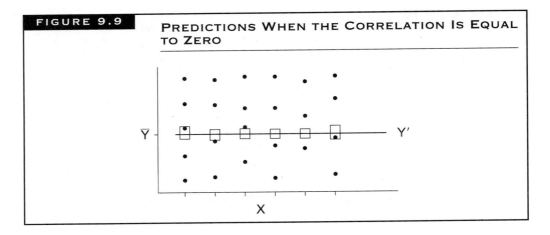

FIGURE 9.9   PREDICTIONS WHEN THE CORRELATION IS EQUAL TO ZERO

Thus, when X and Y are uncorrelated, we end up predicting that every person will be average on Y. Thus, using an uncorrelated X as a predictor variable does not improve the accuracy of our predictions of Y at all, and our predictions are the same as if we had never measured the predictor variable (X) in the first place (see Figure 9-9).

Remember, that when we have *no information* about an individual, our "best guess" is to assume that the individual is average for the population. And while it is true that the concept "best guess" implies that the amount of error in the prediction is *minimized* given the available information, it does not imply that the amount of error is *minimal* (or small). The average error in the predictions when the correlation equals 0.0 (or when we have no predictor variable at all) turns out to be equal to the standard deviation of the Y scores. We can see this by comparing the formulas for the standard deviation of Y to the standard error of the estimate:

$$\text{standard deviation of Y} = s_Y = \sqrt{\frac{\Sigma(Y - \overline{Y})^2}{N - 1}}$$

$$\text{standard error of the estimate} = s_{est} = \sqrt{\frac{\Sigma(Y - Y')^2}{N - 1}}$$

The formulas are identical if Y' is equal to $\overline{Y}$, as it is when Pearson $r = 0.0$. Thus, when there is no correlation between X and Y, the average error in our predictions of Y' will be the same as the average difference between actual Y scores and $\overline{Y}$ (i.e., the standard deviation of Y for the entire sample).

The standard error gives us a rough way of estimating how much more accurate our predictions are when we use the predictor variable (X) in a regression analysis. By comparing the standard error of the estimate to the standard deviation of Y, we can gain some appreciation for how much closer, on average, our predictions are to the actual scores. Look back at the three examples where we predicted IQ scores for family members. For the first example, the standard error of the estimate (s_{est}) was equal to 9.68 and the standard deviation of Y was equal to 13.12 (see Table 9-1). Thus, by using variable X, which had a moderate-to-strong correlation with Y, we reduced the average error in our predictions from 13.12 to 9.68. In the second example, where the correlation was a moderate +.362, we reduced the average error in our predictions from 13.92 (the standard deviation of Y—see Table 9-2) to 12.97 (the standard error of the estimate: s_{est}). Finally, in the third example, where the correlation was a weak +.153, the regression analysis reduced the average error in our predictions only from 18.473 to 18.255—less than one-quarter of an IQ point. Thus, these examples clearly show how the magnitude of the correlation between the predictor variable (X) and the criterion variable (Y) strongly impacts the accuracy of the predictions of Y': As the magnitude of the correlation increases, the accuracy of the predictions also increases. In fact, the relationship between the correlation coefficient and the standard error is so strong that we can compute s_{est} directly from the standard deviation of Y (s_Y) and the correlation. That is, there is a short-cut we can use to measure the accuracy of our predictions.

A Short-Cut for Computing the Standard Error of the Estimate

The formula presented earlier for the standard error of the estimate is a definitional formula, which shows us what the statistic actually measures: the "average difference" between Y and Y'. But instead of having to compute Y' and Y – Y' for each participant, there is a computational formula for the standard error of the estimate that which is very easy to use:

$$\text{Standard error of the estimate} = s_{est} = s_Y\sqrt{1 - r^2}$$

That is, if we know the standard deviation of the actual scores on Y and the correlation between X and Y, we can calculate the standard error of the estimate. Let's use this formula on each of the three sets of IQ data. For the data in Table 9-1, which looked at the relationship between the IQ scores for same-sex fraternal twins, the correlation was equal to +.675 and the standard deviation of the Y-scores (i.e., the IQ scores for the second twin) was equal to 13.12. Therefore:

$$s_{est} = 13.12\sqrt{1 - .675^2}$$
$$= 13.12\sqrt{1 - .455625}$$
$$= 13.12\sqrt{.544375}$$
$$= 13.12(.7378177)$$
$$= 9.6801682$$
$$\approx 9.68$$

which is the same value we computed using the definitional formula in example 1

And for the data in Table 9-2, which looked at the correlation between the IQs of parents and children, the correlation was .362 and the standard deviation of Y was 13.92:

$$s_{est} = 13.92\sqrt{1 - .362^2}$$
$$= 13.92\sqrt{1 - .131044}$$
$$= 13.92\sqrt{.868956}$$
$$= 13.92(.932178)$$
$$= 12.975917$$
$$\approx 12.98$$

which is the same value we computed using the definitional formula in example 2

And, finally, for the data in Table 9-3, which examined the correlation between the IQ scores for step-siblings, where r = .1532 and s_Y = 18.473:

$$s_{est} = 18.473\sqrt{1 - .1532^2}$$
$$= 18.473\sqrt{1 - .0234702}$$
$$= 18.473\sqrt{.9765298}$$
$$= 18.473(.9881952)$$
$$= 18.254929$$
$$\approx 18.25$$

which is the same value we computed using the definitional formula in example 3

Obviously, this computational formula is much easier to use when performing the computations by hand!

z-Scores and Regression Analysis

Let's suppose that performance in high-school math classes is positively correlated with performance on the quantitative section of the Scholastic Aptitude Test (SAT). We would therefore expect students with above-average math grades to have above-average SAT scores, but just how much above average would we predict the SAT scores to be? Recall from Chapter 5 that we can measure how far an individual's score is from the group average by converting the score into a z-score, which measures the difference between scores and $\overline{X}$ in standard deviation units. (That is, if a score is one standard deviation above the mean, it has a z-score of 1; if the score is equal to the mean, it has a z-score of 0, etc.) So if a student's math grades are 2 standard deviations above average (z = +2.0), how many standard deviations above average should we expect him to be on the SATs? It depends on the *magnitude of the correlation* between grades in math classes and SAT scores. If the two variables are perfectly correlated, we would predict that the z-scores for both variables would be equal: If a student scores 2 standard deviations above average in math classes, he also scores 2 standard deviations above average on the SATs ($z_{Math} = z_{SAT} = +2.0$). If the correlation is less than perfect, however, we know that there will be some error in our predictions, so we will try to minimize the error by predicting that the SAT scores will be closer to average than the math grades may be. So if the correlation is strong (e.g., r = +.7), and the student's math grades are 2 standard deviations above average ($z_{Math} = +2.0$), we will predict that the student will score well above average on the SAT, but not quite as far above average as 2 standard deviations. If the correlation is weak or moderate, we will still expect that high math grades will predict above-average SAT scores, but we will be much more cautious in our predictions and stay closer to the mean SAT score. The relationship between correlation coefficients and z-scores is expressed in the following formula, which is an alternate version of the Regression Equation:

$$z_{Y'} = r\, z_X$$

The first step in this "z-score regression" procedure is to convert the scores on X (the predictor variable) to z-scores:

$$z_X = \frac{X - \overline{X}}{s_X}$$

Next, for a particular value of X, we enter the z-score (z_X) into the regression equation above where we multiply it by the correlation coefficient. This gives us the predicted value of z for the criterion variable (Y), which must then be converted into a value of Y'. The z-score formula for Y' is:

$$z_{Y'} = \frac{Y' - \overline{Y}}{s_Y}$$

In order to find the Y' with a given value of z, we use the following "z-to-Y' conversion" formula:

$$Y' = z_{Y'}(s_Y) + \overline{Y}$$

This regression equation produces the same values of Y' as the original formula presented earlier. For example, in Example 1, the Y' for the first pair of twins was found to be equal to 110.80 (see the first value in the third column of Table 9-1). Now let's use the z-score version of the regression equation for the same pair of IQ scores. From the data in Table 9-1, we know that r = +.675, $\overline{X} = 98.47$, $s_X = 14.74$, $\overline{Y} = 100.27$, and $s_Y = 13.12$.

The first step is to compute the z-score for the predictor variable (which is the first twin's IQ score). For the first pair of twins in the data list, the first twin's IQ score is 116, Therefore:

$$z_X = \frac{X - \overline{X}}{s_X}$$

$$= \frac{116 - 98.47}{14.74}$$

$$= \frac{17.53}{14.74}$$

$$= 1.1892808$$

(Thus, the first twin's IQ score of 116 is 1.19 standard deviations above the mean.)

Next, we use the regression equation to find the predicted z-score for the second twin:

$$\text{Regression equation: } z_{Y'} = rz_X$$

$$= (.675)(1.1892808)$$

$$= .8027645$$

Thus, the fraternal twin of a child with an IQ score of 116 (which is 1.19 standard deviations above the group average of 98.47) is expected to be .80 standard deviations above the group mean. What, then, is the second twin's expected IQ score? We apply the conversion formula:

$$\text{Conversion to } Y' \text{: } Y' = z_{Y'}(s_Y) + \overline{Y}$$

$$= .8027645(13.12) + 100.27$$

$$= 10.53227 + 100.27$$

$$= 110.80227$$

$$\approx 110.80$$

Thus, the fraternal twin of a child with an IQ score of 116 is expected to have an IQ score of 110.80—and this is the same value of Y' that was obtained using the original regression equation, as indicated in the third column of Table 9-1.

Coefficient of Determination

A statistic of interest in both correlational studies and simple regression analysis is the **coefficient of determination,** which is the proportion of the variation in Y-scores that is accounted for (or explained) by variation in the predictor variable—that is, how much of the changes in Y systematically "go with" changes in X. To make sense of this statistic, let's go back to the basic concepts of correlation and variance.

Recall that a correlation exists when variation in Y is systematically associated with variation in X. The strongest possible relationship—a perfect correlation—is one in which *every* change in Y is associated with a consistent change in X. In less-than-perfect correlations, however, there are cases where Y changes but X does not, or X changes in the wrong direction, and so forth. That is, there is change in Y that is not systematically related to X. Thus, we can conceptually break the total variability of Y into two components: (1) the variability that is associated with changes in X (which is sometimes called the "explained" or "predicted" variance), and (2) the variability that is not associated with changes in X (the "error" or "unexplained" variance). These two components add up to the total variability in the Y scores:

Total variance of Y = explained variance + error (unexplained) variance

The explained variance can be computed by performing a regression analysis, computing Y′ for every value of X, and then calculating the variance of these predicted scores ($s_{Y'}^2$). The variance of Y′ is the explained variance because the correlation between Y′ and X is perfect: Every unique value of X has its own unique value of Y′, and when X remains the same, so does Y′. Thus, the variation in the predicted values of Y′ is totally accounted for by changes in X.

The "error" variance refers to those changes in Y that are not accounted for by a change in X (such as when the change in Y is larger or smaller than would be expected based on the amount of change in X). This error variance is seen in the difference between Y and Y′ (i.e., the error in our prediction scores), and it is measured by the squaring the standard error of the estimate (s_{est}^2). Therefore, the total variance in Y can be expressed like this:

$$s_Y^2 = s_{Y'}^2 + s_{est}^2$$

The coefficient of determination, as stated above, tells us the proportion of Y-variability that is explained by variation in X, and the definitional formula is:

$$\text{Coefficient of Determination} = \frac{\text{explained variance}}{\text{total Y variance}} = \frac{s_{Y'}^2}{s_Y^2}$$

This formula requires us to perform the regression analysis and compute Y′ and (Y − Y′) for every individual in order to calculate the variance components. Look back at the regression analysis presented in Table 9-2 where we have already computed Y′ for every parent-child pair. The values of Y′, their mean ($\overline{Y}' = 98.93$), and their standard deviation ($s_{Y'} = 5.04$) are presented in the third column. We can compute the explained variance by finding the square of the standard deviation of Y′, and we can compute the total variance by squaring the standard deviation of the actual Y scores (from column 2):

$$\text{explained variance:} \quad s_{Y'}^2 = 5.04^2 = 25.4016$$
$$\text{total variance of Y:} \quad s_Y^2 = 13.92^2 = 193.7664$$

Therefore, the coefficient of determination is:

$$\text{coefficient of determination} = \frac{\text{explained variance}}{\text{total variance}}$$
$$= \frac{25.4016}{193.7664} = 0.13109$$

This coefficient of determination, expressed as a percentage, tells us that 13.1% of the differences among children in IQ are accounted for by differences in their parents' IQ. The remaining 86.9% of the differences among children are not explained by the variation in parental IQ. This *unexplained* variation in Y is known as the **coefficient of non-determination** or the coefficient of alienation. It is equal to:

$$\text{coefficient of nondetermination} = \frac{\text{error variance}}{\text{total variance}} = \frac{s_{est}^2}{s_Y^2}$$

The complexity of the process involved in computing $s_{Y'}^2$ and s_{est}^2 may discourage new researchers from computing the coefficients of determination and non-determination, even though knowing the proportion (or percentage) of the criterion variable explained by the predictor variable can be very useful for researchers and public policy planners. Fortunately, there is a short-cut we can use to calculate these coefficients:

$$\text{coefficient of determination} = r^2$$
$$\text{coefficient of non-determination} = 1 - r^2$$

When we apply the short-cut formulas to the data in Table 9-2, we find the same answers (except for rounding error):

$$\text{coefficient of determination} = r^2 = +.362^2 = .13104 \text{ (or 13.1\%)}$$
$$\text{coefficient of non-determination} = 1 - r^2 = 1 - .13104 = .86896 \text{ (or 86.9\%)}$$

Before moving onto the next topic, we need to make a very important point about how the coefficient of determination is reported. Statisticians commonly use phrases such as "X accounted for 21% of Y" or "33% of Y is explained by changes in X" when they describe the r^2 from correlational or regression analyses, however, students must realize that these phrases are **not** meant to imply that the data demonstrate a causal relationship between X and Y. Instead, the phrases refer only to the systematic covariation between the scores on X and Y, and it is understood that this covariation could be the result of a spurious relationship driven by a third variable. As always, correlational data do not allow us to draw causal conclusions.

Using Venn Diagrams to Illustrate r^2

A **Venn diagram** is a type of graph that is commonly used to visually represent correlations and the coefficient of determination. In the Venn diagrams in Figure 9-10, one circle represents the criterion variable Y (e.g., popularity), and the other circle represents a predictor variable X (e.g., the Social-Problem-Solving Task scores or parents' educational level). The correlation between X and Y and the coefficient of determination are represented by the *overlap* between the circles. If two variables are uncorrelated, the circles do not overlap at all, indicating that *none* of the variability in Y is accounted for by variation in X (both r and r^2 = 0.0). As the magnitude of the correlation increases, the overlapping region increases in size. The proportion of the Y-circle that overlaps with X is meant to approximate the coefficient of determination. For example, in Figure 9-10a, which corresponds to our popularity/social skills example, the correlation between X and Y is 0.60 (so r^2 = .36, indicating that 36% of the differences in popularity is explained by differences in Social-Problem-Solving Task scores), and therefore, approximately 36% of the Y-circle overlaps with the X-circle. In contrast, Figure 9-10b illustrates a situation where the correlation between the variables is only about 0.20 (so r^2 = .04), so that only about 4% of the Y-circle overlaps with the X-circle.

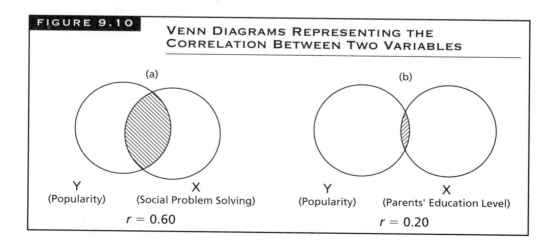

FIGURE 9.10 VENN DIAGRAMS REPRESENTING THE CORRELATION BETWEEN TWO VARIABLES

(a)

Y (Popularity)   X (Social Problem Solving)
r = 0.60

(b)

Y (Popularity)   X (Parents' Education Level)
r = 0.20

The Basic Concepts of Multiple Regression

We began our discussion of simple regression with the example of a kindergarten teacher who wanted to be able to predict how popular children would be by the end of the school year. We saw how the teacher's predictions would become more accurate if she knew how the children performed on a Social-Problem-Solving Task because popularity is correlated with the ability to think of solutions to social dilemmas. We went on to discuss how we could determine the proportion of the variance in popularity that is explained by differences in SPST scores by computing the coefficient of determination.

Now, however, consider a situation in which the teacher has access to lots of different information about each child, such as the parents' socioeconomic status and educational levels, the number of siblings in the household and their ages, the type of preschool experience the children had and their age when they started daycare, ratings of their aggressiveness and shyness at age 3, and measures of their physical characteristics (such as attractiveness and weight). Each of these variables can be the predictor variable (X) in a simple regression analysis, and to the extent that they correlate with popularity, they may improve the teacher's predictions of popularity (compared with having no information at all, where every child would be expected to be average). The teacher could also compute the coefficient of determination for each of these predictor variables and find out which of them explain the most variability in popularity.

Even better, all of these predictor variables can be regressed against popularity *simultaneously* in a process known as **multiple regression**.[2] Multiple regression combines several predictor variables into a single regression equation that follows the general form:

$$Y' = \text{constant} + b_1 X_1 + b_2 X_2 + b_3 X_3 + b_4 X_4 + \ldots$$

where b is the "partial regression weight" for a predictor variable, which essentially measures the *unique* contribution of a given X to the overall prediction of Y.

This equation generates predicted values of Y' that are the *linear combination* of the predictor variables, and this equation is the "best-fitting" equation because the values of Y' form a regression plane which provides the best fit through the multidimensional space by minimizing the differences between the actual Y scores and the predicted values of Y'. The correlation between these predicted values of Y' and the actual values of Y is known as R, and higher values of R indicate greater accuracy in the predictions. The coefficient of determination for multiple regression (R^2) then tells us what proportion of the total variation in Y has been accounted for by the linear combination of the predictor variables.

---

[2]While the computations of multiple regression are well beyond the scope of this text, we have found that a general understanding of the basic *concept* of multiple regression can be useful to students who are reading research reports or conducting their own research.

Several strategies can be used in multiple regression. One strategy, which is called standard regression, includes *all* available predictor variables in the model (or the equation), even those that explain very small amounts of the variability. This strategy is not commonly used by researchers, most of whom instead use multiple regression to identify a *limited set* of predictor variables that maximizes the accuracy of the predictions of the criterion variable (Y). In other words, most researchers want to identify the simplest possible predictive model, which is a regression equation that *accounts for the most variability with the fewest number of predictor variables.* Several strategies are available to these researchers, including forward selection, backward selection, stepwise regression, or hierarchical regression. While these strategies differ in some important ways mathematically, their regression equations share the same basic rule: To be included in the final model, a predictor variable must *significantly increase* R^2 and the accuracy of the predictions. That is, predictors must explain a significant amount of variation that is not already accounted for by the other predictors in the regression equation. The concepts of multiple regression can be illustrated using Venn diagrams.

Using Venn Diagrams to Illustrate Multiple Regression and R^2

As we illustrated earlier, Venn diagrams are visual displays of correlations between pairs of variables, and they can be used to show the proportion of variability in Y that is accounted for by variation in the predictor variable (i.e., the coefficient of determination, r^2). Similarly, in multiple regression, Venn diagrams can be used to illustrate the proportion of Y-variance that is accounted for by the linear combination of the predictor variables (R^2) by having the predictor variables overlap the Y-circle: The amount of overlap represents R^2. A Venn diagram can represent the *unique contributions* of each predictor (referred to as r^2_{unique}) as well as the proportion of variation that is explained by the *combination of the predictors* ($r^2_{combined}$). The total R^2 is equal to the sum of these components. This is illustrated in Figure 9-11, which shows the unique contributions of three predictor variables and the contribution made by the linear combination of the predictors. The total R^2 is represented by the total area of Y that overlaps with the predictors.

Let's suppose that our kindergarten teacher has three pieces of information about each child in the new class and wants to predict the children's future popularity using these three predictor variables. The basic question addressed with multiple regression is: "What is the optimum combination of predictor variables that explains the most variability in Y?" Essentially, there are four possible answers: (a) None of the predictor variables, alone or in combination, significantly improves the accuracy of our predictions of Y; (b) only one of the predictors accounts for a significant proportion of the variance, and adding the others does not improve our ability to predict Y; (c) a combination of two of the predictors accounts for significantly more variance than any single predictor, but adding the third predictor does not significantly improve our predictions; or (d) a combination of all three predictor variables explains significantly more variance than any single predictor alone or any combination of two predictors. Which of these patterns emerges depends on the correlations between Y and each of

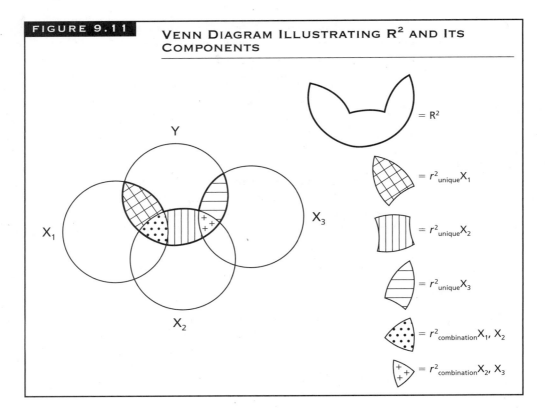

FIGURE 9.11 VENN DIAGRAM ILLUSTRATING R^2 AND ITS COMPONENTS

the predictors and on the correlations among the predictor variables themselves. Let's look at an illustration of each of these possibilities.

Suppose the kindergarten teacher knows how tall each child is (X_1), how much each child weighed at birth (X_2), and how old each child was when he or she learned to walk (X_3). Will these three factors increase the accuracy of the teacher's predictions of how many classmates label a child as "nice?" No, probably not, since these three variables have little or no correlation with popularity. Figure 9-12a presents a Venn diagram illustrating the most likely outcome for this case: None of the three variables (alone or in combination) accounts for a significant portion of the variation in Y. (Note that the diagram indicates that the three predictor variables correlate only slightly with one another, as illustrated by the small amount of overlap among the circles.)

Now let's suppose that the three pieces of information available to the teacher were the children's height (X_1), birthweight (X_2), and Social-Problem-Solving Task score (X_3). Since the SPST scores correlate quite strongly with popularity ($r = +0.60$), this predictor variable will account for a significant portion of the variation

FIGURE 9.12 VENN DIAGRAMS ILLUSTRATING FOUR POSSIBLE OUTCOME PATTERNS

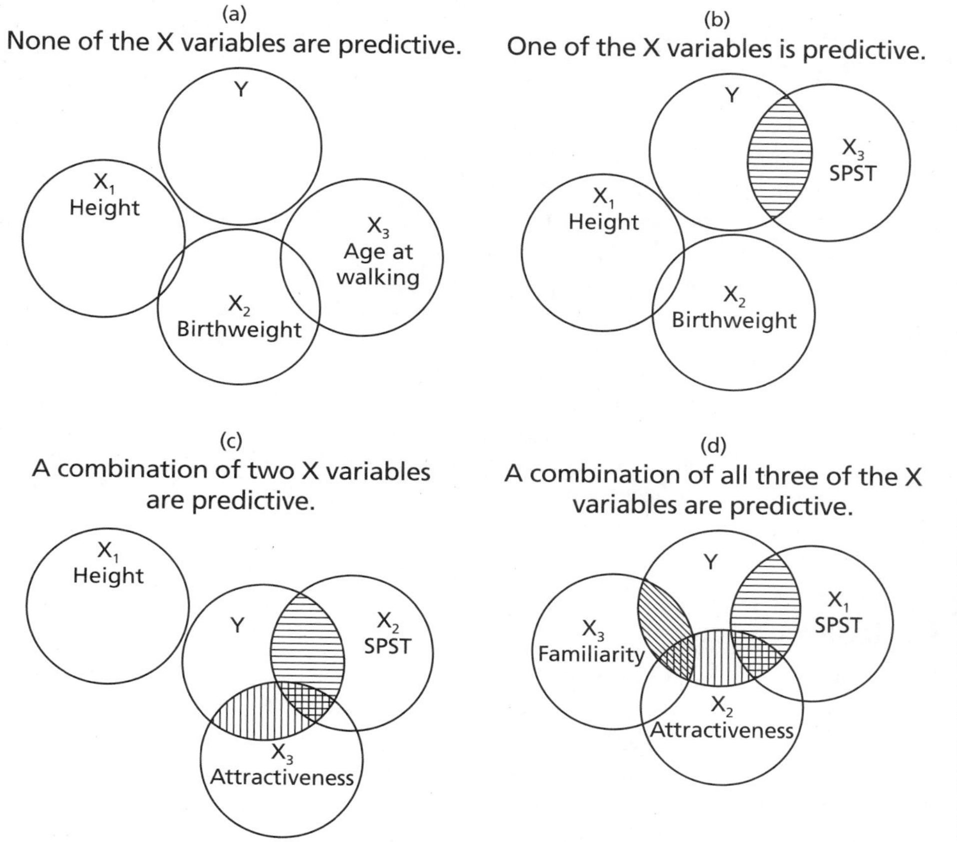

(a) None of the X variables are predictive.

(b) One of the X variables is predictive.

(c) A combination of two X variables are predictive.

(d) A combination of all three of the X variables are predictive.

in Y, while the other two variables, which do not correlate with popularity, will not add anything to the prediction of Y. This situation is illustrated in Figure 9-12b, which also indicates that the three predictor variables are essentially unrelated to one another.

Figure 9-12c illustrates the third possible outcome pattern, where two predictor variables, in combination, account for significantly more variance than either does alone. This would probably be the case if the predictor variables were height (X_1), SPST score (X_2), and the child's physical attractiveness (X_3). Research has demonstrated that "cute" children are more popular with their peers, even as young as age 5, so the correlation between attractiveness and popularity will be significant. (For this example, let's assume the correlation is equal to $+0.40$.) Thus, two of the predictor variables can potentially predict significant proportions of variation in Y. *As long as SPST scores and attractiveness are* not *strongly correlated with each other* (which is assumed in Figure 9-12c), the combination of the two factors will significantly increase R^2.

The fourth possible outcome of a multiple regression analysis with three predictor variables is where all three predictor variables are correlated with Y and the addition of each of the three factors to the model (i.e., the regression equation) significantly increases the proportion of Y-variance that is accounted for. Suppose the teacher's three predictor variables included the Social-Problem-Solving Task scores (X_1), physical attractiveness (X_2), and how many of the children in the class were familiar to the child even before school began (X_3). Familiarity may predict popularity since children are more likely to interact with familiar peers than with strangers, and such interaction may lead to more positive attitudes toward familiar peers. Figure 9-12d illustrates a situation where, despite some correlation between the predictors, they each have some substantial overlap with the Y-circle that is unique. Therefore, a regression equation that includes all three predictors will account for significantly more variance than an equation based on only one or two of the predictors.

Multicollinearity

In each of these examples, we carefully avoided the situation where the predictor variables are highly correlated with one another (a situation known as **multicollinearity**) because when there is a strong correlation between the predictors, the reliability of the regression analysis may be compromised. For example, suppose the kindergarten teacher's predictor variables were the Social-Problem-Solving Task scores (X_1) and the number of years the children had attended a group daycare facility before beginning kindergarten (X_2). Each of these factors is likely to be correlated with popularity, and therefore, in simple regression analyses, they would each significantly improve our predictions (compared with having no predictor variables at all). Figure 9-13 illustrates these simple regressions (using correlation coefficients of $+0.60$ and $+0.59$ for X_1 and X_2, respectively).

However, because attending a group daycare facility gives preschool children the opportunity to encounter many social dilemmas and to practice reaching solutions to those problems, these two predictor variables are also likely to be strongly correlated to each other. Consequently, the variation in popularity that is associated with the ability to solve social problems (SPST scores) may be equally well explained by the differences in years of daycare experience: The two variables are explaining the *same* variance rather than accounting for unique portions of the variability. This is the problem of multicollinearity: Once one of the correlated predictor variables is

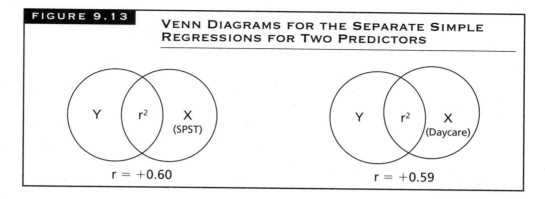

FIGURE 9.13 VENN DIAGRAMS FOR THE SEPARATE SIMPLE REGRESSIONS FOR TWO PREDICTORS

entered into the regression equation, the other predictor factor does not add anything new to R^2. So, despite the high correlation between X_2 and Y, X_2 does *not* improve our ability to predict Y if we are already using X_1 as a predictor. This example of multicollinearity is illustrated in Figure 9-14. There is large degree of overlap between X_1 and X_2, and once the proportion of Y-variance accounted for by X_1 has been identified (and shaded in on the Venn diagram), the additional Y-variance accounted for by X_2 (i.e., r^2_{unique}) is negligible.

Due to multicollinearity, this multiple regression analysis would lead to the conclusion that the ability to solve social dilemmas is the *only* significant predictor. Obviously, this conclusion is highly questionable, as demonstrated by a comparison of the simple r^2s: the SPST scores (X_1) account for 36% of the variance (since $r = +0.60$), while daycare experience (X_2) accounts for almost 35% of the variance (since $r = +0.59$). For all *practical purposes*, it would seem that the two variables are equally good predictors. ●

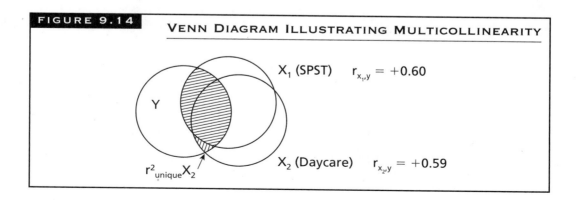

FIGURE 9.14 VENN DIAGRAM ILLUSTRATING MULTICOLLINEARITY

Multicollinearity actually poses a severe threat to the *reliability* (or consistency) of multiple regression analysis because most of the common multiple regression strategies use the absolute value of r to determine which variables are either entered into the equation first (the highest r) or removed from the equation first (the lowest r). In our example, since $+0.60$ is technically larger than $+0.59$, the SPST scores are going to "win" the race against the daycare experience variable. But this slight difference may be due to sampling error. For instance, another kindergarten class (or a different random sample of children from the same class) may have a correlation of $+0.61$ between daycare experience and popularity (instead of $+0.59$) and a correlation of $+0.58$ between SPST scores and popularity (instead of $+0.60$). Since 0.61 is greater than 0.58, daycare experience would enter the equation first, which would lead us to the conclusion that *daycare experience* is the "only significant predictor" of popularity. When two random samples could lead to such different conclusions, the results of the multiple regression analyses must be considered *unreliable*. Consequently, researchers must take the time to examine the pattern of correlations among the predictor variables, looking for evidence of multicollinearity; otherwise, the conclusions they draw from multiple regression can be very misleading.

Exercises

1. An aircraft designer is trying to improve the safety of the plane by giving pilots enough time to shut down the fuel line before an engine fire starts. One of the variables the designer has been testing is the volume (decibel level) of the warning horn. The reaction time (Y) of pilots has been measured under a variety of decibel levels (X) from 45dB to 115dB. The results are below. Graph the relationship. Is regression analysis appropriate? Why or why not?

X	Y	X	Y	X	Y
45	2.0	100	1.3	115	2.2
60	1.3	45	1.8	100	1.6
85	1.2	50	1.7	90	1.3
90	1.2	65	1.5	70	0.9
115	2.0	105	1.5	60	1.5
50	1.6	55	1.6	80	0.9
65	1.4	70	1.1	75	1.1
95	1.6	75	0.8	110	2.0
80	0.8	85	0.8	95	1.4
110	1.8	105	1.7	55	1.8

2. A researcher has tested the ability of college students to recognize 50 familiar objects presented very briefly in their peripheral vision. The angle of presentation (X) ranged from 5° left of center to 50° left of center (with a mean of 31.3° and a standard deviation of 14.4). The mean number of ob-

jects correctly identified ($\overline{Y}$) was 14.1 with a standard deviation of 5.2. The correlation was found to be equal to -0.83.

a. What is the formula for the regression line? Draw a graph of the regression line that shows the slope and the intercept.

b. If the objects are presented 12° left of center, how many objects would we expect to be correctly identified? If the objects are presented 39° left of center, how many objects would we expect to be correctly identified?

c. Compute the standard error of the estimate (using the computational formula). Verbally summarize the information provided by s_{est}.

d. What proportion of the variation in object identification can be accounted for by the variation in angle of presentation? Draw a Venn diagram that illustrates the relationship between these variables.

3. A medical researcher recorded the percentage of calories from fat (X) in the diet of 20 middle-aged women and then measured their baseline (resting) heart rate (Y). The results are presented below.

	X	Y		X	Y		X	Y		X	Y
a	20	50	f	30	58	k	10	46	p	43	58
b	30	54	g	36	60	l	50	50	q	50	62
c	60	70	h	58	60	m	40	58	r	40	57
d	15	50	i	18	55	n	26	53	s	54	58
e	46	55	j	32	65	o	12	40	t	24	62

a. Draw a scatterplot of these data. Estimate the magnitude and the direction of the correlation by looking at the graph.

b. Perform a simple regression analysis on these data: Find the regression equation and calculate the predicted value of Y for X = 24 and for X = 46.

c. What value of Y would be predicted for an individual whose z-score (on X) is equal to $+1.3$?

4. Draw Venn diagrams to represent each of the following correlations:

  a. $r = +0.8$ b. $r = +0.4$ c. $r = -0.5$ d. $r = +0.02$

For questions 5–7, use the following correlation matrix (where Y is the criterion variable and X_1 and X_2 are predictor variables):

	Y	X_1	X_2
Y	1.00	—	—
X_1	+.85	1.00	—
X_2	+.75	+.90	1.00

5. Which of the Venn diagrams in Figure 9-A best represents the correlation between Y and X_1?

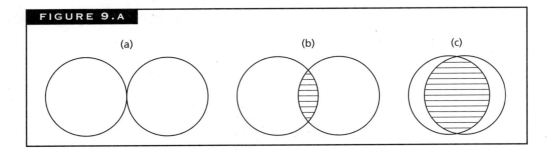

FIGURE 9.A

(a) (b) (c)

6. Does the correlation matrix suggest the possibility of multicollinearity? Explain.

7. Draw a Venn diagram that represents the multiple regression of Y using both predictor variables.

8. Does the amount of time spent surfing the Internet predict the amount of sleep college students get at night? Conduct a correlational study to address this question by surveying at least 20 students and asking them how many minutes they spend on the Internet on a typical weekday (X) and how many hours of sleep they get on a typical night during the week (Y). From the data you collect:

   a. Compute the correlation between X and Y.
   b. Find the regression equation and compute the standard error of the estimate (s_{est}).
   c. Predict the amount of sleep that an individual who spends 45 minutes per day on the Internet would be expected to get.

9. A teacher recorded the number of absences for each student and the number of correct answers each student had on the final exam. The data are below.

Student	Absences	Exam Score
a	3	20
b	5	18
c	6	12
d	2	24
e	1	23
f	4	18
g	3	21
h	2	15
i	7	10
j	5	17

a. Conduct a simple regression analysis, and report the correlation coefficient, the regression equation, and the standard error of the estimate (s_{est}).

b. Using the "original" regression equation, compute Y' for students with 0 absences and 8 absences, and then use the z-score version of the regression equation to predict the exam scores for students with 1 absence and 6 absences.

CHAPTER

10

DESIGNING EXPERIMENTS AND QUASI-EXPERIMENTS

■ ■ ■ ■ ■ ■

In this chapter, you will learn about the basic issues involved in designing an experiment or a quasi-experiment. We discuss the central research questions that can be addressed, the importance of selecting the appropriate variables to answer those questions, and the pros and cons of a variety of design options. You will become familiar with a number of different designs and be able to identify the potential confounds inherent within them.

Look for These Important Terms and Concepts

one-way design
factorial design
two-way factorial design
interactions and main effects
no-treatment control groups
placebo control groups
between-subjects factors
between-subjects designs
within-subjects factors (repeated measures)
within-subjects designs
mixed designs
time-related effects
order effects
demand characteristics
blind procedures

counterbalancing
Latin square
pretest-posttest comparison
differential carryover
matching designs
matched-groups design
matched-pairs design
maturation
history
regression toward the mean
instrumentation
mortality
sensitization
nonreactive measures

Before Reading This Chapter, You May Wish to Review

Chapter 1:
• working hypothesis
• operational definition
• internal validity
Chapter 3:
• experimental control
• causal relationship
• confound
Chapter 6 (and Appendix C):

• power
Chapter 7:
• experiments
• independent, dependent, and controlled variables
• random assignment
• equivalence
• quasi-experiments
• subject variables

The first steps in the research process involve stating the problem and generating hypotheses. If the hypothesis is best stated in the form of a question about *group differences* or *differences between treatments*, the researcher is most likely to adopt an experimental or quasi-experimental research method. You should recall from Chapter 7 that experiments and quasi-experiments are designed to answer questions such as "Is there a difference in performance between participants who receive treatment A and participants who receive treatment B?" The performance (i.e., the dependent variable—DV) is measured for participants under different conditions and the average performance under treatment A is compared to the average performance under treatment B in order to determine whether there is a difference. The treatments or groups being compared constitute the *levels of the independent variable (IV)*. If there *is* a significant difference in performance between the treatments, the researcher concludes that the IV has an effect on the DV.

As you will also recall from Chapter 7, a true experiment requires that the treatment groups be equivalent at the outset of the study. Therefore, when the IV is a *non-subject variable*, and it is possible to randomly assign participants to the treatment conditions, the researcher can conduct an experiment. When the IV is a subject variable, or when random assignment is not possible, the researcher may choose one of the quasi-experimental approaches described in Chapter 7, such as a non-equivalent groups design or a time series design. Quasi-experiments, however, are inherently *confounded* because there are always at least two possible explanations for an observed difference in the dependent variable. (Remember that a confound is created whenever an uncontrolled extraneous variable varies systematically with the levels of the IV.)

For example, suppose a researcher is interested in testing the research question "Do adolescents from divorced families experience more emotional adjustment problems than adolescents from intact families?" The IV would be Family Status, and it would have at least two levels: Divorced versus Intact. The dependent variable would be "emotional adjustment problems" (which would need to be operationally defined). This study would have to be a quasi-experiment since the IV—Family Status—is a subject variable. The adolescent participants would have to be selected from these "pre-existing groups" of interest (i.e., divorced or intact families) instead of being randomly assigned to the conditions, so this study would be an example of a non-equivalent groups design. Without random assignment, we *cannot* presume that all other relevant characteristics are randomly distributed across the conditions, and therefore, we cannot presume that the groups are equivalent. In this case, the adolescents who are from divorced families may differ from adolescents from intact homes in a number of ways, such as socioeconomic status or exposure to parental conflicts, and therefore, any difference between the groups in emotional adjustment problems *cannot* be attributed to the divorce with any degree of certainty. (In fact, as one obvious alternative explanation, it is possible that children with emotional problems cause strain in families, so the divorce may have occurred *after* the children began to display adjustment problems.) Thus, this quasi-experiment is inherently confounded due to nonequivalence (or selection bias). Consequently, no causal conclusions could be drawn from the results from this study.

Having said this, we need to emphasize that the findings from quasi-experiments are important and informative, even if they do not establish causal links between the variables. For instance, it is important to know that adolescents from divorced families are more likely to suffer from emotional adjustment problems because we may be able to enroll them in programs that help them develop effective coping skills before their problems escalate too far—and we can provide these services *without knowing* exactly what causes the emotional adjustment problems. Thus, quasi-experiments help psychologists meet the scientific goals of *description* and *prediction*, which, in turn, can lead to treatments that may *control* behavior (by increasing positive behaviors and decreasing negative behaviors).

One-way Designs

When an experiment or quasi-experiment studies the effect of just *one* independent variable on a dependent variable, it is called a **one-way design.** The researcher selects two or more levels of the IV and compares the average performance of participants under these treatment conditions. The simplest one-way design is a comparison between two groups, as in our example above. The IV was Family Status, and it included only two levels: Divorced versus Intact. This study would allow the researchers to determine whether or not there is a difference in emotional adjustment between these two groups. However, there are more than two possible Family Status conditions, and other status groups may also show emotional adjustment problems. For example, some adolescents are in single-parent homes because a parent has died or their mother was never married. Are adolescents in these families more at risk for emotional adjustment problems, too? If the researcher included *four levels* of Family Status (Divorced vs. Never Married vs. Widowed vs. Intact), the study is still a one-way design because there is only one independent variable: The four groups differ along a single dimension we are calling Family Status.

The benefits of including more than two levels of the independent variable are probably obvious. The four groups of adolescents can be examined to see what kinds (or how many) emotional adjustment problems they have, and then the groups can be compared with one another one at a time to see whether one group of adolescents is at greater risk than other groups. It would be very interesting to know whether children from never-married homes are systematically different from children who experience the breakdown of their family; it would also be very interesting to know whether losing a parent through death is associated with the same emotional problems as when a parent becomes unavailable after a divorce.

Essentially, one-way designs allow us to explore the effects of a single factor. Simple two-group designs answer basic yes-no or either-or questions, such as "Does watching TV violence increase aggressive behavior?" and "Which type of memory task is easier—serial recall or free recall?" The data from these studies are analyzed by simply comparing the average scores from the two groups, using statistics such as Student's *t*, which is presented in Chapter 11. But one-way designs can also be used to explore an independent variable in greater depth by increasing the number of levels of the IV included in the study. The simple yes-no questions of the two-group designs can be expanded to more complex questions, such as: "Do all kinds of TV violence cause increased aggression in viewers?" and the study could compare fistfights, swordfights, gunfights, and bombings to a no-violence condition. The data from these one-way designs are analyzed at two successive levels: First we determine whether the overall difference among the groups is significant, and if it *is* significant (so that the IV has a significant effect overall), we then compare the individual levels of the IV to one another, which will tell us which of the four types of violence lead to more aggression than the no-violence condition, whether fistfights are different from shootings, whether bombings are different from other forms of violence, and so on. Analysis of variance is one of the statistical procedures we can employ when there are more than two treatment conditions in a one-way design (see Chapter 12).

Regardless of the number of levels of the independent variable that are included in the study, one-way designs are still quite limited because they focus only on one IV at a time. Considering the fact that most, if not all, human behaviors are influenced by many different factors simultaneously, the only way for psychologists to fully understand any particular behavior is to study the *joint impact* of these multiple factors. This means that we must design studies that systematically manipulate more than one independent variable. As an illustration, let's return to the question about adolescents' emotional adjustment problems.

The researcher suspects that divorce is related to an adolescent's emotional well-being. Imagine, though, that she *also* suspects that the degree of emotional adjustment problems experienced by adolescents is influenced by whether or not they have a close friend they can turn to when they feel upset or depressed. The researcher might hypothesize, for example, that having a "best friend" or confidant helps adolescents cope with the stresses they face, and therefore, they experience fewer emotional adjustment problems. Now there are *two separate variables* that are suspected of influencing the adolescents' emotional adjustment: "Family Status" and "Having a Best Friend." Although these two hypotheses could be examined in separate one-way design studies, a study that includes both independent variables in the same design will provide *more* information about the effects of divorce and friendship on emotional adjustment than two separate one-way designs. Studies that are designed to compare all combinations of the levels of two or more IVs are known as **factorial designs.** More specifically, in this example, where there are two independent variables (Family Status and Having a Best Friend), the design is a **two-way factorial design.**

Factorial Designs and the Concept of Interaction: "It Depends"

The major advantage of using a factorial design to test the effects of two (or more) IVs on the same dependent variable is that we can examine *how the IVs influence each other.* For example, it is possible that having a best friend in early adolescence might compensate for having parents who are divorced. A true best friend may provide as much social and emotional support to adolescents as does having both parents at home. If this is true, then the difference in emotional adjustment between adolescents from intact families and divorced families will depend on whether the adolescent has a best friend. When one IV's effect on the DV depends on another IV, we say that there is an interaction between the IVs. Obviously, psychologists who want to fully understand the emotional adjustment of adolescents will need to understand how the factors that contribute to emotional adjustment work together, and therefore, they must study the interactions among the variables that influence emotional adjustment. Interactions can be measured only when the study includes the factorial combination of two or more IVs, so let's look more closely at the concept of interaction and issues involved in conducting studies with factorial designs.

Multiple Determinants (or Predictors) of Behavior

Your friend says, as you walk in, "You want the rest of this pepperoni and onion pizza while it's still warm?" How will you reply? If we are to predict your response to that question, it would help to know whether you care for pizza and whether or not you consider yourself a vegetarian. We might also want to know how recently you have eaten, how much, and how you feel about the taste of onions or pepperoni.

The point is that most behaviors are multiply-determined. That is, there is not a single causal factor for the behavior we see. If you say "No, thanks, I'll pass on that one," it might be for any one of several reasons: You're too full (having just finished eating dinner), you don't eat meat, you can't stand onions in your food, or you simply don't like pizza. And these do not exhaust the set of possible determinants—for example, you may have a date in a few minutes with the new love-of-your-life and don't want to have "pizza-with-onion breath." It would not take long to generate even more possible scenarios for why the reply might be "No, thanks."

When psychologists seek to determine the relations among variables, it is important to keep in mind that those relations are not simple one-to-one connections. In correlational research one may find that several other variables can, independently, predict a given behavior. The grade-point-average of members of a college freshman class at the end of that first year may be predictable, to some degree, based on any one of several variables: grades in high school, number of credit hours carried, socioeconomic status of parents, extent to which the student felt he/she "fit in" socially at the college, amount of time spent studying, plus many others. While each variable, by itself, may allow some prediction, a large number of predictor variables, *taken collectively*, may provide much better prediction.[1]

---

[1] There are statistical procedures (e.g., multiple regression analysis, which was introduced in Chapter 9) that can be used to assess the relative strengths of these various sources for prediction, the independence of their contributions to prediction, and the extent of prediction possible from an optimally weighted combination of those predictors. These statistical procedures are beyond the scope of this text, and interested students should ask their instructor for more information or references.

Contingencies Among Determinants: The Essence of Interaction

Suppose that you do like pizza, are not a vegetarian, and do like both pepperoni and onions. With all those variables fixed (remaining constant), then how much you want to eat the pizza your friend has offered may depend on how recently you've eaten: Having recently eaten, you may say, "I don't think so," but having not eaten for many hours, you might reply, "Okay, I'd love it." So far we are describing the effects of something like "level of hunger" on "willingness to eat the pizza." We've seen a simple, lawful relationship: How much you want to eat the pizza depends on how hungry you are. But the extent to which that simple relationship holds true may depend on the current level of another variable: whether or not you are about to go and spend time with the new love of your life. The relationship of hunger to eating behavior may *not* hold in the case where you are about to have that important date but *does* hold when you don't have any expectation of seeing that important someone anytime soon.

Thus, the effect of one independent variable (e.g., hunger level) on the dependent variable (e.g., eating pizza) may depend on the level of *another* variable (e.g., time until you will be with your new love). In such a case we would say that hunger level *interacts* with time-until-seeing-a-loved-one in determining eagerness to eat the pizza such that if it will be a long time, then the hungrier one is, the more eager he/she is to eat, but when it will be a very short time, level of hunger becomes a very poor predictor of how much of the pizza will be eaten. The effect of hunger level on amount eaten is contingent on (depends on) the level of the "time until date" variable.

In general, if we were asked the question: "Does eagerness to eat pizza depend on how hungry the person is?" we would be inclined to answer "yes" since that relationship holds much of the time. The more accurate answer, however, might be "it depends," since under some circumstances (e.g., an imminent date with a new love) the answer may be "no." This is the essence of the concept of interaction: The level of one variable modifies or determines how some other variable affects the behavior of interest. Researchers who want to fully understand the relationship between an IV and a DV will need to look for interactions or the ways that sets of variables have *joint effects* on the behavior in question.

Suppose a researcher is designing a study to look at people's ability to remember a set of unrelated words, and you have agreed to participate. Some participants will be asked to try to remember a list of common (high-frequency) English words, whereas others will try to remember a list of very uncommon (low-frequency) English words. The research question is: Will the number of words that people can remember (DV) differ as a function of frequency of words in the language (IV)? If you are motivated to do well (maybe because you will be paid more for better memory performance), would you rather receive a list of common or uncommon words to study and attempt to remember?

Most people would say they prefer to get the list of common words because they suspect that common words will be easier to remember. However, the more appropriate answer to the question "Which list would you prefer?", as you can guess, would be "it depends." The whole answer might be "it depends; how will memory be tested?" This is the best answer because the effects of word frequency are different depending on whether the memory test is free recall (write down on this blank page as many words from the list as you can recall) or multiple-choice recognition (indicate which of these three words was on the list you studied). In the recall task, most people *will* remember more common than uncommon words; however, if the task was a recognition test where you simply had to pick out the words you studied, performance is typically better for low-frequency words. In this case, one might say "the variable of Word Frequency (high or low) interacts with the variable Type of the Test (free recall versus recognition) in determining amount recalled (DV) such that in a recall test, performance is better for high-frequency words, whereas in a recognition test, performance is better for low-frequency words." This an extreme sort of interaction where the effect of one variable (Word Frequency) is actually *reversed* from one level to another of the second variable (Type of Test). The graph in Figure 10-1 depicts this interaction, which is an example of what is called (for obvious reasons) a cross-over interaction.

From the example above, one might be inclined to conclude that interactions occur only when a change of level of one variable causes a second variable to lose all effects on the behavior or actually reverse its effect. While both those situations do result in clear interactions, one can also have interactions where the effect of one variable is simply to *reduce the magnitude* of the effect of a second variable.

To illustrate an interaction of this kind, consider the following example. Suppose a researcher (Dr. Garcia) was interested in the impact of film editing on the audience's liking of a movie. Dr. Garcia knows that, often, when movies are being shown to certain audiences, some of the scenes are cut, usually those involving off-color language and nudity, and she wanted to know if this makes the audience like the film

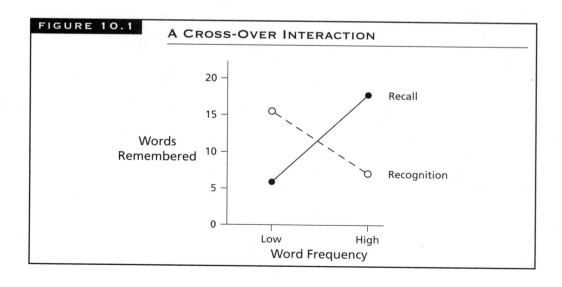

FIGURE 10.1

A CROSS-OVER INTERACTION

better. Furthermore, Dr. Garcia wondered if every audience likes the films to the same degree. Specifically, she wondered if men and women had the same reactions to the film editing. Therefore, she designed a study that would examine the effects of film editing on how much people like the film and determine whether film editing had the same impact on the men and women in the audience. The study had two IVs, each with two levels: Sex (males versus females) and Film Version (cut versus uncut). The factorial combination of these two IVs resulted in four different experimental conditions: men who saw an uncut version, men who saw a cut version, women who saw an uncut version, and women who saw a cut version.

For the study, Dr. Garcia obtained copies of the original and cut versions of a dozen movies, and recruited college students to participate. Each participant saw either the original or the cut version of one of the films, and then filled out a questionnaire that asked them to rate how much they liked the film on a 7-point scale from 1 = "disliked" to 7 = "liked a great deal." Before we present the results of this hypothetical study, we want to make two points about Dr. Garcia's procedure. She used a dozen different movies, because every film is different and cutting footage could have different effects on the plot or continuity of different films. Thus, if her results showed a systematic difference between cut and uncut versions, she could be sure that the effect is generalizable to other films and not limited to one particular film. In contrast, by recruiting college students to participate in the study (probably because they were readily available), Dr. Garcia limited the generalizability of her findings to the population of college students. Even though Dr. Garcia realized that other variables, such as age and education level, might alter the effect of film editing, she did not test these effects in this study.

Now let's consider the results of Dr. Garcia's two-way factorial design. Suppose the mean ratings, as depicted in Figure 10-2, were found to be 6.0 for men who saw originals, 3.0 for men who saw cut versions, 4.1 for women who saw the originals, and 2.9 for women viewing cut versions. You will notice that men and women seemed to like the cut versions equally well (3.0 and 2.9), and both men and women gave higher "liking" ratings to the original versions than cut versions. So it appears that the answer to the question of which version of the films is liked more is clearly "the original," and that cutting a film reduces the audience's liking for the film. But *how much* does cutting reduce liking? The answer to this question, however, is "it depends;" for men the difference in mean ratings of original and cut version was 3.0 (6.0 versus 3.0), whereas for women the difference in mean ratings was only 1.2 (4.1 versus 2.9). The effect of cutting scenes from the movie was to reduce the participants' liking of the films, but this was true *to a greater extent* for men than for women. Because the magnitude of the difference between the two versions of the films is different for the two sexes (3.0 versus 1.2), we would say that "it appears likely that there is an interaction between participant's sex and version of movie in determining the rated liking of the film. The difference in liking for cut versus uncut versions of films is *dependent on* whether one is looking at data for males or data for females: Cutting a film reduces men's ratings of a film more than it reduces women's ratings."

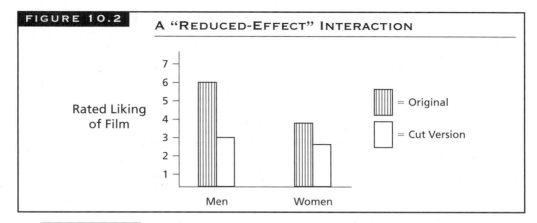

FIGURE 10.2 — A "REDUCED-EFFECT" INTERACTION

Note that the graphs used in Figures 10-1 and 10-2 use different styles. The style used in Figure 10-1, where lines are used to "connect the dots," is appropriate because the variable along the X-axis is a continuous variable (since the frequency of words can increase continuously from low to high), and the line implies that as word frequency increases from low to high, the number of words correctly remembered changes as indicated. In Figure 10-2, however, the variable along the X-axis is a qualitative, categorical variable (men versus women), and there are no "intermediate values" of sex between men and women, so bars are used instead of a continuous line. But if you imagine drawing a line from the top of the men's original-version bar to the top of the women's original-version bar, and then connect the tops of the cut-version bars, you will see that although this is not a cross-over interaction, the lines are not parallel, indicating that there is an interaction.

Terminology and Notation Systems for Factorial Designs

Because interactions represent the way in which the level of one IV alters the effects of a second IV on the measured behavior (DV), they can be explored only in studies where the effects of two or more IVs are being assessed in a single study. If all levels of each IV occur in combination with all levels of any other IV(s), then the research design is referred to as a factorial (or full factorial) design. In the example above, our four research groups represented the factorial combination of the two IVs: each level of one IV (Sex) was combined with every level of the other IV (Film Version). That is, some men saw each type of film and some women saw each type of film. Factorial designs are often labeled using a special *notation system* that uses a string of numbers to tell us how many IVs were included in the study and how many levels each of those IVs had. Each number in the string represents one of the independent variables and the value of the number indicates the number of levels of the IV. For example, a "$2 \times 3 \times 4 \times 2$ factorial design" (which is pronounced: "two by three by four by two") has *four* IVs, as indicated by the fact that the notation string has four numbers. The first IV has two levels, the second IV has three levels, the third IV has four levels, and the last IV has two levels. (Because it has four IVs, this design would be called a *four-way design.*)

Using this notation system, Dr. Garcia's study on the effects of film editing is a *2 × 2 design* (read "two by two"), indicating that there were two IVs and they each had 2 levels. An expanded version of the notation system would include the names of the

IVs in parentheses following the number of levels: "2 (Sex) × 2 (Film Version)." Or it might list the actual levels of the IV in parentheses—especially if the IV does not have an obvious name: "2 (male versus female) × 2 (original versus cut versions)."

In addition to telling us how many IVs were used in a study, this notation system allows us to determine the total number of experimental conditions that complete the full factorial combination of the IVs. By doing the multiplication implied by the notation system, we get the total number of experimental conditions (or treatments or groups) that are included in the factorial design. For example, 2 times 2 equals 4, and as we indicated earlier, Dr. Garcia's 2 × 2 factorial design had 4 experimental groups. A 2 × 3 × 4 × 2 factorial design would have *48* experimental conditions (because *2* times *3* is 6, 6 times *4* is 24, and 24 times *2* is 48). Being able to determine the number of treatment conditions there will be in a factorial design is particularly useful when researchers are planning their studies, because the choice of a specific design may depend on the number of participants available or the number of times you can reasonably test the same group of participants. For example, you may recall from Chapter 6 (or Appendix C) that we need a minimum of 10 participants per group in order to have sufficient power in our analysis, so if we were planning a 2 × 2 factorial design, with 4 experimental groups, we would either need to test each of 10 participants four times or recruit a minimum of 40 participants. If we were planning a four-way design with 48 experimental treatments, our choices range from testing each participant up to 48 times or recruiting a minimum of 480 participants. The advantages and disadvantages of various design options are discussed later in this chapter.

Let's look at another example of the notation system for factorial designs. Suppose we measured the spelling ability of second-, fourth-, and sixth-grade boys and girls, both in the most rural school in a large county and in a school in the urban area, this would be a *three-way design*, which would be called a "2 (Sex) × 3 (Grade Levels) × 2 (Rural versus Urban) factorial design," and data would be gathered for 12 treatment combinations: (1) second-grade boys in the urban school, (2) second-grade boys in the rural school, (3) second-grade girls in the urban school, (4) second-grade girls in the rural school, (5) fourth-grade boys in the urban school, (6) fourth-grade boys in the rural school, (7) fourth-grade girls in the urban school, (8) fourth-grade girls in the rural school, (9) sixth-grade boys in the urban school, (10) sixth-grade boys in the rural school, (11) sixth-grade girls in the urban school, and (12) sixth-grade girls in the rural school. This 2 × 3 × 2 three-way design could be illustrated by drawing a diagram of the design, such as the one below where each box (or "cell") represents one of the factorial combinations of the three IVs:

		Rural School				*Urban School*	
		Boys	**Girls**			**Boys**	**Girls**
	2nd				2nd		
Grade	4th			Grade	4th		
	6th				6th		

Factorial Designs and Confounds

Students often think that factorially combining two or more IVs creates confounds. They remember (from Chapter 7) that a confound exists whenever the groups differ on more than one variable, and a factorial combination seems to fit this definition. For instance, in the example above, the 12 groups are different in sex, grade level, *and* geographical setting, and students often conclude that these IVs are confounded with one another. However, this is not the case. Instead, in a factorial combination, when we are looking at the overall effect of one IV at a time, the other IVs are actually *controlled variables;* that is, they are being held constant across the levels of the IV being examined. To illustrate this point, let's consider an experiment to examine Word Length (6, 9, or 11 letters) and Mode of Response (verbal versus written) as variables (IVs) affecting spelling performance (DV). The study uses a 3 × 2 factorial design (see Table 10-1 for a diagram). One of the working hypotheses says that shorter words will be spelled correctly more often than longer words. A second working hypothesis is that the written mode of response will lead to better spelling performance than verbal, since it reduces the load on working memory and allows a comparison of the appearance of a written response with some mental image of the word. Note that neither of these hypotheses makes any mention of the other variable in this study; these two hypotheses are about the **main effects** of Word Length and Response Mode (that is, they are concerned with the separate, overall effects of the IVs). How can the factorial design allow us to test these working hypotheses when it looks like we had *two* variables being manipulated at once? The answer lies in the fact that when we look at only one IV at a time, the other IV is *constant across levels of the IV being studied.*

For example, to examine the main effect of Word Length, we would compare the number of correct spellings for 6-, 9-, and 11-letter words. Assuming we had randomly but evenly assigned our participants to the experimental treatments, half of the participants who had to spell 6-letter words had to write them out while the other half of the participants had to spell them verbally, and this would be true for the other letter lengths as well. Thus, while Mode of Response was not constant across each *participant*, it *was* a constant across the levels of Word Length (both Response Modes were used equally often with each Word Length). So, if 6-letter

TABLE 10.1		Mean Numbers of Words Spelled Correctly as Function of Word Length and Response Mode			
		IV$_1$ = Word Length			
		6	**9**	**11**	
IV$_2$ = Mode of Response	**Verbal**	18.4	12.5	6.6	$\overline{X}_v = 12.5$
	Written	20.6	16.7	15.8	$\overline{X}_w = 17.7$
		$\overline{X}_6 = 19.5$	$\overline{X}_9 = 14.6$	$\overline{X}_{11} = 11.2$	

words were spelled correctly more often than longer words, it *cannot* be due to a difference in Response Mode. That is, for all three word-length conditions, the average performance is based on *both* written and verbal responses, so Response Mode is *not* a confounding variable.

In a parallel fashion, when looking at the main effect of Response Mode, Word Length becomes a controlled variable, with one-third of the data for each Response Mode coming from 6-letter words, one-third from 9-letter, and one-third from 11-letter words. Any overall difference between the written and verbal response modes *could not* be a result of variation in word length since the distribution of word lengths was the same for both levels of Response Mode.

Thus, factorially combining IVs does not create confounds. Maybe we can further clarify the point this way: How could we manage to create a true confound in this study? If, for some strange reason, the researcher allowed the participants in the 11-letter-word group to write out their responses while the participants in the 6-letter-word group were not allowed to write the words out, there *would* be a confound between Word Length and Response Mode because the response modes are *not evenly distributed* across the word-length conditions. (This would, in fact, be a violation of the very definition of a "factorial" design, which requires that every level of the first IV—Word Length—be combined with every level of the other IV—Response Mode.) Alternatively, a confound could occur in an experiment using the proper factorial combination of the two IVs if some *other relevant extraneous variable* is not controlled. Suppose the 6-letter words all refer to common objects and events while many of the 11-letter words used in the study are uncommon terms (such as "proselytize" or "resplendent"). Participants may do better with the short words simply because they are more familiar with them: The familiarity of the words is confounded with Word Length. (Note, however, that familiarity would *not* be confounded with Response Mode since the familiar and unfamiliar words would be evenly distributed over the written and verbal response modes.)

The Research Questions Addressed in Factorial Designs

Two-way factorial designs allow us to answer *three separate research questions* concerning the effects of the independent variables on performance. The term "effect" refers to a difference in performance on the dependent variable. That is, we say that an IV "has an effect" if the average performance of one level of the IV is significantly different than the average performance of another level of the IV, and we say that the IV "has no effect" if the difference in average performance between the levels of the IV is not significant. When there are two independent variables in a factorial design, the three research questions are: (a) Is there a *main effect* of the first IV? (b) Is there a *main effect* of the second IV? and (c) Is there an *interaction between the IVs*?

Only factorial designs allow us to answer this third question, which is the real advantage of factorial designs over separate one-way designs looking at isolated independent variables. Factorial designs allow us to examine the overall main effects of the IVs and all of the possible interactions among them. For example, a three-way (A × B × C) design answers *seven* separate research questions, including questions about the 3 main effects and 4 possible interactions among the IVs: (1) A × B, where the effect of IV_A depends on the level of IV_B; (2) A × C, where the effect of IV_A depends on the level of IV_C; (3) B × C, where the effect of IV_B depends on the level of IV_C; and A × B × C, where the interaction pattern between IV_A and IV_B depends on the level of IV_C. Higher-order factorial designs such as this are quite complex, so the remainder of our discussion of main effects and interactions uses a hypothetical two-way design.

Table 10-1 presents hypothetical data from a 3 × 2 study on the effects of Word Length and Mode of Response on spelling. The three research questions addressed by this study, which include tests of the two working hypotheses stated above, are: (a) Does the length of a word affect how often it is correctly spelled? That is, are shorter words spelled correctly more often than longer words? If the answer is "yes," there is a main effect of Word Length. (b) Does the mode of response affect spelling performance? That is, does a written response lead to more correct spellings than a verbal response? If the answer is "yes," there is a main effect of Response Mode. (c) Is the difference between written and verbal response modes the same for all word-lengths? If the answer is "no," then there *is* an interaction because the effect of Response Mode (that is, the difference between verbal and written responses) would depend on the length of the words. Let's use the data in Table 10-1 to illustrate, conceptually, how these three research questions are answered.

Table 10-1 presents the mean number of words spelled correctly by the participants in our six experimental treatments as well as the means for each "row" and "column." (The two rows represent the two levels of Response Mode, and the three columns represent the three levels of Word Length.) The statistical analysis that would be appropriate for testing the significance of these two main effects and the interaction effect is called analysis of variance (ANOVA), which is discussed in detail in Chapter 12. Conceptually, what ANOVA does to test for the *main effect of Response Mode* is to determine whether the difference between the *overall means* for performance in verbal and written modes differ enough to make it unlikely that the difference in means is due solely to uncontrolled factors (or chance). That is, we will determine whether there is a *significant difference* between the means of 12.5 (for verbal responses) and 17.7 (for written responses). Similarly, the test for *main effect of Word Length* determines the likelihood that the differences between the overall means for 6-, 9-, and 11-letter words (means of 19.5, 14.6, and 11.2, respectively) could have come about by uncontrolled variation. (These main effects are sometimes said to be tests of the "marginal" means since it is the overall row or column means that are compared rather than the means of the individual cells.)

So far, from just "eyeballing" the row and column means, it would appear that when we address the first two research questions, we find that the two working hypotheses stated earlier have been supported: (a) shorter words are spelled correctly more often than longer words, and as words get longer, they are spelled correctly less and less often (means of 19.5 correct, 14.6 correct, and 11.2 correct for 6-, 9-, and 11-letter words, respectively), and (b) participants in the written response mode group spelled more words correctly than participants in the verbal response mode condition (means of 17.7 correct versus 12.5 correct). What about the third working hypothesis of this factorial design—the question about an interaction? The researcher may have hypothesized that participants in the written response mode condition would perform better than participants in the verbal response mode condition, but only when the length of the words would put a strain on the participant's working memory capacity (which, for normal adults, is typically 5 to 9 items). Thus, when the words contain only 6-letters, we could predict that most adults will experience little difficulty in remembering the letters as they speak them aloud and that writing them down would not add much advantage. Therefore, there may be little difference in performance between participants in the two Response Mode groups when they are trying to spell short words. Words with 9 letters should be more difficult because they exceed the working capacity of many adults, and words with 11 letters should be particularly difficult because they exceed the normal working memory capacity of most adults. Thus, being able to write down the words should provide an advantage for participants in the written response mode condition, but only for the longer words.

Therefore, to test the possibility that there is an *interaction between Word Length and Response Mode*, we need to see whether the differences between verbal responses and written responses are the same for every word length—if the differences *are* the same, then there is *no* interaction. One way to describe an interaction is to say that there is "a significant difference in the differences." By definition, then, *there is an interaction between two IVs when the effect of one IV is not the same at every level of the other IV.* In our example in Table 10-1, the difference between mean spelling performance in the verbal and written modes is quite small for 6-letter words (20.6 versus 18.4 gives a mean difference of only 2.2), but for 11-letter words there is a much larger difference between performance in the two response modes (15.8 versus 6.6 gives a mean difference of 9.2). Thus, in this case, there appears to be an interaction between Word Length and Response Mode in determining spelling performance, and the direction of this change in mean differences provides support for the hypothesized interaction (from the small difference of 2.2 for short words to a larger difference for longer words, 9.2). One would, of course, need to conduct a factorial analysis of variance to establish the statistical significance of this apparent interaction.

Note that the "differences" we are now discussing are *not* the main effects, but what are called *simple effects*—the effect one IV has *at a single level of the other IV.* For example, the difference between the mean for verbal and the mean for written mode for only the 11-letter words is "the simple effect of response mode on spelling accuracy at the 11-letter word length." Therefore, another way of defining an interaction would be to say: *There is an interaction if the simple effect of an IV changes significantly when the level of another IV changes.* For instance, Table 10-1 indicates that the simple effect of response mode increases in magnitude each time the length of the words is increased. For 6-letter words, the simple effect of Response Mode is equal to 2.2 (that is, 18.4 versus 20.6), while for 9-letter words the difference between written and verbal response modes is equal to 4.2 (12.5 versus 16.7), and for 11-letter words, the simple effect is equal to 9.2 (6.6 versus 15.8). Therefore, there appears to be an interaction between the two IVs because the simple effects of Response Mode (across the different levels of Word Length) are not the same.

Let us make one final point about simple effects and interactions. When we are looking for an interaction, it does not matter which set of simple effects are examined, the same conclusion will be reached. That is, if there is an interaction, the simple effects of IV_A will change across the levels of IV_B, and, at the same time, the simple effects of IV_B will change across the levels of IV_A. In our example, we saw that the simple effects of Response Mode changed as the words increased in length. That same interaction is reflected in a difference in the simple effects of Word Length across response modes. For example, the difference between 6-letter words and 9-letter words is equal to 5.9 for the verbal response mode, but it is equal to only 3.9 for the written response mode. Hence, the effect of increased word length depends on the response mode: there *is* an interaction.

Selecting Only the Necessary Independent Variables

Researchers must decide which independent variables they wish to include in a given study. This decision should be based on the specific hypotheses and theoretical issues of interest to the researcher. Given any specific hypothesis, researchers may choose to include a single IV (in a one-way design), or they may choose to include two or more IVs in a factorial design, which allows them to test for potential interactions between or among the IVs. New researchers, however, often find themselves trying to include every potential IV in a single study, because every time they think of another variable that could be related to their dependent variable or that might interact with the primary IVs, they think they must actually test those possibilities. This is not the case.

For instance, students in a graduate class were asked to design a study to test the hypothesis that preschool children are more likely to help when someone clearly expresses a need for help (such as by saying, "I can't do this by myself") and less likely to help if the need for help is expressed only through nonverbal signals (such as a look of frustration or sadness), while middle-school children are equally likely to help in both sets of circumstances. This hypothesis predicts an interaction between the two independent variables of "Age of the Child" and "Type of Help-Me Signal Sent by the Victim." Therefore, the hypothesis calls for a two-way design.

As the students discussed how they would design this study and operationalize the variables, someone pointed out that the age and sex of the "victim" might influence the children's helping responses, and many of the students decided it was necessary to include two new IVs, where the age and sex of the victim would be systematically varied to see whether they made a difference or whether they interacted with the age of the children or the type of "help-me" signal being presented. They had expanded the problem to a *four-way design*. As discussions of the study continued, the students realized that the *type* of help required could *also* make a difference, since preschoolers are capable of things like picking up dropped objects or putting simple puzzles together, but they may not be able to help someone get a toy down from a high shelf while a 9-year-old may be able to do this. Now the students thought it was necessary to add yet another new IV: type of help needed. They were now wrestling with a *five-way design*.

In fact, while it would be important to *control for* these "new" variables, it is *not* necessary to include them all as IVs in a single study. Additional studies should be designed to test the effects and interactions of these other factors. Since the original purpose of the study—as presented in the hypothesis—was to look at the main effects and interactions of age and type of "help me" signal, those are the only necessary IVs, and all other potentially relevant factors need to be controlled in some manner. For example, the researcher could decide to control the sex of the victim by holding it constant across the study, so that every participant (at every age and each treatment condition) encountered a victim of the same sex. Alternatively, the researcher may decide to hold the sex of victim constant across the treatment groups, so that about half of the children at each age and in each condition encountered a female victim, and about half encountered a male victim. Likewise, the age of the victim and the type of help needed could be held constant *across the study* or *across the treatment groups*. Further research could then be designed to examine the effects of age and sex of victim and type of help needed.[2]

Selecting the Necessary Levels of the Independent Variables

After selecting the independent variables required to test the hypothesis, the next critical step is to select the *levels* of those IVs necessary to address the research questions. Consider the following example. A number of years ago, developmental psychologists became concerned about the fate of premature infants. Common medical practice dictated that these tiny infants be placed in incubators or isolettes and touched as little as possible because they were at risk for infection and because being handled would cause stress that could impair their chances of surviving. Normal-weight infants, in contrast, were held and cuddled for several hours per day. The psychologists wondered whether the isolation experienced by premature infants and the consequent lack of loving human touch might help explain why many of these premature children show developmental delays (such as slow weight gain and delays in neurological, motor, and cognitive development).

The psychologists, therefore, hypothesized that if premature babies were touched and cuddled more often, they would develop more rapidly than premature infants who are left in isolation most of the day. To test this hypothesis (which we will call Hypothesis 1), a study was designed where one group of premature infants was treated in the traditional, "hands-off" manner and a second group of premature infants was massaged from head to toe for three 15-minute periods per day for four

---

[2] It may help to remember that for most scientists, research is a career. Completing one study is usually only a prelude to starting another study—often in the same area of interest. Leaving some interesting questions for the next study is simply a way of life.

months. In all other respects, the babies were treated the same way. As the dependent variables, the researchers measured things such as weight gain, how long the babies stayed in the hospital, fine motor development, and cognitive development (such as attentional and memory processes).[3]

Thus, the study included one independent variable with only two levels: Massage versus No Massage. This design provides an appropriate and adequate test of the hypothesis that premature babies who are touched and massaged develop more rapidly than babies who are not massaged. Thus, only one IV is *necessary* and only two levels of the IV are *necessary* to test Hypothesis 1. Consider, however, a variation of the original hypothesis, Hypothesis 2: If premature babies were touched and cuddled more often, they would develop more rapidly than premature infants who are left in isolation most of the day, but *not* as rapidly as normal-weight, full-term infants. This hypothesis requires us to include *three* levels of our IV: premature babies who are massaged, premature babies who are not massaged, and full-term babies.

Consider yet another possible hypothesis (Hypothesis 3): The more extra touch and cuddling premature babies receive, the more rapidly they develop. This hypothesis requires that we systematically manipulate the amount of massage we give to the babies and compare different amounts of massage rather than simply comparing some massage to no massage. We might, for example, design our study to include five treatment groups: no massage; 15 minutes per day; 30 minutes per day; 45 minutes per day (as in the original study above); and 60 minutes per day. All of the infants would be premature, and other than the amount of time spent massaging them, they would be treated alike. Thus, in this example, the study has one IV with five levels. Are these five levels enough? Should we include a group who receives two hours of massage? How about a group that receives three hours of massage? The answer to these specific questions would be based on the researchers' expert knowledge of neonatal development rather than research design principles. However, it is important to understand that this hypothesis (that increasing the amount of massage increases development) could *not* be adequately tested with anything less than three levels (or amounts) of massage. Figures 10-3 and 10-4 illustrate why Hypothesis 3 requires a minimum of three treatment levels.

Figure 10-3 presents hypothetical results from a study that included only two levels of massage: none versus a lot (let's say, 1 hour per day). As you can see, the group that received the massage treatment showed developmental gains. Does this finding provide evidence to support the claim that the more massage the babies receive, the more rapidly they develop? No, it does not. The panels of Figure 10-4 illustrate three of the many possible relationships that could exist between amount of massage and rate of development. Panel 10-4a represents a case where *any amount* (even a small amount) of massage is enough to accelerate development to its maximum level. Panel 10-4b illustrates the case where small amounts of massage have *no effect* on development, but where large amounts of massage trigger an acceleration in development. Panel 10-4c represents the case proposed by our hypothesis where

---

[3] This example is actually a composite based on a variety of studies reviewed in Rosenblith (1992).

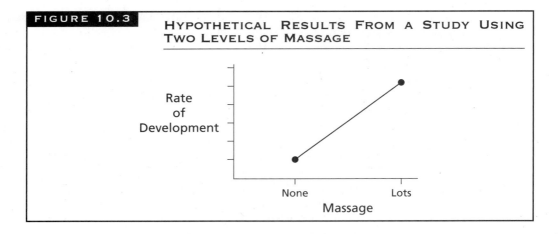

FIGURE 10.3

HYPOTHETICAL RESULTS FROM A STUDY USING TWO LEVELS OF MASSAGE

every increase in the amount of massage results in an incremental acceleration of development. A study with only two levels of the IV *cannot* tell us which of these three patterns (if any of them) is the most accurate portrayal of the effect of massage on development. Minimally, we need one "intermediate" level of massage, such as a group of babies who receive 30 minutes of massage per day, in order to test our hypothesis (and to find out which of the panels of Figure 10-4 more accurately reflects the relationship between amount of massage and development).

The point here is that researchers must include all of the appropriate levels of their independent variables in order to adequately test their hypothesis. We have illustrated how changing the focus of a hypothesis changes the requirements for the design. The original hypothesis simply asked whether massage would influence the rate of development of premature infants, yes or no. Our third hypothesis asked

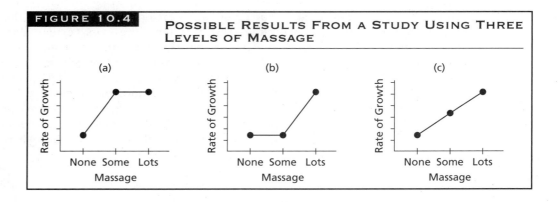

FIGURE 10.4

POSSIBLE RESULTS FROM A STUDY USING THREE LEVELS OF MASSAGE

whether increasing the amount of massage would lead to increases in the rate of development. These hypotheses required different treatment conditions. Researchers, therefore, must carefully tailor their studies to the specific hypothesis being addressed.

No-Treatment Control Group

One specific issue that needs to be addressed is whether or not an experiment needs to include a no-treatment control group as one of the groups. A **no-treatment control group,** as the name implies, is a group of participants who do not receive any experimental treatment before their behavior (the dependent variable) is measured. For instance, in the first and third examples above, the premature babies who do not receive any massage would be considered no-treatment control groups. Are such groups *required?* It depends on the focus of the hypothesis. In order to test the original hypothesis (Hypothesis 1), which asked whether massaging premature babies would increase their rate of development, the no-treatment control group *is* required; it is the group against which the effects of massage are to be compared. It is *implicit* in the hypothesis that massage is expected to increase the rate of development of premature babies *compared with premature babies who do not receive massage*, rather than compared with some other group of babies. (For instance, no one is likely to think that the hypothesis claims that massaged premature babies will develop at a faster rate than normal, full-term infants.)

Hypothesis 3, in contrast, claims that increasing the amount of massage will increase the rate of development. While we included a no-treatment control condition in our example above, it is not necessarily required by this hypothesis. Imagine, for instance, that the first study had already been conducted and adequately replicated and found that massaged premature babies develop faster than non-massaged premature babies. The next reasonable question would be "Does increasing the amount of massage lead to even greater gains in development?" and it would not be necessary to include the no-massage control group, if it has *already been demonstrated* that massage is better than no massage.

As another example, consider research on the effectiveness of different over-the-counter pain relievers. Research has already demonstrated that Advil is better than no treatment in relieving pain, and other research has already demonstrated that Tylenol is also better than no treatment. If we wanted to do a study to find out whether Advil is better than Tylenol, we would not need a no-treatment control group; we would need only a group that takes Advil and a group that takes Tylenol. Imagine, however, that you have just concocted your own home-remedy for pain relief and you want to know whether it works *and* whether it is as good as Advil. Now you would need three conditions in your study: a group that receives your new homemade remedy, a group that receives Advil, and a no-treatment control group. This control group is needed in order to find out whether your home-remedy has any effect at all, even if it is not as good as Advil. To understand why the no-treatment control group is required here (but not in the study comparing

Advil and Tylenol), imagine that you did a study that only compared Advil to your home remedy, and suppose you found that the Advil group experienced significantly greater pain relief than your home-remedy group. Without the no-treatment control group, there are two possible interpretations of this pattern of results: either (1) your home remedy has *no effect* on pain, or (2) your home remedy is better than nothing but less potent than Advil. Put simply, the no-treatment control group is required if the purpose of the study includes determining whether a treatment has any effect at all.

Placebo Control Groups

We should also mention another type of control condition often used in studies designed to test the effectiveness of some new drug or therapy: the **placebo control group.** A placebo is a treatment that is actually meant to have *no* real physiological effect on the participants but that may provide a psychologically soothing effect (Vogt, 1993). For example, in a study to test the effectiveness of a new analgesic (pain reliever), researchers may give the control group pills made out of sugar rather than an active drug. If these sugar pills—the placebo—lead to reduced pain, it is because people often feel better simply because they think they should after taking "medicine"—the so-called placebo effect. In order to determine whether the new analgesic has a beneficial effect on the *physiological level*, we need to demonstrate that it leads to significantly more pain relief than the placebo pills. Thus, this study would require a placebo control group.

Some studies include *both* types of control groups. This allows the researcher to determine, simultaneously, whether the experimental treatment is better than nothing *and* if it is better than a placebo. Additionally, including both types of control groups allows the researcher to compare the two control groups, which provides a measure of the placebo effect itself. That is, the researcher can determine *how much better* people feel simply because they have received what they believe is an experimental treatment.

While many researchers may feel that a treatment cannot be considered effective unless it is significantly more effective than the placebo, it is important to remember that, from a pragmatic standpoint, a placebo effect may be better than nothing at all. Therefore, from the layperson's point of view, where the choice will be to take the medication or not, the comparison between the drug treatment and a no-treatment control group may be the *more realistic test* of the actual benefits of taking the new drug. That is, suppose a study finds that the experimental drug group experiences the same amount of pain relief as the placebo control group, and that both groups show significant improvement over the no-treatment control group. Does this mean that the drug has no beneficial impact on people? No, it means that taking the drug *does* make people feel better. Even if this effect is due solely to the psychological placebo effect, the relief provided by the drug is better than no treatment at all.

Research Designs

Comparisons Between Groups Versus Repeated Measures

In addition to selecting the appropriate IVs and the levels of each IV necessary for testing the hypothesis, the researcher must also decide whether the various levels of the IV will be given to different individuals or to the same individuals. When each level of the IV is administered to a *different* group of individuals, the IV is said to be a **between-subjects (BS) factor,** and if all IVs in a study are BS factors, then the study has employed what is called a **between-subjects (BS) design.** Virtually every independent variable that may be of interest to a researcher can be set up as a BS factor in which different participants are tested under the different levels of the IV. Therefore, researchers always have the option of using a BS design. Alternatively, if *each* participant in the study is tested repeatedly, once under *each* level of an IV, then the IV is a **within-subjects (WS) factor** (or a **repeated measure**). If all IVs in a study are WS factors, then the study has employed what is called a **within-subjects (WS) design.** A third design alternative that is available for factorial designs (i.e., studies with two or more IVs) is a **mixed design,** which includes *both* BS and WS factors in the same study. Within-subjects designs have a number of advantages over between-subjects designs, but there are also a number of disadvantages and potential confounds associated with within-subjects designs. Mixed designs, as you may guess, share some of the advantages and disadvantages of both WS and BS designs. Many IVs cannot be used as repeated measures, as we will explain shortly, so researchers may not have the option of employing WS or mixed designs for their research, despite the advantages these designs have over BS designs.

To illustrate the difference between WS and BS factors, let's return to our example (from Chapter 7) of a study designed to test the effect of background noises on reading. The researcher hypothesizes that people exposed to conversation while they are reading will recall less of the reading material than people who are exposed to instrumental music while they are reading. Therefore, the IV in this study is the type of background noise, and it has two levels: conversation versus instrumental music. In designing this study, the researcher must decide whether the IV will be a WS factor or a BS factor. If the IV is a WS factor, the researcher will have to set up a study where each participant reads a passage while hearing a conversation, takes a memory test, and then *reads a second passage*, this time with music playing in the background, and takes a *second* memory test. Thus, every participant is tested under every level of the IV, which is the definition of a WS factor, and since there is only one IV in the study, the study is a one-way WS design. If, instead, the researcher sets up a study where some people read with the music playing and *other people* read with a conversation in the background, then the IV is a BS factor, and the study is a one-way BS design.

Testing Participants Repeatedly in Within-Subjects Designs

When researchers decide to conduct a within-subjects design, they must arrange to measure the participants' performance on the dependent variable under each of the experimental conditions separately. Some repeated measures designs can be conducted in a single session but others require multiple sessions with the participants, depending on the nature of the dependent variable and the experimental manipulation of the independent variables. For example, if the dependent variable task is long and tedious, it may not be feasible to have participants perform the task more than once in a single session. In a study of helping, for instance, the researcher may want to see how the actions of other people affect the amount of time a participant will spend stuffing envelopes for a charity drive. In one condition, research confederates (i.e., people secretly working for the researcher) will work very steadily on the task, but in the other condition, the confederates will be goofing off, complaining about how boring the task is, and actually stuff very few envelopes. Because some participants may spend several hours on the task, it would not be feasible to expose them to the second experimental manipulation and begin the task again in the same session. Therefore, in order to conduct a within-subjects design, the researcher would need to have the participants return on another day, at which time they would be exposed to the other group of confederates (i.e., the other experimental manipulation), and the amount of time they spend stuffing envelopes would be measured again.

In contrast, in a study of sound localization, where participants must point to the source of a sound, it is easy and efficient to have the participants perform the task under a variety of experimental conditions all in one session. For example, the participants could perform the task in the dark versus in the light, blind-folded versus with eyes open, or sitting up versus lying down. Or the type of sound could be varied from tones to white noise or from adult speech to an infant's cries. After each burst of sound, the participant's localization performance is measured, which takes only a few moments. Hence, participants can be exposed to a number of experimental conditions in the same session.

Just as the nature of the dependent variable affects the feasibility of conducting a within-subjects design in a single session, the nature of the independent variable and the experimental manipulation may also require that participants be tested over the course of multiple sessions. For example, a sleep researcher testing the effectiveness of various sedatives or sleep-inducing programs probably would not administer more than one treatment per night. (Of course, after the participants fall asleep following the first treatment, they could be awakened and given another treatment, but this procedure would seem very unnatural and unrealistic, so the external validity of the study would be questionable.) As another example, suppose a researcher is studying the effect of mood on decision-making. The independent variable is mood state, and the researcher uses a mood-induction technique to make the participants feel either happy or sad before the decision-making task is administered. (The mood induction technique may involve having the participants reminisce aloud about either the happiest or saddest events in their lives for a period of 10 minutes.) Although it is *procedurally* possible to test the participants under both mood states in the same session, it is probably not a good idea because the first mood state may carry over into the mood-induction process for the second condition, making the induction technique less effective, and jeopardizing the internal validity of the study. That is, the induction technique of reminiscing aloud about happy and sad events may make someone feel happy or sad, but only if they are in a neutral mood at the start. For example, reminiscing about happy events may make a sad person feel less sad, but they may not become happy. Therefore, once the participant has undergone the first mood induction procedure, the researcher cannot expect the second mood induction procedure to work as well as it should. That is, the second mood induction technique will not actually produce the desired mood state, so the operational definition of the experimental condition has not been achieved. By waiting for another day, the researcher can reasonably expect that the second mood induction procedure will be as effective as the first in creating the experimental conditions needed to test the hypothesis.

In conclusion, the decision to conduct a within-subjects design in a single session versus multiple sessions is an important one that should be based on a number of considerations. While we have focused on the feasibility of conducting the research in a single session, we should also point out that multiple sessions have their drawbacks as well. From a practical standpoint, it is easier to find volunteers for a one-shot research session; people are less likely to volunteer for a study that requires multiple trips to the laboratory. (Even if they do volunteer, many participants fail to return for the follow-up sessions.) From a procedural point of view, researchers need to be ready to justify asking the participants to return on another day, and this could be problematic in cases where the actual purposes of the study are being hidden in order to avoid reactivity. While the sleep researcher can be completely open with the participants, and explain that they will receive a different sedative each night they come to the sleep lab, the researcher looking at helping behavior could not explain to the participants that they need to return to the office in order to be exposed to a different set of confederates. These participants need to be given some pretext (i.e., a "cover story") that sounds perfectly reasonable, otherwise they may become suspicious, and their behavior may change. We return to the issue of reactivity later in this chapter.

Advantages of Within-Subjects Designs

There are three primary advantages to WS designs. The first is practical in nature: WS designs generally require *fewer participants* to serve in the study. If, for example, a researcher needs to have 20 participants in each treatment group in order to have adequate power for detecting a systematic difference between the treatments, then the researcher needs to recruit only 20 participants for a WS design. For a BS design, however, the researcher would need to recruit 20 participants for *each* experimental condition (so the minimum number would be 40 for a simple two-treatment experiment like the music versus conversation study in our example). Finding 20 volunteers is usually easier than finding 40 (or 60, or 80, and so forth).

The second major advantage of WS designs over BS designs is that when the same people serve in all conditions of the IV, then the whole class of subject variables (that is, all of the personal characteristics the individuals bring with them to our study) *become controlled variables* and the treatment groups are, therefore, equivalent on all of these subject variables. (Indeed, for many of these subject variables, the treatment conditions would be *equal*, not simply equivalent.) Thus, it is often said that the participants in WS designs "serve as their own control group." For example, if we used a WS design in our "music versus conversation" experiment, any differences in memory performance could not be due to differences between the treatment conditions in, say, reading ability or intelligence, because these subject variables would not change as the participants went from one treatment condition to the other. Therefore, the distribution of reading abilities and intelligence would be identical across levels of the IV. Thus, *WS designs minimize the likelihood of selection bias (or non-equivalence) confounds.*

The third major advantage of WS designs is that they have more **power** (or efficiency) than BS designs. *Power* (or efficiency) is the ability of a design to detect a difference between the treatments when, in fact, the treatments are systematically different. In other words, power is related to rejecting the null hypothesis when it *is* false.[4] The power of a design is primarily determined by the amount of *error variance* (or *chance fluctuations*) present in the data. Error variance results from individual differences, random measurement errors, unsystematic experimenter errors, and random fluctuations in participants' performance. The more error variance that is present in the data, the more difficult it is to detect variation between the treatment groups that is systematically due to the independent variable rather than to chance. Thus, large amounts of error variance can lead to Type II errors (where we fail to reject the null hypothesis when it is false).

WS designs are more powerful than BS designs because the primary source of error variance in a WS design is the variation in *an individual's performance over time* while the error variance in a BS design is primarily due to the differences in performance *between different people*, and people are generally *more similar to themselves over time* than they are similar to other people. That is, the chance fluctuations in a participant's behavior across time are *smaller* than the differences between different people. For example, if we measure the intelligence (or reaction time, or personality, or attitudes toward social policy issues, and so forth) of a group of participants at two points of time—without conducting any experimental manipulations to influence performance—we would expect to see that the two scores for the participants would be very similar, while we might expect to see some large differences between the scores of different participants. Thus, the error variance in a within-subjects design will be smaller than the error variance in a between-subjects design, which makes it easier to "see" smaller systematic differences between the treatment conditions. (See Appendix C for a full discussion of power and why within- subjects designs are able to detect smaller systematic effects than between-subjects designs.)

---

[4] One way to think about the power of a test is to compare it with the power of a microscope: A more powerful microscope allows us to see smaller objects, and a more powerful design allows us to detect smaller IV effects or smaller systematic differences between treatments.

Disadvantages of Within-Subjects Designs

Since control of subject variables and increased power would seem very desirable, you may wonder why researchers don't always use a within-subjects design. The reason is that there are several problems that may arise when the same participants are tested in each treatment condition, and sometimes, when the researcher cannot avoid these problems by carefully selecting appropriate procedures and operational definitions, these potential confounds outweigh the benefits of increased power and greater equivalence.

Overstandardization   The first problem that researchers may face when they are designing a within-subjects study is that it is possible to be too standardized. Recall that the scientific method in general, and experiments in particular, require that the only difference between the treatment groups be the level of the IV. Therefore, in our earlier discussion (in Chapter 7) of the relevant variables in our study of reading while either music or a conversation is playing in the background, we had concluded that it would be very desirable to keep the contents of the reading material the *same* for all participants. For example, we proposed that the same new, unpublished short story be used in both experimental conditions so the participants would be *equally unfamiliar* with the contents of the story before they read it in our study. In this way, in a between-subjects design, we control the characteristics of the reading material that may affect its memorability, so that one treatment group does not do better on the memory test simply because the story was easier to remember for some reason. If, however, we design a within-subjects study where the same participants are tested twice (once with music and once with conversation), should we have them read the same story each time? If we keep the story the same, then participants will be more familiar with the story during the second treatment than they were during the first treatment, and consequently, prior familiarity with the reading material—a variable that was being held constant in the BS design—is now *confounded with* the levels of the IV. Thus, by trying to standardize the treatments in our WS design by using the same reading material, we have created another problem.

A common solution to this overstandardization problem would be to select two different novel short stories, but there is the question of whether the two stories are equally easy to comprehend and equally memorable. Researchers may find it necessary to do a series of pilot studies on the materials to empirically establish that a particular pair of stories leads to equal performance on the multiple-choice memory tests that will be used as the dependent variable in the study. If two "equal" stories can be found, then the researcher can conduct a WS design without concern that the IV is confounded with the familiarity, comprehensibility, or memorability of the stories. There may, however, be other differences between the stories that the researcher did not recognize and control. Consequently, there is still the potential for a confound between the IV and characteristics of the story. In order to avoid these confounds, the researcher could use a procedure called *counterbalancing* which is described in detail later in this chapter.

Time-Related Effects   A second major concern for researchers whenever they use a within-subjects design has to do directly with the fact that the participants are exposed to each of the different experimental manipulations. There are a number of potential confounds that are known collectively as **time-related effects** that must be taken into consideration when selecting a research design and research procedures. The first of these time-related effects is known as the **order effect,** which, as the name implies, is concerned with the order in which the participants receive the treatments. An order effect exists whenever there is a *general tendency for the response to change systematically from early in a session to later in a session.* Another name for order effects is "stage of practice" effects, because performance is a function of the number of treatments the participant has received. The systematic changes that occur over time may be positive (where performance improves) or negative (where performance declines).

Performance may improve, for example, as a result of *practice* with the task itself and with being a participant in the study. For instance, since the participants in a WS design perform the dependent variable task at least twice, they may improve simply through practice on the task itself, and the more often they are tested, the better they may become, not because there has been a change in the IV manipulation, but because the task itself has become "easier" due to practice. They may, for instance, during an early session, discover a better task strategy that they use later on, resulting in improved performance in later sessions. Furthermore, a more subtle form of "practice" may occur if the participants become more relaxed and less anxious about participating in research (which is not an everyday experience for most people) so that they are better able to concentrate on the task at hand. Thus, if the participants' performance gets better over time as their anxiety about the situation declines, it might create an order effect. Negative order effects could result if participants' performance declined over time because they became *fatigued or bored* with the task.

Demand Characteristics   The third major disadvantage of within-subjects designs is that they present more (and typically stronger) **demand characteristics** to the participants. Demand characteristics are those cues in a new situation that people interpret as "demands" for particular behaviors. For example, if you go into an unfamiliar building and find yourself in a large, open room with a high-domed ceiling, stained-glass windows, and a large crucifix hanging above a table covered with an ornate cloth, you will probably feel that the room "demands" silence (or only hushed speech). A research setting, whether it is a between-subjects design or a within-subjects design, will also send signals to the participants about what is expected of them. The way the researcher interacts with the participants will, for example, tell the participants whether they are expected to treat the researcher like a new friend or as an aloof, authoritarian figure. Participants will naturally try to identify and interpret whatever cues they find so that they can do their best for the researcher. (They volunteered for the study, after all, so they probably feel some desire to help the researcher get the desired results.) Remember that when participants' behavior changes because they know they are being observed, we call it *reactivity*. If participants react to the demand characteristics in a research setting by engaging in behaviors that are not natural, "real-life" responses, it is a form of reactivity, and it poses a threat to the internal validity of the study. In general, researchers try to minimize the problem of reactivity and demand characteristics by employing **blind procedures.** In a *single blind* study, the participants do not know the hypothesis of the study and do not know what other types of tasks or treatments are being used in the study, and therefore, they are less likely to figure out what the researcher expects them to do. If *both* the participants and research observers who measure the participants' behavior are kept blind, it is called a *double blind procedure.* (Research observers are said to be blind if they are unaware of the treatment condition the participants are in or if they do not even know the hypotheses or details of the research design.) Double blind procedures reduce both reactivity and the potential for observer bias, such as the bias for positive instances (or confirmatory bias) we discussed in Chapter 1.

The demand characteristics in within-subjects designs tend to be greater than between-subjects designs because exposing participants to every experimental condition provides them with more cues about the purposes of the study. Whether the study is conducted in a single session or across multiple sessions, the participants undergo a series of different treatments which makes it more difficult to keep the participants blind to the purposes of the study. Thus, the participants in a WS design are more likely to identify the independent variables and figure out the hypothesis of the study, which may then lead the participants to change their behavior accordingly. Consequently, the effect of the IV (i.e., the difference in average performance under the treatment conditions) may be the result of reactivity to the demand characteristics inherent in receiving different treatments rather than to the IV manipulation itself. While reactivity is not a problem in all cases, and keeping participants blind is not always necessary, researchers who wish to use a WS design may, at times, need to come up with clever disguises (or cover stories) that will keep the participants blind even as they receive different experimental treatments.

In a within-subjects design, since an individual participant must receive one of the conditions first and the other second, levels of the IV will necessarily be confounded with the stage of practice and the demand characteristics for that individual. That is, for any particular individual, we cannot determine whether their performance changed because the IV manipulation changed or because they experienced an order effect or reacted to the demand characteristics generated by the presentation of the different treatment conditions. And if all of the participants receive Treatment A and then receive Treatment B, the entire study is confounded and uninterpretable. Why, then, would researchers ever consider using within-subject designs at all? Fortunately, researchers may be able to prevent time-related effects and demand characteristics from creating confounds by presenting the treatments in counterbalanced order.

Counterbalancing

Counterbalancing the order of treatments involves having some participants receive Treatment A first and other participants receive Treatment B first, and so forth. This procedure turns time-related effects and the impact of demand characteristics into controlled variables by making sure that each treatment condition is *equally exposed* to practice and the demand characteristics inherent in a change of treatment. For example, in the study on the effects of music versus conversation as background noise during reading, a counterbalanced design would have half of the participants receive the music condition first. Therefore, for these participants, practice effects will influence performance under the conversation condition, and, during the second treatment, when the participants notice that this time there is a conversation being broadcast on the radio, if they begin to suspect that the researcher thinks it is harder to read with conversation in the background, they may change their reading performance or not try as hard on the memory test. (They may also be somewhat distracted during the second task when they notice the new experimental condition which could inhibit performance.) For participants who hear the music first, all of these time-related effects and demand characteristics are having an impact on their performance in the conversation condition. The other half of the participants who receive the conversation first will have these same practice effects and demand characteristics impact the music condition. Thus, the two treatment conditions are *equivalent* on these time-related factors, and confounds have been avoided through the use of counterbalancing.

Counterbalancing can also be used to control for the differences between the two stories that we would use in this study: Half of the participants would hear Story A first, while the other half of the participants would hear Story B first, and Story A would be used in the music condition half of the time and in the conversation condition the other half. In this way, if there are any systematic differences between the stories, those differences are *not* confounded with the IV treatments *or* with the order of presentation.

Researchers may use either complete (full) counterbalancing or partial counterbalancing. Complete counterbalancing is when *every possible order of treatments* is included in the study. If there are only two treatments (A and B), there are only two possible orders: AB and BA. For three treatments (A, B, and C), there are six possible orders:

1. ABC

2. ACB

3. BAC

4. BCA

5. CAB

6. CBA

Four experimental treatments (which would be the minimum number for a within-subjects factorial design) have 24 possible orders; five treatments have 120 possible orders; and six treatments have 720 possible orders.[5] As you can guess, complete counterbalancing is generally used only when there are at most four treatments. When there are many possible orders, researchers can use partial counterbalancing, which means they use only *some* of the possible orders. They may select the orders randomly, or they may systematically create what is called a **Latin square,** which is a set of orders that *controls the ordinal position* of each treatment so that the treatments occur in a particular ordinal position (first, second, etc.) the same number of times, so that order effects and demand characteristics affect each treatment equally. The procedure for constructing Latin squares for any possible design is presented in Winer, Brown and Michaels (1991). Here we will illustrate just some of the Latin squares that could be used in studies with three or four treatment conditions.

The number of treatments determines the number of orders in a Latin square. Therefore, for a study with three treatment conditions (referred to as A, B, and C), a Latin square will have three treatment orders. That is, the participants will be assigned to one of three groups and each group receives the treatments in a different sequence. In one possible Latin square, the first group would receive A first, B second, and C last (i.e., ABC), the second group of participants would receive B first, C second, and A last (i.e., BCA), and the third group of participants would receive C first, A second, and B last (i.e., CAB). If you look at the columns in the diagram of this Latin square, you can easily see that each treatment occurs in each ordinal position (first, second, and third) an equal number of times:

$$A \quad B \quad C$$
$$B \quad C \quad A$$
$$C \quad A \quad B$$

A second possible Latin square for a design with three treatments would look like this:

$$A \quad C \quad B$$
$$B \quad A \quad C$$
$$C \quad B \quad A$$

Researchers would select one of these Latin squares for their study, and the participants would be assigned to one of three groups and receive the treatments in the appropriate sequence.

For a design with four treatment conditions (A, B, C, and D), the Latin square will have four different sequences, and therefore, participants will be assigned to one

---

[5] Imagine the reaction of one author who was designing a study with 10 treatments when she realized that there are 3,628,800 possible orders! Needless to say, she opted for a partial counterbalancing of orders instead of complete counterbalancing.

of four groups. In one of the possible Latin squares for a four-treatment design, the first group of participants would receive A first, B second, C third, and D last (i.e., ABCD), the second group of participants would receive C first, A second, D third, and B last (i.e., CADB), the third group of participants would receive B first, D second, A third, and C last (i.e., BDAC), and the fourth group of participants would receive D first, C second, B third, and A last (i.e., DCBA). This Latin square is diagrammed like this:

A	B	C	D
C	A	D	B
B	D	A	C
D	C	B	A

Two other possible Latin squares for a design with four treatments would include:

D	B	C	A		C	B	D	A
B	A	D	C		D	A	B	C
C	D	A	B		B	C	A	D
A	C	B	D		A	D	C	B

Thus, a researcher with four treatments would select one of these Latin squares and assign the participants to one of the four treatment orders. Again, the benefit of using Latin squares as a partial counterbalancing technique is that each treatment appears in each ordinal position (represented by the columns) an equal number of times, and therefore, the time-related effects are held constant across the treatment conditions and potential time-related confounds are avoided.

Counterbalancing, then, is a very powerful technique available to researchers that allows us to take advantage of the benefits of WS designs while avoiding the potential confounds associated with demand characteristics and time-related effects. *Any WS designs and any mixed designs that do not use counterbalancing for the WS factors have to be considered confounded and, therefore, no causal conclusions can be drawn for those non-counterbalanced WS factors.* Certainly, then, researchers should automatically use counterbalancing for any WS factor (including those in mixed designs), right? Well, unfortunately, counterbalancing is not always possible, and there are also specific time-related effects that will create a confound despite counterbalancing.

Limitations of Counterbalancing Suppose a neuropsychologist is studying the function of the hippocampus, which is a structure located within the brain. The neuropsychologist intends to compare the memory performance of rats with an intact hippocampus with the memory performance of rats whose hippocampus has been destroyed. Obviously, because brain cells do not heal, these two levels of the IV (intact versus lesioned hippocampus) can be administered in only one order, intact and then destroyed; counterbalancing is not possible since none of the rats can be first observed with a lesioned (destroyed) hippocampus and then be tested with an intact hippocampus. In this case, then, counterbalancing is simply not feasible: It cannot be done.

Similarly, if a researcher wanted to compare participants' performance from before treatment to after treatment, using a **pretest-posttest** comparison, the order of these treatments, by definition, cannot be counterbalanced: Before always precedes after. Therefore, if every participant is pretested, then treated, and then takes the posttest, the comparison between the before-treatment condition and the after-treatment condition is confounded from the outset by a number of time-related factors. That is, even if the results of a single-group pretest-posttest design indicate that there is a significant change in performance following the onset of the experimental treatment, the researcher cannot be certain that the change was caused by the treatment itself.[6] In order to be able to evaluate the causal impact of a treatment using a pretest-posttest comparison, the researcher needs to switch to a mixed design that includes a group of participants who are pretested and posttested but who do *not* receive any treatment between the tests (i.e., a no-treatment control group). The benefits of including a control group in a pretest-postest design are discussed later in this chapter.

Counterbalancing may be ineffective for other types of experimental manipulations as well. For example, suppose that the IV calls for participants in a memory study to be either given a mental imagery mnemonic (a strategy for learning new material where they are taught to visualize the items on the list in unusual contexts) or simply "left to their own devices" (and not taught an effective memory strategy). While it is clearly possible to first have students perform using their own methods and then perform again after receiving instruction in the imagery mnemonic, it is *not* reasonable to believe that you can do the reverse because once you have instructed the students in how to create mental images and explained why this will help them remember more material, it is not reasonable to think the participants can then be instructed to completely forget this new technique. That is, the researcher cannot "undo" the first treatment and return the participants to their original "state." So even though the researcher can use counterbalancing (by having half of the participants receive the mnemonic condition first while half receive the "no mnemonic" condition first), counterbalancing is not going to be effective in controlling the potential confounds inherent in this experimental IV.

The issue has to do with whether there will be **differential carryover** of the effects of one condition to the other: where performing under Treatment A changes how the participant responds to the later Treatment B but where performing under Treatment B first does *not* have the same influence on the subsequent Treatment A.[7] Here the imagery instruction (Treatment A) is likely to be carried over and still used

---

[6] A single-group pretest-posttest design is an example of a quasi-experimental *time series design*. As discussed in Chapter 7, quasi-experimental designs do not allow us to draw causal conclusions.

[7] In some cases of differential carryover, having A first improves performance on B while having B first *hampers* performance on A. In this case, neither treatment order gives an accurate estimate of the impact of the treatments "in isolation."

when the participant has been left to his/her own devices (Treatment B), whereas there is less likelihood of any carryover of specific activities in the reverse direction (people are less likely to use their own devices after being taught how to use imagery).

The problem that arises from differential carryover (when A affects B but not vice versa) is that the data from the WS design will not give a clear picture of performance under the two treatment conditions, even when the order has been counterbalanced. Participants in one of the order conditions will perform better, overall, than the other participants, even though both groups of participants were exposed to the same treatments. For example, participants who get the mental imagery condition first will have a different, probably higher, average performance during the control ("own devices") condition than participants who performed in the control condition first, but there will be no similar difference in performance for the mental imagery condition.

Let's look at an example. Imagine that we conducted a study on mental imagery and found that the average number of items recalled when the participants were using mental imagery was 15 and the average number of items recalled in the control condition was 9. We employed a WS design and counterbalanced the order of treatments. What effect does the mental imagery mnemonic have on memory performance? That is, how much difference does mental imagery make in memory performance? It appears that mental imagery improves performance by an average of 6 items, which suggests that it is a moderately effective mnemonic technique. Do these overall treatment means provide an accurate assessment of the effectiveness of mental imagery? Not if there has been differential carryover. We may be able to detect evidence of differential carryover by examining the data from the treatment orders separately. Table 10-2 presents hypothetical data from the mental imagery study.

As you can see from the data in Table 10-2, the conclusions we might draw from the study about the relative effectiveness of mental imagery instructions depends on the order of treatments. For the participants who received the control condition first, the difference between mental imagery and the control condition was 9 points (15 versus 6), which would seem to be a substantial effect: Mental imagery looks like a highly effective mnemonic technique. (Remember that, when the data from all participants was combined, the average difference between the treatment means was only a moderate 6 points.) However, for the participants who received the mental imagery condition first, the difference in performance between mental imagery and the control condition was only 3 points (15 versus 12). For these participants,

TABLE 10.2	Hypothetical Mean Number of Correctly Recalled Items	
Treatment Order	**Imagery**	**Own Devices**
AB (Imagery then Control)	15 (done first)	12 (second)
BA (Control then Imagery)	15 (done second)	6 (first)
TREATMENT MEANS	**15**	**9**
NOTE: A = Mental Imagery and B = "own devices" (or Control)		

mental imagery did not appear to be very effective. Why not? It is most likely that, for some of these participants, the mental imagery technique carried over into the control condition. That is, they *continued to use mental imagery* during the control condition, and this carryover reduced the apparent difference in performance between the treatments.

This pattern of results, where the difference between the treatments depends on the order in which the treatments is presented, reflects differential carryover. The carryover from the mental imagery to the control condition for the participants who received the mental imagery instruction first *inflated* their performance during the control condition. Consequently, the difference between the overall treatment means was reduced and we ended up *underestimating* the actual effect of mental imagery as a mnemonic technique. Because counterbalancing cannot prevent the differential carryover problem, researchers who employ within-subject and mixed designs should routinely examine their data for systematic differences in performance between the participants who receive the treatments in different orders.

Summary of Within-Subjects Designs

Compared with between-subjects designs, within-subjects designs are more powerful, require fewer participants, and minimize the likelihood of selection bias (nonequivalence) confounds. While they are also vulnerable to potential confounds due to time-related effects, increased demand characteristics, and overstandardization in an effort to avoid nonstandardization, researchers can use counterbalancing to "spread" these effects evenly across the treatment conditions and thus prevent most of them from actually creating confounds. Counterbalancing, however, has its limits. Specifically, it is not always feasible and it cannot control the effects of differential carryover.

Advantages and Disadvantages of Between-Subjects Designs

The primary advantage of between-subjects designs is that they are not vulnerable to the time-related effects and differential carryover effects that within-subjects designs must worry about. In a BS design, participants are assigned to one and only one experimental condition, and their behavior is measured only once. Therefore, there cannot be any carryover or order effects. For example, all participants are at the same stage of practice (none) and should experience the same amount of fatigue and boredom over the course of the treatment. Since each participant is tested only once, there is no need to find two or more equivalent sets of stimulus materials (such as the short story we would use in the study on music versus conversation). Therefore, it may be easier to maintain standardization in a BS design than in a WS design. Furthermore, since the participants are assigned to only one experimental group, they are not exposed to the demand characteristics associated with a *change* in treatment from one level of the IV to another. That is, while the procedures used in a BS design may present various demand characteristics, the participants are less likely to be able to guess the hypotheses of the study, so any reactivity they exhibit is *less likely* to be systematically confounded with the IV manipulation. In this way, BS designs can be expected to minimize the potential for demand characteristics confounds.

Essentially, then, the major advantage of the BS design is that it is not vulnerable to the disadvantages of the WS design. In turn, the disadvantage of the BS design is that it does not have the advantages of the WS design. BS designs require more participants (since each experimental condition must have a separate group of participants), they are less powerful (since the differences between people are greater than the fluctuations in an individual's performance over time; see the discussion in Appendix C), and they face a greater risk of selection bias (nonequivalence) confounds (since even random assignment will fail to create equivalent groups in about 5% of the between-subjects studies while participants always serve as their own "equivalent control group" when they are tested repeatedly). For example, just by chance, the participants assigned to the music condition may suffer from greater hearing losses than the other group of participants, and this may lead to better memory performance because these participants couldn't hear the background music. The researcher may erroneously conclude that conversation is more distracting than music, but the difference may really be due to the difference in hearing ability between the groups of participants.

Matching Designs

Sometimes, researchers will try to avoid the potential selection bias problems in BS designs by using a **matching design** where participants are assigned to the treatment conditions in such a way that we can be sure that the groups are equivalent on important variables that would create confounds if the groups were not equivalent. For instance, to prevent hearing ability from confounding our study on background noise and memory, we could administer a hearing test to all potential participants and then assign them to our two experimental groups in such a way as to be certain that the hearing ability of each group is the same before we begin our experimental manipulation. Thus, hearing ability is being *directly controlled* through the matching procedure (instead of being probabilistically controlled through random assignment). Participants can, theoretically, be matched on a number of different variables in a single study, thus ensuring equivalence on several potentially-confounding factors at once. (For example, we could also match the participants in our study on intelligence, academic performance, reading ability, and so forth.)

Two procedures can be used for the purpose of matching our groups on potentially confounding variables. One procedure involves simply making sure that the group *means and standard deviations* on the "matching variable" are equal before beginning the experiment. This can be accomplished by randomly assigning *most* of the participants to the groups, checking on the group means and standard deviations, and then *placing* the remaining participants into particular treatment groups in such a way as to keep the means and standard deviations comparable. (This procedure gives us a **matched-groups design.** It is similar to the process a coach may use when putting together teams for a scrimmage: Players with similar abilities are put on different teams so that the teams start out fairly well matched.) The alternative procedure involves pairing participants together because they are equivalent on the matching variable and then randomly assigning one member of the matched pair to each of the experimental treatment conditions. (This procedure gives us a **matched pairs design.**)

While the benefits of matching seem highly desirable, matched-groups designs are fairly uncommon, and most researchers prefer to use completely random assignment. There are a number of reasons for preferring random assignment (which can fail 5% of the time, creating selection bias confounds) over matching, including: (1) matching requires a lot of additional time and effort, both for the researcher and the participants, who need to undergo some form of preliminary testing so that their scores on the matching variable(s) can be determined; and (2) it is virtually impossible to adequately match on more than one or two variables at a time, and so there is still the potential for a selection bias confound from all of the remaining unmatched subject variables. Even more importantly, matched-groups designs are not utilized very often because they are *less powerful* than BS designs that use random assignment (which are referred to as *random-groups designs*). In contrast, matched-pairs designs are more powerful than random-groups (BS) designs because they are analyzed using within-subjects statistical procedures. Appendix C explains why matching the groups causes a *reduction* in power while matching the participants in pairs allows us to employ more powerful statistical procedures.

Some General Confounds: Threats to Internal Validity

The internal validity of a study refers to how well it has addressed its research question. That is, if a study is designed and carried out so that it legitimately answers the question it was supposed to address, the study has internal validity. The central research question addressed by experimental research is "Does the IV cause the DV?," but when an experiment is confounded, it is unable to answer that question. Therefore, confounds are sometimes referred to as threats to internal validity. So far, we have identified some specific confounds that researchers must avoid. These confounds include selection bias, nonstandardization, and cases where demand characteristics or time-related effects (such as stage of practice or carryover effects) are confounded with the levels of the independent variable. There are several other general confounds that must be considered when designing research studies.

Maturation

A **maturation** confound occurs when the participants' behavior undergoes a significant change simply as the result of normal development, not the experimental treatment. For example, we know that children's performance on cognitive or motor tasks will improve over time as they mature, so if researchers conduct studies that take place over a period of time, they must be certain that the experimental treatments are not confounded with time. Suppose, for example, that a researcher wants to compare the effectiveness of two types of swimming instruction for 4-year-old children. If the researcher were to design the study so that the children who attended the swim camp from June 1 to June 15 received Instruction Technique 1, while the children who attended the swim camp from August 15 to August 30 received Instruction Technique 2, the study has the potential for a maturation confound: All children may become better swimmers over the summer when they are 4-years-old, so the children who receive Technique 2 may start out as better swimmers than the children who received Technique 1, simply because one treatment began earlier in time (when the children were younger) than the other treatment.

History

A **history** confound occurs whenever some event occurs outside of the research setting that affects the behavior of the participants when they are being observed or tested by the researcher. For example, researchers who were studying the development of pre-reading skills (such as letter recognition) in preschool children during the early 1970s may have encountered an unexpected pattern of results: 3- and 4-year-old children who had better pre-reading skills than 5- and 6-year-old kindergarten students. The reason: the television program *Sesame Street* went on the air, and many preschoolers began to watch it and learn basic reading skills that the older children did not begin to learn until they started school. Thus, the airing of *Sesame Street* was an "historical" event that influenced participants in one group (the preschoolers) more than it influenced the participants in the other group (the kindergarten students) and thus created a confound with the IV of age.

Consider how other historical events could create confounds by influencing one treatment group more than another treatment group. Suppose the researcher is conducting a study on the power of particular advertising techniques and has designed two television commercials designed to encourage people to call a toll-free number to receive "free information" about a new exercise machine. The first of the two commercials is shown five times a day for a period of four weeks, and the number of calls to the toll-free number are logged. The second commercial is scheduled to be shown at the same times of day and for the same length of time. Imagine, however, that just as the second commercial hits the airwaves, a popular movie star begins to promote a different exercise machine. Now the product being promoted in the researcher's commercials is facing new competition (an "historical" event), but only the second commercial is being affected, and so the relative effectiveness of the two commercials cannot be determined.

Regression Toward the Mean

Measurement devices are seldom, if ever, wholly reliable, so the score a participant receives on any particular occasion contains measurement error of some sort. This means that if the participant were to be tested a second time using the same measurement device, the score may change even if there had been no change in the underlying quality or characteristic being measured. While this measurement error typically affects our research by decreasing the power of our statistical tests, there is a situation when it actually confounds the design. Whenever (a) participants are selected for a study because their pretest scores are extremely high or extremely low, *and* (b) all of the participants receive the experimental treatment prior to a posttest, the researcher must expect the scores on the posttest to be more "moderate" (or more like the population mean) because of a phenomenon known as **regression toward the mean.** Extreme scores are partly due to random measurement error, so if the participants are measured a second time (on a posttest), that particular measurement error is unlikely to occur a second time, and the score is likely to be less extreme and more like the population mean. Thus, any study that selects participants because they have extreme scores (high or low) on a pretest and then compares the pretest scores with scores on a posttest is potentially confounded.

For example, imagine that we have developed a new computerized tutor for a statistics course and we want to assess its effectiveness. We would want to select participants who *need* tutoring to see whether their performance on a statistics exam can be improved by working with our tutoring program. So we could give an exam (as a pretest) in order to identify the students who fail the exam and therefore could be considered "in need of tutoring". If we gave all of these students a series of tutoring sessions with our program and then administered another version of the exam (as a posttest) and found significant improvement, we would not be able to conclude that the tutoring sessions caused the improved performance because there may have been some regression toward the mean where the extremely low scores naturally improved—and would have done so even without the tutoring. For example, some participants may have failed the pretest by accident (carelessness or fatigue, for instance) and did not really need tutoring after all. The improvement in their scores would not be due to the tutoring program but to regression toward the mean.

Instrumentation

An **instrumentation** confound occurs when the recording device used to measure the dependent variable does not remain consistent across the treatment conditions. A "recording device" could be a stopwatch or a human observer. If, for instance, a battery-operated stopwatch becomes inaccurate as the battery loses power, the scores recorded early in the study will be systematically different from the later scores due to the change in the instrument. If the early scores are from one treatment condition and the later scores are from a different treatment condition, then an instrumentation confound has occurred. Likewise, researchers who have to observe a large number of participants engaged in the same tasks may become bored or fatigued, and ultimately less reliable in their recordings. If the first individuals they observed are in one treatment condition while the later individuals are from another treatment condition, the observers' fatigue or boredom will affect the scores for only the second treatment, and thus an instrumentation confound has occurred.

Mortality

A **mortality** confound (which is sometimes called selective attrition or selective subject loss) occurs when participants in one treatment condition drop out of the study more often than do participants in the other treatment conditions because they did not like something about the experiment itself, such as how they felt about their own performance. For example, suppose a researcher is comparing the performance of boys and girls on a spatial skills task where they look at two-dimensional drawings and have to draw the figure from another angle (such as a 180-degree rotation). The study requires the participants to repeat the task several times over a two-week period. This researcher is likely to find that some of the participants stop showing up for their appointments: They have dropped out of the study. This would create an "unequal n problem" for the statistical analysis, and it might also create a mortality confound *if* more girls dropped out than boys, *and if* the girls who dropped out were the ones who knew they were not performing well on the task. If this pattern of drop-outs occurred, the average performance for the girls who completed the study would be higher because the girls with low scores would not be included in the final group average. The results of the study could then lead to a misleading comparison between the boys and the girls.

As another example, consider an experiment to test the effects of rewards versus punishment on learning. Participants who are in the punishment group may be more likely to drop out of the study, especially if they feel their performance is poor (meaning they'll receive more and more punishment). Poorly performing participants in the reward condition, in contrast, may be less likely to drop out of the study, and consequently, the treatment groups are no longer equivalent. Put simply, a mortality confound is like having a selection bias confound occur after the study begins.

Sensitization

When participants must take a test or respond to a questionnaire, the questions themselves may influence the participant's responses by sensitizing them to the issues being studied. Sensitization, then, can lead to reactivity, and the dependent variable itself may serve as a demand characteristic. A **sensitization** confound is created when this reactivity is confounded with the IV manipulation. For example, suppose a researcher designs a study to test the effectiveness of an antidiscrimination TV campaign on people's racial attitudes. Some participants are exposed to the antidiscrimination materials as part of a large set of TV commercials, while other participants see all of the TV commercials except the ones with an antidiscrimination message. Then the participants complete a questionnaire that includes questions about their racial attitudes. Just seeing those questions may sensitize them to the issue of racial discrimination, which may remind them of the commercials they saw, which could lead to responses that are socially desirable. Consequently, it would appear that the commercials had a positive effect in reducing racist attitudes, but in fact, the commercials may have had no effect at all *until* the questionnaire was presented. Therefore, it would not be accurate to conclude that a TV campaign is effective in reducing racist attitudes, because the change in attitude (or at least the change in response to the questionnaire) was really caused by the experience of completing the questionnaire.

A second source of sensitization is a *pretest*. When participants are asked questions during a pretest (in order to establish a baseline of their attitudes or performance), they may become sensitive to the issues included in the pretest. Then when the IV manipulation takes place, the treatment may have an effect only because the participants had become sensitized by the pretest. For example, if a researcher asks participants to report their level of racial prejudice on a pretest questionnaire, and then the researcher presents an antidiscrimination message to the participants, their racial attitudes (as measured on a posttest) may indeed change. However, before we would conclude that the message by itself is effective in reducing racial prejudice, we would have to demonstrate that it works even when participants have not been sensitized by a pretest (or a posttest).

Avoiding sensitization effects can be difficult because it may require **nonreactive measures.** Nonreactive measurement procedures take place without the participants' knowledge. Ethical considerations may prohibit a researcher from using non-reactive procedures since they will almost certainly require some form of deception (or less-than-fully-informed consent). Alternatively, researchers may try to minimize sensitization effects by adding a lot of irrelevant distractors to the IV manipulation, the dependent variable, or both. In the example above, for instance, we implied that the anti-discrimination commercials were only part of a large set of commercials viewed by the subjects. The greater number of different commercials included, the less likely subjects are to be sensitized to just the ones on racial discrimination. Similarly, the questionnaire could ask a lot of questions about a lot of social issues, not just racial attitudes. In this way, the researcher's interest in race has been "buried" in the questionnaire. The cost of these procedures, of course, is that the effect of the anti-discrimination commercials could be diluted by all of the other commercials. The participants may not experience the full impact of the commercials, and the researcher may erroneously conclude that they do not have any positive effects on racial attitudes.

Pretest-Posttest Designs: The Need for a Control Group

Pretest-posttest designs assess the effectiveness of a treatment by comparing scores obtained after the treatment with scores from before the treatment. The independent variable in these designs is typically labeled Time of Test (or Treatment), and the levels of this WS factor are pretest (or before treatment) versus posttest (or after treatment). These designs are intuitively very appealing because they seem perfect for demonstrating the effectiveness of a manipulation. However, as we indicated earlier in this chapter, studies that use a *single group, pretest-posttest design* are confounded at the outset because it is impossible to counterbalance the order of the pretest and posttest conditions, and therefore, these designs are classified as quasi-experimental research designs.

Specifically, in a single-group design, every participant is pretested, given the treatment, and then posttested. Without counterbalancing, these designs are vulnerable to every one of the potential confounds listed above, as well as the time-related effects and demand characteristic effects discussed earlier. That is, when posttest scores are different from the pretest scores, it is impossible to determine whether that difference is the result of the treatment, maturation, history, regression toward the mean, sensitization, mortality, instrumentation, practice effects, carryover, or demand characteristic effects. The only way researchers can draw causal conclusions from a pretest-posttest design is if they use a *mixed design* that includes a no-treatment control group that receives both the pretest and the posttest, but not the experimental treatment. This design is referred to as a *pretest-posttest with control group* design. It is a mixed design because there is a BS factor (Experimental Group: treatment versus no-treatment control) *and* a WS factor (Time of Test: pretest versus posttest).

Participants are assigned to the experimental treatment and no-treatment control groups at random to create equivalent groups, and then all participants are given the pretest. (At this point, researchers can compare the group averages to confirm the groups are equivalent on the pretest.) The treatment group is then exposed to the treatment while the control group does not receive any form of treatment. Then all participants are tested again. If there is a difference between the pretest and posttest scores for the control group it must be the result of one or more of the time-related factors discussed above because those participants did not receive any form of experimental treatment. Thus, the change in performance demonstrated by the no-treatment control group provides a measure of the effects of maturation, sensitization, practice, and so forth. The question of interest to the researcher is whether the experimental treatment group shows either *more or less* change than the control group. If the groups demonstrate the same degree of change, we would have to conclude that the change in performance demonstrated by the experimental group can be accounted for by time-related factors alone. In contrast, if the treatment group's change in performance from the pretest to the posttest is significantly *different* than the change demonstrated by the control group, we would conclude that the experimental treatment had a significant effect. To illustrate this point, let's consider an example.

Suppose a researcher wanted to test the effect of mental imagery training on short-term memory performance using a pretest-posttest with control group design. The dependent variable was the number of items correctly recalled during a digit span memory task. High school students completed a digit span task, and then half of them were selected at random to receive training in the mental imagery mnemonic technique. At the end of the training, all of the students completed the digit span task a second time. Table 10-3 presents hypothetical data from this study. As you can see on the table, the average number of items recalled correctly on the pretest was 7 for both groups, indicating that the groups were equivalent in memory performance prior to the onset of the treatment. The control group's

TABLE 10.3	Hypothetical Data From a Pretest-Pottest With Control Group Design		
Group	Pretest		Posttest
Experimental	7	(mental imagery training)	14
No-Treatment Control	7		10

performance improved by 3 points from the pretest to the posttest, and this change is due to time-related factors such as practice. The treatment group, in contrast, showed a 7-point increase in average memory performance. Thus, there is a 4-point difference between the groups in the amount of improvement they showed between the pretest and the posttest. The experimental group showed more improvement than would be expected simply as a function of time-related factors, and therefore, if the 4-point difference between the posttest scores is statistically significant, we would conclude that mental imagery instruction *did* have an effect on memory.

Another possible pattern of results researchers may encounter is where the experimental treatment group shows significantly *less* change in performance between the pretest and posttest than the control group. This may occur when the repeated testing generates boredom or fatigue, so that performance tends to decline between the pretest and the posttest. When a treatment has a positive effect on performance, but it is combined with boredom and fatigue effects, there may be little change between the pretest and posttest because the gain due to the treatment (such as training in a mnemonic technique) compensates for the decline due to boredom or fatigue. A no-treatment control group, however, would show a decline in performance due to fatigue or boredom. If the treatment group showed significantly *less decline* in performance than the control group, we would conclude that the treatment had a significant effect. Thus, a single group pretest-posttest design would lead to the erroneous conclusion that the treatment had no effect on performance, while the pretest-posttest with control group design would allow us to detect the systematic effect of the treatment.

In summary, including a no-treatment control group in a pretest-posttest design compensates for time-related effects by allowing researchers to compare the amount of improvement demonstrated by the two groups. When the difference between the pretest and posttest scores for the experimental treatment group is significantly different (either greater or smaller) than the difference between the pretest and posttest scores for the control group, we can conclude that the treatment has had an effect on performance. Furthermore, as long as the participants in the two groups (the experimental group and the control group) are tested over the same points in history (rather than all of the participants in the control group being tested in April and all of the experimental group being tested in June, for instance), the researcher can also be fairly certain that the differences between the two groups on the posttest are not due to instrumentation and history.

Selecting Within-Subjects Factors for Mixed Designs

As you should recall, studies that include at least one BS factor and at least one WS factor are known as mixed designs. Mixed designs have some of the advantages and disadvantages of both WS and BS designs. For instance, because they include at least one WS factor, mixed designs have more power than BS designs, and the more WS factors they have, the more powerful they are. However, because they include at least one BS factor, mixed designs have less power than WS designs. As another example, mixed designs include at least one repeated measure, so time-related effects (such as practice) are more likely to create confounds in mixed designs than in BS designs. In contrast, because participants in mixed designs are not exposed to *every* experimental condition, mixed designs have less potential for time-related confounds than WS designs. Essentially, in a mixed design, the BS factors have the advantages of BS designs while the WS factors have the advantages of WS designs. This combination of features makes mixed designs very attractive to many researchers.

Obviously, in order to conduct a mixed design, it must be possible to test the participants at every level of at least one of the IVs, so one of the first steps in planning a mixed design is to decide which independent variable will be the repeated measure, and which will be the BS factor. The nature of the IVs may make this decision easy because some variables (such as sex and race) can never be repeated measures, while other variables (such as a pretest-posttest comparison) are, by definition, always repeated measures. In general, subject variables will always be BS factors, because these personal characteristics tend to be very stable over time, and many of them are permanent. Males are always male, African-Americans are always African-American, and adults who attended a Montessori preschool will always have that as a part of their personal history. Similarly, personality characteristics such as extraversion tend to be highly stable well into late adulthood. Consequently, if one of these subject variables is the IV in a study, it will have to be a BS factor. (Specifically, the study would be a quasi-experiment using a non-equivalent groups design, as discussed in Chapter 7.) Furthermore, you should remember that groups of participants selected on the basis of a subject variable cannot be considered equivalent, and therefore, the main effect of these subject variable IVs cannot be used to draw causal conclusions.

Let's suppose a researcher wants to use a mixed design to compare the effects of visual versus verbal mnemonic training on the memory performance of men versus women. The two IVs are Sex and Type of Mnemonic, and the dependent variable is memory performance. In this mixed design, the BS factor must be Sex, because participants cannot be tested under every level of Sex, and therefore, the Type of Mnemonic will have to be the repeated measure (WS factor). That is, all of the participants will need to be tested under both visual and verbal mnemonic conditions, preferably in counterbalanced order.

The selection of the BS and WS factors for a mixed design is not so easy when all of the IVs are non-subject variables. For instance, suppose a researcher wants to compare the effectiveness of visual versus verbal mnemonic strategies for memorizing lists of nouns versus adjectives. In this case, the IVs are Type of Mnemonic (visual versus verbal) and Type of Word (noun versus adjective), and they are both non-subject variables that could be repeated measures. Therefore, the researcher has a choice between two different mixed designs: a design where Type of Mnemonic is the BS factor and Type of Word is the WS factor, or a design where Type of Word is the BS factor and Type of Mnemonic is the WS factor. Which of these mixed designs is better? There is no hard-and-fast answer to this question other than to say that the best studies are those with fewest potential confounds and the greatest generalizability (i.e., internal and external validity). Therefore, researchers should compare the various mixed designs to determine which IV would present the fewest number of demand characteristics and have the lowest probability of being confounded by time-related effects if it was used as a repeated measure.

In the study on Type of Mnemonic and Type of Word, for example, the researcher may decide that being asked to learn two different mnemonic techniques will present stronger demand characteristics and produce greater reactivity than being asked to recall a list of nouns and then a list of adjectives, and therefore, he would have the Type of Word be the WS factor in the mixed design. That is, the researcher may believe that, while there is no way to disguise a change in training, it is possible to develop a "cover story" for the memory test that would downplay the difference between the types of words so that participants would not realize that the change from nouns to adjectives is an important part of the research. Based on this reasoning, the researcher would randomly assign the participants to one of two groups. The first group would be trained to use the visual mnemonic technique, and the other group would be trained to use the verbal mnemonic technique. (Each subject is trained only once.) After training is complete, each subject would be tested with both lists of words. Thus, the Type of Mnemonic is the BS factor and Type of Word is the WS factor.

As another example, imagine that we are designing a replication of Schachter and Singer's (1962) classic study on the cognitive appraisal of physiological arousal and emotion. Like Schachter and Singer, we will inject the participants with epinephrine (or adrenaline) to create a state of physiological arousal and then expose them to a confederate who acts very happy or very angry. The participants will be blind to the actual purpose of the study, and will be told they are receiving an injection of vitamins. The second independent variable will be the expectations the participants have about the side effects of the injection, and it will have 3 levels: participants will be told the side effects include lethargy and drowsiness; (2) participants will be told the side effects include arousal and energy; or (3) participants will be told the vitamin has no particular side effects. Thus, we are planning a 2 (Confederate's Mood) × 3 (Type of Side Effect Expected) design. The dependent variable will be the participant's self-reported emotional state following exposure to the confederate.

While Schachter and Singer's original study used a BS design, suppose we want to use a more powerful design. Is it possible to use a WS design? Both of the IVs are non-subject variables that can be used as repeated measures. That is, it is procedurally possible to measure participants' response to both happy and angry confederates. It is also procedurally possible to inject each participant on three separate occasions, telling them that they are receiving different vitamins with different side effects. Therefore, it *is* possible to employ a WS design for this study because it is procedurally possible to test every participant under each of the 6 experimental conditions in the 2 × 3 design. It is also possible to use either of two mixed designs (because either of the IVs can be BS factors). Which design should we choose?

In order to answer this question, we need to imagine being a participant in this study. Could we be convinced that there are different vitamins that cause different side effects? Yes, it may be easy to believe that some vitamins will cause drowsiness while others will be stimulating or have no effect at all. Therefore, exposure to different levels of the Type of Side Effect variable may not generate strong demand characteristics and reactivity. What about the other IV? Could we be convinced that it is normal for strangers to behave very angry or very happy in our presence? Well, maybe we could believe it would happen once, maybe twice, but 6 times? In American culture, adults are generally expected to behave with decorum in public places, especially in the presence of strangers. So if it happens two or three times, the participants in our study may notice that every time we give them an injection, we leave them alone with a stranger who then behaves in an unnatural fashion. Unless we have come up with a suitable cover story to make the confederate's behavior look normal, our participants may realize that the actions of the stranger are part of the study, and when we later ask the participants how they feel, they may give us the answer they think we want. Based on this reasoning, if we cannot think of a convincing cover story, we will probably decide that a WS design, where the participants would be exposed to 6 confederates (three acting happy and three acting angry) has too many potential demand characteristics.

So next we would turn our attention to our mixed design options. There are two possible mixed designs for this study. In one case, Confederate's Mood is the BS factor. The participants would be assigned at random to one of the mood conditions and then tested under the three different Side Effect conditions. For example, the first participant has been assigned to the happy confederate condition, so after receiving the first injection and being told to expect drowsiness, the participant is left in a room with a happy confederate and he is later asked to report how he feels. During his next visit, the participant receives another injection, but is told to expect arousal. He is then left in a room with another happy confederate, and his emotional state is measured again. On the third occasion, the participant receives another injection, and is told this vitamin has no side effects. He is left in a room with a happy confederate, and his emotional state is measured a third time. Thus, in this mixed design, Confederate's Mood is a BS factor, which means that once the participants are assigned to one of the Mood conditions, they never see confederates in any other mood. Every time they are tested, it is under the same level of Mood. This mixed design includes two groups of participants, and each participant is tested under three levels of Side Effects.

The other mixed design that we can consider for our study has Type of Side Effect as the BS factor. In this case, participants will be randomly assigned to one of the Side Effect conditions and then tested twice: Once with a happy confederate and once with an angry confederate. For example, the first participant has been assigned to the drowsiness condition, so after receiving the first injection and being told to expect drowsiness, the participant is left in a room with a happy confederate and he is later asked to report how he feels. During his next visit, the participant receives another injection and is again warned to expect drowsiness, and then is left alone with an angry confederate. He is then asked to report how he feels. Thus, in this mixed design, Type of Side Effect is a BS factor, which means that once the participants are assigned to one of the Side Effect conditions, they are never told to expect any other side effect. Every time they are tested, they are told to expect the same side effects. This mixed design includes three groups of participants, and each participant is tested under two levels of Confederate's Mood.

Which of these mixed designs is the better choice? Again we should try to imagine what the participants will be thinking and feeling about the study as they progress through it. In a mixed design for this study, the participants will be tested two or three times, and the question is whether or not we can provide an adequate cover story or pretext that will reduce the demand characteristic of being exposed to two or three confederates acting in what may seem to be an inappropriate manner by being very emotional in public. If we cannot create a convincing cover story, we may need to settle for a BS design in which each participant is tested under only one of the 6 experimental conditions. In a BS design, researchers do not need to try to maintain a cover story over time in order to keep the participants blind to the experimental hypotheses and reduce reactivity. Put simply, we will often decide that it is preferable to use a less powerful design and obtain unconfounded results than to use more powerful designs that produce uninterpretable results.

In conclusion, when selecting any research design, researchers should try to imagine being a participant in the study in order to identify the demand characteristics that may be present, and select the design and procedures that minimizes them. It may be useful for the researcher to consult colleagues or to conduct a pilot study before making a final decision about the design. In a pilot study, for instance, the researcher could do a dry run of both mixed designs, and then interview the participants about the purposes of the research and what they thought the researchers wanted them to say about their emotional state at the end of the session.

The Special Case of Age as an Independent Variable

Before we wrap up this chapter on designing experimental and quasi-experimental research, let's consider the special case of Age as an independent variable. The effect of age on behavior is a central question in psychology. In fact, there is an entire sub-discipline in the field of psychology devoted to the study of how behavior changes with age from infancy through old age. Much of the research conducted by these developmental psychologists includes a comparison between participants of different ages, so the design of studies with age as the IV is one of their specialties. Age, as an explanatory variable and as an independent variable, has some unique properties that we think are important.

Age, of course, is a characteristic of participants that researchers cannot manipulate. Age is a *subject variable*. Researchers cannot, for example, use random assignment to assign participants to the age groups. However, age is a major exception to the general rule we mentioned earlier that says subject variables cannot be WS factors. Age can be *either* a BS factor or a WS factor. For example, suppose a researcher studying language development wants to study children's grammatical development by testing their understanding of a variety of grammatical structures, such as the passive voice in declarative sentences. (That is, understanding that "The car was hit by the truck" has the same meaning as "The truck hit the car.") The researcher believes that grammatical development occurs very rapidly and that most grammatical structures are mastered sometime during the preschool period. Therefore, she plans to include 7 levels of Age in her study: 24 months, 30 months, 36 months, 42 months, 48 months, 54 months, and 60 months. The researcher has the option of letting Age be a BS factor, in which case, she will need to find 7 separate groups of children varying in age—some 24-month-olds, some 30-month-olds, some 36-month-olds, and so forth. Developmental psychologists call this a *cross-sectional design*. Alternatively, the researcher has the option of letting Age be a WS factor, in which case, she will need to find a group of 24-month-old children, test their grammar, wait 6 months and test their grammar again, wait another 6 months and test their grammar a third time, and so forth, until the children have reached the age of 60 months. Thus, every child is tested at every age level—the definition of a WS factor. Developmental psychologists call this a *longitudinal design*.

Cross-sectional and longitudinal designs both allow researchers to test the effect of Age by measuring the difference in performance between the different age levels, and both designs require cautious interpretation. Are developmental changes due to biological growth and physical maturation or are they the result of increased experience, learning, and education? Neither cross-sectional nor longitudinal designs are able to answer this question because these causal mechanisms are inherently confounded with each other and with chronological age. As children get older they become more physically mature and they gain more experience with their environment. Therefore, if we find a significant effect of age in a longitudinal design, where age is a repeated measure, we cannot know whether the change in performance was caused by the natural physical maturation that occurs over time or by the increased learning and experience that also occurs over time. Similarly, cross-sectional designs, where Age is a BS factor, are automatically confounded through *selection bias* (or *non-equivalence*): 2-year-olds are simultaneously less mature and less experienced than 3-year-olds, so the age groups differ on both of these potentially causal dimensions. Thus, like all subject variables, we cannot draw causal conclusions about the variable of age.

Steps in Designing an Experiment or Quasi-Experiment

The steps involved in designing a study are summarized in Table 10-4. The process is very dynamic in that decisions made early in the process often need to be changed as the researcher makes decisions about issues listed later. (Thus, the sequence of

TABLE 10.4	Basic Steps in Designing Experiments

I.   State your hypotheses and select the necessary variables.

II. Operationally define your variables.

   A. Independent variable(s)

   1. Are the IVs non-subject or subject variables?

   2. What levels of the IVs are needed to answer the research question (i.e., test the hypotheses)?

   3. How will you manipulate the experimental setting (or select the participants) in order to make the appropriate comparisons to test the hypotheses?

   B. Dependent variables (decide where and how you will observe and measure the DV—counting behaviors, rating scales, etc.)

   C. Matching variables—*if any* (must correlate with DV)

III. Select a design: BS, WS, or Mixed.

   This will involve asking questions like: Is it *possible* to use a WS design? (If any of the IVs are subject variables or if manipulating the IV would be unethical, the answer will be "no.") Make a preliminary choice for a design and then proceed through the following steps. At any point, you may find that your choice will be confounded or inefficient, etc, in which case, make another choice and repeat the following steps, etc. Note: You may also need to redefine (operationally) your variables.

IV. Select *procedures* for the study (including the control variables).

   A. What will the participants be told about the purposes of the study?

   B. Where and when will the observations take place?

   C. Who will conduct the observations (i.e., score the participants' behaviors) and what will the observers know about:

   1. The purposes of the study?

   2. The treatment condition of any particular participant?

   D. Do you need confederates?

   1. How many?

   2. What roles do they play in the study?

   3. How will they be selected?

   4. What will they know about the purposes of the study?

   E. Write a step-by-step scenario that describes *exactly* what will happen to your participants once the study begins:

   1. How are they recruited?

   2. How is the study described to them?

   3. Where do they go?

   4. What does the researcher say to them?

   5. If there is deception, how is it to be maintained over time (especially in cases of WS or mixed designs)?

   6. How are the participants to be debriefed?

V.   Conduct a *pilot study* to identify any possible "kinks" (or oversights) in your procedures.

steps implied in Table 10-4 is not immutable.) While designing studies, the researcher must always look out for undesirable demand characteristics and potential confounds and avoid them.

Exercises

1. Identify the research design for each of the experimental and quasi-experimental scenarios at the end of Chapter 7. (Note: Scenarios 5, 9, and 10 are correlational studies, not experiments or quasi-experiments.) For factorial designs, use the notation system to summarize the levels of each IV.

Use the following information to answer questions 2–4:

A social psychologist is interested in identifying factors that influence interpersonal judgments. In the next study, the psychologist plans to ask male college students (the participants) to play the role of a company personnel manager who must hire new employees. Each participant will be given a stack of "job applications" to examine, each of which will include a photograph of the applicant. One of these applications will be the "target" for the research; the remainder will be "distractors."

For each file, the participant will be asked to rate the quality of the applicant on a scale from 0 (very poor) to 10 (excellent). The "target" application will have the same résumé and letters of recommendation, but some participants will see a photograph of a very attractive woman, some will see a photograph of an average-looking woman, and the rest will see a photograph of a very unattractive woman.

Furthermore, half of the participants will be led to believe that the "target" applicant is happily married and the others will be told that she is "unattached."

2. What research method is used here?

3. What is the design?

4. Suppose the data from the study revealed the following group averages:

	Married	Unattached
Very Attractive	4	9
Average	6	7
Very Unattractive	7	3

a. Is there a main effect of the attractiveness variable? Verbally describe the effect.

b. Is there a main effect of the marital status ("Availability") variable? Verbally describe the effect.

c. Is there an interaction between the IVs? Describe it.

5. Dr. Smith hypothesizes that as age increases (from about age 5 until early adulthood), racial prejudice increases steadily. To test this hypothesis using a one-way quasi-experiment, what levels of his independent variable should Dr. Smith use? Why?

6. A researcher wants to perform a study to test the effects of punishment on bar-press behavior in trained rats and to see whether the age of the rat influences the effect of punishment. The researcher wants to use two age levels (12 versus 30 months) and three forms of punishment (electric shock versus very loud noise versus a dousing with very cold water). What would be the advantages of using a WS design for this study? What problems would the researcher encounter if he tried to use a WS design?

For problems 7–11, identify the potential confound that is present.

7. A researcher has been studying children's eye-hand coordination and has developed a new training procedure designed to improve children's performance on a mirror-tracing task. Twenty 5-year-olds were randomly selected to participate in the study. First, each child was given the mirror-tracing task to establish a baseline (i.e., current) level of performance. Then each child received 20 minutes of training every other day for 8 weeks. The mirror-tracing task was then administered as a posttest. Performance was measured by counting the number of times the child's tracing line went out of the boundaries of the figure.

8. A school psychologist has conducted a study to test the accuracy of tests that are supposed to predict a child's readiness to begin kindergarten. The teachers at the local Montessori preschool agreed to fill out a teacher's rating scale for each child scheduled to start kindergarten the following year. The owner of the local daycare center agreed to allow the school psychologist to administer the Newgate School Readiness Test to the children attending the daycare. At the end of the children's first 3 months in kindergarten, their performance was evaluated. It was found that the teacher-ratings were more accurate in predicting kindergarten readiness than was the Newgate Test.

9. A developmental psychologist received a 10-year federal research grant to do a longitudinal study of achievement motivation. The Thematic Apperception Test (TAT) was being used to measure achievement motivation, which involves showing participants ambiguous pictures and asking them to tell a story about the people in the pictures. These stories are then "scored" by a research assistant who is looking for indicators of achievement motivation, such as goal-setting, reactions to success or failure, etc. The "intensity" of such indicators are rated on a 7-point scale. For this longitudinal study, 100 participants were given the TAT just after graduating from high school, five years later (at age 23), and again five years after that (at age 28). The TATs were scored immediately after administration by the psychologist's current graduate assistant (thus three different individuals scored the three sets of responses).

10. A taste test was conducted to compare people's preferences for different brands of beer. Participants were randomly selected to taste two beers: Coors Extra-Gold and Miller Lite. The beers were in clear glass mugs in a well-lit room, side by side on the table in front of the participants. (The Coors was a deeper gold in color than the Miller, but no labels were attached to the mugs, and the participants were not told which brands were being compared.) Participants tasted each beer (in counterbalanced order) and then selected the one they felt had "the best beer taste." The results indicated that the majority of participants chose the Coors.

11. A study was conducted to prevent infants from developing insecure attachments with their mothers, which could lead to social and peer problems later in life. The researchers visited 100 families and observed the mother-infant interactions when the babies were three months old. On the basis of these observations, mothers were given scores that represented their "sensitivity" to their infants' needs. Then the 20 women with the lowest sensitivity scores were selected for training. The training included lectures, demonstrations, and role-play exercises, as well as hands-on practice in caring for infants and recognizing their needs. The training took three weeks to complete. When these 20 infants were 12 months old, they were tested in the Ainsworth Strange Situation and their attachment to their mothers was assessed. The results indicated that 13 of the infants had developed secure attachments.

The following is the "method" section from a published research report. Use the information in this method section to answer questions 12–15. (Note: In this research report, published in 1983, the term "subjects" refers to the participants.)

Method

Subjects and Experimenters

Two classrooms each of first-, fourth-, and sixth-grade children participated in the study. The subjects had received written permission to participate from their suburban, middle-class parents and had verbally requested to participate. Two pairs of undergraduate women who were blind to experimental hypotheses portrayed the experimenter and the confederate. Subjects were randomly assigned to experimenters and to experimental conditions.

Design

Like Staub's (1970a) original study, the duration of the experiment was limited to minimize intersubject communication and this resulted, as in Staub's (1970a) work, in an unequal number of subjects per cell ($M = 4.21$, range 3–6). The need to discard potential subjects because of absences due to illness or other commitments ($n = 9$), because equipment malfunctioned ($n = 1$), because subjects failed to accept the existence of the unseen peer ($n = 3$ sixth graders), and because subjects reentered the experimental area before the emergency began ($n = 2$ first graders, 4 fourth graders, and 4 sixth graders) also contributed to unequal cell size. Subject attrition was equal across all experimental categories. One hundred and one children served as subjects: 17 first-grade boys and 17 first-grade girls (M age = 6.54 years), 18 fourth-grade boys and 14 fourth-grade girls (M age = 9.57 years), and 16 sixth-grade boys and 19 sixth-grade girls (M age = 11.51 years).

Procedures

Children participated one at a time in the experiment. The experimental room was divided into three work areas by two solid room dividers (7 ft. high × 9 ft. wide; 2.1m × 2.7m) made of wood paneling. The experimenter led the subjects past the first area into a second area, which contained a table and two chairs. On the table was a gambling game, some chips, a card for betting on, and a smaller card with "reward rules" on it (actually just a table of random numbers). Children were asked to be seated and were introduced to the gambling game. The game was made of three wooden wheels on top of one another, connected in the center with a bolt. The bottom wheel was stationary and was painted into 16 numbered red and black wedges. When the two top wheels, which were separated by a row of nails, were grasped by attached handles and turned in opposite directions, the game made a clicking sound before exposing four numbers and one color through cut out portions of the middle wheel. The object of the game was to bet correctly on a winning number.

While the child looked at the game, the experimenter excused herself and went into the third experimental area beyond the second room divider to "talk to the children who were working there." Subjects in the no-peer-present condition believed the experimenter was visiting with a single same-sex peer (ultimately the "victim" in need of help.) Subjects in the peer-present condition believed the experimenter was conversing with two same-sex peers (ultimately the victim and another bystander/potential donor.) The exact location of the two peers was not specified and there was no mention by the experimenter of their being together. The experimenter briefly inquired if things were going all right and then returned to the subject child. The adult confederate made periodic noises with foot shuffling, paper rustling, etc., to validate the presence of the peer(s).

The rules of the game were explained to the subjects. The subjects could bet one of their 10 chips on a color or a number on the gambling matrix card. The amount won by the bet would be determined by the reward rules card. (In actuality, the experimenter randomly awarded chips such that the subject won about 10 chips in 5 minutes.) Subjects in the no-competence-instruction group heard a simple description of the game. Subjects in the competence group were also told that it was extremely important that they use the handles to turn the wheels and keep their hands away from the spokes. Later, the subjects were told that the experimenter had had some trouble with the game getting stuck and if the children had any trouble like this, they could unstick the game by turning a nut on top of the bolt in the center of the game. The children turned the nut to practice. This training satisfied various definitions of competence that have been offered (e.g., Midlarsky, 1971; Staub, 1978) by ensuring that the children had a relevant skill and some experience with being able to apply this skill. Next, children were asked to explain the game and were asked questions concerning how to play and how to win chips. At this time the experimenter ascertained that the children in the competence group knew how to fix the game should it get stuck. Then, children were allowed to play the game for about 5 minutes and to win 10 chips.

After this, the experimenter glanced at her watch and said she had to leave for a moment; she suggested that she had something the children could play with while she was gone. She allowed the children to select one of several colored pencils and assured the children that they could return to the table to get more pencils if they needed them. This granting of explicit permission to reenter the experimental area had been shown to be important in past research (e.g., Staub, 1971b).

The children were then escorted to the first experimental area next to the door and were given a connect-the-dot picture of a bird that they could color or outline "or whatever you want. It is just something to do while I'm gone." This task was used simply so that children were not wandering around the room during the emergency. The experimenter then returned to the third area and told the peer(s) that she needed to leave for a moment. She then said, "Oh, you didn't get a chance to play with the game? I thought you had. Well, why don't you play with it while I'm gone?" The peer-present group heard the experimenter urge the other (nonvictim) peer to keep working behind the second screen while she was gone. The confederate then entered the middle game area and the experimenter exited past the subject, noting she would be back in a few minutes. Thus, the child victim was apparently between the two peer bystanders, separated from both bystanders with a screen on either side.

After the experimenter had exited, the confederate turned the noisy wheels on the game twice and then stopped the wheels abruptly with a gasp, at the same time turning on a tape recorder. The recorder presented a young child emitting the following distress cues every 15 seconds: "Oh, my finger!" "Oh, rats it really hurts (sob)." "Oh, my hand is hurt, I can't get it out." "I can't get it out, I wish someone would help me." Between verbal cues, labored breathing and a struggle with the machine could be heard. The last cue was delivered 60 sec after the first gasp. The experimenter entered the room 15 seconds later and shuffled papers for 15 seconds to allow the child to report the emergency. If the child had not helped nor reported the problem to the experimenter within 90 seconds, the experimenter entered the game area and spoke to the peer, asking if the peer was all right and expressing pleasure that the peer was fine now.

The experimenter then returned to the subjects and noted that because they had won some chips already, they had won a prize and did not need to play longer. She then asked a number of debriefing questions, beginning with how happy the children felt (using a 5-point scale from "not very happy" to "very happy") prior to playing, right after playing, and currently. She then inquired about anything that may have happened in her absence and, after ascertaining that the children had heard the distress cues, discussed why the children had or had not helped and whether they felt their action was the correct response. The competence-instruction group was again probed to ascertain that they recalled the instructions. Finally, the experimenter offered the children an extra prize if they could guess the number of grooves on the bolt on the inside of the game. The experimenter then told the children there were 33 grooves on the bolt and then repeated this number. This question was used as a probe to assess intersubject communication. Only two of the 101 children in the present experiment guessed the correct number.

From Peterson, L. (1983). Role of donor competence, donor age, and peer presence on helping in an emergency. *Developmental Psychology, 19,* 873–880. Copyright © 1983 by the American Psychological Association. Adapted with permission.

12. Identify Peterson's independent variables. What was the dependent variable and how was it operationally defined?

13. Which research method and which research design did Peterson use in this study?

14. Identify as many directly controlled variables as you can.

15. Generate some hypothetical data for this study that would show an interaction between two of the independent variables. Verbally describe the interaction you have created.

16. Design a study to test the hypothesis that "laughter is the best medicine." Be sure to: (a) select your independent variables and operationally define the levels of the IVs; (b) operationally define the dependent variable; (c) identify the population to be studied, choose the setting where the study will take place, and describe the procedures you will follow. (Your design should include the kinds of information included in Peterson's Method section reprinted above.) Explain the advantages of your design over alternative designs.

CHAPTER

11

THE *z*-TEST AND *t*-TEST: ANALYZING DATA FROM ONE- AND TWO-GROUP DESIGNS

■ ■ ■ ■ ■ ■

In this chapter, you will learn two statistical tests that are used to analyze data from small experimental and quasi-experimental designs. The *z*-test compares the mean from a research sample to the mean of a population, while a *t*-test compares the means from two research samples. Two different applications of the *z*-test are presented, as are three *t*-tests (which are used with different research designs).

Look for These Important Terms and Concepts

directional tests

nondirectional tests

one-tailed tests

two-tailed tests

degrees of freedom

Before Reading This Chapter, You May Wish to Review

Chapter 4:
- interval and ratio scales

Chapter 5:
- sample statistics versus population parameters
- normal distribution
- mean and standard deviation
- z scores
- areas under the normal curve

Chapter 6:
- null hypothesis
- alternate (or research) hypothesis
- standard error
- rejecting the null hypothesis
- alpha (α)
- critical values

Chapter 10:
- between-subjects designs
- within-subjects designs
- matched-pairs designs

In Chapter 10, we discussed how experimental and quasi-experimental research may include one or more independent variables (one-way designs versus factorial designs) and how these IVs may be either between- or within-subjects factors (creating three types of designs: between-subjects, within-subjects, and mixed designs). In the next three chapters, we will cover some of the common statistical tests that are used to analyze the data from these studies. The choice of a statistic is based on the level (or scale) of measurement of the dependent variable and the type of research design. This chapter focuses on the analysis of interval and ratio data from simple designs that include only one or two groups; interval and ratio data from more complex designs can be analyzed using analysis of variance, which is covered in Chapter 12. Chapter 13 covers a variety of statistical procedures that are appropriate for ordinal and nominal data.

The z-Test: When the Population Standard Deviation (σ) Is Known

z-Test: Application 1: When the Population Mean (μ) Is Known

One application of the z-test is to answer the question: "Does the research sample come from a population with a known mean?" In other words, if we know the mean (μ) and standard deviation (σ) of a population, it is possible to examine a single research sample and decide whether or not it comes from that population by comparing the sample mean ($\overline{X}$) to the population mean (μ) relative to the amount of chance fluctuation that occurs among sample means due to random sampling error. This is basically the procedure we used in Chapter 6 to illustrate the principles of hypothesis testing. In the example from Chapter 6, we wanted to know whether prenatal exposure to crack cocaine affects the birthweight of infants, so we found the average birthweight of the population (obtained from birth records from all hospitals), constructed a sampling distribution of all random samples from the population, and compared the average birthweight of a sample of "crack babies" to the critical values (or cut-off points) that indicate which samples are rare when chance alone is operating. This sequence of events is logically equivalent to the steps involved in performing a single-sample z-test.

Step 1 of the z-Test The first step in a z-test is to specify the null and research hypotheses. The null hypothesis (H_0) will almost always state that the sample *does* come from the population with a mean equal to μ_{Null} (i.e., that $\overline{X}$ is representative of μ_{Null}, and that the difference between $\overline{X}$ and μ_{Null} is due to random sampling error). Thus, the null hypothesis can be stated like this:

$$H_0: \mu_{sample} = \mu_{Null}$$

where: μ_{sample} = the mean of the "true" population from which the sample is drawn

μ_{Null} = the known mean of the population, predicted by the null hypothesis

In our study of crack babies, the null hypothesis would state that the mean weight for the population of crack babies is equal to the mean for the population of babies in general:

$$H_0: \mu_{\text{crack babies}} = \mu_{\text{babies}}$$

The research hypothesis (H_1) for a one-sample study will usually state that the sample did *not* come from the known population (i.e., that $\overline{X}$ differs significantly from μ_{Null}, and that the sample comes from a population with a different mean). The research hypothesis can be either directional or nondirectional. A **directional test** specifically asserts that the sample comes from a population with a larger (*or* smaller) mean than the test population, while a **nondirectional test** simply states that the sample comes from a population with a *different value* of μ.

Directional tests are appropriate when theory or empirical observations strongly support them. In our example, for instance, if the researcher had good evidence that prenatal exposure to cocaine delays fetal growth by depriving the fetal tissue of adequate amounts of oxygen, it would be appropriate to predict that "crack babies" will be *smaller* at birth than babies in general, so the directional research hypothesis for this problem would be:

$$H_1: \mu_{\text{crack babies}} < \mu_{\text{babies}}$$

For some research problems, the directional test would predict that the research sample comes from a population with a mean (μ) that is *greater than* the mean predicted by the null hypothesis. For instance, it may be hypothesized that early sensory stimulation of infants (in the form of a variety of interesting sights, sounds, and tactile experiences) will increase their intellectual development, leading to higher IQ scores. Thus, the directional research hypothesis would say that the mean IQ for the population of children who receive early stimulation is *higher than* the mean IQ for the general population:

$$H_1: \mu_{\text{early stimulation}} > \mu_{\text{general population}}$$

To test a directional hypothesis, we set our level of significance by selecting a value of alpha (α) and finding the critical value of the sampling distribution that cuts off the "alpha region" in the appropriate tail. Figure 11-1 illustrates the two possible directional research hypotheses. As you can see in these figures, the region of rejection is found in only one of the tails of the sampling distribution, and therefore, these directional research hypotheses are typically called **one-tailed tests.**

When researchers cannot justify a directional (one-tailed) test on the basis of theory or past research, they will use a nondirectional research hypothesis. A nondirectional test simply states that the sample does not come from the population specified in the null hypothesis. The nondirectional research hypothesis would be stated like this:

$$H_1: \mu_{\text{sample}} \neq \mu_{\text{Null}}$$

where: μ_{sample} = the mean of the "true" population from which the sample is drawn

μ_{Null} = the known mean of the population as predicted by the null hypothesis

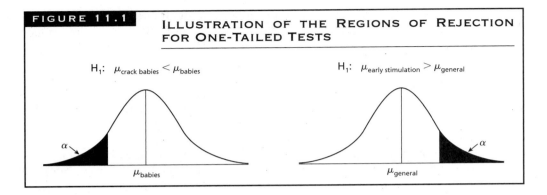

FIGURE 11.1 — ILLUSTRATION OF THE REGIONS OF REJECTION FOR ONE-TAILED TESTS

For example, a researcher may be interested in the effects of a mother's vegetarian diet on the birthweight of her newborn, but there may be no theory or data available to lead the researcher to strongly believe that babies of vegetarians will be either smaller or heavier than average. The research hypothesis, therefore, would be:

$$H_1: \mu_{\text{vegetarian}} \neq \mu_{\text{babies}}$$

To conduct a nondirectional test, we split alpha equally into the two tails of the sampling distribution, identifying the events in each tail as "rare" events, and thus creating two separate regions of rejection. If the mean ($\overline{X}$) of the sample of vegetarian babies falls into *either* of the two tails, the null hypothesis will be rejected. For obvious reasons, then, a nondirectional test is often referred to as a **two-tailed test.** Since a nondirectional test can identify a significant difference in either direction, there are three possible outcomes for a nondirectional test: (1) We may reject the null hypothesis because the vegetarian babies weigh significantly *more* than average; (2) we may reject the null hypothesis because the vegetarian babies weigh significantly *less* than average; or (3) we may fail to reject the null hypothesis because random sampling error frequently produces samples with the mean weight ($\overline{X}$) of the vegetarian babies, and so there is no evidence to support the claim that a vegetarian diet has an effect on birthweight.

In fact, most researchers elect to use nondirectional tests *even when their research hypotheses make specific predictions about the direction of the difference.* Theory and previous research are not always accurate indicators of reality, and sometimes our predictions turn out to be embarrassingly backwards. Sometimes we may find a large difference between the sample $\overline{X}$ and the population μ, but it is in the wrong direction—that is, our sample falls into the "wrong" tail of the sampling distribution, and if we had set up a one-tailed test, we could not reject the null hypothesis despite the large difference. To avoid this problem, researchers typically choose a nondirectional research hypothesis for all studies. For example, in our "crack babies"

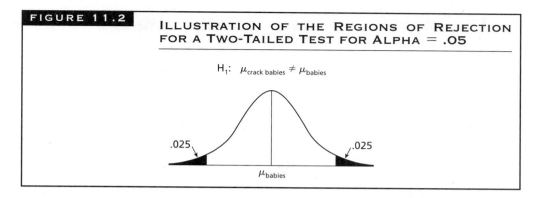

FIGURE 11.2

ILLUSTRATION OF THE REGIONS OF REJECTION FOR A TWO-TAILED TEST FOR ALPHA = .05

H_1: $\mu_{\text{crack babies}} \neq \mu_{\text{babies}}$

.025   .025

μ_{babies}

study, a nondirectional test would allow us to reject the null hypothesis in the event that the "crack babies" turn out—however unexpectedly—to be much heavier than average. Figure 11-2 illustrates a nondirectional (two-tailed) test for our "crack babies" example. Figure 11-2 should look familiar because we used a nondirectional test to illustrate the process of hypothesis testing in Chapter 6.

Step 2 of the z-Test The second step of the z-test is to set our alpha (α) level and look up the critical values of z in the z-Table (Areas Under the Normal Curve—see Table B-1 in Appendix B). If we are making a specific prediction about the direction of the difference between the sample and the population, we could perform a one-tailed test where the region of rejection (i.e., alpha) is all in one tail of the sampling distribution. If we set alpha at .05 for a one-tailed (directional) test, we would look up the value of z that has .05 in the tail beyond it. Looking down the third column of the z-Table (Areas Under the Normal Curve), we find that the proportion closest to .05 is .05050 and that the value of z is 1.64 (see Figure 11-3).

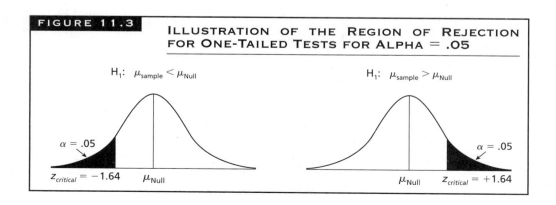

FIGURE 11.3

ILLUSTRATION OF THE REGION OF REJECTION FOR ONE-TAILED TESTS FOR ALPHA = .05

H_1: $\mu_{\text{sample}} < \mu_{\text{Null}}$

H_1: $\mu_{\text{sample}} > \mu_{\text{Null}}$

$\alpha = .05$

$\alpha = .05$

$z_{\text{critical}} = -1.64$ μ_{Null}

μ_{Null} $z_{\text{critical}} = +1.64$

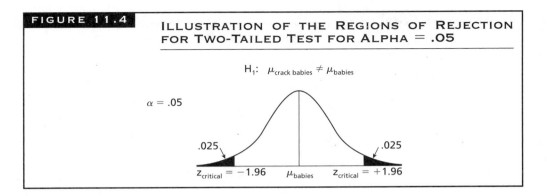

FIGURE 11.4   ILLUSTRATION OF THE REGIONS OF REJECTION FOR TWO-TAILED TEST FOR ALPHA = .05

H_1: $\mu_{\text{crack babies}} \neq \mu_{\text{babies}}$

$\alpha = .05$

.025   .025

$z_{\text{critical}} = -1.96$ μ_{babies} $z_{\text{critical}} = +1.96$

We would use a negative value ($z = -1.64$) if we expect the mean of the sample to be *smaller* than the value of μ that is predicted by the null hypothesis (that is, if our research hypothesis is $\mu_{\text{sample}} < \mu_{\text{Null}}$), and we would use a positive value ($z = +1.64$) if we expect the sample mean to be *larger* than μ (if our research hypothesis is $\mu_{\text{sample}} > \mu_{\text{Null}}$). For a two-tailed (nondirectional) test, we would split alpha in half, so we would look in the third column of the z-Table (Areas Under the Normal Curve) for the proportion .02500, and we will find that the value of z that cuts off 2.5% in each tail is ± 1.96 (see Figure 11-4). Therefore, the values of z_{critical} used most frequently are:

For a Directional Test: If $\alpha = .05$, $z_{\text{critical}} = \pm 1.64$ and if $\alpha = .01$, $z_{\text{critical}} = \pm 2.33$.

For a Nondirectional Test: If $\alpha = .05$, $z_{\text{critical}} = \pm 1.96$ and if $\alpha = .01$, $z_{\text{critical}} = \pm 2.58$.

Step 3 of the z-Test   The next step of the z-test involves calculating the necessary statistics that we will use to evaluate the null hypothesis. At this point, we have two choices: Either we can transform the research sample mean ($\overline{X}$) into a z-score (z_{obtained}) and compare it with the value of z_{critical} from the previous step (e.g., ± 1.64 for a one-tailed test or ± 1.96 for a two-tailed test), *or* we can transform z_{critical} into $\overline{X}_{\text{critical}}$ and compare it with our sample mean ($\overline{X}_{\text{obtained}}$). In either case, if the $\overline{X}$ or z from the research sample falls in the "shaded region" beyond the critical value, we will reject the null hypothesis. Both procedures lead to the same conclusion, as illustrated below using the hypothetical data from Table 6-1 (on page 134), where the average birthweight of the population of babies (μ) is 112 ounces, and the standard deviation (σ) in the population is 8.6. The research sample of four "crack babies" has a mean weight ($\overline{X}$) of 100 ounces. Because we are working with sample means and sampling distributions (rather than individual scores and group means), the formula for z that is used in this hypothesis testing procedure is:

TABLE 11.1	Decision Rules for z-Tests

H_1: $\mu_{sample} > \mu_{Null}$ **(Directional, One-Tailed Test)**

  If $z_{obtained} \geq +z_{critical}$, reject the null hypothesis

  If $\overline{X}_{obtained} \geq \overline{X}_{critical}$, reject the null hypothesis

H_1: $\mu_{sample} < \mu_{Null}$ **(Directional, One-tailed Test)**

  If $z_{obtained} \leq -z_{critical}$, reject the null hypothesis

  If $\overline{X}_{obtained} \leq \overline{X}_{critical}$, reject the null hypothesis

H_1: $\mu_{sample} \neq \mu_{Null}$ **(Nondirectional, Two-tailed Test)**

  If $|z_{obtained}| \geq z_{critical}$, reject the null hypothesis

  (Alternatively: If $z_{obtained} \geq +z_{critical}$, **or** if $z_{obtained} \leq -z_{critical}$, reject the null hypothesis)

  If $\overline{X}_{obtained} \leq \overline{X}_{lower\ critical}$, **or** if $\overline{X}_{obtained} \geq \overline{X}_{upper\ critical}$, reject the null hypothesis

$$z = \frac{\overline{X} - \mu}{\sigma_E}$$

where: $\overline{X}$ = mean of the research sample

  μ = mean of the population

  σ_E = the standard error (i.e., the variability of the sampling distribution—see page 138)

$$\sigma_E = \frac{\sigma}{\sqrt{n}}$$

Step 4 of the z-Test The last step of the z-test is to make a decision about the null hypothesis. The ***decision rules*** for both z-test procedures are presented in Table 11-1.

If we choose to transform the sample mean ($\overline{X}$) into a z-score ($z_{obtained}$), the decision rule for a directional (one-tailed) test is determined by the specific research hypothesis. That is, the different hypotheses have different values of $z_{critical}$. If the research hypothesis predicts that the sample mean will be significantly *less* than the population mean (i.e., if H_1: $\mu_{sample} < \mu_{Null}$), then the appropriate value of $z_{critical}$ will be in the lower tail of the distribution, and in order to be considered significant, the obtained value of z must be equal to or less than the critical value. All values of z below the mean have negative values, so the lower critical value is referred to as $-z_{critical}$. If the research hypothesis predicts that the sample mean will be *greater* than the population mean (i.e., if H_1: $\mu_{sample} > \mu_{Null}$), then the appropriate value of $z_{critical}$ will be in the upper tail of the distribution, and in order to be considered significant, the obtained value of z must be equal to or greater than this value of $+z_{critical}$. For nondirectional (two-tailed) tests, the region of rejection is split into the two tails of the sampling distribution. Therefore, we reject the null hypothesis if $z_{obtained}$ is *either* less than $-z_{critical}$ (and located in the lower tail) *or* if $z_{obtained}$ is greater than $+z_{critical}$ (and located in the upper tail). Because $-z_{critical}$ and $+z_{critical}$ have the same absolute value (which is found on the z-Table), the decision rule for two-tailed tests is frequently expressed in terms of the absolute value of $z_{obtained}$: If the absolute value of $z_{obtained}$ is greater than or equal to the value of $z_{critical}$, we reject the null hypothesis.

Alternatively, if at step 3, you choose to convert the critical value of z ($z_{critical}$) from step 2 into a critical mean ($\overline{X}_{critical}$), the decision will be based on a comparison of the sample mean ($\overline{X}_{obtained}$) to the critical value of the mean ($\overline{X}_{critical}$). If the sample mean is equal to or more extreme than the critical value, we will reject the null hypothesis. That is, if $\overline{X}_{obtained}$ is farther from the predicted value of μ_{Null} than is $\overline{X}_{critical}$ (indicating that the sample mean is "out in the tail" of the sampling distribution), we would reject the null hypothesis. For a one-tailed test, the critical value will be located in only one of the tails, so the decision rule for a directional test depends on the specific research hypothesis. A two-tailed test will have *two separate* values of $\overline{X}_{critical}$, one above μ_{Null} and one below μ_{Null}, so the decision rule for a nondirectional test has a two-part, "either-or" structure, as you can see in Table 11-1.

Numerical Example of the z-Test When $z_{obtained}$ Is Compared to $z_{critical}$ The null hypothesis states that newborn "crack babies" weigh the same as normal babies. Below we perform both one- and two-tailed z-tests to test this hypothesis.[1] (Where the procedures differ, the one-tailed test is presented in the column on the left, and the two-tailed test is presented in the column on the right.)

Summary of Data: $\mu_{babies} = 112$; $\sigma_{babies} = 8.6$; $n = 4$; $\overline{X}_{crack\ babies} = 100$

Step 1:   Choose a one- or two-tailed test, and specify the hypotheses.

One-Tailed (Directional)	Two-Tailed (Nondirectional)
H_0: $\mu_{crack\ babies} = 112$	H_0: $\mu_{crack\ babies} = 112$
H_1: $\mu_{crack\ babies} < \mu_{babies}$	H_1: $\mu_{crack\ babies} \neq \mu_{babies}$

Step 2:   Select alpha and look up critical value of z.

One-Tailed (Directional)	Two-Tailed (Nondirectional)
Let alpha (α) = .05	Let alpha (α) = .05 and $\alpha/2$ = .025
Therefore, $z_{critical} = -1.64$	Therefore, $z_{critical} = \pm1.96$
(As we pointed out earlier, for one-tailed tests with alpha set at .05, $z_{critical}$ always equals ±1.64 because the area under the curve beyond this value of z is equal to .05050. See the third column of the z-Table.)	(As we pointed out earlier, for two-tailed tests with alpha set at .05, $z_{critical}$ always equals ±1.96 because the area under the curve beyond this value of z is equal to .02500. See the third column of the z-Table.)

---

[1] As we indicated in Chapter 5, the numerical examples in this textbook do not include rounding until the final step. The values of the intermediate steps are carried out to the last decimal place on a hand-held calculator. This procedure minimizes the rounding error that could otherwise accumulate when there are several subparts in the computation of the test statistic. The test statistic itself is rounded to the number of decimal places used in the tables of critical values for hypothesis testing and then reported to one significant decimal place.

Step 3:   Transform $\overline{X}_{obtained}$ into $z_{obtained}$

$$z_{obtained} = \frac{\overline{X} - \mu}{\sigma_E} = z_{obtained} = \frac{\overline{X} - \mu}{\dfrac{\sigma}{\sqrt{n}}}$$

$$z_{obtained} = \frac{100 - 112}{\dfrac{8.6}{\sqrt{4}}}$$

$$z_{obtained} = \frac{-12}{\dfrac{8.6}{2}}$$

$$z_{obtained} = \frac{-12}{4.3}$$

$$z_{obtained} = -2.79$$

Step 4:   Make a decision and draw a conclusion.

One-Tailed (Directional):	Two-Tailed (Nondirectional):
H_1: $\mu_{sample} < \mu_{Null}$, therefore: Decision Rule: If $z_{obtained} \leq -z_{critical}$, reject H_0 With $\alpha = .05$, $z_{critical} = -1.64$; $z_{obtained} = -2.79$ -2.79 **is** less than -1.64, therefore, we *reject* the null hypothesis.	H_1: $\mu_{sample} \neq \mu_{Null}$, therefore: Decision Rule: If $\lvert z_{obtained} \rvert \geq z_{critical}$, reject H_0 With $\alpha = .05$, $z_{critical} = 1.96$; $\lvert z_{obtained} \rvert = 2.79$ 2.79 **is** greater than 1.96; therefore we *reject* the null hypothesis.

(In this example, the one- and two-tailed tests reach the same conclusion. This will not always be the case. Specifically, if the value of $z_{obtained}$ is between -1.64 and -1.96, we would reject the null hypothesis in the one-tailed test, but we would fail to reject the null hypothesis in the two-tailed test.)

Conclusion

The z-test indicates that it is unlikely that a sample with a mean of 100 will be drawn at random from a population with a mean of 112 and a standard deviation of 8.6. By rejecting the null hypothesis, we would conclude that our sample of "crack babies" does *not* come from a population with a mean of 112, but is a sample from a separate subpopulation of babies who are *significantly smaller* at birth than babies in general. In other words, newborn "crack babies" weigh significantly less than average.

Numerical Example of the z-Test When $\overline{X}_{obtained}$ Is Compared to $\overline{X}_{critical}$ Now let's test the null hypothesis by transforming $z_{critical}$ into the critical value of $\overline{X}$ and comparing our sample mean ($\overline{X}_{obtained}$) to this value of $\overline{X}_{critical}$. Again we include both one- and two-tailed tests, with the one-tailed test in the column on the left, and the two-tailed test in the column(s) on the right.

Summary of Data: $\mu_{babies} = 112$; $\sigma_{babies} = 8.6$; $n = 4$; $\overline{X}_{crack\ babies} = 100$

Step 1: Choose a one- or two-tailed test, and specify the hypotheses.

One-Tailed (Directional)	Two-Tailed (Nondirectional)
H_0: $\mu_{crack\ babies} = 112$	H_0: $\mu_{crack\ babies} = 112$
H_1: $\mu_{crack\ babies} < \mu_{babies}$	H_1: $\mu_{crack\ babies} \neq \mu_{babies}$

Step 2: Select alpha and look up critical value of z.

One-Tailed (Directional)	Two-Tailed (Nondirectional)
Let alpha (α) = .05	Let alpha (α) = .05; each tail has $\alpha/2$ = .025
Therefore, $z_{critical}$ = -1.64	Therefore, $z_{critical}$ = ± 1.96
(Remember, for one-tailed tests with alpha set at .05, $z_{critical}$ always equals ± 1.64.)	(Remember, for two-tailed tests with alpha set at .05, $z_{critical}$ always equals ± 1.96.)

Step 3: Transform $z_{critical}$ into $\overline{X}_{critical}$.

$$\overline{X}_{critical} = \mu \pm z_{critical}(\sigma_E) \quad \text{or}$$

$$\overline{X}_{critical} = \mu \pm z_{critical}\left(\frac{\sigma}{\sqrt{n}}\right)$$

One-Tailed Test	Two-Tailed Test: Lower Tail	Two-Tailed Test: Upper Tail
$\overline{X}_{critical} = 112 - 1.64\left(\frac{8.6}{\sqrt{4}}\right)$	$\overline{X}_{critical} = 112 - 1.96\left(\frac{8.6}{\sqrt{4}}\right)$	$\overline{X}_{critical} = 112 + 1.96\left(\frac{8.6}{\sqrt{4}}\right)$
$\overline{X}_{critical} = 112 - 1.64\left(\frac{8.6}{2}\right)$	$\overline{X}_{critical} = 112 - 1.96\left(\frac{8.6}{2}\right)$	$\overline{X}_{critical} = 112 + 1.96\left(\frac{8.6}{2}\right)$
$\overline{X}_{critical} = 112 - 1.64(4.3)$	$\overline{X}_{critical} = 112 - 1.96(4.3)$	$\overline{X}_{critical} = 112 + 1.96(4.3)$
$\overline{X}_{critical} = 112 - 7.052$	$\overline{X}_{critical} = 112 - 8.428$	$\overline{X}_{critical} = 112 + 8.428$
$\overline{X}_{critical} = 104.948$	$\overline{X}_{critical} = 103.572$	$\overline{X}_{critical} = 120.428$
$\overline{X}_{critical} \approx 104.9$	$\overline{X}_{critical} \approx 103.6$	$\overline{X}_{critical} \approx 120.4$
(This indicates that, in a population with a mean of 112, only 5% of all random samples will have a $\overline{X}$ of 104.9 or less.)	(This indicates that, in a population with a mean of 112, only 2.5% of all random samples will have a $\overline{X}$ of 103.6 or less.)	(This indicates that, in a population with a mean of 112, only 2.5% of all random samples will have a $\overline{X}$ of 120.4 or higher.)

Step 4: Make a decision and draw a conclusion.

One-Tailed Test	Two-Tailed Test
The decision rule for a one-tailed z-test where the research sample mean is expected to be *less* than the population mean (μ) is:	The decision rule for a two-tailed z-test is:
If $\overline{X}_{obtained} \leq \overline{X}_{critical}$, reject H_0	If $\overline{X}_{obtained} \leq \overline{X}_{lower\ critical}$, or
	If $\overline{X}_{obtained} \geq \overline{X}_{upper\ critical}$, reject H_0
In our data:	In our data:
$\overline{X}_{obtained} = 100, \overline{X}_{critical} = 104.9$	$\overline{X}_{obtained} = 100, \overline{X}_{lower\ critical} = 103.6$, and
	$\overline{X}_{upper\ critical} = 120.4$
100 *is* less than 104.9; therefore, we *reject* the null hypothesis.	100 *is* less than 103.6; therefore, we *reject* the null hypothesis.

Conclusion (just as above): The z-test indicates that it is unlikely that a sample with a mean of 100 will be drawn at random from a population with a mean of 112 and a standard deviation of 8.6. By rejecting the null hypothesis, we would conclude that our sample of "crack babies" does *not* come from a population with a mean of 112 but is a sample from a separate subpopulation of babies who are *significantly smaller* at birth than babies in general.

Thus, the z-test (using either version) would lead us to the conclusion that babies exposed to crack cocaine constitute a distinctly separate subpopulation of infants who are generally smaller at birth than babies who are not exposed prenatally to cocaine.

z-Test: Application 2: When the Population Mean (μ) Is Being Tested

In the "crack babies" example, the mean (μ) and standard deviation (σ) of the population of babies in general was known (through hospital records) and we used it to test a hypothesis about a special group of babies. A z-test can also be used to test a *hypothesis about the value of the population mean*. That is, a second application of the z-test is to answer the question: "Is the population mean really equal to what it is claimed to be?" For instance, if the Chrysler Corporation claims that its newest car gets 42 miles to the gallon, we could test this claim by recording the miles per gallon (mpg) of a sample of cars and using the z-test to decide whether Chrysler's claim (that $\mu = 42$ mpg) seems to be true. Or we may have read advertisements for a new diet pill that claims that people lose an average of 25 pounds in six weeks. If we randomly select a sample of people and have them use the diet pill for six weeks, we can then use a z-test to decide whether the average weight loss for the population of all diet-pill users (μ) actually is 25 pounds. The null hypothesis in these studies would say that the claim about the population mean is *true*, and the research (alternate) hypothesis would say that the research sample does *not* come from a population with the predicted value of mu (μ):

$$H_0: \mu_{\text{actual}} = \mu_{\text{predicted}} \text{ (for example, } H_0: \mu_{\text{actual mpg}} = 42 \text{ mpg or}$$
$$\mu_{\text{actual weight lost}} = 25 \text{ lbs)}$$

$$H_1: \mu_{\text{actual}} \neq \mu_{\text{predicted}} \text{ (for a nondirectional, two-tailed test)}$$

As a concrete example of this application of the z-test, let's suppose that the Kellogg company has designed a new raisin dispenser for packaging Raisin Bran. You have probably heard the advertisements which tell us that every box of Kellogg's Raisin Bran contains "two scoops of raisins"—obviously, the company needs to calibrate its new raisin dispenser to meet the "two scoop" standard. In order to determine whether or not the new machine is putting the correct number of raisins in each box, Kellogg's would want to compare the average from a random sample of boxes to the target population mean of "two scoops" of raisins per box.

To continue with this example, of course, we need to have a clear operational definition of a "scoop" of raisins, so let's suppose that a scoop (like those pictured on the cereal box and used in the TV commercials) contains 200 raisins. Let's further suppose that Kellogg's told us that, because raisins vary a bit in size, which affects the precision of the raisin dispenser, some variation in the number of raisins in each box is unavoidable, and that the old raisin dispenser had produced a standard deviation of 55 raisins. Thus, the goal for the new dispenser is to have a mean (μ) of 400 and a standard deviation (σ) of 55.

In this situation, the null hypothesis would state that the new raisin dispenser puts an average of 400 raisins in each box ($H_0: \mu = 400$). The research hypothesis, however, allows for two possibilities: (a) The new dispenser puts too few raisins in each box, or (b) the dispenser puts too many raisins in each box. Because we have no reason to expect the dispenser to be either more or less generous, it would be appropriate, in this case, to use a two-tailed test where the research hypothesis does not specify a particular direction of difference (so $H_1: \mu \neq 400$).

Let's imagine that we randomly selected 25 boxes of the cereal that have been packaged using the new dispenser and found that the average number of raisins per box was 420 (instead of 400) and the standard deviation was 56. Does the new raisin dispenser need to be recalibrated or does it seem to meet the "two scoop" standard? The nondirectional (two-tailed) z-test for this problem is presented in Figure 11-5. The new dispenser meets the "two scoop" standard.

Requirements for the z-Test

The z-test requires that we know the population standard deviation (σ) and that we know—or suspect—the value of the population mean (μ). We use the z-Table to look up the value of z_{critical}, which assumes that the distribution of random samples forms a normal curve. This assumption, however, may be wrong, in which case, the

FIGURE 11.5

Z-TEST TO DETERMINE WHETHER THERE ARE "TWO SCOOPS" OF RAISINS IN EACH BOX

z-Test comparing $z_{obtained}$ to $z_{critical}$

Step 1 H_0: $\mu_{raisins\ per\ box} = 400$
H_1: $\mu_{raisins\ per\ box} \neq 400$

Step 2 alpha (α) = .05, two-tailed test therefore, $z_{critical} = \pm 1.96$

Step 3 Transform $\overline{X}_{raisins\ per\ box}$ into a z-score (from a sampling distribution)

or:

$$z_{obtained} = \frac{\overline{X} - \mu}{\sigma_E}$$

$$z_{obtained} = \frac{\overline{X} - \mu}{\frac{\sigma}{\sqrt{n}}}$$

$$z_{obtained} = \frac{420 - 400}{\frac{55}{\sqrt{25}}}$$

$$z_{obtained} = \frac{20}{\frac{55}{5}}$$

$$z_{obtained} = \frac{20}{11}$$

$$z_{obtained} = 1.818$$

Decision rule: If $[z_{obtained}] \geq z_{critical}$, reject the null hypothesis.

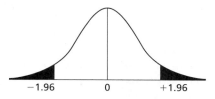

1.818 is less than 1.96; therefore, we cannot reject the null hypothesis.

z-Test comparing $\overline{X}_{obtained}$ to $\overline{X}_{critical}$

Step 1 H_0: $\mu_{raisins\ per\ box} = 400$
H_1: $\mu_{raisins\ per\ box} \neq 400$

Step 2 alpha (α) = .05, two-tailed test therefore, $z_{critical} = \pm 1.96$

Step 3 Transform $z_{critical}$ into $\overline{X}_{critical}$ (from a sampling distribution)

or:

$$\overline{X}_{critical} = \mu \pm z_{critical}(\sigma_E)$$

$$\overline{X}_{critical} = \mu \pm z_{critical}\left(\frac{\sigma}{\sqrt{n}}\right)$$

Lower Critical Value:

$$\overline{X}_{critical} = 400 - 1.96\left(\frac{55}{\sqrt{25}}\right)$$

$$\overline{X}_{critical} = 400 - 1.96\left(\frac{55}{5}\right)$$

$$\overline{X}_{critical} = 400 - 1.96(11)$$

$$\overline{X}_{critical} = 400 - 21.56$$

$$\overline{X}_{critical} = 378.44$$

Upper Critical Value:

$$\overline{X}_{critical} = 400 + 1.96\left(\frac{55}{\sqrt{25}}\right)$$

$$\overline{X}_{critical} = 400 + 1.96\left(\frac{55}{5}\right)$$

$$\overline{X}_{critical} = 400 + 1.96(11)$$

$$\overline{X}_{critical} = 400 + 21.56$$

$$\overline{X}_{critical} = 421.56$$

Decision rule: If $\overline{X}_{obtained}$ is less than or equal to the lower critical value **OR** if $\overline{X}_{obtained}$ is greater than or equal to the upper critical value, reject the null hypothesis.

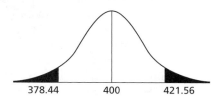

420 ($\overline{X}_{obtained}$) is **between** 378.44 and 421.56; therefore, we cannot reject the null hypothesis.

z-test may be inappropriate. Small samples, for instance, often fail to form a normal distribution. Therefore, most statisticians suggest that the *z*-test be used only when there are at least 25 scores in the sample. When the sample size (n) is less than 25, it may be more appropriate to use the one-sample *t*-test (which is presented below).

The *t*-Test: When the Population Standard Deviation (σ) Is Unknown

In the two applications of the *z*-test illustrated above, we assumed that the standard deviation for the population (σ) was known before the data were collected from the research samples. This allowed us to compute the standard error of the mean (σ_E) directly, and so the *z*-scores are based on an accurate measure of the variability among random samples. The sampling distribution of these *z*-scores usually forms a normal curve, and we can use the *z*-Table to find the cut-off points for any area under the normal curve.

In contrast, when the value of σ is *unknown*, we need to use the standard deviation of the sample as an estimate of σ and compute an *estimate of the standard error*. When we then compare $\overline{X}$ to μ relative to an *estimate* of the standard error, the statistic is called a *t*-score (rather than a *z*-score):

$$\text{estimated } \sigma_E = s_E = \frac{s}{\sqrt{n}}$$

$$t = \frac{\overline{X} - \mu}{\dfrac{s}{\sqrt{n}}}$$

The distribution of *t*-scores, which are based on an estimation of the variability among random samples drawn from a population, is standardized (and known) but does *not* form a normal curve unless the sample size is 120 or more. (Essentially, samples this large provide highly accurate estimates of the standard error.) The *t*-distribution is bell-shaped and symmetrical, but it tends to be "wider and flatter" than a normal distribution. That is, there is more variability among the *t*-scores than among *z*-scores, but because the distribution is standardized, we can still determine the value of $t_{critical}$ that cuts-off the most rare (5% or 1%) sample statistics. Actually, there is a separate *t*-distribution for every sample size (n) so that the value of $t_{critical}$ changes with n, even if our significance level (alpha) remains the same. (This is in contrast to a normal distribution, where a *z*-score of ± 1.64 *always* cuts off 5% of the scores and a *z*-score of ± 1.96 *always* cuts off 2.5% of the scores, regardless of the sample size.) Figure 11-6 presents the *t*-distribution for samples with 2 or 11 scores.

The Student's *t*-Table (Table B-10 in Appendix B) presents the values of $t_{critical}$ that cut off the "regions of rejection" (for both one- and two-tailed tests) for the most commonly used values of α (.05 and .01). To use this table, we need to know the **degrees of freedom,** which are based on the number of participants in the sample. The degrees of freedom for *t* tell us how many scores are "free to vary" or are

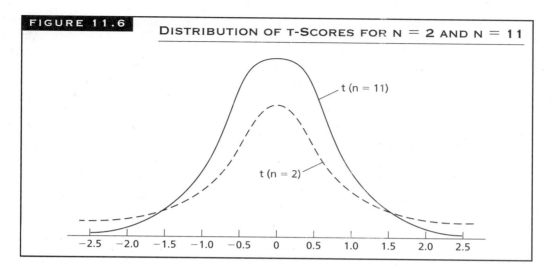

FIGURE 11.6

DISTRIBUTION OF T-SCORES FOR N = 2 AND N = 11

t (n = 11)

t (n = 2)

| −2.5 | −2.0 | −1.5 | −1.0 | −0.5 | 0 | 0.5 | 1.0 | 1.5 | 2.0 | 2.5 |

independent of one another and the group total. Generally, all scores *except the last one* will be free to vary. The last score is constrained: It will have whatever value is left over in the group total. For instance, suppose the three scores in a set add up to 62. Knowing there are three scores with a total of 62, what can you say about the value of the first score? Nothing, since it could be any number from 0 to 62 (i.e., it is free to vary in value, thus we say it has a "degree of freedom"). Suppose the first score is 20; what do you now know about the value of the second score? Again, nothing, since it could be any number from 0 to 42 (so the second score also has a degree of freedom). Suppose the second score is 22; what do you now know about the third (and last) score? It *has to be equal to* 20 since the three scores must add up to 62. This last score cannot vary. Thus, in a set of three scores, there are 2 degrees of freedom. In any data set, the last score is constrained by the values of the other scores. Therefore, the degrees of freedom in a group of scores is equal to the number of scores (n) minus 1:

$$\text{degrees of freedom (df)} = n - 1$$

The *t*-table does not include the values of $t_{critical}$ for all degrees of freedom greater than 30, so there are times when the correct value of degrees of freedom will not be in the table. Whenever this occurs in the problems presented in this text, we have elected to use the *next smaller value* of degrees of freedom (which has a larger value of $t_{critical}$). This is a *conservative* approach, meaning that it is a procedure that reduces the chances of making a Type I error (i.e., rejecting the null hypothesis when it is true) because the difference between the research groups will need to be larger in order to obtain a value of *t* that is greater than or equal to $t_{critical}$. In contrast, other statisticians will estimate the critical value of *t* through a process known as interpolation. (For example, in order to estimate the value of $t_{critical}$ when there are 35 degrees of freedom, they look at the $t_{critical}$ for 30 degrees of freedom and the $t_{critical}$ for 40 degrees of freedom, and estimate that their $t_{critical}$ will be approximately halfway between them.) While this procedure provides a reasonable estimate of $t_{critical}$, it will not be perfectly exact because the relationship between degrees of freedom and $t_{critical}$ is not perfectly linear. Therefore, there will be some error in the researcher's estimated value of $t_{critical}$, but the researcher will be uncertain whether this error increases or decreases the probability of a Type I error. The procedure we have adopted (of simply using the next smaller value of df in the table) means that there is a greater discrepancy between the true value of $t_{critical}$ and the value that we use to make our decision, but we have the advantage of knowing that the risk of Type I error has been decreased. Therefore, if we reject the null hypothesis using the more stringent value of $t_{critical}$, we can place more confidence in that conclusion.

Other than the fact that we are using the *t*-distribution instead of *z*-scores, the basic logic of the *t*-test is the same as the logic of the *z*-test.

One-Sample t-Test

The *t*-test can be used to compare a single research sample to a population mean (μ) in order to answer the nondirectional question "Is this group of participants significantly different than average?" (which would be answered using a two-tailed test). The *t*-test can also answer more specific, directional questions such as "Does this group of participants perform significantly better than average?" or "Does this group of participants perform significantly worse than average?" (both of which would be answered using a one-tailed test). For example, suppose that *The New York Times* reported that a national survey of college students revealed that freshmen males consume an average of 18 cans of beer per week. Further suppose that the standard deviation for the survey respondents was not included in the newspaper article. Thus, the article gives us the value of mu (μ), but sigma (σ) is unknown, and, therefore, we will need to estimate the value of the standard error (σ_E) and use the *t*-distribution.

A researcher may compare the performance of various subgroups to this national average (μ). For example, we may wonder whether the freshman males at a two-year community college drink the same amount of beer as the average freshman from the survey. This would warrant a two-tailed test, since we do not have a theory that specifically predicts that the community college students will drink either more or less than average. Or we may hypothesize that the freshman males whose academic performance makes them eligible for induction into a national honor society (such as Alpha Lambda Delta, which requires a GPA of 3.5 in the first semester of college) drink less beer than the average freshman male. We could test this hypothesis using a one-tailed test, since we have specifically predicted that the honor students drink *less* than average (but remember that most researchers will choose a two-tailed test even when their theory predicts a specific direction of difference).

The formula for *t* for a one-sample *t*-test is structurally equivalent to the formula for the *z*-test: The numerator measures the difference between the sample and population means, and the denominator is a measure of the variability among random samples. In this case, the variability of samples is estimated using the standard deviation of the research sample:

Formula for z:
$$z = \frac{\overline{X} - \mu}{\dfrac{\sigma}{\sqrt{n}}}$$

Formula for t:
$$t = \frac{\overline{X} - \mu}{\dfrac{s}{\sqrt{n}}}$$

The decision rules for t-tests are the same as the decision rules for z-tests with z_{obtained} as the test statistic, and they are presented in Table 11-2.

Numerical Example of a Two-tailed, One-Sample t-Test Let's assume that we surveyed a sample of 25 freshman males from a two-year college in order to see whether they drink the same number of beers per week as do the college students who participated in the national survey. We do not have any specific reason to hypothesize that they drink either more or less than the national average. Suppose we found that our sample of freshman males from two-year colleges reported an average beer consumption of 21 cans per week and that the standard deviation of the

TABLE 11.2	Decision Rules for One- and Two-Sample t-Tests
One-Sample Design	

One-Sample Design

H_1: $\mu_{\text{sample}} > \mu_{\text{Null}}$ **(Directional, One-tailed Test)**
  If $t_{\text{obtained}} \geq +t_{\text{critical}}$, reject the null hypothesis

H_1: $\mu_{\text{sample}} < \mu_{\text{Null}}$ **(Directional, One-tailed Test)**
  If $t_{\text{obtained}} \leq -t_{\text{critical}}$, reject the null hypothesis

H_1: $\mu_{\text{sample}} \neq \mu_{\text{Null}}$ **(Nondirectional, Two-tailed Test)**
  If $|t_{\text{obtained}}| \geq t_{\text{critical}}$, reject the null hypothesis
  (Alternatively: If $t_{\text{obtained}} \geq +t_{\text{critical}}$, **or** if $t_{\text{obtained}} \leq -t_{\text{critical}}$, reject the null hypothesis)

Two-Sample Design

H_1: $\mu_1 > \mu_2$ **(Directional, One-tailed Test)**
  If $t_{\text{obtained}} \geq +t_{\text{critical}}$, reject the null hypothesis

H_1: $\mu_1 < \mu_2$ **(Directional, One-tailed Test)**
  If $t_{\text{obtained}} \leq -t_{\text{critical}}$, reject the null hypothesis

H_1: $\mu_1 \neq \mu_2$ **(Nondirectional, Two-tailed Test)**
  If $|t_{\text{obtained}}| \geq t_{\text{critical}}$, reject the null hypothesis
  (Alternatively: If $t_{\text{obtained}} \geq +t_{\text{critical}}$, **or** if $t_{\text{obtained}} \leq -t_{\text{critical}}$, reject the null hypothesis)

sample was 4. Our first steps are to identify our hypotheses and set an alpha level; then we will compute t and compare it to a value of $t_{critical}$ from the t-Table in Appendix B.

Step 1: H_0: $\mu_{\text{two-year}} = \mu_{\text{all freshmen}}$ H_1: $\mu_{\text{two-year}} \neq \mu_{\text{all freshmen}}$

Step 2: $\alpha = .05$, for a two-tailed test

Step 3: Compute the mean $(\overline{X})$ and standard deviation (s) for the sample data; from the information provided above: $\overline{X} = 21$; s = 4; n = 25

Step 4: Compute the obtained value of t

$$t_{obtained} = \frac{\overline{X} - \mu}{\dfrac{s}{\sqrt{n}}}$$

$$t_{obtained} = \frac{21 - 18}{\dfrac{4}{\sqrt{25}}}$$

$$t_{obtained} = \frac{3}{\dfrac{4}{5}}$$

$$t_{obtained} = \frac{3}{0.8}$$

$$\mathbf{t_{obtained} = 3.75}$$

Step 5: Look up $t_{critical}$ in the t-Table(Table B-10) in Appendix B.

In order to use the t-Table, we need to compute the degrees of freedom (df) for the sample. For a one-sample t-test, df = n − 1 because if we want to assume that the mean for two-year college freshman males has a constant value of 18, then in a set of 25 scores, the first 24 scores are free to take on any values, but the 25th score is determined (it is whatever score is needed to make the group mean equal 18).

$$df = 25 - 1$$
$$= 24$$

Therefore, for a two-tailed test with alpha (α) set at .05: $t_{critical} = \pm 2.064$

Step 6: Make a decision and draw a conclusion.

Compare $t_{obtained}$ to $t_{critical}$, using the following decision rule:

If $|t_{obtained}| \geq t_{critical}$, reject the null hypothesis.

In our example: $|t_{obtained}| = 3.75$; $t_{critical} = 2.064$

3.75 *is* greater than 2.064; therefore, we reject the null hypothesis.

Conclusion: We can conclude that 21 is significantly greater than 18 and that the freshman males attending the two-year school consume significantly more cans of beer per week than the national average reported in the newspaper, and, therefore, they represent a significantly different subgroup of students.

Numerical Example of a One-Tailed, One-Sample *t*-Test   Suppose we hypothesize that honor students drink less beer than the average college student and that we surveyed a sample of 16 freshman males who earned a GPA of 3.5 or higher during their first semester in college, making them eligible for membership in an honor society. Let's assume that the average number of cans of beer consumed by these honors students was 14 per week and that the standard deviation for the sample was 6.

Step 1: H_0: $\mu_{honors} = \mu_{all\ freshmen}$ H_1: $\mu_{honors} < \mu_{all\ freshmen}$

Step 2: $\alpha = .05$, for a one-tailed test

Step 3:   Compute the mean $(\overline{X})$ and standard deviation (s) for the sample data; from the information given above: $\overline{X} = 14$; s = 6; n = 16

Step 4:   Compute $t_{obtained}$

$$t_{obtained} = \frac{\overline{X} - \mu}{\dfrac{s}{\sqrt{n}}}$$

$$t_{obtained} = \frac{14 - 18}{\dfrac{6}{\sqrt{16}}}$$

$$t_{obtained} = \frac{-4}{\dfrac{6}{4}}$$

$$t_{obtained} = \frac{-4}{1.5}$$

$$\mathbf{t_{obtained} = -2.667}$$

Step 5:   Find the degrees of freedom and look up $t_{critical}$ in Appendix B

$$df = 16 - 1$$

$$= 15$$

Therefore, for a one-tailed test with alpha (α) set at .05: $t_{critical} = \pm 1.753$

Step 6:   Make a decision and draw a conclusion

Because we have hypothesized that the sample of honor students drink *less* than average, we will compare $t_{obtained}$ to $-t_{critical}$, using the following decision rule:

If $t_{obtained} \leq -t_{critical}$, reject the null hypothesis

In this example: $t_{obtained} = -2.667$; $-t_{critical} = -1.753$

-2.667 *is* less than -1.753; therefore, we *reject* the null hypothesis.

Conclusion: We can conclude 14 is significantly less than 18 and that freshman males who earn a GPA of 3.5 or higher (and are eligible for an honor society) consume significantly fewer cans of beer per week than the national average reported in the newspaper, and, therefore, the honors students represent a significantly different subgroup of students.

Two-Sample t-Test: Independent Samples From a Between-Subjects Design

In each of the two preceding examples, we compared the mean from a single research sample ($\overline{X}$) to a standard value (μ). Most psychological research, however, involves the comparison of two or more research samples to each other. The typical research question is: "Are the samples significantly different from each other?" (Or: "Do the samples come from populations with equal means?") Also typically, the sample standard deviations (s) must be used to estimate the variability among samples (σ_E) because the population parameters (σ) are unknown. For this *t*-test, the relevant sampling distribution is the sampling distribution of the difference between means (sometimes referred to as the *empirical sampling distribution*), which is constructed by drawing pairs of random samples and calculating the difference between the sample means ($\overline{X}_1 - \overline{X}_2$). When the pairs of samples are drawn from the same population, the average difference between the pairs of means will be equal to 0 (since each sample will be representative of—and similar to—μ), but the variability among the difference scores (i.e, the standard error of the sampling distribution of $\overline{X}_1 - \overline{X}_2$) will depend on the size of the samples (since larger samples are more alike while smaller samples can be very different from each other).

The steps involved in a two-group *t*-test are conceptually the same as in the one-sample *t*-tests described above, but the computations are somewhat more complex since we have to estimate the standard error (σ_E) of the sampling distribution using data from two samples instead of one. That is, we have the standard deviation from two separate samples, so we must pool them together in order to have a measure of variability that we can use as an estimate of the standard error. Furthermore, the degrees of freedom must be based on two samples instead of one.

Step 1:   Specify the hypotheses.

Typically, the null hypothesis will state that there is *no* difference between the group means, claiming that the samples come from populations with equal means. The research hypothesis will either be directional or nondirectional.

Two-tailed test: H_0: $\mu_1 = \mu_2$ and H_1: $\mu_1 \neq \mu_2$

One-tailed test: H_0: $\mu_1 = \mu_2$ and H_1: $\mu_1 < \mu_2$

or $\qquad\qquad$ H_0: $\mu_1 = \mu_2$ and H_1: $\mu_1 > \mu_2$

Step 2: Select an alpha level (α)

Step 3: Compute the means ($\overline{X}$) and standard deviations (s) for each group of scores

Step 4: Calculate the *pooled variance* (s^2_{pooled}) for the two samples:

$$s^2_{pooled} = \frac{(n_1 - 1)s^2_1 + (n_2 - 1)s^2_2}{(n_1 - 1) + (n_2 - 1)}$$

where: n_1 = the number of participants in the first group
$\qquad\quad$ n_2 = the number of participants in the second group
$\qquad\quad$ s^2_1 = the variance (i.e., the standard deviation squared) of the first group
$\qquad\quad$ s^2_2 = the variance (i.e., the standard deviation squared) of the second group

Step 5: Estimate the standard error (estimated σ_E) using the pooled variance:

$$\text{estimated } \sigma_E = s_{\overline{X}-\overline{X}} = \sqrt{\frac{s^2_{pooled}}{n_1} + \frac{s^2_{pooled}}{n_2}}$$

Step 6: Calculate $t_{obtained}$:

$$t_{obtained} = \frac{(\overline{X}_1 - \overline{X}_2) - (\mu_1 - \mu_2)}{s_{\overline{X}-\overline{X}}}$$

In this formula, the numerator measures the difference between the difference we *observed* between the research groups ($\overline{X}_1 - \overline{X}_2$) and the difference we would *expect* to see if the null hypothesis is true ($\mu_1 - \mu_2$). Since the null hypothesis typically predicts that the population means are equal to each other (so that $\mu_1 - \mu_2 = 0$), the numerator of the *t* formula is usually going to be reduced to simply $\overline{X}_1 - \overline{X}_2$. That is, the formula for *t* will typically be abbreviated to:

$$t = \frac{(\overline{X}_1 - \overline{X}_2)}{s_{\overline{X}-\overline{X}}}$$

Step 7: Find the degrees of freedom and look up $t_{critical}$ in Appendix B.

$$df = (n_1 - 1) + (n_2 - 1) \quad \textbf{or} \quad df = n_1 + n_2 - 2$$

Find $t_{critical}$ by using the alpha level and type of test (from steps 1 and 2), select the appropriate column on the Table of Critical Values, and read down until you find the appropriate degrees of freedom.

Step 8: Make a decision and draw a conclusion.

Compare $t_{obtained}$ to $t_{critical}$ using the applicable decision rule from Table 11-2:

Nondirectional test: H_1: $\mu_1 \neq \mu_2$: If $|t_{obtained}| \geq t_{critical}$, reject the null hypothesis

Directional tests: For H_1: $\mu_1 > \mu_2$: If $t_{obtained} \geq +t_{critical}$, reject the null hypothesis

or For H_1: $\mu_1 < \mu_2$: If $t_{obtained} \leq -t_{critical}$, reject the null hypothesis

If the decision is to reject the null hypothesis, we will conclude that there is a significant difference between the two research groups. For a true experiment, we would conclude that our experimental treatment had a significant effect on performance. For a quasi-experiment, we would conclude that the two groups represent distinctly separate sub-populations with different values of μ.

Numerical Example of a One-Tailed, Independent Samples *t*-Test   Let's suppose that we conducted a simple two-group experiment to test the hypothesis that having vocal music playing in the background during study interferes with memory performance. Two groups of participants were given 3 minutes to study the information presented in a 6-paragraph passage, where each paragraph presented 8 facts about a historical event. The 20 participants in the experimental group ($n_1 = 20$) studied the passage with popular soft-rock songs being played at a loudness level of 60dB (just about the loudness of a normal conversation). The 15 participants in the control group ($n_2 = 15$) studied the passage in a quiet room. After 3 minutes of study, the participants wrote down as much information as they could recall from the passage, and the researcher counted how many facts they correctly recalled (from the total of 48). The research hypothesis stated that the experimental (Music) group would recall significantly fewer facts than the control (Quiet) group. This is a directional hypothesis, and therefore, a one-tailed test could be appropriate.

Let's suppose that the Music group recalled an average of 12 facts, with a standard deviation of 3.1, while the Quiet group recalled an average of 16 facts, with a standard deviation of 4.7. Is there a significant difference in memory performance between these two groups?

Step 1: Specify the hypotheses.

H_0: $\mu_{Music} = \mu_{Quiet}$

H_1: $\mu_{Music} < \mu_{Quiet}$

Step 2: Select an alpha level (α).

Let $\alpha = .05$

Step 3: Compute the means ($\overline{X}$) and standard deviations for each group of scores.

For this example, the following data were provided:

	Music Group	Quiet Group
Sample Size (n)	$n_1 = 20$	$n_2 = 15$
Mean ($\overline{X}$)	$\overline{X}_1 = 12$	$\overline{X}_2 = 16$
Standard Deviation (s)	$s_1 = 3.1$	$s_2 = 4.7$

Step 4: Calculate the pooled variance (s^2_{pooled}) for the two samples:

$$s^2_{pooled} = \frac{(n_1 - 1)s^2_1 + (n_2 - 1)s^2_2}{(n_1 - 1) + (n_2 - 1)}$$

$$s^2_{pooled} = \frac{(20 - 1)(3.1)^2 + (15 - 1)(4.7)^2}{(20 - 1) + (15 - 1)}$$

$$s^2_{pooled} = \frac{19(9.61) + 14(22.09)}{19 + 14}$$

$$s^2_{pooled} = \frac{182.59 + 309.26}{33}$$

$$s^2_{pooled} = \frac{491.85}{33}$$

$$s^2_{pooled} = 14.904545$$

Step 5: Estimate the standard error ($s_{\overline{X}-\overline{X}}$) using the pooled variance:

$$s_{\overline{X}-\overline{X}} = \text{estimated } \sigma_E = \sqrt{\frac{s^2_{pooled}}{n_1} + \frac{s^2_{pooled}}{n_2}}$$

$$s_{\overline{X}-\overline{X}} = \sqrt{\frac{14.904545}{20} + \frac{14.904545}{15}}$$

$$s_{\overline{X}-\overline{X}} = \sqrt{0.7452272 + 0.9936363}$$

$$s_{\overline{X}-\overline{X}} = \sqrt{1.7388635}$$

$$s_{\overline{X}-\overline{X}} = 1.3186597$$

Step 6: Calculate $t_{obtained}$:

$$t_{obtained} = \frac{(\overline{X}_1 - \overline{X}_2) - (\mu_1 - \mu_2)}{s_{\overline{X} - \overline{X}}}$$

$$t_{obtained} = \frac{(12 - 16) - 0.0}{1.3186597}$$

$$t_{obtained} = \frac{(-4) - 0.0}{1.3186597}$$

$$t_{obtained} = \frac{-4}{1.3186597}$$

$$t_{obtained} = -3.033383$$

$$t_{obtained} \approx -3.033$$

Step 7: Find the degrees of freedom and look up $t_{critical}$ in the t-Table on page B-16.

$$df = (n_1 - 1) + (n_2 - 1)$$
$$df = (20 - 1) + (15 - 1)$$
$$= (19) + (14)$$
$$= 33$$

When we look at the Table of Critical Values of t in Appendix B, we find that the critical values for a sampling distribution with 33 degrees of freedom are not presented. Therefore, we use the next smaller value (which is df = 30). For a one-tailed test with α set at .05, we read down the second column.

$$t_{critical} \ (df = 30) = \pm 1.697$$

Step 8: Make a decision and draw a conclusion.

Compare $t_{obtained}$ to $t_{critical}$, using the following decision rule:

If $t_{obtained} \leq -t_{critical}$, reject the null hypothesis

$t_{obtained} = -3.033; \ -t_{critical} = -1.697$

-3.033 *is* less than -1.697; therefore, we will reject the null hypothesis.

Conclusion: We conclude that the participants in the experimental group (who heard songs playing during their study time) recalled significantly fewer facts from the passage than the participants in the control group (who studied in a quiet room). If we had conducted an experiment where the participants had been assigned to the treatment conditions at random, we could conclude that it is very likely that the exposure to the music caused the reduction in memory performance.

Numerical Example of a Two-Tailed, Independent Samples *t*-Test   Suppose a researcher was interested in "sensitivity to criticism" as an important personality dimension and wondered whether individuals who are high in their sensitivity to criticism would be less likely to seek out feedback than individuals who are low in their sensitivity to criticism. Suppose the researcher conducted a study where college students whose mid-semester grades in a public speaking class were C– or below served as participants. Each student completed a Sensitivity to Criticism Scale (like that developed by Atlas, 1994), which classified them as either high or low in sensitivity. The students in these two groups were then offered the opportunity to attend up to 12 special "tutoring sessions," which would involve being videotaped while they gave short speeches to a group of peers and then being critiqued by the professor and their peers. The researcher counted how many times each student attended one of these sessions. Let's suppose that the 20 students in the High Sensitive group attended an average of 3.1 tutoring sessions (with a standard deviation of 1.43) while the 24 students in the Low Sensitive group attended an average of 5.4 sessions (with a standard deviation of 2.01). Without a firm theory or data to support a specific prediction that the High Sensitive people are more likely to avoid feedback than other people, the researcher should probably choose to perform a two-tailed (nondirectional) test that simply predicts a difference between the groups.

Step 1:   Specify the hypotheses.

$H_0: \mu_1 = \mu_2$

$H_1: \mu_1 \neq \mu_2$

Step 2:   Select an alpha level (α).

Let $\alpha = .05$

Step 3:   Compute the means ($\overline{X}$) and standard deviations for each group of scores. For this example, the following data were provided:

	High Sensitivity Group	Low Sensitivity Group
Sample Size (n)	$n_1 = 20$	$n_2 = 24$
Mean ($\overline{X}$)	$\overline{X}_1 = 3.1$	$\overline{X}_2 = 5.4$
Standard Deviation(s)	$s_1 = 1.43$	$s_2 = 2.01$

Step 4:   Calculate the pooled variance (s^2_{pooled}) for the two samples:

$$s^2_{pooled} = \frac{(n_1 - 1)s^2_1 + (n_2 - 1)s^2_2}{(n_1 - 1) + (n_2 - 1)}$$

$$s^2_{pooled} = \frac{(20 - 1)(1.43)^2 + (24 - 1)(2.01)^2}{(20 - 1) + (24 - 1)}$$

$$s^2_{pooled} = \frac{19(2.0449) + 23(4.0401)}{19 + 23}$$

$$s^2_{pooled} = \frac{38.8531 + 92.9223}{42}$$

$$s^2_{pooled} = \frac{131.7754}{42}$$

$$s^2_{pooled} = 3.1375095$$

Step 5:   Estimate the standard error (estimated σ_E) using the pooled variance:

$$s_{\overline{X}-\overline{X}} = \text{estimated } \sigma_E = \sqrt{\frac{s^2_{pooled}}{n_1} + \frac{s^2_{pooled}}{n_2}}$$

$$s_{\overline{X}-\overline{X}} = \sqrt{\frac{3.1375095}{20} + \frac{3.1375095}{24}}$$

$$s_{\overline{X}-\overline{X}} = \sqrt{0.1568754 + 0.1307295}$$

$$s_{\overline{X}-\overline{X}} = \sqrt{0.2876049}$$

$$s_{\overline{X}-\overline{X}} = 0.536288$$

Step 6:   Calculate $t_{obtained}$:

$$t_{obtained} = \frac{(\overline{X}_1 - \overline{X}_2) - (\mu_1 - \mu_2)}{s_{\overline{X}-\overline{X}}}$$

$$t_{obtained} = \frac{(3.1 - 5.4) - 0.0}{0.536288}$$

$$t_{obtained} = \frac{(-2.3) - 0.0}{0.536288}$$

$$t_{obtained} = \frac{-2.3}{0.536288}$$

$$t_{obtained} = -4.2887403$$

$$t_{obtained} \approx -4.289$$

Step 7:   Find the degrees of freedom and look up $t_{critical}$ in the t-Table (Table B-10).

$$df = (n_1 - 1) + (n_2 - 1)$$
$$df = (20 - 1) + (24 - 1)$$
$$= (19) + (23)$$
$$= 42$$

When we look at the Table of Critical Values of t in Appendix B, we find that the critical values for a sampling distribution with 42 degrees of freedom are not presented. Therefore, we will use the next smaller value (which is df = 40). For a two-tailed test with α set at .05, we read down the third column.

$$t_{critical} \ (df = 40) = \pm2.021$$

Step 8:   Make a decision and draw a conclusion.

Compare $t_{obtained}$ to $t_{critical}$, using the following decision rule:

If $|t_{obtained}| \geq t_{critical}$, reject the null hypothesis

$|t_{obtained}| = 4.289; t_{critical} = 2.021$

4.289 *is* greater than 2.021; therefore, we will reject the null hypothesis.

Conclusion: We conclude that the participants who have a high sensitivity to criticism are significantly different from participants who have a low sensitivity to criticism. Examining the means, we see that the High Sensitive participants attended fewer tutoring sessions (where they would receive feedback about their performance) than the Low Sensitive participants. This is a quasi-experiment (since sensitivity to criticism is a subject variable), and therefore, we cannot say that sensitivity to criticism *caused* the difference in attendance; we can only describe the significant difference between the groups that suggests high and low sensitive people come from distinctly separate subpopulations.

Two-Sample t-Test: Related Samples From a Within-Subjects or Matching Design

When the researcher uses within-subjects or matched-pairs designs, the two group means are going to be related to each other (rather than being independent), and the analysis will focus on the ***difference scores*** for the individuals (or matched pairs of respondents) rather than on the difference between the means. The sampling distribution for the related-samples t-test is the distribution of difference scores. This sampling distribution of difference scores is constructed by drawing all random samples from a population, testing each participant twice *without performing any manipulation* (so that the two scores are obtained under identical conditions), calculating the difference between the pairs of scores ($D = X_1 - X_2$), and then computing the average difference score for each sample ($\overline{D}$). This sampling distribution has a mean of 0 ($\mu_{\overline{D}} = 0.0$) because the differences are due solely to chance. (That is, while many people will have the same score when they are retested, some people will show a random increase in their score, while others show a random decrease. Therefore, in the population, the difference scores average out to 0.) The standard error (or variability) of this sampling distribution depends on the size of the samples (n) and can be estimated using the standard deviation of the difference scores in the sample (s_D).

The formula for the related-samples t compares the mean of the difference scores in the sample to the difference we expect to see when the null hypothesis is true, adjusted for the variability among difference scores that occurs by chance. Conceptually, then:

$$t = \frac{\text{obtained average difference score} - \text{expected average difference}}{\text{standard error of difference scores}}$$

Symbolically, the formula can be expressed like this:

$$t = \frac{\overline{D} - \mu_{\overline{D}}}{s_{\overline{D}}}$$

where $s_{\overline{D}}$ is an estimate of the standard error

Let's imagine that we have data from a simple experiment testing the effect of the motives for televised violence on the aggressiveness of children. In one videotape, the violence is motivated by greed, while in the other videotape, the same violent actions are performed in self-defense. A group of five-year-olds watched the two videotapes on separate occasions (in counterbalanced order), and after each tape, they were observed in a playroom and the number of aggressive actions they performed in a 15-minute period was recorded:

Subject	Greed	Self-Defense
a	14	15
b	8	6
c	2	2
d	5	8
e	6	10
f	4	9
g	3	11
h	0	2
i	11	7
j	8	9

The null hypothesis for this study would claim that the experimental manipulation of the motivation for violence had no effect on children's aggressiveness. That is, it would predict that there is no systematic difference between the scores children received in the first treatment and the scores they received in the second treatment. Thus, the null hypothesis predicts that if a difference score (D) is computed for each child by subtracting the second score from the first score (which indicates how much the child's performance changed from one treatment to the other), the average of these difference scores will equal 0. Therefore, the formula for t can be simplified into:

$$t = \frac{\overline{D}}{s_{\overline{D}}}$$

The variability of the sampling distribution of difference scores (i.e., the standard error) can be estimated using the standard deviation of the sample difference scores, using the following formula:

$$\text{estimated standard error} = s_{\overline{D}} = \frac{s_D}{\sqrt{n}}$$

where: s_D = standard deviation of the difference scores
n = the number of participants (or pairs of scores)

Numerical Example of a Two-Tailed, Related Samples *t*-Test Let's use the data from our hypothetical experiment on motivations for violence to illustrate the steps in computing the related-samples *t*-test:

Step 1: Specify the hypotheses.

H_0: $\mu_1 = \mu_2$

H_1: $\mu_1 \neq \mu_2$

This will be a nondirectional (two-tailed) test that does not predict which treatment will have the higher mean.

Step 2: Select an alpha level (α).

Let $\alpha = .05$

Step 3: Calculate the difference (D) for each pair of scores.

Participant	Greed	Self-Defense	D
a	14	15	−1
b	8	6	2
c	2	2	0
d	5	8	−3
e	6	10	−4
f	4	9	−5
g	3	11	−8
h	0	2	−2
i	11	7	4
j	8	9	−1

Step 4:   Calculate the mean difference score ($\overline{D}$).

Participant	Greed	Self-Defense	D
a	14	15	−1
b	8	6	2
c	2	2	0
d	5	8	−3
e	6	10	−4
f	4	9	−5
g	3	11	−8
h	0	2	−2
i	11	7	4
j	8	9	−1
			$\Sigma D = -18$

$$\overline{D} = \frac{\Sigma D}{N} = \frac{-18}{10} = -1.8$$

Step 5:   Calculate the standard deviation of the difference scores (s_D).

The computational formula for the standard deviation of difference scores is:

$$s_D = \sqrt{\frac{\Sigma D^2 - \frac{(\Sigma D)^2}{n}}{n - 1}}$$

To use this formula, we need to compute D^2 for each participant:

Participant	Greed	Self-Defense	D	D^2
a	14	15	−1	1
b	8	6	2	4
c	2	2	0	0
d	5	8	−3	9
e	6	10	−4	16
f	4	9	−5	25
g	3	11	−8	64
h	0	2	−2	4
i	11	7	4	16
j	8	9	−1	1
			$\Sigma D = -18$	$\Sigma D^2 = 140$

Now we have the values needed for the standard deviation formula:

$$s_D = \sqrt{\frac{140 - \frac{(-18)^2}{10}}{10 - 1}}$$

$$s_D = \sqrt{\frac{140 - \frac{324}{10}}{9}}$$

$$s_D = \sqrt{\frac{140 - 32.4}{9}}$$

$$s_D = \sqrt{\frac{107.6}{9}}$$

$$s_D = \sqrt{11.955556}$$

$$s_D = 3.4576807$$

Step 6: Compute the estimated standard error ($s_{\overline{D}}$).

$$s_{\overline{D}} = \frac{s_D}{\sqrt{n}}$$

$$s_{\overline{D}} = \frac{3.4576807}{\sqrt{10}}$$

$$s_{\overline{D}} = \frac{3.4576807}{3.1622776}$$

$$s_{\overline{D}} = 1.0934146$$

Step 7: Compute the obtained value of t for related samples.

$$t_{obtained} = \frac{\overline{D}}{s_{\overline{D}}}$$

$$t_{obtained} = \frac{-1.8}{1.0934146}$$

$$t_{obtained} = -1.646219$$

$$t_{obtained} \approx -1.646$$

Step 8: Find the degrees of freedom and look up $t_{critical}$ in the t-Table (Table B-10.

$$df = n - 1 \qquad \textbf{(where n is the number of participants or pairs of scores)}$$

$$df = 10 - 1$$

$$df = 9$$

For a two-tailed test with alpha set at .05, we look in the third column of the t-Table:

$$t_{critical} \ (df = 9) = 2.262$$

Step 9:   Make a decision and draw a conclusion.

Compare $t_{obtained}$ to $t_{critical}$, using the following decision rule:

$$\text{If } |t_{obtained}| \geq t_{critical}, \text{ reject the null hypothesis}$$

$|t_{obtained}| = 1.646; \ t_{critical} = 2.262$

1.646 is less than 2.262; therefore, we fail to reject the null hypothesis.

Conclusion: We conclude that there is no significant difference in the amount of aggressiveness displayed by five-year-olds after they have watched violence motivated by greed versus violence motivated by self-defense. (Recall from Chapter 6, that a failure to reject the null hypothesis cannot be interpreted as evidence that the null hypothesis is *true* because the probability of a Type II error may be very high. Different motivations for violence may, in fact, have an effect on children's aggression, but this particular experiment may have had insufficient power to detect the effect. For example, the sample size (n = 10) may have been too small. The only conclusion we can draw is that the difference between the groups did not reach statistical significance.)

The Limited Applicability of z- and t-Tests

In this chapter we have described two inferential statistical tests that can test hypotheses about one or two samples. The z-test can be used to determine whether or not a research sample comes from a population whose parameters (μ and σ) are known, and the one-sample t-test can be used when the population parameters must be estimated using the research sample data. Two-sample t-tests can be used to determine whether or not two research samples are significantly different from each other, and therefore, this test is appropriate for simple designs that compare two treatment conditions. In practice, however, the z-test is not commonly employed in psychological research because the population parameters are usually unknown, and relatively few studies include only two experimental conditions. As you may recall from Chapter 10, one-way designs frequently require three or more treatments in order to answer the research question, and factorial designs must have a minimum of four conditions in order to investigate the possible interaction between independent variables. Therefore, t-tests cannot be the primary statistical test in the majority of studies. However, while the overall analysis of these designs requires other statistical tests, the t-test is often used as a follow-up procedure comparing two treatment groups at a time. The basic principles of this kind of *post hoc analysis* are discussed in Chapter 12 following the presentation of analysis of variance (ANOVA), one of the most popular tests for analyzing data from experimental and quasi-experimental designs.

Exercises

1. When the American Association of University Professors (AAUP) published the results of its national survey on college salaries, it indicated that the national average (μ) for associate professors in liberal arts was $40,000 with a standard deviation (σ) of $3600. At Belmore Liberal Arts College, nine female associate professors began to wonder whether they were the victims of discrimination, since their average salary ($\overline{X}$) was only $38,000. Are the women being paid significantly less than average?

   a. Set alpha at .05 and conduct a one-tailed test. What conclusion would you draw about the salaries of female faculty at Belmore College?

   b. Now set alpha at .05 and conduct a two-tailed test and verbally summarize the results.

   c. Compare the results of the two tests.

2. The national average (μ) on the Verbal subtest of the Scholastic Aptitude Test (SAT-V) is 500 with a standard deviation (σ) of 100. If a sample of 36 students who were home-schooled had an average SAT-V score of 540, should we conclude that home-schooled students have significantly higher verbal skills? Set alpha at .05 and conduct the appropriate two-tailed statistical test. Verbally summarize the results.

3. A researcher wanted to know whether married men are healthier than never-married bachelors, so the age at time of death was recorded for a sample of married men and a sample of never-married bachelors. The results are below. Set alpha at .05 and conduct the appropriate two-tailed statistical test. Verbally summarize the results.

Married	Bachelors
78	69
75	70
83	75
79	74
71	64
77	73
86	81
79	72
68	78

4. At 36 months of age, the average child can put 3.6 words together in a sentence. (This is known as the *mean length of utterance*, or MLU.) If the

average MLU for a sample of 12 abused children was found to be 2.9 with a standard deviation of 0.76, would we conclude that abused children's language development is significantly delayed? Set alpha at .05 and conduct the appropriate two-tailed statistical test. Verbally summarize the results.

5. In a study on the effects of alcohol on sperm cells, a researcher collected two sperm samples from a group of volunteers. One sperm sample was collected after a two-week period when no alcohol was consumed, and the second sperm sample was collected after a two-week period during which the men had consumed three beers per day. (The order of treatments was counterbalanced.) The percentage of sperm cells that contained genetic defects was recorded. The results are presented below. Set alpha at .05 and conduct the appropriate two-tailed statistical test. Verbally summarize the results.

No Alcohol	Alcohol
23	29
18	24
22	27
24	30
9	13
16	18
17	14
32	36
20	22
26	23

6. A psychologist wanted to examine the effects of diet on learning in rats. Newborn rats were randomly assigned to one of two diets: standard Purina Rat Chow or a supplemented diet where vitamins and minerals were added to the Rat Chow. After six months, each rat was tested on a discrimination problem, and the researcher recorded the number of errors each animal made before it solved the problem. The data are below. Set alpha at .01 and conduct the appropriate two-tailed statistical test. Verbally summarize the results.

Regular Rat Chow	Special Rat Chow
13	9
11	8
12	7
13	8
11	9
9	10
12	7
10	8
12	9
14	6
10	8
12	10

7. A nutritionist began to suspect that the artificial sweeteners used in diet co-
    las actually served to increase appetites. Therefore, she measured the daily
    caloric intake of 25 adults who drink diet cola, and found an average ($\overline{X}$) of
    3,100 calories per day with a standard deviation (s) of 600. If the national
    average (μ) is known to be 2,800 calories per day, do diet cola drinkers take
    in significantly more calories than average? Perform the appropriate
    directional (one-tailed) test with alpha set at .05, and verbally summarize the
    results.

8. After her examination of her original sample of diet cola drinkers, the nutri-
    tionist (from problem 7 above) decided to conduct a study in which 10
    normal-weight volunteers would drink diet cola for a week and drink regular
    cola for a week (in counterbalanced order). The nutritionist hypothesized
    that the average daily caloric intake for the participants would be higher
    while they were drinking diet cola. The data are below. Conduct the
    appropriate directional (one-tailed) test with alpha set at .05, and verbally
    summarize the results.

Participant	Diet Cola	Regular Cola
a	3416	2929
b	2257	2004
c	4097	3099
d	3845	3273
e	3631	3155
f	3690	3106
g	2119	2208
h	3304	2495
i	3082	2551
j	2731	3128

CHAPTER

12

ANALYSIS OF VARIANCE

■ ■ ■ ■ ■ ■

In this chapter, you will learn how to perform one of the most versatile statistical tests for experimental and quasi-experimental research: Analysis of variance (ANOVA). Each of the steps involved in the procedure are explained and detailed examples of ANOVAs for one-way between-subjects and within-subjects designs are presented. Additionally, an example of an ANOVA for a factorial between-subjects design shows you how to test for main effects and interactions.

Look for These Important Terms and Concepts

F-ratio
error term
sources of variability
between-subjects (BS) ANOVA
within-subjects (RM) ANOVA
sum of squares (SS)

degrees of freedom (df)
mean squares (MS)
post hoc analyses
Dunn's multiple comparisons test
critical range (CR)

Before Reading This Chapter, You May Wish to Review

Chapter 3:
• confound

Chapter 4:
• interval and ratio scales

Chapter 5:
• variance and standard deviation

Chapter 6:
• random sampling error (chance)

Chapter 10:
• one-way and factorial designs
• main effects and interactions
• between-subjects designs
• within-subjects designs

• rejecting the null hypothesis
• critical values

Experimental and quasi-experimental designs which employ interval or ratio scales of measurement for the dependent variable may be analyzed using a statistical procedure known as analysis of variance, which is nicknamed ANOVA. While the two statistics covered in Chapter 11 z and t are limited to simple one- or two-group designs, ANOVA can be used for designs with two or more groups, including one-way and factorial designs. In designs with only two groups, t-tests and ANOVA are conceptually equivalent, and they reach the same conclusion. (In fact, the ANOVA F for a two-group design is equal to t^2).

ANOVA measures two types of variability in the data set: (1) the differences among individual scores *within the same treatment groups* that can be attributed to chance fluctuations (i.e., individual differences, measurement error, and experimenter error), and (2) the variability *between or among the group means (or totals)*, which would include systematic effects of the independent variable as well as the chance fluctuations associated with random sampling or changes within individuals over time. ANOVA then calculates the ratio of these two measures of variability (calling it the "F ratio"):

$$F = \frac{\text{IV} + \text{chance fluctuations}}{\text{chance fluctuations alone}}$$

The denominator of F, which measures "chance fluctuations," is referred to as the **error term**.

If the IV has no systematic effect (so that the difference between the groups is no larger than chance fluctuations alone), the value of F will approximate 1.00. If the IV *does* have an effect, F will be larger than 1.00, and as the effect of the IV gets stronger, the value of F increases.

There are a number of steps involved in computing the ANOVA F, so it is customary to keep track by setting up an "ANOVA summary table" and filling it in as we complete the separate computations. Table 12-1 illustrates a summary table for a one-way between-subjects design, both before the computations begin and after they have been completed.

As you can see in Table 12-1, an ANOVA summary table consists of 5 columns, beginning with a list of the "sources" of variation among the scores in the data set, including the variability attributable to the IVs ("BG") and the variability attributable to chance alone ("WG"). The second column is where we record the sums of squares

TABLE 12.1					An ANOVA Summary Table, Before and After the Computations				
Source	SS	df	MS	F	Source	SS	df	MS	F
BG					BG	345	3	115.0	4.00*
WG					WG	1035	36	28.75	
Total					Total	1380	39		
								*p < .05	

(a measure of variability) for each of these sources. The next column contains the degrees of freedom (df) for each of the sum of squares which tell us how many independent scores are involved in the sum of squares, and these degrees of freedom are used to compute mean squares (MS), which provide a measure of the average variability for each source. Finally, the *F* ratios—the actual test statistics—are computed (using mean squares) and recorded in the fifth column of the summary table.

Sources of Variation

Between-Subjects Designs

Let's suppose that a study has been conducted where 100 participants were assigned to one of four groups so that each group had 25 participants. This one-way between-subjects design would result in a data set including 100 scores (one score from each of the participants). If we measure the variability among these 100 scores, it would give us the **total variability** for the data. What we then need to do is identify the separate sources of variation that comprise this total variability.

One source of variation among these 100 scores would be the difference in treatment for the four groups. In other words, if the independent variable has had an effect, it would explain why one group of 25 scores tends to be different from the other groups of scores. Thus, one source of variation in the set of 100 scores is the IV manipulation. This is called the **between-groups variability.**

A second source of variation among the scores is simply referred to as "chance fluctuations," which includes all of the variation among the scores that is not systematically related to the researcher's treatment. (Individual differences, measurement error, and experimenter error are all components of "chance.") We can see these chance fluctuations when we look at the 25 scores for the participants in one of the four treatment groups: The differences among these 25 scores cannot be attributed to the IV because the participants were all given the same treatment. The differences among these scores, then, are due to chance. We refer to these chance fluctuations as the **within-group variability** and we use a measure of the within-group variability as the denominator of *F* (i.e., as the **error term**) when we conduct an ANOVA on data from a between-subjects design.

In a one-way between-subjects design, then, there are only two sources of variation: chance fluctuations (or error) and the effect of the IV. Therefore, the first column for the ANOVA for this study would look like this:

Source
BG (or IV)
WG (error)
Total

When we have a between-subjects design and we are breaking the total variability down into these sources of variability, we say that we are conducting a **between-subjects analysis of variance (BS-ANOVA).**

Within-Subjects Designs

If our study, however, had used a within-subjects design where each of 25 participants were observed under each of the four different treatments, the sources of variability would be a little different. Again, we have a total of 100 scores (four scores for each of 25 participants) and we could measure the total variability among these 100 scores. Why are these scores different? One potential source of variation is, of course, the independent variable manipulation: 25 of the scores were obtained under one experimental treatment while the other scores were observed under three other treatment conditions. Thus, like in the between-subjects design described above, the independent variable is one of the components (i.e., one of the sources) of the total variation among the scores in a within-subjects design.

Since participants are observed under every treatment condition, within-subjects designs allow us to compute the average scores for each participant across the four treatments. This average performance can be viewed as an estimate of the individual's general ability to perform the task. (For example, if we are measuring memory performance under four treatment conditions, Joshua's average score across the four tests represents his overall memory ability.) Thus, individual differences in basic performance ability are the second component of the total variability among the scores in a within-subjects design. We can measure this "source" of variation by calculating an average score for each participant and measuring the variability among these average scores. This source of variation is called the *subjects* component.

The third and final source of variability among the scores in the data set can be observed when you compare one individual's *pattern* of performance across the treatments to another individual's pattern of performance under the different treatments. One participant, for example, may show only small changes in behavior from one treatment to another, while another participant may show large changes. Different patterns of performance will be due to a combination of random changes in temporary states (such as mood or fatigue levels) and individual differences in more permanent characteristics which may affect performance at different points in time or under different circumstances. (For example, an individual with attention deficit disorder may do well on memory tasks conducted in a quiet room but perform poorly when there are distractions nearby.) In technical terms, then, there is an *interaction* between the independent variable and the participants. As you may recall from Chapter 10, an interaction exists when the effect of one variable is not the same for every level of another variable. Here we are describing a case where the effects of the experimental treatments are not the same for every individual participant, so there is a "treatment × subjects" interaction. Certainly, the fact that the treatments may affect individual participants in different ways is not surprising; it is simply a reflection of the individual differences among people that we label "chance fluctuations." This treatment × subjects interaction is the measure of "chance fluctuations" that we will use when we compute the ANOVA *F* for a within-subjects design. That is, the treatment × subjects interaction is the *error term* for the ANOVA.

Thus, in a one-way within-subjects design, the total variability has three components and the first column of the ANOVA summary table would look like this:[1]

Source
Treatment
Subjects
Treatment × Subjects
Total

When we break the total variability down into these sources, we are conducting what we call a **repeated-measures analysis of variance (RM-ANOVA)**.

Factorial Designs

In designs with two or more independent variables, the overall variability among the treatment conditions (or experimental groups) is the sum of the variability due to the separate components of the research design. That is, the overall variability among the experimental conditions can be broken down into the *main effects* of the IVs and the *interactions* among the IVs. This allows us to determine whether the first IV has a systematic impact on behavior, whether the second IV has a systematic effect, and whether the effect of the first IV depends upon the level of the second IV. These are, you'll recall from Chapter 10, the three research questions that are addressed in a two-way factorial design. Each of these research questions is answered by its own unique value of F.

For example, in a two-way design, there are two main effects (A and B) and one interaction (A × B), so *three* separate F-ratios will be computed. A three-way design has three main effects (A, B, and C), three two-way interactions (A × B; A × C; and B × C), and one three-way interaction (A × B × C). Each of these effects and interactions require their own F-ratio, so a three-way ANOVA will involve *seven* F-ratios. A four-way design has four main effects (A, B, C, and D), six two-way interactions (A × B; A × C; A × D; B × C; B × D; and C × D), four three-way interactions (A × B × C; A × B × D; A × C × D; and B × C × D), and one four-way interaction (A × B × C × D), so it requires *fifteen* separate F-ratios. Figure 12-1 illustrates the breakdown of sources of variation for the different types of designs using "ANOVA Trees." The last branches from an ANOVA tree are included in the list of sources (column 1) of the ANOVA summary table (see Figure 12-1).

Mixed Designs

Mixed designs include both between-subject factors and within-subjects factors, and therefore, the total variability among the scores is composed of *both* types of error

---

[1] In an ANOVA summary table for a within-subjects design, the term "Treatment" refers to the independent variable. The term "Conditions" may be used instead, or the name of the IV may be used on the table (such as "Age" or "Type of Therapy" or "Amount of Violence" and so forth).

FIGURE 12.1 ANOVA "TREES" AND SOURCES OF VARIABILITY

(a) One-way BS-ANOVA

$SS_{Total} \begin{cases} SS_{BG} \\ SS_{WG} \end{cases}$

Sources	SS	df	MS	F
BG				4.0
WG				[NOTE: WG is the Error Term for F]
Total				

(b) Two-way BS-ANOVA

$SS_{Total} \begin{cases} SS_{BG} \begin{cases} SS_A \\ SS_B \\ SS_{A \times B} \end{cases} \\ SS_{WG} \end{cases}$

Sources	SS	df	MS	F
A				3.2
B				4.6
A × B				2.5
WG				[NOTE: WG is the Error Term for all 3 Fs]
Total				

(c) Three-way BS-ANOVA

$SS_{Total} \begin{cases} SS_{BG} \begin{cases} SS_A \\ SS_B \\ SS_C \\ SS_{A \times B} \\ SS_{A \times C} \\ SS_{B \times C} \\ SS_{A \times B \times C} \end{cases} \\ SS_{WG} \end{cases}$

Sources	SS	df	MS	F
A				2.4
B				3.5
C				3.4
A × B				4.1
A × C				2.7
B × C				4.8
A × B × C				3.1
WG				[NOTE: WG is the Error Term for all 7 Fs]
Total				

(d) One-way RM-ANOVA

$SS_{Total} \begin{cases} SS_{Treatment \ (or \ Condition)} \\ SS_{Subjects} \\ SS_{Treatment \times Subjects} \end{cases}$

Sources	SS	df	MS	F
Treatment (T)				4.6
Subjects (S)				
T × S				[NOTE: T × S is the Error Term for F]
Total				

(e) Two-way RM-ANOVA

$SS_{Total} \begin{cases} SS_{Treatment} \begin{cases} SS_A \\ SS_B \\ SS_{A \times B} \end{cases} \\ SS_{Subjects} \\ SS_{Treatment \times Subjects} \begin{cases} SS_{A \times Subjects} \\ SS_{B \times Subjects} \\ SS_{A \times B \times Subjects} \end{cases} \end{cases}$

Sources	SS	df	MS	F
A				4.0
B				3.6
A × B				2.7
Subjects (S)				
A × S				[NOTE: A × S is the Error Term for F_A]
B × S				[NOTE: B × S is the Error Term for F_B]
A × B × S				[NOTE: A × B × S is the Error Term for $F_{A \times B}$]
Total				

variance: The random sampling error which results from having different participants receiving different treatments, *and* the individual differences in how participants react to changes in treatment. The between-subjects factors are, initially, analyzed separately from the within-subjects factors, but then they are combined in
order to measure their interactions. Doing a mixed ANOVA by hand, therefore, is
quite complicated and very time-consuming, so consequently, the computations will
not be included in this text. Interested students should see Keppel and Zedeck (1989)
for the formulas for mixed ANOVAs.

Computing Sums of Squares

The measure of variability used in ANOVA is called the **sum of squares**, which is
short for "sum of the squared deviations of X from the mean": $\Sigma(X - \overline{X})^2$. You
should recognize this as the numerator of the definitional formula for the standard
deviation. Thus, a sum of squares (SS) is a measure of the differences among scores.
The SS_{Total} measures the differences among all of the individual scores in the data set;
that is, it measures the deviation of the individuals from the grand mean ($\overline{\overline{X}}$) of the
entire data set. This *total variability* will be divided into the unique components
which represent the variation that is due to the systematic effects of the IV treatments, individual differences in ability, or chance alone. Each sum of squares has its
own formula because they each measure a different source of variability among the
scores.

Before we begin presenting the formulas for sums of squares, we want to point
out that there are three features of the data set that you will need to know to perform
ANOVA. These include the number of treatment conditions (k), the number of
scores in each treatment condition (n), and the total number of scores in the data set
(N). The total sample size (N) will always be equal to the sum of the condition sizes
(n). That is, $\Sigma n = N$. Furthermore, if the treatment conditions have an equal number of scores, then $N = k \times n$.

One-way BS-ANOVA

We will use the following data set to illustrate the computations of the sums of
squares for a one-way BS-ANOVA. (A complete one-way BS-ANOVA is presented
in Appendix 12-A, beginning on page 373.)

Treatment A	Treatment B	Treatment C
2	5	7
4	4	3
3	6	6

This data set has three treatment conditions (so k = 3). Each group has three scores
in it (so there is equal n, and n = 3), and therefore, there are 9 scores altogether
(N = 9). (A small data set like this is sufficient to illustrate the computations, but

researchers need to have more participants to test their hypotheses with sufficient power.)

Measuring the Total Variability in the Data Set   The *definitional formula* for the "Total Sum of Squares" is:

$$SS_{Total} = \Sigma\Sigma(X - \overline{\overline{X}})^2$$

where $\Sigma\Sigma$ indicates a "Grand Total" which is the sum of all N scores and $\overline{\overline{X}}$ is the mean of all N scores.

As you can see, this formula asks us to compute a deviation score—from the grand mean—for each participant, square it, and then find the sum of the squared deviation scores. Applying this formula is tedious, so we recommend that you use the *computational formula* because it is easier to use when calculating the SS_{Total}:

$$SS_{Total} = \Sigma\Sigma X^2 - \frac{(\Sigma\Sigma X)^2}{N}$$

To use this version of the SS_{Total} formula, simply square every score in the data set, find the sum of the raw scores (i.e., the grand total $= \Sigma\Sigma X$) and the sum of the squared Xs ($\Sigma\Sigma X^2$), and solve for SS_{Total}. (N is the total number of scores in the data set.) The first piece of this formula instructs us to square the individual scores and add them together ($\Sigma\Sigma X^2$). The numerator of the second component of the formula requires us to find the *grand total* of the scores ($\Sigma\Sigma X$). The most efficient procedure is to get the ΣX and ΣX^2 for each group, and then add the groups together as part of the first step in solving the formula.

Treatment		Treatment		Treatment	
A	**X^2**	**B**	**X^2**	**C**	**X^2**
2	4	5	25	7	49
4	16	4	16	3	9
3	9	6	36	6	36
$\Sigma X = 9$	$\Sigma X^2 = 29$	$\Sigma X = 15$	$\Sigma X^2 = 77$	$\Sigma X = 16$	$\Sigma X^2 = 94$

Therefore:

$$SS_{Total} = (29 + 77 + 94) - \frac{(9 + 15 + 16)^2}{9}$$

Measuring the Variability Due to the Independent Variable   The effect of the IV in a one-way between-subjects design is measured with the "between-groups sum of squares" ($SS_{Between\ Groups}$ or SS_{BG}). The *definitional formula* for SS_{BG} is:

$$SS_{Between\ Groups} = n\Sigma(\overline{X} - \overline{\overline{X}})^2$$

This formula technically measures the squared deviations of each treatment mean ($\overline{X}$) from the grand mean ($\overline{\overline{X}}$). It tells us to compute the difference between a group mean and the grand mean, square this deviation, add the squared deviations together across the groups, and then multiply by the number of participants in the experimental conditions (n).[2] Just like the SS_{Total} definitional formula, this formula for SS_{BG} is difficult to use for hand-computations. Therefore, we recommend that you use the *computational formula*:

$$SS_{BG} = \sum \frac{(\Sigma X)^2}{n} - \frac{(\Sigma \Sigma X)^2}{N}$$

The first piece of the computational SS_{BG} formula asks us to: (1) take a group total (ΣX), square it and divide by the number of participants in that group, and (2) after doing step 1 for each group, add the groups together. The second piece asks us to square the grand total and divide it by N. Let's apply this formula to the data set.

	X scores	
Treatment A	Treatment B	Treatment C
2	5	7
4	4	3
3	6	6
$\Sigma X = 9$	$\Sigma X = 15$	$\Sigma X = 16$

$$SS_{BG} = \left(\frac{9^2}{3} + \frac{15^2}{3} + \frac{16^2}{3} \right) - \frac{(9 + 15 + 16)^2}{9}$$

There is also a useful short-cut that we can apply when the treatment groups are the same size. When there is equal n, the first piece of the SS_{BG} formula can be re-written so that the numerators are added together before the division by n. (That is, we only need to divide by n once.)

$$SS_{BG} = \frac{\Sigma(\Sigma X)^2}{n} - \frac{(\Sigma \Sigma X)^2}{N}$$

$$SS_{BG} = \frac{9^2 + 15^2 + 16^2}{3} - \frac{(9 + 15 + 16)^2}{9}$$

You may have noticed that the second piece of this formula is identical to the second piece in the SS_{Total} formula: It asks us to square the grand total and divide by the total number of scores in the data set. This piece of the formulas is referred to as the *correction factor* and it only needs to be computed once: After this piece has been computed for the SS_{Total} formula, it can be immediately inserted into the SS_{BG} formula. Consequently, the only difference between the two sums of squares formulas is the first component. In the SS_{Total} formula, the first piece of the formula asked us to square each individual score (X), while the first piece of the SS_{BG} formula asks us to square each group total (ΣX). As a result, the SS_{Total} formula measures the variability among the individual scores, and the SS_{BG} formula measures the variability

---

[2] Note that this formula assumes that there is an equal number of participants in each treatment group. That is, that $n_1 = n_2 = n_3 = \cdots$

among the group totals and serves as a measure of the variability due to the independent variable. (If the IV has had a systematic effect on the performance of the participants, then the total score for one group will be higher than the total score for the other groups, and SS_{BG} will be larger.)

Measuring the Chance Fluctuations: The Error Term   The last sum of squares that we need to calculate for a one-way BS-ANOVA measures the differences among the participants within the *same* treatment groups. That is, we can look at the scores from just one experimental group and calculate the variability among the participants in that group. This within-group variability is a measure of the chance fluctuations among the scores (i.e., individual differences, measurement error, or experimenter error) rather than systematic effects from the IV since the participants in the group received the *same* experimental treatment. As the *definitional formula* indicates, the within-group sum of squares (SS_{WG}) is simply the sum of the within-group variabilities for all of the experimental groups:

$$SS_{WG} = \Sigma[\Sigma(X - \overline{X})^2]$$

This definitional formula can, of course, be re-written into a more useful *computational formula*:

$$SS_{WG} = \Sigma\left(\Sigma X^2 - \frac{(\Sigma X)^2}{n}\right)$$

This formula still requires us to compute the variability for each group separately and then add them together. Fortunately, there is an even easier formula that does not require tedious computations for every group of scores. Recall that the variability due to the independent variable and chance fluctuations are the two components that account for the total variability among the scores in the data set. This means that these two sources of variability must *add up to* the total variability, and therefore, once we have computed SS_{Total} and SS_{BG}, we can find the within-group sum of squares (SS_{WG}) through simple subtraction:

$$SS_{WG} = SS_{Total} - SS_{BG}$$

After each of the sum of squares is computed, it is entered into the ANOVA summary table which was prepared in advance. When we complete the computations for the sums of squares for our sample data set, and enter them into an ANOVA summary table, we find the following values:

Source	SS
BG	9.55555
WG	12.66667
Total	22.22222

Another numerical example for each sums of squares is presented as part of a complete one-way BS-ANOVA, starting on page 373.

Two-way BS-ANOVA

We will use the following data set to illustrate the computations of the sums of squares for a two-way BS-ANOVA. (A complete two-way BS-ANOVA is presented in Appendix 12-B, beginning on page 379.)

IV$_B$

	B$_1$	B$_2$
A$_1$	2 5 3	5 4 6
IV$_A$ A$_2$	1 3 2	3 6 1
A$_3$	5 6 3	7 5 8

This 3 × 2 design has a total of six treatment conditions (so k = 6). The first independent variable (A) has three levels and the second independent variable (B) has two levels. The symbol for the number of levels of an IV is k_{IV}, therefore, in this design, $k_A = 3$ and $k_B = 2$. Each treatment group has three scores in it (i.e., n = 3), and therefore, there are 18 scores altogether (N = 18).

The first three sums of squares that we compute in a two-way BS-ANOVA are identical to the sums of squares in a one-way BS-ANOVA. Therefore, in order to use the computational formulas to compute SS$_{Total}$ and SS$_{BG}$, we need to square each score and then find the group totals for X and X^2 (i.e., ΣX and ΣX^2):

IV$_B$

	B$_1$		B$_2$	
	X	X^2	X	X^2
A$_1$	2 5 3	4 25 9	5 4 6	25 16 36
	$\Sigma X=10$	$\Sigma X^2=38$	$\Sigma X=15$	$\Sigma X^2=77$
IV$_A$ A$_2$	1 3 2	1 9 4	3 6 1	9 36 1
	$\Sigma X=6$	$\Sigma X^2=14$	$\Sigma X=10$	$\Sigma X^2=46$
A$_3$	5 6 3	25 36 9	7 5 8	49 25 64
	$\Sigma X=14$	$\Sigma X^2=70$	$\Sigma X=20$	$\Sigma X^2=138$

Therefore, the group totals are:

	ΣX			ΣX^2	
	B_1	B_2		B_1	B_2
A_1	10	15		38	77
A_2	6	10		14	46
A_3	14	20		70	138

Now we plug these values into the computational formulas:

$$SS_{Total} = \Sigma\Sigma X^2 - \frac{(\Sigma\Sigma X)^2}{N}$$

$$SS_{Total} = (38 + 77 + 14 + 46 + 70 + 138) - \frac{(10 + 15 + 6 + 10 + 14 + 20)^2}{18}$$

And, because the groups have equal n:

$$SS_{BG} = \frac{\Sigma(\Sigma X)^2}{n} - \frac{(\Sigma\Sigma X)^2}{N}$$

$$SS_{BG} = \frac{10^2 + 15^2 + 6^2 + 10^2 + 14^2 + 20^2}{3} - \frac{(10 + 15 + 6 + 10 + 14 + 20)^2}{18}$$

The total variability in a two-way design is equal to the sum of the variability due to the systematic difference between the groups and the random variation among the participants within the groups. Therefore, as in the one-way BS-ANOVA, the within-group sum of squares in a two-way design can be found through subtraction:

$$SS_{WG} = SS_{Total} - SS_{BG}$$

Measuring the Main Effects of the Independent Variables   Two-way factorial designs, of course, include two independent variables, each of which may have a unique effect on the dependent variable. Therefore, the next step in the two-way BS-ANOVA involves calculating the sums of squares for the main effects of the independent variables. The main effects and the interactions are separate components of the SS_{BG} (and together, the main effects and interactions *add up to* the SS_{BG}).

As you may recall from Chapter 10, an independent variable has a *main effect* if there is a difference in the overall performance of the participants who received different levels of the IV. In order to measure the *overall performance* for the levels of an independent variable in a two-way factorial design, we re-write the data matrix so that it includes only the row (or column) totals from the original data set. Essentially, then, we pretend that there was only one IV in the design. This process is called "collapsing" the data, and we say we "collapse across variable B" in order to assess the main effect of variable A, and vice versa. We then measure the variability among these "collapsed groups" using the formula that measures the difference among group totals (i.e., the SS_{BG} formula). Let's illustrate the process of collapsing the data and computing the sums of squares for the main effects in our 3×2 data set.

Original data matrix (where the numbers are the group totals):

	B_1	B_2
A_1	10	15
A_2	6	10
A_3	14	20

n = 3

Collapsing the data matrix in order to find the main effect of A (i.e., "collapsing across B"):

A_1	10 + 15
A_2	6 + 10
A_3	14 + 20

$\Rightarrow$

A_1	25
A_2	16
A_3	34

NOTE: These collapsed groups have 6 scores each, therefore, n = 6

Sum of Squares for the Main Effect of A:

$$SS_A = \frac{25^2 + 16^2 + 34^2}{6} - \frac{(25 + 16 + 34)^2}{18}$$

Next, we would collapse the original data matrix into the main effect of B (i.e., we would collapse across A). This new matrix would have *two* groups (since there are only two levels of variable B) and each group would have 9 scores:

B_1	B_2
10 + 6 + 14	15 + 10 + 20

$\Rightarrow$

B_1	B_2
30	45

NOTE: n = 9

Sum of squares for the main effect of B:

$$SS_B = \frac{30^2 + 45^2}{9} - \frac{(30 + 45)^2}{18}$$

These main effects measure the unique impact of the IVs on the dependent variable. Next we need to measure the interaction between the IVs. That is, we want to measure the extent to which the effect of one IV varies from one level of the other

IV to another. Therefore, the next (and last) sum of squares we need to compute in a two-way BS-ANOVA will be a measure of the interaction between IV_A and IV_B. This $A \times B$ interaction (read: "A by B") is the third component of the overall SS_{BG} (see Figure 12-1b). That is, SS_{BG} is equal to the sum of the main effects and the interaction, and therefore, we can calculate the sum of squares for the interaction using subtraction:

$$SS_{A \times B} = SS_{BG} - SS_A - SS_B$$

When we complete the computations for the sums of squares for this 3×2 data set, and enter the values into an ANOVA summary table, we find the following values:

Source	SS
A	27.00
B	12.50
A × B	0.333333
WG	30.666667
Total	70.50

Another numerical example of the computations of these sums of squares is presented, as part of a complete two-way BS-ANOVA, in Appendix 12-B starting on page 379.

One-way RM-ANOVA

To illustrate the computation of the sum of squares for a one-way RM-ANOVA, we'll use the small data set below. In this design, two participants were exposed to each of three different treatments, so that we have a total of 6 scores in the data set. Thus, $n = 2$, $k = 3$, and $N = 6$.

	X scores		
Subject	Treatment A	Treatment B	Treatment C
a	2	5	7
b	3	6	6
	$\Sigma X = 5$	$\Sigma X = 11$	$\Sigma X = 13$

As we discussed earlier in this chapter, the total variability in a within-subjects design has three separate components: The systematic difference between the experimental treatments, the individual differences in overall ability to perform the task, and random variation in how the different treatments affect the individual participants (i.e., differences in their patterns of performance). The formula for the total sum of squares in a RM-ANOVA is the same as in BS-ANOVA, so the *Computational Formula* is:

$$SS_{Total} = \Sigma\Sigma X^2 - \frac{(\Sigma\Sigma X)^2}{N}$$

Therefore:

Subject	Treatment A	X^2	Treatment B	X^2	Treatment C	X^2
a	2	4	5	25	7	49
b	3	9	6	36	6	36
	$\Sigma X = 5$	$\Sigma X^2 = 13$	$\Sigma X = 11$	$\Sigma X^2 = 61$	$\Sigma X = 13$	$\Sigma X^2 = 85$

$$SS_{Total} = (13 + 61 + 85) - \frac{(5 + 11 + 13)^2}{6}$$

Measuring the Effect of the Independent Variable   The systematic difference between the treatments is measured the same way in both BS- and RM-ANOVAs: The treatment totals (ΣXs) are compared to each other (i.e., to the grand mean). Therefore, the formula for the $SS_{Treatment}$ is identical to the formula for SS_{BG}, except we do not refer to this effect as a difference between "groups" because there was only one group of participants tested repeatedly under different treatment conditions. The *computational formula* is:

$$SS_{Treatment} = \Sigma \frac{(\Sigma X)^2}{n} - \frac{(\Sigma \Sigma X)^2}{N}$$

We have equal n, so we can use the shortcut version of the formula. Therefore, the $SS_{Treatment}$ for our example is:

$$SS_{Treatment} = \frac{5^2 + 11^2 + 13^2}{2} - \frac{(5 + 11 + 13)^2}{6}$$

Measuring the Individual Differences in Overall Ability   Suppose we measured memory performance under three different conditions using a within-subjects design. The average of Maria's three scores will reflect her basic memory skills (although there may be some variation among her three scores due to the effects of different experimental treatments), and Maria's average score is likely to be different than the average memory performance of someone else. We measure these individual differences in ability by computing the **sum of squares of subjects ($SS_{Subjects}$).** The *definitional formula* is:

$$SS_{Subjects} = k\Sigma(\text{Subject Average} - \overline{\overline{X}})^2$$

This formula tells us to subtract the grand mean (of all scores in the data set) from the mean score for each individual participant, square the deviations, add them up, and multiply by the number of treatments (k, which is the number of times each participant was measured). As we have pointed out before, working with deviation scores is quite tedious, so we recommend that you use the *computational formula:*

$$SS_{\text{Subjects}} = \sum \frac{(\text{Subject Total})^2}{k} - \frac{(\Sigma\Sigma X)^2}{N}$$

You will notice the second piece of this formula is familiar: It is the second piece from the computational formulas for both SS_{Total} and $SS_{\text{Treatment}}$. (This is the same *correction factor* that we saw in the sums of squares from the BS-ANOVA.) It is not necessary to compute the correction factor a second time — once it has been calculated as part of the SS_{Total}, it can simply be inserted into the computations for the other sum of squares.

To compute the SS_{Subjects} for the data from our small within-subjects design example, we need to compute the total score for each participant (or "subject"), square these subject totals, and add them together:

| | X scores | | | | |
Subject	Treatment A	Treatment B	Treatment C	Subject Total	(Subject Total)²
a	2	5	7	14	196
b	3	6	6	15	225
	$\Sigma X = 5$	$\Sigma X = 11$	$\Sigma X = 13$		$\Sigma(\text{Subject Total})^2 = 421$

These values are entered into the formula:

$$SS_{\text{Subjects}} = \left(\frac{196}{3} + \frac{225}{3} \right) - \frac{(5 + 11 + 13)^2}{6}$$

Because each participant was tested an equal number of times (so n is the same for each treatment condition), we can use an "equal n version" of the formula:

$$SS_{\text{Subjects}} = \frac{\Sigma(\text{Subject Total})^2}{k} - \frac{(\Sigma\Sigma X)^2}{N}$$

The first piece of this formula has already been calculated: It is the sum of the column of squared subject totals (see the column on the right). Therefore:

$$SS_{\text{Subjects}} = \frac{421}{3} - \frac{(5 + 11 + 13)^2}{6}$$

Measuring the Random Variability in Reactions to the Independent Variable
The final component of the total variability in a one-way within-subjects design is known as the *treatment × subjects interaction* and it measures the variability among the participants' individual patterns of response to the changing treatments. These individual differences in responsiveness to the levels of the independent variable are due entirely to chance, and therefore, the treatment × subjects interaction will be the

error term for the *F*-ratio. As we have pointed out, in RM-ANOVA, the total variability is equal to the sum of the three separate variance components ($SS_{Treatment}$, $SS_{Subjects}$, and $SS_{Treatment \times Subjects}$), and therefore, we can compute the $SS_{Treatment \times Subjects}$ using subtraction:

$$SS_{Treatment \times Subjects} = SS_{Total} - SS_{Treatment} - SS_{Subjects}$$

When we complete the computations for the sums of squares for this one-way repeated measures design, and enter the values into an ANOVA summary table, we find the following values:

Source	SS
Treatment	17.333333
Subjects	0.166667
Treatment × Subjects	1.333333
Total	18.833333

Another example of these computations is presented, as part of a complete RM-ANOVA, starting on page 391.

Degrees of Freedom

In analysis of variance, **degrees of freedom** (df) are the number of scores in a sum of squares that are independent of each other and the total (ΣX). For example, suppose a sum of squares is measuring the variability among 100 scores that add up to 650. What is the value of the first score? We do not know because it can be any value from 0 to 650, so we say that it has a degree of freedom. Suppose the first score has a value of 20, what is the value of the second score? Again, we do not know. The second score can be anything from 0 to 630, so it has another degree of freedom. Suppose the second number is 30, what is the value of the third score? We don't know. . . . Eventually we will reach a point where the previous scores *will* tell us what the next score must be, and the value of this score will not be free to vary. Specifically, when we reach the end of the data set, we will find that the last score in the set is constrained by the other scores and the group total and does *not* have any freedom to vary. For example, if 100 scores add up to 650, then the value of the 100th score is determined by the values of the first 99 scores. If the first 99 scores add up to 625, then the 100th score must be equal to 25. The last score in a set must be whatever value is necessary to bring the sum of the scores up to the specified total, so the last score is dependent on the values of the other scores. The degrees of freedom for a sum of squares is the number of scores whose values cannot be determined by looking at the other scores in the data set. Each sum of squares measures the variability among a different set of scores, so each sum of squares has its own degrees of freedom.

The total sum of squares (SS_{Total}) measures the variability among the individual scores in the entire data set. The total number of scores in the data set is equal to N, and therefore, the formula for the **total degrees of freedom** (for SS_{Total}) is:

$$\textbf{df}_{\textbf{Total}} = \textbf{N} - \textbf{1} \quad \text{(where N = the total number of scores)}$$

The sum of squares for the IV (SS_{BG} or $SS_{Treatment}$) measures the variation among the treatment totals (ΣXs). If there are 4 experimental treatments, and the grand total of the treatments is 650, what was the total for the first treatment? It has a degree of freedom. And so forth. The last treatment total can be determined once we know the first 3 treatment totals, and therefore, the last group total is *not* free to vary. The number of treatment conditions is equal to k, and therefore, the formula for the **degrees of freedom for the experimental conditions** (for SS_{BG} *and* $SS_{Treatment}$) is:

$$\textbf{df}_{\textbf{BG}} = \textbf{df}_{\textbf{Treatment}} = \textbf{k} - \textbf{1} \quad \text{(where k = the number of conditions)}$$

In BS-ANOVA, the SS_{WG} is a measure of the variability among individuals within the same treatment groups. The variability for each group is measured separately and SS_{WG} is the sum of these measures of chance fluctuations. The degrees of freedom for this sum of squares are equal to the number of scores in the data set that are independent of their own group totals. Each group total will contain one score that is not free to vary because the last score in each group total will be constrained. That is, for every group in the design, we "lose" one degree of freedom from the total N, so the formula for the **degrees of freedom for the within group variability** is:

$$\textbf{df}_{\textbf{WG}} = (\textbf{n}_1 - \textbf{1}) + (\textbf{n}_2 - \textbf{1}) + (\textbf{n}_3 - \textbf{1}) + \ldots + (\textbf{n}_k - \textbf{1}) \quad \text{or} \quad \textbf{df}_{\textbf{WG}} = \textbf{N} - \textbf{k}$$

The sum of squares for subjects (in a within-subjects design's RM-ANOVA) measures the difference among participants in overall ability by computing the total performance for each individual across the treatment conditions. If there were 25 participants, and the grand total of their individual total scores must equal 650, then all but the last participant's total are free to vary; the last participant's total would have to be whatever was "left over" to give us a grand total of 650. The number of participants in a within-subjects design is equal to n, and therefore, the formula for the **degrees of freedom for subjects** (for $SS_{Subjects}$) is:

$$\textbf{df}_{\textbf{Subjects}} = \textbf{n} - \textbf{1} \quad \text{(where n = the number of participants)}$$

The sum of squares for the main effect of one independent variable in a factorial design measures the difference between the total scores for the different levels of the IV (after collapsing across all other IVs in the design). For example, suppose a 4×2 study included four levels of age (4-, 6-, 8-, and 10-year-olds) and two levels of sex (male versus female). To compute the sum of squares for the main effect of Age, we would collapse across Sex by putting all of the 4-year-olds in one group, all of the 6-year-olds in a second group, and so forth. Each group would contain both boys and girls. There are four levels of Age in the study (which is expressed as $k_{age} = 4$), so when we collapse across Sex, we end up with four group totals, and the SS_{Age} would be measuring the variability among these four group totals. If the grand total is 650, how many of the age group totals would be free to vary? All but the last one. Similarly, for the the main effect of Sex, we would collapse across Age by putting all of the boys in one group and all of the girls in another group (so $k_{sex} = 2$), and the sum of squares would measure the difference between the total score for the boys and the total score for the girls. If the grand total is 650, only one of these group totals would have a degree of freedom. For the main effects in a factorial design, then, when we collapse across the other IVs, we end up with a group total for each level of the IV. The number of levels for an independent variable is equal to k_{IV}, and therefore, the **degrees of freedom for a main effect** are equal to:

$$df_{IV} = k_{IV} - 1 \quad \text{where } k_{IV} = \text{the number of levels of the IV}$$

For example, in a 3 × 5 design, where the variables are called A and B respectively, the factorial notation tells us there are three levels of A and five levels of B, and therefore, $k_A = 3$ and $k_B = 5$. Thus, the degrees of freedom for the main effects of variables A and B would be:

$$df_A = k_A - 1 = 3 - 1 = 2 \quad \text{and} \quad df_B = k_B - 1 = 5 - 1 = 4$$

So far, the degrees of freedom for the sums of squares have all been equal to the number of scores minus one. The degrees of freedom for an interaction, however, are somewhat more complex because two variables are involved. Consider the simple 3 × 2 design below, where there are six treatments (so $k = 6$). There is an interaction if the effect of B is not the same for every level of A (or vice versa), and therefore, to test for an interaction, we need to examine the pattern of scores within the rows (or columns). That is, if the pattern in the first row is repeated in every row (or if the pattern in the first column is repeated in every column), there is no interaction between the variables. Therefore, the sum of squares for the interaction measures the differences among the six group totals, but only as they relate to their particular row (or column). As you can see from the data table, the grand total is 25, the total for treatment A_1 is 7, the total for treatment B_1 is 10, and so forth. Given these row and column totals, how many of the group totals are free to vary?

	B_1	B_2	Row Total
A_1	?	?	7
A_2	?	?	9
A_3	?	?	9
Column Total	10	15	25 = Grand Total

The first group total (for condition A_1B_1) is free to vary from 0 to 7. (It cannot be greater than its row total.) Let's suppose the total for the A_1B_1 is equal to 5; what is the total for treatment A_1B_2? It *must* be equal to 2 in order to give us a row total of 7. Therefore, the first row has one degree of freedom. Now consider the second row.

What is the total for group A_2B_1? It is free to vary from 0 to 5, but cannot be greater than 5 because $A_1B_1 = 5$ and the column total is 10. Let's suppose the total for A_2B_1 is equal to 3; what is the total for treatment A_2B_2? It *must* be equal to 6 in order to give us a row total of 9. Therefore, the second row has one degree of freedom. Now consider the third row. What is the total for group A_3B_1? It *must* be equal to 2 in order to give us a column total of 10. Finally, the total for the last group (A_3B_2) *must* be equal to 7 in order to give us a row total of 9 and a column total of 15. The third row has no degrees of freedom at all. Thus, a 3×2 design has six group totals but only two degrees of freedom. While the procedure we just used to determine the number of degrees of freedom may seem complicated, there is an easier way. Let's look at the design again, making note of the group totals that were free to vary:

	B_1	B_2	Row Total
A_1	5*	2	7
A_2	3*	6	9
A_3	2	7	9
Column Total	10	15	25

* = group total with a degree of freedom

Notice that the last group in each row and each column were not free to vary because they were constrained by the row and column totals. That is, at every level of B, the total for A_3 is determined by the totals at A_1 and A_2 and the overall total for variable B at that level. Similarly, at every level of A, the value of B_2 is determined by the total of B_1 and the overall total for variable A at that level. This, of course, brings us back to the general rule for degrees of freedom: The last value in the set is not free to vary, and for an interaction, the "set" refers to the rows and columns. Therefore, the rule, as it applies to a two-way interaction, can be written as follows:

$$df_{A \times B} = (\text{number of rows} - 1) \times (\text{number of columns} - 1)$$

In our 3×2 example, where we logically reasoned that two of the group totals would be free to vary, using the formula looks like this:

$$df_{A \times B} = (3 - 1) \times (2 - 1) = 2 \times 1 = 2$$

Because each row corresponds to a level of the first independent variable (IV_A) and each column corresponds to a level of the second independent variable (IV_B), the formula can be also be expressed as:

$$df_{A \times B} = (k_A - 1) \times (k_B - 1)$$

And this is equivalent to:

$$\mathbf{df_{A \times B} = df_A \times df_B}$$

TABLE 12.2   **Computing Degrees of Freedom**

BS-ANOVA	RM-ANOVA

BS-ANOVA

2×3 BS-designs with 3 scores per group:

	B_1	B_2	B_3
A_1	4 5 3	5 2 4	2 3 1
A_2	4 7 7	7 8 10	4 2 4

$$N = 18 \quad k = 6 \quad n = 3$$

SS_{Total} measures the variability among all of the individual scores, therefore:

$$df_{Total} = N - 1$$
$$= 18 - 1 = 17$$

SS_{BG} measures the variability among the totals for the six groups, therefore:

$$df_{BG} = k - 1$$
$$= 6 - 1 = 5$$

SS_{WG} measures the variability within each of the six groups separately and then adds them together, therefore:

$$df_{WG} = N - k$$
$$= 18 - 6 = 12$$

In a factorial design, SS_{BG} is broken into the main effects and interactions(s):

SS_A measures the difference between the total scores for levels of A, therefore:

$$df_A = \text{\# of levels of A} - 1 \text{ (or } k_A - 1)$$
$$= 2 - 1 = 1$$

SS_B measures the difference between the total scores for levels of B, therefore:

$$df_B = \text{\# of levels of B} - 1 \text{ (or } k_B - 1)$$
$$= 3 - 1 = 2$$

The degrees of freedom for any interaction are equal to the product of the degrees of freedom for the main effects of each variable in the interaction, therefore:

$$df_{A \times B} = df_A \times df_B$$
$$= 1 \times 2 = 2$$

RM-ANOVA

2×3 WS-design with 3 participants (a, b, c):

	A_1			A_2		
	B_1	B_2	B_3	B_1	B_2	B_3
a	3	4	2	6	5	3
b	4	5	2	4	7	4
c	5	2	3	7	8	2

$$N = 18 \quad k = 6 \quad n = 3$$

SS_{Total} measures the variability among all of the individual scores, therefore:

$$df_{Total} = N - 1$$
$$= 18 - 1 = 17$$

$SS_{Treatment}$ measures the variability among the totals for the six treatments, therefore:

$$df_{Treatment} = k - 1$$
$$= 6 - 1 = 5$$

$SS_{Subjects}$ measures the variability among the total scores for each individual, therefore:

$$df_{Subjects} = n - 1$$
$$= 3 - 1 = 2$$

$SS_{Treatment \times Subjects}$ is an interaction, and the degrees of freedom for an interaction is the product of the separate degrees of freedom, therefore:

$$df_{Treatment \times Subjects} = df_{Treatment} \times df_{Subjects}$$
$$= 5 \times 2 = 10$$

In a factorial design, $SS_{Treatment}$ is broken into the main effects and interaction(s):

For SS_A:

$$df_A = \text{\# of levels of A} - 1 \text{ (or } k_A - 1)$$
$$= 2 - 1 = 1$$

For SS_B:

$$df_B = \text{\# of levels of B} - 1 \text{ (or } k_B - 1)$$
$$= 3 - 1 = 2$$

For $SS_{A \times B}$:

$$df_{A \times B} = df_A \times df_B$$
$$= 1 \times 2 = 2$$

The error terms for a factorial RM-ANOVA are the IV $\times$ Subjects interaction terms. Therefore the degrees of freedom are:

$$df_{A \times Subjects} = df_A \times df_{Subjects}$$
$$= 1 \times 2 = 2$$
$$df_{B \times Subjects} = df_B \times df_{Subjects}$$
$$= 2 \times 2 = 4$$
$$\text{and } df_{A \times B \times Subjects} = df_A \times df_B \times df_{Subjects}$$
$$= 1 \times 2 \times 2 = 4$$

Therefore, the degrees of freedom for the interaction are equal to the product of the degrees of freedom for the main effects. In fact, we can compute the degrees of freedom for *any* interaction by multiplying the degrees of freedom for the main effects of the variables involved in the interaction. The following examples illustrate this principle:

$$df_{B \times C} = df_B \times df_C$$

$$df_{A \times B \times C \times D} = df_A \times df_B \times df_C \times df_D$$

$$df_{Treatment \times Subjects} = df_{Treatment} \times df_{Subjects}$$

$$df_{A \times Subjects} = df_A \times df_{Subjects}$$

Table 12-2 illustrates the computation of degrees of freedom for ANOVAs.

Mean Squares

If one sum of squares measures the variability among 4 group totals, but another sum of squares measures the variability among 100 individual scores, it is not possible to make direct comparisons between these two SSs. Consider the following analogy:

Imagine that John and David are engaged in a semester-long dart-throwing contest. The bartender at a local pub is keeping score, and every time John or David throws a dart, the bartender records whether or not it was a "bull's eye." At midsemester, John has a score of 10 bull's eyes, while David only has 6. Is it fair to say John is ahead? Only if John and David have thrown the same number of darts. Suppose John has been to the pub more often than David, and has thrown a total of 100 darts, while David has so far only thrown 30 darts. In order to make a legitimate comparison between John and David at midsemester, we would want to "correct for" the fact that John had more throws than David by calculating a "mean bull's eye" score for each of the contestants. Only then can we compare their current scores. John's current standing is 10 bull's eyes out of 100 attempts, so his mean score would be equal to .10 (or 10%). David's score is 6 out of 30, which equals .2 (or 20%). David is actually outperforming John at this point in the competition.

Comparing one sum of squares to another would be as misleading as comparing John's 10 bull's eyes to David's 6 bull's eyes. They are based on different numbers of scores, so we must first "correct for" this by dividing each sum of squares by its own degrees of freedom (which is a measure of the number of independent scores involved in the SS). This gives us a measure of the average amount of variability among the independent scores in the sum of squares. Then we can make direct comparisons among these so-called **mean squares (MS)**. The formula for every mean square is the same:

$$MS = \frac{SS}{df}$$

For instance, for BS-ANOVA, the mean squares used to compute the F-ratios are:

$$MS_{BG} = \frac{SS_{BG}}{df_{BG}} \qquad MS_{WG} = \frac{SS_{WG}}{df_{WG}}$$

$$MS_A = \frac{SS_A}{df_A} \qquad MS_B = \frac{SS_B}{df_B} \qquad MS_{A \times B} = \frac{SS_{A \times B}}{df_{A \times B}}$$

And for a one-way RM-ANOVA, the mean squares used to compute the F-ratio are:

$$MS_{Treatment} = \frac{SS_{Treatment}}{df_{Treatment}} \qquad MS_{Treatment \times Subjects} = \frac{SS_{Treatment \times Subjects}}{df_{Treatment \times Subjects}}$$

The *F*-Ratio

In order to determine whether an independent variable had a systematic effect on the participants' performance, we compute the statistic called **F** by creating a ratio with the variability due to the IV in the numerator and the variability due to chance alone in the denominator. The effect of the IV is first measured using the SS_{IV} (or $SS_{Treatment}$ or SS_{BG}) and then we compute MS_{IV} (or $MS_{Treatment}$ or MS_{BG}) which we use as the numerator of the F-ratio. Our measure of chance in a BS-ANOVA is the measure of variability among the individuals who are in the same treatment group (SS_{WG}), so our denominator for F in a BS-ANOVA is the MS_{WG}.

For BS-ANOVAs: $\qquad F = \dfrac{MS_{IV}}{MS_{WG}} = \dfrac{\text{effect of the IV + chance}}{\text{chance fluctuations alone}}$

The MS_{WG} is the error term for *every* F in a BS-ANOVA. That is, the main effects of each IV and the interaction terms in BS factorial designs all have MS_{WG} in the denominator of the F-ratio.

In a within-subjects design, the error term (or measure of chance) is the treatment × subjects ($MS_{IV \times Subjects}$) interaction term, which measures the differences among individuals in their *pattern* of performance across the treatments (that is, how different participants reacted to the changes in the treatments). Each independent variable will interact in unique ways with the participants' characteristics and, therefore, there is a separate "treatment × subjects" interaction term for each IV. For example, in an A × B two-way design, we measure the individual differences in reaction to IV_A by computing a sum of squares for the "A × subjects" interaction, and we measure the individual differences in reaction to IV_B by computing a sum of squares for the "B × subjects" interaction. Additionally, we measure the individual differences in how the participants reacted to the *factorial combination* of the two IVs by computing a sum of squares for the "A × B × subjects" interaction. These three interaction terms are all measures of random variability (chance fluctuations) among the participants, and, therefore, are used as the error terms for the F-ratios in a factorial RM-ANOVA. Put simply, in a factorial RM-ANOVA, each F-ratio has its *own* error term. Thus, for RM-ANOVAs, the formula for F depends on the effect being tested:

One-way RM-ANOVA (one IV):

$$F = \frac{MS_{IV}}{MS_{IV \times Subjects}}$$

Two-way RM-ANOVA (A × B design):

$$F_A = \frac{MS_A}{MS_{A \times Subjects}} \qquad F_B = \frac{MS_B}{MS_{B \times Subjects}} \qquad F_{A \times B} = \frac{MS_{A \times B}}{MS_{A \times B \times Subjects}}$$

(The error terms for each F in a variety of designs are also listed in the summary tables outlined in Figure 12-1 on page 348.)

Testing the Significance of *F*

After we compute the **F-ratio(s)** for our analysis, we need to test the null hypothesis. In ANOVA, the null hypothesis says that the independent variables had no effect on performance. As you can see in the conceptual formula for F below, the H_0 predicts that F (in the population) is equal to 1.00:

$$F = \frac{IV + chance}{chance} = \frac{0 + chance}{chance} = \frac{chance}{chance} = 1.00$$

That is, the null hypothesis predicts that the difference between the treatments is equivalent to the differences that can be attributed to chance alone. Thus, the null hypothesis states that the F-ratio obtained from our research data is nothing more than a chance fluctuation from the population parameter of 1.00.

In order to test this hypothesis, we need to look up the critical value(s) of F on the ANOVA table (Table B-6 in Appendix B). To use the F table, we need to know the degrees of freedom for the mean square in the numerator of the F-ratio, and the degrees of freedom for the mean square in the denominator of the F-ratio, both of which can be found on the ANOVA summary table. The F table gives us the critical values for $\alpha = .05$ and $\alpha = .01$. The decision rule is:

If $F_{obtained}$ is greater than or equal to $F_{critical}$, reject the null hypothesis

The F table does not include the values of $F_{critical}$ for all degrees of freedom, so there are times when the correct value of degrees of freedom will not be in the table.[3] Whenever this occurs in the problems presented in this text, we have elected to use the *next smaller value* of degrees of freedom (which has a larger value of $F_{critical}$). This is a *conservative* approach, meaning that it is a procedure that reduces the chances of making a Type I error (i.e., rejecting the null hypothesis when it is true) because the difference between the research groups will need to be larger in order to obtain a value of F that is greater than or equal to $F_{critical}$. In contrast, other statisticians will estimate the critical value of F through a process known as interpolation. (For example, in order to estimate the value of $F_{critical}$ when there are 35 degrees of freedom in the denominator, they look at the $F_{critical}$ for 30 degrees of freedom and the $F_{critical}$ for 40 degrees of freedom, and estimate that their $F_{critical}$ will be approximately halfway between them.) While this procedure provides a reasonable estimate of $F_{critical}$, it will not be perfectly exact because the relationship between degrees of freedom and $F_{critical}$ is not linear. Therefore, there will be some error in the researcher's estimated value of $F_{critical}$, but the researcher will be uncertain whether this error increases or decreases the probability of a Type I error. The procedure we have adopted (of simply using the next smaller value of df in the table) means that there is a greater discrepancy between the true value of $F_{critical}$ and the value that we use to make our decision, but we have the advantage of knowing that this discrepancy has reduced the risk of Type I error. Therefore, if we reject the null hypothesis using the more stringent value of $F_{critical}$, we can place more confidence in that conclusion.

Post Hoc Analyses

When we conduct an analysis of variance or various other inferential statistical procedures, we end up with an "omnibus" statistic (such as F) that provides us with an *overall analysis* of the data. If the omnibus statistic is significant, it indicates that the independent variables had systematic effects on performance. However, if the study included more than two experimental treatments, the overall finding will not address all of the specific hypotheses of the study. For example, in a one-way design with 4 experimental conditions, a significant ANOVA F tells us that the four groups are *not* all equivalent. However, that significant F does *not* tell us whether treatment #1 is different than treatment #2, or if treatment #3 is different than treatment #4, and so forth. For example, imagine a study that compared the effectiveness of four different types of treatment for depression: Psychoanalysis, rational-emotive therapy, cognitive-behavioral therapy, and drug therapy. If the overall ANOVA resulted in a significant omnibus F, it would indicate there is difference in effectiveness among the types of treatment, but F would *not* tell us specifically if rational-emotive therapy is more effective than psychoanalysis or if cognitive-behavioral therapy is more effective than

---

[3] If this paragraph sounds familiar, it is because the same problem arose in Chapter 11 when we discussed *t*-tests and the *t*-table. Because our solution to the problem is the same for *t*-tests and ANOVA, our reasoning is also the same.

drug therapy. The researcher, however, is probably very interested in finding out exactly which therapies are more effective than others, so in order to make these specific comparisons between individual treatment conditions, the significant ANOVA must be followed up using **post hoc analyses** that explore the effect of the independent variables by looking at the treatment means one pair at a time, in what are referred to as *simple comparisons* among means.

A number of different post hoc tests are available, such as the Scheffé, Tukey, Newman-Keuls, Dunnett, Dunn, and *t*-tests. The primary difference among these tests has to do with how they handle the increased likelihood of making Type I errors when post hoc comparisons are conducted. For example, a two-sample *t*-test procedure makes no adjustment at all, and sets the lowest possible criterion for rejecting the null hypothesis. Consequently, the odds of making Type I errors increase with every post hoc comparison that is made with the *t*-tests. In contrast, the Scheffé test assumes that the researcher will conduct every possible post hoc comparison, and sets a very stringent criterion for rejecting the null, which increases the odds of Type II errors. We prefer to use a post hoc test that falls between these two extremes. **Dunn's multiple comparisons** procedure adjusts its error rate on the basis of the number of comparisons actually included in the analysis, thus maintaining a reasonable balance between Type I and Type II errors.

Dunn's Multiple Comparisons Procedure

Dunn's post hoc procedure allows us to make comparisons between and among the treatment means by computing a **critical range** (CR) which tells us how much difference there is likely to be between two means as a result of random sampling error. Random differences between means form a normal sampling distribution around 0.0, and, when alpha is set at .05, the Dunn CR is the cut-off point between the common difference scores (that occur in 95% of all random samples) and the rare difference scores (that occur in only 5% of all random samples). In other words, when the null hypothesis is true (and alpha is set at .05), 95% of random samples will have a difference score that is somewhere between 0.0 and ±CR; only 5% of all random samples will have a difference score equal to or greater than ±CR just by chance. Therefore, if our research means have a difference score that is greater than or equal to the Dunn critical range, we will reject the null hypothesis and conclude that the means are significantly different from one another. (See Figure 12-2 for an illustration of CR as the cut-off point for the region of rejection.)

The first step in calculating the Dunn critical range (CR) is to make a list of the simple comparisons of interest to us. Remember, we design studies to compare the effects of specific experimental conditions, so we need to make sure we test the hypotheses by making the relevant comparisons. The comparisons that are relevant for one main effect will be different than the comparisons for other main effects and interactions, so the list of comparisons we make for the Dunn post hoc test will depend on which omnibus F is being analyzed. For example, in a 3×2 factorial design, if the main effect of IV_A is significant, the post hoc comparisons will include A_1 versus A_2, A_1 versus A_3, and A_2 versus A_3. Thus, the post hoc analysis of the main effect of A

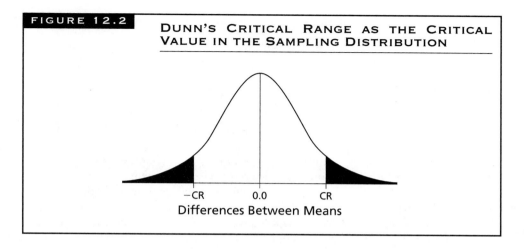

FIGURE 12.2 DUNN'S CRITICAL RANGE AS THE CRITICAL VALUE IN THE SAMPLING DISTRIBUTION

would include 3 simple comparisons. The means used in these post hoc comparisons are the means used to compute SS_A (where we collapsed across IV_B). In contrast, if the main effect of IV_B is significant, we do *not* conduct any post hoc comparisons because IV_B has only two levels, and the omnibus F for this main effect indicates that the mean for B_1 is significantly different than the mean for B_2. There are no other simple comparisons to be made for IV_B. If the A × B interaction in a 3 × 2 design is significant, we need to make a number of simple comparisons among the *six* original (uncollapsed) treatment means.

Therefore, the rule is that post hoc comparisons are required when F finds a significant difference among *three or more* means. No post hoc comparisons are needed when there are only two levels of an independent variable. As another general rule, the list of simple comparisons should include only *unconfounded* pairwise comparisons (where groups differ on only one independent variable). To illustrate the concept of unconfounded post hoc comparisons, let's look at some examples.

Suppose we conducted a study comparing four types of treatment for depression, and obtained the following hypothetical means for the conditions in our one-way design:

Type of Therapy

Psychoanalysis	Rational-Emotive	Cognitive-Behavioral	Drug
$\overline{X} = 31$	$\overline{X} = 26$	$\overline{X} = 23$	$\overline{X} = 19$

To conduct a post hoc analysis on this data, the list of all possible unconfounded pairwise comparisons would include:

1. psychoanalysis ($\overline{X} = 31$) versus rational-emotive therapy ($\overline{X} = 26$)
2. psychoanalysis ($\overline{X} = 31$) versus cognitive-behavioral therapy ($\overline{X} = 23$)

3. psychoanalysis ($\overline{X} = 31$) versus drug therapy ($\overline{X} = 19$)

4. rational-emotive therapy ($\overline{X} = 26$) versus cognitive-behavioral therapy ($\overline{X} = 23$)

5. rational-emotive therapy ($\overline{X} = 26$) versus drug therapy ($\overline{X} = 19$)

6. cognitive-behavioral therapy ($\overline{X} = 23$) versus drug therapy ($\overline{X} = 19$)

This list includes a comparison of each form of therapy against each other form of therapy. Since Type of Therapy is the only independent variable in this one-way design, these pairwise comparisons are all unconfounded (i.e., the groups differ only on the type of therapy being administered to the participants).

Now suppose that, instead of a one-way design, our study on the effectiveness of different therapies also included Type of Depression as a second independent variable, where we compared the effectiveness of the therapies for people suffering from major depression versus people who suffer from bipolar disorder (formerly called manic-depression). Our study would be a 4 (Type of Therapy) × 2 (Type of Depression) between-subjects design and there would be eight experimental groups (labeled *a* through *b* in the following table):

	Psychoanalysis	Rational-Emotive	Cognitive-Behavioral	Drug Therapy
Major Depression	*a*	*b*	*c*	*d*
Bipolar Disorder	*e*	*f*	*g*	*b*

If the ANOVA revealed a significant main effect of Type of Depression, no post hoc tests would be necessary because there are only two levels of Type of Depression. The results of this omnibus F tells us that there is a significant difference between major depression and bipolar disorder. In contrast, if the main effect of Type of Therapy is significant, post hoc comparisons are required because this F tells us that the four types of therapy are not equivalent, but we need to make pairwise comparisons among the (collapsed) means in order to find out which type of therapy is most effective. The list of post hoc comparisons for this main effect is the same as the list for a one-way design with Type of Therapy as the only independent variable:

1. psychoanalysis ($a + e$) versus rational-emotive therapy ($b + f$)

2. psychoanalysis ($a + e$) versus cognitive-behavioral therapy ($c + g$)

3. psychoanalysis ($a + e$) versus drug therapy ($d + b$)

4. rational-emotive therapy ($b + f$) versus cognitive-behavioral therapy ($c + g$)

5. rational-emotive therapy ($b + f$) versus drug therapy ($d + b$)

6. cognitive-behavioral therapy ($c + g$) versus drug therapy ($d + b$)

If the ANOVA revealed a significant Therapy × Depression interaction and we were performing the Dunn multiple comparisons procedure, the list of unconfounded simple (or pairwise) comparisons would include the following:

1. *a* versus *b*	5. *b* versus *d*	9. *e* versus *h*	13. *a* versus *e*
2. *a* versus *c*	6. *c* versus *d*	10. *f* versus *g*	14. *b* versus *f*
3. *a* versus *d*	7. *e* versus *f*	11. *f* versus *h*	15. *c* versus *g*
4. *b* versus *c*	8. *e* versus *g*	12. *g* versus *h*	16. *d* versus *h*

(The first six of these comparisons look at the effects of therapy on people suffering from major depression, while the next six comparisons look at the effects of therapy on people suffering from bipolar disorder. The remaining comparisons look at the difference between major depression and bipolar disorder under the four different forms of therapy.)

These comparisons are unconfounded because the means in each pair differ from each other on only one of the independent variables. For example, comparison #1 looks at groups *a* and *b* which had different types of therapy, but they had the same type of depression. Similarly, comparison #15 looks at groups *c* and *g* which each received the same type of therapy (cognitive-behavioral), but they suffered from different forms of depression. Because these comparisons are unconfounded, we are able to *interpret their meanings*. For instance, if comparison #1 is significant, we can conclude that psychoanalysis and rational-emotive therapy are not equally effective for people suffering from a major depression. That is, we can attribute the observed difference in performance to the difference in therapy. Likewise, if comparison #15 is significant, we can conclude that clients suffering from a major depression versus bipolar disorder are not equally depressed, even when both groups are receiving the cognitive-behavioral therapy. Thus, the observed difference is attributed to the type of depressive disorder.

In contrast, suppose we compared group *c* to group *f*. This is a confounded comparison because the two groups are different on both independent variables (i.e., they are in different rows *and* different columns). We cannot interpret the results of this comparison. For instance, if group *c* displays more depression than group *f*, we could not know whether it was because a major depression is worse than bipolar disorder *or* if cognitive-behavioral therapy is less effective in reducing depression than rational-emotive therapy. Thus, there are two possible explanations for the observed difference between groups *c* and *f* (which is the definition of a confound) and therefore, the finding will have little or no theoretical value for us. This is true of almost all confounded comparisons, and therefore, post hoc comparisons will typically be made only on unconfounded, interpretable pairs of means.

The next step in the post hoc procedure is to test the significance of the differences between the means in the pairwise comparisons. In order to do so, we need to compute Dunn's critical range (CR), which tells us how different two means are likely to be just by chance. The formula for CR includes the mean square for the error term (i.e., the denominator of *F*) as a measure of the chance fluctuations among the scores, so we look up the appropriate MS in our ANOVA summary table and enter it into the formula. The CR formula also contains an adjustment factor (d) that we must look up in Dunn's multiple comparisons table, which is presented in Appendix B (Table B-7). To find the appropriate d on the Dunn table, we must know how many unconfounded pairwise comparisons we plan to make (c), and we need to know the degrees of freedom for the error term used to compute the significant F (df_{Error}). (Remember, the error term is the denominator for F, and its degrees of freedom can be found in our ANOVA summary table.) The Dunn table includes a value of d for both the .05 and the .01 levels of significance which allows us to compute two critical ranges. After we find the appropriate value(s) of d on the Dunn table, we compute the critical range:

$$CR_{Dunn} = d\sqrt{2\frac{MS_{Error}}{n}}$$

where: (1) d comes from the Dunn table;

(2) MS_{Error} is the denominator of F (the error term) and is found on the ANOVA summary table; and

(3) n is the number of scores used to compute the $\overline{X}s$ for the conditions being compared.[4]

The final step of the post hoc test is to test each of the simple comparisons. We compare the obtained difference scores (e.g., $\overline{X}_{Psychoanalysis} - \overline{X}_{Drug Therapy}$) to CR, and if the absolute value of the obtained difference is equal to or greater than CR, we reject the null hypothesis and conclude that the difference between the two groups is significant.

It is important to remember that each significant F with three or more groups requires a *separate* Dunn analysis. The critical range for the main effect of IV_A will *not* be the same as the CR for the main effect of IV_B. Furthermore, as we demonstrated earlier, the pairwise comparisons for one independent variable are different than the comparisons for another independent variable. Therefore, it is conceivable that post hoc comparisons may be required for every main effect and interaction in the design, and each of these post hoc tests must start with a list of the relevant pairwise comparisons.

Examples of the Dunn multiple comparisons procedure are presented as the final step in the complete ANOVAs found in the Appendices at the end of this chapter. In Appendix 12-A, the Dunn test is performed on a significant F from a one-way BS-ANOVA (see Step 10 on page 377). A Dunn analysis of a significant two-way

---

[4]This formula is used when all of the means in the list of pairwise comparisons are based on an equal number of scores. If the groups are not equal in size, the *harmonic mean* of n ($\tilde{n}$) is substituted for n in the formula for CR, where $\tilde{n}$ is:

$$\tilde{n} = \frac{k}{(1/n_1) + (1/n_2) + (1/n_3) + \cdots}$$

interaction (from a BS-ANOVA) is presented in Appendix 12-B (see Step 15 on page 387). Finally, a significant F from a one-way RM-ANOVA is analyzed in Appendix 12-C (see Step 11 on page 397).

Appendix 12-A

EXAMPLE OF A ONE-WAY BS-ANOVA

To study the effects of common drugs on cognitive performance, a researcher randomly assigned college students to one of three conditions. One group of students was served two cans of beer, another group was served two cups of coffee, and the third group (the control group) was served two glasses of orange juice. Then each participant was given a test of logical reasoning and the number of errors was recorded.

Alcohol	Caffeine	No Drug (Control)
15	9	6
20	8	4
10	10	10
12	13	11
13	12	6

Step 1: Organize preliminary information and set up ANOVA Summary Table:

$$n = 5$$
$$k = 3$$
$$N = 15$$

$$SS_{Total} \begin{cases} SS_{BG} \\ \\ SS_{WG} \end{cases}$$

Sources	SS	df	MS	F
BG				
WG				
Total				

Step 2: Compute SS_{Total}:

$$SS_{Total} = \Sigma\Sigma X^2 - \frac{(\Sigma\Sigma X)^2}{N}$$

Alcohol	X^2	Caffeine	X^2	No Drug (Control)	X^2
15	225	9	81	6	36
20	400	8	64	4	16
10	100	10	100	10	100
12	144	13	169	11	121
13	169	12	144	6	36
$\Sigma X = 70$	$\Sigma X^2 = 1038$	$\Sigma X = 52$	$\Sigma X^2 = 558$	$\Sigma X = 37$	$\Sigma X^2 = 309$

(continued)

Appendix 12-A *(continued)*

$$SS_{Total} = (1038 + 558 + 309) - \frac{(70 + 52 + 37)^2}{15}$$

$$= 1905 - \frac{(159)^2}{15}$$

$$= 1905 - \frac{25281}{15}$$

$$= 1905 - 1685.4$$

$$= 219.6 \qquad \text{This value is entered into the summary table:}$$

Sources	SS	df	MS	F
BG				
WG				
Total	219.6			

Step 3: Compute SS_{BG}:

$$SS_{BG} = \sum \frac{(\Sigma X)^2}{n} - \frac{(\Sigma \Sigma X)^2}{N}$$

(**Note:** The second piece of this formula is the same as the second piece in the SS_{Total} formula. It is known as the correction factor, and although we re-compute it below, it is not necessary to do so.)

$$SS_{BG} = \left(\frac{70^2}{5} + \frac{52^2}{5} + \frac{37^2}{5} \right) - \frac{(70 + 52 + 37)^2}{15}$$

because we have equal n:
$$= \frac{70^2 + 52^2 + 37^2}{5} - \frac{(159)^2}{15}$$

$$= \frac{4900 + 2704 + 1369}{5} - \frac{25281}{15}$$

$$= \frac{8973}{5} - 1685.4$$

$$= 1794.6 - 1685.4$$

$$= 109.2 \qquad \text{This value is entered into the summary table:}$$

Sources	SS	df	MS	F
BG	109.2			
WG				
Total	219.6			

(continued)

Appendix 12-A *(continued)*

Step 4: Compute SS_{WG}:

$$SS_{WG} = SS_{Total} - SS_{BG}$$
$$= 219.6 - 109.2$$
$$= 110.4 \quad \text{This value is entered into the summary table:}$$

Sources	SS	df	MS	F
BG	109.2			
WG	110.4			
Total	219.6			

Step 5: Compute the degrees of freedom:

$$df_{Total} = N - 1 \qquad df_{BG} = k - 1 \qquad df_{WG} = N - k$$
$$= 15 - 1 \qquad\qquad = 3 - 1 \qquad\qquad = 15 - 3$$
$$= 14 \qquad\qquad\quad = 2 \qquad\qquad\quad = 12$$

Enter the degrees of freedom in the summary table:

Sources	SS	df	MS	F
BG	109.2	2		
WG	110.4	12		
Total	219.6	14		

Note: Double-check your degrees of freedom by making sure that $df_{BG} + df_{WG} = df_{Total}$

Step 6: Compute mean squares:

$$MS_{BG} = \frac{SS_{BG}}{df_{BG}} \qquad\qquad MS_{WG} = \frac{SS_{WG}}{df_{WG}}$$
$$= \frac{109.2}{2} \qquad\qquad\qquad = \frac{110.4}{12}$$
$$= 54.6 \qquad\qquad\qquad\quad = 9.2$$

(continued)

Appendix 12-A *(continued)*

Enter these values into the summary table:

Sources	SS	df	MS	F
BG	109.2	2	54.6	
WG	110.4	12	9.2	
Total	219.6	14		

Step 7: Compute F:

$$F = \frac{MS_{BG}}{MS_{WG}}$$

$$= \frac{54.6}{9.2}$$

$= 5.9348$ Round this value to two decimal places and enter it into the summary table:

Sources	SS	df	MS	F
BG	109.2	2	54.6	5.93
WG	110.4	12	9.2	
Total	219.6	14		

Step 8: Look up $F_{critical}$:

Numerator = MS_{BG}, therefore df for the numerator = df_{BG} = 2
Denominator = MS_{WG}, therefore df for the denominator = df_{WG} = 12
Therefore: **$F_{crit\,(.05)}$ (2, 12) = 3.89** and **$F_{crit\,(.01)}$ (2, 12) = 6.93**

Note: If the F table does not include your degrees of freedom, use the next **smaller** value.

Step 9: Test the significance of F and state your preliminary conclusions:

Decision Rule: **If $F_{obtained} \geq F_{critical}$, reject the null hypothesis**

$F_{obtained}$ = 5.93
$F_{critical\,(.05)}$ = 3.89
$F_{critical\,(.01)}$ = 6.93

Sources	SS	df	MS	F
BG	109.2	2	54.6	5.93*
WG	110.4	12	9.2	
Total	219.6	14		

*$p < .05$

5.93 > 3.89, therefore we reject the null hypothesis at the .05 level (but not at .01).

(continued)

Appendix 12-A *(continued)*

Note: We indicate our decision by using asterisks next to F on the summary table. One asterisk indicates significance at .05, two asterisks indicate significance at .01. Non-significant Fs either have no symbol next to them, or the abbreviation "n.s." is used to indicate non-significance.

Conclusion (preliminary): The IV (Type of Drug) has a significant effect on performance on the logical reasoning task. (We are 95% certain this difference is not due solely to chance.)

Step 10: Perform post hoc analyses, if necessary:

a. Determine if post hocs are necessary:

    1. Is F significant? If not, post hocs are not necessary. If F is significant, ask:

    2. How many groups/treatments are being compared in the numerator of F?

If there are only two groups involved in that F, post hocs are **not** needed because the F tells us that the two groups are significantly different from each other. If the F compares three or more groups, then post hoc comparisons are required.

Here the F is significant and it is comparing three different experimental conditions (alcohol, caffeine, and a no drug control condition), therefore post hoc comparisons *are* needed.

b. Conduct the post hoc analyses

Dunn Multiple Comparisons Test:

Dunn's Step A: Calculate the means for the treatment groups:

Alcohol	Caffeine	No Drug (Control)
$\Sigma X = 70$	$\Sigma X = 52$	$\Sigma X = 37$
$n = 5$	$n = 5$	$n = 5$
$\overline{X} = 14.0$	$\overline{X} = 10.4$	$\overline{X} = 7.4$

Dunn's Step B: List (and count) the comparisons to be made:

    Alcohol vs. Caffeine

    Alcohol vs. No Drug (Control)

    Caffeine vs. No Drug (Control)   **c (number of comparisons)** $= 3$

(continued)

Appendix 12-A *(continued)*

Dunn's Step C: Calculate the differences between the means:

Comparisons	Obtained Differences
Alcohol vs. Caffeine	$14.0 - 10.4 = 3.6$
Alcohol vs. No Drug (Control)	$14.0 - 7.4 = 6.6$
Caffeine vs. No Drug (Control)	$10.4 - 7.4 = 3.0$

Dunn's Step D: Look up the adjustment factor (d) on the Dunn table:

To use the Dunn table, you need to know how many comparisons you will be making (from Step B above) and the degrees of freedom for the denominator of F (df_{error}), which can be found on the ANOVA summary table.

For this problem, $c = 3$ and $df_{error} = df_{WG} = 12$. Therefore: $\mathbf{d_{.05} = 2.78}$ and $\mathbf{d_{.01} = 3.65}$

Dunn's Step E: Compute the critical range(s):

$$CR_{Dunn\,(.05)} = d_{.05}\sqrt{2\left(\frac{MS_{Error}}{n}\right)} \qquad CR_{Dunn\,(.01)} = d_{.01}\sqrt{2\left(\frac{MS_{Error}}{n}\right)}$$

$$= 2.78\sqrt{2\left(\frac{9.2}{5}\right)} \qquad\qquad = 3.65\sqrt{2\left(\frac{9.2}{5}\right)}$$

$$= 2.78\sqrt{2(1.84)} \qquad\qquad = 3.65\sqrt{2(1.84)}$$

$$= 2.78\sqrt{3.68} \qquad\qquad = 3.65\sqrt{3.68}$$

$$= 2.78\,(1.9183326) \qquad\qquad = 3.65\,(1.9183326)$$

$$= 5.3329646 \approx 5.3 \qquad\qquad = 7.0019139 \approx 7.0$$

Note: The Dunn critical range tells us how different two means need to be in order to be considered significantly different from each other. In this example, then, if the null hypothesis is true (and the groups are not significantly different and $\mu_1 - \mu_2 = 0.0$), the $CR_{.05}$ indicates that 95% of all random samples will have means that are less than 5.3 points apart. Only 5% of all random samples would have a difference of 5.3 or more just by chance. The $CR_{.01}$ indicates that only 1% of all random samples would have a difference of 7.0 or more just by chance. (See Figure 12-2 on page 369.)

Dunn's Step F: Compare the obtained differences between the means to the CR(s):

Decision Rule: If Obtained Difference $\geq$ CR, reject the null hypothesis

(continued)

Appendix 12-A *(continued)*

Alcohol ($\overline{X} = 14$) vs. Caffeine ($\overline{X} = 10.4$):   3.6 is not $\geq$ 5.3, therefore we cannot
reject H_0

Alcohol ($\overline{X} = 14$) vs. Control ($\overline{X} = 7.4$):   6.6 is $\geq$ 5.3, therefore reject H_0 at .05
(But 6.6 is *not* greater than 7.0, so it is not significant at .01)

Caffeine ($\overline{X} = 10.4$) vs. Control ($\overline{X} = 7.4$):   3.0 is not $\geq$ 5.3, therefore we cannot reject H_0

Step 11 (ANOVA): Verbally summarize the results of the study:

The logical reasoning scores were entered into a one-way BS-ANOVA which revealed a significant effect for Type of Drug [$F(2, 12) = 5.93, p < .05$]. Dunn multiple comparisons indicated that participants who drank two cans of beer made significantly more errors on the logical reasoning task than participants who drank orange juice (means were 14.0 and 7.4, respectively). Participants who drank two cups of coffee (mean = 10.4) were not significantly different than either of the other two groups. These results indicate that alcohol has a significantly detrimental impact on logical reasoning compared to the No Drug condition. Caffeine appeared to have a weaker effect on performance (with an "intermediate" number of errors which was not significantly different than either the Alcohol or the No Drug Control conditions).

(**Note:** This verbal summary follows the APA-format for reporting results in a research report. More conversationally, we would summarize the results by saying that alcohol leads to more errors than no drug at all, and caffeine seems to have a milder negative effect on performance than alcohol.)

Appendix 12-B

EXAMPLE OF A 2 × 3 (TWO-WAY) BS-ANOVA

A researcher randomly assigned participants to either "win" a desirable prize or to "lose" the prize in an effort to manipulate the participants' mood. ("Winners" were expected to be in a good mood while "losers" were expected to be in a bad mood). Shortly after winning or losing the prize, the participants were asked to make a monetary donation to a charity. For one-third of the participants, the recipient of the charity (the "victim") was portrayed as being in deep distress (i.e., starving), for one-third of the participants the victim was in moderate

(continued)

Appendix 12-B *(continued)*

distress (i.e., lost their home during a tornado), and the remaining one-third of the participants saw a victim who is experiencing mild distress (i.e., needs airfare to visit relatives for the holidays). The dependent variable was the amount of money (in dollars) each participant donated to the distressed victim.

		Victim's Distress Level		
		Mild	Moderate	Deep
	just won (good mood)	12	15	27
		16	21	24
		19	20	26
		19	26	26
		19	17	19
		20	25	23
Mood	just lost (bad mood)	11	11	13
		14	17	6
		12	14	6
		12	11	2
		11	12	15
		16	6	8

DESIGN:
2×3 BS

$k = 6$
$n = 6$
$N = 36$

Step 1: Organize preliminary information and set up ANOVA summary table:

Design = $A \times B$ (Mood $\times$ Distress)
$k = 6$ $n = 6$ $N = 36$
$k_{Mood} = 2$ $k_{Distress} = 3$

$$SS_{Total} \begin{cases} SS_{BG} \begin{cases} SS_A \\ SS_B \\ SS_{A \times B} \end{cases} \\ SS_{WG} \end{cases}$$

Sources	SS	df	MS	F
Mood (M)				
Distress (D)				
M $\times$ D				
WG				
Total				

Step 2: Compute SS_{Total}:

$$SS_{Total} = \Sigma\Sigma X^2 - \frac{(\Sigma\Sigma X)^2}{N}$$

(continued)

Appendix 12-B *(continued)*

Victim's Distress Level

		Mild		Moderate		Deep	
	X	X²	X	X²	X	X²
	12	144	15	225	27	729
just won	16	256	21	441	24	576
(good	19	361	20	400	26	676
mood)	19	361	26	676	26	676
	19	361	17	289	19	361
	20	400	25	625	23	529
	ΣX = 105	ΣX² = 1883	ΣX = 124	ΣX² = 2656	ΣX = 145	ΣX² = 3547
	X	X²	X	X²	X	X²
	11	121	11	121	13	169
just lost	14	196	17	289	6	36
(bad	12	144	14	196	6	36
mood)	12	144	11	121	2	4
	11	121	12	144	15	225
	16	256	6	36	8	64
	ΣX = 76	ΣX² = 982	ΣX = 71	ΣX² = 907	ΣX = 50	ΣX² = 534

Mood labels appear at left: *just won (good mood)* for the top block, *just lost (bad mood)* for the bottom block.

$$SS_{Total} = (1883 + 2656 + 3547 + 982 + 907 + 534) - \frac{(\Sigma\Sigma X)^2}{N}$$

$$= 10509 - \frac{(105 + 124 + 145 + 76 + 71 + 50)^2}{36}$$

$$= 10509 - \frac{(571)^2}{36}$$

$$= 10509 - \frac{326041}{36}$$

$$= 10509 - 9056.6944$$

$$= 1452.306 \quad \text{This value is entered into the Summary Table:}$$

Sources	SS	df	MS	F
Mood (M)				
Distress (D)				
M × D				
WG				
Total	1452.306			

Step 3: Compute SS_{BG}:

$$SS_{BG} = \sum \frac{(\Sigma X)^2}{n} - \frac{(\Sigma\Sigma X)^2}{N}$$

(continued)

Appendix 12-B *(continued)*

(**Note:** The second piece of this formula is the same as the second piece in the SS_{Total} formula. It is the correction factor, and we already know the grand total.)

$$SS_{BG} = \left(\frac{105^2}{6} + \frac{124^2}{6} + \frac{145^2}{6} + \frac{76^2}{6} + \frac{71^2}{6} + \frac{50^2}{6} \right) - \frac{(571)^2}{36}$$

because we have equal n:

$$= \frac{105^2 + 124^2 + 145^2 + 76^2 + 71^2 + 50^2}{6} - \frac{(571)^2}{36}$$

$$= \frac{11025 + 15376 + 21025 + 5776 + 5041 + 2500}{6} - \frac{326041}{36}$$

$$= \frac{60743}{6} - 9056.6944$$

$$= 10123.833 - 9056.6944$$

$$= 1067.139 \quad \text{This value is } not \text{ entered into the summary table, but set aside to be used later.}$$

Step 4: Compute SS_{WG}:

$$SS_{WG} = SS_{Total} - SS_{BG}$$
$$= 1452.306 - 1067.139$$
$$= 385.167 \quad \text{This value is entered into the summary table:}$$

Sources	SS	df	MS	F
Mood (M)				
Distress (D)				
M × D				
WG	385.167			
Total	1452.306			

Step 5: Collapse across variable B to find main effect of variable A (Mood):

Just Won (Good Mood)	Just Lost (Bad Mood)
105 + 124 + 145 = **374** n = 18	76 + 71 + 50 = **197** n = 18

(continued)

Appendix 12-B *(continued)*

Step 6: Calculate the sum of squares for the main effect of variable A (SS_{Mood}):

$$SS_A = \sum \frac{(\Sigma X)^2}{n} - \frac{(\Sigma\Sigma X)^2}{N}$$

(**Note:** The second piece of this formula is the same as the second piece in the SS_{Total} formula. It is the correction factor, and although we re-compute it below using the totals from the collapsed groups, it is not necessary to do so.)

$$SS_{Mood} = \left(\frac{374^2}{18} + \frac{197^2}{18} \right) - \frac{(374 + 197)^2}{36}$$

because we have equal n:

$$= \frac{139876 + 38809}{18} - \frac{571^2}{36}$$

$$= \frac{178685}{18} - \frac{326041}{36}$$

$$= 9926.9444 - 9056.6944$$

$$= 870.250 \quad \text{This value is entered into the summary table:}$$

Sources	SS	df	MS	F
Mood (M)	870.250			
Distress (D)				
M × D				
WG	385.167			
Total	1452.306			

Step 7: Collapse across variable A to find main effect of variable B (Victim's Distress Level):

Mild Distress	Moderate Distress	Deep Distress
105 + 76 = **181** n = 12	124 + 71 = **195** n = 12	145 + 50 = **195** n = 12

Step 8: Calculate the sum of squares for the main effect of variable B ($SS_{Distress}$):

$$SS_B = \sum \frac{(\Sigma X)^2}{n} - \frac{(\Sigma\Sigma X)^2}{N}$$

(continued)

Appendix 12-B *(continued)*

(**Note:**   The second piece of this formula is the same as the second piece in the SS_{Total} formula. It is the correction factor, and although we re-compute it below using the totals from the collapsed groups, it is not necessary to do so.)

$$SS_{Distress} = \left(\frac{181^2}{12} + \frac{195^2}{12} + \frac{195^2}{12} \right) - \frac{(181 + 195 + 195)^2}{36}$$

because we have equal n:
$$= \frac{32761 + 38025 + 38025}{12} - \frac{571^2}{36}$$

$$= \frac{108811}{12} - \frac{326041}{36}$$

$$= 9067.5833 - 9056.6944$$

$$= 10.889 \quad \text{This value is entered into the summary table:}$$

Sources	SS	df	MS	F
Mood (M)	870.250			
Distress (D)	10.889			
M × D				
WG	385.167			
Total	1452.306			

Step 9:   Calculate the sum of squares for the interaction ($SS_{Mood \times Distress}$):

The interaction is the last component of the SS_{BG}, so it can be found by subtraction:

$$SS_{M \times D} = SS_{BG} - SS_{Mood} - SS_{Distress}$$

$$= 1067.139 - 870.250 - 10.889$$

$$= 186.000 \quad \text{This value is entered into the summary table:}$$

Sources	SS	df	MS	F
Mood (M)	870.250			
Distress (D)	10.889			
M × D	186.000			
WG	385.167			
Total	1452.306			

Step 10:   Compute the degrees of freedom and enter them into the summary table:

(continued)

Appendix 12-B *(continued)*

Note: N = the total number of scores k_{Mood} = the number of levels of
= 36   Mood = 2

  k = the experimental groups $k_{Distress}$ = the number of levels of
= 6   Distress = 3

a. $df_{Total} = N - 1$ b. $df_{BG} = k - 1$
   $= 36 - 1$ $= 6 - 1$
   $= 35$ $= 5$

c. $df_{WG} = N - k$ d. $df_{Mood} = k_{Mood} - 1$
   $= 36 - 6$ $= 2 - 1$
   $= 30$ $= 1$

e. $df_{Distress} = k_{Distress} - 1$ f. $df_{M \times D} = df_{Mood} \times df_{Distress}$
   $= 3 - 1$ $= 1 \times 2$
   $= 2$ $= 2$

Sources	SS	df	MS	F
Mood (M)	870.250	1		
Distress (D)	10.889	2		
M × D	186.000	2		
WG	385.167	30		
Total	1452.306	35		

Step 11: Compute the mean squares:

$$MS_{Mood} = \frac{SS_{Mood}}{df_{Mood}} = \frac{870.250}{1} = 870.250$$

$$MS_{Distress} = \frac{SS_{Distress}}{df_{Distress}} = \frac{10.889}{2} = 5.4445$$

$$MS_{Mood \times Distress} = \frac{SS_{Mood \times Distress}}{df_{Mood \times Distress}} = \frac{186.000}{2} = 93.000$$

$$MS_{WG} = \frac{SS_{WG}}{df_{WG}} = \frac{385.167}{30} = 12.8389$$

(continued)

Appendix 12-B *(continued)*

These values are entered into the summary table:

Sources	SS	df	MS	F
Mood (M)	870.250	1	870.250	
Distress (D)	10.889	2	5.4445	
M × D	186.000	2	93.000	
WG	385.167	30	12.8389	
Total	1452.306	35		

Step 12: Compute *F* for each main effect and the interaction:

> **Note:** In a BS-ANOVA, the error term (denominator of F) is *always* the MS_{WG}.

$$F_{Mood} = \frac{MS_{Mood}}{MS_{WG}} = \frac{870.250}{12.8389} = \mathbf{67.782}$$

$$F_{Distress} = \frac{MS_{Distress}}{MS_{WG}} = \frac{5.4445}{12.8389} = \mathbf{0.424}$$

$$F_{Mood \times Distress} = \frac{MS_{Mood \times Distress}}{MS_{WG}} = \frac{93.00}{12.8389} = \mathbf{7.244}$$

These values (rounded to two decimal places) are entered into the summary table:

Sources	SS	df	MS	F
Mood (M)	870.250	1	870.250	67.78
Distress (D)	10.889	2	5.4445	0.42
M × D	186.000	2	93.000	7.24
WG	385.167	30	12.8389	
Total	1452.306	35		

Step 13: Look up $F_{critical}$ for each *F*:

For the main effect of **Mood:**   Numerator $= MS_{Mood}$, so $df_{numerator} = df_{Mood} = 1$

Denominator $= MS_{WG}$, so $df_{denominator} = df_{WG} = 30$

Therefore: $F_{crit\,(.05)}\,(1, 30) = 4.17$ and $F_{crit\,(.01)}\,(1, 30) = 7.56$

(continued)

Appendix 12-B *(continued)*

For the main effect of **Distress:**

$$\text{Numerator} = MS_{\text{Distress}}, \text{ so } df_{\text{numerator}} = df_{\text{Distress}} = 2$$

$$\text{Denominator} = MS_{\text{WG}}, \text{ so } df_{\text{denominator}} = df_{\text{WG}} = 30$$

$$\text{Therefore: } F_{\text{crit (.05)}} (2, 30) = 3.32 \text{ and } F_{\text{crit (.01)}} (2, 30) = 5.39$$

For the **Mood** × **Distress** Interaction:

$$\text{Numerator} = MS_{M \times D}, \text{ so } df_{\text{numerator}} = df_{M \times D} = 2$$

$$\text{Denominator} = MS_{\text{WG}}, \text{ so } df_{\text{denominator}} = df_{\text{WG}} = 30$$

$$\text{Therefore: } F_{\text{crit (.05)}} (2, 30) = 3.32 \text{ and } F_{\text{crit (.01)}} (2, 30) = 5.39$$

Step 14: Test the significance of the Fs and state your preliminary conclusions:

Decision Rule: If $F_{\text{obtained}} \geq F_{\text{critical}}$, **reject the null hypothesis**

F_{mood} (67.78) is greater than the $F_{\text{crit (.01)}}$ (1,30) of 7.56, therefore we reject the null at .01

F_{distress} (0.42) is not greater than the $F_{\text{crit (.05)}}$ (2,30) of 3.32, therefore we cannot reject H_0

$F_{M \times D}$ (7.24) is greater than the $F_{\text{crit (.01)}}$ (2,30) of 5.39, therefore we reject the null at .01

Sources	SS	df	MS	F
Mood (M)	870.250	1	870.250	67.78 **
Distress (D)	10.889	2	5.4445	0.42 n..s.
M × D	186.000	2	93.000	7.24 **
WG	385.167	30	12.8389	
Total	1452.306	35		** $p < .01$

Conclusion (preliminary): There is a significant main effect of Mood and a significant Mood × Distress interaction. The main effect of Victim's Distress Level was not significant.

Step 15: Perform post hoc analyses, if necessary:

a. For each F separately, determine if post hocs are necessary:
   1. Is F significant? If not, post hocs are not necessary. If F is significant, ask:
   2. How many groups/treatments are being compared in the numerator of F?

(continued)

Appendix 12-B *(continued)*

If there are only two groups involved in that F, post hocs are **not** needed because the F tells us that the two groups are significantly different from each other. If the F compares three or more groups, then post hoc comparisons are required.

b. Conduct the post hoc analyses

For the **main effect of Mood:**

F_{mood} is significant but it is comparing only two different experimental conditions (Good versus Bad Mood conditions), therefore post hoc comparisons are not needed.

This significant main effect tells us that the participants in the Good Mood (Just Won) condition donated significantly more money (a total of $374) than did participants in the Bad Mood (Just Lost) condition (a total of only $197).

For the **main effect of Victim's Distress Level:**

$F_{distress}$ was not significant, and therefore post hoc comparisons are not needed.

This non-significant main effect tells us that the Victim's Distress Level did not have an overall effect on the amount of money donated. That is, the differences among the three group totals ($181, $195, and $195 for Mild, Moderate, and Deep Distress, respectively) are not significant.

For the **Mood $\times$ Distress Interaction:**

$F_{M \times D}$ is significant and it involves **six** groups (since it is a 2×3 interaction), therefore post hoc comparisons *are* required.

Important: The post hoc comparisons we make on the significant interaction are critical to the interpretation of the results of this study. The preliminary conclusions stated earlier about the main effects of Mood and Distress are **superseded** by this significant interaction, which by definition, tells us that the effect of Mood is not the same for every Distress level. (That is, the effect of the victim's distress level depends on the donor's mood). Therefore, when discussing the results of this study, we will deemphasize the main effect of Mood because it is "qualified" by the interaction. The significant interaction is the primary finding of the study.

Dunn Multiple Comparisons Test

Dunn's Step A: Calculate the means for the treatment groups:

(continued)

Appendix 12-B *(continued)*

	Mild Distress	**Moderate Distress**	**Deep Distress**
Just Won (Good Mood)	$\Sigma X = 105$ $n = 6$ $\bar{X} = 17.50$	$\Sigma X = 124$ $n = 6$ $\bar{X} = 20.67$	$\Sigma X = 145$ $n = 6$ $\bar{X} = 24.17$
Just Lost (Bad Mood)	$\Sigma X = 76$ $n = 6$ $\bar{X} = 12.67$	$\Sigma X = 71$ $n = 6$ $\bar{X} = 11.83$	$\Sigma X = 50$ $n = 6$ $\bar{X} = 8.33$

Dunn's Step B: List (and count) the unconfounded comparisons of interest:

For Good Mood:	Mild vs. Moderate
	Mild vs. Deep
	Moderate vs. Deep
For Bad Mood:	Mild vs. Moderate
	Mild vs. Deep Therefore, c = 9
	Moderate vs. Deep
For Mild Distress:	Good Mood vs. Bad Mood
For Moderate Distress:	Good Mood vs. Bad Mood
For Deep Distress:	Good Mood vs. Bad Mood

Dunn's Step C: Calculate the differences between the means:

Comparisons		Obtained Differences
For Good Mood:	Mild vs. Moderate	17.50 vs. 20.67 = 3.17
	Mild vs. Deep	17.50 vs. 24.17 = 6.67
	Moderate vs. Deep	20.67 vs. 24.17 = 3.50
For Bad Mood:	Mild vs. Moderate	12.67 vs. 11.83 = 0.84
	Mild vs. Deep	12.67 vs. 8.33 = 4.34
	Moderate vs. Deep	11.83 vs. 8.33 = 3.50
For Mild:	Good Mood vs. Bad Mood	17.50 vs. 12.67 = 4.83
For Moderate:	Good Mood vs. Bad Mood	20.67 vs. 11.83 = 8.84
For Deep:	Good Mood vs. Bad Mood	24.17 vs. 8.33 = 15.84

Dunn's Step D: Look up the adjustment factor (*d*) on the Dunn table:

To use the Dunn table, you need to know how many comparisons you will be making (from Step B above) and the degrees of freedom for the denominator of F (df_{error}), which can be found on the ANOVA summary table.

For this problem, c = 9 and $df_{error} = df_{WG} = 30$. Therefore: $\mathbf{d_{.05} = 2.99}$ and $\mathbf{d_{.01} = 3.61}$

(continued)

Appendix 12-B *(continued)*

Dunn's Step E: Compute the critical range(s):

$$CR_{Dunn\ (.05)} = d_{.05}\sqrt{2\left(\frac{MS_{Error}}{n}\right)} \qquad\qquad CR_{Dunn\ (.01)} = d_{.01}\sqrt{2\left(\frac{MS_{Error}}{n}\right)}$$

$$= 2.99\sqrt{2\left(\frac{12.8389}{6}\right)} \qquad\qquad = 3.61\sqrt{2\left(\frac{12.8389}{6}\right)}$$

$$= 2.99\sqrt{2(2.1398)} \qquad\qquad = 3.61\sqrt{2(2.1398)}$$

$$= 2.99\sqrt{4.2796} \qquad\qquad = 3.61\sqrt{4.2796}$$

$$= 2.99\ (2.0687) \qquad\qquad = 3.61\ (2.0687)$$

$$= 6.185413 \approx 6.19 \qquad\qquad = 7.468007 \approx 7.47$$

Note: The Dunn critical range tells us how different two means need to be in order to be considered significantly different from each other. In this example, then, if the null hypothesis is true (and the groups are not significantly different and $\mu_1 - \mu_2 = 0.0$), the $CR_{.05}$ indicates that 95% of all random samples will have means that are less than 6.19 points apart. Only 5% of all random samples would have a difference of 6.19 or more just by chance. The $CR_{.01}$ indicates that only 1% of all random samples would have a difference of 7.47 or more just by chance. (See Figure 12-2 on page 369.)

Dunn's Step F: Compare the obtained differences between the means to the CR(s):

Decision Rule: If obtained difference ≥ CR, reject the null hypothesis

(In this example, we indicate the decision by placing asterisks next to the significant differences and "n.s." next to the non-significant comparisons. One asterisk indicates significance at the .05 level, and two asterisks indicate significance at the .01 level.)

	Comparisons	Obtained Differences	Significance
For Good Mood:	Mild vs. Moderate	17.50 vs. 20.67 = 3.17 ≱ 6.19	n.s.
	Mild vs. Deep	17.50 vs. 24.17 = 6.67 ≥ 6.19	*
	Moderate vs. Deep	20.67 vs. 24.17 = 3.50 ≱ 6.19	n.s.
For Bad Mood:	Mild vs. Moderate	12.67 vs. 11.83 = 0.84 ≱ 6.19	n.s.
	Mild vs. Deep	12.67 vs. 8.33 = 4.34 ≱ 6.19	n.s.
	Moderate vs. Deep	11.83 vs. 8.33 = 3.50 ≱ 6.19	n.s.
For Mild:	Good Mood vs. Bad Mood	17.50 vs. 12.67 = 4.83 ≱ 6.19	n.s.
For Moderate:	Good Mood vs. Bad Mood	20.67 vs. 11.83 = 8.84 ≥ 7.47	**
For Deep:	Good Mood vs. Bad Mood	24.17 vs. 8.33 = 15.84 ≥ 7.47	**

$^* p < .05$
$^{**} p < .01$

(continued)

Appendix 12-B *(continued)*

Step 16 (ANOVA): Verbally summarize the results of the study:

The donation scores were entered into a 2 (Mood) × 3 (Victim's Distress Level) BS-ANOVA. The ANOVA revealed a significant main effect of Mood [$F(1, 30) = 67.78, p < .01$] which indicated that people in a good mood donated significantly more money than people in a bad mood (means: $20.78 > $10.94). The main effect of Victim's Distress Level was not significant [$F(2, 30) = 0.42, p > .05$]. However, there was a significant Mood × Distress Level interaction [$F(2, 30) = 7.24, p < .01$] and Dunn Multiple Comparisons indicated that people in a good mood donate more money than people in a bad mood only when the victims are suffering moderate (means: $20.67 > $11.83, p < .01$) or deep distress (means: $24.17 > $8.33, p < .01$); there is no difference in donations between people in good and bad moods when the victim was experiencing only mild distress (means: $17.50 versus $12.67, p > .05$).

Dunn post hoc comparisons also revealed significantly higher donations for victims in deep distress versus victims in mild distress, but only for people in a good mood (means: $24.17 > $17.50, p < .05$). For people in a bad mood, the victim's level of distress did not have an impact on donations (means: $12.67 versus $11.83 versus $8.33, for mild, moderate and deep, respectively; $p > .05$).

Note: This verbal summary follows the APA-format for reporting results in a research report. More conversationally, we would conclude that a donor's mood (good versus bad) influences the amount of the donation only when the victims are experiencing at least a moderate level of distress and that the level of a victim's distress only affects the donations of people in a good mood. (People in a bad mood give generally low donations regardless of the victim's plight.)

Appendix 12-C

EXAMPLE OF A ONE-WAY RM-ANOVA

A researcher observed 14-month-old infants in a strange situation and measured how long they spent crying (in seconds) during each of 4 experimental conditions (each lasting 120 seconds). In one condition, the infants were observed in the presence of their mothers. In a second condition, the infants were alone in the room. In the third condition, a stranger was in the room with the infants, and in the last condition, both mom and a stranger were in the room with the baby. The order of treatments was counterbalanced.

Infants	With Mom	Alone	With Stranger	With Mom & Stranger	
a	57	118	96	76	
b	2	109	81	58	k = 4
c	43	96	91	59	n = 6
d	34	106	96	60	N = 24
e	58	101	107	66	
f	31	104	96	55	

(continued)

Appendix 12-C *(continued)*

Step 1: Organize preliminary information and set up ANOVA summary table:

Sources	SS	df	MS	F
Treatment (T)				
Subjects (S)				
T × S				
Total				

$$k = 4$$
$$n = 6$$
$$N = 24$$

$$SS_{Total} \begin{cases} SS_{Treatment} \\ SS_{Subjects} \\ SS_{Treatment \times Subjects} \end{cases}$$

Step 2: Compute SS_{Total}:

$$SS_{Total} = \Sigma\Sigma X^2 - \frac{(\Sigma\Sigma X)^2}{N}$$

With Mom	X^2	Alone	X^2	With Stranger	X^2	Mom & Stranger	X^2
57	3249	118	13924	96	9216	76	5776
2	4	109	11881	81	6561	58	3364
43	1849	96	9216	91	8281	59	3481
34	1156	106	11236	96	9216	60	3600
58	3364	101	10201	107	11449	66	4356
31	961	104	10816	96	9216	55	3025

$\Sigma X = 225$ $\Sigma X^2 = 10583$ $\Sigma X = 634$ $\Sigma X^2 = 67274$ $\Sigma X = 567$ $\Sigma X^2 = 53939$ $\Sigma X = 374$ $\Sigma X^2 = 23602$

$$SS_{Total} = \Sigma\Sigma X^2 - \frac{(\Sigma\Sigma X)^2}{N}$$

$$= (10583 + 67274 + 53939 + 23602) - \frac{(225 + 634 + 567 + 374)^2}{24}$$

$$= 155398 - \frac{1800^2}{24}$$

$$= 155398 - \frac{3240000}{24}$$

$$= 155398 - 135000$$

$$= 20398.00 \quad \text{This value is entered into the summary table:}$$

Sources	SS	df	MS	F
Treatment (T)				
Subjects (S)				
T × S				
Total	20398.00			

(continued)

Appendix 12-C *(continued)*

Step 3: Compute $SS_{Treatment}$:

$$SS_{Treatment} = \sum \frac{(\Sigma X)^2}{n} - \frac{(\Sigma\Sigma X)^2}{N}$$

(**Note:** The second piece of this formula is the same as the second piece in the SS_{Total} formula. It is known as the correction factor, and although we re-compute it below, it is not necessary to do so.)

$$SS_{Treatment} = \left(\frac{225^2}{6} + \frac{634^2}{6} + \frac{567^2}{6} + \frac{374^2}{6} \right) - \frac{(225 + 634 + 567 + 374)^2}{24}$$

because we
equal n
$$= \frac{(50625 + 401956 + 321489 + 139876)}{6} - \frac{(1800)^2}{24}$$

$$= \frac{913946}{6} - \frac{3240000}{24}$$

$$= 152324.33 - 135000$$

$$= 17324.33 \quad \text{This value is entered into the summary table:}$$

Sources	SS	df	MS	F
Treatment (T)	17324.33			
Subjects (S)				
T × S				
Total	20398.00			

Step 4: Compute $SS_{Subjects}$:

$$SS_{Subjects} = \sum \frac{(Subject\ Total)^2}{k} - \frac{(\Sigma\Sigma X)^2}{N}$$

because we have
no missing scores
(so k is the same):
$$= \frac{\Sigma(Subject\ Total)^2}{k} - \frac{(\Sigma\Sigma X)^2}{N}$$

(**Note:** The second piece of this formula is the same as the second piece in the SS_{Total} formula. It is known as the correction factor, and although we re-compute it below, it is not necessary to do so.)

(continued)

Appendix 12-C *(continued)*

Infant	With Mom	Alone	With Stranger	With Mom & Stranger	Subject Total	(Subj. Tot)^2
a	57	118	96	76	347	120409
b	2	109	81	58	250	62500
c	43	96	91	59	289	83521
d	34	106	96	60	296	87616
e	58	101	107	66	332	110224
f	31	104	96	55	286	81796
	$\Sigma = 225$	$\Sigma = 634$	$\Sigma = 567$	$\Sigma = 374$	$\Sigma\Sigma = 1800$	$\Sigma = 546066$

$$SS_{Subjects} = \frac{546066}{4} - \frac{1800^2}{24}$$

$$= 136516.5 - \frac{3240000}{24}$$

$$= 136516.5 - 135000$$

$$= 1516.5 \quad \text{This value is entered into the summary table:}$$

Sources	SS	df	MS	F
Treatment (T)	17324.33			
Subjects (S)	1516.50			
T × S				
Total	20398.00			

Step 5:   Compute $SS_{Treatment \times Subjects}$:

The interaction is the last component of the SS_{Total}, so it can be found by subtraction:

$$SS_{T \times S} = SS_{Total} - SS_{Treatment} - SS_{Subjects}$$

$$= 20398.00 - 17324.33 - 1516.5$$

$$= 1557.17 \quad \text{This value is entered into the summary table:}$$

Sources	SS	df	MS	F
Treatment (T)	17324.33			
Subjects (S)	1516.50			
T × S	1557.17			
Total	20398.00			

(continued)

Appendix 12-C *(continued)*

Step 6: Compute the degrees of freedom:

$$df_{Total} = N - 1 \qquad df_{Treatment} = k - 1 \qquad df_{Subjects} = n - 1 \qquad df_{T\times S} = df_T \times df_S$$
$$= 24 - 1 \qquad\qquad = 4 - 1 \qquad\qquad = 6 - 1 \qquad\qquad = 3 \times 5$$
$$= 23 \qquad\qquad\quad = 3 \qquad\qquad\quad = 5 \qquad\qquad\quad = 15$$

The values of the degrees of freedom are entered into the summary table:

Sources	SS	df	MS	F
Treatment (T)	17324.33	3		
Subjects (S)	1516.50	5		
T × S	1557.17	15		
Total	20398.00	23		

Step 7: Compute the mean squares and enter them into the summary table:

$$MS_{Treatment} = \frac{SS_{Treatment}}{df_{Treatment}} \qquad MS_{T\times S} = \frac{SS_{T\times S}}{df_{T\times S}}$$
$$= \frac{17324.33}{3} \qquad\qquad = \frac{1557.17}{15}$$
$$= 5774.7767 \qquad\qquad = 103.81133$$

(**Note:** We do not compute the $MS_{Subjects}$ because it is not used to compute F.)

Sources	SS	df	MS	F
Treatment (T)	17324.33	3	5774.7767	
Subjects (S)	1516.50	5	—	
T × S	1557.17	15	103.81133	
Total	20398.00	23		

Step 8: Compute F:

For a one-way RM-ANOVA, there is only one F to be computed, and its error term is the Treatment × Subjects interaction term:

$$F = \frac{MS_{Treatment}}{MS_{T\times S}}$$
$$= \frac{5774.7767}{103.81133}$$
$$= 55.627615$$

(continued)

Appendix 12-C *(continued)*

This value is rounded to two decimals and entered into the summary table:

Sources	SS	df	MS	F
Treatment (T)	17324.33	3	5774.7767	55.63
Subjects (S)	1516.50	5	—	
T × S	1557.17	15	103.81133	
Total	20398.00	23		

Step 9: Look up $F_{critical}$:

Numerator = $MS_{Treatment}$, therefore df for the numerator = $df_{Treatment}$ = 3

Denominator = $MS_{T \times S}$, therefore df for the denominator = $df_{T \times S}$ = 15

Therefore: $\mathbf{F_{crit\ (.05)}\ (3,\ 15) = 3.29}$ and $\mathbf{F_{crit\ (.01)}\ (3,\ 15) = 5.42}$

Note: If the *F* table does not include your degrees of freedom, use the next **smaller** value.

Step 10: Test the significance of *F* and state your preliminary conclusions:

Decision Rule: If $\mathbf{F_{obtained} \geq F_{critical}}$, **reject the null hypothesis**

$F_{obtained} = 55.63$

$F_{critical\ (.05)} = 3.29$

$F_{critical\ (.01)} = 5.42$

55.63 > 5.42, therefore we reject the null hypothesis at .01.

Sources	SS	df	MS	F
Treatment (T)	17324.33	3	5774.7767	55.63**
Subjects (S)	1516.50	5	—	
T × S	1557.17	15	103.81133	
Total	20398.00	23		

** $p < .01$

Note: We indicate our decision by using asterisks next to *F* on the summary table: one would indicate significance at .05, two asterisks indicate significance at .01. Nonsignificant *F*s either have no symbol next to them, or the abbreviation "n.s." is used to indicate nonsignificance

Conclusion (preliminary): The presence of mom or an unfamiliar adult has a significant effect on infants' crying behavior. (We are 99% certain that this difference is not due solely to chance.)

(continued)

Appendix 12-C *(continued)*

Step 11: Perform post hoc analyses, if necessary:

a. Determine if post hocs are necessary:

   1. Is F significant? If not, post hocs are not necessary. If F is significant, ask:
   2. How many groups/treatments are being compared in the numerator of F?

If there are **only two** groups involved in that F, post hocs are **not** needed because the F tells us that the two groups are significantly different from each other. If the F compares three or more groups, then post hoc comparisons are required. Here the F is significant and it is comparing four different experimental conditions (With Mom, Alone, With a Stranger, or With both Mom & a Stranger), therefore post hoc comparisons are needed.

b. Conduct the post hoc analyses

Dunn Multiple Comparisons Test

Dunn's Step A: Calculate the means for the treatment groups:

With Mom	Alone	With Stranger	With Mom & Stranger
$\Sigma X = 225$	$\Sigma X = 634$	$\Sigma X = 567$	$\Sigma X = 374$
$n = 6$	$n = 6$	$n = 6$	$n = 6$
$\overline{X} = 37.5$	$\overline{X} = 105.67$	$\overline{X} = 94.5$	$\overline{X} = 62.33$

Dunn's Step B: List (and count) the comparisons to be made:

Mom vs. Alone
Mom vs. Stranger
Mom vs. Mom & Stranger   **c (number of comparisons) = 6**
Alone vs. Stranger
Alone vs. Mom & Stranger
Stranger vs. Mom & Stranger

Dunn's Step C: Calculate the differences between the means:

Comparisons	Obtained Differences
Mom vs. Alone	37.5 vs. 105.67 = 68.17
Mom vs. Stranger	37.5 vs. 94.5 = 57.00
Mom vs. Mom & Stranger	37.5 vs. 62.33 = 24.83
Alone vs. Stranger	105.67 vs. 94.5 = 11.17
Alone vs. Mom & Stranger	105.67 vs. 62.33 = 43.34
Stranger vs. Mom & Stranger	94.5 vs. 62.33 = 32.17

(continued)

Appendix 12-C *(continued)*

Dunn's Step D: Look up the adjustment factor (d) on the Dunn table:

To use the Dunn table, you need to know how many comparisons you will be making (from Step B above) and the degrees of freedom for the denominator of F (df_{error}), which can be found on the ANOVA summary table.

For this problem, c = 6 and df_{error} = $df_{T \times S}$ = 15. Therefore: $\mathbf{d_{.05}}$ = **3.04** and $\mathbf{d_{.01}}$ = **3.82**

Dunn's Step E: Compute the critical range(s):

$$CR_{Dunn\ (.05)} = d_{.05}\sqrt{2\left(\frac{MS_{Error}}{n}\right)} \qquad CR_{Dunn\ (.01)} = d_{.01}\sqrt{2\left(\frac{MS_{Error}}{n}\right)}$$

$$= 3.04\sqrt{2\left(\frac{103.81133}{6}\right)} \qquad\qquad = 3.82\sqrt{2\left(\frac{103.81133}{6}\right)}$$

$$= 3.04\sqrt{2(17.301888)} \qquad\qquad = 3.82\sqrt{2(17.301888)}$$

$$= 3.04\sqrt{34.603777} \qquad\qquad = 3.82\sqrt{34.603777}$$

$$= 3.04\,(5.8824975) \qquad\qquad = 3.82\,(5.8824975)$$

$$= 17.882792 \approx 17.88 \qquad\qquad = 22.47114 \approx 22.47$$

Note: The Dunn critical range tells us how different two means need to be in order to be considered significantly different from each other. In this example, then, if the null hypothesis is true (and the groups are not significantly different and $\mu_1 - \mu_2 = 0.0$), the $CR_{.05}$ indicates that 95% of all random samples will have means that are less than 17.88 points apart. Only 5% of all random samples would have a difference of 17.88 or more just by chance. The $CR_{.01}$ indicates that only 1% of all random samples would have a difference of 22.47 or more just by chance. (See Figure 12-2 on page 369.)

Dunn's Step F: Compare the obtained differences between the means to the CR(s):

Decision Rule: If Obtained Difference ≥ CR, reject the Null

(In this example, we indicate the decision by placing asterisks next to the significant differences and "n.s." next to the non-significant comparisons. One asterisk indicates significance at the .05 level, and two asterisks indicate significance at the .01 level. Remember that $CR_{Dunn\ (.05)}$ = 17.88 and $CR_{Dunn\ (.01)}$ = 22.47.)

(continued)

Appendix 12-C *(continued)*

Comparisons	Obtained Differences	Significance
Mom vs. Alone	37.5 vs. 105.67 = 68.17	**
Mom vs. Stranger	37.5 vs. 94.5 = 57.00	**
Mom vs. Mom & Stranger	37.5 vs. 62.33 = 24.83	**
Alone vs. Stranger	105.67 vs. 94.5 = 11.17	n.s.
Alone vs. Mom & Stranger	105.67 vs. 62.33 = 43.34	**
Stranger vs. Mom & Stranger	94.5 vs. 62.33 = 32.17	**

$** p < .01$

Step 12 (ANOVA): Verbally summarize the results of the study:

The crying duration scores were entered into a one-way RM-ANOVA with Adult Presence as the repeated measure. The ANOVA revealed a significant effect of the experimental manipulation [$F (3, 15) = 55.63, p < .01$]. Dunn multiple comparisons indicated that infants in an unfamiliar room showed significantly less distress when they were just with mom than any of the other three experimental conditions (means: 37.5 vs. 62.33, 94.5, and 105.67, all p s $< .01$). The infants showed a significant increase in crying when the stranger entered the room, even if mom is still with them (means: $37.5 < 62.33, p < .01$). When mom left the infants either alone or with the stranger, there was another significant increase in crying (respective means: 105.67 and $94.5 > 62.33$, both p s $< .01$). There was no difference in the amount of crying between being left with a stranger and being left alone in the room (respective means: 94.5 vs. 105.67, $p > .05$).

(**Note:** This verbal summary follows the APA-format for reporting results in a research report. More conversationally, we would conclude that the presence of strangers or separation from mom generates anxiety in 14-month-old infants in unfamiliar situations, and we would point out that the presence of a stranger does not comfort an infant who has been separated from his/her mother.)

Exercises

For problems 1–6, conduct the appropriate ANOVA and test the significance of F. Conduct Dunn's multiple comparisons, if necessary. Verbally summarize the results.

1. A psychologist wanted to examine the effects of diet on learning in rats. Newborn rats were randomly assigned to one of two diets: standard Purina Rat Chow or a supplemented diet where vitamins and minerals were added to the Rat Chow. After six months, each rat was tested on a discrimination problem and the researcher recorded the number of errors each animal made before it solved the problem.

Regular Rat Chow	Special Rat Chow
13	9
11	8
12	7
13	8
11	9
9	10
12	7
10	8
12	9
14	6
10	8
12	10

2. A program was developed to prevent infants from developing insecure attachments with their mothers. To test its effectiveness, researchers visited 100 families and observed the mother-infant interactions when the babies were three weeks old. On the basis of these observations, mothers' sensitivity to their infants' needs was measured. Two groups of women were identified to participate in the study itself: the 10 women with the highest sensitivity scores and the 20 women with the lowest sensitivity scores. Half of the "low sensitive" mothers were randomly assigned to a no-treatment control group, and half were randomly assigned to receive intensive parenting training. The training included lectures, demonstrations, and role-play exercises, as well as hands-on practice in caring for infants and recognizing their needs. The training took five weeks to complete.

   Ten months later, when the infants from all groups were 12 months old, they were observed for two minutes in an unfamiliar setting with two unfamiliar peers (other 12-month-old babies). The researchers recorded the number of seconds the infants spent in physical contact with their mothers during the two-minute period.

High Sensitivity	Low Sensitivity/ No-Treatment Control	Low Sensitivity/ Training
51	43	31
32	44	18
25	61	49
52	24	61
43	100	26
8	82	49
19	42	44
39	39	61
30	49	62
15	77	27

3. In a study on the effectiveness of anti-smoking campaigns, a researcher compared three different strategies for persuading teenagers to stop smoking. He was also interested in the possibility that males and females react in different ways to various approaches. The first strategy (I) involved having the participants read the complete reports from the Surgeon General's office. The second strategy (II) gave the participants information on the financial costs of smoking over a period of years (including the cost of cigarettes and medical insurance, etc.). The third strategy (III) was to emphasize how smoking affected the participants' personal appearance and attractiveness to their peers (including the smelly clothes, bad breath, yellowed teeth and fingers, etc.) The researcher randomly assigned the teenagers to one of the three strategies and recorded the number of times the participants refused to accept a cigarette offered to them by confederates over a two-week period following the anti-smoking session. (Every participant was offered a total of 10 cigarettes by a variety of confederates during the 2-week test period.)

| | | STRATEGY | | |
		I	II	III
		2	3	7
		3	4	7
	Males	4	6	6
		1	5	6
		2	2	8
SEX				
		2	3	5
		3	4	6
	Females	1	4	8
		2	5	7
		3	5	5

4. A researcher has conducted a study to examine the effects of role-play training (where children act out peer-conflict situations) on their ability to generate possible solution strategies for hypothetical conflicts. The researcher included 3rd-graders who had been identified as liked, disliked, or neither by their classmates. Half of the children in each popularity status group received two-weeks of daily role-play training while the others were assigned to a no-treatment control group. Two months after the training was completed, the children were assessed using the interpersonal cognitive problem-solving test (ICPS) and the number of socially-acceptable conflict solutions they spontaneously generated was recorded.

| | POPULARITY STATUS | | |
	Liked	Disliked	Neutral
Trained	5	7	9
	7	4	7
	9	2	11
	14	5	3
	2	6	8
TRAINING			
Control	4	1	6
	6	3	5
	9	4	12
	10	2	9
	5	5	5

5. A clinical psychologist conducted an experiment to test the effects of a counselor's comments on the success of the therapy for severely depressed people. A counselor was trained to use three types of comments: (1) self-disclosing comments (i.e., telling clients about personal past experiences similar to the clients': "I flunked stats the first time I took it, too"); (2) client-focused comments (i.e., comments about how the client's behaviors make the counselor feel: "I feel very good that you were able to stand up to your roommate about having overnight guests during finals week"); and (3) neutral comments (similar to the reflection and restatement techniques used by Rogerian therapists: "So you are saying that you were annoyed at your roommate."). Eight clients saw the counselor for a total of 18 weeks. For the first six weeks, the counselor used one type of comments, then he switched and used a different type of comments for the next six weeks, etc. The order of comments was counterbalanced across the clients. At the end of each six-week therapy period, each client was interviewed by a blind psychologist (supposedly their counselor's supervisor) who recorded the number of depressive statements made by each client.

TYPE OF COMMENTS

Client	Self-Disclosing	Client-Focused	Neutral
a	12	10	15
b	8	3	12
c	13	4	12
d	10	6	16
e	13	5	9
f	7	2	13
g	9	7	12
h	11	10	11

6. In a longitudinal study of children's antisocial behavior toward peers, a researcher was able to track the changes in children's behavior as their family status underwent the transition from the intact nuclear family to a stepfamily. The number of antisocial behaviors recorded by observers during four time periods were recorded. The "intact" scores were obtained at least 12 months before the parents decided to get divorced. The "divorcing" scores were obtained within 1 month of the parents' announcement that they were getting divorced. The "single parent" scores were obtained at least 12 months after the divorce (and before the custodial parent became openly involved with anyone new). The "remarried" scores were obtained at least 6 months after the custodial parent remarried.

Child	Intact Family	Divorcing	Single Parent	Remarried (Stepfamily)
a	5	13	9	8
b	8	12	6	9
c	10	12	9	7
d	7	10	9	9
e	5	11	13	9
f	12	13	13	14
g	6	10	11	3
h	5	13	4	8
i	9	13	12	13
j	10	14	11	10

7. The following data are from a between-subjects design:

	B_1	B_2	B_3	B_4
A_1	2	4	6	1
	3	1	4	2
	1	3	5	1
A_2	5	4	3	2
	4	5	3	1
	2	3	1	1

a. What is N?

b. What is k?

c. What is n?

d. How many degrees of freedom are there for the within-groups term (df_{WG})? How many degrees of freedom are there for the main effect of variable A (df_A)? How many degrees of freedom are there for the A × B interaction ($df_{A \times B}$)?

  e. How many *F*s will be computed?

  f. If all *F*s are significant, which would require post hocs?

8. Suppose a researcher conducted a 5 × 2 × 3 between-subjects design with 10 participants in each experimental condition. If α is set at .01, what is the critical value of *F* (from the *F* Table) for the A × C interaction term?

For each of the following ANOVA summary tables, complete the analysis and answer the following questions (which require that you work backwards from the information given to the various formulas, etc.):

  a. What research design was used? (e.g., one-way BS; 2 × 3 × 5 WS, etc.)

  b. How many experimental conditions were in the study?

  c. How many people participated in the study?

  d. How many times was each participant tested?

  e. Are post hoc analyses required? For which effects?

9.

Source	Sum of Squares	df	Mean Squares	F
Treatment	60	3		
Subjects	70	9		
T × S				
Total	210			

10.

Source	Sum of Squares	df	Mean Squares	F
Therapy	560	5		
WG		24		
Total	690			

11.

Source	Sum of Squares	df	Mean Squares	F
Outcome	50	2		
Motive	90	3		
O × M	100			
WG				
Total	500	119		

12.

Source	Sum of Squares	df	Mean Squares	F
Instructions	60	3		
Materials	40	2		
I × M	90			
Within Group				
Total	382	59		

13.

Source	Sum of Squares	df	Mean Squares	F
Grade	75	3		
Subjects	20	4		
G × S				
Total	167			

14.

Source	Sum of Squares	df	MS	F
A	50	2		
B	60	3		
C	90	1		
A × B	180			
A × C	120			
B × C	75			
A × B × C	240			
WG				
Total	2975	239		

15.

Source	Sum of Squares	df	MS	F
Type of Task	100	4		
Emotional State	80	2		
Task × Emotion	48			
Subjects	380	19		
Task × Ss	304			
Emotion × Ss	190			
T × E × Ss	912			
Total				

16.

Source	Sum of Squares	df	MS	F
A	50	2		
B	60	3		
C	90	1		
A × B	180			
A × C	120			
B × C	75			
A × B × C	240			
Subjects	480	4		
A × Ss	560			
B × Ss	720			
C × Ss	640			
A × B × Ss	1152			
A × C × Ss	880			
B × C × Ss	360			
A × B × C × Ss	320			
Total				

CHAPTER

13

NONPARAMETRIC TESTS FOR EXPERIMENTS AND QUASI-EXPERIMENTS

■ ■ ■ ■ ■ ■

In this chapter, you will learn how to conduct five statistical procedures that are appropriate for experiments and quasi-experiments with data on nominal or ordinal scales. Three of the tests are used to analyze data from between-subjects designs, while the other two tests are used for within-subjects designs.

Look for These Important Terms and Concepts

Chi-Square (χ^2)
parametric tests
nonparametric tests
chi-square (χ^2) goodness-of-fit test
chi-square (χ^2) test for contingency tables

Cochran's Q
Wilcoxon Rank Sum test (Wilcoxon-Mann-Whitney T)
Kruskal-Wallis H
Wilcoxon W (or Signed Ranks test)

Before Reading This Chapter, You May Wish to Review

Chapter 4:
• nominal and ordinal scales

Chapter 5:
• frequency
• joint probability

Chapter 6:
• null hypothesis
• α and rejecting the null hypothesis
• critical values

Chapter 8:
• rank scores
• tied ranks procedure

Chapter 10:
• between-subjects designs
• within-subjects designs
• matched-pairs designs
• one-way and factorial designs

Chapter 12:
• degrees of freedom
• post hoc analyses

Analysis of variance (Chapter 12) and *t*-tests (Chapter 11) are often referred to as **parametric tests** because they are based on specific assumptions about the characteristics, or parameters, of the underlying population. For instance, the independent samples *t*-test and BS-ANOVA assume that the scores in the population are normally distributed and that the treatment groups come from populations with similar variances. Furthermore, these assumptions can be met only if the scores correspond closely with the underlying variable, and therefore, *t*-tests and ANOVA are appropriate only for experiments and quasi-experiments with dependent variables on interval or ratio scales. You should recall from Chapter 4 that scores with interval and ratio levels of measurement have equal intervals, so that a one-point difference in score always represents the same amount of difference in the underlying quantity (e.g., one inch is always equal to the same distance, a minute is always equal to the same amount of time, and one bar-press response is always the same amount of bar-pressing behavior). Consequently, for interval and ratio scales, the difference between two scores or means is an accurate measurement of the difference in the underlying quantity, and parametric tests are appropriate. The Pearson *r*, which we presented in Chapter 8, is another parametric test because it is designed to measure the correlation between variables on interval and ratio scales.

Nominal and ordinal scales, in contrast, do not have the property of "equal intervals," and generally cannot be assumed to be normally distributed in the population. Therefore, when the level of measurement for the dependent variable from an experiment or quasi-experiment is nominal or ordinal, the parametric tests are not appropriate. So just like we used the Spearman *r* or the phi coefficient, instead of the Pearson *r*, to measure correlations among ordinal and nominal variables, we should analyze ordinal and nominal data from experiments and quasi-experiments with tests that do not assume equal intervals among the scores or make assumptions about the population parameters. Such tests are referred to as **nonparametric tests.**

Ordinal scales, as you'll recall, measure the ordering or ranking of the individuals within a group. That is, they indicate the relative positions of the scores from highest to lowest or from most to least. They do not tell us *how much* difference there is between individuals. (For example, Ann is the tallest child in her second-grade class while Connie is the next tallest: how much taller than Connie is Ann? The ordinal ranking scores do not answer this question.) Nominal scales, you'll recall, simply form categories or classes that are qualitatively different from each other. Each value on a nominal scale represents a unique category, and these categories generally cannot be ordered in a meaningful fashion. For example, the variable of religious affiliation forms a nominal scale with values such as Jewish, Catholic, Hindu, and Presbyterian, and it is not possible to rank order these groups as "more" or "less" religious—they are simply different religions. Nominal data sets are generally presented in the form of the number of individuals who belong in particular categories. That is, after each participant has been classified into one of the categories, the number of participants in each category is determined. For example, the number of male nurses, the number of female nurses, the number of male doctors, and the number of female doctors on staff at a major hospital could be measured for a study on sex-role stereotyping. The analysis of nominal data looks at the frequency counts for each category.

Before we proceed with our discussion of nonparametric tests, we should point out that the distinction between nominal and ordinal scales can sometimes become blurred by exceptions to the general principle that says nominal categories cannot be put in meaningful order. For example, the scale of measurement will be ambiguous in cases where performance on *quantitative* variables is dichotomized so that each participant is categorized into one of two groups that are considered to be qualitatively distinct, such as when a test is measured on a pass/fail basis. While it is accurate to say that students who passed an exam did "better" than those who failed, the degree of ordering among the individuals is extremely limited, with no distinction made among participants who had no errors at all and participants who made errors on 39% of the test items, and so forth. When the ordering among the scores is minimal, the power of the nonparametric tests for ordinal data is reduced, so simple dichotomies (and some trichotomies where participants are categorized into one of three groups) are typically treated as nominal scales even if the underlying variable is quantitative and the categories do have an inherent order to them.

In this chapter, we present some of the more common nonparametric procedures used with ordinal and nominal scales. Table 13-1 indicates the nonparametric test which is appropriate for different types of experimental and quasi-experimental designs.

TABLE 13.1	Appropriate Nonparametric Statistical Procedures	
	Nominal Level of Measurement	**Ordinal Level of Measurement**
BS Designs (Independent Groups Designs)	Chi Square (χ^2)	Wilcoxon Rank Sum Test (aka Wilcoxon-Mann-Whitney T) (for only 2 groups) or Kruskal-Wallis H
WS Designs or Paired Matching (Related Samples)	McNemar Test* (for only 2 treatments) or Cochran's Q	Wilcoxon Signed Ranks Test (aka Wilcoxon W) (for only 2 treatments) or

*The computations for these two tests are not included in this edition. Interested readers are referred to David Sheskin's *The Handbook of Parametric and Non-Parametric Statistical Procedures (1997).*

Nominal Scales

Between-Subjects Designs: Chi-Square (χ^2)

When the data to be analyzed from a BS design are on a nominal scale, where the participants' values on the dependent variable represent their membership in a particular category, the most common test is the chi-square test. The symbol for this statistic is χ^2. This statistic compares the observed frequencies for each category to the frequencies that would be expected if the null hypothesis is true. For instance, if we were to toss a coin 100 times, we would expect to get 50 heads and 50 tails, assuming the coin is fair. If we actually observed 42 heads and 58 tails, would we conclude that the coin was biased or is the difference between 50-50 and 42-58 a common event just by chance? How many samples of 100 fair coin tosses result in a split that is so far from 50-50? The χ^2 statistic measures the difference between the expected and the observed frequencies, and the sampling distribution for χ^2 allows us to determine what values of χ^2 are rare by chance alone.

Chi-square can be used with one-way designs (where there is a single independent variable) to compare the frequency distribution we observe in the research sample to the frequency distribution that is predicted by the null hypothesis, which predicts that the independent variable has no effect on behavior or categorical membership. The χ^2 test allows us to determine whether or not the observed frequency distribution is equivalent to the distribution expected by the null hypothesis. (By definition, two distributions are equivalent if the differences between them are random and attributable solely to chance.) This application of chi-square to one-way designs is known as the **chi-square goodness-of-fit test**. The χ^2 statistic can also be used to test for an interaction between two nominal (or categorical) variables. That is, we can compare the frequencies to determine whether or not the distributions across one IV are the same at every level of the other IV. This application of chi-square to two-way designs is known as the **chi-square test for contingency tables**. (Often, these two tests are nicknamed the one-way χ^2 and the two-way χ^2, respectively.)

One-way χ^2 Goodness-of-Fit Test To illustrate the steps involved in the one-way χ^2 goodness-of-fit test, let's use the following example. A researcher sent a survey to 150 people and asked them to identify which brand of pain reliever they would purchase if there was no difference in cost. The results were as follows:

Bayer Aspirin	Tylenol	Advil
38	58	54

$$N = 150$$

The null hypothesis for this problem would be that there is no preference for one brand of pain reliever over any other. In order to test this hypothesis, we first need to calculate the cell frequencies that we would expect to see if the null hypothesis is correct. The symbol for these expected cell frequencies is E, and the formula is:

$$E = \frac{N}{k}$$

where: N = the total number of scores

k = the number of categories

[Note: To minimize potential computation errors, we round the expected cell frequencies in the chi-square test to *one* decimal place, if necessary. This is a rare case where we round before we reach the final step in the computation of the statistic.]

For our example, the expected cell frequencies are equal to:

$$E = \frac{N}{k}$$

$$= \frac{150}{3}$$

$$= 50$$

Thus, the null hypothesis predicts that the sample would be evenly divided and that each of the three brands of pain relievers would be preferred by 50 participants. We now want to compare these expected cell frequencies (E) to the cell frequencies we observed in our survey results (O):

Bayer Aspirin	Tylenol	Advil
38	58	54
50	50	50

$$N = 150$$

We measure the difference between the observed (O) and expected (E) cell frequencies using the χ^2 formula:

$$\chi^2 = \sum \frac{(O - E)^2}{E}$$

This formula tells us to subtract E from O, square the difference, and divide by E. We do this for each group separately, and then add them together. While this is the official χ^2 formula, the one-way goodness-of-fit test can use an algebraic shortcut because the expected cell frequencies in this one-way χ^2 goodness-of-fit test are the same for every group. In this shortcut, the squared deviations between O and E are summed across the groups, and then the sum is divided by E. The shortcut formula would be written like this:

$$\chi^2 = \frac{\sum(O - E)^2}{E}$$

If we apply this formula for χ^2 to our example, we get:

$$\chi^2 = \frac{(38 - 50)^2 + (58 - 50)^2 + (54 - 50)^2}{50}$$

$$\chi^2 = \frac{(-12)^2 + (8)^2 + (4)^2}{50}$$

$$\chi^2 = \frac{144 + 64 + 16}{50}$$

$$\chi^2 = \frac{224}{50}$$

$$\chi^2 = 4.48$$

To test the significance of our obtained value of χ^2, we must look up $\chi^2_{critical}$ on the table of critical values (Table B5 in Appendix B). In order to use the table, we need to compute the *degrees of freedom* for our data set. In chi-square tests, the degrees of freedom refer to the number of independent cell frequencies that are in N. In other words, if there are 150 participants in three categories, how many will fall into the first category? Anywhere from 0 to 150, so the first cell frequency is "free to vary" (and is independent of the other frequencies). Suppose the first cell frequency is 38; how many participants are in the second category? Anywhere from 0 to 112, so this cell frequency has a "degree of freedom." If the second cell frequency is equal to 58, how many people are in the third (and last) category? It must be 54. This cell frequency is not independent of the other cell frequencies and the total N, so it has no freedom to vary. Thus, with 3 categories, we find we have 2 degrees of freedom. The degrees of freedom for a one-way χ^2 goodness-of-fit test, then, can be expressed with the formula:

df = k − 1   where k = 5 the number of categories

With 2 degrees of freedom, and setting our alpha level to .05, the table of χ^2s indicates that the *critical value* of χ^2 is **5.991**. The decision rule is:

If $\chi^2_{obtained}$ is greater than or equal to $\chi^2_{critical}$, reject the H_0

Our obtained value of χ^2 (4.48) is less than 5.991, so we *cannot* reject the null hypothesis. This failure to reject the null indicates that the difference in frequencies that we observed in our sample is a common random event when the null hypothesis is true. Therefore, we must conclude that our data provide no evidence of a significant preference for one brand of pain reliever over the others. Thus, our results suggest that, if the pain relievers cost the same, they are preferred by about the same numbers of people. However, it is possible that we have made a Type II error, so the study should be replicated in order to confirm the findings.

Two-way χ^2 Test for Contingency Tables   The χ^2 test for contingency tables can be used to test for an interaction between two categorical variables. For example, is sex related to hyperactivity? If there is no relationship between sex and hyperactivity, then a group of boys will have the same number (or proportion) of hyperactive children as does a group of girls. Likewise, if the two variables are unrelated, there should be the same percentage of male hyperactive children as there are female hyperactive children. However, if boys are significantly more at risk for hyperactivity, then a comparison between boys and girls should reveal a larger percentage of hyperactive boys than girls. The χ^2 test for contingency tables (which is nicknamed a "two-way χ^2") allows us to decide whether the variables are related.

To illustrate this use of χ^2, let's use the following example. A sociologist wanted to see if there is a systematic relationship between the sex of a defendant and the verdict rendered in a murder trial. He collected data from a sample of 120 murder trials where a verdict had been reached. The results are as follows:

	Guilty	Not Guilty	
Male	30	25	55
Female	20	45	65
	50	70	N = 120

The first step in the χ^2 contingency tables test is to calculate the expected cell frequency (E) for each of the groups. For a contingency (two-way) table, the expected frequency for any particular cell is based on the *joint probability* that a participant drawn at random would be in that particular row and that particular column. For example, if one murder trial is selected at random from the 120 trials in our sample, what is the probability that the trial would have a female defendant? What is the probability that the randomly selected trial would have resulted in a guilty verdict? The probability that the one trial selected at random would have both a female defendant and a guilty verdict is called the joint probability, and it is equal to the product of the two separate probabilities of being female and being found guilty. (This computation of joint probability assumes that the two variables are independent of each other, which is exactly what the null hypothesis asserts.) Joint probability was discussed in Chapter 5.

In the sample data for murder trials, the probability that one trial selected at random would have a female defendant is equal to $65/120 = .542$ or 54.2%. This is determined by counting the total number of trials with female defendants $(20 + 45)$ and dividing by the total number of trials $(N = 120)$. The probability that a trial selected at random would have resulted in a guilty verdict can be determined by getting the total number of guilty verdicts (30 + 20 = 50) and dividing by N. Thus, the probability of selecting a trial with a guilty verdict is equal to 50/120 = .417 or 41.7%. The joint probability that a single trial selected at random would have both a female defendant and a guilty verdict, therefore, is:

$$p_{(female)} \times p_{(guilty)} = .542 \times .417 = .226 \text{ (or } 22.6\%)$$

This probability, then, tells us what proportion of the population is expected to fall into the category of "guilty females" just by chance when the variables are not truly related to each other (and the null is true). If 22.6% of the population is expected to be in this cell, then we can calculate how many (out of our sample of 120) should be in that cell:

$$120 \times .226 = 27.1$$

Thus, by chance alone, if the null is true, the expected cell frequency for the guilty female cell is equal to 27.1.

Fortunately, there is an easier procedure for calculating the expected cell frequencies for contingency tables:

$$\mathbf{E} = \frac{\textbf{(row total) (column total)}}{\mathbf{N}}$$

Let's apply this formula to the guilty female cell:

$$E = \frac{(65)(50)}{120}$$

$$= \frac{3250}{120}$$

$$= 27.1$$

Thus, we get the same expected cell frequency without having to directly compute the separate probabilities and the joint probabilities, and so forth.

Now we need to compute the Es for each of the other cells. If we apply the formula to each cell, we get the following:

Guilty Males:	**Not Guilty Females:**	**Not Guilty Males:**
$E = \dfrac{(55)(50)}{120}$	$E = \dfrac{(65)(70)}{120}$	$E = \dfrac{(55)(70)}{120}$
$= \dfrac{(2750)}{120}$	$= \dfrac{(4550)}{120}$	$= \dfrac{(3850)}{120}$
$= 22.9$	$= 37.9$	$= 32.1$

(As noted earlier, expected cell frequencies are rounded to one decimal place.)

By using the formula for E to compute the expected cell frequency for each of the cells, we find that the null hypothesis predicts that 22.9 of the 120 trials should have male defendants who are found guilty, while 37.9 of the trials should have female defendants who are found not guilty, and 32.1 trials should have male defendants who are found not guilty. (Of course, as we found earlier, 27.1 of the trials should have female defendants who are found guilty.) While the E formula is much easier to use than the joint probability procedure, there is another shortcut that we can use to find some expected cell frequencies. This shortcut is based on the fact that the expected cell frequencies in a row must add up to the row total, and the expected cell frequencies in a column must add up to the column total. Therefore, the last cell in a row or column can be found by subtraction. For example, when we used the formula for E to compute the cell frequency for the guilty male cell, we found that E = 22.9. So if there were a total of 55 males in the sample, and 22.9 of them are expected to be guilty, how many males are expected to be not guilty? When we subtract 22.9 from 55, we get 32.1, which is exactly the same as the value of E that we computed using the formula. Similarly, if the expected cell frequency for the guilty male cell is 22.9, and there was a total of 50 guilty verdicts, how many females are expected to be guilty? Subtracting 22.9 from 50 gives us 27.1—the same value we found when we applied the E formula *and* when we computed the actual joint probabilities for guilty females.

After we have computed the expected cell frequency for each cell, we enter them into the data table and compute χ^2:

	Guilty		Not Guilty	
Male	30		25	
		22.9		32.1
Female	20		45	
		27.1		37.9

N = 120

$$\chi^2 = \frac{(30 - 22.9)^2}{22.9} + \frac{(25 - 32.1)^2}{32.1} + \frac{(20 - 27.1)^2}{27.1} + \frac{(45 - 37.9)^2}{37.9}$$

$$\chi^2 = \frac{(7.1)^2}{22.9} + \frac{(-7.1)^2}{32.1} + \frac{(-7.1)^2}{27.1} + \frac{(7.1)^2}{37.9}$$

$$\chi^2 = \frac{(50.41)}{22.9} + \frac{(50.41)}{32.1} + \frac{(50.41)}{27.1} + \frac{(50.41)}{37.9}$$

$$\chi^2 = 2.20131 + 1.570405 + 1.8601476 + 1.3300792$$

$$\chi^2 = 6.9619418$$

$$\chi^2 \approx 6.962$$

This is our obtained value of χ^2 and we now need to test its significance by looking up $\chi^2_{critical}$ on the table of critical values (Table B5 in Appendix B). To use this table, we need to know the degrees of freedom for the data set. For a two-way χ^2 test for contingency tables, the formula for degrees of freedom is:

$$\textbf{df = (\# of rows } -1)(\textbf{\# of columns } -1)$$

This formula gives us the degrees of freedom for a two-way interaction. The number of rows is equal to the number of levels of the first categorical IV (k_A), so when we subtract one from the number of rows, it gives us the degrees of freedom for the main effect of the first IV. The number of columns is equal to the number of levels of the second IV (k_B), so when we subtract one from the number of columns, it gives us the degrees of freedom for the main effect of the second IV. Because the degrees of freedom for any interaction are equal to the product of the degrees of freedom for the main effects, this formula can be written as:

$$
\begin{aligned}
\textbf{df} &= \textbf{(k}_A - \textbf{1)(k}_B - \textbf{1)} \\
&= (2 - 1)(2 - 1) \\
&= 1 \times 1 \\
&= 1
\end{aligned}
$$

If alpha is set at .05, we find that the critical value of χ^2 is equal to 3.841. Because 6.962 is larger than 3.841, we can reject the null hypothesis. (If we take a peek at the critical value of χ^2 for $\alpha = .01$, we see that we can also reject the null at the .01 level: $6.962 > 6.635$. We would probably report the "stronger" result, using the .01 level.)

The results of this analysis indicate that the verdict in a murder trial is systematically and significantly related to (or interacts with) the sex of the defendant. There is a significantly different pattern of verdicts for men and women: While more men are found guilty, more women are found not guilty. Note that this conclusion simply describes the pattern of results without trying to explain them. While it would be tempting to conclude that our jury system is biased in favor of women, we must remember this hypothetical study employed a *quasi-experimental design*, and both IVs are subject variables. Therefore, we cannot draw any causal conclusions from the results. An alternative explanation of the results is that men commit murder more often than women, and are, in fact, guilty more often than women. The results may reflect a real sex difference in the commission of the crime rather than a judicial bias in favor of women.

Within-Subjects Designs: Cochran's Q

An appropriate test for one-way within-subjects designs or matched-pairs designs with two or more treatments is known as **Cochran's Q,** which is a special application of the chi-square distribution that compares the frequencies of two possible outcomes. That is, when performance on the dependent variable can be classified into two and only two categories, such as pass/fail, we can count how many times these outcomes occurred under each of the experimental treatments and use Cochran's Q to determine whether there is a significant difference in the frequency of these outcomes across the treatment conditions. Cochran's Q is appropriate when the dependent variable is a *dichotomous* variable, where there are only two possible scores. Some other common examples of dichotomous measurements include for/against and yes/no. When responses to the dependent variable are recorded, Cochran's Q requires that they be *assigned scores of 0 and 1.* To illustrate the computation of Q, let's consider the following example.

Suppose a researcher is interested in subliminal perception. A visual "subliminal" message is a stimulus that is presented so briefly that people are not able to consciously describe what they saw, and may deny seeing anything at all. In order to test the effectiveness of different types of subliminal messages, the researcher made three videos in which an "actor" is auditioning for a part in a play, and the contents of each of the videos were the same. One video, however, had the words "Hershey's Chocolate" flash by 10 times during the 15-minute tape. Another video flashed a photograph of a Hershey's chocolate candy bar (still in its wrapper) 10 times during the tape. The words and the photograph were flashed at the same points in the two videos. The third video had no subliminal messages in it.

Participants were told that they were to help select the best "actor" for the part in the play. After viewing each one of the videotaped "auditions," the participants were offered a candy bar from a tray which contained Hershey candy bars and Nestlé candy bars of the same size. The videos were presented in counterbalanced order and the researcher recorded whether or not the participant selected the Hershey bar. The null hypothesis for this study would be that there is no difference in the number of participants who select the Hershey bar under the three video conditions. The results are presented in the following table, where 1 = selected the Hershey bar, and 0 = did not select the Hershey bar.

Viewer	Hershey's	Photograph	Control
a	0	1	0
b	1	0	1
c	1	1	1
d	0	1	0
e	0	1	0
f	1	1	0
g	1	1	1
h	0	0	0
i	1	1	0
j	1	1	0
k	0	1	1
l	1	0	0
m	0	1	0
n	1	1	0
o	0	1	0

The formula is:

$$Q = \frac{(k-1)[k(\Sigma C^2) - T^2]}{kT - \Sigma R^2}$$

Where: k = the number of experimental conditions
C = a condition total or the sum of the scores in a treatment condition
R = a row total or the total score for a particular participant (or matched pair)
T = the grand total of all scores

To apply this formula to our data, we need to compute the condition totals, the row totals, and the grand total:

Viewer	Hershey's	Photograph	Control	R (row tot)
a	0	1	0	1
b	1	0	1	2
c	1	1	1	3
d	0	1	0	1
e	0	1	0	1
f	1	1	0	2
g	1	1	1	3
h	0	0	0	0
I	1	1	0	2
j	1	1	0	2
k	0	1	1	2
l	1	0	0	1
m	0	1	0	1
n	1	1	0	2
o	0	1	0	1
	C = 8	C = 12	C = 4	T = 24

The denominator of the Q formula includes the sum of the squared row totals, and the easiest way to get that sum is to create a new column of R^2s and find its sum:

Viewer	Hershey's	Photograph	Control	R (row tot)	R^2
a	0	1	0	1	1
b	1	0	1	2	4
c	1	1	1	3	9
d	0	1	0	1	1
e	0	1	0	1	1
f	1	1	0	2	4
g	1	1	1	3	9
h	0	0	0	0	0
i	1	1	0	2	4
j	1	1	0	2	4
k	0	1	1	2	4
l	1	0	0	1	1
m	0	1	0	1	1
n	1	1	0	2	4
o	0	1	0	1	1
	C = 8	C = 12	C = 4	T = 24	$\Sigma R^2 = 48$

Now we are ready to plug the numbers into the formula and solve for Q. Three computational rules that you need to remember are: (1) computations inside parentheses or brackets are done first; (2) summation (Σ) is done last; and (3) multiplication is done before subtraction. Therefore, the numerator for Q tells us to square each condition total, add them together, multiply the sum by k, subtract T^2, and then multiply by k minus 1. The denominator instructs us to multiply k times T and subtract the sum of the squared row totals we computed above. When we follow these computational steps, we get:

$$Q = \frac{(k - 1)\,[k(\Sigma C^2) - T^2]}{kT - \Sigma R^2}$$

$$= \frac{(3 - 1)[3(8^2 + 12^2 + 4^2) - 24^2]}{3(24) - 48}$$

$$= \frac{2[3(64 + 144 + 16) - 576]}{72 - 48}$$

$$= \frac{2[3(224) - 576]}{24}$$

$$= \frac{2(672 - 576)}{24}$$

$$= \frac{2(96)}{24}$$

$$= \frac{192}{24}$$

$$= 8.000$$

Thus, our obtained value of Q is 8.000 and we need to decide whether a value of 8.000 is a common event just by chance or whether it is a rare event that would allow us to reject the null hypothesis.

Because Q is a special version of χ^2, we use the chi-square table to find our critical value, and we compare Q to $\chi^2_{critical}$. (See Table B5 in Appendix B.) In order to use the χ^2 table, we need to calculate the degrees of freedom (df). In a one-way design, the formula for the degrees of freedom for Cochran's Q is:

df = k − 1   where k = the number of treatments

Therefore, for our problem which compared three videos conditions (k = 3):

df = 3 − 1 = 2

Thus, the critical values of χ^2, with 2 degrees of freedom, are 5.991 (at the .05 level) and 9.210 (at the .01 level). The decision rule for Q is the same as the rule for the chi-square test itself:

If Q ≥ $\chi^2_{critical}$, reject the null hypothesis

Therefore, we would reject the null hypothesis at the .05 level because 8.000 is greater than 5.991. We conclude that there is a significant difference among the three video conditions in the number of participants who chose the Hershey's bar. An examination of the condition totals indicates that the participants selected the Hershey's bar most often when they were exposed to the subliminal presentation of a photograph ($C_{Photograph} = 12$), and they selected the Hershey's bar least often when they were exposed to the film with no subliminal messages ($C_{Control} = 4$). When they were subliminally exposed to the words "Hershey's Chocolate," the condition total was between the other conditions ($C_{Word} = 8$). The analysis tells us the difference between the highest and lowest condition totals is significant. We cannot, however, on the basis of the omnibus Q statistic, draw any conclusions about the effect of a subliminal presentation of the words "Hershey's Chocolate" compared to the other two conditions. That is, we cannot assume that the 4-point differences between the word condition and the photograph and control conditions are significant. We need to conduct *post hoc analyses* in order to determine whether: (1) subliminal presentation of pictures is more effective than presentation of words, and (2) whether subliminal presentation of words has any effect on behavior at all (compared to a control condition).

Post hoc analyses for a significant Cochran's Q, when there are three or more treatment conditions, involve performing Cochran's Q tests for *every pair* of treatments. These comparisons should address the research questions the study was designed to answer. For our example, our study was designed to answer three questions about the relative impact of subliminal messages. Therefore, we would be interested in making three pairwise comparisons: (1) a comparison of the control and the photograph conditions in order to determine whether the subliminal presentation of a photograph influences behavior at all; (2) a comparison of the word and control conditions, in order to determine whether the subliminal presentation of a printed word influences behavior at all; and (3) a comparison of the photograph and word conditions, in order to compare the relative effectiveness of the two types of subliminal messages.

We can expect the post hoc comparison between the photograph and control conditions to be significant because the omnibus Q was significant and the difference between those conditions was larger than any other pair of treatments. And, in fact, when we conduct Cochran's Q on those two treatments, we find that Q is equal to 6.4 and the critical value of χ^2 (at the .05 level with 1 degree of freedom) is equal to 3.841, indicating that the participants selected a Hershey's bar significantly more often after they were subliminally exposed to the photograph of a Hershey's bar than when they were in the control condition. The other two post hoc comparisons are presented on page 421.

Post Hoc Comparison: Word versus Control			
Words	**Control**	**R**	**R^2**
0	0	0	0
1	1	2	4
1	1	2	4
0	0	0	0
0	0	0	0
1	0	1	1
1	1	2	4
0	0	0	0
1	0	1	1
1	0	1	1
0	1	1	1
1	0	1	1
0	0	0	0
1	0	1	1
0	0	0	0
C = 8	C = 4	T = 12	ΣR^2 = 18

$$Q = \frac{(2-1)[2(8^2 + 4^2) - 12^2]}{2(12) - 18}$$

$$= \frac{1[2(64 + 16) - 144]}{24 - 18}$$

$$= \frac{2(80) - 144}{6}$$

$$= \frac{160 - 144}{6}$$

$$= \frac{16}{6}$$

$$= 2.667$$

$$df = k - 1 = 2 - 1 = 1$$

$$\chi^2_{critical\,(.05)}\,(df = 1) = 3.841$$

Decision: Q (2.667) is less than $\chi^2_{critical}$ (3.841), so we *cannot reject* the null hypothesis.

Post Hoc Comparison: Word versus Photograph			
Words	**Photo**	**R**	**R^2**
0	1	1	1
1	0	1	1
1	1	2	4
0	1	1	1
0	1	1	1
1	1	2	4
1	1	2	4
0	0	0	0
1	1	2	4
1	1	2	4
0	1	1	1
1	0	1	1
0	1	1	1
1	1	2	4
0	1	1	1
C = 8	C = 12	T = 20	ΣR^2 = 32

$$Q = \frac{(2-1)[2(8^2 + 12^2) - 20^2]}{2(20) - 32}$$

$$= \frac{1[2(64 + 144) - 400]}{40 - 32}$$

$$= \frac{2(208) - 400}{8}$$

$$= \frac{416 - 400}{8}$$

$$= \frac{16}{8}$$

$$= 2.000$$

$$df = k - 1 = 2 - 1 = 1$$

$$\chi^2_{critical\,(.05)}\,(df = 1) = 3.841$$

Decision: Q (2.0) is less than $\chi^2_{critical}$ (3.841), so we *cannot reject* the null hypothesis.

In summary, the analyses indicate that the presentation of the photograph led to significantly more selections of the Hershey's bar than the control condition, but the presentation of the words "Hershey's Chocolate" did not have the same significant effect. The post hoc comparisons, however, also indicated that the difference between the two types of subliminal messages was not significant. Our overall conclusion for this study would be that the subliminal presentation of photographs has a significant influence on people's behavior, but the effect of subliminally presented words is less certain. There was no difference between the "words" condition and *either* of the other two conditions. This pattern of results suggests the possibility that subliminally presented words may indeed have an effect on behavior that our study was unable to detect. That is, our design and analysis may have lacked sufficient power to detect the effect of subliminally presented words. Alternatively, the significant effect of the photograph may reflect a Type I error. Replication of the study is very important for our interpretation of the data.

Ordinal Scales

Between-Subjects Designs: The Wilcoxon Rank Sum Test and the Kruskal-Wallis H

Two statistical tests appropriate for one-way between-subjects designs with ordinal data are the Wilcoxon Rank Sum test and the Kruskal-Wallis H test. Like the *t*-test for interval and ratio data, the Wilcoxon Rank Sum test (which is also known as the Wilcoxon-Mann-Whitney T) is limited to designs with two groups. The Kruskal-Wallis H, in contrast, can be used with two or more groups, making it more versatile than the Wilcoxon Rank Sum T. Let's look at examples of each of these statistical procedures.

Wilcoxon Rank Sum Test (a.k.a. Wilcoxon-Mann-Whitney T)   The **Wilcoxon Rank Sum test** is appropriate for ordinal data collected using one-way between-subjects designs with two and only two treatment groups. This statistic measures the difference in *rank-order scores* for the participants in the two treatment groups. The null hypothesis would say that there is no difference in performance between two groups, and if that is true, and we put all of the participants in order according to their performance, the participants from the two groups should be randomly "mixed" in the list; if the null is false, then the participants from one group will tend to be higher on the list of ranks than the participants from the other group. Let's use the following scenario to illustrate the computation of T.

A researcher wanted to test the effectiveness of a new program designed to prevent young adolescents from using drugs. Junior high school students were assigned at random to one of two groups, a control group and a group who participated in a debate on whether drugs should be legalized. The students in the debate group were required to do research in the library on the physiological, psychological, and social effects of drugs. Six weeks after the debate, all participants were asked to indicate (on a 7-point scale) whether they would try cocaine if someone offered them a free sample. On the scale, 1 meant "definitely would not try the cocaine" and 7 meant "definitely would try the cocaine." The data were as follows:

Control group (n = 13):
3, 4, 5, 2, 3, 1, 6, 5, 2, 7, 6, 6, 7
Debate group (n = 10):
1, 2, 1, 3, 2, 3, 1, 1, 1, 2

FIGURE 13.1		ASSIGNING RANK SCORES		

Ordinal Position	Student's Score	Treatment Group	Assigned Rank Score	
1)	1	Control	3.5 ⎫	There are 6 students with
2)	1	Debate	3.5 ⎪	a score of 1, and they are
3)	1	Debate	3.5 ⎪	in the first 6 positions, so
4)	1	Debate	3.5 ⎬	they each get a rank score of 3.5,
5)	1	Debate	3.5 ⎪	which is the average of position
6)	1	Debate	3.5 ⎭	numbers 1, 2, 3, 4, 5, and 6.
7)	2	Control	9 ⎫	
8)	2	Control	9 ⎪	The five students with scores of 2 are in
9)	2	Debate	9 ⎬	positions 7 through 11, and the
10)	2	Debate	9 ⎪	average of 7, 8, 9, 10, and 11 is a rank
11)	2	Debate	9 ⎭	of 9.
12)	3	Control	13.5 ⎫	
13)	3	Control	13.5 ⎪	A rank of 13.5 is the average of
14)	3	Debate	13.5 ⎬	positions 12, 13, 14, and 15.
15)	3	Debate	13.5 ⎭	
16)	4	Control	16	
17)	5	Control	17.5 ⎫	A rank of 17.5 is the average of
18)	5	Control	17.5 ⎭	positions 17 and 18.
19)	6	Control	20 ⎫	
20)	6	Control	20 ⎬	A rank of 20 is the average of 19, 20,
21)	6	Control	20 ⎭	and 21
22)	7	Control	22.5 ⎫	A rank of 22.5 is the average of
23)	7	Control	22.5 ⎭	positions 22 and 23.

Because the data are on an ordinal level, the analysis is conducted on the *rank-order scores* instead of the original values of the dependent variable. Thus, the first step in conducting the Wilcoxon Rank Sum Test is to find the rank score for each participant, while keeping track of the participants' treatment group. Ranking should be done from low to high (so that the smallest value of X is assigned a rank score of 1). Whenever there are tied scores, the tied ranks procedure presented in Chapter 8 should be employed (see page 200). Figure 13-1 presents the results of the ranking procedure for the data from our hypothetical study on the effects of debating the legalization of drugs. As you can see in Figure 13-1, there are numerous tied scores in the data set, and a systematic procedure for keeping track of the ordinal positions of the scores is essential.

After the original scores have been converted to rank scores, the next step in the Wilcoxon Rank Sum Test is to compute the sum of the rank scores (ΣR) for each of the treatment groups:

Control	Ranks	Debate	Ranks
3	13.5	1	3.5
4	16	2	9
5	17.5	1	3.5
2	9	3	13.5
3	13.5	2	9
1	3.5	3	13.5
6	20	1	3.5
5	17.5	1	3.5
2	9	1	3.5
7	22.5	2	9
6	20		
6	20		$\Sigma R = 71.5$
7	22.5		$n_1 = 10$
	$\Sigma R = 204.5$		
	$n_2 = 13$		

At this point, we need to ask if we have equal numbers of participants in each group. If the answer is "Yes," then we have completed the computations, and the value of the Wilcoxon Rank Sum statistic (T) is equal to the ΣR with the smaller value. (If we had equal numbers of participants in our two groups, our obtained value of T would be 71.5 because it is smaller than 204.5.)

Thus, for samples of equal size: $T_{obtained} =$ **the smaller ΣR**

When there are unequal sample sizes, as in our example, we must then compute a statistic called T' ("T-prime") which allows us to make adjustments based on the fact that one group has more scores in it than the other:

$$T' = n_1(n_1 + n_2 + 1) - \Sigma R_{n1}$$

where: $n_1 =$ the number of scores in the smaller group of participants
   $n_2 =$ the number of scores in the larger group of participants
   $\Sigma R_{n1} =$ the ΣR for the group with the fewer number of participants

For our example,

$$T' = 10(10 + 13 + 1) - 71.5$$

$$= 10(24) - 71.5$$

$$= 240 - 71.5$$

$$= 168.5$$

Now we compare T' to ΣR_{n1} and let the obtained value of T be equal the smaller of these two values. So for this example, $T_{obtained} = 71.5$ (because it is less than 168.5).

Thus for samples of unequal sizes:

$$T_{obtained} = \text{the smaller of } T' \text{ and } \Sigma R_{n1}$$

The smaller sum of ranks provides a test of the null hypothesis because when the null hypothesis is true, the sums of ranks for the two groups are very similar, but when the null hypothesis is false, the sums of ranks will differ, with the smaller sum of ranks approaching the minimum possible value. The smallest possible value of a sum of ranks is the sum of numbers from 1 to n because every score in the group is assigned a rank score and each rank score is included in the sum. The only time ΣR will have the minimum possible value is when every member of one group scores above every member of the other group, so $\Sigma R = 1 + 2 + \cdots + n$. Thus, a small value of T indicates that the rank scores in one group are lower than the rank scores for the other group.

After we compute T, we need to look up $T_{critical}$. The critical values for T are presented in Appendix B (in Table B-8). The T-table actually consists of separate tables for each alpha level for one- and two-tailed tests. Therefore, if we are using a two-tailed (nondirectional) test and we set alpha to be equal to .05, we need to use part "b" of the table and for a two-tailed test with alpha = .01, we'd use part "a" of the table. Across the top of the table is the sample size of the smaller group and down the side is the sample size of the larger group. When we read across to n_1 and down to n_2, we find the critical value of T. Therefore, for our example, with 10 scores in one group and 13 scores in the second group:

$$T_{critical (.05, two-tailed)} = 88 \text{ and } T_{critical (.01, two-tailed)} = 79$$

The decision rule for the Wilcoxon Rank Sum test (a.k.a. Wilcoxon-Mann-Whitney T) is:

If $T_{obtained}$ is less than or equal to $T_{critical}$, reject the null hypothesis

It is very important to note that this decision rule is "backwards" compared to every other statistic covered so far. In order to be significant, our obtained value of T must be smaller than the critical value of T. (This is because the value of T is determined by the smaller sum of ranks rather than the larger sum.)

In our example, then:

$$T_{obtained} (71.5) \text{ is less than } T_{critical} (79), \text{ therefore we reject the null at .01}$$

We can conclude that participating in debates about legalizing drugs (and doing research on the effects of drugs) significantly reduced students' reported willingness to try cocaine.

Kruskal-Wallis H Another appropriate test for one-way between-subjects designs with ordinal data is the **Kruskal-Wallis H** (which is another special use of the χ^2 distribution). The Kruskal-Wallis H, like the Wilcoxon Rank Sum test (T), analyzes the pattern of rank scores for the participants in the treatment groups, but unlike the Rank Sum test, the Kruskal-Wallis H can be used with any number of treatment conditions. The first two computational steps for the Kruskal-Wallis H are the same as the steps for the Wilcoxon Rank Sum T: all of the participants are put in order and assigned rank scores, and the sum of the rank scores is computed for each treatment group. Then H is computed and compared to a critical value of χ^2. To illustrate the computation of H, let's suppose that the Coordinator for Greek Life at a small private university was looking at the academic performance of three fraternities. The registrar's office provided data on the students' class rank (an ordinal scale where smaller numbers indicate better academic performance; i.e., being ranked #1 is best):

Omega Mu	Rho Gamma	Alpha Beta
2	301	198
87	188	208
60	244	247
43	102	186
61	123	265
55	243	300
154	206	284
170		
137		

The first step is to put all of the scores in order and assign rank scores to each participant, starting with the smaller values first. If there are tied scores, use the tied ranks procedure (described in Chapter 8, on page 200). Be sure to keep track of which group the scores are from, too.

Class Rank	Frat	Rank Score
2	OM	1
43	OM	2
55	OM	3
60	OM	4
61	OM	5
87	OM	6
102	RG	7
123	RG	8
137	OM	9
154	OM	10
170	OM	11
186	AB	12
188	RG	13
198	AB	14
206	RG	15
208	AB	16
243	RG	17
244	RG	18
247	AB	19
265	AB	20
284	AB	21
300	AB	22
301	RG	23

The next step is to calculate the Sum of Ranks (ΣR) for each of the three groups of participants:

Omega Mu	Rho Gamma	Alpha Beta
1	7	12
2	8	14
3	13	16
4	15	19
5	17	20
6	18	21
9	23	22
10		
11		
$\Sigma R = 51$	$\Sigma R = 101$	$\Sigma R = 124$
n = 9	n = 7	n = 7

Now we calculate the Kruskal-Wallis H using the following formula:

$$H = \left[\frac{12}{N(N + 1)} \Sigma \frac{(\Sigma R^2)}{n} \right] - 3(N + 1)$$

where: N = total number of scores in the study
n = the number of participants in a group

$$H = \left[\frac{12}{23(24)} \left(\frac{51^2}{9} + \frac{101^2}{7} + \frac{124^2}{7} \right) \right] - 3(24)$$

$$= \left[\frac{12}{552} \left(\frac{2601}{9} + \frac{10201}{7} + \frac{15376}{7} \right) \right] - 72$$

$$= [(.0217391) (289 + 1457.2857 + 2196.5714)] - 72$$

$$= [(.0217391) (3942.8571)] - 72$$

$$= 85.714165 - 72$$

$$= 13.714165$$

$$\approx 13.714$$

To test the significance of the Kruskal-Wallis H, we compare it to a critical value of χ^2, which means that we need to compute the degrees of freedom. Since this is a one-way design:

df = k − 1   where k = the number of groups

Therefore, for this problem, where we are comparing three fraternities ($k = 3$), our degrees of freedom are equal to 2 and the χ^2 table (Tabnle B-5) indicates that the critical value of χ^2, at the .01 level, with 2 degrees of freedom is equal to 9.210. The decision rule for H is:

If H $\geq \chi^2_{critical}$, reject the null hypothesis

For our example, H = 13.714 which is greater than $\chi^2_{critical}$ = 9.210, therefore we will reject the null hypothesis with alpha set at .01, and conclude that there is a significant difference in academic performance among the three fraternities. Does this indicate that the academic performance of the Rho Gamma brothers is significantly different than the performance of the Alpha Beta brothers? The omnibus H does not answer this question, so post hoc analyses are required in order to make specific comparisons among pairs of fraternity houses. (Remember that post hoc comparisons will be required whenever the omnibus statistic is significant and there are three or more groups in the design.) Post hoc comparisons can be made by computing a new Kruskal-Wallis H for two groups of scores at a time, just like we computed a new Cochran's Q for each pair of treatments in an earlier example. If you compute H separately for each of the three pairwise comparisons in this design, you will find that academic ranks of the Omega Mu brothers are significantly higher than the ranks of both Rho Gamma ($H = 7.286$, $p < .01$) and Alpha Beta ($H = 11.118$, $p < .01$) brothers. (In fact, every Omega Mu brother ranked higher than all of the Alpha Beta brothers, so the value of H is at its maximum for a design with 16 scores.) The difference between Rho Gamma and Alpha Beta brothers is not significant ($H = 1.180$, $p > .05$).

Within-Subjects Designs: Wilcoxon Signed Ranks Test (a.k.a. the Wilcoxon W)

The **Wilcoxon W** (or **Signed Ranks Test**) is used for one-way within-subjects designs or one-to-one paired matching designs when the dependent variable is on an ordinal scale of measurement. The test is limited to those designs that have only two experimental treatments, and the Wilcoxon W ranks the participants based on the amount of change they exhibited from the first treatment to the next and compares the rank scores for participants who showed an increase in performance to those who showed a decrease in performance.

To illustrate this procedure, let's suppose that college students on the Student Activities Board were trying to choose between two bands to invite to campus for a concert. Each of the 10 members of the board listened to an album by each of the two bands and gave each band a rating of how much they enjoyed the music. The ratings were on a 15-point scale where higher numbers represented greater enjoyment. The students listened to the bands in counterbalanced order. The ratings scores are:

Students	Band A	Band B
a	7	8
b	9	12
c	10	10
d	1	3
e	4	3
f	4	8
g	7	5
h	8	12
i	6	12
j	5	5

The first step is to calculate the difference score for each participant: $X_1 - X_2$ (this is how much the participant's score changed from treatment 1 to treatment 2). The direction of change is crucial, so you must keep track of any negative signs in the difference scores.

Step 1:

Students	Band A	Band B	Diff
a	7	8	−1
b	9	12	−3
c	10	10	0
d	1	3	−2
e	4	3	1
f	4	8	−4
g	7	5	2
h	8	12	−4
i	6	12	−6
j	5	5	0

The second step is to throw out any participant with a difference score of zero. So in this case:

Step 2:   Participants "c" and "j" are deleted and N now equals 8.

The third step in calculating W is to put the absolute values of the difference scores in rank order (from low to high) and assign a **rank score** to each participant, using the tied-ranks procedure as necessary (see page 200). The smallest difference score receives the smallest rank score of 1.

Step 3:

Ordinal Position	Diff	Rank	
1	1	1.5	(using the tied score procedure)
2	1	1.5	
3	2	3.5	
4	2	3.5	
5	3	5	
6	4	6.5	
7	4	6.5	
8	6	8	

Thus:

Students	Band A	Band B	Diff	Rank
a	7	8	−1	(−)1.5
b	9	12	−3	(−)5
c	10	10	0	—
d	1	3	−2	(−)3.5
e	4	3	1	(+)1.5
f	4	8	−4	(−)6.5
g	7	5	2	(+)3.5
h	8	12	−4	(−)6.5
i	6	12	−6	(−)8
j	5	5	0	—

The fourth step is to sort the rank scores into two groups: participants whose difference scores were positive and those whose difference scores were negative. In this example, positive difference scores indicate a preference for Band A while negative difference scores indicate a preference for Band B. (Large difference scores, in either direction, reflect a strong preference for the music of one band over the other.) Once we have sorted the difference scores into positive and negative scores, we compute the total rank score (ΣR) for each of these groups.

Step 4:

Positive		Negative	
Students	Rank	Students	Rank
e	1.5	a	1.5
g	3.5	b	5
	$\Sigma R = 5$	d	3.5
		f	6.5
		h	6.5
		i	8
			$\Sigma R = 31$

The next step is to find $W_{obtained}$: the **Wilcoxon W is equal to the smaller ΣR**.

Step 5:

$$W_{obtained} = 5 \text{ (since } \Sigma R = 5 \text{ is less than } \Sigma R = 31)$$

The remaining steps are to test the null hypothesis by looking up a critical value of W and applying the appropriate decision rule. The critical value of W is found on Table B9 in Appendix B. It is important to remember that two of the original participants were dropped because their scores showed no change from treatment one to treatment two (i.e., they rated the bands equally), so the value of N that we use to look up $W_{critical}$ is now 8 rather than 10. The decision rule for W is:

If $W_{obtained}$ is **less than or equal to** $W_{critical}$, reject the null hypothesis

Just like the Wilcoxon Rank Sum test, the decision rule for the Wilcoxon W is "backwards" compared to the decision rules for most inferential statistics because the value of W is determined by the *smaller* ΣR rather than the larger one. (Note that if the null hypothesis is true, the ΣRs will be approximately equal. At the other extreme, if the IV has a systematic effect on every participant so they all show change and their scores all change in the same direction, W will equal 0.0. Essentially, the decision rule asks if W is "small enough"—close enough to zero—to conclude that the IV has had a systematic effect on the participants.) Returning to our example:

Step 6: Look up $W_{critical}$ on table, using the correct N (N = 8):

$$W_{critical\,(.05)} = 3$$

Step 7: Make a Decision

$W_{obtained}$ (5) is **not** less than or equal to $W_{critical}$ (3), so we cannot reject H_0

The conclusion we reach based on these data is that the students on the Student Activities Board did not show a significant preference for one band over the other.

A Cautionary Note about *When* to Select the Appropriate Statistic

There are a number of nonparametric tests available to analyze data that are on nominal or ordinal scales. For nominal scales, chi-square and Cochran's Q examine the frequencies for the treatment conditions; for ordinal scales, the Wilcoxon tests and the Kruskal-Wallis H analyze the rank scores. Researchers need to select the test that is most suitable for their data and their design and they must do so *before* they actually conduct the study. The statistical analysis of the data must be considered very early because not all combinations of designs and measurements are analyzable with the common tests covered in most statistics texts. For instance, there is no test available to analyze a mixed design when the data are on a nominal scale. It is better for the researcher to know this ahead of time rather than to discover at the end of the study that the research hypotheses cannot be tested statistically. Therefore, the process of designing a study should include the selection of an appropriate statistical test. If a suitable test is not available it may be necessary to change the design or the level of measurement for the dependent variable.

Exercises

For each problem, conduct the appropriate test and verbally summarize the results.

1. A researcher was interested in the effects of incentive on people's willingness to volunteer to perform a boring task that would take hours. A total of 210 college students were randomly assigned to three groups, and each group was offered one of three monetary incentives. The researcher recorded whether or not the students agreed to perform the task, and the number of students who agreed to participate are as follows:

   ### INCENTIVE

$5	$10	$15
24	32	56

2. The researcher from the problem above then conducted another study to test for an interaction between the level of incentive offered for participation in a boring task and whether the participants believed they would be alone during the task or with other people. So participants were randomly assigned to be offered one of three incentive levels and were either told that there would be other people helping them or were left to believe they would be working alone. The numbers of people who agreed to participate in each condition are below:

   ### INCENTIVE LEVEL

	$5	$10	$15
Alone	8	9	15
Not Alone	7	11	25

3. In a study investigating the relationship between recognition memory and altered states of consciousness, a group of participants saw two videotapes

depicting a "mugging" and were asked to pick the muggers out of police-like line-ups. In one condition, the participants saw the tape under "normal consciousness" (i.e., they were awake and sober). In the second condition, the participants saw the tape after drinking three cans of beer in 40 minutes. The dependent variable was simply whether or not the participants correctly identified the mugger. The data are as follows:

Participant	Sober	Drunk
a	yes	no
b	yes	no
c	yes	yes
d	no	no
e	no	no
f	yes	no
g	no	no
h	yes	yes
i	yes	no
j	yes	no
k	yes	no
l	yes	no

4. In a study on the development of prosocial behavior in young children, mothers were asked to rate their children's helpfulness when the children were 3 years old and again when they were 5 years old. On the 10-point scale, 1 = "not at all helpful" and 10 = "very helpful." The data are as follows:

Child	3 Years Old	5 Years Old
a	2	4
b	3	7
c	1	2
d	2	5
e	4	4
f	1	7
g	6	1
h	2	10
i	2	7
j	3	4
k	3	8
l	5	9

5. A sports medicine researcher is interested in the effectiveness of a new exercise machine that claims to be better at reducing back pain than traditional flexibility exercises. The researcher recruited participants suffering from back pain and assigned them at random to one of three conditions: the new machine, a flexibility exercise regimen, or a relaxation training treatment.

After 4 weeks, the participants were asked to indicate the level of pain they experienced on a 20-point scale (where 1 = little pain and 20 = lots of pain). The results were as follows:

Machine	Flexibility	Relaxation
13	9	7
11	18	9
12	7	13
13	8	15
11	9	9
9	10	8
12	7	12
10	8	13
12	9	6
14	16	15
10	8	10
12	10	11

6. A doctor wrote a new pamphlet that described the dangers of AIDS and recommended consistent, conscientious use of condoms. To test the effectiveness of the pamphlet, the doctor gave a copy of the pamphlet to patients from different environments and SES levels, who had been matched one-to-one on the basis of age, sex, marital status, and sexual history. Three months later, the doctor asked each patient: "Do you regularly use condoms while having sex?" The following results were obtained from the three groups of subjects:

Matched Trio	Urban-Upper SES	Rural-Low SES	Urban-Low SES
a	yes	no	no
b	yes	no	no
c	yes	yes	yes
d	yes	no	no
e	yes	yes	yes
f	no	no	no
g	yes	no	no
h	yes	yes	no
i	no	no	no
j	yes	yes	yes
k	yes	yes	no
l	yes	yes	no
m	yes	no	no
n	no	no	no
o	yes	yes	yes

7. Based on interviews with parents, a researcher identified a group of preschool children who frequently watched *Mr. Rogers* on television, and a

group who never watched the program. The researcher then asked the children's preschool teachers to rate them on their helpfulness toward others, using a scale from 1 to 7 (where 7 means very helpful). The researcher wanted to find out if the children who watch *Mr. Rogers* frequently are more helpful than children who do not watch the program.

Watch	Do Not
4	3
7	2
3	4
5	3
1	5
6	2
7	3
4	1
2	
6	

8. Tellers at the local off-track betting office suspected that many bettors choose horses solely on the basis of their name. Horses with names that imply speed and endurance seem to be bet on more often than horses with other names. To test this hypothesis, the tellers kept a record of the number of bettors who placed wagers on three horses with equal performance records. The results were that 65 people bet on "Surefire," 43 people bet on "McDugan," and 12 people bet on "Also-Ran."

9. Teachers at a school for autistic children wanted to measure the amount of improvement in social responsiveness shown by the children in a special social skills training class. Blind observers rated each child's responsiveness during interpersonal interactions (using a scale from 0 = "completely unresponsive" to 15 = "fully responsive") on the 1st day of the class and again on the last day of training, 6 weeks later.

Child	1st Day	Last Day
a	8	7
b	3	5
c	4	4
d	5	8
e	4	8
f	4	9
g	3	9
h	6	2
i	2	9
j	6	6
k	3	11
l	5	15
m	12	11

10. During an experiment on the effects of persuasion on people's attitudes, a researcher randomly selected two groups of participants and asked them to read one of the two short speeches asking people to support a ban on objects made of ivory. One of the speeches included very emotional, graphic descriptions of how elephants are slaughtered by poachers. The other speech gave a very logical, technical account of the importance of elephants to the ecology. After reading the speech, participants were asked to indicate their opinion on the ivory ban using a 15-point rating scale where 1 = very much opposed and 15 = very much in favor. The results are as follows:

Type of Speech

Emotional	Logical
14	10
12	1
9	2
11	7
12	4
8	13
	15
	3
	5

11. A researcher did a study on attitudes about the legal drinking age. Adults who were either "Children of Alcoholics" or not were asked if they supported legislation increasing the drinking age. The researcher wanted to know if adults with a family history of alcoholism had the same pattern of attitudes toward the legislation as people with no history of alcoholism in their family. The frequencies for the four conditions are as follows:

Attitude About Increasing the Drinking Age

	Favor	Oppose
Child of Alcoholics	26	14
Non-Alcoholic Parents	18	22

12. A psychologist is interested in the effects of parental loss on children's behavior in school. The researcher has surveyed third-grade teachers and asked them to rate the likelihood that the children in their classes would be referred to the school psychologist for counseling at some time within the next two years. (On the rating scale, higher rating scores indicated a stronger likelihood that the child will be referred.) The ratings for six children whose parents have divorced, six children

who have been orphaned, and eight children from intact families are as follows:

Intact	Orphan	Divorce
3	8	7
2	3	5
5	4	4
1	5	8
4	4	9
3	4	9
1		
6		

CHAPTER

14

ESTIMATION AND CONFIDENCE INTERVALS

■ ■ ■ ■ ■ ■

In this chapter, you will learn how to use sample data to estimate the most likely range of values of various population parameters, including means, proportions, and correlations. Confidence intervals provide us with an alternative method for testing our research hypotheses. You will see how this approach differs from traditional null hypothesis testing, and why we favor using a combination of these techniques when interpreting the results of a study.

Look for These Important Terms and Concepts

point estimation and confidence intervals
confidence intervals for the mean
maximum error of the estimate
confidence level

confidence interval for proportions (or percentages)
confidence intervals for the Pearson r
minimum difference between means

Before Reading This Chapter, You May Wish to Review

Chapter 6:
- sampling distributions
- standard error
- α and critical values
- power (or see Appendix C)
- alternatives to null hypothesis testing

Chapter 8:
- Pearson r
- $r - to - z^*$ transformation

Chapter 10:
- between-subjects and within-subjects designs

Chapter 11:
- z-scores and t-scores
- one-tailed and two-tailed tests

Chapter 12:
- ANOVA
- Dunn multiple comparisons

In Chapter 6, we discussed the basic logic involved in testing the null hypothesis, and in subsequent chapters we illustrated the hypothesis-testing process with correlation coefficients, z- and t-tests, ANOVA, and non-parametric statistics. In each of these statistical procedures, a statistic is calculated from a sample of data, and if the probability of that statistic occurring by chance is very low (.05 or less), we decide to reject the null hypothesis, and conclude that, in the population, there is a significant relationship between the variables (or a significant difference between the groups). Essentially, the decision to reject the null hypothesis only tells us that the sample statistic seems to come from a population where the null hypothesis is false. For example, in a two-group experiment, the null hypothesis says there is no difference between the group means, but if we reject the null hypothesis (because our value of t or F is significant), we are concluding that, in the population, the difference between the groups is not zero. The next logical question, then, is: "What is the difference between the groups?" This question asks us to estimate the value of the population parameter.

Random samples, because they are generally representative of their populations, provide us with our best estimates of population parameters. That is, the mean of a random sample ($\overline{X}$) is an estimate of the population mean (μ), the standard deviation in the sample (s) provides an estimate of the population standard deviation (σ), a sample correlation (r) is an estimate of the population correlation (ρ), and the difference between two sample means ($\overline{X}_1 - \overline{X}_2$) is an estimate of the difference between two population means ($\mu_1 - \mu_2$). Therefore, once we reject the null hypothesis, we can use the characteristics of our research sample as estimates of the characteristics of the population. When we use our sample statistic as an estimate of the population parameter, we are using a procedure known as **point estimation.**

However, point estimation does not take into consideration the fact that our sample cannot be an exact replica of the population.[1] Recall, for example, that the size of the samples influences their representativeness, where small samples tend to be less representative of the population while large samples tend to be more representative. However, even large random samples show variation from the population (and from each other). Therefore, when we use the sample as our estimate of the population, we must understand that our estimate is likely to be "off" at least a little.

We can measure just how far off our estimates are likely to be. This is possible because we can measure how much random variation occurs among random samples by computing the standard error (σ_E) of the sampling distribution. You may remember (from Chapter 6) that the standard error is a measure of the average difference between a random sample and the population. Therefore, when we draw a random sample, we can use the standard error as an indicator of how far off our sample

---

[1]Because samples do not include the entire set of scores from the population, there are unknown values in the population which we can only estimate, and therefore, the population parameters are necessarily going to be different than sample statistics. For example, the population includes both the highest and the lowest possible scores, but few samples would include either or both of these scores. Therefore, the variability of the population will be greater than the variability of a sample. Essentially, the only "perfectly representative" sample would be one that contained each and every member of the population.

statistic is likely to be from the population parameter. Consequently, it is possible for us to report our best estimate and a margin of error using **confidence intervals.** A confidence interval is a range of values in which the population parameter is likely to fall. That is, the confidence interval tells us the lowest and highest likely values of the parameter. For example, suppose the results of a poll (of 200 American voters) indicated that 30% of the respondents feel the president's foreign policy is "totally misguided." If the margin of error is found to be 3%, then these results tell us that the percentage of American voters who feel the president's foreign policy is "totally misguided" is somewhere between 27% and 33%, and this range of values is our confidence interval. Basically, confidence intervals are equal to:

$$\text{Confidence Interval} = \text{"Best Estimate"} \pm \text{Margin of Error}$$

Confidence intervals can be computed for just about any statistic that we wish to estimate for the population, including the means, the difference between means, percentages or proportions, correlations, and standard deviations. The procedures for each of these are based on the same underlying logic, so we will present the basic concepts in detail as we discuss confidence intervals for the population mean (μ). Later in this chapter, we will also describe the procedures for finding confidence intervals for population proportions (or percentages), population correlations, and the minimum difference between the means of separate populations. We will also discuss how confidence intervals can be used as an alternative to testing the null hypothesis to compare group means.

Confidence Intervals for the Mean

Let's imagine that a child psychologist is asked if a two-year-old's frequent tantrum behavior is "normal" or not. Before attempting to answer this question about an individual child, the psychologist would need to know how many tantrums are "normal" for two-year-olds. That is, we need to know the average number of tantrums thrown by the population of two-year-old children. If we selected a random sample of two-year-olds and calculated the average number of tantrums ($\overline{X}$), we could use this sample $\overline{X}$ as our best estimate of the population average (μ). However, because we know that $\overline{X}$ is unlikely to be exactly equal to μ, we would need to find the "margin of error." The margin of error is equal to the largest difference between $\overline{X}$ and μ that is likely to happen by chance alone, and it is measured with a statistic called the **maximum error of the estimate (E_{max}).** In order to understand the computation of E_{max}, we need to review the basic concept of chance fluctuations among random samples.

Finding the Margin of Error: The Maximum Error of the Estimate

Remember that a sampling distribution is created by drawing all random samples from a population and calculating a statistic (such as $\overline{X}$) for each sample. These

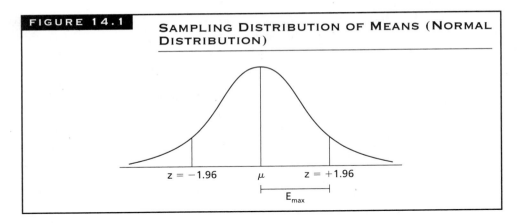

FIGURE 14.1   SAMPLING DISTRIBUTION OF MEANS (NORMAL DISTRIBUTION)

sample statistics form a standardized distribution around the population parameter and the variability among the sample statistics can be measured using the standard error (σ_E). For example, the sample means ($\overline{X}$s) will distribute themselves around the population mean (μ), and the variability among the $\overline{X}$s depends on the size of the samples (where large samples are less variable than small samples). Because the distribution of samples is standardized, it is possible for us to find the critical values of $\overline{X}$ which cut off the most rare 5% or 1% of the sample means by finding either $z_{critical}$ or $t_{critical}$. (As you may recall from Chapter 11, we can convert sample means to z-scores if σ, the population standard deviation, is known. These z-scores form a normal distribution when there are at least 25 scores in the sample. When σ must be estimated using the sample standard deviation *or* when the sample size is less than 25, we can compute t-scores instead of z-scores.)

When the sampling distribution forms a normal curve, we know that a z-score of ± 1.96 cuts off 5% of the samples (2.5% in each tail). These critical values tell us that 95% of all random samples drawn from this population will have a mean ($\overline{X}$) with a z-score somewhere between -1.96 and $+1.96$ (see Figure 14-1). Any sample mean with a z-score equal to or greater than $z_{critical}$ is considered to be a non-random, significant event, and therefore, the largest value of the mean that will occur "by chance" is found just below the cut-off point. Consequently, the largest difference between $\overline{X}$ and μ that is likely to occur by chance—the **maximum error of the estimate (E_{max})**—is equal to the distance between the mean of the sampling distribution and the critical value (cut-off point) which indicates where the "non-random" events begin.

Similarly, for non-normal sampling distributions which fit Student's t-distribution, we can look up the value of $t_{critical}$ for any particular sample size and this will allow us to locate 95% or 99% of the random samples. For example, for samples with 20 participants (so the distribution has 19 degrees of freedom), a two-tailed t-score of ± 2.093 cuts off the most rare 5% of the samples. This tells us that

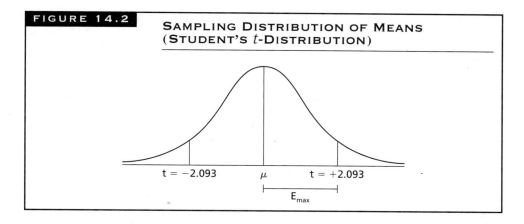

FIGURE 14.2 SAMPLING DISTRIBUTION OF MEANS (STUDENT'S *t*-DISTRIBUTION)

95% of the sample means will have a *t*-score between -2.093 and $+2.093$. Like *z*-scores, *t*-scores are based on the variability among random samples, so this t_{critical} indicates that 95% of the sample means are no more than 2.093 "standard error units" from μ. Therefore, if we draw one sample of twenty scores at random from the population, we can be 95% certain that our sample $\overline{X}$ will be no more than 2.093 standard error units away from the population mean (μ). Again, the maximum error of the estimate (E_{max}) is equal to the distance between the mean of the sampling distribution and the critical value (or cut-off point). (See Figure 14-2.)

Note that the maximum error of the estimate (E_{max}) is based on how far a single random sample mean is likely to be from the mean of its population. That is, E_{max} tells us we can be 95% certain that a sample mean will fall somewhere between $-t_{\text{critical}}$ and $+t_{\text{critical}}$. However, E_{max} can also be interpreted in the other direction: that is, it also tells us that we can be 95% certain that the population mean (μ) is no more than 2.093 standard error units away from our sample mean ($\overline{X}$). This turn around is the logical basis for being able to use $\overline{X}$ to determine that μ lies within a particular range of likely values — that is, a confidence interval.

The maximum error of the estimate (E_{max}) is computed by following these steps:

Step 1: Calculate the standard error (σ_E) or estimate the standard error (s_E) using the standard deviation of the scores in the research sample:

$$\sigma_E = \frac{\sigma}{\sqrt{n}}$$
where σ = population standard deviation

OR

$$\text{estimated } \sigma_E = s_E = \frac{s}{\sqrt{n}}$$
where s = sample standard deviation

Step 2: Select a Confidence Level (CL)—typically .95 (95%) or .99 (99%)

Step 3: Using the appropriate table in Appendix B, find the two-tailed value of $z_{critical}$ or $t_{critical}$ with $\alpha = 1 - CL$ (i.e., typically, $\alpha = .05$ or .01)

NOTE: We use z when the standard deviation of the population (σ) is known and when n is 25 or more. We use t when σ is unknown or when n is less than 25. The degrees of freedom for $t_{critical}$ are equal to:

$$df = n - 1$$

Step 4: Compute the maximum error of the estimate:

$$E_{max} = t_{critical} (s_E) \quad \text{or} \quad E_{max} = z_{critical} (\sigma_E)$$

Numerical Example of the Maximum Error of the Estimate   To illustrate this procedure, let's suppose that Table 14.1 presents the results of a study where thirty 2-year-olds were observed for a week and the number of tantrums they threw was recorded. The mean of this sample ($\overline{X}$) is 14 tantrums, so our best estimate of the population mean (μ) is also 14. Now we need to determine our margin of error (E_{max}). First we need to compute the standard deviation for the sample (s) so we can use it to compute an estimate of the standard error (s_E) (Step 1 above). When we calculate s, using the formula on page 99, we find that the standard deviation for our sample of thirty 2-year-olds is equal to 8.416. Now we are ready to compute E_{max}:

Step 1: Calculate (or estimate) the standard error:

In our hypothetical study of tantrums, the standard deviation of the population (σ) of two-year-olds is unknown, so we'll be using the t-statistic and need to

TABLE 14.1		The Number of Tantrums Thrown in a Week from a Hypothetical Sample of Thirty 2-Year-Olds			
Child	Tantrums	Child	Tantrums	Child	Tantrums
a	20	k	2	u	15
b	24	l	22	v	0
c	0	m	9	w	17
d	8	n	29	x	17
e	5	o	16	y	26
f	2	p	13	z	25
g	22	q	21	aa	17
h	10	r	22	bb	16
i	19	s	1	cc	11
j	6	t	17	dd	8

compute an estimate of the standard error:

$$\text{estimated } \sigma_E = s_E = \frac{s}{\sqrt{n}} = \frac{8.416}{\sqrt{30}}$$

$$\text{estimated } \sigma_E = s_E = \frac{8.416}{5.4772256}$$

$$= 1.5365443$$

Steps 2 and 3: Select a confidence level and look up $t_{critical}$ for a two-tailed test:

If we select a 95% confidence level, we look up $t_{critical}$ for a two-tailed test with alpha equal to .05 (or 5%) in Table B-10 in Appendix B. The degrees of freedom for $t_{critical}$ are equal to 29 (because df $= n - 1$) and, therefore:

Let CL $= 95\%$ (so $\alpha = .05$)

Therefore: $t_{critical} = 2.045$

Step 4: Compute the maximum error of the estimate

$$E_{max} = t_{critical} (s_E)$$
$$= 2.045 (1.5365443)$$
$$= 3.142233$$
$$\approx 3.1$$

This statistic (E_{max}) tells us that we can be 95% certain that the difference between our sample mean and the population mean (i.e., $\overline{X} - \mu$) is no more than 3.1. That is, our best estimate of μ is no more than 3.1 points "off."

Confidence Interval: The Range of Likely Values of the Population Mean

Now we are ready to compute a **confidence interval (CI)** for our estimate of the population mean. As indicated earlier, confidence intervals tell us the highest and lowest likely values of the population parameter, based on our best estimate and our "margin of error:"

CI $=$ best estimate $\pm$ margin of error

More specifically, the confidence interval for the estimate of the mean is equal to:

Confidence Interval of the Mean $= \overline{X} \pm E_{max}$

Therefore, for our study on tantrums, we would compute our confidence interval to be:

Lower value of the CI $= \overline{X} - E_{max}$ Upper value of the CI $= \overline{X} + E_{max}$
$= 14 - 3.1$ $= 14 + 3.1$
$= 10.9$ $= 17.1$

The 95% confidence interval for the mean is 10.9 to 17.1. Thus, we can be 95% certain that the mean number of tantrums thrown per week by 2-year-old children is somewhere between 10.9 and 17.1 (or 14 ± 3.1). In other words, our best estimate of the population average is 14, but it could be "off" by 3.1 points in either direction due to random sampling error.

Reporting and Interpreting Confidence Intervals   When researchers report confidence intervals, they typically choose one of two formats. Confidence intervals may be expressed in the form of the equation "best estimate plus or minus the margin of error" or the upper and lower values of the confidence interval may be reported. In either case, the confidence level is also included. For instance, in our study of tantrum behavior, we could report our results as "$CI_{95\%} = 14 \pm 3.1$" or as "$CI_{95\%} = 10.9$ to 17.1." Of course, our interpretation of the confidence intervals is more important than the format we use for reporting them. Many researchers are likely to interpret this confidence interval by concluding that: "There is a 95% chance that μ lies somewhere between 10.9 and 17.1 tantrums per week." However, Huck and Cormier (1996) point out that the proper interpretation of confidence intervals is subtly different than this. They explain confidence intervals this way:

> After a sample has been extracted from a population and then measured, the confidence interval around the sample's statistic either will or will not "cover" the value of the parameter. Hence, the probability that the parameter lies between the end points of a confidence interval is either 0 or 1. Because of this fact, a confidence interval should never be considered to specify the chances (or probability) that the parameter is "caught" by the interval.
>
> The proper way to interpret a confidence interval is to *imagine* that (1) many, many samples of the same size are extracted from the same population; and (2) a 95 percent confidence interval is constructed separately around the statistic computed from each sample's data set. Some of these intervals would "capture" the parameter—that is, the interval's end points would be such that the parameter would lie within the interval. On the other hand, some of these confidence intervals would *not* capture the parameter. Looked at collectively, it would turn out that 95 percent of these 95 percent confidence intervals contain the parameter. Accordingly, when you see a 95 percent confidence interval, you should consider that the chances are 95 out of 100 that the interval you are looking at is one of those that does, in fact, capture the parameter. Likewise, when you encounter a 99 percent confidence interval, you can say to yourself that the chances are

even higher (99 out of 100) that the interval in front of you is one of the many possible intervals that would have "caught" the parameter. (1996, p. 140)

Thus, according to Huck and Cormier (1996), the proper way to interpret the confidence interval for our hypothetical study of tantrums is to say: "We are 95% certain that the interval from 10.9 to 17.1 includes the population parameter." This conclusion is warranted because 95% of all intervals constructed around random sample statistics will, in fact, "capture" the value of the parameter.

Summary: Steps in Computing the Confidence Interval for the Mean

To summarize, we can estimate the value of the population mean by selecting a random sample and computing a confidence interval for the mean. The steps in this process are:

Step 1: Compute mean ($\overline{X}$) and standard deviation (s) for the sample of scores

Step 2: Identify the appropriate critical statistic: z or t

We use z-scores if σ is known and n is 25 or more. We use t-scores if σ is unknown or if n is less than 25.

Step 3: Compute the standard error (σ_E) or the estimated standard error (s_E)

$$\sigma_E = \frac{\sigma}{\sqrt{n}} \qquad\qquad s_E = \frac{s}{\sqrt{n}}$$

$\qquad\quad$**(used with z-scores)** $\qquad\qquad$ **(used with t-scores)**

Step 4: Select a confidence level ($1 - \alpha$)

Step 5: Look up the two-tailed critical value for the appropriate statistic. Find $z_{critical}$ on the areas under the normal curve table (Table B-1) by looking in the third column for half of α. Find the two-tailed $t_{critical}$ for α using the Student's t-table (Table B-10), with df $= n - 1$.

Step 6: Compute the maximum error of the estimate

$$E_{max} = z_{critical}\,(\sigma_E) \quad \text{or} \quad E_{max} = t_{critical}\,(s_E)$$

Step 7: Find the confidence interval

$$CI = \overline{X} \pm E_{max}$$

Confidence Intervals for Proportions (or Percentages)

Accurately estimating the population mean can be very informative. Equally useful is being able to accurately estimate proportions or percentages. For example, in developing strategic budget plans, and in order to properly allocate resources, educators may need to accurately estimate what percentage of children are dyslexic or learning disabled. If 20% of children are dyslexic, the school board will need to allocate their resources differently than if only 5% of the population are dyslexic. Or a congressman who hopes to be re-elected may need to know what percentage of the voters are opposed to a new legislative proposal. If only 2% of the voters oppose the new law, then the congressman can vote in favor of the proposal without much fear of being unseated in the next election, whereas, if 30% are opposed, the congressman's chances of being re-elected may be substantially reduced if he votes in favor of the proposal.

Just as the mean of a representative sample provides us with an estimate of the population mean, the proportions of a random sample provide us with our best estimates of the population proportions. Furthermore, the variability among random samples can be used to measure the margin of error in our estimates. In other words, we can use a random sample to estimate population proportions or percentages and establish confidence intervals around that estimate. The steps involved in finding the confidence intervals for proportions are essentially the same as the steps involved in finding a confidence interval for the mean, except that the formula for computing the "margin of error" (or the maximum error of the estimate) is based on the distribution of percentages rather than means. The formula for the standard error for a distribution of proportions is:

$$\text{standard error of proportions} = \sqrt{\frac{p(1 - p)}{n}} \quad \textbf{where p = the proportion from the sample data}$$

The first step in finding the confidence interval for a percentage or proportion is to randomly select a sample from the population and find out what proportion of the sample meets the "target criterion" (e.g., being dyslexic or being opposed to the new legislation). This sample proportion (p) provides us with our best estimate of the population proportion. Next we select a confidence level, look up the critical value of z, and compute E_{max}:

$$E_{max} = z_{critical}\sqrt{\frac{p(1 - p)}{n}}$$

Finally, we compute the confidence interval:

$$CI = \text{Best Estimate} \pm E_{max}$$
$$= p \pm E_{max}$$

Numerical Example of Confidence Intervals for Proportions (or Percentages)

To illustrate the procedure for finding confidence intervals for estimates of proportions, let's assume we are interested in the transgenerational transmission of child abuse. Specifically, let's say we are interested in knowing what percentage of physically abused children, later in life, use harsh physical punishment with their own children. Imagine that we had access to court records from twenty-five years ago and could identify children who had been abused by a parent (who was tried and convicted for the crime). If we randomly selected a sample of these victims and tracked them down, we could then measure their disciplinary practices to determine how many of them use harsh forms of physical punishment (which may be defined as hitting children with their fists or with objects such as belts).

Let's pretend that we tracked down a sample of 250 individuals who had been abused by their parents and who now have at least one child under the age of 7. Suppose we interviewed them about their parenting styles, and found that 80 of them responded "yes" to the question: "Have you spanked your child with a belt (or other object) at least once in the past week?" We would compute the proportion (or percentage) of the sample who report using harsh forms of punishment:

$$p = \frac{80}{250}$$

$$p = .32$$

Thus, 32% of our random sample reported spanking their child with a belt or other object sometime within the previous week. The sample proportion (.32) is our best estimate of the population proportion (and would be our point estimate). We would then measure the variability among random samples, calculate a margin of error for our estimate, and establish a confidence interval around our estimate.

First we choose a confidence level (CL), which is typically 95% or 99%, and then look up the two-tailed z-score for the alpha level associated with our confidence level (for a 95% CL, two-tailed $\alpha = .025$; for a 99% CL, two-tailed $\alpha = .005$):

For 95% confidence interval, the two-tailed $z_{\text{critical}} = \pm 1.96$

Next we compute the maximum error of the estimate (E_{max}):

$$E_{\text{max}} = z_{\text{critical}} \sqrt{\frac{p(1-p)}{n}} \qquad \textbf{where p = the proportion from the sample data}$$

$$E_{\text{max}} = \pm 1.96 \sqrt{\frac{.32(1-.32)}{250}}$$

$$E_{\text{max}} = \pm 1.96 \sqrt{\frac{.32(.68)}{250}}$$

$$E_{\text{max}} = \pm 1.96 \sqrt{\frac{.2176}{250}}$$

$$E_{\text{max}} = \pm 1.96 \sqrt{.0008704}$$

$$E_{\text{max}} = \pm 1.96 \,(.0295025)$$

$$E_{\text{max}} = \pm .057825$$

$$E_{\text{max}} \approx \pm .058$$

This tells us that our sample percentage is probably within 5.8% of the actual population percentage. Finally, we find the confidence interval for the estimated proportion (or percentage):

$$CI = p \pm E_{max}$$

Lower CI $= .32 - .058$ Upper CI $= .32 + .058$

$\approx .262$ (or 26.2%) $\approx .378$ (or 37.8%)

Thus, we could be 95% certain that the percentage of abused children who will grow up to use harsh forms of punishment with their own children is somewhere between 26.2% and 37.8% (i.e., 32% $\pm$ 5.8%).

Limitations of Confidence Intervals for Proportions (or Percentages)

The procedure above assumes that the sampling distribution of sample proportions from random samples is normally distributed (and hence the formula for E_{max} uses $z_{critical}$ in the computation of the margin of error). This assumption cannot be made if the number of participants involved in the sample proportion is less than 5 or if the number of participants not included in the sample proportion is less than 5. For instance, in our previous example, the sample proportion included the abused children who grew up to use harsh forms of punishment with their own children. Abused children who do *not* use harsh punishment on their children are not in the sample proportion. In order to use this confidence interval procedure, we must have at least 5 people in each of these categories. Therefore, the rule is we cannot use this confidence interval procedure if:

$$(n)(p) < 5 \quad \text{or} \quad n(1 - p) < 5$$

For example, suppose we surveyed 75 adults and found that 5% of them claim they were abducted by aliens. Can we establish confidence intervals for this percentage using the formula above? Let's check:

The rule is: If $(n)(p) < 5$, we cannot assume a normal distribution

Since $(75)(.05) = 3.75$, we have to assume that the z-distribution is not appropriate so we cannot establish confidence intervals for this percentage.

However, if we had surveyed 150 people and found that 5% of them claim they were abducted by aliens, we could establish confidence intervals using the z-distribution, because:

$(150)(.05) = 7.5$, which is greater than 5, so we can assume a normal distribution

Therefore, we could legitimately use the formula above to calculate E_{max} and then construct a confidence interval for the proportion of people who claim to have been abducted by aliens:

$$E_{max} = z_{critical}\sqrt{\frac{p(1-p)}{n}}$$

where p = the proportion from the sample data

$$E_{max} = \pm 1.96\sqrt{\frac{.05(1-.05)}{150}}$$

$$E_{max} = \pm 1.96\sqrt{\frac{.05(.95)}{150}}$$

$$E_{max} = \pm 1.96\sqrt{\frac{.0475}{150}}$$

$$E_{max} = \pm 1.96\sqrt{.0003166}$$

$$E_{max} = \pm 1.96(.0177932)$$

$$E_{max} = \pm .0348746$$

$$E_{max} = \pm .035$$

Therefore, the confidence interval for the estimated proportion (or percentage) is:

$$CI = p \pm E_{max}$$

Lower CI = .05 − .035   Upper CI = .05 + .035

$\approx$ .015   (or 1.5%) $\approx$ .085   (or 8.5%)

We would be 95% certain that the percentage of people (in the population) who claim they were abducted by aliens is somewhere between 1.5% and 8.5%.

Confidence Intervals for Pearson Correlations

The Pearson correlation coefficient (r) for a random sample of data can be used as our best (point) estimate of the population correlation (ρ) and a confidence interval can be established. If the population correlation coefficient is equal to zero, the sampling distribution of sample coefficients (r) will be normal. But as the magnitude of the population correlation (ρ) increases, the sampling distribution will be more and more skewed (as illustrated in Figure 14-3). Consequently, because the population correlation may not be equal to zero, we cannot simply presume that the distribution of sample correlations is normal. We can, however, transform sample correlations into z scores using the r-to-z transformation table (on Table B-4 in Appendix B). (When we look up a z-score for a correlation coefficient on this table, the z-score is referred to as z^*.) The values of z^* form a normal distribution, so we can use $z_{critical}$ to

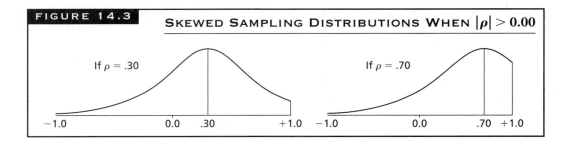

FIGURE 14.3 SKEWED SAMPLING DISTRIBUTIONS WHEN $|\rho| > 0.00$

If $\rho = .30$

If $\rho = .70$

compute the confidence interval for z^*, and after we do so, we can convert z^* back into values of r, which gives us the confidence interval for the correlation coefficient. The formulas for the standard error, the maximum error of the estimate, and the confidence intervals are:

$$\text{standard error of } r = \sigma_E = \sqrt{\frac{1}{n-3}}$$

$$E_{max} = z_{critical}(\sigma_E)$$

$$CI_z = z^* \pm E_{max}$$

Three steps in the computation can be combined into a single step if the formula for the confidence interval is re-written, substituting the formulas for σ_E and E_{max}:

$$CI_z = z^* \pm z_{critical}\sqrt{\frac{1}{n-3}}$$

Therefore, the steps involved in finding confidence intervals for the Pearson r are as follows:

Step 1: Calculate the correlation coefficient (r) for a random sample of participants.

Step 2: Convert the sample r to a value of z^*, using the r-to-z transformation table (on Table B-4 in Appendix B).

Step 3: Select a confidence level $(1 - \alpha)$.

Step 4: Find $z_{critical}$ for a two-tailed test. For the standard confidence levels of 95% or 99%, where α is set at .05 or .01, the values of $z_{critical}$ are ± 1.96 and ± 2.58, respectively. For any other confidence level, we find the appropriate two-tailed value of $z_{critical}$ on the areas under the normal curve table (on Table B-1 in Appendix B) by looking in the third column for half of α (that is, $\alpha/2$).

Step 5:   Compute the confidence interval for z^*:

$$\text{CI}_z = z^* \pm z_{\text{critical}}\sqrt{\frac{1}{n-3}}$$

Step 6:   Convert the upper CI_z limit and the lower CI_z limit to values of r, using the r-to-z transformation table (on Table B-4 in Appendix B). If your exact value of z^* is not on the table, use the value that is *closest*.

Numerical Example of Confidence Intervals for the Pearson Correlation

To illustrate the steps involved in finding the confidence interval for a Pearson r, let's assume that we are interested in the relationship between parents' use of corporal punishment (spanking) and their children's aggressiveness with their peers. Suppose we randomly selected thirty 7-year-old children to participate in our study and we observed the children for a week. During home observations, we recorded the number of times the child was spanked, and at school, we counted the number of times the child behaved aggressively toward others during recess. Let's assume that the Pearson correlation for this sample was equal to $+.40$ (indicating that children who are spanked more often tend to behave aggressively more often). Our best point estimate, then, would be that the population correlation (ρ) is equal to $+.40$. Now, let's establish the confidence interval for this estimate:

Step 1:   Calculate the correlation coefficient (r) for a random sample of participants.

For this example, n = 30   and $r = +.40$

Step 2:   Convert the sample r to a value of z^*, using the r-to-z transformation table (on Table B-4 in the Appendix)

For $r = +.40$, $z^* = .4236$

Step 3:   Select a confidence level $(1 - \alpha)$

Let's use the 95% confidence level. Therefore, $\alpha = .05$

Step 4:   Look up the two-tailed critical value of z_{critical}

$z_{\text{critical}} = \pm 1.96$

Step 5:   Compute the confidence interval for z^*

$$CI_z = z^* \pm z_{critical}\sqrt{\frac{1}{n-3}}$$

$$CI_z = .4236 \pm 1.96\sqrt{\frac{1}{30-3}}$$

$$CI_z = .4236 \pm 1.96\sqrt{\frac{1}{27}}$$

$$CI_z = .4236 \pm 1.96\sqrt{.037037}$$

$$CI_z = .4236 \pm 1.96\,(.1924499)$$

$$CI_z = .4236 \pm .3772018$$

Therefore:

Lower $CI_z = .4236 - .3772018$	Upper $CI_z = .4236 + .3772018$
$= .0463982$	$= .8008018$
$\approx .0464$	$\approx .8008$

Step 6:   Convert the upper CI_z limit and the lower CI_z limit (which are values of z^*) into values of r, using the r-to-z transformation table (on Table B-4 in Appendix B):

Lower $CI_z = .0464$, therefore, the closest value of $r = .05$

Upper $CI_z = .8008$, therefore, the closest value of $r = .66$

Therefore, we can be 95% certain the population correlation (ρ) between being spanked and behaving aggressively is somewhere between .05 and .66.

This example illustrates two things. First, notice that the sample correlation coefficient ($r = +.40$) is not in the center of the confidence interval. This is due to the skew in a sampling distribution where the ρ does not equal zero. Second, you may notice that the confidence interval is quite wide, indicating that our point estimate of ρ may be very imprecise (and therefore, may be very inaccurate). With such a wide range of possible values of ρ, what conclusions would we be able to draw about the relationship between being spanked and being aggressive? If ρ equals .05, we would probably conclude that the relationship between the variables is so negligible that it can be safely ignored. In contrast, if the correlation is really equal to .66, we may want to launch a public service campaign designed to convince parents to stop using corporal punishment in hopes that children's aggressiveness may also decline.[2]

This wide confidence interval is a "symptom" of the small sample size used in the study. For correlation coefficients, the variability among small samples is substantial, and that is why statisticians typically recommend that researchers include a minimum of 75 participants in a correlational study. If our example had been based on 75 participants, the 95% confidence interval would be +.19 to +.57, and if we had 100 participants, the 95% CI would be +.22 to +.55. Generally, as sample size increases, the confidence intervals become narrower and our estimate of the likely values of ρ becomes more precise. However, even very large sample sizes do not have very narrow confidence intervals for correlations. For example, if our study on spanking and aggression had included 200 participants, the 95% confidence interval would still be +.28 to +.51.

Minimum Differences Between Treatment Means

When the results of an experiment lead researchers to reject the null hypothesis, they are able to conclude that there is a significant difference between the treatment groups. As we suggested at the beginning of this chapter, the next logical step may be to ask just how much difference exists between the groups. For example, studies may indicate that infant boys are significantly more active than infant girls. When we hear these results, should we get a mental picture of infant boys in perpetual motion while infant girls are still and motionless? Or is the difference between boys and girls actually relatively small, so that, despite the statistical difference, they are more alike than they are different? In order to get a sense of the magnitude of differences between groups, we can use point estimation and confidence intervals for **differences between means** $(\mu_1 - \mu_2)$.

Specifically, we can use the difference between the means of our two samples $(\overline{X}_1 - \overline{X}_2)$ as our best point estimate of the difference between the population means, and we can establish a confidence interval around this estimate. To find this confidence interval, we will use an estimate of the standard error of the sampling distribution (s_E or $s_{\overline{X} - \overline{X}}$) and $t_{critical}$ to compute our margin of error or the maximum error of the estimate. The sampling distribution that is relevant here is the distribution of differences between means, which is known as the *empirical sampling distribution*. It is constructed by drawing all possible pairs of samples and calculating the difference between the means $(\overline{X}_1 - \overline{X}_2)$ for each pair.

If the null hypothesis is true, the mean of the empirical sampling distribution will equal 0.0, and 95% of all pairs of random samples will have confidence intervals that cover, or include, the difference score of 0.0. Therefore, if 0.0 does *not* fall

---

[2]This public service campaign would be based on the assumption that being spanked causes children to adopt aggressive behaviors when interacting with others. The study, of course, does not provide any evidence for this causal conclusion. However, public policy is often based on the possibility that a causal link exists between two correlated variables.

within the confidence interval, we can be at least 95% certain that there is a differ-ence between the population means of the treatment groups, and we can use the CI limit with the lower absolute value as our estimate of the *smallest* likely difference be-tween them. That is, if the CI tells us that the difference between the population means ($\mu_1 - \mu_2$) is somewhere between the lower and upper limits of the CI, then it also tells us that the difference between the population means is unlikely to be less than the smaller of these values. Hence the smaller CI limit can be interpreted as the **minimum difference**. For example, if the 95% CI is 3 to 8, then the minimum dif-ference is 3 (indicating that μ_1 is likely to be at least 3 points *higher than* μ_2); and if the 95% CI is -2 to -10, then the minimum difference is 2 (indicating that μ_1 is likely to be at least 2 points *less than* μ_2).

Let's illustrate these procedures with some concrete problems. First we will show how to find the minimum difference for a between-subjects design with two groups and then we will show how to find the minimum difference for a related-samples design with two groups. (Related-samples designs include within-subjects and matched-pairs designs). As you may recall from Chapters 11 and 12 or Appendix C, between-subjects and related-samples designs have different measures of error vari-ance, so the formulas for the standard error of the empirical sampling distribution and the margin of error are not the same.

Minimum Differences in Two-Group Between-Subjects Designs

To find the confidence interval for the difference between means in a between-subjects design, we start by computing the means and standard deviations for the research samples. Next we use the sample data to estimate the standard error of the sampling dis-tribution ($s_{\overline{X} - \overline{X}}$), just as we did for independent-samples *t*-tests (which were presented in Chapter 11.) The estimate of the standard error is used to compute the margin of error (E_{max}), which, in turn, is used to calculate the upper and lower limits of the confidence interval. Finally, once we have the confidence interval, we will be able to estimate the smallest difference between the means that is likely to occur due solely to chance.

After we have the means and standard deviations for our groups, we follow these steps:

Step 1:   Select a confidence level (and its associated level of α)

Step 2:   Compute the degrees of freedom and look up $t_{critical}$ for a two-tailed test:

$$df = (n_1 - 1) + (n_2 - 1)$$

Step 3:   Compute an estimate of the standard error ($s_{\overline{X} - \overline{X}}$):

a.   First, calculate the pooled variance (s^2_{pooled}) for the two samples:

$$s^2_{pooled} = \frac{(n_1 - 1)s^2_1 + (n_2 - 1)s^2_2}{(n_1 - 1) + (n_2 - 1)}$$

b. Then estimate the standard error (estimated σ_E) using the pooled variance:

$$s_{\overline{X} - \overline{X}} = \text{estimated } \sigma_E = \sqrt{\frac{s^2_{pooled}}{n_1} + \frac{s^2_{pooled}}{n_2}}$$

Step 4: Compute the maximum error of the estimate (E_{max})

$$E_{max} = t_{critical}\,(s_{\overline{X} - \overline{X}})$$

Step 5: Find the confidence interval

$$CI = (\overline{X}_1 - \overline{X}_2) \pm E_{max}$$

Step 6: Find the minimum difference:

Ask the question: "Does 0.0 lie within the confidence interval?"

If *yes*, zero falls within the confidence interval, we must conclude that the two population means may not be different from each other (and that the minimum difference between them may be 0.0).

If *no*, zero falls outside the confidence interval, we can be at least 95% certain that the two population means are different from each other, and that the smallest likely difference (i.e., the minimum difference) between them is equal to the CI limit with the smaller absolute value.

Numerical Example of the Minimum Difference for a Between-Subjects Design   Let's assume that we observed 22 newborn boys and 20 newborn girls, and measured their activity level by recording the number of times their movements trigger a motion sensor mounted above their cribs during a 15-minute period when they are awake and not crying. Suppose we found that the mean number of movements for the boys was 570 (with a standard deviation of 50), while the mean for the girls was 510 (with a standard deviation of 56).[3]

Step 1: Select a confidence level (and its associated level of α):

Let's use the 95% confidence level (so $\alpha = .05$)

Step 2: Compute the degrees of freedom and look up $t_{critical}$ for a two-tailed test:

---

[3]On average, infants produce 2000 movements per hour when they are awake and alert and up to 12,000 movements per hour when they are crying (Rosenblith, 1992).

$$df = (n_1 - 1) + (n_2 - 1)$$
$$= (22 - 1) + (20 - 1)$$
$$= 21 + 19$$
$$= 40$$

Therefore: for a two-tailed test with $\alpha = .05$

$$t_{critical} = 2.021$$

Step 3: Compute an estimate of the standard error $(s_{\overline{X}-\overline{X}})$:

a. Calculate the pooled variance (s^2_{pooled}) for the two samples:

$$s^2_{pooled} = \frac{(n_1 - 1)s^2_1 + (n_2 - 1)s^2_2}{(n_1 - 1) + (n_2 - 1)}$$

$$s^2_{pooled} = \frac{(22 - 1)(50)^2 + (20 - 1)(56)^2}{(22 - 1) + (20 - 1)}$$

$$s^2_{pooled} = \frac{21\,(2500) + 19\,(3136)}{21 + 19}$$

$$s^2_{pooled} = \frac{52500 + 59584}{40}$$

$$s^2_{pooled} = \frac{112084}{40}$$

$$s^2_{pooled} = 2802.1$$

b. Estimate the standard error (estimated σ_E) using the pooled variance:

$$s_{\overline{X}-\overline{X}} = \text{estimated } \sigma_E = \sqrt{\frac{s^2_{pooled}}{n_1} + \frac{s^2_{pooled}}{n_2}}$$

$$s_{\overline{X}-\overline{X}} = \sqrt{\frac{2802.1}{22} + \frac{2802.1}{20}}$$

$$s_{\overline{X}-\overline{X}} = \sqrt{127.36818 + 140.105}$$

$$s_{\overline{X}-\overline{X}} = \sqrt{267.47318}$$

$$s_{\overline{X}-\overline{X}} = 16.354607$$

Step 4:   Compute the maximum error of the estimate (E_{max}):

$$E_{max} = t_{critical} (s_{\overline{X} - \overline{X}})$$
$$= 2.021 \, (16.354607)$$
$$= 33.05266$$
$$\approx 33.1$$

Step 5:   Find the confidence interval:

$$CI = (\overline{X}_1 - \overline{X}_2) \pm E_{max}$$

Lower Limit   Upper Limit

$$\text{of CI} = (\overline{X}_1 - \overline{X}_2) - E_{max} \qquad\qquad \text{of CI} = (\overline{X}_1 - \overline{X}_2) + E_{max}$$
$$= (570 - 510) - 33.1 \qquad\qquad\qquad = (570 - 510) + 33.1$$
$$= 60 - 33.1 \qquad\qquad\qquad\qquad\quad = 60 + 33.1$$
$$= 26.9 \qquad\qquad\qquad\qquad\qquad\quad = 93.1$$

Therefore, we can be 95% certain that the difference in activity level between newborn boys and girls is somewhere between 26.9 and 93.1 movements per quarter-hour.

Step 6:   Find the minimum difference: Ask "Does 0.0 lie within the confidence interval?"

No. The confidence interval indicates that there is a 95% chance that the difference between the population means is *not* less than 26.9; therefore, we can be 95% certain that the minimum difference between the means is 26.9 movements per quarter-hour.

Interpreting the Minimum Difference Between Means   A *t*-test analysis of these hypothetical data indicates the difference between infant boys and girls is highly significant [t (df = 40) = 3.669, $p < .001$]. The confidence interval analysis confirms the conclusion that there is a difference in activity level between boys and girls. However, the minimum difference indicated by the confidence interval is only 26.9 movements. This is not a particularly large difference when we consider the facts that: (1) both boys and girls move around a lot (as indicated by the fact that the average number of movements is 510 for girls and 570 for boys), and (2) there is a lot of random variability among individual babies (as indicated by the fact that the standard deviations for the groups are 56 and 50).

Seen in the context of the means and standard deviations, the minimum difference of about 27 points between the group means, although statistically significant, should not be interpreted to mean that there are substantial differences in performance between the groups. The difference may, in fact, have little practical

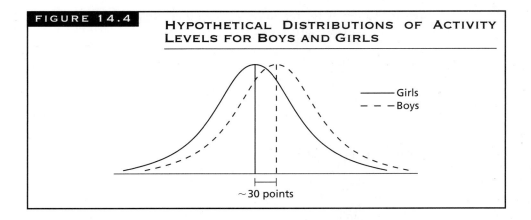

FIGURE 14.4

HYPOTHETICAL DISTRIBUTIONS OF ACTIVITY LEVELS FOR BOYS AND GIRLS

—— Girls
– – – Boys

~30 points

significance. Imagine, for instance, that you are simply watching babies (without special recording devices), and you see the babies move over 500 times during a 15-minute period. You may only notice that babies move a lot and that some babies move a lot more often than others—you probably will not notice those 27 additional movements made by baby boys compared to baby girls. (Figure 14-4 illustrates this situation, where the null hypothesis is false and the two populations have different means, but where the actual difference between the populations is relatively small so that many baby girls are actually more active than many baby boys.)

Minimum Differences in Two-Treatment Related-Samples Designs

If a researcher uses a within-subjects design or a matched-pairs design, the treatment means will be related to each other (rather than independent) and the analysis focuses on the change (or difference) in scores across the treatments. For example, in the related-samples *t*-test which we presented in Chapter 11, the first steps were to calculate a difference score (D) for each participant (or each matched pair), and then average these difference scores together ($\overline{D}$). Therefore, the relevant sampling distribution would be the distribution of the average difference scores ($\overline{D}$). The standard error of this distribution is estimated using the following formula:

$$\text{estimated standard error} = s_{\overline{D}} = \frac{s_D}{\sqrt{n}}$$

where: s_D = standard deviation of
difference scores for
individual participants
or matched pairs

n = the number of participants
(or pairs of scores)

This standard error is used to calculate the margin of error (E_{max}) for our confidence interval, from which we determine the minimum difference:

$$E_{max} = t_{critical}(s_{\overline{D}})$$

And: Confidence Interval (CI) $= \overline{D} \pm E_{max}$

And then: If 0.0 does not lie within the CI, the CI limit with the *smallest absolute value* can be interpreted as the minimum difference between the means

To summarize, the specific steps involved in this analysis are:

Step 1:   Calculate the difference score for each participant (D).

Step 2:   Compute the mean of the difference scores ($\overline{D}$).

Step 3:   Compute the standard deviation of the difference scores (s_D).

Step 4:   Calculate the estimated standard error of the sampling distribution ($s_{\overline{D}}$).

Step 5:   Choose a confidence level and its associated α.

Step 6:   Find the degrees of freedom: df $=$ n $-$ 1

Step 7:   Look up the two-tailed $t_{critical}$ for your selected value of α.

Step 8:   Compute the maximum error of the estimate (E_{max}).

Step 9:   Compute the lower and upper limits of the confidence interval.

Step 10:   Ask: "Does 0.0 lie within the confidence interval?" If 0.0 lies within the CI, then conclude that the means may not differ from each other. If 0.0 does not lie within the CI, then the CI limit with the smaller absolute value is the minimum difference between the means.

Numerical Example of the Minimum Difference for a Related-Samples Design
Let's suppose that a researcher wanted to determine which type of building fund male alumni are more willing to support, so he *matched* pairs of male alumni on the basis of their professions, graduation date, and the amount of their contribution to the university the previous year and then sent each of them a brochure describing the university's new fund-raising campaign and asking them to consider increasing their donation for the year. Each brochure listed four long-range goals (or building projects) for the campaign, but the project listed first was either a new theatre or a new gymnasium. The brochures were identical in all other respects, and one member of each matched pair received a "theatre first" brochure and the other member of the pair received the "gymnasium first" brochure. The researcher then recorded how

much money (in dollars) each participant donated to the campaign and the hypothetical data are as follows:[4]

Pair	Theatre	Gymnasium
a	77	86
b	57	62
c	32	50
d	28	40
e	68	73
f	29	40
g	39	73
h	40	56
i	75	64
j	47	50

The first three steps in finding the minimum difference are to calculate the difference scores (D) for each matched-pair and find the mean and standard deviation for these difference scores:

Pair	Theatre	Gymnasium	Difference (D)	D^2
a	77	86	-9	81
b	57	62	-5	25
c	32	50	-18	324
d	28	40	-12	144
e	68	73	-5	25
f	29	40	-11	121
g	39	73	-34	1156
h	40	56	-16	256
i	75	64	$+11$	121
j	47	50	-3	9
			$\Sigma D = -102$	$\Sigma D^2 = 2262$

Step 1:   Refer to the Difference column in the preceding table.

Step 2:   The mean of the difference scores $(\overline{D})$ is equal to:

$$\overline{D} = \frac{-102}{10} = -10.2$$

Step 3:   The standard deviation of the difference scores (s_D) is equal to:

$$s_D = \sqrt{\frac{2262 - \dfrac{-102^2}{10}}{10 - 1}}$$

---

[4]For ethical reasons, of course, all of the money received from the alumni must be used just as described in the brochure.

$$s_D = \sqrt{\dfrac{2262 - \dfrac{10404}{10}}{9}}$$

$$s_D = \sqrt{\dfrac{2262 - 1040.4}{9}}$$

$$s_D = \sqrt{\dfrac{1221.6}{9}}$$

$$s_D = \sqrt{135.73333}$$

$$s_D = 11.650465$$

Next, we find the confidence interval by computing an estimate of the standard error of the difference scores, calculating the maximum error of the estimate (E_{max}), and looking up the appropriate value of $t_{critical}$:

Step 4: The estimated standard error ($s_{\overline{D}}$) is equal to:

$$s_{\overline{D}} = \dfrac{s_D}{\sqrt{n}}$$

$$s_{\overline{D}} = \dfrac{11.650465}{\sqrt{10}}$$

$$s_{\overline{D}} = \dfrac{11.650465}{3.1622776}$$

$$s_{\overline{D}} = 3.6842005$$

Steps 5–7: Select a confidence level and look up the two-tailed $t_{critical}$:

Step 5: Let's use the 95% confidence level, so $\alpha = .05$

Step 6: The degrees of freedom are equal to:

$$df = n - 1 \qquad \textbf{where n = the number of}$$
$$= 10 - 1 \qquad \textbf{participants or the number}$$
$$= 9 \qquad \textbf{of matched pairs}$$

Step 7: Therefore, the two-tailed $t_{critical}$ (with df = 9 and $\alpha = .05$) is equal to:

$$t_{critical} = 2.262$$

Step 8: Calculate the maximum error of the estimate (E_{max}):

$$E_{max} = t_{critical}\,(s_{\overline{D}})$$
$$= 2.262\,(3.6842005)$$
$$= 8.3336615$$
$$\approx 8.33$$

Step 9:   Find the confidence interval:

$$CI = \overline{D} \pm E_{max}$$
$$= -10.2 \pm 8.33$$

Lower Limit $= -10.2 - 8.33$ Upper Limit $= -10.2 + 8.33$

$= -18.53$ $= -1.87$

The average difference score ($\overline{D}$) and the confidence limits are negative, indicating that the donations in the Theatre First condition were less than the donations in the Gymnasium First condition, but the theatre scores were arbitrarily presented in the first column of data. Because the negative signs reflect nothing more than an arbitrary arrangement of the scores into the data columns, the confidence levels are interpreted in terms of absolute values. Therefore, this confidence interval tells us that we can be 95% certain that the average difference in donations between men who see a theatre listed first and men who see a gymnasium listed first is somewhere between $1.87 and $18.53. This confidence interval could be diagrammed as follows:

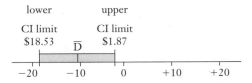

Step 10:   Identify the minimum difference by asking if 0.0 lies within the confidence interval. If 0.0 is within the CI, then conclude that the means may not differ from each other. If 0.0 is not within the CI, then the CI limit with the smaller absolute value is the minimum difference between the means:

Conclusion: 0.0 is not between -1.87 and -18.53, therefore, the minimum difference in donations is 1.87. That is, we can be 95% certain that the average donation from men who see a gymnasium listed first is at least $1.87 more than the average donation from men who see a theatre listed first.

Once again, an analysis using a confidence interval leads us to conclude that there is most likely some difference between the two population means (where men who see a gymnasium at the top of the list donate more than men who see a theatre at the top of the list), but the minimum difference (of $1.87) is quite small. However, from a fund-raiser's point of view, an extra $1.87 per donor might have "practical significance."

Confidence Intervals Versus Significance Testing

A typical experiment is designed to test a research hypothesis (H_1) that says manipulating the independent variable will produce a systematic difference in the dependent variable. For example, a social psychology experiment may test the hypothesis that the presence of others causes a delay in helping responses during a potential emergency. Let's imagine that the psychologist staged an "emergency" in which smoke began to seep from under the door of a locked room, and recorded the time it took for a bystander to pull the fire alarm. Suppose the participants had been randomly assigned to one of three levels of the independent variable: (1) alone when the emergency starts; (2) with one research confederate (who reacts to the smoke with only mild concern); or (3) with five confederates (all of whom show only mild curiosity about the smoke and its dangers). Based on a social psychology theory known as "diffusion of responsibility," the research hypothesis of this experiment would be that participants would be slower to pull the fire alarm when other people are present than when they are alone, and that the more people present, the slower they will be to respond. Thus, the research hypothesis predicts that the mean response times will follow a specific pattern of significant differences, while the null hypothesis says that, in the population, the presence of others has no systematic effects on behavior, so there will be no difference among the three treatment conditions:

$$H_1: \mu_{\text{Alone}} < \mu_{\text{One Other}} < \mu_{\text{Five Others}}$$

$$H_0: \mu_{\text{Alone}} = \mu_{\text{One Other}} = \mu_{\text{Five Others}}$$

Most researchers would test this null hypothesis by entering the data into a one-way analysis of variance (ANOVA) and performing appropriate post hoc comparisons if the null hypothesis is rejected (see Chapter 12). If the null hypothesis is rejected with alpha set at .05, we can be 95% certain that the difference between the treatment means is not due to random sampling error. If the null hypothesis is not rejected, we have to conclude the difference between the treatment means could be due solely to chance fluctuations or random sampling error. Confidence intervals provide an increasingly popular alternative to this traditional null hypothesis significance testing approach.

Earlier in this chapter we saw that we can use the mean from a sample ($\overline{X}$) as an estimate of the population mean (μ) and then compute a confidence interval for our estimate which tells us the range of likely values of μ. In our hypothetical experiment, we have three sample $\overline{X}$s (one for each of our treatment conditions) and we could compute confidence intervals for each of these means separately. For example, we could use the first treatment mean as an estimate of the mean for the population of individuals who are alone when an emergency arises and we could use the second treatment mean as an estimate of the mean for the population of individuals who are with one other person when an emergency arises, and so on.

The research hypothesis (H_1) states that our treatment groups are, in fact, from three separate populations, while the null hypothesis (H_0) states that the three sample means are from a single population (or three populations with equal means) because the independent variable has no effect on the dependent variable. We can choose between these two possibilities by comparing the confidence intervals which estimate the population means for the separate treatment conditions. *If the confidence intervals for treatment means do not overlap with each other, we can be quite certain the treatment groups come from populations with different means.* For example, if the

95% confidence interval for one treatment group is 23 to 29 (26 ± 3) and the 95% CI for another treatment condition is 32 to 40 (36 ± 4), we could be 95% certain that the treatments come from different populations, because the mean of the first population (μ) is unlikely to be greater than 29 while the mean of the second population (μ) is unlikely to be less than 32. If the confidence intervals *do* overlap, however, we cannot reasonably conclude that the samples come from separate populations. For example, if the 95% confidence interval for one treatment group is 23 to 29 (26 ± 3) and the 95% CI for another treatment condition is 27 to 35 (31 ± 4), there is a reasonable possibility that both sample means (26 and 31) come from a population where μ is some value between 27 and 29. Two examples of using confidence intervals in place of traditional null-hypothesis-significance-testing—one for CIs that do not overlap and one for CIs that do overlap—are presented below.

Numerical Example of Confidence Intervals That Do Not Overlap

Let's imagine that we conducted the "diffusion of responsibility" experiment described above and recorded the time (in seconds) it took the participants to pull the fire alarm after the smoke began to seep from under the locked door. The hypothetical data is presented in Table 14-2.

The first step is to find confidence intervals for each sample mean, using the procedure summarized on page 447. Table 14-3 presents these computations.

If we compare these three confidence intervals, we see that there is no overlap among them. We see that the population mean for the "Alone" condition (μ_{Alone}) is unlikely to be higher than 49.2, while the population mean for the "One

TABLE 14.2	Hypothetical Data Set #1 from the Diffusion of Responsibility Experiment: Nonoverlapping CIs (Scores = number of seconds to pull fire alarm)		

Alone	One Other	Five Others
30	88	112
59	81	96
30	100	95
35	78	121
46	79	83
37	61	96
51	88	91
47	77	118
51	68	79
34	85	117
$\overline{X} = 42.0$	$\overline{X} = 80.5$	$\overline{X} = 100.8$
$s = 10.1$	$s = 10.91$	$s = 15.13$
$n = 10$	$n = 10$	$n = 10$

TABLE 14.3	Computing the 95% Confidence Intervals for Each Treatment Group		

Alone	One Other	Five Others
$s_E = \dfrac{s}{\sqrt{n}}$	$s_E = \dfrac{s}{\sqrt{n}}$	$s_E = \dfrac{s}{\sqrt{n}}$
$s_E = \dfrac{10.1}{\sqrt{10}}$	$s_E = \dfrac{10.91}{\sqrt{10}}$	$s_E = \dfrac{15.13}{\sqrt{10}}$
$s_E = \dfrac{10.1}{3.1622776}$	$s_E = \dfrac{10.91}{3.1622776}$	$s_E = \dfrac{15.13}{3.1622776}$
$s_E = 3.1939004$	$s_E = 3.4500449$	$s_E = 4.7845261$
For CL = 95%, $\alpha = .05$	For CL = 95%, $\alpha = .05$	For CL = 95%, $\alpha = .05$
df = $n - 1 = 10 - 1 = 9$	df = $n - 1 = 10 - 1 = 9$	df = $n - 1 = 10 - 1 = 9$
therefore, $t_{critical} = 2.262$	therefore, $t_{critical} = 2.262$	therefore, $t_{critical} = 2.262$
$E_{max} = t_{critical}\,(s_E)$	$E_{max} = t_{critical}\,(s_E)$	$E_{max} = t_{critical}\,(s_E)$
$E_{max} = 2.262\,(3.1939004)$	$E_{max} = 2.262\,(3.4500449)$	$E_{max} = 2.262\,(4.7845261)$
$E_{max} = 7.2246027$	$E_{max} = 7.8040016$	$E_{max} = 10.822598$
$E_{max} \approx 7.2$	$E_{max} \approx 7.8$	$E_{max} \approx 10.8$
$CI = \overline{X} \pm E_{max}$	$CI = \overline{X} \pm E_{max}$	$CI = \overline{X} \pm E_{max}$
lower CI = 42.0 − 7.2	lower CI = 80.5 − 7.8	lower CI = 100.8 − 10.8
= 34.8	= 72.7	= 90.0
upper CI = 42.0 + 7.2	upper CI = 80.5 + 7.8	upper CI = 100.8 + 10.8
= 49.2	= 88.3	= 111.6
$CI_{95\%}$: 34.8 to 49.2	$CI_{95\%}$: 72.7 to 88.3	$CI_{95\%}$: 90.0 to 111.6

Other" condition ($\mu_{One\ Other}$) is unlikely to be less than 72.7, therefore, we can be 95% certain these conditions represent distinctly separate populations. Likewise, while the population mean for the "One Other" treatment ($\mu_{One\ Other}$) is unlikely to be more than 88.3, the population mean for the "Five Others" condition ($\mu_{Five\ Others}$) is unlikely to be less than 90.0, so again, we can be 95% certain that these treatments represent different populations. And, of course, we can be 95% certain that the "Alone" treatment population is different than the "Five Others" condition (a maximum of 49.2 versus a minimum of 90.0). These findings are consistent with the results of traditional null-hypothesis testing on the data from this hypothetical experiment. A one-way BS-ANOVA revealed a significant effect [$F\,(2,27) = 59.49$, $p < .01$] and post hoc analyses using Dunn's multiple comparisons indicated that each of the treatments means are significantly different from the others (all $ps < .01$).

Numerical Example of Confidence Intervals That Overlap

Now let's change the data from our hypothetical experiment on "diffusion of responsibility" in order to illustrate a situation where the confidence intervals show some overlap. The new set of data is presented in Table 14-4.

TABLE 14.4	Hypothetical Data Set #2 from the Diffusion of Responsibility Experiment: Overlapping CIs (Scores = number of seconds to pull fire alarm)		

Alone	One Other	Five Others
39	69	61
45	59	59
30	33	120
50	47	65
30	58	68
45	30	90
57	56	87
50	59	56
46	50	91
34	69	62
$\overline{X} = 42.6$	$\overline{X} = 53.0$	$\overline{X} = 75.9$
s = 9.09	s = 13.3	s = 20.47
n = 10	n = 10	n = 10

As in the earlier example, the first step is to find confidence intervals for each sample mean, using the procedure summarized on page 447. Table 14-5 presents these computations.

When we compare the confidence intervals for the "Alone" and "One Other" conditions, we see that they do overlap: the population mean for the "Alone" treatment (μ_{Alone}) condition can be as high as 49.1, while the population mean for the "One Other" condition ($\mu_{\text{One Other}}$) can be as low as 43.5. Therefore, we should conclude that these treatment conditions may represent populations with equal means. However, when we compare the confidence intervals for the "Alone" condition to the CI for the "Five Others" condition, we see that there is no overlap, since the population mean for the "Alone" group (μ_{Alone}) is unlikely to be higher than 49.1 and the population mean for the "Five Others" condition ($\mu_{\text{Five Others}}$) is unlikely to be lower than 61.3. Therefore, it is reasonable to conclude that these treatment conditions represent two distinctly different populations. At this point, we would conclude that the presence of just one other person may have no effect on performance (and the response time to the emergency is equivalent to the response time when the participants are alone), but that the presence of five other people increases response times compared to being alone.

However, if we also compare the confidence intervals for the "One Other" condition to the CI for the "Five Others" condition, we see that there is overlap (since the population mean for the "One Other" group can be as high as 62.5 and the population mean for the "Five Others" condition can be as low as 61.3). This suggests that there may be no difference between being with only one person versus being with five people. Yet this conclusion would contradict our earlier conclusion

TABLE 14.5	Computing the 95% Confidence Intervals for Each Treatment Group	
Alone	**One Other**	**Five Others**
$s_E = \dfrac{s}{\sqrt{n}}$	$s_E = \dfrac{s}{\sqrt{n}}$	$s_E = \dfrac{s}{\sqrt{n}}$
$s_E = \dfrac{9.09}{\sqrt{10}}$	$s_E = \dfrac{13.3}{\sqrt{10}}$	$s_E = \dfrac{20.47}{\sqrt{10}}$
$s_E = \dfrac{9.09}{3.1622776}$	$s_E = \dfrac{13.3}{3.1622776}$	$s_E = \dfrac{20.47}{3.1622776}$
$s_E = 2.8745104$	$s_E = 4.2058293$	$s_E = 6.4731824$
For CL = 95%, α = .05	For CL = 95%, α = .05	For CL = 95%, α = .05
df = n − 1 = 10 − 1 = 9	df = n − 1 = 10 − 1 = 9	df = n − 1 = 10 − 1 = 9
therefore, $t_{critical}$ = 2.262	therefore, $t_{critical}$ = 2.262	therefore, $t_{critical}$ = 2.262
$E_{max} = t_{critical}\,(s_E)$	$E_{max} = t_{critical}\,(s_E)$	$E_{max} = t_{critical}\,(s_E)$
E_{max} = 2.262 (2.8745104)	E_{max} = 2.262 (4.2058293)	E_{max} = 2.262 (6.4731824)
E_{max} = 6.5021425	E_{max} = 9.5135858	E_{max} = 14.642338
$E_{max} \approx 6.5$	$E_{max} \approx 9.5$	$E_{max} \approx 14.6$
$CI = \overline{X} \pm E_{max}$	$CI = \overline{X} \pm E_{max}$	$CI = \overline{X} \pm E_{max}$
lower CI = 42.6 − 6.5	lower CI = 53.0 − 9.5	lower CI = 75.9 − 14.6
= 36.1	= 43.5	= 61.3
upper CI = 42.6 + 6.5	upper CI = 53.0 + 9.5	upper CI = 75.9 + 14.6
= 49.1	= 62.5	= 90.5
$CI_{95\%}$: 36.1 to 49.1	$CI_{95\%}$: 43.5 to 62.5	$CI_{95\%}$: 61.3 to 90.5

that being with one person is equivalent to being alone (since these CIs overlap), which is different than being with five people (since these CIs do not overlap). How can being with one person be the same as being alone and simultaneously be the same as being with five people?

Obviously, it cannot be both, but the confidence intervals do not allow us to decide which conclusion to draw concerning the effect of being with one person compared to the other conditions. In fact, this "dilemma" illustrates one of the primary differences between this type of analysis and traditional null hypothesis significance testing. Traditional statistical tests, such as ANOVA, allow us to make "all-or-none" decisions about the effects of our variables: either there is a significant effect or there isn't one. That is, for each comparison of interest, we will either reject the null hypothesis or we will not. For example, the one-way BS-ANOVA on the data in Table 14-4 reveals a significant overall effect [F (2,27) = 12.83, $p < .01$] and post hoc analyses using Dunn's multiple comparisons indicates that being with one other person is *not* significantly different from being alone ($p > .10$) but it *is* significantly different than being with five other people ($p < .05$). Unlike the confidence interval analysis, the results of this null hypothesis significance testing procedure allow an unambiguous interpretation: being with five people significantly delays participants' response to the smoke, while being with only one person is the same as being alone.

While the results of the ANOVA and the post hoc comparisons may be appealing to us because they seem to be less ambiguous and more definitive compared to the contradictory and confusing confidence interval analysis, it is important to remember that ANOVA and other traditional null hypothesis significance testing procedures essentially treat the sample means as *point estimates* of population means, and they do not take into account the "margin of error" around each $\overline{X}$ which tells us that the actual value of μ may be somewhat larger or smaller than $\overline{X}$. The Dunn multiple comparisons test, for example, calculates a critical range that represents the largest difference between two specific values of $\overline{X}$ that is likely to occur by chance alone, and if the difference between the sample means is equal to or greater than the critical range, we reject the null hypothesis. The critical range (with $\alpha = .05$) for this hypothetical data is equal to 17.4, indicating that 95% of samples drawn at random from the same population will have means that are within 17.4 points of each other; only 5% of the samples will differ by 17.4 or more. The mean for the "One Other" condition is 53 and the mean for the "Five Others" group was 75.9, and the difference of 22.9 points is larger than the critical range (17.4), so we conclude the difference is significant (and that the two experimental conditions represent separate populations).

However, the 95% confidence intervals for the sample means indicate that the population mean for the "One Other" condition could actually be anything from 43.5 to 62.5 and the population mean for the "Five Others" condition could actually be anything from 61.3 to 90.5. Earlier we interpreted this "overlap" between the confidence intervals to mean that there is a reasonable likelihood that these samples each come from the same population (where μ is somewhere between 61.3 and 62.5), and we concluded that the two treatment groups may represent the same population. This conclusion implies that the significant difference we found using the Dunn multiple comparisons test might be the result of a Type I Error (where we rejected the null hypothesis when it is true.)

But is this interpretation of the overlapping confidence intervals the correct one? Not necessarily, since the margins of error around these sample means are relatively wide ($E_{max} = 9.5$ for the "One Other" condition and $E_{max} = 14.6$ for the "Five Others" condition), it might be argued that the research design lacked adequate power (as discussed in the next section of this chapter). For example, there were only ten participants in each group, and it is possible there is a true systematic difference between the populations, but this difference was "lost" amid the large degree of random variation among small samples (as measured by the confidence intervals). Thus, overlapping confidence intervals do not provide conclusive proof that the populations are not different from each other, just as a decision to reject the null hypothesis because the statistic reaches "significance" does not guarantee the populations are different.

In summary, confidence intervals can be used as an alternative to traditional null hypothesis significance testing, but they do not necessarily lead to more accurate conclusions. It may be most useful and informative for researchers to report the results of both forms of analysis. When the results of a significance test is confirmed by an examination of the confidence intervals, it may allow us to place greater confidence in our conclusions. For instance, the Dunn multiple comparisons test indicated a significant difference between the "Alone" and "Five Others" conditions, and this difference was confirmed by the confidence intervals analysis (which found no overlap between the CIs), so we can confidently conclude that the presence of five other people delays participants' reactions to the potential fire emergency. In contrast, the two analyses lead to contradictory conclusions in the case of "One Other" and "Five Others" conditions. Therefore, if we report that the difference is significant (based on the ANOVA and post hoc comparison), we may want to also acknowledge that there is some possibility that this difference is due to chance, as indicated by the overlapping confidence intervals. Reporting both analysis—even if the two sets of results appear contradictory—will provide other researchers with a more accurate picture of the results of the study.

Confidence Intervals and Statistical Power

Another reason that confidence intervals are becoming increasingly popular with researchers is that the "width" of a confidence interval (or the margin of error in an estimate) can be used as a rough indicator of statistical power. Power, you may recall from Chapter 6 and Appendix C, is the ability of the statistical test to correctly reject the null hypothesis when there is a systematic effect present. That is, increasing power reduces the probability of Type II errors and makes it possible to detect smaller and smaller systematic effects. Whenever a researcher fails to reject the null hypothesis, there are two possibilities: (1) the null hypothesis is really true and there is no systematic effect, or (2) the null hypothesis is actually false, but the test did not have sufficient power to detect the effect. An examination of the confidence intervals may give us a general sense about the relative likelihoods of these two possibilities, because tests with high power will typically have narrow confidence intervals while tests with low power will typically have wide confidence intervals.

As an illustration, let's compare the data from two hypothetical studies. The first study observed forty 9-year-old children in the classroom during a geography lesson and compared the time-on-task (or attention span) of boys and girls. (The percent of time-on-task was measured for each child, and these scores are presented in Table 14-6.) These data indicate that girls were on-task an average of 71.15% of the time (and the 95% confidence interval is $71.15 \pm 2.22\%$). Boys were on-task an average of 69.20% of the time (and the 95% confidence interval is $69.20 \pm 2.17\%$). A t-test on these data results in a non-significant value of t ($p > .05$), so the null hypothesis is not rejected.

Our second hypothetical study compared the social acceptance of normal and hyperactive children. Forty 9-year-old children were observed on their first day at a summer camp and their interactions with other children were coded as positive,

TABLE 14.6	Percentage of Time On-Task	
Boys		**Girls**
76		75
69		71
71		72
65		75
70		65
67		68
64		74
72		66
64		64
74		75
61		72
66		71
77		72
75		70
64		65
70		69
72		71
68		67
74		83
65		78
$\overline{X} = 69.20$		$\overline{X} = 71.15$
$n = 20$		$n = 20$
$s = 4.63$		$s = 4.75$
$s_E = 1.035$		$s_E = 1.062$
for $\alpha = .05$, df $= 19$		for $\alpha = .05$, df $= 19$
$t_{critical} = 2.093$		$t_{critical} = 2.093$
$E_{max} = 2.17$		$E_{max} = 2.22$
$CI_{95\%} = 69.20 \pm 2.17$		$CI_{95\%} = 71.15 \pm 2.22$
CI: 67.03 to 71.37		CI: 68.93 to 73.37

$$t(38) = 1.31, p > .05$$

The difference between boys and girls is not significant

negative or neutral, and the percentage of interactions coded as positive was recorded (see Table 14-7). These data indicate that, for normal children, an average of 74.25% of their peer interactions are positive (with a 95% confidence interval of 74.25 ± 11.07%), while for hyperactive children, an average of 71.55% of their peer interactions are positive (with a 95% confidence interval of 71.55 ± 9.56%). A t-test on these data results in a non-significant value of t ($p > .05$), so the null hypothesis is not rejected.

In both of these hypothetical studies, the null hypothesis is not rejected when we employ a t-test, and this conclusion is confirmed when we examine the confidence intervals. In both studies, the CIs overlap, which would lead us to conclude that there is a reasonable likelihood that the samples come from the same population. How

TABLE 14.7	**Percentage of Positive Interactions with Peers**	
Normal		**Hyperactive**
90		88
78		92
81		75
36		100
77		86
100		100
52		88
62		65
100		25
36		68
94		61
60		77
54		69
85		59
100		95
26		32
100		68
80		68
99		52
75		63
$\overline{X} = 74.25$		$\overline{X} = 71.55$
n = 20		n = 20
s = 23.66		s = 20.42
$s_E = 5.291$		$s_E = 4.566$
for $\alpha = .05$, df = 19		for $\alpha = .05$, df = 19
$t_{critical} = 2.093$		$t_{critical} = 2.093$
$E_{max} = 11.07$		$E_{max} = 9.56$
$CI_{95\%} = 74.25 \pm 11.07$		$CI_{95\%} = 71.55 \pm 9.56$
CI: 63.18 to 85.32		CI: 61.99 to 81.11

$$t(38) = 0.39, p > .05$$

The difference between normal and hyperactive children is not significant

should these outcomes be interpreted? Should we conclude that there is truly no difference between the attention spans of boys and girls and no difference between normal and hyperactive children in social acceptance? Or are there systematic differences between the groups that our studies failed to detect due to a lack of sufficient power? We can tentatively answer these questions by examining the size of the confidence intervals, because increased power is generally associated with smaller confidence intervals. That is, small confidence intervals typically indicate high statistical power, while large confidence intervals indicate low statistical power.

Look at the graphs presented in Figure 14-5, which present the means and confidence intervals for these two studies. The confidence intervals for the study on attention span (Figure 14-5a) are quite small (or narrow), suggesting a high degree of

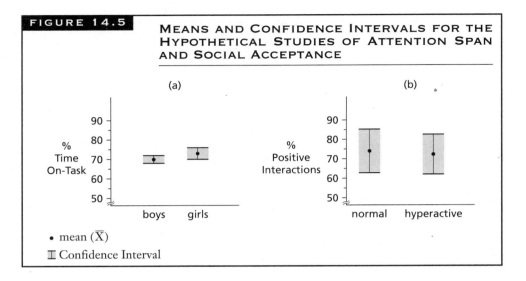

FIGURE 14.5

MEANS AND CONFIDENCE INTERVALS FOR THE HYPOTHETICAL STUDIES OF ATTENTION SPAN AND SOCIAL ACCEPTANCE

power. We can be 95% certain that the average time-on-task span of boys is between 67.03 and 71.37% and the average time-on-task for girls is between 68.93 and 73.37%. Even if we assume both sample means are off to the maximum degree of random error (so that the population mean for boys is actually equal to its lowest likely value of 67.03%, and the population mean for girls is actually equal to its highest likely value of 73.37%), then the *largest likely difference* between boys and girls is only 6.34%. This "maximum difference," which is illustrated in Figure 14-6a, is

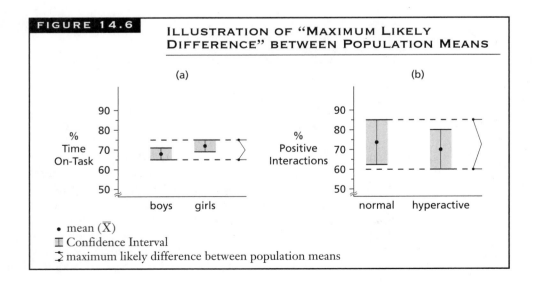

FIGURE 14.6

ILLUSTRATION OF "MAXIMUM LIKELY DIFFERENCE" BETWEEN POPULATION MEANS quite small, so it seems reasonable to interpret the non-significant *t*-test as an indication that, for all intents and purposes, there is little or no difference in attention span between boys and girls.

In contrast, the confidence intervals for the study on social acceptance of normal and hyperactive children are quite large (or wide), suggesting that the study had a low degree of power (see Figure 14-5b). We can be 95% certain that between 63.18 and 85.32% of normal children's peer interactions are positive and between 61.99 and 81.11% of hyperactive children's peer interactions are positive. Again, if we assume both samples means are off to the maximum degree of random error (so that the population mean for normal children is actually equal to its maximum likely value of 85.32% and the population mean for hyperactive children is equal to its minimum likely value of 61.99%), then the largest likely difference between the groups is 23.33%. This "maximum difference," illustrated in Figure 14-6b, is quite large. This raises the possibility that there truly is a systematic difference between the populations means, but the study lacked sufficient power to detect it. In other words, the wide confidence intervals indicate that there is a good chance that a Type II Error has occurred here. Therefore, unlike the study on sex differences in attention span, these data do not convincingly support a claim that normal and hyperactive children experience the same levels of social acceptance. Instead, because of the wide confidence intervals, and the low degree of power, we are unable to confidently interpret the nonsignificant findings.

Renewing the Call for Compromise: Combining the Approaches

Confidence intervals can be very informative. They allow researchers to estimate the range of likely values for population parameters and can be used to compare treatment conditions. Additionally, they give us some indication about the degree of statistical power present in the data which helps us interpret the findings, particularly when the results are not statistically significant. While some statisticians have recently argued that confidence intervals should *replace* traditional null hypothesis testing procedures, such as *t*-tests and analysis of variance (e.g., Loftus, 1996), we believe that using them *together* may provide researchers with a more complete understanding of their data. We learn something important when we compare the results of traditional significance tests and confidence interval analyses, even if these results are contradictory.

Exercises

1. A survey of 100 high school sophomores revealed that 19% of them had experimented with marijuana in the past 30 days. Estimate the percentage of the population of sophomores using marijuana using a 95% confidence interval.

2. Based on records from 1995, the New York State Police Accident Investigation Team reported that 31 out of 74 fatal car accidents involved at least one driver under 21 years of age. Using a 95% confidence interval, estimate the percentage of fatal accidents that involve young drivers annually.

3. Fifty college students completed a test of creative thinking and an IQ test. The Pearson correlation between IQ and creativity was found to be $r = +0.21$. Using a 99% confidence interval, estimate the value of the population correlation coefficient (ρ).

4. Sixty fourth-grade children were asked to identify photographs of familiar objects as rapidly as possible. The correlation between the amount of time required to identify photographs of foods and the children's weight was found to be $r = -0.32$. Using a 95% confidence interval, estimate the value of the population correlation coefficient (ρ).

5. A sample of 18 counselors with master's degrees earn an average of $8.65 per hour (with a standard deviation of $2.03) while a sample of 24 counselors with bachelor's degrees earn an average of $7.80 per hour (with a standard deviation of $1.98). How much does having a master's degree affect earnings?

   a. Calculate the 95% confidence interval for the means of each of the groups of counselors.
   b. Calculate the minimum difference in hourly wages using the 95% confidence level.

6. In a study on the effect of season of year on the depression among hospitalized mental patients, the staff recorded the number of hours the patients spent alone during 48-hour periods in December and June. The results were:

Patient	December	June
a	21	16
b	18	16
c	27	28
d	14	8
e	16	14
f	20	17
g	17	20
h	19	27
i	18	17
j	23	26

   a. Calculate the 95% confidence interval for the means of each of the treatments.
   b. Calculate the minimum difference between the means using the 99% confidence interval.

7. A researcher presented young adults, middle-aged adults, and elderly adults with two lists of 24 words. After one list, the participants were asked to recall as many of the words as they could (Recall Task). After the other list, the participants were given a Recognition Task in which they were given 5 words and had to say which of them had been on the list. (This was repeated for each of the 24 words on the list.) The researcher recorded the number of words the participant remembered correctly and the means and 95% Confidence Intervals are presented in the graph below. What conclusions can be drawn from these results regarding the difference between Recognition and Recall at different age levels?

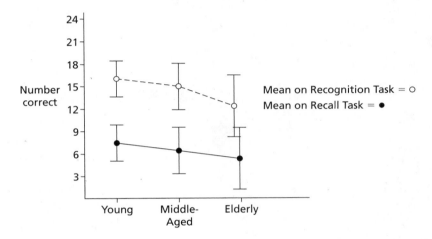

CHAPTER

15

SINGLE-SUBJECT RESEARCH DESIGN[1]

In this chapter, you will learn about research techniques that are particularly useful in the study of individual differences, such as clinical or applied research where the goal may be to test the effectiveness of treatments for behavioral problems. The strengths and potential weaknesses of single-subject (or small N) designs, as well as the basic approaches to the analysis of data from these designs, are presented.

Look for These Important Terms and Concepts

single-subject versus group designs
frequency
event recording
rate of occurrence
partial versus whole interval recording
time sampling
duration
intensity
latency
baseline and treatment phases

confounds
implementation integrity
functional control
AB and ABAB designs
changing conditions designs
multiple baseline designs
changing criterion designs
alternating treatment designs
mixed designs
trend analysis

Before Reading This Chapter, You May Wish to Review

Chapter 1:
• operational definition
• internal validity

Chapter 3:
• confound

Chapter 4:
• behavioral observations
• behavioral ratings
• ordinal scales

Chapter 5:
• mean and median
• variability and standard deviation
• outliers

Chapter 7:
• quasi-experiments
• time series designs

Chapter 9:
• simple regression
• slope of a line

Chapter 10:
• threats to internal validity
• no-treatment control groups
• counterbalancing
• pretest-posttest designs

[1]The original draft of this chapter was written by Dr. Mark Fugate, Division of School Psychology, at Alfred University. We are very grateful to him for lending his expertise in the area of single-subject designs to this textbook.

So far, research designs and methods of data analyses that require groups of participants have been presented. Yet, there are occasions when conducting research with groups of individuals might be difficult (because a sufficient number of suitable participants are not available) or inappropriate (because the goal of the study is to describe, predict or control the behavior of specific individuals rather than to identify the average performance of a group). Under these circumstances, single-subject or "small N" designs may be the method of choice. For instance, consider the fact that not all behaviors or mental processes of interest to psychologists are demonstrated by large numbers of people. As a result, it might be difficult to find enough research participants to use a group research design. For example, a researcher might want to study the effectiveness of a new treatment for children who exhibit autistic behaviors. Unfortunately for this researcher, autism occurs so rarely within the general population that it could be difficult to find more than a few autistic children to work with.

Furthermore, the primary purpose of group designs is to compare the typical or normative responses of the research participants who are in different research conditions, but this norm-referenced (or *nomothetic*) approach may not adequately account for individual differences within the group. That is, knowing about the average performance of the group does not necessarily predict the response of a particular individual within the group, yet there are instances when these individual differences need to be the focus of research, such as in clinical research where the goal may be to predict or control the behavior of specific individuals. For example, a researcher who uses a group design to study the effectiveness of a treatment for depression may conclude that the treatment is ineffective because the difference between the experimental groups is non-significant. Yet there may be a number of participants in the treatment group for whom the treatment was, in fact, completely, or partially, effective. (These individual differences would be treated as "error variance" in the analysis of the group data.) Understanding the conditions under which the treatment is effective for some individuals may be just as important, if not more important, than concluding that, on the whole, the treatment is generally ineffective. The ability to focus on individual differences, which is called the *idiographic* approach, is a major advantage of a single-subject research design.

In this chapter we will discuss several single-subject designs and the major issues involved in the interpretation of their results. While we primarily rely on clinical examples to illustrate the principles of single-subject research design (where the goal is to find an effective treatment for an individual who displays behavior problems), these designs are commonly used in other areas of applied research (such as industrial-organizational and educational psychology) and they can be used in basic (non-applied) research as well. Brief non-clinical examples are presented later in this chapter.

Key Elements of Single-Subject Research

There are two general research strategies which involve studying a single individual (or case) in hopes of detecting some general principles that can be generalized to other cases: Case studies and single-subject designs. Case studies are in-depth descriptions of a wide range of an individual's behaviors and experiences, and they typically do not involve systematic observations or careful measurements. Instead, case studies often use *qualitative research* techniques such as those described in the next chapter. In contrast, single-subject designs focus on one or a few carefully defined behaviors, which are systematically observed under controlled conditions. Essentially, a single-subject design is a within-subjects quasi-experiment conducted on a single participant. (Specifically, single-subject designs are time series designs, as described in Chapter 7.) Some texts refer to these designs as "single-case experiments," but since they are not true experiments, we prefer the terms single-subject designs or single-subject research.

The key elements of single-subject research design include: choice of measurement technique; design phases; visual representation of data; and the threats to validity that are common to single-subject research. We will illustrate each of these concepts by applying them to a hypothetical case: "Cameron."

Cameron   Cameron is a three-year-old boy who attends a specialized preschool program for children with serious behavior disorders. It has been observed that Cameron is often oppositional (e.g., refuses to do as he is asked by his parents and his teachers), disruptive, exhibits frequent temper tantrums, and is quite aggressive with other children. Dr. Jacobs, the consulting psychologist for the day care program, recently attended a workshop for the treatment of noncompliant children. As a result, she has developed new treatment ideas for helping Cameron develop more positive behaviors.

Elements of Measurement

The roots of single-subject research are found in behavioral psychology and applied behavioral analysis. As a result, this research is most often oriented toward documenting changes in specific behaviors in response to a treatment or intervention. Therefore, this discussion of measurement issues will focus on the selection and measurement of target behaviors.

Most single-subject research uses direct observation of selected behaviors as the primary mode of data collection, and behavioral rating techniques (such as behavior checklists and rating scales) are also quite common. Whichever data-gathering technique is chosen, developing clear *operational definitions* is an essential element in the process of selecting target behaviors. The accuracy of an observation (or data-gathering) system is determined by how well the definition of targeted behavior matches the actual behavior of concern, and how effectively the observed behaviors are transformed into numbers or scores. Good operational definitions tell us, clearly and precisely, which behaviors to record and how to score our observations.

Initially, it is important to note that the target behavior must be *observable*. If the behavior is not defined in clearly observable and unambiguous terms, it will be difficult to measure the behavior reliably. Furthermore, a good definition will be well focused, in an effort to distinguish between the target behavior and other closely related behaviors. However, the definition will also need to be broad enough to include all or most occurrences of the target behavior. Maintaining this balance between breadth and focus will also facilitate consistent and more reliable measurement. For example, as Dr. Jacobs develops a measure of Cameron's aggressive behavior, she needs to consider all the typical occurrences of the behavior (e.g., hitting, biting, or name calling) while distinguishing between the nonoccurrences of the behavior (e.g., knocking down his block tower during play time).

Another step in defining target behavior is deciding which dimensions of the behavior will be measured. There are four dimensions that are commonly used: frequency, duration, intensity, and latency. Let's look at each of them separately.

Measuring the Frequency of Behavior **Frequency** is a measure of how often a behavior occurs. There are two common methods for measuring how often behaviors occur: event recording and interval recording (which includes partial interval, whole interval, and time sampling techniques). In **event recording** (or *event sampling*), the observer makes a note (like a hash-mark on a sheet of paper) each time the target behavior occurs during a period of observation. This allows the observer to determine the total number of times the behavior took place as well as the **rate of occurrence** for the specified behavior, which is calculated by taking the total number of occurrences and dividing by the elapsed time of the observation period. For example, if Cameron throws a total of seven tantrums over a five-day observation period:

$$\text{rate of occurrence} = \frac{\text{number of occurrences}}{\text{elapsed time}} = \frac{7}{5} = 1.4 \text{ tantrums per day}$$

Thus, we could report that Cameron had 1.4 tantrums per day. When using event recording it is necessary to be able to accurately determine exactly when a behavior starts and stops. Behaviors that are difficult to define with such precision or that occur in quick flurries of activity are events that will be difficult to record accurately using event sampling. In our example, Dr. Jacobs has decided to use event recording to count the number of aggressive behaviors Cameron exhibits each day.

The frequency of a behavior can also be measured using **interval recording** techniques. The first step in interval recording is to divide the observation time block into intervals of a given length (e.g., 5 minutes is divided into twenty 15-second intervals) and then the occurrence of the target behavior is recorded interval-by-interval. There are three variations of interval recording: Partial interval recording, whole interval recording, and time sampling. With **partial interval recording** a behavior is recorded *once* (e.g., with a single hash-mark for the interval) if it occurs at any time within the interval, even if the target behavior actually occurred multiple times during the interval. (Thus, this technique does not provide a frequency count of the total number of occurrences.) Partial interval recording is especially useful when recording noncontinuous or discrete behaviors that sporadically appear during the observation session. In contrast, **whole interval recording** requires that the target behavior occur continuously throughout the entire interval to be recorded.

That is, the behavior must be in progress when the interval begins and continue non-stop until the interval (e.g., 15 seconds) is over. This method is, of course, most useful when the target behaviors are continuous and of long duration rather than discrete and brief. For example, whole interval recording may be appropriate for measuring the crying behavior of an infant, but it would not be appropriate for measuring the frequency of hiccoughs or eye-blinks.

The third form of interval recording is **time sampling,** which is sometimes referred to as momentary recording. Time sampling requires the observer to note whether the target behavior was present (occurring) or absent (not occurring) at the exact moment when a timed interval either begins or ends. With this technique, behaviors that occur at any point during the interval are essentially ignored, and only the behavior that is occurring at the moment of observation is recorded. Time sampling is useful for measuring behaviors that are not necessarily continuous, but have a relatively long duration. For example, an adolescent's nail-biting behavior could be effectively measured using time sampling or momentary recording, because a nail-biting episode may last several seconds at a time, but it is less likely to persist over long intervals.

Each of these interval recording methods allows the observer to compute the percentage of intervals in which the behavior occurred across the observation period. Partial interval recording counts the number of intervals during which the target behavior occurred at all; whole interval recording counts the number of intervals that were completely full of the behavior; and time sampling counts the number of intervals which began (or ended) with the behavior in progress. This percentage-of-intervals measure provides an estimate of how often a behavior occurs, but should not be confused with (or misrepresented as) a measure of the total number of times a behavior occurred within the observation period. Furthermore, the percentage of intervals does **not** measure the *duration* of the behavior (i.e., the amount of time the individual spends engaged in the target behavior), which we turn to shortly.

It is also possible to combine event recording and interval recording techniques in the same study using a procedure that is called Event-By-Interval Recording. Essentially, this procedure uses event recording, where every episode of the target behavior is recorded, but the observation period is divided into intervals, and each event is noted within the specific time interval in which it occurred. In this way, observers will be able to determine whether the behavior occurs in a steady "stream" across time or in "flurries" (or bursts) separated by long pauses. For example, an Event x Interval Recording procedure may help a school psychologist recognize that one child's disruptive behaviors occur steadily throughout the school day while another child's disruptive behaviors occur frequently during math class but infrequently during science class. This information may assist the psychologist in identifying possible environmental factors that "trigger" the behavior and this could be useful in designing an effective treatment plan for the child.

Measuring the Duration of Behavior   The **duration** of a behavior is another type of response that can be measured. In this measure, the researcher simply notes the length of time from the beginning of the behavioral response until it ends. Measures of duration work well when behavioral responses are complex and difficult to define discretely, but where the starting and ending points of the behavior can be defined with precision. For example, **duration recording** might be the measurement of choice for Cameron's temper tantrum behavior since temper tantrums are complex behavioral responses (involving both verbal and motor actions) that generally have well-defined beginning and ending points.

The duration of the target behavior is most commonly presented as either the **total duration** or **average duration** of all the behavioral occurrences during the observation period. If Cameron has three tantrums per day of about 20 to 30 minutes each, this behavior could be reported as an average duration of 25 minutes per tantrum, or a total duration of 75 minutes of tantrum behavior per day. An advantage of using duration recording in this case, rather than event recording, is that duration recording may be a more sensitive measure of behavior *change*. For example, it is quite possible that as the intervention is introduced, Cameron will continue to have three tantrums per day (event recording) but they will only last an average of 5 minutes per tantrum (or 15 minutes per day). Thus, event recording would suggest no change in the target behavior while duration recording would demonstrate a substantial change in tantrum behavior.

Measuring the Intensity of a Behavior   In contrast, instead of being concerned by the number of tantrums Cameron has, the teacher may be concerned because the one tantrum Cameron has per day tends to be very destructive, even though it is of short duration. In this case, the intensity of the behavior may be of more concern than its duration. **Intensity** is an estimate of the force of a behavior. Describing the intensity of a behavior is often a subjective process. There are few direct measures of the force of a behavior, so the only option is to use indirect estimates of its intensity. These indirect measures will then lack precision and, as a result, the reliability of the measurements will decrease. For example, we may ask two of Cameron's preschool teachers to rate the intensity of his tantrums on a ten-point scale. Because each teacher has a different level of tolerance for problem behavior, one teacher may give a score of ten while the other rates the behavior as a six.

Behavior rating scales of this kind, which we briefly discussed in Chapter 4, are often used to measure the intensity of a behavior. Behavior rating scales typically consist of a series of items that ask about related behaviors, and people who are close to the individual are asked to use a Likert scale to rate the individual on each item. For example, a depression rating scale may ask teachers to use four-point rating scales to answer questions about a child's depressive symptoms, such as:

"How sad is (s)he?"	1	2	3	4
	(Very)	(Moderately)	(Mildly)	(Not At All)
"How often does (s)he smile spontaneously?"	1	2	3	4
	(Never)	(Rarely)	(Once in a While)	(Often)

The ratings for the items on the scale are then compiled into a single score, which represents an estimate of the severity of the target behavior. Scores from such behavior rating scales are often used as though they provided a *precise measure* of a target behavior, but as we discussed in Chapter 4, Likert Scales (like all ordinal scales) do not have fixed intervals between numbers and do not have an absolute zero point. Therefore, scores from Likert Scales are not absolute and are subject to the bias of the individual doing the rating. At best, such behavior rating scales represent one person's perception of the behavior. If possible, more direct measures of a behavior are preferable as they will allow for more reliable measurement.

Measuring the Latency of a Behavior   Another measurable dimension of behavior is the latency of response. **Latency** is the length of time that elapses between the instructions to perform a behavior and the occurrence of that behavior. Similar to duration recording, latency is frequently reported in terms of **average latency** or **total latency.** Latency would be a possible measure for Cameron's oppositional or disobedient behavior since oppositional behavior is often characterized by a failure to comply to requests within a reasonable amount of time, if at all. Dr. Jacobs might choose to evaluate the severity of Cameron's oppositional behavior by recording the amount of time that elapses between a parent or teacher request and when Cameron begins the task.

Sensitivity   It is important to select measures that are *sensitive to change*. The essential element of the single-subjects research designs we are going to discuss is repeated measurements of the target behavior over time. Because changes in behavior can often be gradual, rather than dramatic, it is important to choose measures that will sensitively measure small, perhaps incremental, changes in behavior. While this is not usually a problem with a well-developed behavioral observation system with a clear operational definition, items on Behavior Rating Scales and other norm-referenced measures may be either too limited in scale or too broadly defined to allow for sensitive measurement of the target behavior. Consider, for example, how much improvement there would have to be in a child's mood before a teacher's perception would change from "Very Sad" to "Moderately Sad" or how much more often the child would have to smile to have the teacher change her rating from "Once in a While" to "Often." Thus, our hypothetical depression rating scale would probably not be very sensitive to small improvements (or declines) in depressive symptoms because the 4-point scale is too limited in its range of values.

As another example, let's consider math ability. A typical measurement procedure used in norm-referenced, group designs would involve the administration of a math test consisting of a set of problems and the dependent variable would be the number of correct answers. These scores are then interpreted as precise measures of the target behavior, which is math ability. However, with the exception of items testing basic math facts, successful completion of a mathematics problem often involves a complex, multistage process. Over time, people often learn to successfully solve complex problems *in stages* rather than all at once. That is, over time, they will be able to successfully complete more and more of the steps correctly, but this improvement will not be reflected in their scores on the math test because, until they are able to successfully complete all of the steps, their final answer will be incorrect. Therefore, a more sensitive measure of math performance would be one that accounts for increased success in solving pieces of the problem, rather than one that is dependent upon successful completion of the entire problem.

Design Phases in Single-Subject Research Designs

There are two phases which make up the basic design elements of single-subject research. These are the **baseline** and **treatment** phases. During these phases, data are gathered by making multiple observations of the target behavior (the dependent variable) over time. Baseline, also known as the "A" phase, is a period in the study where the researcher measures the current frequency, duration, latency, or intensity of the target behavior under normal conditions when no treatment is being applied. (Essentially, baseline data describe the current level of the target behavior and can be used to predict the level of future behavior if no intervention is applied.) The baseline measurement of the target behaviors will then be used as the basis for comparison to evaluate the effects of the treatment, similar to the way in which a no-treatment control condition is used in between-subjects designs, or how a pretest is used in within-subjects or time series designs (see Chapters 7 and 10). In the case of Cameron, who is exhibiting several problem behaviors, Dr. Jacobs will want to establish baselines of behavior by measuring Cameron's activity level, oppositional behavior, and aggressiveness toward others prior to the beginning of the new treatment plans.

During the treatment phase, or **"B"** phase, the target behaviors are observed in conjunction with the administration of an intervention. In the simplest single-subject design, there is typically one treatment phase, and the design is designated as an **AB design.** However, in more complex research designs there may be more than one treatment. In these designs, treatment phases are generally labeled "**C**", "**D**", and so on. For instance, a two-treatment design would be referred to as an **ABC design,** indicating that the baseline (phase A) was followed by the first treatment (phase B), which was followed by the second treatment (phase C). The effect of intervention (the independent variable) is then evaluated by looking for changes from the baseline to the treatment phases in the target behavior's frequency, duration, latency or intensity. Similar to the baseline phase, the primary purposes of the treatment phase are to describe the current level of behavior and predict future behavior if the intervention were to continue.

Presentation of Data

Although there are a few statistical procedures (such as trend analysis) which may be applied to data from single-subject designs, the most common form of data analysis relies on *visual inspection*. Therefore, data from the various phases of a single-subject research design are characteristically presented in graphic form (usually using standard line graphs), although the data are occasionally presented in a table rather than

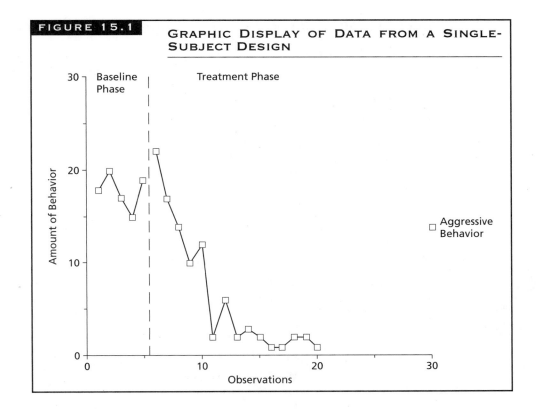

FIGURE 15.1 — GRAPHIC DISPLAY OF DATA FROM A SINGLE-SUBJECT DESIGN

on a graph. Whichever form of data presentation is used, it is important that the data be presented in a way that makes it easy to compare the baseline and treatment phases.

To illustrate how the data can be analyzed by visually inspecting graphs, let's return to Dr. Jacobs' case study of Cameron. Because of the potential danger that it posed, Dr. Jacobs chose to treat Cameron's aggressiveness as the first target behavior and asked the preschool teacher to count the number of aggressive outbursts that occurred each school day for four weeks. Baseline data were collected during the first week (days 1 to 5), and the treatment was put in place during the final three weeks (days 6 to 20) of the case study. The hypothetical results of this AB (time series) design are presented in Figure 15-1. The number of aggressive outbursts for each day is plotted on the vertical (Y) axis while the time element of the design is reflected on the horizontal (X) axis where the data for each day are plotted progressively from left to right. Note that a *phase line* has been incorporated into the graph to mark the boundary between the baseline and treatment phases. The graph clearly shows a difference in Cameron's behavior between the two phases of the case study.

Threats to the Validity of Data from Single-Subject Designs

Looking at the data presented in Figure 15-1 it would be easy to conclude that the reduction in Cameron's aggressive behavior was due to the intervention. Unfortunately, this conclusion is not necessarily correct. As you will recall, one of the essential tasks in the interpretation of data is to rule out plausible alternative hypotheses before drawing causal conclusions. Just like quasi-experimental time series designs (Chapter 7) and single-group, pretest-posttest designs (Chapter 10), the results of an AB design are open to a variety of plausible alternative hypotheses, and consequently there are many threats to the valid interpretation of this data. That is, single-subject AB designs are faced with many of the same potential **confounds** discussed in Chapter 10.

Single-subject research is especially susceptible to measurement-related confounds, such as *instrumentation*, because they involve so many repeated measurements. An instrumentation confound occurs when the calibration of a measurement instrument changes over time, resulting in unreliable data collection. In studies using direct behavioral observation techniques such as event sampling or interval recording, where an observer records the ongoing behavior of the participant, instrumentation typically takes one of two forms: observer drift and topographical drift. *Observer drift* occurs when observers make changes in how target behaviors are defined across (or even *within*) observation sessions. *Topographical drift* occurs when the definition of the target behavior differs over time or across people, so that what is an adequate definition at one time (or for one person) may prove to be inadequate at another time (or for another person). For example, let's suppose that, originally, Cameron's disruptive behavior was operationally defined as getting out of his seat and interfering with the educational progress of the class (the teacher's primary concern). If, over time, Cameron begins to stay in his seat but he continues to disrupt students in his area of the classroom, his new behavior fails to meet the "topographical" requirements of the operational definition but it is none the less disruptive. The dilemma for the researcher is obvious: sticking with the original definition of "disruptiveness" will overestimate the degree of improvement that Cameron will show over the treatment phase, while changing the operational definition of the target behavior makes the validity of a comparison between the phases of the study questionable.

Another potential measurement problem is the *reactive effect* of being observed or tested. As we have pointed out before, it is not uncommon for an individual's behavior to change if they suspect that they are the target of observation. This reaction to being observed may result in changes in the target behavior which are not caused by the treatment or intervention. Reactivity also can occur with other behavioral measures. For example, the questions on a behavior rating scale may cause parents to think about their child's behavior differently and, as a result, the parents may now notice (even actively look for) behaviors that were previously ignored. Consequently, any changes in behavior the parents report may be due to changes in the parents' changed sensitivity to the behavior rather than any real differences in the target behavior itself. (This is similar to the sensitization confound discussed in Chapter 10.)

Reactivity poses yet another threat to the internal validity of the single-subject research design in the form of *practice effects*. Repeated exposure to the same test items may result in an increased ability to respond correctly to those items. Thus, test performance improves even though the underlying ability to perform the task may remain relatively unchanged. To avoid practice effects in time series research, it may be necessary to develop equivalent, alternative forms of measurement.

An additional area of concern in single-subject research is implementation integrity. **Implementation integrity** refers to the accuracy with which an intervention is administered. Without implementation integrity, it is impossible to form conclusions about treatment effects. It is now common practice in single-subject research to report implementation integrity data. Often a checklist of the rules and steps of treatment implementation will be developed and an observer will then make periodic checks to evaluate how accurately the treatment has been administered. Implementation integrity data are then reported as either (a) the percentage of intervention steps which were appropriately administered, or (b) the percentage of intervention steps that were not appropriately administered.

For example, suppose Dr. Jacobs' treatment plan for Cameron included two parts, each based on standard behavior modification techniques. The teachers have been instructed to ignore Cameron's tantrums (i.e., unless they endanger him or others) and to reward his compliant and cooperative behaviors by praising him as a very good boy. During the first week of the treatment phase, Cameron was to receive praise if he complied with a teacher's request within one minute, but during the second week, Cameron would only be praised if he complied within thirty seconds, and in the third week of the treatment phase, Cameron needed to respond within fifteen seconds in order to receive praise. The implementation integrity of this treatment plan could be assessed by having an observer visit the classroom periodically during the treatment phase and observe the teachers' responses to Cameron's tantrums and compliant behaviors. The observer would have a checklist of specific items to look for, such as whether the teacher recognized occurrences of opposition or compliance, whether she gave the appropriate initial response to the behavior, and whether she provided the appropriate consequence or reinforcer for the behavior. The percentage of (non-dangerous) tantrums which were ignored (as they were supposed to be) could then be computed, as could the percentage of compliant behaviors that were praised according to the specified criteria. (Alternatively, the percentage of tantrums that were not ignored, as they were supposed to be, and the percentage of compliant behaviors that were not praised could be computed.) If the teachers are not actually following the treatment plan, the data from the study obviously cannot be interpreted as evidence for or against the effectiveness of the treatment.

Finally, maturation, history, and placebo effects each pose an additional threat to the validity of an AB design. *Maturation* occurs when variables related to the passage of time (e.g., increasing age or fatigue) produce effects that are confounded with the effect of an experimental variable. For example, a possible alternative explanation for a reduction in Cameron's aggressive behavior following several weeks of treatment might be that he simply grew out of the "terrible twos" during the case study. The confounding effect of *history* occurs when specific events other than the experimental stimulus or the treatment influence the experimental outcome. For example, Cameron's behavior might change if a new child joins his preschool class or if Cameron gets the opportunity to engage in more interesting classroom activities as the curriculum changes over the semester. *Placebo effects* occur when the target behavior changes, not as a response to a specific intervention, but as a response to being intervened upon. That is, for example, Cameron's aggressive behavior might decrease simply because he knows that his behavior is supposed to change because he is receiving treatment for that behavior. The specific treatment introduced by Dr. Jacobs may not actually matter at all.

Specific Research Designs

Ruling out the effects of confounding variables such as instrumentation, reactivity and history is necessary in order to demonstrate that the target behavior is under the **functional control** of the experimental condition. Although it may not be entirely possible to rule out all plausible alternative hypotheses, it is possible to make these alternative hypotheses less plausible with some additions to the basic AB research design. In each of the following designs, functional control of the target behavior is demonstrated through the *replication* of both baseline behavior and the treatment effect.

ABAB Designs

ABAB designs involve the repeated administration and withdrawal of the treatment or independent variable. As the name of the design suggests, a basic reversal design starts with an initial "A" or baseline phase which is followed by a "B" or treatment phase. Then the treatment is removed so there is a return to baseline (another "A" phase) which is then followed by the reinstitution of the treatment or "B" phase. If the target behavior is, indeed, under the **functional control** of the treatment, then that behavior will change appropriately during the first treatment phase, return to near baseline levels during the second baseline phase, and change appropriately *again* when the treatment is reinstituted during the second treatment phase. If the target behavior responds in this manner, rival hypotheses, such as history and maturation, become less plausible. On the other hand, if the behavior does not return to baseline levels during the second "A" phase or if the treatment effect is not replicated during the second "B" phase, we would not be able to conclude that the treatment effectively controls the behavior. Let's look at an example of an ABAB design.

Realizing the limitations of the original case study (AB) design, Dr. Jacobs decided to institute an ABAB design to demonstrate the effectiveness of her intervention for Cameron. (As before, the teachers counted the number of aggressive outbursts Cameron exhibited each day.) The first baseline phase lasted five school days, and the first treatment phase took place over the next 15 days. After this intervention period, Dr. Jacobs returned to 5 days of no intervention, followed by another 10 days of treatment. The hypothetical results of this design are found in Figure 15-2.

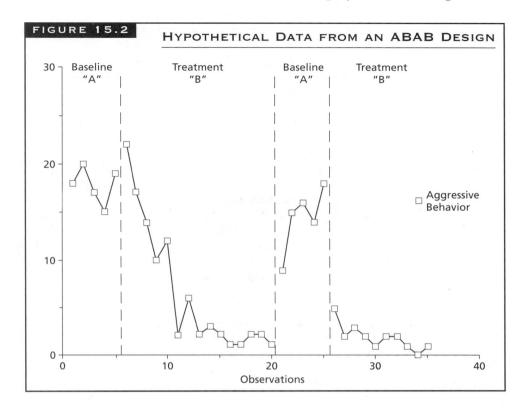

FIGURE 15.2 HYPOTHETICAL DATA FROM AN ABAB DESIGN

As you can see from the data in Figure 15-2, Cameron's aggressive behavior showed a clear decline during the first treatment phase compared to the baseline phase. More importantly, during the reversal to baseline procedures, Cameron's aggressive behavior returned to a level approximating the original baseline data. Furthermore, there was also an immediate and sustained decrease in Cameron's aggressive behavior following the reintroduction of the intervention in the second "B" phase, replicating the effectiveness of the intervention. Thus, the data suggest that Cameron's aggression is, indeed, under the functional control of the treatment.

Excited as Dr. Jacobs might be to demonstrate control of the target behavior, Cameron's pre-school teacher will not be too happy to experience another week of his aggressive behavior in her classroom. One disadvantage of an ABAB design is that the withdrawal of treatment may not be appropriate if the target behavior is negative or disruptive. In fact, it may be unethical to remove a treatment if it is providing control for a behavior that is harmful to self or others. Assuming it is ethical to do so, an alternative to an extended return to baseline is an abbreviated return to baseline of only one or two observation periods. An abbreviated baseline phase will only be an effective test if the target behavior responds quickly to the withdrawal and reinstatement of treatment. For example, while the number of aggressive outbursts per day can increase or decrease quickly, other behaviors, such as stuttering, will show more gradual changes over time. Therefore, an abbreviated baseline phase may be suitable when the target behavior is aggression, but not stuttering.

Another limitation of the ABAB design that must be considered is the fact that some behaviors, by their very nature, are resistant to reversal once they have been changed. In such cases, the target behavior will not revert to baseline levels once the intervention is removed, and without the return to baseline during the second "A" phase, there can be no replication of the treatment effect during the second "B" phase. Therefore, the evidence for functional control is weakened and other interpretations (such as maturation and history) become more plausible. For example, let's suppose that Cameron has had difficulty with "potty training" and has been having "accidents" in school. For most children, once these skills are learned, the change in behavior is quite permanent. Therefore, if an intervention for teaching toileting skills is successful during the first treatment phase of an ABAB design, it is quite unlikely that Cameron will lose these skills when the intervention is discontinued. A different single-subject research design is needed to demonstrate control over these kinds of behaviors.

Variations on the ABAB Design   Similar to group research designs, single-subject research designs are quite flexible and can be modified in many ways to meet the specific demands of the setting or target behavior. As a result there are many variations of the basic ABAB design that have been developed. In one popular variant, the second "A" phase is replaced with a treatment that is known to be ineffective, rather than returning to a baseline condition without intervention. This is a particularly good method to use when placebo effects are a concern, because if the target behavior appears to improve during the "ineffective treatment" phase, we would be fairly certain that a placebo effect is influencing the behavior. For example, suppose Dr. Jacobs plans to treat Cameron's aggressive behavior by reinforcing nonaggressive behaviors, a technique referred to as differential reinforcement of other behavior (DRO). Thus, when Cameron responds with any behavior other than an aggressive one, he will be reinforced. (Let's presume the reinforcer is a colorful sticker.) However, Dr. Jacobs is concerned that Cameron may respond to something other than the differential reinforcement, so rather than return to baseline conditions, she might choose to include a phase in which Cameron receives stickers at random points during the day, regardless of his current behavior. This is known as noncontingent reinforcement, and it is well-known that it is generally an ineffective strategy for behavior management. Thus, Dr. Jacobs is planning an ABCB design, where the baseline (phase A) is followed by DRO treatment (phase B), which is then followed by the "placebo" noncontingent reinforcement treatment (phase C), and then the DRO treatment is reinstituted (the second phase B). Imagine that Cameron's aggression decreased during the first treatment phase (B). If the DRO treatment is truly controlling Cameron's aggression, we would expect to see his aggressive behavior return to baseline levels during the noncontingent reinforcement period (phase C). If the aggressive behavior does not return to baseline levels during the C phase, we would be unable to conclude that the DRO treatment had functional control over the behavior.

Variations of the ABAB design also can be used to assess the effects of two or more different treatments (including the combination of treatments) during the same research project by adding additional phases (e.g., "C", "D", "E", etc.) to the basic design. When the treatments are presented sequentially (one at a time), such as in an ABCBCBCAC design, it is possible to make comparisons among the treatments, much like the comparisons we make among the levels of an independent variable in group designs. This variation of an ABAB design is known as the **changing conditions design.**

Suppose that as Dr. Jacobs looked at the original data from the AB case study, she was pleased with the change in the target behavior but was still concerned that Cameron's aggressive behavior continued to occur one or two times per day. Although this represents a substantial improvement in his behavior, there is zero tolerance for aggressive behavior in the classroom, so the goal of treatment would be to eliminate Cameron's aggressive outbursts altogether. To this end, Dr. Jacobs has chosen to add an additional treatment (a "C" phase) to Cameron's intervention plan. Now, in addition to the differential reinforcement of other, nonaggressive behaviors (the DRO treatment), Cameron will lose some play privileges when his behavior is aggressive. That is, every time Cameron behaves aggressively, he will lose 3 minutes of time in the playroom. This treatment is referred to as a response cost (RC), so phase "C" in the design will be a DRO + RC condition.

Therefore, the new design started with a five-day baseline period (phase A), followed by twenty days of the differential reinforcement (DRO) treatment (phase B), and this phase was followed by ten days of the DRO + RC intervention (phase C). In order to be able to demonstrate the functional control of the combination treatment over the target behavior, Dr. Jacobs then instituted a brief, two-day return to baseline (phase A) followed by an eight-day replication of the DRO + RC condition (phase C). The hypothetical results of this ABCAC design are found in Figure 15-3. As you can see in Figure 15-3, as Dr. Jacobs hoped, adding a response cost to the DRO treatment (phase C) brought the number of aggressive outbursts down from one or two per day to near zero. There was a striking return of Cameron's aggressive behavior during the second "A" phase, but it dropped again to near zero when the DRO + RC treatment was reinstituted in the second "C" phase. This pattern of results offers a clear demonstration of the treatment's functional control over Cameron's aggressive behavior, and suggests that a combination of differential reinforcment of nonaggressive behaviors and a response cost may be an effective technique for eliminating aggressive behavior.

Multiple-Baseline Designs

Multiple-baseline designs allow researchers to evaluate the effectiveness of an intervention by applying the intervention to a series of dependent variables (or "tar-

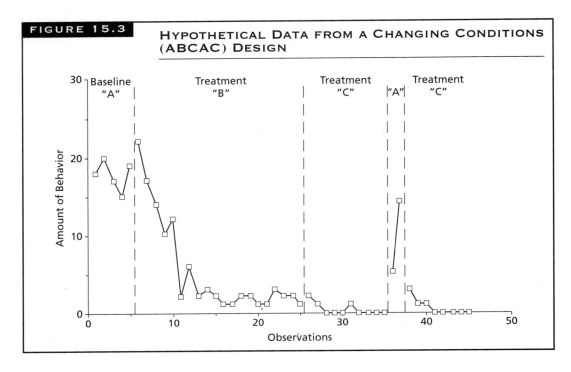

FIGURE 15.3

HYPOTHETICAL DATA FROM A CHANGING CONDITIONS (ABCAC) DESIGN

gets") at different points in time. These targets may be different behaviors, different settings, or different people.[2] For instance, the intervention may be first applied to a child's aggressive behavior, then to her disruptive behavior, and then to her inattentiveness. Or, the intervention may be first applied to Jill, then Renee, and then Terrence; or it may be first applied in the classroom, then in the lunchroom, and then at home. Whether the study compares different behaviors, settings, or people, the basic steps in a multiple-baseline design are always the same: (1) multiple targets are selected and are started in baseline phases simultaneously; (2) the treatment is then administered to one of the targets while the other(s) remain in the baseline phase; (3) the treatment is then administered to a second target while the first target continues to receive the treatment and the remaining targets continue in baseline; and (4) then the treatment is administered to another target, and the pattern continues until all the targets have been exposed to the treatment. In this design the extended baseline of the as-yet-untreated targets allows the researcher to monitor for possible history and maturation effects, while the replication of the treatment effect across multiple

---

[2]While it is customary among single-subject researchers to use the term "dependent variables" when referring to the multiple behaviors, people, or settings in a multiple-baseline design, other researchers (particularly those of us familiar with group research methods) may think these different targets more closely resemble levels of an *independent* variable. Therefore, we have chosen to use the term targets in order to minimize the potential confusion.

targets provides for a demonstration of functional control. Because the treatment is not withdrawn during a multiple-baseline design, the researcher is not faced with the ethical dilemma of ABAB designs, and multiple-baseline designs can be used for behaviors that would not be expected to return to baseline if the intervention were to be withdrawn. Another positive feature, of this single-subject research design is that a treatment can be applied across multiple behaviors, persons, or settings in relatively quick succession. Let's take a look at an example.

Suppose that while planning an intervention strategy for Cameron, Dr. Jacobs realized that it might be in everybody's best interest to try to address all four of his behavior problems at the same time, rather than in succession. She noted that it would, for example, take eight weeks to conduct the ABCAC changing conditions design described above to effectively control just one of Cameron's problem behaviors, and during that time, Cameron's other behaviors could become increasingly disruptive. Another benefit to applying a multiple-baseline design in Cameron's case is that his preschool teacher would not be required to learn a new intervention strategy for each problem behavior. Therefore, after consulting with the teacher, Dr. Jacobs designed a single intervention she believed would be effective in treating Cameron's four problem behaviors, and she decided to test the effectiveness of this single intervention strategy by using a multiple-baseline design.

Let's suppose that Dr. Jacobs decided to treat Cameron using a variation of the differential reinforcement of other behaviors technique in which the teacher systematically reinforced Cameron when he was cooperative (or compliant), nonaggressive, nondisruptive, and calm (rather than throwing a tantrum). These behaviors are all incompatible with Cameron's problem behaviors, so the treatment technique is referred to as differential reinforcement of incompatible responses (DRI). The hope is that, because even Cameron cannot perform two incompatible behaviors at one time, an increase in the desirable behaviors due to the reinforcement should result in a decrease in, and possibly the complete elimination of, the problem behaviors. Let's also suppose that Dr. Jacobs and the teacher prioritized Cameron's problems and decided that the most dangerous behavior (aggression) would receive the intervention first, while the least problematic behavior (temper tantrums) would be held in baseline for the longest period of time. The hypothetical data for this multiple-baseline design are presented in Figure 15-4.

As you can see in Figure 15-4, each of the four target behaviors showed improvement when the differential reinforcement of incompatible behaviors (DRI) treatment was instituted. Hence, the effectiveness of the treatment was replicated across the target behaviors. Furthermore, with the exception of tantrum behaviors, the target behaviors had remained relatively stable throughout their baseline phase and the substantial change in behavior occurred only after the introduction of the treatment. This pattern would be interpreted as evidence that the intervention (DRI) had functional control over the target behaviors since other hypotheses, such as history or maturation, offer less plausible alternative explanations. For example, if a historical event in the classroom caused the improvement in Cameron's aggressive behavior during the first week of treatment, we would wonder why it did not have any noticeable impact on the other target behaviors (whose baseline rates remained

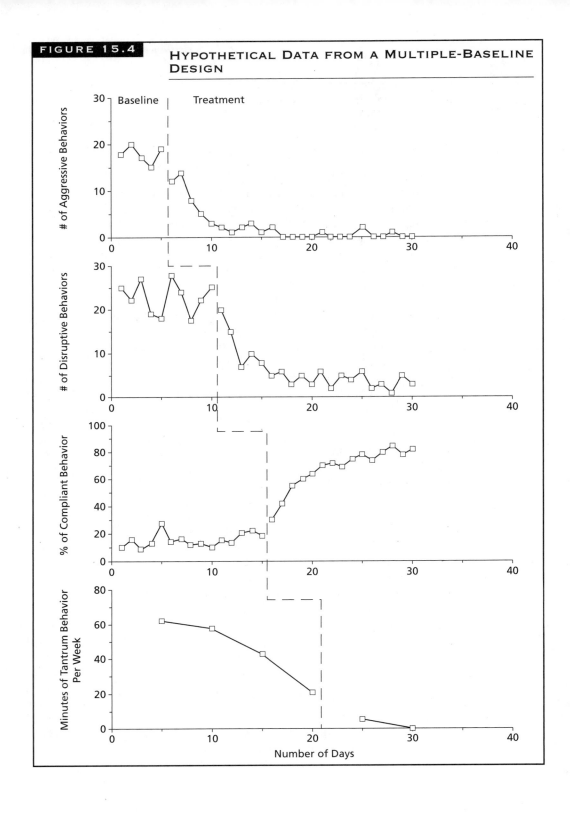

FIGURE 15.4 HYPOTHETICAL DATA FROM A MULTIPLE-BASELINE DESIGN

relatively stable during that time). Even if it could be argued that some historical event could have had an impact solely on Cameron's aggressiveness, we would have to ask about the likelihood that two other historical events, one which only affected Cameron's disruptive behavior and the other which only affected his compliance behaviors, just happened to take place when the DRI treatment was being instituted for these target behaviors. Such a series of coincidences seems implausible, and it seems more likely that the change in these three target behaviors was due to the introduction of the DRI intervention.

The data for the tantrum behavior, however, illustrates a potential problem with multiple-baseline designs. Although the introduction of the DRI intervention was followed by a noticeable decline of tantrum behavior, there had been a substantial decrease in tantrum behavior prior to the administration of the treatment. That is, as Cameron's behavior improved in the other three areas, his tantrum behavior was also decreasing, even though it was still in the baseline phase, which suggests that these target behaviors are correlated with each other, so the effect of the treatment for one of the behaviors carries over to the other behaviors, and this carry-over effect will ultimately confound the interpretation of the results of the experiment. Therefore, when a researcher is considering the use of a multiple-baseline design it is important to consider the relationship between the settings, behaviors, or persons across which the intervention is to be applied; if the target variables are not independent of each other, there is an increased risk of carry-over effects.

Furthermore, carryover is not the only alternative explanation for the pattern of changes in Cameron's tantrums. The tantrum data presented here closely resemble the example of a quasi-experimental time series design presented in Figure 7-2c on page 174. Both graphs show a steady improvement in performance *prior* to the onset of the experimental manipulation that must be due to factors such as maturation. When behavior is steadily improving even before the treatment begins, we cannot attribute *continued* improvement to the experimental manipulation.

Another disadvantage of a multiple-baseline research design involves potential problems surrounding the extended baseline of the targets variables which are the last to receive treatment. There may be occasions when a target behavior is potentially dangerous, or particularly disruptive, and maintaining the behavior in a lengthy baseline would be unethical, or at best, programmatically difficult. In this example, Dr. Jacobs knew (based on the design of the study) that Cameron's tantrum behavior would be maintained in baseline for 20 days, or almost a month, of preschool. If those tantrums were potentially harmful in their intensity, it would be difficult for Dr. Jacobs to justify an extended baseline of almost one month in length.

Measuring the Target Behaviors: Some Alternative Scoring Procedures If you look closely at the four panels of the multiple-baseline design presented in Figure 15-4, you will notice that three different operational definitions were employed in this study: aggression and disruptiveness were both measured by recording the total number of behaviors in a day (i.e., basic event recording); compliant behavior was measured by recording the percentage of behavior in a day; and tantrum behavior was measured by recording the amount of time over a week. The difference among these measurements, in part, reflects some important differences among the behaviors themselves.

For instance, aggressive and disruptive behaviors are essentially under the control of the individual, in that they can occur at almost any time, while oppositional behavior is more dependent on the opportunities to be oppositional, and these opportunities are usually presented by others. For instance, Cameron may display oppositional behavior by refusing to put a toy truck away and join the rest of the class for reading circle when asked to do so by his teacher. If, however, the teacher does not make the request, Cameron has no opportunity to be either compliant or oppositional. Therefore, oppositional behavior can only occur if another person (such as a parent or teacher) makes a request or gives the child an instruction, and the number of opportunities to comply can vary greatly from day to day. Therefore, basic event recording of this target behavior would lack validity, so it makes more sense to translate event data into a percentage (where the number of times compliance occurs is divided by the total number of teacher requests). In addition, rather than present the data as the percentage of oppositional behavior, these data are presented as the percentage of compliant behavior (the incompatible alternative behavior). Presenting data in this way provides a record of increasing appropriate behavior rather than a record of decreasing inappropriate behavior (i.e., it emphasizes the positive even though the results of the two approaches are objectively identical).

Behaviors that occur inconsistently can create highly variable data, which can lead to difficulties in interpretation of the data. As such, the measurement of Cameron's tantrum behavior creates another hypothetical problem for Dr. Jacobs. Tantrum behavior often does not occur daily, and the duration or intensity of a tantrum might vary greatly from one episode to the next. (Consequently, the data points on our graph will "bounce up and down" seemingly at random, which will make it difficult to tell whether systematic changes are taking place during the treatment phases.) Therefore, researchers will typically try to smooth out the graph by recording some type of summary of the behavior. In this example, as indicated on the vertical (Y) axis of Figure 15-4, Dr. Jacobs chose to monitor Cameron's tantrum behavior by reporting the total minutes of tantrum behavior that occurred over a week, rather than in a single day. This summary measure gives Dr. Jacobs a more stable, less variable estimate of Cameron's tantrum behavior. To compensate for the fact that Dr. Jacobs was only going to get one data point per week (instead of five), she decided that Cameron's tantrum behavior should be the last to receive the treatment so there would be an opportunity to establish a consistent baseline of the summary (i.e., weekly) data. It is generally accepted that a minimum of three stable data points are required to establish a reliable estimate of an individual's level of performance.

The Changing Criterion Design

The **changing criterion design** is a technique that is used to change an individual's behavior in small, gradual, attainable steps, until the final behavioral goal is reached. (The step-by-step process of a changing criterion design closely resembles the process known as *shaping by successive approximations*, the operant conditioning procedure B. F. Skinner used to teach rats to press a bar and pigeons to play simple tunes on a toy piano.) For example, when Walter wanted to quit smoking, he decided to start by cutting down from his usual 20 cigarettes per day to 15 per day, and as an incentive, on days when he successfully limited himself to only 15 cigarettes, he would treat himself to a new compact disc (CD). Although it took awhile, Walter eventually was able to limit himself to 15 cigarettes for four days in a row. At that point, Walter allowed himself to buy a new CD only if he limited himself to 10 cigarettes per day. Thus, Walter had changed the criterion of his own treatment plan: at first, the reinforcer was awarded for 15-cigarette days, but then it was only awarded for 10-cigarette days. And once Walter reached this new intermediate goal (by limiting his smoking to 10 cigarettes per day for four days in a row), he changed the criterion to 5 cigarettes per day, and so on until he ultimately reached his final goal of zero cigarettes per day.

In general, then, the changing criterion design involves the following steps: (1) a baseline of behavior is determined; (2) the final goal of intervention is established; (3) intermediate goals for behavior are established; (4) intervention is administered until the first intermediate goal is reached; and when behavior stabilizes at this intermediate goal, (5) the next goal is introduced, and the process repeats itself until the final behavioral goal is reached. If the target behavior does indeed change to meet the ever progressing behavioral goals of the changing criterion, it provides evidence that the treatment has functional control of the target behavior. (Furthermore, each change in behavior in response to a change in criterion serves as a replication of the treatment effect.) Let's look at an example involving another one of Dr. Jacob's cases.

Shana When Dr. Jacobs was consulting with the preschool teacher about Cameron's many behavior problems, the teacher raised some concerns about 4-year-old Shana. It seems that Shana was scheduled to go to a very academically-oriented kindergarten (Belmore Preparatory Academy) during the next year, but with only two months to go in the preschool program, she was having trouble with some of the early academic skills that she would need to be successful in that new setting. Although Shana's behavior was socially appropriate and she consistently demonstrated many teacher-pleasing behaviors, she was having difficulty learning to write her name and recognize letters of the alphabet. The teacher told Dr. Jacobs that the curriculum at Belmore Academy made it very difficult for children to be successful if they could not write their names and recognize at least 40 of the 52 upper- and lower-case letters in the English alphabet before they enrolled. Of greatest concern to the teacher was that Shana could only recognize about ten letters.

After some discussion, Dr. Jacobs and the teacher decided to use a changing criterion design to improve Shana's letter recognition capabilities by giving her flash-card drills for an extra ten minutes per day and rewarding her with extra play time at the sand table (her favorite activity) on days when she met a pre-determined letter recognition criteria. A four-day baseline phase indicated that Shana was recognizing fewer than ten letters, and the final goal was set at 40 upper- and lower-case letters. In order to reach the final goal in the eight remaining weeks of the school year, it was decided that the first intermediate goal would be to firmly establish Shana's

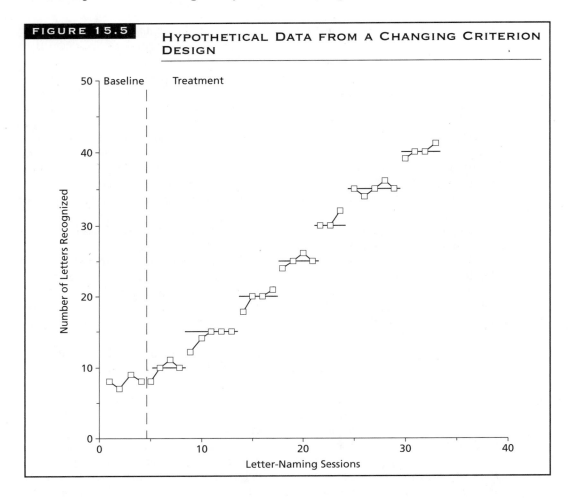

FIGURE 15.5

HYPOTHETICAL DATA FROM A CHANGING CRITERION DESIGN

performance at ten recognized letters and then reset the goals at intervals of five letters whenever Shana's performance was at or above the goal for three consecutive days. The hypothetical results of this treatment plan are presented in Figure 15-5. (On this graph, the intermediate goals are represented by the series of successively higher horizontal lines. New intermediate goals were implemented when Shana's performance met or exceeded the goal three days in a row.) The functional control of the intervention over the target behavior is demonstrated by the consistency with which the goals are met and the stability of the behavior at each level. Furthermore, because Shana's performance increased to meet each new goal, the effect of the treatment has been replicated without having to return to a baseline phase.

Thus, one of the advantages of a changing criterion design is that, similar to the multiple-baseline design, it does not require a withdrawal of treatment. However, a minimum of two criterion changes are required to determine that the behavior is appropriately matching the criteria, and that the intervention is responsible for the change in target behavior. In Shana's case there were six criterion changes (and Walter, our former 20 cigarettes-per-day smoker, would have undergone three criterion changes if he consistently reset his goals at intervals of 5 cigarettes: the change from 15 to 10, from 10 to 5, and from 5 to 0).

Another nice feature of the changing criterion design is the flexibility it offers: the criterion levels can be adapted to each individual and they can be refined during the course of treatment. For example, if Walter is unable to go four days in a row smoking only 15 cigarettes per day, the initial intermediate goal can be adjusted to a more attainable level, such as 17 cigarettes per day, and the criterion shifts can be reduced from 5 to 3 cigarettes. A word of caution is in order, however, concerning the number and size of the criterion shifts that are planned. While these designs usually include several criterion shifts, researchers should avoid using a large number of very small shifts (such as reducing Walter's smoking by only one cigarette at a time) because the results may be unable to provide a clear demonstration of the treatment effect. Ideally, the intermediate criterion levels should be spaced far enough apart to clearly demonstrate that the treatment has a noticeable impact on the behavior, yet close enough to allow the behavior shaping process to actually begin. For instance, if Walter was a very heavy smoker who smoked 60 cigarettes per day, it would be unrealistic to set the first intermediate goal at 20 since it is unlikely that the promise of a new CD would be powerful enough to induce a behavior change of such magnitude.

Alternating Treatment Designs

Earlier in this chapter, we presented the changing conditions design (i.e., ABCAC) to illustrate how the basic ABAB design can be expanded to evaluate the effects of more than one intervention (independent variable) upon a single target behavior (dependent variable). Another common multiple treatment design is the **alternating treatments design.** In an alternating treatments design, the interventions are simultaneously presented during the same treatment phase, rather than in sequential phases as in the changing conditions design. That is, over the course of the treatment phase, two or more different interventions are administered in an alternating (or rotating) fashion. For example, to test two treatments for an infant who has a tantrum every time she is placed in her crib, the first intervention may be applied before the afternoon nap while the second treatment can be applied at bedtime, and the next day, the treatments are reversed. This alternation of interventions will prevent a confound between specific treatments and specific times of the day. Thus, data can be gathered for both treatments during the same treatment phase.

The steps in an alternating treatments design are: (1) defining a target behavior, (2) developing the (multiple) interventions, (3) collecting baseline data, and (4) administering the interventions in an alternating or balanced rotation during the treatment phase. Depending on the specific characteristics of the target behavior (such as when it typically occurs) and the interventions themselves (such as how long they take), the multiple treatments can be administered within a single session, during sessions at different times of the day, or across days. In addition, if the observations suggest that one treatment is more effective than the other, it is common practice to add a treatment phase in which that intervention is administered exclusively.

As an example of an alternating treatments design, let's suppose that Dr. Jacobs had developed two interventions designed to reduce Cameron's oppositional behavior: differential reinforcement of incompatible responses (DRI) and response cost (RC). For the DRI intervention, the teacher differentially reinforced Cameron for being cooperative and compliant, and for the RC intervention, Cameron lost three minutes of playtime whenever he displayed oppositional behavior. According to the teacher, Cameron's oppositional behavior seemed to peak at three distinctly different times during the day: around mid-morning, shortly after lunch, and again shortly after the afternoon nap. Therefore, Dr. Jacobs decided to alternately apply the two interventions and a no-intervention control condition in a balanced rotation across the each time period during the alternating treatments phase. That is, she set up a schedule where, on the first day of treatment, the DRI intervention was used in the morning, the RC intervention was used after lunch, and the no-treatment control condition was implemented after the afternoon nap period. The following day, the control condition was applied in the morning, the DRI intervention was used after lunch, and the RC intervention was used after the nap. On the third day, the RC intervention was used in the morning, the control condition was applied after lunch, and the DRI was implemented after the nap. This cycle of three days was repeated through the treatment phase of the study.

Baseline data were collected across five days during each of three time periods, and then the alternating treatments were implemented over a ten-day treatment phase. During this treatment phase, it became apparent that differential reinforcement of incompatible responses (the DRI intervention) was most effective in increasing Cameron's compliant behavior, so Dr. Jacobs added a five-day DRI-only phase (in which DRI was used at all three periods during the day). The hypothetical data from this study are presented in Figure 15-6. In the first and third panels of this graph (i.e., the "Baseline" and "DRI" phases), the three lines represent Jimmy's behavior during the three time periods—mid-morning, after lunch, and after naptime. In the "Alternating Treatments" panel of the graph, the three lines represent the three separate treatment conditions.

As you can see, Cameron's compliant behavior was consistently low across all three time periods during the baseline phase (indicating that he was quite oppositional at all three points during the day, just as the teacher had predicted). During the alternating treatments phase, Cameron's oppositional behavior during the no-treatment time periods remained consistent with his baseline behavior, but both interventions resulted in increases in compliant behavior, especially the DRI treatment. The effectiveness of differential reinforcement of incompatible responses (DRI) is then further demonstrated in the final phase of the design when this intervention was administered across all three time periods, and it was found that Cameron was very compliant throughout the day for the entire week.

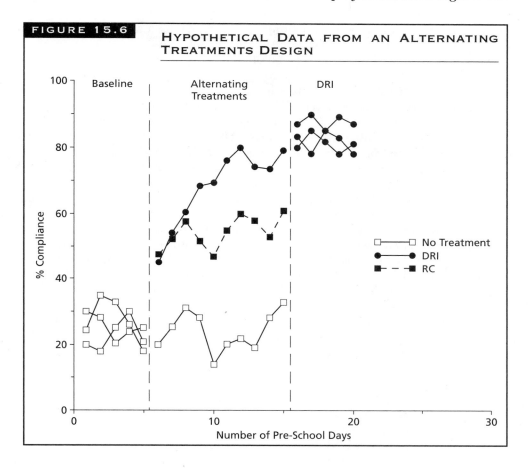

FIGURE 15.6 HYPOTHETICAL DATA FROM AN ALTERNATING TREATMENTS DESIGN

In this example, the functional control of the interventions over the target behavior is demonstrated by Cameron's increased compliance as compared to his continuing oppositional behavior during the no-treatment control condition in the alternating treatments phase. By the end of the alternating treatments phase, Cameron was displaying three distinctly different patterns of behavior each day, and these patterns were consistent with the different interventions: when the treatment changed, so did Cameron's behavior. Hence, the effectiveness of the treatments was being replicated during the alternating treatments phase. And, of course, the effectiveness of DRI was further replicated in the final phase.

An advantage of an alternating treatments design is that this design permits us to compare two or more interventions. In the hypothetical data presented in Figure 15-6, both interventions were effective, but DRI was better. Had Dr. Jacobs only used the response cost (RC) intervention with Cameron (e.g., in an ABAB design), she would not have become aware of the greater effectiveness of differential reinforcement (DRI). Furthermore, as the example demonstrates, it is sometimes possible to include a no-treatment control condition (which serves as a continuing baseline) in the balanced rotation of the treatments, and this additional experimental control helps rule out potential confounds.

There are some important limitations for alternating treatments designs. First, they rely on changes in behaviors over short periods of time (e.g., from mid-morning to just after lunch), and therefore, they can only be effectively employed for target behaviors which tend to show quick shifts. Behaviors that tend to persist over time and change only gradually are not suitable for these designs because they will not show an immediate response to the session-by-session changes in treatment. Second, these designs are only suitable when the interventions are likely to have relatively immediate effects on behavior. If the treatment is not capable of generating a rapid response, the effect of the treatment will be lost when the next treatment is applied in the balanced rotation. Third, in order for the alternating treatments design to detect differences in the effectiveness of the treatments, the treatments cannot be too much alike. That is, the participants need to be able to discriminate between them. Finally, the interventions must be free of carryover effects. If the effects of one treatment do not degrade quickly, it becomes confounded with the next treatment in the rotation, and even a balanced rotation of the treatments cannot completely control for the possibility of such carryover effects, although it may make their presence easier to detect. (This is similar to the problem of differential carryover as a limitation of counterbalancing for within-subjects designs as discussed in Chapter 10.)

Mixed Designs

Up to this point, single-subject research designs have been presented in their simple form. However, elements of different designs can be combined in the same study in what is called a **mixed design**. Combining elements from different designs can add strength or clarity to an investigation, since the strengths of one design may be able to offset the weaknesses of another. For instance, the reversal to baseline, which is the defining characteristic of the ABAB design, is frequently mixed into other designs in order to make the demonstration of functional control over the target behavior more clear. Similarly, multiple-baselines are often added to designs where there is a concern about the wisdom (or ethics) of withdrawing a treatment after it has begun to affect the target behavior, especially if multiple settings or participants are available. While the decision to mix design elements typically occurs before the data are collected (as part of the effort to design the best possible study by controlling for anticipated problems), researchers may add new elements to an ongoing study in an attempt to control for the unforeseen complications which occur frequently in applied research settings (and create possible history confounds). Let's look at an example of a mixed design which illustrates both a planned mix of elements and a design change that was necessitated by unexpected events.

Dr. Jacobs, our by now quite famous psychological consultant, also works with a physician who has recently diagnosed Daniel, a second-grader, with Attention Deficit Hyperactivity Disorder (ADHD). Daniel's impulsiveness and his inattentive behavior was interfering with his progress in school, so the physician wanted to prescribe a minimum dose of stimulant medication as a treatment for the ADHD behaviors. However, Daniel's parents, while not opposed to medication, wanted to explore additional options before making a decision, so Dr. Jacobs was asked to evaluate treatment options. After observing Daniel in school, Dr. Jacobs determined that his inattentive behavior was particularly disruptive during the structured exercises of math class and noted that he responded well to positive reinforcement from his teacher. This suggested to Dr. Jacobs that differential reinforcement of on-task behavior, which is incompatible with inattentiveness, may be an effective approach with Daniel, but there was still the question of whether stimulant medication would be a better choice. Therefore, after consulting with Daniel's parents, teacher, and physician, Dr. Jacobs decided to try three interventions: differential reinforcement of on-task behavior (DRI); a minimum amount of stimulant medication; and a combination of DRI and stimulant medication.

Because everyone was interested in finding an effective treatment in a timely manner, Dr. Jacobs decided to use an alternating treatments design. She realized, however, that while stimulant medication is generally a fast acting treatment, DRI often results in a slower response to intervention. This could make the stimulant medication appear to be more effective than DRI simply because its effects occur sooner. Dr. Jacobs decided to avoid this obstacle by adding a DRI-only training phase prior to the alternating treatments phase. Thus, the mixed design included elements from a changing conditions design and an alternating treatments design. The design started with five-day baseline (phase A) during which Daniel's on-task behavior during math class was recorded. This was followed by five days when the teacher differentially reinforced Daniel's on-task behavior (phase B), and then the alternating treatments phase was implemented over a period of 13 days. (The three treatments were administered on alternating days, in partially counterbalanced order, during math class.) The hypothetical data for this study are presented in Figure 15-7.

During the alternating treatments phase, it quickly became clear that the combination of DRI with stimulant medication was the most effective intervention. However, during a routine interview with Daniel's parents on the twentieth day of the study, Dr. Jacobs discovered that Daniel had gotten a puppy for his birthday early in the DRI-only phase (B) and had immediately become much less impulsive at home. This unanticipated event created a potentially confounding variable for the design, since Daniel's improvement in impulsiveness at home might have carried over into increased on-task behavior in school, so there was a question of how much of Daniel's improvement at school was actually due to the introduction of the puppy (rather than the experimental interventions). To control for this potential confound, Dr. Jacobs extended the design in order to conduct a replication of the effects of the stimulant medications-plus-DRI intervention by instituting a brief three-day return to baseline (A) phase, followed by a five-day period where Daniel received the combination of DRI and the stimulant medication. As you can see in Figure 15-7, the data from these last two phases provided confirmation of the finding that the DRI plus medication intervention was very effective. With this data in hand, Dr. Jacobs,

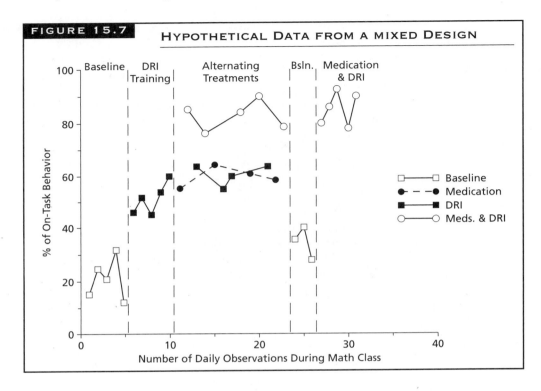

FIGURE 15.7   HYPOTHETICAL DATA FROM A MIXED DESIGN

Daniel's parents, and the physician were able to agree on an intervention that they believed was best for Daniel.

Single-Subject Designs for Applied and Basic Research Questions

As we indicated earlier, the usefulness of single-subject research designs is not limited to clinical applications where the goal is to change the behavior of specific individuals. Instead, single-subject designs can be used to address both basic and applied research questions about general phenomena. Let's look at some brief examples.

During the 1980s and 1990s, a new style of corporate management became fashionable, and millions of dollars were spent training managers in what was called "Total Quality Management" (or TQM). The question for a researcher would naturally be: "Does TQM training improve the productivity of a company?" We might first consider using an ABAB design where, following a baseline phase during which productivity is carefully defined and measured, the managers of the company undergo TQM training and begin to apply those principles at work. After some period of time (such as six months), the managers could be instructed to return to their pre-TQM management styles for a second baseline phase, and then TQM could be reintroduced.

The problem with this design that immediately comes to mind is the possibility of carryover. If the managers who received the TQM training came to believe in its benefits, they may not completely give it up during the second baseline phase, and consequently, productivity levels may not return to baseline levels, and the pattern of data would not clearly demonstrate that TQM had functional control over productivity. Therefore, we may consider using a multiple-baseline design instead of an ABAB design. The multiple targets in this study could be different branch offices of the company or different departments within the same office. All of these target settings are started on baseline simultaneously, and then TQM training is instituted for the managers of one of the target units while the other targets stay at baseline. Then a second target receives TQM training, and later the third target receives the training, and so on until all units are using TQM. If TQM had functional control over productivity levels, we would see that each unit showed increases in productivity when TQM was implemented within their branch office or department.

This hypothetical study on the effectiveness of TQM management principles is an example of applied research. As an example of how single-subject designs can be used to address basic research questions, let's suppose that a psychologist is interested in the effects of caffeine consumption on normal sleep cycles and the number of dream periods (known as REM sleep) a person experiences at night. In order to determine whether or not drinking caffeine during the day has any influence on REM sleep, the psychologist could use an ABAB design where the baseline phase involves an average amount of caffeine consumption during the day and the treatment phase involves drinking only decaffeinated beverages. The participants could sleep in the researcher's laboratory where recordings of brain wave activity (using an electroencephalograph—EEG) and muscle tone (using an electromyograph—EMG) could identify periods of REM sleep. If caffeine influences dream sleep, there should be a change in the number of REM sleep cycles during the treatment phase, a return to baseline levels during the second phase A, and another change in REM sleep when the treatment is reintroduced. If the evidence from the ABAB design suggests that caffeine indeed has an effect on dream sleep, the design could then be expanded to further explore the relationship between the variables. For instance, the effects of increased amounts of caffeine could be explored in an ABABCAC design where phase C involves higher levels of caffeine consumption than phase B. For these studies, it would be important that the researcher establish the implementation integrity of the treatment by measuring accidental intake of caffeine (such as eating chocolate, taking diet pills, or drinking various soft drinks, including some so-called sports drinks).

Evaluation of Data from Single-Subject Designs

Thus, single-subject designs can be used to explore the general effects of an experimental manipulation as well as to test the effectiveness of an intervention for specific individuals. These two types of research have different goals, and therefore, the data may be evaluated from different perspectives. If the purpose of the study is to simply determine if the treatment has an effect, then the researcher will compare performance under the baseline (no treatment condition) to the treatment phase, and if there is a systematic difference between the two conditions, we say that an *experimental criterion* has been met. However, when the therapeutic value of the intervention is the focus of the study, finding systematic differences may not be enough. For example, the intervention implemented by Dr. Jacobs in the original case study (see Figure 15-1) decreased Cameron's aggressive behavior from an average of 18 outbursts per day during the baseline phase, to one or two outbursts per day by the end of the treatment phase. This difference certainly meets an experimental criterion, but if Cameron's one or two aggressive outbursts are potentially harmful to him or others, then, from a therapeutic standpoint, the treatment has not been effective *enough*. In Cameron's case, the intervention isn't considered "effective" unless it meets a *therapeutic criterion* (such as a reduction in aggressive behavior to zero occurrences). The rest of this chapter describes the techniques commonly used to evaluate the results of single-subject research designs.

Visual Inspection

Just as we have done in each of our examples thus far, the effect of an intervention in single-subject research is usually evaluated by visually inspecting a graph of the data points. Put simply, we look to see if the introduction of the intervention was followed by a change in the target behavior that would not have occurred if the intervention had not been administered. Although this visual inspection process may sound very subjective and open to bias compared to the statistical tests used to analyze data from group designs (such as ANOVA), in reality this method is generally quite objective. For example, an intervention effect needs be to quite potent in order to be seen during a visual inspection of the data from single-subjects designs, while statistical analysis of group research data sometimes indicates that very small effects are statistically significant, especially if the size of the group is large. Thus, while group research may not distinguish between the statistical significance and the meaningfulness of an effect, visual inspection of single-subjects data tends to identify only the more powerful (and potentially meaningful) effects.

During visual inspection of the data, the researcher compares the level of performance during the phases of the design. Typically, the researcher will use one of two approaches in evaluating the data: (1) judging the *magnitude* of the differences in behavior between phases, or (2) comparing changes in *trend* across phases.

Magnitude of Change   One method for evaluating the magnitude of change is to compare changes in the means, or average rates of performance, across design phases. A comparison of phase means provides an indication of whether the target behavior responded to the intervention as expected. Figure 15-8 presents a hypothetical example of an ABAB design with the mean of each phase indicated by a solid

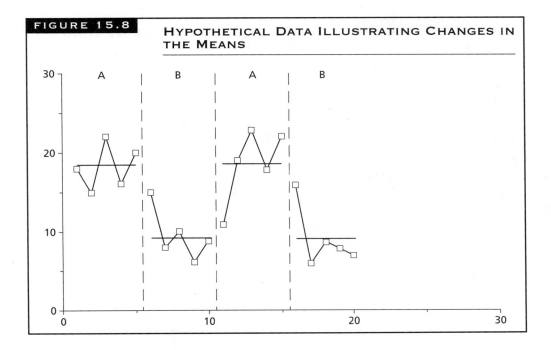

FIGURE 15.8 HYPOTHETICAL DATA ILLUSTRATING CHANGES IN THE MEANS

horizontal line. The figure demonstrates consistent changes in behavior across the baseline and treatment phases as represented by the changes in phase means.

A second method for assessing the magnitude of change between phases is to evaluate *changes in level* of performance between phases. The change in level refers to how quickly the target behavior reacts to the onset of a new treatment condition. That is, we compare the level of performance at the end of one phase to the level of performance at the beginning of the next phase. The hypothetical data in Figure 15-9 demonstrates a clear change of level between phases in an ABAB design: the behavior shows a distinct and immediate response to changes in the phases. In contrast, the shifts between phases in Figure 15-8 are more gradual and there is some overlapping of data points between phases.

Trend Analysis   Sometimes the rate of change is a more important feature of the data than is the magnitude of change. In these situations it is more appropriate to compare changes in *trends* between the phases. The rate of change is represented by the slope of the "line" that connects the data points on the graph.[3] The steeper the line (i.e., the higher the slope), the faster behavior is changing, since performance reaches higher levels in a shorter period of time. If we compare the slopes (or trends)

---

[3]See Chapter 9 for a brief review of the slope of straight lines.

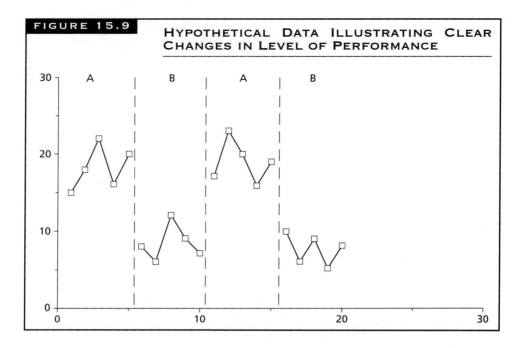

FIGURE 15.9

HYPOTHETICAL DATA ILLUSTRATING CLEAR CHANGES IN LEVEL OF PERFORMANCE

in each phase, we may be able to detect systematic differences in the rate of change that can be attributed to the treatment.

In some cases, we may see opposing trends when we compare the phases, such as when performance steadily deteriorates during baseline (resulting in a decreasing trend), but steadily improves during the treatment phase (resulting in an increasing trend). Obviously, these opposing trends are easy to detect and simple to evaluate. However, there are many cases where the trends are in the same direction, but the rate of increase or decrease (that is, the slope) changes between phases. This situation is illustrated in Figure 15-10, which presents hypothetical data from an intervention to improve the reading skill of a first-grade student. In this example, the increasing trend during the baseline phase would be expected because, even without the intervention, a first-grader's reading skill is likely to improve over time as a function of normal classroom experiences. The goal of the intervention, then, is to increase the rate of learning. If you examine the data in Figure 15-10, you will see that the rate of increase in reading skill during the intervention phase appears to be about three times faster than the rate of change during baseline. That is, over the course of the six days of the first baseline phase, the reading scores changed from approximately 21 to 26, while over the next six days of treatment, the scores improved from 30 to 47. (If you imagine drawing a straight line through the data points for each of the four phases in Figure 15-10, you will see that the lines in the "B"

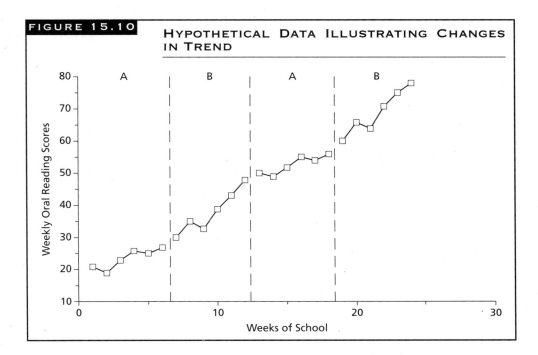

FIGURE 15.10 — HYPOTHETICAL DATA ILLUSTRATING CHANGES IN TREND

phases have steeper slopes than the lines for the "A" phases.) Unfortunately, trends are not always so easy to judge and additional methods for determining slope must be employed.

One relatively quick method for estimating the slope for a treatment phase is the median split technique. This technique splits the treatment phase in half and calculates the median score for each half, as illustrated in see Figure 15-11a (where a vertical dashed line shows the mid-point of the 14-day treatment phase and the median scores for each half of the phase are circled). A **trend line** is then drawn connecting these two median data points (Figure 15-11b) and the slope of that line can be determined. The disadvantage of the median split technique is that it only provides an estimate of the slope, so some researchers will choose to perform a simple regression analysis instead.[4]

Simple regression analysis using the least-squares method of regression (LSM, which is presented in detail in Chapter 9) measures the slope of a data set much more precisely than the median split technique, and if you have an appropriate computer-based statistics or spread sheet program, the analysis will not take much time. Figure 15-11c presents the results of an LSM trend analysis for the hypothetical data from a 14-day treatment phase, and Figure 15-11d shows us the difference between

---

[4]The median is discussed in Chapter 5, and the slope of a line and regression analysis are presented in Chapter 9.

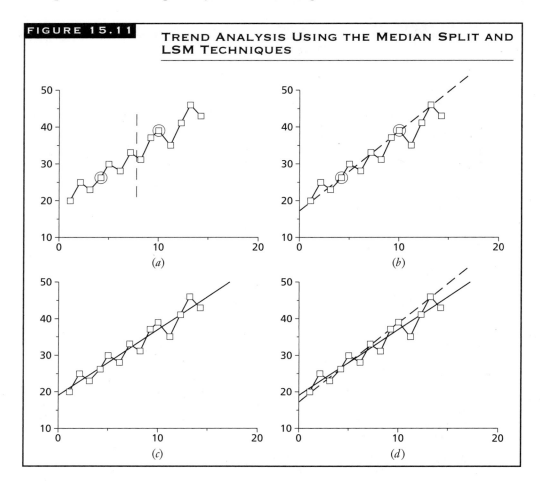

FIGURE 15.11

TREND ANALYSIS USING THE MEDIAN SPLIT AND LSM TECHNIQUES

the trend lines generated by the two techniques. (For these data, the median split technique provides an overestimate of the rate of change during the treatment phase; that is, the slope of the trend line from the median split technique is steeper than the trend line from the regression analysis.)

Variability   There are times when the goal of an intervention is to stabilize highly variable behavior. For example, treatment for a person with bipolar disorder (i.e., manic depression) may be designed to replace the wild mood swings which are characteristic of the disorder with a calmer, more stable, and less variable behavior pattern. In such cases, the effectiveness of an intervention will be evident in a shift from a highly variable pattern of behavior during baseline to a more controlled, less variable pattern of behavior during treatment. Figure 15-12 presents hypothetical data

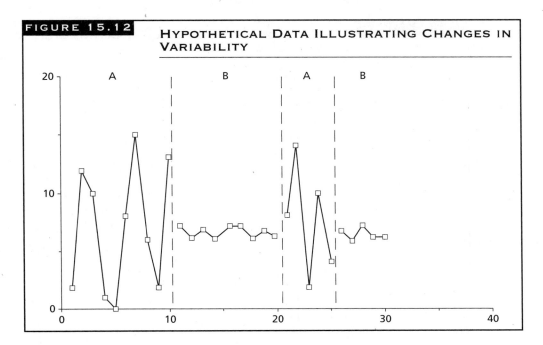

FIGURE 15.12

HYPOTHETICAL DATA ILLUSTRATING CHANGES IN VARIABILITY

from an ABAB design in which the intervention effectively reduces the variability in behavior. (This figure also illustrates how easy it is to detect changes in variability between phases through visual inspection of the data.)

Unfortunately, highly variable behavior often will not stabilize as clearly as it did in the hypothetical data in Figure 15-12, and variability in the data can make a change in level difficult to assess.[5] When variability in the data creates an interpretation problem, changes in level can sometimes be analyzed by calculating the **percentage of overlap** for adjacent design phases. The four steps in calculating the percentage of overlapping data points are: (a) determining the range of scores in the first phase; (b) finding the number of data points in the second phase that fall within the range of scores for phase one; (c) counting the total number of data points in phase two; and then (d) dividing the number of overlapping data points by the total number of data points in phase two and multiplying the quotient by 100. If there is a high degree of overlap between phases, it suggests that the treatment is not having a meaningful effect on the target behavior. A low percentage of overlapping data

---

[5]It is important to understand that an unexpectedly high degree of variability in the data set might be an indicator of error in the measurement procedure. If the researcher detects an unusual amount of variability in the target behavior, he or she should look closely at the operational definitions and the implementation integrity of the design. Greater standardization in the administration of the experimental conditions may be required.

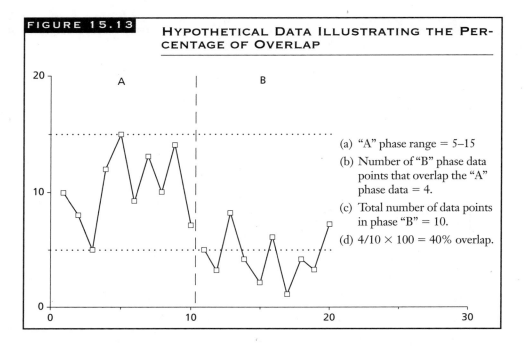

FIGURE 15.13

HYPOTHETICAL DATA ILLUSTRATING THE PERCENTAGE OF OVERLAP

(a) "A" phase range = 5–15

(b) Number of "B" phase data points that overlap the "A" phase data = 4.

(c) Total number of data points in phase "B" = 10.

(d) 4/10 × 100 = 40% overlap.

points, in contrast, is considered to be an indicator of a meaningful treatment effect. Having said this, we need to point out that there are no specific rules that define the cut-off points for "high" and "low" percentages of overlap. The researcher will need to use good judgment if the results fall in the gray areas between obviously high and obviously low percentages of overlap. The procedure for computing the percentage of overlap is illustrated in Figure 15-13.

In the example presented in Figure 15-13: (a) the scores in phase one range from 5 to 15; (b) the number of data points in phase two that fall within the range of scores from phase one is 4; (c) the total number of data points in phase two is 10; and therefore, (d) the percentage of overlapping data points = 4/10 × 100 or 40%.

Interpreting the Data from Single-Subject Research

So far, we have illustrated the single-subject designs with idealized hypothetical data that are easily interpreted as evidence that the treatment indeed has functional control of the behavior, and that this effect is replicated. And as long as the obvious potential confounding factors such as history, maturation, and instrumentation have been ruled out through appropriate controls, it is easy to argue that a causal interpretation of the data—the treatment actually causes the change in behavior—is highly

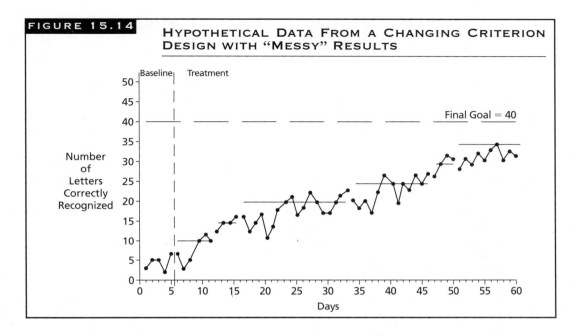

FIGURE 15.14

HYPOTHETICAL DATA FROM A CHANGING CRITERION DESIGN WITH "MESSY" RESULTS

plausible. Thus, when the data from a single-subject design are clean and neat, as they have been in our examples, the clinicians and researchers who rely on these designs are satisfied that they have met the criteria for causality. However, the data from single-subjects designs are sometimes pretty "messy" rather than clean and neat. For example, let's assume that the data in Figure 15-14 is from a Changing Criterion Design with Shana, the little girl who needed to learn to recognize most of the upper- and lower-case letters in order to be successful in the academically-oriented Belmore Preparatory Academy's kindergarten. (As you'll recall, Shana was tested with flash-card drills each day, and if she met the predetermined daily criterion for letter-recognition, she was rewarded with extra time playing at the sand table—her favorite activity. The criterion level was increased when Shana met or exceeded the daily criterion for three consecutive days.)

The data in Figure 15-14 indicate that although Shana's performance did improve gradually over the 60 days of the study, she did not achieve the final goal (of 40 correct), and she did not respond consistently to intermediate changes in the criterion. That is, at times she seemed to respond rapidly to the new criterion, but at other times, she was very slow to meet the new criterion, and she showed a lot of variability from day to day. From this data, is it reasonable to conclude that the reward (extra play time) had functional control over Shana's letter-recognition behavior? Certainly, we would be less willing to reach this conclusion based on the results presented in Figure 15-14 than we were for the data in Figure 15-5, because there are any number of alternative explanations for these "messy" data. For instance, the gradual improvement over the 60 days may be due to continued exposure to reading materials in general rather than the treatment (which would be an example of a history confound).

Since single-subject research is quasi-experimental in nature and because it may be impossible to rule out every possible alternative explanation for the observed results, many researchers insist that single-subject designs not be interpreted like true experiments, even when the data are very neat and clean. While the controversy over the appropriate interpretation of these designs will not be resolved in this text, we think students should be aware of the basic arguments involved. Many proponents of single-subject research are clinical or applied psychologists who are trying to help specific individuals, and if they find that a particular treatment has replicable, functional control over the target behavior, they can apply this knowledge immediately, hopefully to the direct benefit of their client. Furthermore, multiple-baseline designs which compare the treatment across different individuals can help applied psychologists identify those individuals for whom a particular treatment is effective and those for whom the treatment is ineffective. This may help them tailor treatments to the individual needs of different clients. Basically, then, the needs of clinical or applied research may be adequately met with single-subject designs, even though they do not meet the strict criteria for true experimental research.

Potential Confounds and Problems in the Visual Interpretation of Data

As we have indicated, there are many potential confounds or problems to overcome in the visual interpretation of data from single-subject designs. In this section three of these potential problems will be presented: cyclical patterns of behavior (cyclicity); carryover effects; and outliers.

At times, *cycles of behavior* (cyclicity) will be exhibited in a set of data points. If these cycles of behavior occur in an ABAB design, as illustrated in Figure 15-15, interpretation of the results becomes quite difficult. When a cyclical pattern appears in the graphed data points, it is important to consider the possibility of plausible alternative hypotheses. For instance, in the study presented in Figure 15-15, it is possible that the target behavior is being influenced by any of three possible factors other than the treatment: a naturally occurring schedule of reinforcement within the institutional setting; a complex pattern of chained responses; or internal biological (circadian) rhythms.

Carryover effects occur when the effects of an intervention continue beyond the point at which the intervention is discontinued. If the focus of the intervention is therapeutic, carryover of an effective treatment would be a positive outcome of intervention. However, when the focus of the study is experimental, carryover effects create a confound in multiple treatment designs and interfere with a return to baseline in an ABAB design. A balanced rotation of the treatments in a multiple treatment design might be able to control for carryover effects, but not necessarily. In most cases, then, when carryover is a threat to the design, the best cure for carryover effects is to choose a design, such as multiple baseline design, in which a withdrawal of treatment is not required.

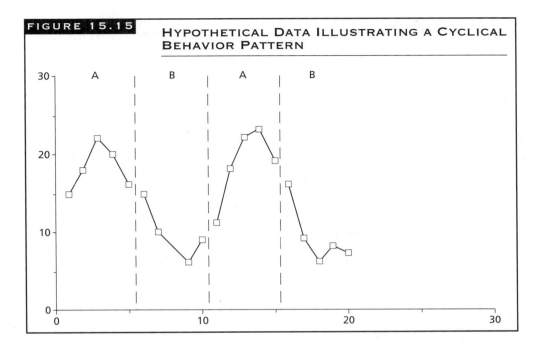

FIGURE 15.15

HYPOTHETICAL DATA ILLUSTRATING A CYCLICAL BEHAVIOR PATTERN

Temporary carryover effects can sometimes cause a delayed response to the treatment. This is referred to as a *latency of response*. Latency is exhibited in a set of data points when the target behavior responds gradually, rather than immediately, to the introduction of an intervention, and it can also occur if a target behavior is resistant to change, or if a treatment has an accumulating effect. Figure 15-16 provides hypothetical data in which latency of response creates a problem for interpretation. Although it is clear in this example that there is a change in the magnitude of the target behavior (as indicated by a change in means and a change in level) between the baseline and treatment phase, there is also a gradual increase of behavior during baseline, followed by a slow response to the intervention. This pattern of response makes it more difficult to determine whether the change in behavior is an effect of the intervention or another confounding variable that appears later in the treatment phase.

An *outlier* is a data point that appears to be discrepant from the trend, or level, established by the other data points in the set, and if they occur with some frequency, they can create problems in the interpretation of the data. Therefore, it is important to be able to recognize outliers, and if at all possible, to try to identify their probable cause. Although outliers are sometimes nothing more than a random, spurious data point, they are often caused by experimental error or an uncontrolled, confounding variable. When outliers occur during an intervention phase, a common suspect is a lack of treatment integrity in the implementation of the intervention.

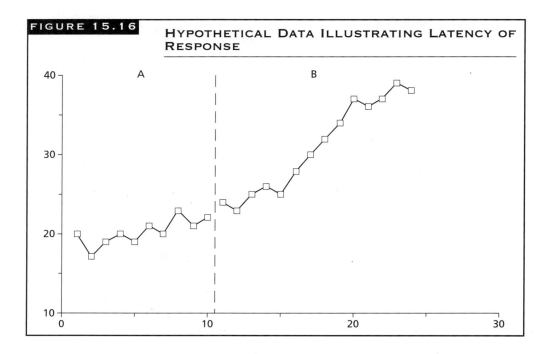

FIGURE 15.16

HYPOTHETICAL DATA ILLUSTRATING LATENCY OF RESPONSE

Outliers may be identified through visual inspection of the data. Since, by definition these points fall outside of the general shape of the data set, it is often quite obvious when an outlier is present. However, if there is a lot of variability within the data set, visual inspection may be less effective at detecting outliers, so other techniques may be needed. For instance, outliers may be more precisely defined and identified by using the standard deviation of the data set. For example, any score that falls more than two standard deviations above or below the mean may be considered to be outliers. Figure 15-17 demonstrates the use of standard deviations in determining outliers. In this figure, the mean of the data set is represented by the solid line; the dashed line is one standard deviation from the mean; and the dotted line is two standard deviations away from the mean. In this case, there are two data points which lie more than two standard deviations below the mean, and they would be considered to be the obvious outliers. This technique of using standard deviation units to evaluate outliers is particularly helpful if there is fair amount of variability in the data set.

Resources for Further Study

Visual inspection is generally a reliable and valid approach for evaluating the results of single-subject research. Although there is still some debate on the value of various statistical methods in analyzing single-subject research data, statistical verification of

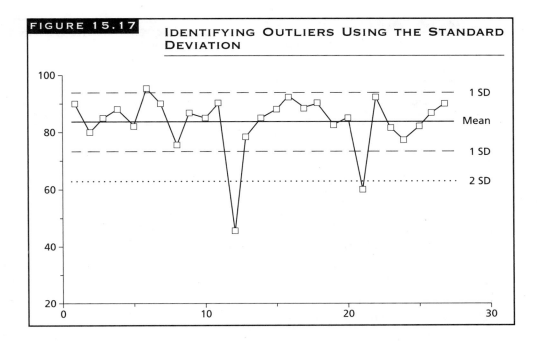

FIGURE 15.17   IDENTIFYING OUTLIERS USING THE STANDARD DEVIATION

effects is becoming more common. Statistical analysis may be most helpful when the effects of the intervention are less clear or when there are trends in the baseline which hinder visual interpretation of the data. For a more comprehensive presentation of the issues surrounding the use of statistics in single-subject research, as well as detailed discussions on many of the other concepts introduced in this chapter, interested students are referred to Franklin, Allison, and Gorman (1996), Kazdin (1982), or Kratochwill and Levin (1992).

Exercises

1. A psychologist videotaped a client suffering from obsessive-compulsive disorder for 6 minutes during which the client engaged in several episodes of ritualistic contamination behavior. The diagram in Figure 15-18 is an "analog" of the videotape, with each of the six minutes divided into 10-second intervals. The shaded boxes represent the episodes of ritualistic behavior (and the actual duration of each episode is indicated below the box).

   Measure the frequency of the client's ritualistic behavior using: (a) event recording (or event sampling); (b) partial interval recording (using the 10-second intervals); (c) whole interval recording (again

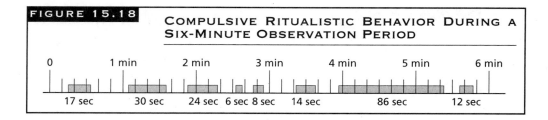

FIGURE 15.18

COMPULSIVE RITUALISTIC BEHAVIOR DURING A SIX-MINUTE OBSERVATION PERIOD

using the 10-second intervals); (d) time sampling using the beginning of a 10-second interval as the "moment" being recorded; and (e) duration. Do each of these techniques seem to convey the same information about the frequency of the behavior? Explain.

2. For each of the following designs, describe how the **functional control** of the target behavior is established: (a) ABAB designs; (b) changing conditions designs; (c) multiple baseline designs; (d) changing criterion designs; and (e) alternating treatment designs.

3. The ABAB and changing conditions designs each involve a return to the baseline phase which allows the researcher to replicate the treatment effect. How do multiple baseline designs and changing criterion designs (which do not include a return to baseline) demonstrate replication of the treatment effects?

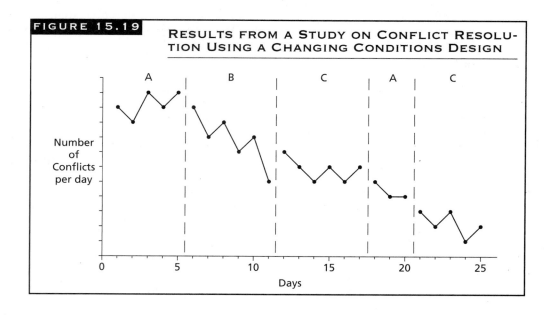

FIGURE 15.19

RESULTS FROM A STUDY ON CONFLICT RESOLUTION USING A CHANGING CONDITIONS DESIGN

4. For each of the following designs, identify the potential confounds (such as history effects) which pose the greatest threats to the validity of the interpretation of the design and explain why you think so. (a) ABAB designs; (b) changing conditions designs; (c) multiple baseline designs; (d) changing criterion designs; and (e) alternating treatment designs.

5. The graph in Figure 15-19 presents hypothetical data from a changing conditions design. An industrial-organizational psychologist was working with employees who were constantly engaged in disruptive conflicts with their co-workers and decided to try to reduce these conflicts by providing conflict resolution training alone (Phase B) or in combination with an anger management program (Phase C). What conclusions would you draw from the data?

6. A 3-year-old autistic child had begun to use the bathroom sporadically, but the parents wanted to speed up the learning process so that the child would be allowed to attend preschool the following year. They decided to use positive reinforcement (by giving the child some of his favorite candy each time he successfully used the bathroom), and the results of their ABAB toilet-training study are presented in Figure 15-20. What technique could be used to determine whether the treatment successfully increased the rate

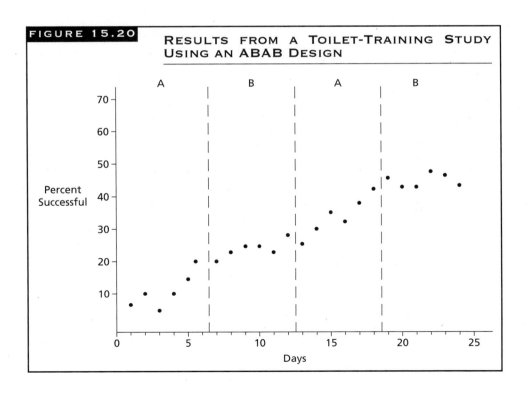

FIGURE 15.20 RESULTS FROM A TOILET-TRAINING STUDY USING AN ABAB DESIGN

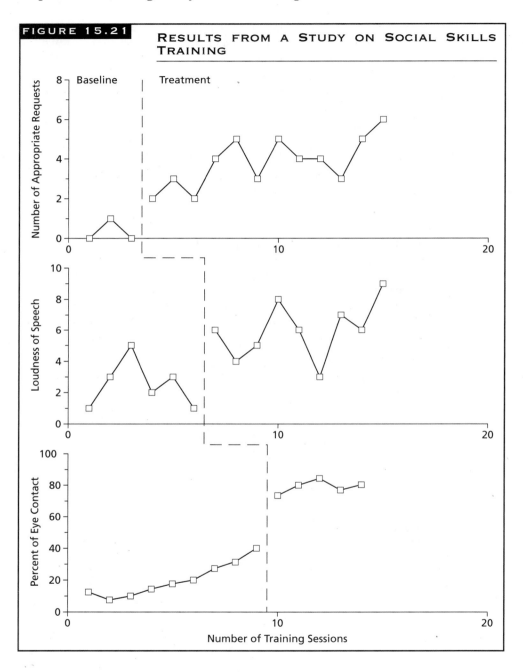

FIGURE 15.21 RESULTS FROM A STUDY ON SOCIAL SKILLS TRAINING

of learning? Using that technique, what conclusion would you draw from these data?

7. Figure 15-21 presents the results of a social skills training study with a 12-year-old girl. Identify the type of research design and provide an interpretation of the results.

8. Suppose you wanted to design a single-subjects study to assess the effectiveness of an intervention being administered to an inattentive and impulsive 11-year-old boy.

   a. Choose a design and determine what steps you would need to follow before the intervention could actually be implemented.

   b. Create a graph presenting hypothetical results of your design that suggest that the intervention has been successful.

   c. Create a second graph presenting hypothetical results of your design that suggest that the intervention has not been successful (or where there is a potential confound which prevents a clear interpretation of the findings).

   d. Identify a second possible design you could have chosen. What difference would it make if you had selected this second design rather than the first?

CHAPTER

16

QUALITATIVE RESEARCH METHODS AND ANALYSIS

■ ■ ■ ■ ■ ■

In this chapter, you will be introduced to the principles of qualitative research which focuses on behavior as it occurs in complex, natural settings. This contextual approach is characterized by a distinct flexibility in data-gathering that is in direct contrast to the systematic, standardized procedures we have emphasized throughout this text. You will see how this approach may have much to offer to psychologists trying to understand human behavior.

Look for These Important Terms and Concepts

qualitative research
contextual approach
quantitative research
unobtrusive observation
participant observation
unstructured interviews

structured interviews
textual analysis
archival materials (or texts)
transcription
triangulation of methods

Before Reading This Chapter, You May Wish to Review

Chapter 1:
• internal and external validity
• convergence of evidence

Chapter 2:
• ethical principles
• informed consent and privacy

Chapter 4:
• data-gathering techniques
• reliability and validity

Chapter 7:
• naturalistic observation
• reactive behavior

The principal aim of **qualitative research** is to gain an interpretive understanding of human experience, using a naturalistic approach. This means that questions are formulated within a specific context, and the information is almost always gathered in a naturally occurring setting. One reason qualitative research methods are being used more frequently by psychologists is the growing interest in how the social and physical environment influences human development and behavior, and this quite naturally leads researchers out of the controlled laboratory and into the field. This **contextual approach** requires the researcher to confront and explore the complexity of the many and varied influences that everyday life has on behavior, which is in contrast with laboratory studies that strive to simplify the environment by controlling the situation.

Of course, there is a tradeoff: In naturalistic settings there is a loss of control over other variables, some of which are relevant to the behavior or situation of interest, and hence, there are potential confounds. At the same time, the qualitative researcher is obtaining a more realistic picture of how people behave in the complexity of natural settings, even if the relevant aspects of the setting are not all known. The resulting qualitative data usually consist of rich and detailed information relating to a small number of persons or events, rather than the abstracted quantitative information usually collected from a large sample. As an example, imagine that we wanted to understand more about how members of the wait staff of a restaurant (that is, the waiters and waitresses, who we will henceforth refer to, collectively, as "waiters") interact on the job. Specifically, we might wish to focus on a few questions, such as: "How do waiters' communication patterns change when a restaurant is more or less crowded?" and "Are waiters more likely to make errors on orders when the restaurant is crowded or when it is late in their shift?" and "Do certain waiters play a consistent role in the communication and organization of tasks?" We will return to this example throughout the chapter to illustrate various aspects of qualitative research.

Unlike the research questions addressed by quantitative research (the primary focus of this book so far), qualitative research is generally focused on aspects of behaviors, settings or experiences that may not be rigorously measured, if measured at all, in terms of their amount, intensity, frequency, time, or quantity. Qualitative methods do not completely forego counting and numbers, but they are more focused on the *presence* or *absence* of phenomena. But like quantitatively focused researchers, qualitative researchers induce and then test hypotheses based on theory, using a set of appropriate methods and statistics. These qualitative methods are used in many disciplines in the humanities, social and physical sciences.

Qualitative Methods for Gathering Data

A variety of methods are used in qualitative research, and some of them are the same as those employed in quantitative research. However, the manner in which they are employed, and the interpretations of the resulting data, can be strikingly different. Four of the most commonly used qualitative methods are *observation, interviews,*

TABLE 16.1	**Four Research Methods in Qualitative and Quantitative Research**	
Method	**Qualitative Methodology**	**Quantitative Methodology**
Observation	Crucial to understanding the group or culture under study. Used to help focus the research questions. A major data-collection method.	Often used at the preliminary stages, prior to organized research. Behavioral Observation used in many different types of studies.
Interviews	Used with small samples and usually conducted in person. Open-ended questions are presented in either a structured or unstructured format. Interviewer has the flexibility to pursue unexpected topics of interest.	Used with large samples. Fixed-response surveys or questionnaires presented often by phone or mail. Face-to-face interviews are typically highly structured.
Textual Analysis	Explores the range of categories (e.g., events or themes) that are meaningful to the participants.	Usually used for purposes of a "content analysis" where items are sorted into pre-determined categories and counted.
Transcription	The structure of verbalizations can be analyzed (in addition to a textual or a "content analysis" of the conversation).	Relatively infrequent. Used to check interviews for standardization or preparing data for content analysis.

Adapted from Silverman (1993).

archival or *textual analysis*, and *transcription*. Qualitative researchers do not believe that any particular data-gathering strategy is superior to others, but rather believe that all methods can provide valuable information. Frequently, a variety of methods are used in conjunction with each other in a single qualitative study as a way to provide increased validity for the findings. This strategy is called *triangulation*.

Table 16-1 emphasizes some of the key differences between the way qualitative and quantitative researchers use the four most common methods, and each will be addressed briefly as the methods are described in further detail.

Observation

Observation is the primary method used by qualitative researchers to collect information about a person, group or event in a particular context.[1] There are two major kinds of observation: unobtrusive observation and participant observation. **Unobtrusive observations** are those in which the subjects of observation (e.g., persons,

---

[1]The direct observation of ongoing behavior is also a common technique in quantitative research. See Chapter 4 for a review of behavioral observation as a data-gathering technique, and see Chapter 7 for a review of naturalistic observation as it is employed in correlational research.

animals, or events) are unaware that they are being observed. Consequently, as long as the presence of the observer does not alter the behaviors under study, the behavior is *nonreactive* and the internal validity of the study is increased. For example, if a researcher sits on the side of the road at an intersection and counts the number (or color or make) of cars that go through a yellow light, or sits in the library and records where people sit while studying (e.g., away from or near the windows; close to or as far away from other studiers as possible; in groups or alone), the researcher is conducting unobtrusive observation. This requires a systematic recording of specific target behaviors from a useful observation post. Observations also can be recorded on a map of the observation area (such as a floor plan of the library that indicates all the tables and study carrels), giving information about spatial patterns of behaviors. Going back to our plans to study waiters, imagine that we have chosen a restaurant named *Joe's* as the context for a study of the communication among and the behaviors of waiters. Unobtrusive observations of the waiters who work at *Joe's* can tell us any number of interesting things. For example, do the waiters spend much time talking with each other? Do they help each other out when the restaurant is busy? When and where do they tend to interact with each other? What sorts of errors do the waiters make? Over a number of visits to *Joe's*, an unobtrusive observer can gather quite a bit of information that could be interpreted alone, or used to generate more specific questions that serve as an "advanced organizer" for the next phase of our qualitative investigation.

While many behaviors can be studied through unobtrusive observation, there are clearly many potentially relevant pieces of information that might be missed. For example, observers may not be able to determine the sex of the drivers passing through the intersection from the observation point, and they certainly cannot know if there are extenuating circumstances that may explain a driver's decision to go through the yellow light rather than stop. Similarly, from our vantage point in *Joe's* restaurant, we may not be able to tell much about the *content* of the waiters' interactions with each other. Are they complaining about the customers at their tables? Are they comparing their tips? Are they discussing their private lives? To answer these sorts of questions we need to "get closer" to the subject of our interest, and we may be able to do that using the second major observational technique: **participant observation.**

Participant observation is a technique where the researcher becomes a member of the group under study and, consequently, is able to interact directly with others as they engage in the natural activities of the group. For instance, participant observers may move to a new locale and live within a new culture or subculture, possibly for years, perhaps learning a new language, and recording vast amounts of information about what they see, hear and experience. On a smaller scale, participant observation may be conducted in any naturally occurring setting. For example, a participant observer might work as a basketball team assistant in order to observe coach-player interactions, or live with a native tribe in New Guinea in order to observe the impact of religious beliefs on everyday interactions. In our study of the behavioral patterns of waiters, a participant observer could take a job as a waiter at *Joe's*, where they would be close enough to know if waiters complain about customers, compare tips, or discuss their private lives as they go about their work. This participatory method of gaining understanding of a group, culture or event has been used at least since the time of the ancient Greeks. More recently the technique has been used by anthropologists studying non-western groups, and by sociologists, clinical psychologists and others to gain a rich, detailed picture of their specific subject matter.

Early in an observational study (either unobtrusive or participative), the information observers record in their "field notes" is generally quite broad and exploratory (often including records of who was present, what behaviors they engaged in, and what the physical setting was like). This initial data set is then examined for patterns and hypotheses are generated to explain those patterns. Decisions are then made about how to test these hypotheses in the next wave of observations; that is, a method is selected and specific target behaviors or events are identified. For example, during two days of unobtrusive observation at *Joe's*, the researcher may begin to suspect that waiters are more helpful toward each other if they have received decent tips from their own tables. Therefore, in order to collect information about the tips being left for the waiters, the researcher could stop the diners as they leave the restaurant and ask them how much they tipped their waiter, and keep track of this information on a "time table" that will indicate the timing of both tips and helping behavior.

Once the relevant hypotheses and questions are chosen, a coding scheme (based on the narrowed set of questions) can be developed to record relevant information in the field. This recorded qualitative data can later be categorized or otherwise analyzed to answer the questions of interest. It is useful to employ as many senses as possible; in particular, Silverman (1993) suggests that people often forget to record information about what they see and focus almost exclusively on what they hear. Depending on the questions of interest, of course, recording nonverbal behaviors may be the key to reaching useful conclusions. To accomplish this, it is sometimes possible to use audio- or video-taping methods to more thoroughly capture both verbal and non-verbal behaviors and other aspects of the situation such as the use of artifacts, but once again the issue of reactivity is important to consider. How might it affect those you are observing to have a tape-recorder or video-camera present? If their behavior is likely to be less "natural" (and more *reactive*), is the extra information recorded on the tape going to be worth the loss of generalizability? This is a decision that needs to be made for each specific situation, based—among other issues—on the topic of the investigation and the feelings of the participants.

It may take longer to collect enough qualitative data to produce clear results than it would to collect similar amounts of quantitative data because a large amount of information is often recorded for each case, and more than one or two cases are usually needed as evidence for a given hypothesis. Yet recording everything that is observed may be counterproductive. When recording data in the field, it is important to keep the hypotheses in mind and to concentrate on gathering relevant information. While qualitative methods facilitate case studies and allow researchers to gather a great deal of detailed information, the quantity of information gathered is less important than the nature of the information. Sifting through massive amounts of data is extremely tedious, and if much of the data are irrelevant to the hypothesis, the effort required to identify the important patterns in the data would be wasted if the same pattern could be detected in a smaller, well-focused study. Therefore, you should record only as much relevant information as is necessary to answer the questions at hand, unless something extremely compelling occurs.

For example, in a study of mother-infant interactions, after a number of preliminary observations designed to identify the most relevant dimensions of these interactions, the researcher might decide to record only a limited number of infant behaviors directed at the mother (such as touching, vocalizing, smiling, looking, and fussing/crying) and a limited number of maternal behaviors directed at the infant (such as looking, smiling, vocalizing, and touching/holding). Additionally, the researcher may ask the observer to make notes about the auditory qualities of the events, such as the loudness of an infant's cries or the tone of voice the mother uses when addressing the infant. Thus, the observers will have a checklist of these behaviors. Furthermore, if the coding sheet is designed so that it resembles a "time line" of the observation period (similar to those used in partial- or whole-interval recording procedures, as discussed in Chapter 15), it would be possible to detect patterns in the sequences of events during the interactions. Figure 16-1 illustrates an example of a behavioral observation coding sheet that could be adapted for a qualitative research study to help the observers concentrate on gathering only relevant information. The number of specific behaviors to be recorded will, of course, vary from study to study, and as the number of target behaviors increases, it becomes more difficult for an observer to record them as they are occurring. Consequently, when there are many different behaviors to be recorded, researchers may find videotapes of the observation sessions extremely valuable.

The Question of Ethics   Does observational research violate the basic ethical rights of the participants? Some critics believe it does, especially the right to informed consent and the right to privacy. Unobtrusive procedures, in particular, could be an invasion of privacy because the researchers do not get the informed consent of the people they observe, and although participant observation does have the consent of the people being studied, it runs the risk of being too intrusive. However, many researchers argue that observational research can be conducted ethically, as long as the researchers take special precautions against the invasion of privacy.

As we outlined in Chapter 2, the American Psychological Association's (APA) Ethical Principles and Code of Conduct (see Appendix A) provide clear guidelines for studies that collect data without fully informed consent. According to the APA, informed consent is not necessary if the following conditions are met: (a) the behavior being recorded is naturally-occurring, and it is neither particularly revealing nor potentially embarrassing; and (b) the individuals are, and remain, anonymous. While the unobtrusive observation of drivers passing through yellow lights at an intersection, or of students choosing seats in a library would seem to meet these criteria easily, unobtrusive observation of other behaviors would be more controversial. Hence, researchers who want to use unobtrusive observation bear a special burden: they must take the responsibility of protecting the rights of their anonymous participants, even if doing so interferes with the scientific goals of the research. Essentially, the researchers must consider whether reasonable people would agree to be observed, and if the honest answer is "no," the study should not be conducted.

FIGURE 16.1 · A SAMPLE CODING SHEET FOR OBSERVING MOTHER-INFANT INTERACTIONS

	1 – 10 seconds	11 – 20 seconds	21 – 30 seconds	31 – 40 seconds	41 – 50 seconds	51 – 60 seconds
min 1	Baby: L S V T F/C Mom: L S V T/H notes:	Baby: L S V T F/C Mom: L S V T/H notes:	Baby: L S V T F/C Mom: L S V T/H notes:	Baby: L S V T F/C Mom: L S V T/H notes:	Baby: L S V T F/C Mom: L S V T/H notes:	Baby: L S V T F/C Mom: L S V T/H notes:
min 2	Baby: L S V T F/C Mom: L S V T/H notes:	Baby: L S V T F/C Mom: L S V T/H notes:	Baby: L S V T F/C Mom: L S V T/H notes:	Baby: L S V T F/C Mom: L S V T/H notes:	Baby: L S V T F/C Mom: L S V T/H notes:	Baby: L S V T F/C Mom: L S V T/H notes:
min 3	Baby: L S V T F/C Mom: L S V T/H notes:	Baby: L S V T F/C Mom: L S V T/H notes:	Baby: L S V T F/C Mom: L S V T/H notes:	Baby: L S V T F/C Mom: L S V T/H notes:	Baby: L S V T F/C Mom: L S V T/H notes:	Baby: L S V T F/C Mom: L S V T/H notes:
min 4	Baby: L S V T F/C Mom: L S V T/H notes:	Baby: L S V T F/C Mom: L S V T/H notes:	Baby: L S V T F/C Mom: L S V T/H notes:	Baby: L S V T F/C Mom: L S V T/H notes:	Baby: L S V T F/C Mom: L S V T/H notes:	Baby: L S V T F/C Mom: L S V T/H notes:
min 5	Baby: L S V T F/C Mom: L S V T/H notes:	Baby: L S V T F/C Mom: L S V T/H notes:	Baby: L S V T F/C Mom: L S V T/H notes:	Baby: L S V T F/C Mom: L S V T/H notes:	Baby: L S V T F/C Mom: L S V T/H notes:	Baby: L S V T F/C Mom: L S V T/H notes:

KEY: L = looking
S = smiling
V = vocalizing
T = touching
F/C = fussing or crying
T/H = touching or holding

Participant observation, in contrast, requires informed consent because the people being studied are not anonymous. Researchers seeking permission from other people to participate in their lives need to: (a) explain the general outlines of why the observer wants to be there; (b) describe the sorts of data that will be collected; and (c) assure the people that any observations collected about them will not be used with their name or other identifying traits. Under these conditions, participant research will meet the basic ethical guidelines set forth by the APA.

A number of unobtrusive and participant observational studies conducted in the past are now considered unethical, typically because the experimenter did not tell the people being observed that they were being observed for research purposes, or because the studies were an invasion of privacy. (That is, the behaviors that were observed were private or confidential, and it is unlikely that the individuals would have consented to the observation, had they been asked.) Today, if the APA's ethical guidelines are strictly followed, thus protecting the participants' right to privacy, most researchers feel that observational research—using both unobtrusive and participant observer techniques—can be ethically acceptable. As a general rule, then, you should remember that plans for all research should be submitted to an Institutional Review Board (IRB) for approval, even research as seemingly straightforward as unobtrusive observation. Furthermore, as an added safe-guard, researchers should make sure that there is no information in their data records that could be used by others to identify any individuals who have been or are being observed.

Interviews

Interviews, which are a form of self-report data-gathering (as we discussed in Chapter 4), are used in qualitative research to gather answers to specific questions from small samples of individuals. The success of any self-report technique depends heavily on how the questions are posed to the respondents. There are five general types of questions that are used for interviews, questionnaires or surveys, and examples of each type are presented in Table 16-2. The most common errors made in constructing questions for self-report instruments are summarized in Table 16-3.

The goal of qualitative research is to gain a genuine understanding of a person or situation, and therefore, qualitative interviews typically center around open-ended questions. Responses to open-ended interview questions are not necessarily predictable and may suggest new lines of inquiry for the researcher interested in exploring the topic in depth. (This is unlike a fixed-choice survey that forces respondents to select an answer from a list of choices generated in advance by the researcher, possibly based on a narrowly-focused hypothesis.) There are at least five kinds of information that can be gathered in an interview setting: *facts* (including basic demographic or biographical information about the individual, or information about events); *self-reported behaviors* (including current, past or planned behaviors); *attitudes or beliefs* (including attitudes about the self or others, and beliefs about events and future courses of action); *feelings and motivations*; and *reasons* for the respondents' answers to the above kinds of questions (for example, "Why do you feel this way?" or "What life experiences have led you to believe in the supernatural?").

| TABLE 16.2 | Common Formats for Interview and Survey Questions |

1. **Fill-In-the-Blank Questions (for questions with a single factual answer, or a short list of factual answers):**

Interview Format:
"How many times have you been skiing?"
"What health problems have you experienced in the past 12 months?"

Questionnaire/Survey Format:
How many times have you been skiing?
List the health problems you have experienced in the past 12 months: _____
_____
_____
_____

2. **Multiple Choice Questions (with a limited list of answers to choose from):**

a. True/False or Yes/No Questions

Interview Format:
"For each of the following statements, please indicate whether the statement is true or false:
I am interested in learning how to ski.
I have experienced serious health problems in the last 12 months."

"Are you interested in learning to ski?"

Questionnaire/Survey Format:
I am interested in learning how to ski.
_____True _____False

I have experienced serious health problems in the last 12 months.
_____True _____False
Are you interested in learning to ski?
_____Yes _____No

b. Multiple Choice Questions with more than two possible answers

Interview Format:
Which of the following cities is the capital of Greece? Istanbul, Ithaca, Athens, Sparta, or Troy?

Which of the following sports do you most enjoy? Football, Baseball, Basketball, Skiing, Tennis, or Golf? Is there another sport that you enjoy more than these sports?

Questionnaire/Survey Format:
Which city is the capital of Greece?
_____Istanbul _____Sparta
_____Ithaca _____Troy
_____Athens
Which sport do you enjoy most? (check one)
_____Football _____Skiing
_____Baseball _____Tennis
_____Basketball _____Golf
_____Other (please specify: _____)

3. **Rank Ordering a Set of Items:**

Interview Format:
"I'm going to list a variety of sports and I would like you to tell me which sport you enjoy most and which you prefer second, and third, and so forth. Football, Baseball, Basketball, Skiing, Tennis, and Golf. Which of these sports is your favorite? Which is your next favorite? . . . " [Note: the interviewer may need to repeat the list periodically.]

Questionnaire/Survey Format:
Please rank the following sports in order of your preference (where 1 = most favorite and 6 = least favorite):
_____Football _____Skiing
_____Baseball _____Tennis
_____Basketball _____Golf

(continued)

TABLE 16.2   *(continued)*

"What do you think is the most important benefit of a college education? . . . What do you think is the next most important benefit of a college education? . . . What is the third major benefit of a college education? . . ."	Please list, in order, the three most important benefits of a college education: 1. _____ 2. _____ 3. _____

4. Rating Scales

Interview Format:	Questionnaire/Survey Format:
"Would you describe your health over the last 12 months as very good, good, fair, poor, or very poor?"	How would you rate your health over the past 12 months? (circle one) Very Good Fair Poor Very Good Poor
"Using a scale from 1 to 7, where 1 means very poor and 7 means very good, how would you rate your health over the last 12 months?"	How would you rate your health over the past 12 months? (circle one) 1 2 3 4 5 6 7 Very Very Poor Good
"Do you think the sale of handguns should be unrestricted, somewhat restricted or highly restricted?"	The sale of handguns should be: (circle one) Not at All Somewhat Highly Restricted Restricted Restricted

5. Open-Ended Questions

Interview Format:	Questionnaire/Survey Format:
"What do you like to do for recreation?"	What do you like to do for recreation? _____ _____
"What do you think could be done to improve the American political system?"	What could be done to improve the American political system? _____ _____ _____ _____

TABLE 16.3   **Common Errors in the Construction of Questions for Interviews, Questionnaires, and Surveys**

1. Using compound questions that ask about two or more separate issues:

For example, how should a non-smoker who drinks alcohol respond to the following question?

I drink and smoke (circle one):   *0*   *1*   *2*   *3*

                                  never   *occasionally*   *frequently*   *constantly*

(continued)

TABLE 16.3   *(Continued)*

Solution: Only address one issue or idea in a single question.

(e.g., *I drink:*	*0*	*1*	*2*	*3*
	never	*occasionally*	*frequently*	*constantly*
I smoke:	*0*	*1*	*2*	*3*
	never	*occasionally*	*frequently*	*constantly*)

2. **Using jargon or technical language that may not be understood by the respondents:**

For example, how many people would be able to respond to the following question?

What, if any, perinatal complications did the neonate exhibit in the first 12 hours postpartum?

Solution: Use simple, straightforward language, and avoid slang.
(e.g., *Did your newborn baby experience any medical problems during the 12 hours right after birth?*)

You should consider pilot testing the questions with people who are similar to your respondents and make sure that they understand the questions.

3. **Asking leading questions that reflect the researcher's bias or suggest an answer the researcher feels is appropriate:**

For example, the following question suggests that the respondent *must* agree to at least some extent:

How strongly do you agree with the statement: "Abortion is a mistake for women."?
Very Strongly   Moderately   Somewhat   A Little   Not at All

Solution: Write the questions in as neutral a form as possible.
(e.g., *How do you feel about abortion?*)

4. **Using negatives and double negatives:**

For example, the following question is unnecessarily difficult to understand: How should a respondent who is in favor of campaign finance reform respond to this statement?

I will not vote for candidates who do not endorse the proposed anti-campaign-finance-fund-abuse plan. _____True _____ False

Solution: Use positive or neutral terms, and be as straightforward as possible.
(e.g., *I will vote for candidates who support campaign finance reform legislation.* _____True _____False)

5. **Not including the choice of "other" for multiple choice questions where an exhaustive list is not provided:**

For example, how should a respondent who is of mixed racial heritage (such as Hispanic/Native American) respond to the following item?

Race (check one): _____*Caucasian* _____ *African American* _____ *Asian American*
_____ *Hispanic* _____ *Native American*

Solution: Include a space for respondents to fill in their racial identity if it is not on the list.
(e.g., *Race (check one):* _____ *Caucasian* _____ *African American*
_____ *Asian American* _____*Hispanic* _____ *Native American*
_____ *other (please specify:* _____)

In qualitative interviews, the questions are usually asked orally, in person, and the respondent is free to answer any way they wish. This is called "open-ended responding." Furthermore, in qualitative interviews, the goal is often to establish rapport so that the interview resembles a conversation between equals, rather than an interrogation where the interviewer reveals nothing and only asks questions. This procedure is expected to elicit more information from the respondents. In contrast, quantitative research is more likely to use other self-report techniques, such as surveys or questionnaires that are highly standardized. Quantitative studies are more likely to use a fixed-response format for the questions (such as Yes/No, True/False, Multiple-Choice, or a Likert Rating Scale) and to administer the survey or questionnaire to a large sample in a non-personal manner (such as a group setting or by mail—both of which ask respondents to reply in writing). These fixed responses are easy to count and analyze, and the use of a large sample size decreases concern about the representativeness of the resultant conclusions. Qualitative researchers, however, are often more interested in detail and individual contexts than ease of analysis, so interviews with a small number of representative individuals are well-suited to their purpose.

There are two main types of interviews, each used in different situations to elicit slightly different kinds of information. **Unstructured interviews** are typically used when a researcher is just beginning to explore a topic and does not yet know what specific questions will be most relevant to their general hypotheses. In these cases, the interviewer may select a few general topics for discussion, and will allow the interview to proceed in whatever direction(s) seem useful. The broad, unstructured information that is elicited from the respondents can be used to develop specific questions addressing the hypotheses of interest. **Structured interviews** are used when the researcher already has some idea of the most important questions to ask in order to address the hypotheses. In structured interviews, the questions and the order in which they are presented stay the same for every respondent, much like an oral questionnaire. Structured interviews, by definition, do not allow the interviewer much flexibility so they tend to deviate less from the pre-chosen topics. Sometimes, in order to give the interviewer the opportunity to explore an interesting or unexpected response, the structured interview schedule includes open-ended *probing* questions, where the respondent is asked to "Tell me more about that."

For example, in a study of waiters, a researcher may start by conducting unstructured interviews that include general exploratory questions such as: "What are the things you like and dislike about working as a waiter here at *Joe's*?" and "How do the waiters generally get along on the job?" and "Do you ever help the other waiters with their tables? When are you likely to do that?" Questions like these will help the researcher identify potentially important factors involved in the experience of being a waiter. These specific factors could be further explored by becoming a participant observer by getting a job as a waiter at *Joe's*. After several months on the job, the researcher will have collected quite a bit of data and generated a number of hypotheses about the behaviors of and interactions among waiters, and these hypotheses could be tested using structured interviews. This combination of techniques within a single qualitative research study—unstructured interviews, participant observation, and structured interviews—can provide researchers with vast amounts of information.

(This is an example of *triangulation*, which we will discuss in detail later in this chapter.) A consistent pattern of results from each phase of the study (that is, a *convergence of evidence*) would suggest that the conclusions are reliable and valid.

Tips on Conducting Successful Interviews

The Questions   To prepare for a successful interview, you should begin by creating an interview schedule relevant to the hypotheses of interest. For a structured interview, this schedule will be a list of specific questions, all of which are presented to every interviewee in exactly the same order. For unstructured or exploratory interviews, the schedule will be a list of topics or very general questions. You also may want to have a *script*, which is a predetermined "commentary" that you can use before and between questions as a way to give the interview context and make it flow together. Except for the demographic questions (e.g., name, age, sex, number of years on the job), the questions should be designed to elicit answers that go beyond simple one-word responses (such as "yes" or "no"), or, if necessary, there should be follow-up probes that will elicit more information from the respondent. Table 16-4 presents a sample interview schedule and a script for an unstructured interview exploring communication among waiters at *Joe's*.

When constructing interview questions, researchers should avoid "leading" questions that somehow convey to the respondent what they want to hear. For example, the question "How much do you resent other waiters when they get a few good tippers while you work harder than they do but get fewer tips?" makes it clear that waiters are expected to be resentful of their co-workers. This presents a *demand characteristic* that is likely to elicit a socially- or situationally-acceptable response. In contrast, carefully-constructed non-leading questions such as "What are the rules about keeping tips here at *Joe's*?" can be used to elicit the waiters' feelings about well-tipped co-workers without cueing them to say they are or are not resentful toward them.

It is also important for interviewers to get a sense of how the respondent understands the questions. It is crucial that you understand or at least have a record of their definitions of the concepts involved in the questions. For example, if you are discussing "the relationship between alcohol consumption and unsafe sex," it is important to know what they consider unsafe, what they would call "drunk," and so forth. If their definitions are sufficiently different from yours, the resulting interpretation of the answers could be quite skewed. Knowledge of how the respondent views the terms and concepts involved is crucial to interpretation of data.

Recording the Responses   You should have a coding sheet to record answers in brief, but it is also desirable to tape record the interview so that the exact wording and other details can be extracted later. As mentioned earlier, videotaping an interview can provide even more information than audiotapes, and if the participants are comfortable with the idea (and/or the topic is not too confidential), you may gain further valuable data. Taped records are extremely valuable in unstructured interviews, where no two people are asked the same set of questions. They also are useful to have in structured

TABLE 16.4	A Sample Interview Schedule and Script for an Unstructured Interview

For a Study of Communications among Waiters at *Joe's* Restaurant:

Interview Schedule (i.e., topics to focus on):

> Do waiters talk mostly about work-related topics or do they discuss their personal lives?
> Do waiters discuss the customers at their tables?
> Do waiters give each other advice on how to handle rude customers?
> Do waiters offer to help each other when things get busy?

Script (including some specific questions and some probes):

> "In my research, I am interested in exploring the relationships among co-workers in various jobs, and today I would like to ask you some questions about your job here at *Joe's*. Before we begin, let me just get a few basic facts about you. How long have you worked as a waiter? . . . How long have you been a waiter here at *Joe's*? . . . Which shift do you typically work (breakfast, lunch or dinner)? . . .
>
> Okay, now let me ask you a few questions about your conversations with the other waiters while you're at work: What kinds of things do you usually talk about with your co-workers? . . . Would you say that you spend more time discussing the job and the customers, or more time talking about other things? . . . How do these discussions about the job and the customers help you or the other waiters? . . . Can you think of any other benefits of being able to talk about the job to your co-workers? . . .
>
> Now let me ask a more specific question: Have you and the other waiters ever discussed strategies for dealing with rude customers? . . . Tell me about your first weeks on the job. . . . Now that you've had some experience, what kinds of advice would you give a new waiter about handling difficult customers? . . . And one last specific question: Are waiters expected to help each other when they can? . . . How and when are waiters most likely to help each other out? . . . Can you tell me more about situations where waiters do or do not help each other out? . . .
>
> Well, I guess that's about it for now. Thank you very much for your time. . . ."

interviews because it may become necessary to deviate from the interview schedule if the respondents misunderstand a question or if their answers are not complete or clear. It may be necessary, in such cases, to add questions to the interview schedule "on the fly" to make sure you understand the respondent's answers. Some researchers will try to anticipate situations like this, and prepare a set of follow-up questions or comments designed to elicit a more complete or relevant response, but occasionally interviewers have to invent questions on the spot to deal with unexpected answers to previous questions. It is important to have a record of these new questions because the interpretation of the answers may depend heavily on the exact phrasing of the questions. If a tape recorder is not available, researchers need to write down the exact text of any new questions they ask.

Timing   The length of the list of questions should be, of course, based on how long the interviewee will be available. Ideally, there will be enough time to ask all of the questions, and follow up any important issues raised that are not on the standard list of questions. Having a standard set of questions allows us to compare answers between participants, and leaving enough time for unstructured questions allows a greater understanding of what lies behind the interviewee's answers.

Textual Analysis

Textual analysis covers a wide range of methods for investigating existing sources of written information about a culture or context. Two kinds of materials are used in both qualitative and quantitative research: archival materials and textual materials produced by respondents specifically for some study. **Archival materials** include any pre-existing records or documents (including books, articles, newspapers, songs, cartoons, art, and other images) that are usually publicly available. Textual materials produced by the participants in a research project include things like diaries, journals, or sets of route directions. Qualitative researchers analyze these materials in order to understand a culture from the point of view of its members; that is, to find out how the culture categorizes or gives meaning to their world. Textual analysis may take the form of a "content analysis" that counts the number of occurrences of specific predetermined categories of things, such as the number of cartoons that ridicule prominent politicians, or the number of references to the findings of a specific research report. (Content analysis is used in both quantitative and quantitative research.) Alternatively, textual analysis may involve the identification of the items or concepts that represent meaningful categories to the members of the culture. For example, a researcher may try to determine when and where the phrase "political correctness" first appeared in the textual materials of American culture, how quickly it became commonplace, and why.

The study of **archival texts** or other existing cultural materials can give us insight into what the members of a group or culture find important (such as the major themes of editorials, songs, art), and it can reveal information about countercultures. The attitudes, beliefs or values that support creation of various cultural artifacts can be explored through analysis of these pre-existing materials. For example, in one study researchers were interested in whether there were differences in the frequency with which men and women were portrayed as patients in medical advertising, and what that might say about our society. In a preliminary study, it was found that men and women were portrayed in equal numbers. However, a closer look at the type of medications advertised using male and female models showed a sex-based stereotyping: Men appeared mainly in advertisements about physical injuries or illnesses, while women appeared mainly in advertisements about psychological ailments such as depression or anxiety (Prather & Fidell, 1975). This finding represents one way to observe a culturally significant difference in the way males and females were seen in the eyes of the medical community, and by the larger society.[2]

---

[2]But remember that the role of *context* is the central focus of qualitative methods. This study was published in 1975, and our culture has changed in many ways since then, so the sex-based stereotyping that was evident at that time may no longer be the case.

Similarly, texts may be produced for a specific study, such as journals about time spent on various aspects of office work or student diaries recording the difficulties encountered while studying for different types of classes. Each of these gives the qualitative researcher a source of information that would otherwise be uncollectible, either due to time, resources or privacy issues. The waiters at *Joe's* restaurant might be asked to keep journals of the interactions they had with other waiters, and their feelings about those interactions, and from these journals the researcher may find out when the other waiters are helpful or distracting, how frequently the waiters interact, whether the interactions are generally pleasant or unpleasant, and so on.

Transcription

The last qualitative method we will introduce is known as **transcription**. This technique was originally developed by linguists for recording conversations, interviews, and other oral behaviors, but it is now used in many disciplines where verbal data are important. It is used to organize the data from oral interviews, the taped narratives of an unobtrusive observer recording an ongoing event, participant observations, or any other source of oral data. The *verbatim* transcript holds an important place in qualitative research because it records every aspect of the verbal information produced, rather than the summary that is often used in quantitative research. Transcripts also may contain records of the nonverbal elements of an interaction, such as when the researcher videotapes the episode or when their audiotaped narratives include references to the nonverbal events that form the background for the conversation. For example, the following excerpt is from an observer's day-long narrative recording of the daily routine of 3-year-old Winton, who is just sitting down to dinner with his family:

> Winton looks down at his food just to see what is there.
> The father points to the stewed tomatoes in Winton's dish.
> The father says, "That's an apple," in an amused tone.
> Greg looks over with amusement too, but he does not have any interaction with Winton.
> Winton starts to take a whole tomato up in his spoon.
> The mother looks over at him and says crossly, "Winton, *cut* that tomato up."
> She is still standing.
> "That's an apple," says Greg with amusement to the mother as if she does not understand.
> "Well, apple then," says the mother flatly, without amusement.
> Immediately Winton sticks his spoon into the tomato and saws it back and forth to cut some of it up.

(Schoggen and Schoggen, 1971, as quoted in Schoggen, 1991, p. 287)

TABLE 16.5	Interview at *Joe's* Restaurant

I = Interviewer (also a participant observer)	J = Interviewee
notation: (..) = pause	[= overlapping

I: So what do *you* find hardest about communicating with the other waiters?
J: Well sometimes they are too (.) too (...)
I: too(..) [what?
J: Oh you know, they start thinking about what they need to be doing and they forget to think about things like (...) like what would be, you know, helpful for other [people.
I: Right! And that makes it harder to communicate [with them.
J: Oh definitely. I mean, I haven't been here very long so there's a lot of questions that I want to ask or sometimes I could *really* use a little [help
I: uh huh, uh huh.
J: but no one seems to be paying attention.
I: Yeah, I know what you mean. Like when someone gets too many tables and [they just push
J: Yes, exactly!
I: you out of the way at the coffee [machine.
J: That always drives me [crazy.
I: I know. Then you can't even talk to them, or get their help when it would be useful.
J: And I hate (...) nooo, it's not that bad, I mean sometimes it's frustrating but I just (..)
I: Just what?
J: Well (...) it sounds crazy. I just wish they would realize that I'm new. They ask me to do things I don't know how to [do and I feel silly.
I: That's frustrating.
J: Yeah, (.) I guess that's it. I get frustrated. But I think it will get better with time.

This observer used ordinary, everyday language to describe the child's activities and the contexts in which they occurred. The narrative included descriptions of some of the nonverbal elements of the family interaction, including some inferences about emotional states based on the speaker's tone of voice and facial expression. These running narratives (which are sometimes called specimen records) are very hard work and require a lot of training, but they provide a "full, rich, word picture" of behavior and its context (Schoggen, 1991, p. 286).

A transcript also allows us see the *flow* of information between two or more parties. That is, transcripts can allow researchers to focus on the *structure* of an interaction (as well as its content) by coding various elements of the interchange, such as interruptions and pauses. In this way, the underlying processes or social interaction can be explored as a meaningful addition to the specific knowledge gained in the interview. To illustrate this technique, Table 16-5 presents a hypothetical interview conducted by the participant observer at *Joe's* with a fairly new waiter. You will notice that the interchange was not a neat and tidy interaction, with clear complete sentences and polite "turn-taking." This transcript shows where the speakers paused in their speech and where they interrupted each other.

Reliability and Validity in Qualitative Research

Each of the four key methods for gathering qualitative data—interviews, observation, textual analysis, and transcription—have their limitations. In fact, qualitative research is often criticized on the grounds that it suffers from problems with both reliability and validity. As you must have noticed in our presentation of the qualitative research process, there may be little consistency in the data-gathering "instruments" across the study since researchers may change their methods and hypotheses, which raises doubts about the reliability of the data. However, proponents of qualitative research point out that any study (qualitative or quantitative) is reliable if it consistently and systematically records whatever is the focus of the study (whether it is words, behaviors, or events) and that as long as the researcher can demonstrate the *inter-rater reliability* of the data coding, then the study is reliable. For example, with textual analysis, transcripts, or certain observational data, we would want to see that: (a) multiple researchers would record a behavior or answer in the same way, which is sometimes called *synchronic reliability* (which means that two people give the same interpretation of an event at the same point in time); and (b) the same researcher would record a verbal answer or behavior in the same way from day to day or participant to participant, which is called *diachronic reliability* (which is similar to test-retest reliability in that the same observer gives the same interpretation of a similar event at two different times). Qualitative studies that do not assess these forms of reliability are as questionable as quantitative studies that use unreliable measurement techniques.

The inherent belief among psychologists who take a contextual approach is that events can be explained only in terms of the particular context in which they occur. To the extent that this theoretical position is true, it would mean there could be little or no external validity for any given study. That is, the findings of one particular study could not be generalized to anything except identical settings. If, as the contextualists claim, we are only learning about what occurs in one context, how can we ever hope to generalize our conclusions? (This argument, of course, can be applied to experimental studies as well.) There is, however, sufficient reason to believe there are some stable properties of the physical and social world that are constant across similar situations. Consequently, there are detectable patterns in behavior from one setting to another, so it is not impossible to generalize the findings from one study to another, as long as the settings share the relevant properties in common. Furthermore, proponents of qualitative research methods argue that any study carried out in a naturalistic setting may be more realistic than, and therefore at least as generalizable as, a study of the same phenomenon performed in an artificially controlled laboratory.

Fielding and Fielding (1986) bring up two important mistakes often made by qualitative researchers that decrease the external validity of their findings. These are: (a) selecting data that fit into a preconceived theory (often called experimenter bias), and (b) ignoring commonplace findings in favor of a focus on extreme or novel outcomes. The second of these issues, in particular, causes problems for external validity. If the less exciting but more stable findings are ignored in favor of rare events, the generalizability of the reported events is necessarily decreased. Again, this suggests a need for a systematic collection of data relevant to some hypotheses or areas of interest, rather than simply a mass of anecdotal data with no internal organization or focus.

One important method for maximizing the validity of qualitative research is choosing representative cases. Since qualitative research is frequently done with a small number of cases, and the cases are not usually chosen randomly, the generalizability of the findings can be increased if we can show that the cases we have chosen are not different from the population of interest in any significant way. The researcher should start by identifying the relevant dimensions of the population of interest (such as age, occupation, and sex) and then select cases that are comparable to the population along those dimensions. If the researcher can show that there are very few differences between their nonrandomly chosen cases and the population, there is a greater chance that generalization of findings is appropriate. For example, to show that the waiters at *Joe's* do not differ from other waiters in other restaurants in any important way, we would need to identify the general factors that influence the interpersonal communications among waiters, such as level of experience, age, sex, restaurant setting, or number of waiters working at the time. If the sample of waiters from *Joe's* does not differ significantly on the demographic variables from other groups of waiters, and the restaurant itself is not significantly different from other restaurant settings, we can be more confident about generalizing our findings to waiters at other restaurants. In whatever ways the waiters at *Joe's* are different from the "average" waiter, or the extent to which *Joe's* may be different from the average restaurant setting (e.g., in size, prices, or location), we would have to place some limits on the generalizability of our conclusions.

Triangulation of Methods: Increasing the Validity

A second technique that can help deal with questions of validity in qualitative research is **triangulation**: using multiple research methods to examine the same question of interest. Earlier we described a triangulation of observation and interview techniques in the study of waiters at *Joe's*, and we also indicated that we could use transcription in that study as well. Thus, several qualitative methods can be combined in a single study. Furthermore, quantitative techniques (such as field experiments) could be triangulated with qualitative methods to further explore the hypotheses of the study. (For instance, the researcher may arrange to have an obstreperous customer give a particularly hard time to a new waiter in order to observe the reactions of the experienced waiters.) When triangulation leads to a convergence of evidence (i.e., similar conclusions) from a variety of different research methods, it is more likely that the conclusions are valid than if they are based on a single method.

Researchers should consider using a variety of qualitative methods, perhaps in addition to quantitative methods, to help answer questions about how things happen in natural settings. While the conclusions that can be drawn are more contextually bound, they are almost always more complete depictions of behaviors in their complex environmental settings. The following overview of a case study of a third-grade classroom nicely captures the richness of the data that can be collected using a triangulation of qualitative research methods.

A Case Study Illustrating Triangulation of Qualitative Research Methods

To test the hypothesis that a socio-cultural approach to language education may be very effective, Luis C. Moll and Kathryn F. Whitmore (1993) conducted a case study of a third-grade bilingual classroom from the southwestern U.S.[3] They collected data during weekly classroom observations over a two-year period, and they begin their presentation of the study by describing a "typical day" in the classroom:

> The classroom community includes 27 children (12 boys and 15 girls) who come from either the neighborhood or "barrio" surrounding the school (16 children) or who travel from other neighborhoods in the city (11 children) . . . . Fifteen of the children are monolingual English speakers . . . nine children are bilingual. . . . Acuzena is a monolingual Spanish speaker. She arrived in the United States from Mexico in the spring and reads only Spanish.
>
> . . . Each day for this classroom begins in the patio area of the school, where children, staff, and faculty meet to share announcements, sing, and recite the Pledge of Allegiance. After this morning ritual, the children enter the classroom, noisily put away their things, greet each other in English and Spanish, and move to the group meeting area in the center of the room. The teacher finds a chair, and the group quiets for announcements, calendar and weather information, and a discussion of the schedule for the day. She reads aloud to the children in either English or Spanish at least once each day.
>
> . . . This classroom is a functionally organized setting. There are several large tables in the room that, along with the ample amount of carpeted floor area, provide work space for the children and adults. Cubicles and cupboards are used by the children as storage space for their personal belongings, but the school supplies (pencils, papers, crayons, and the like) are shared by the classroom community.
>
> . . . [L]iterature studies transform into a writing workshop (WW) with a quiet direction or by turning off and on the lights. . . . At the piano bench, Rachael and Lupita finish a conference with the student teacher about spelling and return to the publication process.

---

[3]The "socio-cultural approach" to learning and development is based on the theories of Lev Vygotsky, a Russian psycholgist. The details of this theoretical model are not our concern here; the research methods and types of data they collected are. Students interested in the findings of the study are encouraged to read Moll and Whitmore's chapter in Forman, Minick, and Stone (1993).

. . . Jaime and Roberto are nestled under the loft. They are busy writing letters during WW time. . . . Meanwhile, Susana and the teacher are at the computer, putting a story on the word processor for final publication. Across the room a group of girls sit at a table covered with final projects deeply involved in an author's circle, reading their writing to one another, asking each other questions, and making revisions in their texts. (Moll & Whitmore, 1993, pp. 21–28).

In this excerpt, you can see how the researchers used the observation method and recorded information about the physical and social aspects of the classroom as well as the events that took place. They recorded information about the specific children and adults in the classroom, and kept track of the interactions among all of the participants. They prepared verbatim transcripts of classroom or group activities and examined them for specific interaction patterns that were relevant to their hypotheses. For example, they used the following transcript as an example of how the teacher is explicit about her own goals for the children:

T: What did you say in your log about the story when you wrote in your log yesterday?
Richard: That it was a good book.
T: Why would you say this was a good story?
Richard: I don't know.
T: I guess what I want is for kids to know why they think something is a good story. (Moll & Whitmore, 1993, p. 25).

Moll and Whitmore also used interviews in this case study. For example, they interviewed the teacher and presented a verbatim transcript of her comments about her emphasis on writing as a process:

. . . She describes the process of attending to traditional skills within a classroom emphasizing writing as a process:

I keep almost everything that the kids write, so that I'm real aware of what things they are trying out when they are writing. If I see a lot of children exploring something, then I will do a short class lesson [about a skill]. We did that with quotation marks. . . .
(Moll & Whitmore, 1993, p. 29)

And finally, as a form of **textual analysis**, Moll and Whitmore present samples of the children's written work that can be used to illustrate their progress over the school year or to assess how often and how well the children are writing in their second language.

In summary, Moll and Whitmore provide an example of a triangulation of methods in a qualitative research study. They are able to paint for us a rich, detailed portrait of the classroom and its inhabitants, and the variety of data gives them the opportunity to demonstrate a convergence of evidence, which would increase the validity of their conclusions.

Statistics for Qualitative Data

The statistical techniques used for dealing with qualitative data are not substantially different from those used with quantitative data; in fact, a subset of the statistical techniques you have already learned are most commonly applied. The key quality of most qualitative data is, as mentioned above, the presence or absence of certain phenomenon of interest. For this reason, the data are mostly of a categorical nature. Observations, texts, and interviews are all coded for the presence (or absence) of predetermined events, behaviors, or other phenomena of interest. Accordingly, the statistics used to examine qualitative data are those used with nominal data: frequencies, percentages, modes, chi-squares or other statistics appropriate to nominal data. We said before that the goal of qualitative research was to gain an interpretive understanding of human experience. Statistical analysis of the data collected in qualitative research allows us to reach empirically based conclusions regarding our research questions.

According to Huberman and Miles (1994), there are three inter-linked steps in analysis of qualitative data: data reduction, data display, and conclusion drawing/verification. "Data reduction" refers to the process of limiting data collection to only some subset of information that is available in the universe of potentially collectible information (e.g., every behavior and setting component during an observation session, or every word in a text or interview). Instead of recording everything, only a manageable amount of information is recorded. (This process is analogous to the process of operationally defining the variables of interest in quantitative studies. For example, after deciding to define aggression as the average rating received from classmates, the researcher only records those peer ratings; no other information is recorded.)

Most data reduction techniques used in qualitative studies focus on (1) choosing a subset of potential materials to gather or watch for before actual data collection begins, and (2) developing coding schemes that can be applied during or after data collection to place the data in a finite number of relevant categories. These techniques allow categorization of the resulting data into relevant groups, to be used in display and analysis. For example, in the study at *Joe's* restaurant, the observer knows to focus only on the communicative behaviors and events relating to the waiters, and not other behaviors or other restaurant personnel. By recording only the pre-selected behaviors and events, the total amount of data is reduced.

Once the researcher has "reduced" the universe of data to a manageable subset of relevant behaviors or events, the data collection can begin. Once some data have been collected, it is possible to "display" the information in a variety of ways, including graphically or in terms of descriptive and inferential statistics. The specific display techniques that are most helpful will depend on the format of your data and the questions you are hoping to answer. For instance, scatterplots could be constructed showing the relationship between pairs of events (such as the number of communicative statements between waiters and the number of customers present), or a sequence of events could be plotted on a time-line. These preliminary displays of the early data may help the researcher refine the hypotheses and identify "holes" in the observations. For example, if the early examination of waiters' conversations suggests that tips are a common theme, the observer at *Joe's* could be instructed to start recording the amount of money diners leave as tips for the waiters. As more data are collected, the data displays are updated and further refinements are made as necessary.

The displays of the complete data set are then used to draw conclusions about questions of interest. This process is not substantially different from that of quantitative research, except that significance tests are rarely the basis on which conclusions are drawn. For example, a qualitative researcher who has data on the number of customers present and the number of communicative statements between waiters during the lunch hour can prepare a scatterplot and calculate a correlation coefficient. However, the "null hypothesis" is not tested by comparing the correlation coefficient to a critical value. Rather, the correlation between these variables that was observed among the waiters at *Joe's* is not interpreted as an individual "fact," but, instead becomes part of the "mosaic" that is pieced together from all of the data that were collected. The researcher examines the data, seeking verification of patterns that can be interpreted in meaningful ways so that they illuminate the behaviors, processes, or events being investigated.

The process of drawing conclusions or verifying patterns, and indeed the whole qualitative research process, is considerably more flexible than quantitative research. In particular, the process of qualitative research is iterative; that is, it occurs in a (relatively small) number of repeating loops. As certain regularities are found in data, decisions are made about further data collection (e.g., reducing or increasing the categories of things to be included in data, or a realization that another instrument might be better suited to data gathering). This is quite different from quantitative research, where changes in the protocol used are very rare once the research has begun. The ability to change various aspects of both the procedure and the focus during research increases the external validity of the qualitative study by allowing the collection of data on increasingly relevant aspects of the situation.

Computer Programs   Many computer programs have been written specifically to assist with the analysis of qualitative data. Miles and Huberman (1994, Appendix A) review a number of existing packages. These programs can be very useful in helping to make sense of the very complex data that often results from qualitative data collection. In particular, these computer programs can often detect patterns that are not easily visible. They also can help determine if a pattern or trend a researcher believes to be present is "real," that is, it is unlikely to have occurred by chance. This can help alleviate the potential problem of confirmation bias (or the bias for positive instances described in Chapter 1). Computers also can cross-reference large amounts of material in ways that would be far more difficult by hand. For example, a method called code-and-retrieve allows a researcher to code each observation, text passage, interview segment or other piece of data with one or more codes that relevantly categorizes their content. The retrieval program then provides a way to find all content (e.g., passages or observations) that are coded in the same way. In this way, huge sets of data can be analyzed more efficiently than would be possible if researchers needed to re-read every text or transcript repeatedly in order to locate all instances of the relevant events.

Finally, the methods used in qualitative research are extremely varied, so standardizing how to describe them for other researchers in a research report may be difficult. Huberman and Miles (1994) suggest that a research report should contain the following "minimum set" of information: (a) sampling decisions, both within and across cases; (b) the instrumentation and data collection methods; (c) a summary of the database, including its size and how it was produced; (d) information on any software that may have been used; (e) an overview of the strategies used for data analysis; and (f) data displays that support the main conclusions. Clarity in such reporting can give weight to your conclusions, and help dispel some potential concerns about the reliability and validity of the qualitative methods.

The Future of Qualitative Methods

Qualitative research has often been accused of being "soft" research by those who work solely with quantitative methods, and in the past, the debates between proponents of quantitative and qualitative methods were often quite heated. However, in recent years many traditionally quantitative researchers have begun to include elements of qualitative methods in their research because it is becoming clear that both can contribute to most any topic of research. Seen as complements to each other, a judicious use of both quantitative and qualitative methods can produce strong arguments for (or against) any hypothesis. We expect to see increasing emphasis placed on qualitative research methods in psychology in the future and hope that this brief introduction will encourage students to add qualitative methods to their "bag of tricks."

Suggestions for Further Reading

Denzin, N. K., & Lincoln, Y. S. (1994). *Handbook of qualitative research*. Thousand Oaks, CA: Sage Publications.

Kirk, J., & Miller, M. L. (1986). *Reliability and validity in qualitative research*. Beverly Hills, CA: Sage Publications.

Mertens, D. M. (1998). *Research methods in education and psychology: Integrating diversity with quantitative & qualitative approaches*. Thousand Oaks, CA: Sage Publications.

Miles, M. B., & Huberman, A. M. (1994). *Qualitative data analysis: An expanded sourcebook* (2nd ed.). Newbury Park, CA: Sage.

Silverman, D. (1993). *Interpreting qualitative data: Methods for analysing talk, text, and interaction*. London: Sage Publications.

Exercises

1. What is the goal of triangulation in qualitative research? How do quantitative researchers typically attempt to meet that goal?

2. How, if at all, does the "Scientific Method" as defined in Chapter 1 need to be changed to incorporate qualitative research methods? What are the potential consequences—both good and bad—of changing our conception of scientific research?

3. What sorts of research questions do you think may be more appropriately addressed by the qualitative methods described in Chapter 16 than the quantitative methods covered in the earlier chapters? What research questions may be best addressed using quantitative methods? Explain your answers.

4. Exercises 12–15 at the end of Chapter 10 refer to the Method section of a published quantitative research study on children's helping behavior. Design a study that uses *qualitative* methods to address Dr. Peterson's research questions. Do you think your qualitative approach is more or less appropriate than Peterson's quantitative approach? Explain.

5. What types of archival materials do you think would be useful and informative for a qualitative textual analysis of risk-taking behavior among adolescents?

6. Suppose you want to explore how parents discipline children of different ages and you have chosen a participant observation design for your study (where you will live with the family for a period of six months). Write a script that you would use to explain your purpose to the parents and children in an effort to get their permission to move in and study them, and make a list of the things you think would be most important to record as you interact with the parents and children. Be sure to indicate the setting(s) you would use and the specific procedure you would use to record this information while ensuring that your presence and the act of recording what you see are not too intrusive.

7. Now suppose you want to explore how parents' discipline practices change as children grow older but you have chosen the interview method for your study. Prepare a script to read to the participating parents before the interview and create a set of at least 10 interview questions that collect relevant demographic and behavioral information. (Your questions should not include slang, technical jargon, ambiguous language or compound questions.)

8. What benefits would there be if you included interviews with children in your study of how parental disciplinary practices change as children get older? Create a set of six questions you could ask children of different ages that would generate relevant information.

ETHICAL PRINCIPLES OF PSYCHOLOGISTS AND CODE OF CONDUCT

■ ■ ■ ■ ■ ■

CONTENTS

Introduction

The American Psychological Association's (APA's) Ethical Principles of Psychologists and Code of Conduct (hereinafter referred to as the Ethics Code) consists of an Introduction, a Preamble, six General Principles (A–F), and specific Ethical Standards. The Introduction discusses the intent, organization, procedural considerations, and scope of application of the Ethics Code. The Preamble and General Principles are *aspirational* goals to guide psychologists toward the highest ideals of psychology. Although the Preamble and General Principles are not themselves enforceable rules, they should be considered by psychologists in arriving at an ethical course of action and may be considered by ethics bodies in interpreting the Ethical Standards. The Ethical Standards set forth *enforceable* rules for conduct as psychologists. Most of the Ethical Standards are written broadly, in order to apply to psychologists in varied roles, although the application of an Ethical Standard may vary depending on the context. The Ethical Standards are not exhaustive. The fact that a given conduct is not specifically addressed by the Ethics Code does not mean that it is necessarily either ethical or unethical.

Membership in the APA commits members to adhere to the APA Ethics Code and to the rules and procedures used to implement it. Psychologists and students, whether or not they are APA members, should be aware that the Ethics Code may be applied to them by state psychology boards, courts, or other public bodies.

This version of the APA Ethics Code was adopted by the American Psychological Association's Council of Representatives during its meeting, August 13 and 16, 1992, and is effective beginning December 1, 1992. Inquiries concerning the substance or interpretation of the APA Ethics Code should be addressed to the Director, Office of Ethics, American Psychological Association, 750 First Street, NE, Washington, DC 20002-4242.

This Code will be used to adjudicate complaints brought concerning alleged conduct occurring on or after the effective date. Complaints regarding conduct occurring prior to the effective date will be adjudicated on the basis of the version of the Code that was in effect at the time the conduct occurred, except that no provisions repealed in June 1989, will be enforced even if an earlier version contains the provision. The Ethics Code will undergo continuing review and study for future revisions; comments on the Code may be sent to the above address.

The APA has previously published its Ethical Standards as follows:

American Psychological Association. (1953). *Ethical standards of psychologists*. Washington, DC: Author.
American Psychological Association. (1958). Standards of ethical behavior for psychologists. *American Psychologist, 13*, 268–271.
American Psychological Association. (1963). Ethical standards of psychologists. *American Psychologist, 18*, 56–60.
American Psychological Association. (1968). Ethical standards of psychologists. *American Psychologist, 23*, 357–361.
American Psychological Association. (1977, March). Ethical standards of psychologists. *APA Monitor*, pp. 22–23.
American Psychological Association. (1979). *Ethical standards of psychologists*. Washington, DC: Author.
American Psychological Association. (1981). Ethical principles of psychologists. *American Psychologist, 36*, 633–638.
American Psychological Association. (1990). Ethical principles of psychologists (Amended June 2, 1989). *American Psychologist, 45*, 390–395.

Request copies of the APA's Ethical Principles of Psychologists and Code of Conduct from the APA Order Department, 750 First Street, NE, Washington, DC 20002-4242, or phone (202) 336-5510.

This Ethics Code applies only to psychologists' work-related activities, that is, activities that are part of the psychologists' scientific and professional functions or that are psychological in nature. It includes the clinical or counseling practice of psychology, research, teaching, supervision of trainees, development of assessment instruments, conducting assessments, educational counseling, organizational consulting, social intervention, administration, and other activities as well. These work-related activities can be distinguished from the purely private conduct of a psychologist, which ordinarily is not within the purview of the Ethics Code.

The Ethics Code is intended to provide standards of professional conduct that can be applied by the APA and by other bodies that choose to adopt them. Whether or not a psychologist has violated the Ethics Code does not by itself determine whether he or she is legally liable in a court action, whether a contract is enforceable, or whether other legal consequences occur. These results are based on legal rather than ethical rules. However, compliance with or violation of the Ethics Code may be admissible as evidence in some legal proceedings, depending on the circumstances.

In the process of making decisions regarding their professional behavior, psychologists must consider this Ethics Code, in addition to applicable laws and psychology board regulations. If the Ethics Code establishes a higher standard of conduct than is required by law, psychologists must meet the higher ethical standard. If the Ethics Code standard appears to conflict with the requirements of law, then psychologists make known their commitment to the Ethics Code and take steps to resolve the conflict in a responsible manner. If neither law nor the Ethics Code resolves an issue, psychologists should consider other professional materials[1] and the dictates of their own conscience, as well as seek consultation with others within the field when this is practical.

The procedures for filing, investigating, and resolving complaints of unethical conduct are described in the current Rules and Procedures of the APA Ethics Committee. The actions that APA may take for violations of the Ethics Code include actions such as reprimand, censure, termination of APA membership, and referral of the matter to other bodies. Complainants who seek remedies such as monetary damages in alleging ethical violations by a psychologist must resort to private negotiation, administrative bodies, or the courts. Actions that violate the Ethics Code may lead to the imposition of sanctions on a psychologist by bodies other than APA, including state psychological associations, other professional groups, psychology boards, other state or federal agencies, and payors for health services. In addition to

---

[1]Professional materials that are most helpful in this regard are guidelines and standards that have been adopted or endorsed by professional psychological organizations. Such guidelines and standards, whether adopted by the American Psychological Association (APA) or its Divisions, are not enforceable as such by this Ethics Code, but are of educative value to psychologists, courts, and professional bodies. Such materials include, but are not limited to, the APA's *General Guidelines for Providers of Psychological Services* (1987), *Specialty Guidelines for the Delivery of Services by Clinical Psychologists, Counseling Psychologists, Industrial/Organizational Psychologists, and School Psychologists* (1981), *Guidelines for Computer Based Tests and Interpretations* (1987), *Standards for Educational and Psychological Testing* (1985), *Ethical Principles in the Conduct of Research With Human Participants* (1982), *Guidelines for Ethical Conduct in the Care and Use of Animals* (1986), *Guidelines for Providers of Psychological Services to Ethnic, Linguistic, and Culturally Diverse Populations* (1990), and *Publication Manual of the American Psychological Association* (3rd ed., 1983). Materials not adopted by APA as a whole include the APA Division 41 (Forensic Psychology)/American Psychology–Law Society's *Specialty Guidelines for Forensic Psychologists* (1991).

actions for violation of the Ethics Code, the APA Bylaws provide that APA may take action against a member after his or her conviction of a felony, expulsion or suspension from an affiliated state psychological association, or suspension or loss of licensure.

Preamble

Psychologists work to develop a valid and reliable body of scientific knowledge based on research. They may apply that knowledge to human behavior in a variety of contexts. In doing so, they perform many roles, such as researcher, educator, diagnostician, therapist, supervisor, consultant, administrator, social interventionist, and expert witness. Their goal is to broaden knowledge of behavior and, where appropriate, to apply it pragmatically to improve the condition of both the individual and society. Psychologists respect the central importance of freedom of inquiry and expression in research, teaching, and publication. They also strive to help the public in developing informed judgments and choices concerning human behavior. This Ethics Code provides a common set of values upon which psychologists build their professional and scientific work.

This Code is intended to provide both the general principles and the decision rules to cover most situations encountered by psychologists. It has as its primary goal the welfare and protection of the individuals and groups with whom psychologists work. It is the individual responsibility of each psychologist to aspire to the highest possible standards of conduct. Psychologists respect and protect human and civil rights, and do not knowingly participate in or condone unfair discriminatory practices.

The development of a dynamic set of ethical standards for a psychologist's work-related conduct requires a personal commitment to a lifelong effort to act ethically; to encourage ethical behavior by students, supervisees, employees, and colleagues, as appropriate; and to consult with others, as needed, concerning ethical problems. Each psychologist supplements, but does not violate, the Ethics Code's values and rules on the basis of guidance drawn from personal values, culture, and experience.

General Principles

Principle A: Competence

Psychologists strive to maintain high standards of competence in their work. They recognize the boundaries of their particular competencies and the limitations of their expertise. They provide only those services and use only those techniques for which they are qualified by education, training, or experience. Psychologists are cognizant of the fact that the competencies required in serving, teaching, and/or studying groups of people vary with the distinctive characteristics of those groups. In those areas in which recognized professional standards do not yet exist, psychologists exercise careful judgment and take appropriate precautions to protect the welfare of those with whom they work. They maintain knowledge of relevant scientific and professional information related to the services they render, and they recognize the need for ongoing education. Psychologists make appropriate use of scientific, professional, technical, and administrative resources.

Principle B: Integrity

Psychologists seek to promote integrity in the science, teaching, and practice of psychology. In these activities psychologists are honest, fair, and respectful of others. In describing or reporting their qualifications, services, products, fees, research, or teaching, they do not make statements that are false, misleading, or deceptive. Psychologists strive to be aware of their own belief systems, values, needs, and limitations and the effect of these on their work. To the extent feasible, they attempt to clarify for relevant parties the roles they are performing and to function appropriately in accordance with those roles. Psychologists avoid improper and potentially harmful dual relationships.

Principle C: Professional and Scientific Responsibility

Psychologists uphold professional standards of conduct, clarify their professional roles and obligations, accept appropriate responsibility for their behavior, and adapt their methods to the needs of different populations. Psychologists consult with, refer to, or cooperate with other professionals and institutions to the extent needed to serve the best interests of their patients, clients, or other recipients of their services. Psychologists' moral standards and conduct are personal matters to the same degree as is true for any other person, except as psychologists' conduct may compromise their professional responsibilities or reduce the public's trust in psychology and psychologists. Psychologists are concerned about the ethical compliance of their colleagues' scientific and professional conduct. When appropriate, they consult with colleagues in order to prevent or avoid unethical conduct.

Principle D: Respect for People's Rights and Dignity

Psychologists accord appropriate respect to the fundamental rights, dignity, and worth of all people. They respect the rights of individuals to privacy, confidentiality, self-determination, and autonomy, mindful that legal and other obligations may lead to inconsistency and conflict with the exercise of these rights. Psychologists are aware of cultural, individual, and role differences, including those due to age, gender, race, ethnicity, national origin, religion, sexual orientation, disability, language, and socioeconomic status. Psychologists try to eliminate the effect on their work of biases based on those factors, and they do not knowingly participate in or condone unfair discriminatory practices.

Principle E: Concern for Others' Welfare

Psychologists seek to contribute to the welfare of those with whom they interact professionally. In their professional actions, psychologists weigh the welfare and rights of their patients or clients, students, supervisees, human research participants, and other affected persons, and the welfare of animal subjects of research. When conflicts occur among psychologists' obligations or concerns, they attempt to resolve these conflicts and to perform their roles in a responsible fashion that avoids or minimizes harm. Psychologists are sensitive to real and ascribed differences in power between themselves and others, and they do not exploit or mislead other people during or after professional relationships.

Principle F: Social Responsibility

Psychologists are aware of their professional and scientific responsibilities to the community and the society in which they work and live. They apply and make public their knowledge of psychology in order to contribute to human welfare. Psychologists are concerned about and work to mitigate the causes of human suffering. When undertaking research, they strive to advance human welfare and the science of psychology. Psychologists try to avoid misuse of their work. Psychologists comply with the law and encourage the development of law and social policy that serve the interests of their patients and clients and the public. They are encouraged to contribute a portion of their professional time for little or no personal advantage.

Ethical Standards

1. General Standards

These General Standards are potentially applicable to the professional and scientific activities of all psychologists.

1.01 Applicability of the Ethics Code

The activity of a psychologist subject to the Ethics Code may be reviewed under these Ethical Standards only if the activity is part of his or her work-related functions or the activity is psychological in nature. Personal activities having no connection to or effect on psychological roles are not subject to the Ethics Code.

1.02 Relationship of Ethics and Law

If psychologists' ethical responsibilities conflict with law, psychologists make known their commitment to the Ethics Code and take steps to resolve the conflict in a responsible manner.

1.03 Professional and Scientific Relationship

Psychologists provide diagnostic, therapeutic, teaching, research, supervisory, consultative, or other psychological services only in the context of a defined professional or scientific relationship or role. (See also Standards 2.01, Evaluation, Diagnosis, and Interventions in Professional Context, and 7.02, Forensic Assessments.)

1.04 Boundaries of Competence

(a) Psychologists provide services, teach, and conduct research only within the boundaries of their competence, based on their education, training, supervised experience, or appropriate professional experience.

(b) Psychologists provide services, teach, or conduct research in new areas or involving new techniques only after first undertaking appropriate study, training, supervision, and/or consultation from persons who are competent in those areas or techniques.

(c) In those emerging areas in which generally recognized standards for preparatory training do not yet exist, psychologists nevertheless take reasonable steps to ensure the competence of their work and to protect patients, clients, students, research participants, and others from harm.

1.05 Maintaining Expertise

Psychologists who engage in assessment, therapy, teaching, research, organizational consulting, or other professional activities maintain a reasonable level of awareness of current scientific and professional information in their fields of activity, and undertake ongoing efforts to maintain competence in the skills they use.

1.06 Basis for Scientific and Professional Judgments

Psychologists rely on scientifically and professionally derived knowledge when making scientific or professional judgments or when engaging in scholarly or professional endeavors.

1.07 Describing the Nature and Results of Psychological Services

(a) When psychologists provide assessment, evaluation, treatment, counseling, supervision, teaching, consultation, research, or other psychological services to an individual, a group, or an organization, they provide, using language that is reasonably understandable to the recipient of those services, appropriate information beforehand about the nature of such services and appropriate information later about results and conclusions. (See also Standard 2.09, Explaining Assessment Results.)

(b) If psychologists will be precluded by law or by organizational roles from providing such information to particular individuals or groups, they so inform those individuals or groups at the outset of the service.

1.08 Human Differences

Where differences of age, gender, race, ethnicity, national origin, religion, sexual orientation, disability, language, or socioeconomic status significantly affect psychologists' work concerning particular individuals or groups, psychologists obtain the training, experience, consultation, or supervision necessary to ensure the competence of their services, or they make appropriate referrals.

1.09 Respecting Others

In their work-related activities, psychologists respect the rights of others to hold values, attitudes, and opinions that differ from their own.

1.10 Nondiscrimination

In their work-related activities, psychologists do not engage in unfair discrimination based on age, gender, race, ethnicity, national origin, religion, sexual orientation, disability, socioeconomic status, or any basis proscribed by law.

1.11 Sexual Harassment

(a) Psychologists do not engage in sexual harassment. Sexual harassment is sexual solicitation, physical advances, or verbal or nonverbal conduct that is sexual in nature, that occurs in connection with the psychologist's activities or roles as a psychologist, and that either: (1) is unwelcome, is offensive, or creates a hostile workplace environment, and the psychologist knows or is told this; or (2) is sufficiently severe or intense to be abusive to a reasonable person in the context. Sexual harassment can consist of a single intense or severe act or of multiple persistent or pervasive acts.

(b) Psychologists accord sexual-harassment complainants and respondents dignity and respect. Psychologists do not participate in denying a person academic admittance or advancement, employment, tenure, or promotion, based solely upon their having made, or their being the subject of, sexual-harassment charges. This does not preclude taking action based upon the outcome of such proceedings or consideration of other appropriate information.

1.12 Other Harassment

Psychologists do not knowingly engage in behavior that is harassing or demeaning to persons with whom they interact in their work based on factors such as those persons' age, gender, race, ethnicity, national origin, religion, sexual orientation, disability, language, or socioeconomic status.

1.13 Personal Problems and Conflicts

(a) Psychologists recognize that their personal problems and conflicts may interfere with their effectiveness. Accordingly, they refrain from undertaking an activity when they know or should know that their personal problems are likely to lead to harm to a patient, client, colleague, student, research participant, or other person to whom they may owe a professional or scientific obligation.

(b) In addition, psychologists have an obligation to be alert to signs of, and to obtain assistance for, their personal problems at an early stage, in order to prevent significantly impaired performance.

(c) When psychologists become aware of personal problems that may interfere with their performing work-related duties adequately, they take appropriate measures, such as obtaining professional consultation or assistance, and determine whether they should limit, suspend, or terminate their work-related duties.

1.14 Avoiding Harm

Psychologists take reasonable steps to avoid harming their patients or clients, research participants, students, and others with whom they work, and to minimize harm where it is foreseeable and unavoidable.

1.15 Misuse of Psychologists' Influence

Because psychologists' scientific and professional judgments and actions may affect the lives of others, they are alert to and guard against personal, financial, social, organizational, or political factors that might lead to misuse of their influence.

1.16 Misuse of Psychologists' Work

(a) Psychologists do not participate in activities in which it appears likely that their skills or data will be misused by others, unless corrective mechanisms are available. (See also Standard 7.04, Truthfulness and Candor.)

(b) If psychologists learn of misuse or misrepresentation of their work, they take reasonable steps to correct or minimize the misuse or misrepresentation.

1.17 Multiple Relationships

(a) In many communities and situations, it may not be feasible or reasonable for psychologists to avoid social or other nonprofessional contacts with persons such as patients, clients, students, supervisees, or research participants. Psychologists must always be sensitive to the potential harmful effects of other contacts on their work and on those persons with whom they deal. A psychologist refrains from entering into or promising another personal, scientific, professional, financial, or other relationship with such persons if it appears likely that such a relationship reasonably might impair the psychologist's objectivity or otherwise interfere with the psychologist's effectively performing his or her functions as a psychologist, or might harm or exploit the other party.

(b) Likewise, whenever feasible, a psychologist refrains from taking on professional or scientific obligations when preexisting relationships would create a risk of such harm.

(c) If a psychologist finds that, due to unforeseen factors, a potentially harmful multiple relationship has arisen, the psychologist attempts to resolve it with due regard for the best interests of the affected person and maximal compliance with the Ethics Code.

1.18 Barter (with Patients or Clients)

Psychologists ordinarily refrain from accepting goods, services, or other nonmonetary remuneration from patients or clients in return for psychological services because such arrangements create inherent potential for conflicts, exploitation, and distortion of the professional relationship. A psychologist may participate in bartering *only* if (1) it is not clinically contraindicated, *and* (2) the relationship is not exploitative. (See also Standards 1.17, Multiple Relationships, and 1.25, Fees and Financial Arrangements.)

1.19 Exploitative Relationships

(a) Psychologists do not exploit persons over whom they have supervisory, evaluative, or other authority such as students, supervisees, employees, research participants, and clients or patients. (See also Standards 4.05–4.07 regarding sexual involvement with clients or patients.)

(b) Psychologists do not engage in sexual relationships with students or supervisees in training over whom the psychologist has evaluative or direct authority, because such relationships are so likely to impair judgment or be exploitative.

1.20 Consultations and Referrals

(a) Psychologists arrange for appropriate consultations and referrals based principally on the best interests of their patients or clients, with appropriate consent, and subject to other relevant considerations, including applicable law and contractual obligations. (See also Standards 5.01, Discussing the Limits of Confidentiality, and 5.06, Consultations.)

(b) When indicated and professionally appropriate, psychologists cooperate with other professionals in order to serve their patients or clients effectively and appropriately.

(c) Psychologists' referral practices are consistent with law.

1.21 Third-Party Requests for Services

(a) When a psychologist agrees to provide services to a person or entity at the request of a third party, the psychologist clarifies to the extent feasible, at the outset of the service, the nature of the relationship with each party. This clarification includes the role of the psychologist (such as therapist, organizational consultant, diagnostician, or expert witness), the probable uses of the services provided or the information obtained, and the fact that there may be limits to confidentiality.

(b) If there is a foreseeable risk of the psychologist's being called upon to perform conflicting roles because of the involvement of a third party, the psychologist clarifies the nature and direction of his or her responsibilities, keeps all parties appropriately informed as matters develop, and resolves the situation in accordance with this Ethics Code.

1.22 Delegation to and Supervision of Subordinates

(a) Psychologists delegate to their employees, supervisees, and research assistants only those responsibilities that such persons can reasonably be expected to perform competently, on the basis of their education, training, or experience, either independently or with the level of supervision being provided.

(b) Psychologists provide proper training and supervision to their employees or supervisees and take reasonable steps to see that such persons perform services responsibly, competently, and ethically.

(c) If institutional policies, procedures, or practices prevent fulfillment of this obligation, psychologists attempt to modify their role or to correct the situation to the extent feasible.

1.23 Documentation of Professional and Scientific Work

(a) Psychologists appropriately document their professional and scientific work in order to facilitate provision of services later by them or by other professionals, to ensure accountability, and to meet other requirements of institutions or the law.

(b) When psychologists have reason to believe that records of their professional services will be used in legal proceedings involving recipients of or participants in their work, they have a responsibility to create and maintain documentation in the kind of detail and quality that would be consistent with reasonable scrutiny in an adjudicative forum. (See also Standard 7.01, Professionalism, under Forensic Activities.)

1.24 Records and Data

Psychologists create, maintain, disseminate, store, retain, and dispose of records and data relating to their research, practice, and other work in accordance with law and in a manner that permits compliance with the requirements of this Ethics Code. (See also Standard 5.04, Maintenance of Records.)

1.25 Fees and Financial Arrangements

(a) As early as is feasible in a professional or scientific relationship, the psychologist and the patient, client, or other appropriate recipient of psychological services reach an agreement specifying the compensation and the billing arrangements.

(b) Psychologists do not exploit recipients of services or payors with respect to fees.

(c) Psychologists' fee practices are consistent with law.

(d) Psychologists do not misrepresent their fees.

(e) If limitations to services can be anticipated because of limitations in financing, this is discussed with the patient, client, or other appropriate recipient of services as early as is feasible. (See also Standard 4.08, Interruption of Services.)

(f) If the patient, client, or other recipient of services does not pay for services as agreed, and if the psychologist wishes to use collection agencies or legal measures to collect the fees, the psychologist first informs the person that such measures will be taken and provides that person an opportunity to make prompt payment. (See also Standard 5.11, Withholding Records for Nonpayment.)

1.26 Accuracy in Reports to Payors and Funding Sources

In their reports to payors for services or sources of research funding, psychologists accurately state the nature of the research or service provided, the fees or charges, and where applicable, the identity of the provider, the findings, and the diagnosis. (See also Standard 5.05, Disclosures.)

1.27 Referrals and Fees

When a psychologist pays, receives payment from, or divides fees with another professional other than in an employer-employee relationship, the payment to each is based on the services (clinical, consultative, administrative, or other) provided and is not based on the referral itself.

2. Evaluation, Assessment, or Intervention

2.01 Evaluation, Diagnosis, and Interventions in Professional Context

(a) Psychologists perform evaluations, diagnostic services, or interventions only within the context of a defined professional relationship. (See also Standard 1.03, Professional and Scientific Relationship.)

(b) Psychologists' assessments, recommendations, reports, and psychological diagnostic or evaluative statements are based on information and techniques (including personal interviews of the individual when appropriate) sufficient to provide appropriate substantiation for their findings. (See also Standard 7.02, Forensic Assessments.)

2.02 Competence and Appropriate Use of Assessments and Interventions

(a) Psychologists who develop, administer, score, interpret, or use psychological assessment techniques, interviews, tests, or instruments do so in a manner and for purposes that are appropriate in light of the research on or evidence of the usefulness and proper application of the techniques.

(b) Psychologists refrain from misuse of assessment techniques, interventions, results, and interpretations and take reasonable steps to prevent others from misusing the information these techniques provide. This includes refraining from releasing raw test results or raw data to persons, other than to patients or clients as appropriate, who are not qualified to use such information. (See also Standards 1.02, Relationship of Ethics and Law, and 1.04, Boundaries of Competence.)

2.03 Test Construction

Psychologists who develop and conduct research with tests and other assessment techniques use scientific procedures and current professional knowledge for test design, standardization, validation, reduction or elimination of bias, and recommendations for use.

2.04 Use of Assessment in General and with Special Populations

(a) Psychologists who perform interventions or administer, score, interpret, or use assessment techniques are familiar with the reliability, validation, and related standardization or outcome studies of, and proper applications and uses of, the techniques they use.

(b) Psychologists recognize limits to the certainty with which diagnoses, judgments, or predictions can be made about individuals.

(c) Psychologists attempt to identify situations in which particular interventions or assessment techniques or norms may not be applicable or may require adjustment in administration or interpretation because of factors such as individuals' gender, age, race, ethnicity, national origin, religion, sexual orientation, disability, language, or socioeconomic status.

2.05 Interpreting Assessment Results

When interpreting assessment results, including automated interpretations, psychologists take into account the various test factors and characteristics of the person being assessed that might affect psychologists' judgments or reduce the accuracy of their interpretations. They indicate any significant reservations they have about the accuracy or limitations of their interpretations.

2.06 Unqualified Persons

Psychologists do not promote the use of psychological assessment techniques by unqualified persons. (See also Standard 1.22, Delegation to and Supervision of Subordinates.)

2.07 Obsolete Tests and Outdated Test Results

(a) Psychologists do not base their assessment or intervention decisions or recommendations on data or test results that are outdated for the current purpose.

(b) Similarly, psychologists do not base such decisions or recommendations on tests and measures that are obsolete and not useful for the current purpose.

2.08 Test Scoring and Interpretation Services

(a) Psychologists who offer assessment or scoring procedures to other professionals accurately describe the purpose, norms, validity, reliability, and applications of the procedures and any special qualifications applicable to their use.

(b) Psychologists select scoring and interpretation services (including automated services) on the basis of evidence of the validity of the program and procedures as well as on other appropriate considerations.

(c) Psychologists retain appropriate responsibility for the appropriate application, interpretation, and use of assessment instruments, whether they score and interpret such tests themselves or use automated or other services.

2.09 Explaining Assessment Results

Unless the nature of the relationship is clearly explained to the person being assessed in advance and precludes provision of an explanation of results (such as in some organizational consulting, preemployment or security screenings, and forensic evaluations), psychologists ensure that an explanation of the results is provided using language that is reasonably understandable to the person assessed or to another legally authorized person on behalf of the client. Regardless of whether the scoring and interpretation are done by the psychologist, by assistants, or by automated or other outside services, psychologists take reasonable steps to ensure that appropriate explanations of results are given.

2.10 Maintaining Test Security

Psychologists make reasonable efforts to maintain the integrity and security of tests and other assessment techniques consistent with law, contractual obligations, and in a manner that permits compliance with the requirements of this Ethics Code. (See also Standard 1.02, Relationship of Ethics and Law.)

3. Advertising and Other Public Statements

3.01 Definition of Public Statements

Psychologists comply with this Ethics Code in public statements relating to their professional services, products, or publications or to the field of psychology. Public statements include but are not limited to paid or unpaid advertising, brochures, printed matter, directory listings, personal resumes or curricula vitae, interviews or comments for use in media, statements in legal proceedings, lectures and public oral presentations, and published materials.

3.02 Statements by Others

(a) Psychologists who engage others to create or place public statements that promote their professional practice, products, or activities retain professional responsibility for such statements.

(b) In addition, psychologists make reasonable efforts to prevent others whom they do not control (such as employers, publishers, sponsors, organizational clients, and representatives of the print or broadcast media) from making deceptive statements concerning psychologists' practice or professional or scientific activities.

(c) If psychologists learn of deceptive statements about their work made by others, psychologists make reasonable efforts to correct such statements.

(d) Psychologists do not compensate employees of press, radio, television, or other communication media in return for publicity in a news item.

(e) A paid advertisement relating to the psychologist's activities must be identified as such, unless it is already apparent from the context.

3.03 Avoidance of False or Deceptive Statements

(a) Psychologists do not make public statements that are false, deceptive, misleading, or fraudulent, either because of what they state, convey, or suggest or because of what they omit, concerning their research, practice, or other work activities or those of persons or organizations with which they are affiliated. As examples (and not in limitation) of this standard, psychologists do not make false or deceptive statements concerning (1) their training, experience, or competence; (2) their academic degrees; (3) their credentials; (4) their institutional or association affiliations; (5) their services; (6) the scientific or clinical basis for, or results or degree of success of, their services; (7) their fees; or (8) their publications or research findings. (See also Standards 6.15, Deception in Research, and 6.18, Providing Participants with Information About the Study.)

(b) Psychologists claim as credentials for their psychological work, only degrees that (1) were earned from a regionally accredited educational institution or (2) were the basis for psychology licensure by the state in which they practice.

3.04 Media Presentations

When psychologists provide advice or comment by means of public lectures, demonstrations, radio or television programs, prerecorded tapes, printed articles, mailed material, or other media, they take reasonable precautions to ensure that (1) the statements are based on appropriate psychological literature and practice, (2) the statements are otherwise consistent with this Ethics Code, and (3) the recipients of the information are not encouraged to infer that a relationship has been established with them personally.

3.05 Testimonials

Psychologists do not solicit testimonials from current psychotherapy clients or patients or other persons who because of their particular circumstances are vulnerable to undue influence.

3.06 In-Person Solicitation

Psychologists do not engage, directly or through agents, in uninvited in-person solicitation of business from actual or potential psychotherapy patients or clients or other persons who because of their particular circumstances are vulnerable to undue influence. However, this does not preclude attempting to implement appropriate collateral contacts with significant others for the purpose of benefiting an already engaged therapy patient.

4. Therapy

4.01 Structuring the Relationship

(a) Psychologists discuss with clients or patients as early as is feasible in the therapeutic relationship appropriate issues, such as the nature and anticipated course of therapy, fees, and confidentiality. (See also Standards 1.25, Fees and Financial Arrangements, and 5.01, Discussing the Limits of Confidentiality.)

(b) When the psychologist's work with clients or patients will be supervised, the above discussion includes that fact, and the name of the supervisor, when the supervisor has legal responsibility for the case.

(c) When the therapist is a student intern, the client or patient is informed of that fact.

(d) Psychologists make reasonable efforts to answer patients' questions and to avoid apparent misunderstandings about therapy. Whenever possible, psychologists provide oral and/or written information, using language that is reasonably understandable to the patient or client.

4.02 Informed Consent to Therapy

(a) Psychologists obtain appropriate informed consent to therapy or related procedures, using language that is reasonably understandable to participants. The content of informed consent will vary depending on many circumstances; however, informed consent generally implies that the person (1) has the capacity to consent, (2) has been informed of significant information concerning the procedure, (3) has freely and without undue influence expressed consent, and (4) consent has been appropriately documented.

(b) When persons are legally incapable of giving informed consent, psychologists obtain informed permission from a legally authorized person, if such substitute consent is permitted by law.

(c) In addition, psychologists (1) inform those persons who are legally incapable of giving informed consent about the proposed interventions in a manner commensurate with the persons' psychological capacities, (2) seek their assent to those interventions, and (3) consider such persons' preferences and best interests.

4.03 Couple and Family Relationships

(a) When a psychologist agrees to provide services to several persons who have a relationship (such as husband and wife or parents and childern), the psychologist attempts to clarify at the outset (1) which of the individuals are patients or clients and (2) the relationship the psychologist will have with each person. This clarification includes the role of the psychologist and the probable uses of the services provided or the information obtained. (See also Standard 5.01, Discussing the Limits of Confidentiality.)

(b) As soon as it becomes apparent that the psychologist may be called on to perform potentially conflicting roles (such as marital counselor to husband and wife, and then witness for one party in a divorce proceeding), the psychologist attempts to clarify and adjust, or withdraw from, roles appropriately. (See also Standard 7.03, Clarification of Role, under Forensic Activities.)

4.04 Providing Mental Health Services to Those Served by Others

In deciding whether to offer or provide services to those already receiving mental health services elsewhere, psychologists carefully consider the treatment issues and the potential patient's or client's welfare. The psychologist discusses these issues with the patient or client, or another legally authorized person on behalf of the client, in order to minimize the risk of confusion and conflict, consults with the other service providers when appropriate, and proceeds with caution and sensitivity to the therapeutic issues.

4.05 Sexual Intimacies with Current Patients or Clients

Psychologists do not engage in sexual intimacies with current patients or clients.

4.06 Therapy with Former Sexual Partners

Psychologists do not accept as therapy patients or clients persons with whom they have engaged in sexual intimacies.

4.07 Sexual Intimacies with Former Therapy Patients

(a) Psychologists do not engage in sexual intimacies with a former therapy patient or client for at least two years after cessation or termination of professional services.

(b) Because sexual intimacies with a former therapy patient or client are so frequently harmful to the patient or client, and because such intimacies undermine public confidence in the psychology profession and thereby deter the public's use of needed services, psychologists do not engage in sexual intimacies with former therapy patients and clients even after a two-year interval except in the most unusual circumstances. The psychologist who engages in such activity after the two years following cessation or termination of treatment bears the burden of demonstrating that there has been no exploitation, in light of all relevant factors, including (1) the amount of time that has passed since therapy terminated, (2) the nature and duration of the therapy, (3) the circumstances of termination, (4) the patient's or client's personal history, (5) the patient's or client's current mental status, (6) the likelihood of adverse impact on the patient or client and others, and (7) any statements or actions made by the therapist during the course of therapy suggesting or inviting the possibility of a posttermination sexual or romantic relationship with the patient or client. (See also Standard 1.17, Multiple Relationships.)

4.08 Interruption of Services

(a) Psychologists make reasonable efforts to plan for facilitating care in the event that psychological services are interrupted by factors such as the psychologist's illness, death, unavailability, or relocation or by the client's relocation or financial limitations. (See also Standard 5.09, Preserving Records and Data.)

(b) When entering into employment or contractual relationships, psychologists provide for orderly and appropriate resolution of responsibility for patient or client care in the event that the employment or contractual relationship ends, with paramount consideration given to the welfare of the patient or client.

4.09 Terminating the Professional Relationship

(a) Psychologists do not abandon patients or clients. (See also Standard 1.25, under Fees and Financial Arrangements.)

(b) Psychologists terminate a professional relationship when it becomes reasonably clear that the patient or client no longer needs the service, is not benefiting, or is being harmed by continued service.

(c) Prior to termination for whatever reason, except where precluded by the patient's or client's conduct, the psychologist discusses the patient's or client's views and needs, provides appropriate pretermination counseling, suggests alternative service providers as appropriate, and takes other reasonable steps to facilitate transfer of responsibility to another provider if the patient or client needs one immediately.

5. *Privacy and Confidentiality*

These Standards are potentially applicable to the professional and scientific activities of all psychologists.

5.01 Discussing the Limits of Confidentiality

(a) Psychologists discuss with persons and organizations with whom they establish a scientific or professional relationship (including, to the extent feasible, minors and their legal representatives) (1) the relevant limitations on confidentiality, including limitations where applicable in group, marital, and family therapy or in organizational consulting, and (2) the foreseeable uses of the information generated through their services.

(b) Unless it is not feasible or is contraindicated, the discussion of confidentiality occurs at the outset of the relationship and thereafter as new circumstances may warrant.

(c) Permission for electronic recording of interviews is secured from clients and patients.

5.02 Maintaining Confidentiality

Psychologists have a primary obligation and take reasonable precautions to respect the confidentiality rights of those with whom they work or consult, recognizing that confidentiality may be established by law, institutional rules, or professional or scientific relationships. (See also Standard 6.26, Professional Reviewers.)

5.03 Minimizing Intrusions on Privacy

(a) In order to minimize intrusions on privacy, psychologists include in written and oral reports, consultations, and the like, only information germane to the purpose for which the communication is made.

(b) Psychologists discuss confidential information obtained in clinical or consulting relationships, or evaluative data concerning patients, individual or organizational clients, students, research participants, supervisees, and employees, only for appropriate scientific or professional purposes and only with persons clearly concerned with such matters.

5.04 Maintenance of Records

Psychologists maintain appropriate confidentiality in creating, storing, accessing, transferring, and disposing of records under their control, whether these are written, automated, or in any other medium. Psychologists maintain and dispose of records in accordance with law and in a manner that permits compliance with the requirements of this Ethics Code.

5.05 Disclosures

(a) Psychologists disclose confidential information without the consent of the individual only as mandated by law, or where permitted by law for a valid purpose, such as (1) to provide needed professional services to the patient or the individual or organizational client, (2) to obtain appropriate professional consultations, (3) to protect the patient or client or others from harm, or (4) to obtain payment for services, in which instance disclosure is limited to the minimum that is necessary to achieve the purpose.

(b) Psychologists also may disclose confidential information with the appropriate consent of the patient or the individual or organizational client (or of another legally authorized person on behalf of the patient or client), unless prohibited by law.

5.06 Consultations

When consulting with colleagues, (1) psychologists do not share confidential information that reasonably could lead to the identification of a patient, client, research participant, or other person or organization with whom they have a confidential relationship unless they have obtained the prior consent of the person or organization or the disclosure cannot be avoided, and (2) they share information only to the extent necessary to achieve the purposes of the consultation. (See also Standard 5.02, Maintaining Confidentiality.)

5.07 Confidential Information in Databases

(a) If confidential information concerning recipients of psychological services is to be entered into databases or systems of records available to persons whose access has not been consented to by the recipient, then psychologists use coding or other techniques to avoid the inclusion of personal identifiers.

(b) If a research protocol approved by an institutional review board or similar body requires the inclusion of personal identifiers, such identifiers are deleted before the information is made accessible to persons other than those of whom the subject was advised.

(c) If such deletion is not feasible, then before psychologists transfer such data to others or review such data collected by others, they take reasonable steps to determine that appropriate consent of personally identifiable individuals has been obtained.

5.08 Use of Confidential Information for Didactic or Other Purposes

(a) Psychologists do not disclose in their writings, lectures, or other public media, confidential, personally identifiable information concerning their patients, individual or organizational clients, students, research participants, or other recipients of their services that they obtained during the course of their work, unless the person or organization has consented in writing or unless there is other ethical or legal authorization for doing so.

(b) Ordinarily, in such scientific and professional presentations, psychologists disguise confidential information concerning such persons or organizations so that they are not individually identifiable to others and so that discussions do not cause harm to subjects who might identify themselves.

5.09 Preserving Records and Data

A psychologist makes plans in advance so that confidentiality of records and data is protected in the event of the psychologist's death, incapacity, or withdrawal from the position or practice.

5.10 Ownership of Records and Data

Recognizing that ownership of records and data is governed by legal principles, psychologists take reasonable and lawful steps so that records and data remain available to the extent needed to serve the best interests of patients, individual or organizational clients, research participants, or appropriate others.

5.11 Withholding Records for Nonpayment

Psychologists may not withhold records under their control that are requested and imminently needed for a patient's or client's treatment solely because payment has not been received, except as otherwise provided by law.

6. Teaching, Training Supervision, Research, and Publishing

6.01 Design of Education and Training Programs

Psychologists who are responsible for education and training programs seek to ensure that the programs are competently designed, provide the proper experiences, and meet the requirements for licensure, certification, or other goals for which claims are made by the program.

6.02 Descriptions of Education and Training Programs

(a) Psychologists responsible for education and training programs seek to ensure that there is a current and accurate description of the program content, training goals and objectives, and requirements that must be met for satisfactory completion of the program. This information must be made readily available to all interested parties.

(b) Psychologists seek to ensure that statements concerning their course outlines are accurate and not misleading, particularly regarding the subject matter to be covered, bases for evaluating progress, and the nature of course experiences. (See also Standard 3.03, Avoidance of False or Deceptive Statements.)

(c) To the degree to which they exercise control, psychologists responsible for announcements, catalogs, brochures, or advertisements describing workshops, seminars, or other non-degree-granting educational programs ensure that they accurately describe the audience for which the program is intended, the educational objectives, the presenters, and the fees involved.

6.03 Accuracy and Objectivity in Teaching

(a) When engaged in teaching or training, psychologists present psychological information accurately and with a reasonable degree of objectivity.

(b) When engaged in teaching or training, psychologists recognize the power they hold over students or supervisees and therefore make reasonable efforts to avoid engaging in conduct that is personally demeaning to students or supervisees. (See also Standards 1.09, Respecting Others, and 1.12, Other Harassment.)

6.04 Limitation on Teaching

Psychologists do not teach the use of techniques or procedures that require specialized training, licensure, or expertise, including but not limited to hypnosis, biofeedback, and projective techniques, to individuals who lack the prerequisite training, legal scope of practice, or expertise.

6.05 Assessing Student and Supervisee Performance

(a) In academic and supervisory relationships, psychologists establish an appropriate process for providing feedback to students and supervisees.

(b) Psychologists evaluate students and supervisees on the basis of their actual performance on relevant and established program requirements.

6.06 Planning Research

(a) Psychologists design, conduct, and report research in accordance with recognized standards of scientific competence and ethical research.

(b) Psychologists plan their research so as to minimize the possibility that results will be misleading.

(c) In planning research, psychologists consider its ethical acceptability under the Ethics Code. If an ethical issue is unclear, psychologists seek to resolve the issue through consultation with institutional review boards, animal care and use committees, peer consultations, or other proper mechanisms.

(d) Psychologists take reasonable steps to implement appropriate protections for the rights and welfare of human participants, other persons affected by the research, and the welfare of animal subjects.

6.07 Responsibility

(a) Psychologists conduct research competently and with due concern for the dignity and welfare of the participants.

(b) Psychologists are responsible for the ethical conduct of research conducted by them or by others under their supervision or control.

(c) Researchers and assistants are permitted to perform only those tasks for which they are appropriately trained and prepared.

(d) As part of the process of development and implementation of research projects, psychologists consult those with expertise concerning any special population under investigation or most likely to be affected.

6.08 Compliance with Law and Standards

Psychologists plan and conduct research in a manner consistent with federal and state law and regulations, as well as professional standards governing the conduct of research, and particularly those standards governing research with human participants and animal subjects.

6.09 Institutional Approval

Psychologists obtain from host institutions or organizations appropriate approval prior to conducting research, and they provide accurate information about their research proposals. They conduct the research in accordance with the approved research protocol.

6.10 Research Responsibilities

Prior to conducting research (except research involving only anonymous surveys, naturalistic observations, or similar research), psychologists enter into an agreement with participants that clarifies the nature of the research and the responsibilities of each party.

6.11 Informed Consent to Research

(a) Psychologists use language that is reasonably understandable to research participants in obtaining their appropriate informed consent (except as provided in Standard 6.12, Dispensing with Informed Consent). Such informed consent is appropriately documented.

(b) Using language that is reasonably understandable to participants, psychologists inform participants of the nature of the research; they inform participants that they are free to participate or to decline to participate or to withdraw from the research; they explain the foreseeable consequences of declining or withdrawing; they inform participants of significant factors that may be expected to influence their willingness to participate (such as risks, discomfort, adverse effects, or limitations on confidentiality, except as provided in Standard 6.15, Deception in Research); and they explain other aspects about which the prospective participants inquire.

(c) When psychologists conduct research with individuals such as students or subordinates, psychologists take special care to protect the prospective participants from adverse consequences of declining or withdrawing from participation.

(d) When research participation is a course requirement or opportunity for extra credit, the prospective participant is given the choice of equitable alternative activities.

(e) For persons who are legally incapable of giving informed consent, psychologists nevertheless (1) provide an appropriate explanation, (2) obtain the participant's assent, and (3) obtain appropriate permission from a legally authorized person, if such substitute consent is permitted by law.

6.12 Dispensing with Informed Consent

Before determining that planned research (such as research involving only anonymous questionnaires, naturalistic observations, or certain kinds of archival research) does not require the informed consent of research participants, psychologists consider applicable regulations and institutional review board requirements, and they consult with colleagues as appropriate.

6.13 Informed Consent in Research Filming or Recording

Psychologists obtain informed consent from research participants prior to filming or recording them in any form, unless the research involves simply naturalistic observations in public places and it is not anticipated that the recording will be used in a manner that could cause personal identification or harm.

6.14 Offering Inducements for Research Participants

(a) In offering professional services as an inducement to obtain research participants, psychologists make clear the nature of the services, as well as the risks, obligations, and limitations. (See also Standard 1.18, Barter [with Patients or Clients].)

(b) Psychologists do not offer excessive or inappropriate financial or other inducements to obtain research participants, particularly when it might tend to coerce participation.

6.15 Deception in Research

(a) Psychologists do not conduct a study involving deception unless they have determined that the use of deceptive techniques is justified by the study's prospective scientific, educational, or applied value and that equally effective alternative procedures that do not use deception are not feasible.

(b) Psychologists never deceive research participants about significant aspects that would affect their willingness to participate, such as physical risks, discomfort, or unpleasant emotional experiences.

(c) Any other deception that is an integral feature of the design and conduct of an experiment must be explained to participants as early as is feasible, preferably at the conclusion of their participation, but no later than at the conclusion of the research. (See also Standard 6.18, Providing Participants with Information About the Study.)

6.16 Sharing and Utilizing Data

Psychologists inform research participants of their anticipated sharing or further use of personally identifiable research data and of the possibility of unanticipated future uses.

6.17 Minimizing Invasiveness

In conducting research, psychologists interfere with the participants or milieu from which data are collected only in a manner that is warranted by an appropriate research design and that is consistent with psychologists' roles as scientific investigators.

6.18 Providing Participants with Information About the Study

(a) Psychologists provide a prompt opportunity for participants to obtain appropriate information about the nature, results, and conclusions of the research, and psychologists attempt to correct any misconceptions that participants may have.

(b) If scientific or humane values justify delaying or withholding this information, psychologists take reasonable measures to reduce the risk of harm.

6.19 Honoring Commitments

Psychologists take reasonable measures to honor all commitments they have made to research participants.

6.20 Care and Use of Animals in Research

(a) Psychologists who conduct research involving animals treat them humanely.

(b) Psychologists acquire, care for, use, and dispose of animals in compliance with current federal, state, and local laws and regulations, and with professional standards.

(c) Psychologists trained in research methods and experienced in the care of laboratory animals supervise all procedures involving animals and are responsible for ensuring appropriate consideration of their comfort, health, and humane treatment.

(d) Psychologists ensure that all individuals using animals under their supervision have received instruction in research methods and in the care, maintenance, and handling of the species being used, to the extent appropriate to their role.

(e) Responsibilities and activities of individuals assisting in a research project are consistent with their respective competencies.

(f) Psychologists make reasonable efforts to minimize the discomfort, infection, illness, and pain of animal subjects.

(g) A procedure subjecting animals to pain, stress, or privation is used only when an alternative procedure is unavailable and the goal is justified by its prospective scientific educational, or applied value.

(h) Surgical procedures are performed under appropriate anesthesia; techniques to avoid infection and minimize pain are followed during and after surgery.

(i) When it is appropriate that the animal's life be terminated, it is done rapidly, with an effort to minimize pain, and in accordance with accepted procedures.

6.21 Reporting of Results

(a) Psychologists do not fabricate data or falsify results in their publications.

(b) If psychologists discover significant errors in their published data, they take reasonable steps to correct such errors in a correction, retraction, erratum, or other appropriate publication means.

6.22 Plagiarism

Psychologists do not present substantial portions or elements of another's work or data as their own, even if the other work or data source is cited occasionally.

6.23 Publication Credit

(a) Psychologists take responsibility and credit, including authorship credit, only for work they have actually performed or to which they have contributed.

(b) Principal authorship and other publication credits accurately reflect the relative scientific or professional contributions of the individuals involved, regardless of their relative status. Mere possession of an institutional position, such as Department Chair, does not justify authorship credit. Minor contributions to the research or to the writing for publications are appropriately acknowledged, such as in footnotes or in an introductory statement.

(c) A student is usually listed as principal author on any multiple-authored article that is substantially based on the student's dissertation or thesis.

6.24 Duplicate Publication of Data

Psychologists do not publish, as original data, data that have been previously published. This does not preclude republishing data when they are accompanied by proper acknowledgment.

6.25 Sharing Data

After research results are published, psychologists do not withhold the data on which their conclusions are based from other competent professionals who seek to verify the substantive claims through reanalysis and who intend to use such data only for that purpose, provided that the confidentiality of the participants can be protected and unless legal rights concerning proprietary data preclude their release.

6.26 Professional Reviewers

Psychologists who review material submitted for publication, grant, or other research proposal review respect the confidentiality of and the proprietary rights in such information of those who submitted it.

7. *Forensic Activities*

7.01 Professionalism

Psychologists who perform forensic functions, such as assessments, interviews, consultations, reports, or expert testimony, must comply with all other provisions of this Ethics Code to the extent that they apply to such activities. In addition, psychologists base their forensic work on appropriate knowledge of and competence in the areas underlying such work, including specialized knowledge concerning special populations. (See also Standards 1.06, Basis for Scientifc and Professional Judgments; 1.08, Human Differences; 1.15, Misuse of Psychologists' Influence; and 1.23, Documentation of Professional and Scientific Work.)

7.02 Forensic Assessments

(a) Psychologists' forensic assessments, recommendations, and reports are based on information and techniques (including personal interviews of the individual, when appropriate) sufficient to provide appropriate substantiation for their findings. (See also Standards 1.03, Professional and Scientific Relationship; 1.23, Documentation of Professional and Scientific Work; 2.01, Evaluation, Diagnosis, and Interventions in Professional Context; and 2.05, Interpreting Assessment Results.)

(b) Except as noted in (c), below, psychologists provide written or oral forensic reports or testimony of the psychological characteristics of an individual only after they have conducted an examination of the individual adequate to support their statements or conclusions.

(c) When, despite reasonable efforts, such an examination is not feasible, psychologists clarify the impact of their limited information on the reliability and validity of their reports and testimony, and they appropriately limit the nature and extent of their conclusions or recommendations.

7.03 Clarification of Role

In most circumstances, psychologists avoid performing multiple and potentially conflicting roles in forensic matters. When psychologists may be called on to serve in more than one role in a legal proceeding—for example, as consultant or expert for one party or for the court and as a fact witness—they clarify role expectations and the extent of confidentiality in advance to the extent feasible, and thereafter as changes occur, in order to avoid compromising their professional judgment and objectivity and in order to avoid misleading others regarding their role.

7.04 Truthfulness and Candor

(a) In forensic testimony and reports, psychologists testify truthfully, honestly, and candidly and, consistent with applicable legal procedures, describe fairly the bases for their testimony and conclusions.

(b) Whenever necessary to avoid misleading, psychologists acknowledge the limits of their data or conclusions.

7.05 Prior Relationships

A prior professional relationship with a party does not preclude psychologists from testifying as fact witnesses or from testifying to their services to the extent permitted by applicable law. Psychologists appropriately take into account ways in which the prior relationship might affect their professional objectivity or opinions and disclose the potential conflict to the relevant parties.

7.06 Compliance with Law and Rules

In performing forensic roles, psychologists are reasonably familiar with the rules governing their roles. Psychologists are aware of the occasionally competing demands placed upon them by these principles and the requirements of the court system, and attempt to resolve these conflicts by making known their commitment to this Ethics Code and taking steps to resolve the conflict in a responsible manner. (See also Standard 1.02, Relationship of Ethics and Law.)

8. Resolving Ethical Issues

8.01 Familiarity with Ethics Code

Psychologists have an obligation to be familiar with this Ethics Code, other applicable ethics codes, and their application to psychologists' work. Lack of awareness or misunderstanding of an ethical standard is not itself a defense to a charge of unethical conduct.

8.02 Confronting Ethical Issues

When a psychologist is uncertain whether a particular situation or course of action would violate this Ethics Code, the psychologist ordinarily consults with other psychologists knowledgeable about ethical issues, with state or national psychology ethics committees, or with other appropriate authorities in order to choose a proper response.

8.03 Conflicts Between Ethics and Organizational Demands

If the demands of an organization with which psychologists are affiliated conflict with this Ethics Code, psychologists clarify the nature of the conflict, make known their commitment to the Ethics Code, and to the extent feasible, seek to resolve the conflict in a way that permits the fullest adherence to the Ethics Code.

8.04 Informal Resolution of Ethical Violations

When psychologists believe that there may have been an ethical violation by another psychologist, they attempt to resolve the issue by bringing it to the attention of that individual if an informal resolution appears appropriate and the intervention does not violate any confidentiality rights that may be involved.

8.05 Reporting Ethical Violations

If an apparent ethical violation is not appropriate for informal resolution under Standard 8.04 or is not resolved properly in that fashion, psychologists take further action appropriate to the situation, unless such action conflicts with confidentiality rights in ways that cannot be resolved. Such action might include referral to state or national committees on professional ethics or to state licensing boards.

8.06 Cooperating with Ethics Committees

Psychologists cooperate in ethics investigations, proceedings, and resulting requirements of the APA or any affiliated state psychological association to which they belong. In doing so, they make reasonable efforts to resolve any issues as to confidentiality. Failure to cooperate is itself an ethics violation.

8.07 Improper Complaints

Psychologists do not file or encourage the filing of ethics complaints that are frivolous and are intended to harm the respondent rather than to protect the public.

APPENDIX

B

STATISTICAL TABLES

■ ■ ■ ■ ■ ■

TABLE B.1		Areas Under the Normal Curve (z Table)			
Z	Area Between Mean and Z	Area Beyond Z	Z	Area Between Mean and Z	Area Beyond Z
0.00	0.00000	0.50000	0.34	0.13307	0.36693
0.01	0.00400	0.49600	0.35	0.13684	0.36316
0.02	0.00798	0.49202	0.36	0.14058	0.35942
0.03	0.01198	0.48802	0.37	0.14432	0.35568
0.04	0.01595	0.48405	0.38	0.14803	0.35197
0.05	0.01995	0.48005	0.39	0.15174	0.34826
0.06	0.02392	0.47608	0.40	0.15542	0.34458
0.07	0.02791	0.47209	0.41	0.15911	0.34089
0.08	0.03188	0.46812	0.42	0.16276	0.33724
0.09	0.03587	0.46413	0.43	0.16641	0.33359
0.10	0.03983	0.46017	0.44	0.17003	0.32997
0.11	0.04381	0.45619	0.45	0.17366	0.32634
0.12	0.04776	0.45224	0.46	0.17724	0.32276
0.13	0.05173	0.44827	0.47	0.18083	0.31917
0.14	0.05567	0.44433	0.48	0.18439	0.31561
0.15	0.05963	0.44037	0.49	0.18794	0.31206
0.16	0.06356	0.43644	0.50	0.19146	0.30854
0.17	0.06751	0.43249	0.51	0.19498	0.30502
0.18	0.07142	0.42858	0.52	0.19847	0.30153
0.19	0.07536	0.42464	0.53	0.20195	0.29805
0.20	0.07926	0.42074	0.54	0.20540	0.29460
0.21	0.08318	0.41682	0.55	0.20885	0.29115
0.22	0.08706	0.41294	0.56	0.21226	0.28774
0.23	0.09096	0.40904	0.57	0.21567	0.28433
0.24	0.09483	0.40517	0.58	0.21904	0.28096
0.25	0.09872	0.40128	0.59	0.22242	0.27758
0.26	0.10257	0.39743	0.60	0.22575	0.27425
0.27	0.10643	0.39357	0.61	0.22908	0.27092
0.28	0.11026	0.38974	0.62	0.23237	0.26763
0.29	0.11410	0.38590	0.63	0.23566	0.26434
0.30	0.11791	0.38209	0.64	0.23891	0.26109
0.31	0.12173	0.37827	0.65	0.24216	0.25784
0.32	0.12552	0.37448	0.66	0.24537	0.25463
0.33	0.12931	0.37069	0.67	0.24858	0.25142

(continued)

TABLE B.1		Areas Under the Normal Curve (z Table)—(continued)			
Z	Area Between Mean and Z	Area Beyond Z	Z	Area Between Mean and Z	Area Beyond Z
0.68	0.25175	0.24825	1.09	0.36215	0.13785
0.69	0.25491	0.24509	1.10	0.36433	0.13567
0.70	0.25804	0.24196	1.11	0.36651	0.13349
0.71	0.26116	0.23884	1.12	0.36864	0.13136
0.72	0.26424	0.23576	1.13	0.37077	0.12923
0.73	0.26732	0.23268	1.14	0.37286	0.12714
0.74	0.27035	0.22965	1.15	0.37494	0.12506
0.75	0.27338	0.22662	1.16	0.37698	0.12302
0.76	0.27637	0.22363	1.17	0.37901	0.12099
0.77	0.27936	0.22064	1.18	0.38100	0.11900
0.78	0.28230	0.21770	1.19	0.38299	0.11701
0.79	0.28525	0.21475	1.20	0.38493	0.11507
0.80	0.28814	0.21186	1.21	0.38687	0.11313
0.81	0.29104	0.20896	1.22	0.38877	0.11123
0.82	0.29389	0.20611	1.23	0.39066	0.10934
0.83	0.29674	0.20326	1.24	0.39251	0.10749
0.84	0.29955	0.20045	1.25	0.39436	0.10564
0.85	0.30235	0.19765	1.26	0.39617	0.10383
0.86	0.30511	0.19489	1.27	0.39797	0.10203
0.87	0.30786	0.19214	1.28	0.39973	0.10027
0.88	0.31057	0.18943	1.29	0.40149	0.09851
0.89	0.31328	0.18672	1.30	0.40320	0.09680
0.90	0.31594	0.18406	1.31	0.40491	0.09509
0.91	0.31860	0.18140	1.32	0.40658	0.09342
0.92	0.32121	0.17879	1.33	0.40825	0.09175
0.93	0.32383	0.17617	1.34	0.40988	0.09012
0.94	0.32639	0.17361	1.35	0.41150	0.08850
0.95	0.32895	0.17105	1.36	0.41309	0.08691
0.96	0.33147	0.16853	1.37	0.41467	0.08533
0.97	0.33399	0.16601	1.38	0.41621	0.08379
0.98	0.33646	0.16354	1.39	0.41775	0.08225
0.99	0.33892	0.16108	1.40	0.41924	0.08076
1.00	0.34134	0.15866	1.41	0.42074	0.07926
1.01	0.34376	0.15624	1.42	0.42220	0.07780
1.02	0.34614	0.15386	1.43	0.42365	0.07635
1.03	0.34851	0.15149	1.44	0.42507	0.07493
1.04	0.35083	0.14917	1.45	0.42648	0.07352
1.05	0.35315	0.14685	1.46	0.42785	0.07215
1.06	0.35543	0.14457	1.47	0.42923	0.07077
1.07	0.35770	0.14230	1.48	0.43056	0.06944
1.08	0.35993	0.14007	1.49	0.43190	0.06810

(continued)

TABLE B.1 **Areas Under the Normal Curve (z Table)**—(continued)

Z	Area Between Mean and Z	Area Beyond Z	Z	Area Between Mean and Z	Area Beyond Z
1.50	0.43319	0.06681	1.92	0.47257	0.02743
1.51	0.43449	0.06551	1.93	0.47321	0.02679
1.52	0.43574	0.06426	1.94	0.47381	0.02619
1.53	0.43700	0.06300	1.95	0.47442	0.02558
1.54	0.43822	0.06178	1.96	0.47500	0.02500
1.55	0.43944	0.06056	1.97	0.47559	0.02441
1.56	0.44062	0.05938	1.98	0.47615	0.02385
1.57	0.44180	0.05820	1.99	0.47672	0.02328
1.58	0.44295	0.05705	2.00	0.47725	0.02275
1.59	0.44409	0.05591	2.01	0.47780	0.02220
1.60	0.44520	0.05480	2.02	0.47831	0.02169
1.61	0.44631	0.05369	2.03	0.47883	0.02117
1.62	0.44738	0.05262	2.04	0.47932	0.02068
1.63	0.44846	0.05154	2.05	0.47983	0.02017
1.64	0.44950	0.05050	2.06	0.48030	0.01970
1.65	0.45054	0.04946	2.07	0.48078	0.01922
1.66	0.45154	0.04846	2.08	0.48124	0.01876
1.67	0.45255	0.04745	2.09	0.48170	0.01830
1.68	0.45352	0.04648	2.10	0.48214	0.01786
1.69	0.45450	0.04550	2.11	0.48258	0.01742
1.70	0.45543	0.04457	2.12	0.48300	0.01700
1.71	0.45638	0.04362	2.13	0.48342	0.01658
1.72	0.45728	0.04272	2.14	0.48382	0.01618
1.73	0.45820	0.04180	2.15	0.48423	0.01577
1.74	0.45907	0.04093	2.16	0.48461	0.01539
1.75	0.45995	0.04005	2.17	0.48501	0.01499
1.76	0.46080	0.03920	2.18	0.48537	0.01463
1.77	0.46165	0.03835	2.19	0.48575	0.01425
1.78	0.46246	0.03754	2.20	0.48610	0.01390
1.79	0.46328	0.03672	2.21	0.48646	0.01354
1.80	0.46407	0.03593	2.22	0.48679	0.01321
1.81	0.46486	0.03514	2.23	0.48714	0.01286
1.82	0.46562	0.03438	2.24	0.48745	0.01255
1.83	0.46639	0.03361	2.25	0.48779	0.01221
1.84	0.46712	0.03288	2.26	0.48809	0.01191
1.85	0.46785	0.03215	2.27	0.48841	0.01159
1.86	0.46856	0.03144	2.28	0.48870	0.01130
1.87	0.46927	0.03073	2.29	0.48900	0.01100
1.88	0.46995	0.03005	2.30	0.48928	0.01072
1.89	0.47063	0.02937	2.31	0.48957	0.01043
1.90	0.47128	0.02872	2.32	0.48983	0.01017
1.91	0.47194	0.02806	2.33	0.49011	0.00989

(continued)

TABLE B.1   **Areas Under the Normal Curve (z Table)**—(continued)

Z	Area Between Mean and Z	Area Beyond Z	Z	Area Between Mean and Z	Area Beyond Z
2.34	0.49036	0.00964	2.75	0.49703	0.00297
2.35	0.49062	0.00938	2.76	0.49711	0.00289
2.36	0.49086	0.00914	2.77	0.49721	0.00279
2.37	0.49112	0.00888	2.78	0.49728	0.00272
2.38	0.49134	0.00866	2.79	0.49738	0.00262
2.39	0.49159	0.00841	2.80	0.49744	0.00256
2.40	0.49180	0.00820	2.81	0.49753	0.00247
2.41	0.49203	0.00797	2.82	0.49760	0.00240
2.42	0.49224	0.00776	2.83	0.49768	0.00232
2.43	0.49246	0.00754	2.84	0.49774	0.00226
2.44	0.49266	0.00734	2.85	0.49782	0.00218
2.45	0.49287	0.00713	2.86	0.49788	0.00212
2.46	0.49305	0.00695	2.87	0.49796	0.00204
2.47	0.49325	0.00675	2.88	0.49801	0.00199
2.48	0.49343	0.00657	2.89	0.49808	0.00192
2.49	0.49362	0.00638	2.90	0.49813	0.00187
2.50	0.49379	0.00621	2.91	0.49820	0.00180
2.51	0.49397	0.00603	2.92	0.49825	0.00175
2.52	0.49413	0.00587	2.93	0.49832	0.00168
2.53	0.49431	0.00569	2.94	0.49836	0.00164
2.54	0.49446	0.00554	2.95	0.49842	0.00158
2.55	0.49462	0.00538	2.96	0.49846	0.00154
2.56	0.49477	0.00523	2.97	0.49852	0.00148
2.57	0.49493	0.00507	2.98	0.49856	0.00144
2.58	0.49506	0.00494	2.99	0.49862	0.00138
2.59	0.49521	0.00479	3.00	0.49865	0.00135
2.60	0.49534	0.00466	3.02	0.49874	0.00126
2.61	0.49548	0.00452	3.04	0.49882	0.00118
2.62	0.49560	0.00440	3.06	0.49889	0.00111
2.63	0.49574	0.00426	3.08	0.49896	0.00104
2.64	0.49585	0.00415	3.10	0.49903	0.00097
2.65	0.49599	0.00401	3.12	0.49910	0.00090
2.66	0.49609	0.00391	3.14	0.49916	0.00084
2.67	0.49622	0.00378	3.16	0.49921	0.00079
2.68	0.49632	0.00368	3.18	0.49926	0.00074
2.69	0.49644	0.00356	3.20	0.49931	0.00069
2.70	0.49653	0.00347	3.25	0.49943	0.00057
2.71	0.49665	0.00335	3.30	0.49952	0.00048
2.72	0.49674	0.00326	3.35	0.49961	0.00039
2.73	0.49684	0.00316	3.40	0.49966	0.00034
2.74	0.49693	0.00307	3.45	0.49973	0.00027

(continued)

TABLE B.1	Areas Under the Normal Curve (z Table)—(continued)

Z	Area Between Mean and Z	Area Beyond Z	Z	Area Between Mean and Z	Area Beyond Z
3.50	0.49977	0.00023	3.80	0.49993	0.00007
3.60	0.49984	0.00016	3.90	0.49995	0.00005
3.70	0.49989	0.00011	4.00	0.49997	0.00003

From *Statistics in the Behavioral Sciences: A Conceptual Introduction*, by R. S Lehman. Copyright © 1995 Brooks/Cole Publishing Company, Pacific Grove, CA 93950, a division of International Thomson Publishing Inc. By permission of the publisher and the author.

TABLE B.2	Critical Values of the Spearman r (Spearman Rank Order Correlation Coefficient)

Number of pairs	Level of Significance		
	.10	.05	.01
5	.900	1.000	—
6	.829	.886	1.000
7	.714	.786	.929
8	.643	.738	.881
9	.600	.683	.833
10	.564	.648	.794
12	.506	.591	.777
14	.456	.544	.715
16	.425	.506	.665
18	.399	.475	.625
20	.377	.450	.591
22	.359	.428	.562
24	.343	.409	.537
26	.329	.392	.515
28	.317	.377	.496
30	.306	.364	.478

Tabled values compiled by the first author using Sums of Squares from Olds, E. G. (1938). Distributions of sums of squares of rank differences for small numbers of individuals. *Annals of Mathematical Statistics, 9*, 113–148, and Olds, E. G. (1949). The 5% significance levels for sums of squares of rank differences and a correction. *Annals of Mathematical Statistics, 20*, 117–118.

| TABLE B.3 | | Critical Values of the Pearson r (Pearson Product Moment Correlation Coefficient) | |

| | *Level of Significance* | | |
Number of Pairs Minus Two	.10	.05	.01
1	.98769	.99692	.999877
2	.90000	.95000	.990000
3	.8054	.8783	.95873
4	.7293	.8114	.91720
5	.6694	.7545	.8745
6	.6215	.7067	.8343
7	.5822	.6664	.7977
8	.5494	.6319	.7646
9	.5214	.6021	.7348
10	.4973	.5760	.7079
11	.4762	.5529	.6835
12	.4575	.5324	.6614
13	.4409	.5139	.6411
14	.4259	.4973	.6226
15	.4124	.4821	.6055
16	.4000	.4683	.5897
17	.3887	.4555	.5751
18	.3783	.4438	.5614
19	.3687	.4329	.5487
20	.3598	.4227	.5368
25	.3233	.3809	.4869
30	.2960	.3494	.4487
35	.2746	.3246	.4182
40	.2573	.3044	.3932
45	.2428	.2875	.3721
50	.2306	.2732	.3541
60	.2108	.2500	.3248
70	.1954	.2319	.3017
80	.1829	.2172	.2830
90	.1726	.2050	.2673
100	.1638	.1946	.2540

From Table VII in *Statistical Tables for Biological, Agricultural, and Medical Research (6th Ed)*, by Sir R. A. Fisher and F. Yates. Copyright © 1963. Reprinted by permission of Addison Wesley Longman, Ltd.

TABLE B.4   *r*-to-*z* Transformation

r	*z*	*r*	*z*	*r*	*z*
0.00	0.0000	0.36	0.3769	0.71	0.8872
0.01	0.0100	0.37	0.3884	0.72	0.9076
0.02	0.0200	0.38	0.4001	0.73	0.9287
0.03	0.0300	0.39	0.4118	0.74	0.9505
0.04	0.0400	0.40	0.4236	0.75	0.9730
0.05	0.0500	0.41	0.4356	0.76	0.9962
0.06	0.0601	0.42	0.4477	0.77	1.0203
0.07	0.0701	0.43	0.4599	0.78	1.0454
0.08	0.0802	0.44	0.4722	0.79	1.0714
0.09	0.0902	0.45	0.4847	0.80	1.0986
0.10	0.1003	0.46	0.4973	0.81	1.1270
0.11	0.1104	0.47	0.5101	0.82	1.1568
0.12	0.1206	0.48	0.5230	0.83	1.1881
0.13	0.1307	0.49	0.5361	0.84	1.2212
0.14	0.1409	0.50	0.5493	0.85	1.2562
0.15	0.1511	0.51	0.5627	0.86	1.2933
0.16	0.1614	0.52	0.5763	0.87	1.3331
0.17	0.1717	0.53	0.5901	0.88	1.3758
0.18	0.1820	0.54	0.6042	0.89	1.4219
0.19	0.1923	0.55	0.6184	0.90	1.4722
0.20	0.2027	0.56	0.6328	0.91	1.5275
0.21	0.2132	0.57	0.6475	0.92	1.5890
0.22	0.2237	0.58	0.6625	0.93	1.6584
0.23	0.2342	0.59	0.6777	0.94	1.7380
0.24	0.2448	0.60	0.6931	0.95	1.8318
0.25	0.2554	0.61	0.7089	0.96	1.9459
0.26	0.2661	0.62	0.7250	0.97	2.0923
0.27	0.2769	0.63	0.7414	0.98	2.2976
0.28	0.2877	0.64	0.7582	0.99	2.6467
0.29	0.2986	0.65	0.7753		
0.30	0.3095	0.66	0.7928		
0.31	0.3205	0.67	0.8107		
0.32	0.3316	0.68	0.8291		
0.33	0.3428	0.69	0.8480		
0.34	0.3541	0.70	0.8673		
0.35	0.3654				

NOTE: The table shows positive values; the transformed value takes the sign of the original r (e.g. $r = 0.81$ becomes 1.1270, and $r = -0.81$ becomes -1.1270).

From *Statistics in the Behavioral Sciences: A Conceptual Introduction*, by R. S. Lehman. Copyright © 1995 Brooks / Cole Publishing Company, Pacific Grove, CA 93950, a division of International Thomson Publishing Inc. By permission of the publisher and the author.

| TABLE B.5 | Critical Values of Chi squares (X^2) |

Degrees of Freedom df	Two-tail levels			
	p = .10	.05	.02	.01
1	2.706	3.841	5.412	6.635
2	4.605	5.991	7.824	9.210
3	6.251	7.815	9.837	11.341
4	7.779	9.488	11.668	13.277
5	9.236	11.070	13.388	15.086
6	10.645	12.592	15.033	16.812
7	12.017	14.067	16.622	18.475
8	13.362	15.507	18.168	20.090
9	14.684	16.919	19.679	21.666
10	15.987	18.307	21.161	23.209
11	17.275	19.675	22.618	24.725
12	18.549	21.026	24.054	26.217
13	19.812	22.362	25.472	27.688
14	21.064	23.685	26.873	29.141
15	22.307	24.996	28.259	30.578
16	23.542	26.296	29.633	32.000
17	24.769	27.587	30.995	33.409
18	25.989	28.869	32.346	34.805
19	27.204	30.144	33.687	36.191
20	28.412	31.410	35.020	37.566
21	29.615	32.671	36.343	38.932
22	30.813	33.924	37.659	40.289
23	32.007	35.172	38.968	41.638
24	33.196	36.415	40.270	42.980
25	34.382	37.652	41.566	44.314
26	35.563	38.885	42.856	45.642
27	36.741	40.113	44.140	46.963
28	37.916	41.337	45.419	48.278
29	39.087	42.557	46.693	49.588
30	40.256	43.773	47.962	50.892

TABLE B.6   **Critical Values of F (ANOVA)**

df for denom.	p	1	2	3	4	5	6	7	8	9	10
						df for numerator					
1	.05	161	200	216	225	230	234	237	239	241	242
2	.05	18.5	19.0	19.2	19.2	19.3	19.3	19.4	19.4	19.4	19.4
	.01	98.5	99.0	99.2	99.2	99.3	99.3	99.4	99.4	99.4	99.4
3	.05	10.1	9.55	9.28	9.12	9.10	8.94	8.89	8.85	8.81	8.79
	.01	34.1	30.8	29.5	28.7	28.2	27.9	27.7	27.5	27.3	27.2
4	.05	7.71	6.94	6.59	6.39	6.26	6.16	6.09	6.04	6.00	5.96
	.01	21.2	18.0	16.7	16.0	15.5	15.2	15.0	14.8	14.7	14.5
5	.05	6.61	5.79	5.41	5.19	5.05	4.95	4.88	4.82	4.77	4.74
	.01	16.3	13.3	12.1	11.4	11.0	10.7	10.5	10.3	10.2	10.1
6	.05	5.99	5.14	4.76	4.53	4.39	4.28	4.21	4.15	4.10	4.06
	.01	13.7	10.9	9.78	9.15	8.75	8.47	8.26	8.10	7.98	7.87
7	.05	5.59	4.74	4.35	4.12	3.97	3.87	3.79	3.73	3.68	3.64
	.01	12.2	9.55	8.45	7.85	7.46	7.19	6.99	6.84	6.72	6.62
8	.05	5.32	4.46	4.07	3.84	3.69	3.58	3.50	3.44	3.39	3.35
	.01	11.3	8.65	7.59	7.01	6.63	6.37	6.18	6.03	5.91	5.81
9	.05	5.12	4.26	3.86	3.63	3.48	3.37	3.29	3.23	3.18	3.14
	.01	10.6	8.02	6.99	6.42	6.06	5.80	5.61	5.47	5.35	5.26
10	.05	4.96	4.10	3.71	3.48	3.33	3.22	3.14	3.07	3.02	2.98
	.01	10.0	7.56	6.55	5.99	5.64	5.39	5.20	5.06	4.94	4.85
11	.05	4.84	3.98	3.59	3.36	3.20	3.09	3.01	2.95	2.90	2.85
	.01	9.65	7.21	6.22	5.67	5.32	5.07	4.89	4.74	4.63	4.54
12	.05	4.75	3.89	3.49	3.26	3.11	3.00	2.91	2.85	2.80	2.75
	.01	9.33	6.93	5.95	5.41	5.06	4.82	4.64	4.50	4.39	4.30
13	.05	4.67	3.81	3.41	3.18	3.03	2.92	2.83	2.77	2.71	2.67
	.01	9.07	6.70	5.74	5.21	4.86	4.62	4.44	4.30	4.19	4.10
14	.05	4.60	3.74	3.34	3.11	2.96	2.85	2.76	2.70	2.65	2.60
	.01	8.86	6.51	5.56	5.04	4.69	4.46	4.28	4.14	4.03	3.94
15	.05	4.54	3.68	3.29	3.06	2.90	2.79	2.71	2.64	2.59	2.54
	.01	8.68	6.36	5.42	4.89	4.56	4.32	4.14	4.00	3.89	3.80
16	.05	4.49	3.63	3.24	3.01	2.85	2.74	2.66	2.59	2.54	2.49
	.01	8.53	6.23	5.29	4.77	4.44	4.20	4.03	3.89	3.78	3.69
17	.05	4.45	3.59	3.20	2.96	2.81	2.70	2.61	2.55	2.49	2.45
	.01	8.40	6.11	5.18	4.67	4.34	4.10	3.93	3.79	3.68	3.59
18	.05	4.41	3.55	3.16	2.93	2.77	2.66	2.58	2.51	2.46	2.41
	.01	8.29	6.01	5.09	4.58	4.25	4.01	3.84	3.71	3.60	3.51
19	.05	4.38	3.52	3.13	2.90	2.74	2.63	2.54	2.48	2.42	2.38
	.01	8.18	5.93	5.01	4.50	4.17	3.94	3.77	3.63	3.52	3.43
20	.05	4.35	3.49	3.10	2.87	2.71	2.60	2.51	2.45	2.39	2.35
	.01	8.10	5.85	4.94	4.43	4.10	3.87	3.70	3.56	3.46	3.37
22	.05	4.30	3.44	3.05	2.82	2.66	2.55	2.46	2.40	2.34	2.30
	.01	7.95	5.72	4.82	4.31	3.99	3.76	3.59	3.45	3.35	3.26

(continued)

| TABLE B.6 | | Critical Values of F (ANOVA) | | | | | | | | | |

df for numerator

df for denom.	p	1	2	3	4	5	6	7	8	9	10
24	.05	4.26	3.40	3.01	2.78	2.62	2.51	2.42	2.36	2.30	2.25
	.01	7.82	5.61	4.72	4.22	3.90	3.67	3.50	3.36	3.26	3.17
26	.05	4.23	3.37	2.98	2.74	2.59	2.47	2.39	2.32	2.27	2.22
	.01	7.72	5.53	4.64	4.14	3.82	3.59	3.42	3.29	3.18	3.09
28	.05	4.20	3.34	2.95	2.71	2.56	2.45	2.36	2.29	2.24	2.19
	.01	7.64	5.45	4.57	4.07	3.75	3.53	3.36	3.23	3.12	3.03
30	.05	4.17	3.32	2.92	2.69	2.53	2.42	2.33	2.27	2.21	2.16
	.01	7.56	5.39	4.51	4.02	3.70	3.47	3.30	3.17	3.07	2.98
40	.05	4.08	3.23	2.84	2.61	2.45	2.34	2.25	2.18	2.12	2.08
	.01	7.31	5.18	4.31	3.83	3.51	3.29	3.12	2.99	2.89	2.80
60	.05	4.00	3.15	2.76	2.53	2.37	2.25	2.17	2.10	2.04	1.99
	.01	7.08	4.98	4.13	3.65	3.34	3.12	2.95	2.82	2.72	2.63
120	.05	3.92	3.07	2.68	2.45	2.29	2.17	2.09	2.02	1.96	1.91
	.01	6.85	4.79	3.95	3.48	3.17	2.96	2.79	2.66	2.56	2.47
200	.05	3.89	3.04	2.65	2.42	2.26	2.14	2.06	1.98	1.93	1.88
	.01	6.76	4.71	3.88	3.41	3.11	2.89	2.73	2.60	2.50	2.41
∞	.05	3.84	3.00	2.60	2.37	2.21	2.10	2.01	1.94	1.88	1.83
	.01	6.63	4.61	3.78	3.32	3.02	2.80	2.64	2.51	2.41	2.32

| TABLE B.7 | | Values of d (Dunn Multiple Comparisons Test) | | | | | | | | | | | |

Number of comparisons (C)	α	df_{error}											
		5	7	10	12	15	20	24	30	40	60	120	∞
2	.05	3.17	2.84	2.64	2.56	2.49	2.42	2.39	2.36	2.33	2.30	2.27	2.24
	.01	4.78	4.03	3.58	3.43	3.29	3.16	3.09	3.03	2.97	2.92	2.86	2.81
3	.05	3.54	3.13	2.87	2.78	2.69	2.61	2.58	2.54	2.50	2.47	2.43	2.39
	.01	5.25	4.36	3.83	3.65	3.48	3.33	3.26	3.19	3.12	3.06	2.99	2.94
4	.05	3.81	3.34	3.04	2.94	2.84	2.75	2.70	2.66	2.62	2.58	2.54	2.50
	.01	5.60	4.59	4.01	3.80	3.62	3.46	3.38	3.30	3.23	3.16	3.09	3.02
5	.05	4.04	3.50	3.17	3.06	2.95	2.85	2.80	2.75	2.71	2.66	2.62	2.58
	.01	5.89	4.78	4.15	3.93	3.74	3.55	3.47	3.39	3.31	3.24	3.16	3.09
6	.05	4.22	3.64	3.28	3.15	3.04	2.93	2.88	2.83	2.78	2.73	2.68	2.64
	.01	6.15	4.95	4.27	4.04	3.82	3.63	3.54	3.46	3.38	3.30	3.23	3.15
7	.05	4.38	3.76	3.37	3.24	3.11	3.00	2.94	2.89	2.84	2.79	2.74	2.69
	.01	6.36	5.09	4.37	4.13	3.90	3.70	3.61	3.52	3.43	3.34	3.27	3.19
8	.05	4.53	3.86	3.45	3.31	3.18	3.06	3.00	2.94	2.89	2.84	2.79	2.74
	.01	6.56	5.21	4.45	4.20	3.97	3.76	3.66	3.57	3.48	3.39	3.31	3.23
9	.05	4.66	3.95	3.52	3.37	3.24	3.11	3.05	2.99	2.93	2.88	2.83	2.77
	.01	6.70	5.31	4.53	4.26	4.02	3.80	3.70	3.61	3.51	3.42	3.34	3.26
10	.05	4.78	4.03	3.58	3.43	3.29	3.16	3.09	3.03	2.97	2.92	2.86	2.81
	.01	6.86	5.40	4.59	4.32	4.07	3.85	3.74	3.65	3.55	3.46	3.37	3.29
15	.05	5.25	4.36	3.83	3.65	3.48	3.33	3.26	3.19	3.12	3.06	2.99	2.94
	.01	7.51	5.79	4.86	4.56	4.29	4.03	3.91	3.80	3.70	3.59	3.50	3.40
20	.05	5.60	4.59	4.01	3.80	3.62	3.46	3.38	3.30	3.23	3.16	3.09	3.02
	.01	8.00	6.08	5.06	4.73	4.42	4.15	4.04	3.90	3.79	3.69	3.58	3.48
25	.05	5.89	4.78	4.15	3.93	3.74	3.55	3.47	3.39	3.31	3.24	3.16	3.09
	.01	8.37	6.30	5.20	4.86	4.53	4.25	4.1*	3.98	3.88	3.76	3.64	3.54
30	.05	6.15	4.95	4.27	4.04	3.82	3.63	3.54	3.46	3.38	3.30	3.22	3.15
	.01	8.68	6.49	5.33	4.95	4.61	4.33	4.2*	4.13	3.93	3.81	3.69	3.59
35	.05	6.36	5.09	4.37	4.13	3.90	3.70	3.61	3.52	3.43	3.34	3.27	3.19
	.01	8.95	6.67	5.44	5.04	4.71	4.39	4.3*	4.26	3.97	3.84	3.73	3.63
40	.05	6.56	5.21	4.45	4.20	3.97	3.76	3.66	3.57	3.48	3.39	3.31	3.23
	.01	9.19	6.83	5.52	5.12	4.78	4.46	4.3*	4.1*	4.01	3.89	3.77	3.66
45	.05	6.70	5.31	4.53	4.26	4.02	3.80	3.70	3.61	3.51	3.42	3.34	3.26
	.01	9.41	6.93	5.60	5.20	4.84	4.52	4.3*	4.2*	4.1*	3.93	3.80	3.69
50	.05	6.86	5.40	4.59	4.32	4.07	3.85	3.74	3.65	3.55	3.46	3.37	3.29
	.01	9.68	7.06	5.70	5.27	4.90	4.56	4.4*	4.2*	4.1*	3.97	3.83	3.72
100	.05	8.00	6.08	5.06	4.73	4.42	4.15	4.04	3.90	3.79	3.69	3.58	3.48
	.01	11.04	7.80	6.20	5.70	5.20	4.80	4.7*	4.4*	4.5*		4.00	3.89
250	.05	9.68	7.06	5.70	5.27	4.90	4.56	4.4*	4.2*	4.1*	3.97	3.83	3.72
	.01	13.26	8.83	6.9*	6.3*	5.8*	5.2*	5.0*	4.9*	4.8*			4.11

*Obtained by graphical interpolation.

From Dunn, O. J. (1961). Multiple comparisons among means. *Journal of the American Statistical Association, 56*, 52–64. Reprinted with permission from *Journal of the American Statistical Association* and the author. Copyright © 1961 by the American Statistical Association. All rights reserved.

TABLE B.8   Critical Values of T (Wilcoxon-Mann-Whitney Rank Sum Test)

a. Two-tailed Test, $\alpha = .01$ or   One-tailed Test, $\alpha = .005$

n_1 (size of the smaller sample)

n_2	1	2	3	4	5	6	7	8	9	10	11	12	13	14	15	16	17	18	19	20
3																				
4																				
5				15																
6			10	16	23															
7			10	16	24	32														
8			11	17	25	34	43													
9		6	11	18	26	35	45	56												
10		6	12	19	27	37	47	58	71											
11		6	12	20	28	38	49	61	73	87										
12		7	13	21	30	40	51	63	76	90	105									
13		7	14	22	31	41	53	65	79	93	109	125								
14		7	14	22	32	43	54	67	81	96	112	129	147							
15		8	15	23	33	44	56	69	84	99	115	133	151	171						
16		8	15	24	34	46	58	72	86	102	119	136	155	175	196					
17		8	16	25	36	47	60	74	89	105	122	140	159	180	201	223				
18		8	16	26	37	49	62	76	92	108	125	144	163	184	206	228	252			
19	3	9	17	27	38	50	64	78	94	111	129	147	168	189	210	234	258	283		
20	3	9	18	28	39	52	66	81	97	114	132	151	172	193	215	239	263	289	315	

b. Two-tailed Test, $\alpha = .05$ or   One-tailed Test, $\alpha = .025$

n_1 (size of the smaller sample)

n_2	1	2	3	4	5	6	7	8	9	10	11	12	13	14	15	16	17	18	19	20
3																				
4				10																
5			6	11	17															
6			7	12	18	26														
7			13	20	27	36														
8		3	8	14	21	29	38	49												
9		3	8	14	22	31	40	51	62											
10		3	9	15	23	32	42	53	65	78										
11		3	9	16	24	34	44	55	68	81	96									
12		4	10	17	26	35	46	58	71	84	99	115								
13		4	10	18	27	37	48	60	73	88	103	119	136							
14		4	11	19	28	38	50	62	76	91	106	123	141	160						
15		4	11	20	29	40	52	65	79	94	110	127	145	164	184					
16		4	12	21	30	42	54	67	82	97	113	131	150	169	190	211				
17		5	12	21	32	43	56	70	84	100	117	135	154	174	195	217	240			
18		5	13	22	33	45	58	72	87	103	121	139	158	179	200	222	246	270		
19		5	13	23	34	46	60	74	90	107	124	143	163	182	205	228	252	277	303	
20		5	14	24	35	48	62	77	93	110	128	147	167	188	210	234	258	283	309	337

TABLE B.8 — Critical Values of T (Wilcoxon-Mann-Whitney Rank Sum Test)—

(continued)

c. Two-tailed Test, $\alpha = .10$ or   One-tailed Test, $\alpha = .05$

n_2	1	2	3	4	5	6	7	8	9	10	11	12	13	14	15	16	17	18	19	20
3		6																		
4		6	11																	
5	3	7	12	19																
6	3	8	13	20	28															
7	3	8	14	21	29	39														
8	4	9	15	23	31	41	51													
9	4	9	16	24	33	43	54	66												
10	4	10	17	26	35	45	56	69	82											
11	4	11	18	27	37	47	59	72	86	100										
12	5	11	19	28	38	49	62	75	89	104	120									
13	5	12	20	30	40	52	64	78	92	108	125	142								
14	5	13	21	31	42	54	67	81	96	112	129	147	166							
15	6	13	22	33	44	56	69	84	99	116	133	152	171	192						
16	6	14	24	34	46	58	72	87	103	120	138	156	176	197	219					
17	6	15	25	35	47	61	75	90	106	123	142	161	182	203	225	249				
18	7	15	26	37	49	63	77	93	110	127	146	166	187	208	231	255	280			
19	1	7	16	27	38	51	65	80	96	113	131	150	171	192	214	237	262	287	313	
20	1	7	17	28	40	53	67	83	99	117	135	155	175	197	220	243	268	294	320	348

From Table L in Tate, M. W. & Clelland, R. C. (1975). *Nonparametric and Shortcut Statistics in the Social, Biological, and Medical Sciences*. Danville, IL: Interstate Printers and Publishers, Inc. Reprinted with permission from the author.

TABLE B.9				**Critical Values of W (Wilcoxon Signed Ranks Test)**					
Two Tails	0.10	0.05	0.02	0.01	Two Tails	0.10	0.05	0.02	0.01
One Tail	0.05	0.025	0.01	0.005	One Tail	0.05	0.025	0.01	0.005
N					N				
4					28	130	116	101	91
5	0				29	140	126	110	100
6	2	0			30	151	137	120	109
7	3	2	0		31	163	147	130	118
8	5	3	1	0	32	175	159	140	128
9	8	5	3	1	33	187	170	151	138
10	10	8	5	3	34	200	182	162	148
11	13	10	7	5	35	213	195	173	159
12	17	13	9	7	36	227	208	185	171
13	21	17	12	9	37	241	221	198	182
14	25	21	15	12	38	256	235	211	194
15	30	25	19	15	39	271	249	224	207
16	35	29	23	19	40	286	264	238	220
17	41	34	27	23	41	302	279	252	233
18	47	40	32	27	42	319	294	266	247
19	53	46	37	32	43	336	310	281	261
20	60	52	43	37	44	353	327	296	276
21	67	58	49	42	45	371	343	312	291
22	75	65	55	48	46	389	361	328	307
23	83	73	62	54	47	407	378	345	322
24	91	81	69	61	48	426	396	362	339
25	100	89	76	68	49	446	415	379	355
26	110	98	84	75	50	466	434	397	373
27	119	107	92	83					

From McCornack, R. L. (1965). Extended tables of the Wilcoxon matched pair signed rank statistic. *Journal of the American Statistical Association, 60*, 864–871. Reprinted with permission from *Journal of the American Statistical Association*. Copyright © 1965 by the American Statistical Association. All rights reserved.

TABLE B.10		Critical Values of Student's *t*-Distribution			

	Level of Significance for One-tailed Test					
df	*.10*	*.05*	*.025*	*.01*	*.005*	*.0005*
	Level of Significance for Two-tailed Test					
	.20	*.10*	*.05*	*.02*	*.01*	*.001*
1	3.078	6.314	12.706	31.821	63.657	636.619
2	1.886	2.920	4.303	6.965	9.925	31.598
3	1.638	2.353	3.182	4.541	5.841	12.941
4	1.533	2.132	2.776	3.747	4.604	8.610
5	1.476	2.015	2.571	3.365	4.032	6.859
6	1.440	1.943	2.447	3.143	3.707	5.959
7	1.415	1.895	2.365	2.998	3.499	5.405
8	1.397	1.860	2.306	2.896	3.355	5.041
9	1.383	1.833	2.262	2.821	3.250	4.781
10	1.372	1.812	2.228	2.764	3.169	4.587
11	1.363	1.796	2.201	2.718	3.106	4.437
12	1.356	1.782	2.179	2.681	3.055	4.318
13	1.350	1.771	2.160	2.650	3.012	4.221
14	1.345	1.761	2.145	2.624	2.977	4.140
15	1.341	1.753	2.131	2.602	2.947	4.073
16	1.337	1.746	2.120	2.583	2.921	4.015
17	1.333	1.740	2.110	2.567	2.898	3.965
18	1.330	1.734	2.101	2.552	2.878	3.992
19	1.328	1.729	2.093	2.539	2.861	3.883
20	1.325	1.725	2.086	2.528	2.845	3.850
21	1.323	1.721	2.080	2.518	2.831	3.819
22	1.321	1.717	2.074	2.508	2.819	3.792
23	1.319	1.714	2.069	2.500	2.807	3.767
24	1.318	1.711	2.064	2.492	2.797	3.745
25	1.316	1.708	2.060	2.485	2.787	3.725
26	1.315	1.706	2.056	2.479	2.779	3.707
27	1.314	1.703	2.052	2.473	2.771	3.690
28	1.313	1.701	2.048	2.467	2.763	3.674
29	1.311	1.699	2.045	2.462	2.756	3.659
30	1.310	1.697	2.042	2.457	2.750	3.646
40	1.303	1.684	2.021	2.423	2.704	3.551
60	1.296	1.671	2.000	2.390	2.660	3.460
120	1.289	1.658	1.980	2.358	2.617	3.373
∞	1.282	1.645	1.960	2.326	2.576	3.291

INTRODUCTION TO STATISTICAL POWER

■ ■ ■ ■ ■ ■

In Chapter 6, we presented hypothesis-testing, the process by which we make inferences about relationships among variables in the population based on our sample statistics. For example, as you will recall, when our sample statistic has a low probability of occurring by chance alone, we reject the null hypothesis, with the understanding that we might have made a Type I Error. Because the goals of psychological research are to accurately describe the relationships among variables and discover facts about behavior, it is important that we understand how the hypothesis-testing process works, and one of its most crucial elements is **power**.

As we defined it in Chapter 6, power is the probability that a test will reject the null hypothesis when, in fact, it is false. That is, it is the ability to detect a systematic relationship between the variables amidst all of the random variation that exists due to measurement error, experimenter error, and individual differences—which are collectively referred to as "chance fluctuations" or "error variance." The power of a test, then, depends on the relative amounts of systematic and random variation within the data set. A small degree of systematic variability created by an experimental manipulation will be lost in a large pool of error variance but may be easily detected in a small pool of random variation. For instance, if prenatal exposure to crack cocaine reduces the fetal growth rate by just a small amount so that newborn crack babies weigh, on average, 6 ounces less than normal infants, this small effect may go undetected if the typical difference between normal infants is large (say 11 or 12 ounces). However, if the random variability in birthweight among normal infants is small (such as 3 or 4 ounces), a systematic difference of 6 ounces is more likely to be detected by the analysis. The power of a design or a statistical test is the ability to detect a systematic difference when one exists, and like microscopes, some designs and tests are more powerful than others and can detect smaller effects because they have "greater magnification"—that is, less error variance.

Two Variances

To illustrate the relationship between power and the degree of chance fluctuations in the data, let's look at a hypothetical data set from a simple between-subjects design comparing three treatment conditions: Tutoring (T), Computer-Assisted Instruction (CAI), and a Control (C) group.[1]

---

[1]Most researchers would include more than five participants in each treatment condition because small samples are less powerful than larger samples, as explained later in this Appendix.

T	CAI	C
77	96	18
56	72	35
32	45	39
28	50	74
68	83	58
$\Sigma X = 261$	$\Sigma X = 346$	$\Sigma X = 224$
$\overline{X} = 52.2$	$\overline{X} = 69.2$	$\overline{X} = 44.8$
$s = 21.6$	$s = 21.6$	$s = 21.6$

This data set includes a total of 15 exam scores (N) and the grand mean of these scores is equal to 55.4. The standard deviation of these 15 scores, which tells us the average deviation of the scores from the grand mean, is equal to 22.7. This is known as the *total* variability, and it is made up of two separate components that measure the variability from different sources: (1) the variation that is due to the experimental manipulation (or the "effect of the independent variable"), and (2) the variation that is not the result of the systematic manipulation of the independent variable, but is instead due to chance (i.e, the error variance).

The systematic effect of the independent variable (if there is one) can be seen by measuring the variability among the group means: the mean score for the Tutoring group is 52.2, the mean score for the CAI group is 69.2, and mean score for the Control group is 44.8. The standard deviation among these means is equal to 12.5, indicating that the group means differ from the grand mean by an average of 12.5 points, so the question is: Why are these means so different from each other? One obvious source of difference between the group means is the experimental manipulation: one group received tutoring, while another group received computer-assisted instruction, and the third group received a control treatment. If tutoring improves performance, then the scores in the tutoring group should be systematically higher than the scores in the control condition, and so forth. Thus, the effect of the IV is measured by examining the variability *between* the group means. However, we must also admit that the difference between the group means may include random variation, including individual differences, measurement error, and experimenter error. For example, some of the people who received tutoring may have simply been smarter than the people in the control group, so the mean for the tutoring group would have been higher even without the tutoring, and therefore, the difference among the group means—that is, the "Between-Group Variance"—is actually the sum of two subcomponents: the effect of the IV plus some chance fluctuations:

between-group variance = IV + chance

The second source of variability in a between-subjects design data set is error variance or *chance* and it can be seen by looking at just one condition at a time. For instance, the five scores from the Tutoring condition are not equal to each other, even though they were measured under identical experimental circumstances. There-

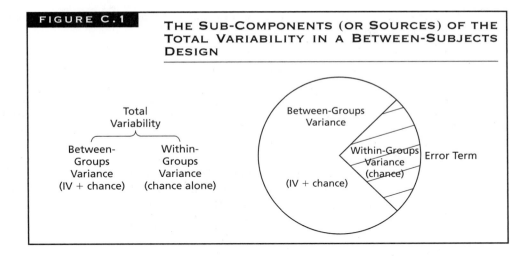

FIGURE C.1

THE SUB-COMPONENTS (OR SOURCES) OF THE TOTAL VARIABILITY IN A BETWEEN-SUBJECTS DESIGN

Total Variability

Between-Groups Variance (IV + chance)

Within-Groups Variance (chance alone)

Between-Groups Variance (IV + chance)

Within-Groups Variance (chance)

Error Term

fore, the differences between these five scores are not due to the manipulation of the independent variable, but instead must be due to some combination of individual differences, measurement errors, and experimenter errors—that is, chance. The standard deviation of these five scores indicate that, just by chance alone, scores on the exam will vary from the group mean by approximately 21.6 points when participants receive tutoring. Similarly, if we look at the five scores in the CAI condition or at the five scores in the Control condition, we see that scores obtained under identical circumstances vary substantially just by chance alone. (In this illustration, these groups also have standard deviations equal to 21.6, but in real data sets, there will be some differences in variability among the groups). Thus, the error variance is measured by examining the scores *within* the treatment groups, and this variance component is sometimes called the *within-group variance*. Figure C-1 illustrates the breakdown of the total variability into the between-groups and within-groups variances.[2]

Using the Two Variances to Test the Null Hypothesis

Thus far we have identified two sources of variability that can be "pulled out" of the total variation in the data set: the between-group variance (measuring the effect of the IV plus chance fluctuations) and the within-group variance (measuring chance fluctuations). In order to determine whether or not the IV has had a systematic effect, we need a way to cancel out the chance fluctuations that are present in the

---

[2]Note that this discussion is only intended to provide a conceptual understanding of the relationship between power and error variability; specific statistical tests and computational rules for the different variance components can be found in the appropriate chapters.

between-group variance. We can accomplish this by creating a test ratio between our two types of variability:

$$\text{Test Ratio} = \frac{\text{between-group variance}}{\text{within-group variance}} = \frac{\text{IV} + \text{chance}}{\text{chance}}$$

(There are several statistical tests that use a ratio of this sort, including the *t*-test and analysis of variance, which are presented in Chapters 11 and 12, respectively. The denominator of this ratio is known as the "error term." The error term always refers to a measure of random, unexplained variability.)

If this test-ratio is equal (or close) to 1.00, it would suggest that all of the difference between the means is due to chance fluctuations and that the IV has had no systematic effect on the scores (so that the IV added nothing to the value of the between-group variance):

$$\text{Test Ratio} = \frac{\text{between-group variance}}{\text{within-group variance}} = \frac{0 + \text{chance}}{\text{chance}} = \frac{\text{chance}}{\text{chance}} = 1.0$$

Thus, when the null hypothesis is true (and the independent variable has no effect), the value of the test-ratio will approximate 1.00. In contrast, if the null hypothesis is false and the IV does have a systematic effect on performance (so the scores for one group are systematically higher than the scores for another group), then the value of this test-ratio will be greater than 1.00: the between-group variance will be greater than the within-group variance because the systematic effect of the IV will be added to the chance fluctuations that already exist. As the effect of the IV increases, the value of the test-ratio increases. For example, let's suppose the chance fluctuations are equal to 10, and compute the test-ratio for IVs that systematically increase scores by 2 points, 8 points, and 14 points:

Effect of IV = +2:

$$\text{Test-Ratio} = \frac{\text{between-group variance}}{\text{within-group variance}} = \frac{2 + 10}{10} = \frac{12}{10} = 1.2$$

Effect of IV = +8:

$$\text{Test-Ratio} = \frac{\text{between-group variance}}{\text{within-group variance}} = \frac{8 + 10}{10} = \frac{18}{10} = 1.8$$

Effect of IV = +14:

$$\text{Test-Ratio} = \frac{\text{between-group variance}}{\text{within-group variance}} = \frac{14 + 10}{10} = \frac{24}{10} = 2.4$$

As you can see, the value of the test-ratio increases as the effect size increases. Thus, this test-ratio gives us a way to test the null hypothesis by contrasting the relative amounts of systematic and random variability, and the general rule is if the test-ratio is equal to (or close to) 1.00, we cannot reject the null hypothesis, but if the test-ratio is significantly larger than 1.00, we will reject the null, and conclude that the IV has had an effect.

Statistical Power

How do these variance components and this test-ratio relate to the concept of statistical power? In order to continue with this explanation of power, we need to remind you of two things: (1) power is defined as the probability that a test will reject the null hypothesis when a systematic difference between treatments actually exists, so our discussion of power must be based on the premise that the IV does have an effect and rejecting the null hypothesis is the correct decision; and (2) in order to reject the null hypothesis, the sample statistic must be equal to or greater than the critical value and lie in the region of rejection of the sampling distribution. Therefore, to continue with our explanation of power, we will need to identify a hypothetical critical value for the test-ratio. If the test-ratio is equal to or greater than the critical value, we will reject the null hypothesis, indicating the test has sufficient power to detect the systematic effect of the IV.

Imagine a study using a between-subjects design to compare the Graduate Record Examination (GRE) scores of a control group to those of an experimental group who attended *Dr. Smith's Magic Tutoring Course* one week before taking the GREs. Let's presume that attending this course systematically increases GRE scores by 21 points (so that the "effect of the independent variable" is equal to 21 points). Now imagine that we have a table of critical values for our test-ratio statistic and it indicates that the critical value (with alpha set at .05) is 4.00. (This means that we will reject the null hypothesis only if our obtained test-ratio statistic is equal to or greater than 4.00.) If we succeed in rejecting the null, then our study has adequate power, but if our obtained statistic is less than 4.00, we would not reject the null hypothesis, and the systematic effect of the tutoring course would be missed. (You may recall from Chapter 6 that this is what we call a Type II Error—failing to reject the null hypothesis when it is false.)

Will we reject the null hypothesis when the effect of the IV is equal to 21? That is, do we have enough power to detect this 21-point increase in GRE scores? From the previous discussion, you should realize that it depends on the amount of error variance or chance fluctuations that are present in the data set. For example, suppose the within-group variance (or error variance) is equal to 10 points. The test-ratio would be:

$$\text{Test-ratio} = \frac{\text{between-group variance}}{\text{within-group variance}} = \frac{\text{IV} + \text{chance}}{\text{chance}} = \frac{21 + 10}{10} = \frac{31}{10} = 3.1$$

Based on this statistical test, we will not reject the null hypothesis because our obtained test-ratio is only equal to 3.1, which does not reach significance (i.e., it is not equal to or greater than the critical value of 4.00). Thus, our test is not powerful enough to detect a 21-point difference between the two groups when the chance fluctuations are equal to 10 points (and therefore, we end up making a Type II error). However, if the within-group variance in the data set is only 7 points, we will reject the null hypothesis because our test-ratio will reach significance:

$$\text{Test-ratio} = \frac{\text{between-group variance}}{\text{within-group variance}} = \frac{\text{IV} + \text{chance}}{\text{chance}} = \frac{21 + 7}{7} = \frac{28}{7} = 4.00$$

In both cases, the IV had the same impact on GRE scores (increasing them by 21 points), but when there was a lot of random variation among scores (so that the error variance was larger than 7 points), our test was not powerful enough to detect that systematic effect. In fact, when the error variance is equal to 10, in order to reject the null hypothesis, *Dr. Smith's Magic Tutoring Course* would have to increase GRE scores by at least 30 points, because anything less will not reach the critical value of 4.00:

$$\text{Test-ratio} = \frac{\text{between-group variance}}{\text{within-group variance}} = \frac{\text{IV} + \text{chance}}{\text{chance}} = \frac{30 + 10}{10} = \frac{40}{10} = 4.00$$

Using the microscope analogy, when the error variance equals 10 points, our test is only powerful enough to see effects that are 30 points or larger; anything smaller would remain "invisible" to us.

Failing to detect systematic effects due to a lack of power can be costly, to individuals and to society. Consider, for example, research on the possible carcinogenic effects of second-hand smoke. If exposure to second-hand smoke can cause cancer in non-smokers, it is important to identify this effect in order to educate people about the risks. If the research has insufficient power, so that it fails to detect the impact of second-hand smoke, an untold number of people will develop cancer because the appropriate warnings were not issued. Similarly, pharmaceutical research designed to test the effectiveness of new drug therapies must be concerned with the degree of power in the studies. For example, when they tested the drug Tamoxifen as a preventive treatment for breast cancer, they needed to have enough power to detect even small reductions in cancer rates among women taking the drug. Insufficient power in the research could deprive women of a potentially life-saving drug. At the same time, studies needed to be conducted which tested for any unwanted side-effects of Tamoxifen, such as endometrial cancer. Again, if the studies had insufficient power, an untold number of women would develop endometrial cancer because they were taking a drug to prevent breast cancer—which would be doubly tragic if Tamoxifen, in fact, does not significantly reduce the risk of breast cancer.[3]

---

[3]In cases like this, the potential benefits of the drug must be weighed against the possible risks of side effects. For instance, women who are at high risk for breast cancer may be willing to increase their risk of endometrial cancer by 3% if taking Tamoxifen reduces the risk of breast cancer by 50%, but if Tamoxifen only reduces the risk of breast cancer by 6%, the increased risk of endometrial cancer may not be worth it. In either case, the research on the side-effects of Tamoxifen needs to have sufficient power to detect even small effects so that people can make informed decisions about their health and life-style.

Maximizing the Power in a Study

As we have indicated, the power of a test primarily depends on the amount of chance fluctuations present in the data: Greater error variance means less power, so that IV effects must be larger in order to be detected. Consequently, if researchers can reduce the degree of chance fluctuations within the data, they will increase the power of the test and improve their ability to successfully detect smaller experimental effects. Exerting experimental control over relevant extraneous variables in the research setting may be the first and foremost technique researchers apply in order to increase the power of their study. That is, controlling extraneous factors in the study, by holding them constant, reduces random variation in the data, making it easier to detect systematic effects due to the manipulation of the independent variable. (Other issues involved in the experimental control of extraneous variables are discussed in Chapters 7 and 10.) In addition to direct control of extraneous variables, there are basically three things a researcher can do to maximize the likelihood that the effect of the independent variable is successfully detected: use adequate sample sizes; increase the significance level (alpha); and select appropriate research designs that, inherently, have more power.

Adequate Sample Size

When we discussed the variability of sampling distributions in Chapter 6, we pointed out that there is less random variation among large samples drawn from the same population because large samples tend to be more representative of the population, and are, therefore, more similar to each other. So as sample size increases, the variability of the sampling distribution decreases. Therefore, if the null hypothesis is actually false, increasing the sample size reduces β (the probability of a Type II Error, which is represented by the overlap between the common region of the sampling distribution and the real population) and this produces an *increase in power*. Figure C-2 illustrates the relationship between sample size (n) and β.

As you can see, when the sample size is large, a greater proportion of samples from the real population lie beyond the critical value and fall in the sampling distribution's region of rejection. (These samples result in the correct decision to reject the null hypothesis and they form what we refer to as the "power region"). Because more large samples fall in the region of rejection, there is a greater chance that a large random sample drawn from the real population will be from the power region, which means there is an increased probability of correctly rejecting the null hypothesis. By definition, then, larger samples have more power. This raises an important practical question: just how many participants does the researcher need to include in a study in order to have adequate power?

Minimum Sample Sizes   A widely accepted guideline is that, for experiments and quasi-experiments, there should be between 15 to 20 scores in each treatment condition or group. Ten participants per group is usually considered the absolute minimum sample size because studies with smaller sample sizes are generally unable to

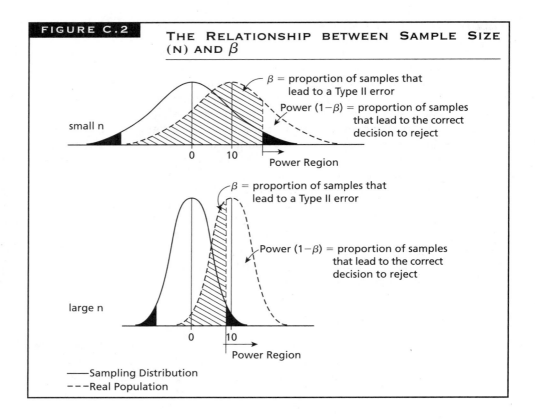

FIGURE C.2 THE RELATIONSHIP BETWEEN SAMPLE SIZE (N) AND β

detect anything but huge effects. With thirty participants per group, the variability of the sampling distribution has essentially reached its minimum possible value, so running additional participants does not appreciably increase the power of the design.

Correlational studies generally require a larger number of participants than experiments or quasi-experiments, especially if the correlation you can reasonably expect to find is in the low-to-moderate range of magnitude (e.g., if the population parameter, *rho* (ρ), is .40 or below). For example, if the relationship between reading speed and reading comprehension in the population of college students has a Pearson correlation (ρ) equal to 0.3000, a perfectly representative research sample (with $r = 0.3000$) would have to have more than 42 participants in order to reject the null hypothesis at the .05 level. You can see this by examining the table of critical values (Table B-3 in Appendix B) which indicates that, if there are only 42 participants, the sample r needs to be .3044 or greater in order to reject the null. Of course, if the population parameter is $\rho = .3000$, approximately half of the random samples drawn from the population would have correlations smaller than .3000 so there is a pretty high probability we will select a sample that would lead to a Type II error. Therefore, in order to have enough power to detect a systematic relationship of low-to-moderate magnitude, the sample size needs to be quite large. Table B-3, as well as the tables of critical values for other statistical tests, clearly illustrate the relationship between sample size and power: The smaller the sample size, the larger the critical value. Thus, small samples are unlikely to detect low-to-moderate correlations (or small treatment effects) because the sample statistics are unlikely to reach significance. So if we wish to successfully identify low- or moderate-relationships or small differences between groups, we must use large samples.

Lower Significance (α) Levels

As indicated in Chapter 6, the conventional level of significance used to reject the null hypothesis is an alpha (α) of .05 or less. (That is, we will reject the null hypothesis if our research outcome would be expected to occur by chance alone only 5% of the time or less.) Researchers who adopt a less-stringent Type I error rate, and set alpha to be something greater than .05 (such as .08 or .10), will increase the power of their test. That is, as long as the null hypothesis is actually false, tests with α set at .08 or .10, and so on, are more powerful than a test with alpha set at the traditional value of .05. This relationship is fairly easy to understand by looking at diagrams such as those in Figure C-2. If the regions of rejection become larger (due to an increase in α), it is apparent that beta (β) will get smaller, and a reduction in β means an increase in power. In other words, increasing α increases the probability of rejecting the null hypothesis, so we are more likely to find an effect if it is there.

At this point, you may be wondering why researchers continue to adopt the fairly stringent significance level of .05 or less when we could increase power simply by choosing higher levels of α. The reason is that this increase in power only applies when there is a systematic effect to be found (so rejecting the null hypothesis is the correct decision). Adjusting α does not increase our chances of reaching the correct decision when the null hypothesis is actually true. In fact, to the contrary, when there is no systematic relationship in the population, increasing α increases the likelihood that we will mistake random sampling error for a non-existent effect, thus increasing the probability of a Type I Error. Essentially, then, if we use a less stringent significance level, such as $\alpha = .10$, we are more likely to reject the null hypothesis even if it is actually true. Yet we will be less certain than usual about whether the results reflect a true systematic effect or a Type I Error, because with alpha set at .10, we can only be 90% certain that the null hypothesis is really false, whereas with $\alpha = .05$, we can be 95% certain that a significant outcome is due to a real effect. Thus, the gain in power we can achieve by increasing the significance level is, at best, a mixed blessing, and most researchers prefer to use other techniques to increase the power of their research designs and analyses.

Selecting Designs with More Inherent Power

As discussed in detail earlier in this appendix, the power of a test depends on the relative amounts of systematic and random variation within the data set. Within-subjects (or repeated measures) designs are more powerful than other experimental designs because there is less random variability inherent in them. These designs take advantage of the fact that, in general, the random variability in one person's behavior across time is less than the variability due to individual differences between people. That is, even though Raymond's behavior does not remain perfectly consistent across time, the difference in his behavior from situation to situation, and over time, will generally be less than the differences between Raymond, Irvin, Paul, and Arnie. So even though Raymond may experience changes in states such as mood and motivation, other central characteristics such as intelligence, personality, race, sex, and family background will remain largely unchanged over the course of a within-subjects experiment. Therefore, there are fewer chance fluctuations in the data set when we conduct repeated measures on the same individuals than when we make comparisons between different people who have been assigned to different treatments.

Additionally, within-subjects designs are more powerful because they allow us to break the total variability within the data into three separate variance components, not just two, and this reduces the error term of the test-ratio (because there is less "unexplained variance"). For instance, suppose we have conducted a simple one-way within-subjects design where each participant performed a perception test (reading lists of words printed in blue ink) under three different conditions: against a white background, against a pink background, and against a gray background. The amount of time (in seconds) required to read the words aloud was recorded:

Participant	White	Pink	Gray
Roberto	5	7	8
Will	2	6	9
Charlie	4	8	10
Danny	3	4	6

The total variability among these 12 scores can be subdivided into the variation between the individual participants (between-subjects variance) and the variation within the participants as they moved from one treatment condition to another (within-subjects variance). Then the within-subjects variance can be further subdivided into two components: the variability that is due to the difference in treatments (between-conditions variance) and the individual differences in how the participants reacted to the treatments (a condition × subjects interaction). Figure C-3 illustrates the breakdown of the variability in a within-subjects data set.

In the data set from our hypothetical perception study, we have three scores for each of the participants and we could average these scores together to obtain an estimate of their overall perceptual performance. In this case, Roberto's average performance was 6.67, Will's was 5.67, Charlie's was 7.33, and Danny's was 4.33. The between-subjects variance is the variability among the average scores of the participants, and it provides a measure of individual differences in overall perceptual ability.

The within-subjects variance measures how much the participants' scores in the treatment conditions differ from their overall average performance. That is, it

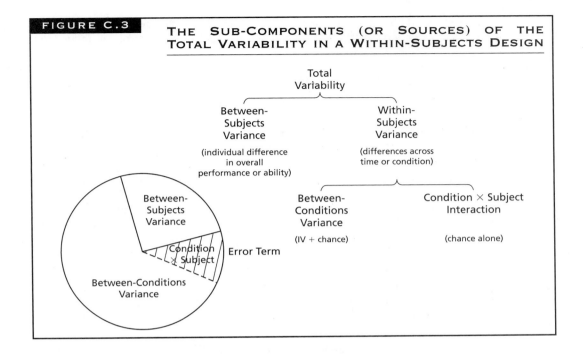

FIGURE C.3

THE SUB-COMPONENTS (OR SOURCES) OF THE TOTAL VARIABILITY IN A WITHIN-SUBJECTS DESIGN

compares Roberto's three scores (5, 7, and 8) to his average score of 6.67, compares Will's three scores (2, 6, and 9) to his average of 5.67, and so forth. This variance component has two sub-parts. The between-conditions variance measures the effect of the independent variable by calculating the variability among the three condition means ($\overline{X}_{White} = 6.25$ versus $\overline{X}_{Pink} = 3.50$ versus $\overline{X}_{Gray} = 8.25$). This is exactly comparable to the between-groups variance from a between-subjects design (as we described earlier in this appendix), and it is a measure of the effect of the independent variable *plus* chance fluctuations in individuals over time:

between-conditions variance = IV + random variation over time

The second part of the within-subjects variance is the condition × subjects interaction that compares the patterns of performance of the participants across the treatments and measures the differences among those patterns. For example, if we compare the white and pink background treatments, we see that while Roberto's performance declined by 2 points when the background changed from white to pink, Will showed a 4-point decline, and Danny's score only declined by 1 point. The different patterns of response among the participants are due to the random changes in temporary states (such as mood and motivation), as well as individual differences among people in more permanent characteristics (such as visual acuity and information-processing abilities) that may affect their perceptual performance at different points in time. This interaction is a measure of random variation over time and it is used as the error term in the test-ratio when we assess the effect of the independent variable:

$$\text{Test ratio} = \frac{\text{between-condition variance}}{\text{condition} \times \text{subjects}} = \frac{\text{IV} + \text{random variability over time}}{\text{random variability over time}}$$

This formula provides a more powerful test than the formula presented earlier for between-subjects designs because the between-subjects variance (the variability due to differences in ability among the participants) has been controlled by removing it from the total variability so that the amount of random variability that is unexplained is reduced. Therefore, the error term in the within-subjects design (the condition × subjects interaction) is smaller than the error term would be if the data were from a between-subjects design (the within-groups variance), which makes the value of the test-ratio larger and more likely to reach significance. Consequently, the within-subjects design has more power because the effect of the independent variable is easier to see against a backdrop of random variation in performance across time than against a backdrop that includes both variation over time and variability in overall memory ability among individuals.

Increasing Power in Between-Subjects Designs Through Matching   In Chapter 10, we identified a number of potential confounds in within-subjects designs, so, while within-subjects designs are, inherently, the most powerful designs, there are many reasons why a researcher may elect to use a between-subjects design. After making this choice, certainly, the researcher will want to maximize the power of the test by having a sufficient sample size. Furthermore, if the effect of the independent variable is expected to be relatively small, the researcher may be tempted to reduce the random variation between the groups—and thereby increase power—by **matching** them on potentially confounding subject variables before introducing the experimental manipulation. As we discussed in Chapter 10, there are two general matching procedures that force the treatment groups to be more alike than they necessarily would be following random assignment, but one of these procedures—the matched-groups design—is misleading because it does not actually increase the power of the test while the matched-pairs design is, in fact, more powerful than a between-subjects design which assigns participants to the conditions totally at random (i.e., a random-groups design).

Matched-Groups Design   A **matched-groups design** is one where the researcher places constraints on the assignment of participants to the experimental conditions so that groups start out with the same average score on the matching variable. For example, suppose a teacher wants to find out if one type of homework assignment is more effective than another type of assignment for preparing students for the unit tests, but she wants to be certain that the groups start out with the same average test grades. (Thus, in this example, test grades are both the matching variable and the dependent variable.) The teacher could use random assignment with most of the children, but then she would compute preliminary averages for each group and decide where to assign the last several children into groups based upon their grades: a child with high test grades would be placed in the group with the lower preliminary mean, and a child with low grades would be placed in the group with the higher preliminary mean, and so forth.

When this matching process is complete, the group means on the matching variable will be the same or very similar. Of course, this is not a truly random assignment, but the teacher will know that the two groups started out with equivalent performance on the dependent variable, and she is likely to presume she has a better chance of detecting a systematic difference between the homework assignments if there is one. However, in actuality, if there is an effect, matching the groups in this fashion has the opposite effect. To understand why this is the case, let's look at what this group matching process actually does.

Matching groups on the dependent variable prior to the manipulation of the IV reduces the random differences between the groups, making it less likely that we will mistake random variation for a *non-existent* systematic effect. That is, if the null hypothesis is actually true, matching the groups reduces the likelihood of a Type I error. However, whenever we decrease the probability of a Type I error, we automatically increase the likelihood of a Type II error, which means that when the null hypothesis is actually false—and there really is a systematic effect—we are less likely to detect the effect. Thus, matching the groups decreases the power of the design.[4]

It may help to consider what the group-matching process does to the value of our test-ratio. By selecting participants for one group at random, the within-group variability—the denominator of the ratio—should be the same as it would be in a random-groups design (i.e., a between-subjects design that uses totally random assignment). However, the chance fluctuations that would ordinarily occur between the groups is being reduced by the matching process, so the numerator of the test-ratio is being reduced. This reduces the value of the test-ratio, making it less likely that it will reach significance, and increasing the chances of making a Type II error and decreasing power:

$$\text{Test-ratio} = \frac{\text{between-groups variance}}{\text{within-group variance}} = \frac{\text{IV} + (\text{chance} - \text{the matching effect})}{\text{chance}}$$

Matched-Pairs Design The matching procedure in a **matched-pairs design** is also intended to make sure that the groups start out the same on some potentially-confounding variable. However, instead of simply making sure the groups had

---

[4]Of course, if a researcher uses a matched-groups design and still finds a significant effect, it suggests that the effect is real and robust: it was detected even with the "deck stacked against it."

the same average on the matching variable, the matched-pairs design makes sure that the groups are the same, participant by participant. That is, the researcher selects pairs of participants who have the same (or very similar) scores on the matching variable and then randomly assigns one member of each pair to the treatments. This procedure allows the researcher to be certain that the groups are equivalent—if not equal—on the matching variable before the manipulation begins. Like the matched-groups design, this matching procedure reduces the random variability between the treatment groups (which reduces the numerator of the test-ratio). However, because the pairs of participants were selected because they have the same scores on the matching variable, we can isolate the variability that is due to differences in the matching variable and remove it from our error term, thus reducing the denominator of the test-ratio. This is the same statistical procedure used with within-subjects designs: the total variability is divided into *three* sub-components rather than two, and this gives the statistical test more power. Hence, matched-pairs designs are no less powerful—and are potentially more powerful—than random-groups designs. The major drawback to matched-pairs designs is the effort required to perform the matching procedure: a large pool of potential participants will need to be tested on the matching variable in order to identify a sufficient number of matched pairs who will then participate in the study. Random-groups designs are much more common in the psychological literature than matched-pairs designs, indicating that researchers are willing to sacrifice some power in order to avoid the difficulties and expenses involved in matching.

In summary, within-subjects designs are inherently more powerful than between-subjects designs (and mixed designs, which we describe in Chapter 10, fall between them). Of the various types of between-subjects designs, matched-pairs designs are more powerful than random-groups designs, and random-groups designs are more powerful than matched-groups designs.

Power Analysis

As part of the growing concern over the validity of the null-hypothesis-testing procedures, particularly the frequent misinterpretation of non-significant results (see Chapter 6), researchers are increasingly concerned with trying to estimate the probability that a statistical test will reach the correct decision when the null hypothesis is false. This is known as **power analysis**. Essentially, the goal of power analysis is to estimate the size of β and power (which is equal to 1 minus β) by determining the proportion of samples that will lead to a Type II error and the proportion of samples that will lead to the correct decision to reject the null hypothesis. An increasing number of researchers consider power analysis to be a critical part of data analysis, and they recommend that power analyses become part of the normal routine. Currently, however, power analysis is not routinely conducted because it requires us to make a specific prediction about the value of the population parameter, and many researchers are uncomfortable with having to specify the effect size even before they conduct the study. They point out that the purpose of the study is to

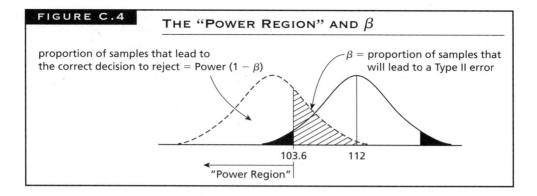

FIGURE C.4   THE "POWER REGION" AND β

proportion of samples that lead to
the correct decision to reject = Power $(1 - \beta)$

β = proportion of samples that
will lead to a Type II error

103.6   112

"Power Region"

determine whether an effect even exists, and that they cannot know what the effect size is in advance. In any event, understanding the principles of power analysis can be very useful. Therefore, let's illustrate the concepts underlying power analysis by considering a simple, single-sample design in which we compare a sample mean to a known population mean.[5]

Let's return to the example we used in Chapter 6 to present the basic concepts of hypothesis-testing: the effects of "crack" cocaine on the birthweight of newborn babies. It was hypothesized that prenatal exposure to crack causes a delay in development and growth, resulting in smaller birthweights compared to normal, non-exposed infants. In that example, we assumed that the population of newborn infants is known to have a mean weight (μ) equal to 112 ounces and a standard deviation (σ) of 8.6. The null hypothesis states that "crack babies" are not different than normal babies, so they also are expected to have a mean weight of 112. If we conduct a nondirectional (two-tailed) test, which is the preferred procedure (see Chapter 11), the research hypothesis (H_1) states that the newborn crack babies are different than average:

$$H_0: \mu_{crack} = \mu_{babies}$$

$$H_1: \mu_{crack} \neq \mu_{babies}$$

Suppose we have a sample of four infants (n = 4) who were exposed to crack cocaine during pregnancy: Power analysis asks "what are our chances of successfully rejecting the null hypothesis if, in fact, exposure to crack cocaine has reduced the growth rate of these babies?" Essentially, we want to know what proportion of samples from the real population falls in the sampling distribution's region of rejection because these are the samples that will lead to the correct decision to reject the null hypothesis. Figure C-4 illustrates this "power region" (which is equal to $1 - \beta$).

---

[5]The procedures used in power analyses for other statistical tests (such as *t*-tests, Pearson correlations and analysis of variance) all follow the same logic of the power analysis we present here using a single-sample *z*-test. Interested students will find the formulas in texts such as Howell (1997).

Our power analysis for this single-sample design is based on a z-test because we know both μ and σ for the population and the scores are normally distributed. Because the cut-off point for the "power region" is the same as the cut-off point for the region of rejection in the sampling distribution, the first step in the power analysis is to find that cut-off point — $\overline{X}_{critical}$ — using the z-test procedures presented in Chapter 11:

$$\overline{X}_{critical} = \mu \pm z_{critical}(\sigma_E) \qquad \text{where} \qquad \sigma_E = \frac{\sigma}{\sqrt{n}}$$

From the z-table (Table B-1), we find that $z_{critical}$ for a nondirectional (two-tailed) test with alpha set at .05 is equal to ± 1.96. Therefore:

$$\text{lower } \overline{X}_{critical} = 112 - 1.96\frac{8.6}{\sqrt{4}} \qquad\qquad \text{upper } \overline{X}_{critical} = 112 + 1.96\frac{8.6}{\sqrt{4}}$$

$$= 112 - 1.96\frac{8.6}{2} \qquad\qquad\qquad = 112 + 1.96\frac{8.6}{2}$$

$$= 112 - 1.96\,(4.3) \qquad\qquad\qquad\;\; = 112 + 1.96\,(4.3)$$

$$= 112 - 8.428 \qquad\qquad\qquad\qquad\;\; = 112 + 8.428$$

$$= 103.572 \qquad\qquad\qquad\qquad\qquad\;\; = 120.428$$

$$\approx 103.6 \qquad\qquad\qquad\qquad\qquad\qquad \approx 120.4$$

Thus, 95% of all random samples drawn from a population with a mean of 112 and a standard deviation of 8.6 will have means between 103.6 and 120.4 Using these critical values, we will reject the null hypothesis if the research sample has a mean weight of 103.6 or less or 120.4 or higher. If the null hypothesis is actually false, and the average weight of the population of crack babies is less than 112, the power region will overlap with the lower region of rejection of the sampling distribution, as illustrated in Figure C-4. Remember that the power region consists of the samples from the real population that lead to a correct decision to reject the null hypothesis. Therefore, the power of the test is equal to the proportion of samples from the real population that lie in the tail beyond the critical value, and the purpose of the power analysis is to estimate this proportion.

After determining the critical values, the next step in our power analysis is to make a specific prediction about the value of the population mean (μ) for babies exposed to crack cocaine. Let's assume that, in our expert opinion, we believe prenatal exposure to crack cocaine reduces the growth rate by 10%, so the average crack baby weighs 100.8 ounces (instead of the 112 ounces of normal infants). Thus, the research hypothesis could be written like this:

$$H_1: \mu_{crack} = 100.8$$

The power analysis now asks: If 100.8 ounces is the value of the mean for the true population of crack babies, what proportion of random samples of 4 infants drawn from this population will have a mean weight less than or equal to 103.6, thus falling in the region of rejection and allowing us to correctly reject the null hypothesis?

Because the distribution of all random samples of crack babies fits the normal distribution where the mean equals the median, we know that 50% of the samples of crack babies will have means of 100.8 or less, so we need to determine what percentage of samples lie between 100.8 and 103.6. We can find out by calculating the z-score for 103.6 in a population with a mean of 100.8 and then using the z-table (Table B-1) to find the proportion of samples that fall between the mean and z. In computing the value of $z_{critical}$, the standard error of the real population is assumed to be equal to the standard error of the sampling distribution because the sample size remains the same; only the means of the two distributions are different.

$$z_{critical} = \frac{\overline{X}_{critical} - \text{predicted value of } \mu \text{ for population}}{\sigma_E}$$

$$z_{critical} = \frac{103.6 - 100.8}{4.3}$$

$$= \frac{2.8}{4.3}$$

$$= 0.651162791$$

$$\approx 0.65$$

From the second column of Table B-1, we find that the area under the normal curve between the mean and $z = 0.65$ is equal to .24216. Thus, 24.2% of the random samples will have a mean between 100.8 and 103.6. When we add the fact that half of the samples (.50 or 50%) will have means less than 100.8, the power region encompasses an area equal to .74216, and therefore, we can conclude that, *if* the actual mean birthweight of crack babies is 100.8 ounces, 74.2% of all random samples of four babies will lead us to correctly reject the null hypothesis. That is, the power of the test is equal to .74216 or 74.2%.

The power analysis indicates that our chance of correctly rejecting the null hypothesis with a sample of 4 infants is just over 74% if, in fact, crack cocaine reduces the growth rate by 10 percent. From this, we can determine the probability of a Type II error where we fail to reject the null hypothesis and miss the systematic impact of prenatal exposure to cocaine on birthweight. The probability of a Type II error, which is known as β, is equal to the proportion of samples from the real population that lie in the common region of the sampling distribution, and together, β and power add up to 1.0 (or 100%). Therefore, if the power of our test is equal to .74216 (or 74.2%), then β must be equal to .25784 (or 25.8%). This tells us the chance that we will *miss* a ten-percent decrease in birthweight is almost 26% if our sample includes only 4 babies. Figure C-5 illustrates the results of this power analysis.

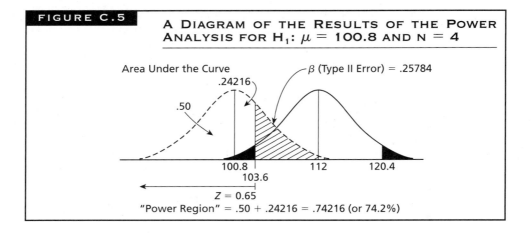

FIGURE C.5 **A DIAGRAM OF THE RESULTS OF THE POWER ANALYSIS FOR H$_1$: μ = 100.8 AND N = 4**

Note that in this example, our predicted value for the real population mean ($\mu = 100.8$ ounces) fell in the region of rejection (that is, it was less than the critical value of 103.6). Consequently, we needed to find the area under the curve *between* the predicted mean and the critical value from the sampling distribution and add it to the 50% of samples from the other side of the mean. However, in cases where the predicted value of μ lies within the common region of the sampling distribution, the power of the test is simply equal to the area *beyond* the critical value. For example, if we predicted that crack reduced growth by only 6% so the mean weight of crack babies is 105.3 ounces, the power of the analysis would be equal to the proportion of samples from a population with $\mu = 105.3$ that have mean equal to 103.6 or less.

We would compute the z-score for 103.6 and look up the area of the normal curve beyond that value of z:

$$z_{\text{critical}} = \frac{103.6 - 105.3}{4.3}$$

$$= \frac{-1.7}{4.3}$$

$$= -0.3953488$$

$$\approx -0.40$$

From the z-table, we find that the area under the normal curve in the tail beyond $z = \pm 0.40$ is .34458. Thus, if crack reduces growth by 6%, the power of our test using a sample of 4 crack babies is equal to 34.5%. We have a 34.5% chance of correctly concluding that crack babies are systematically smaller than normal infants. The chance of missing the effect and making a Type II error (β) is .65542 or 65.5%. (You should not be surprised to see that when the effect size was reduced, from 10% to 6%, the power of the test decreased as well.) Figure C-6 presents this power analysis.

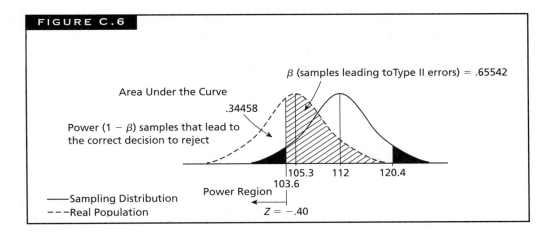

FIGURE C.6

Having performed a power analysis based upon an educated guess about the size of the effect of exposure to crack on the fetal growth rate, the next question must be: Do we have enough power? Unlike the standards that have been adopted for setting alpha levels and Type I error rates, similar standards for setting power levels and Type II error rates have not been established, and consequently, different researchers have adopted different criteria. However, the most common practice has been to set the acceptable level of power at 80% or higher, which means that we are willing to risk missing real effects—and make Type II errors—20% of the time. Under this criterion, a study with 4 crack babies, with power just over 74%, is not powerful enough to reliably detect a 10-percent decrease in birthweight. We could then ask: "How many participants do we need in order to have power that is equal to or greater than 80%?" We answer this question by substituting different values of n into the power analysis until we reach the criterion. When we go through this exercise, we find that a minimum of 5 babies would be required in order to have this level of power.

You may be wondering whether we have just contradicted our earlier position that the minimum sample size for experiments and quasi-experiments is $n = 10$ because smaller samples sizes are generally unable to detect anything but huge effects. In fact, a 10-percent decline in human prenatal growth probably is a huge effect. Prenatal growth is primarily determined by genetic factors and there is relatively little individual variation that is due to environmental factors. So it may actually be unlikely that exposure to crack cocaine will have such a strong effect on the fetus. Consequently, we may want to ask if our research design has enough power to detect a smaller effect size, such as a 6-percent decrease in birthweight (in which case, we would hypothesize that the population of crack babies would have a mean weight equal to 105.28 ounces). A power analysis where we try various sample sizes reveals that we would need a minimum of 13 crack babies in our sample in order to have a power level of at least 80% to detect a 6% decrease in weight using a nondirectional, two-tailed test with alpha set at .05.

We could, of course, reason that even a 6-percent decline in growth rate is unlikely to occur as a result of prenatal exposure to crack cocaine. Therefore, we could hypothesize that the effect of exposure is to reduce birthweight by 4 percent, or 3 percent, or 1 percent, and so forth, and we could conduct power analyses to determine how much power a test would have as a function of sample size. That is, we could determine how many participants we would need to have a sufficient amount of power to detect any given effect size. For example, with 52 babies, we would have enough power to detect a 3-percent decline in birthweight at the 80% criterion (where the average weight of the crack babies would be 108.6 ounces). The smaller the effect we are trying to detect, the more participants we will need.

Practical Significance   Theoretically, any effect—however small—can be detected if the sample size is large enough. However, we want to caution students that not all effects are worth detecting. That is, we should consider the practical significance of the findings. Let's suppose for example, that prenatal exposure to crack cocaine causes a 1-percent decline in birthweight. These babies would weigh an average of 110.9 ounces, which is only just over one ounce below the weight of normal infants. If this difference in birthweight has no real impact on the lives of these children, then the statistical significance of the difference in birthweight may not be worth the costs involved in conducting the research. Similarly, systematic, but low-magnitude correlations (e.g., 0.10 or less) may be detected if the sample size is large enough, but we need to ask if finding a very low correlation has any practical value. For instance, suppose a study involving a large national sample finds that the correlation between performance in a parenting course during junior high school and parenting skills during young adulthood is statistically significant but very small: $r = +0.10$. The coefficient of determination (r^2; see Chapter 9) tells us that variation in course grades only accounts for 1% of the variation in later parenting skills, so should the government spend millions of dollars on a new school curriculum that requires junior high students to take the parenting course? No, because improving the performance of the young teens will have very little impact on their adult behavior, and there may be more effective programs that should be funded. Put simply, statistical significance does not guarantee that the findings are useful or meaningful.

Exercises

Use the following information to answer questions 1–4:

Suppose there is sex discrimination in American circuses, so that women circus performers are paid systematically less than average. Further suppose that the American Association of Clowns and Things (AACT) reported that the national average salary (μ) for circus clowns was $40,000 with a standard deviation (σ) of $3600.

1. Assume there is a 4% difference between the women's salary and the national average (where women are paid less than average). Would a sample of 10 women circus clowns be powerful enough to detect this difference? Perform a power analysis for a sample size of 10, using a two-tailed test with alpha set a .05, and set the power criterion at 80%.

2. How big would the difference in salary need to be in order to be detected with a sample of 10 women (with the power criterion set at 80%)?

3. What is the minimum sample size needed to detect a systematic 4% difference in salary for women if the power criterion is 80%?

4. How, if at all, does the variability in the population affect the power of a test? To find out, perform the power analysis again, once assuming that the standard deviation for the salaries of clowns is $\sigma = \$1600$ (rather than $3600), and then assuming the standard deviation is $\sigma = \$6400$. (In each case, the mean remains at $\mu = \$40,000$, the effect size is 4%, and the sample size is equal to 10.)

For each of the following effect sizes, find the minimum sample size needed to have adequate power (i.e., to meet an 80% criterion) in a two-tailed test. (Assume normal distributions.)

5. A 20-point increase in SAT-Verbal scores following completion of a Humanities course. The mean SAT-Verbal score is $\mu = 500$, and the standard deviation is $\sigma = 100$.

6. A 65% decrease in disruptive behaviors in the classroom for attention deficit disorder children after they begin to take the stimulant drug Ritalin. Assume the mean number of disruptive behaviors per day is $\mu = 12$, and the standard deviation is $\sigma = 4$.

7. A 6% increase in total brain weight for rats raised in enriched environments. Assume the mean brain weight is $\mu = 13$ grams and the standard deviation is $\sigma = 2$ grams.

8. A 500-calorie reduction in daily food intake following hypnosis therapy for obesity. Assume the mean caloric intake is $\mu = 2800$ and the standard deviation is $\sigma = 750$.

REPORTING THE RESEARCH

■ ■ ■ ■ ■ ■

The broad purpose of conducting psychological research is to add to our store of knowledge, and the value of good research lies in the knowledge gained. Science is a public endeavor and the value of research is very limited if only the researcher is aware of the research effort and the results obtained. It must become known to others so dissemination of the knowledge is a vital part of the research process. For example, suppose that a researcher determined that some particular intervention helps students with dyslexia learn to read more readily. The value of that research would not be fully realized until these findings were known to those involved directly in the education of dyslexic students and to those involved in the training of teachers of such students, and ultimately to parents of the students. Many psychological researchers feel that part of their job is to "give away" psychological information to those who could bene-fit from it.

As a public exercise, science requires detailed reporting of research. In one sense, the "truth" of any phenomenon is determined by the extent to which it can be repli-cated by others. Replication, of course, requires precise knowledge of what was done in a given study. The procedures used, the measures taken, the analyses conducted, and the logical inferences made must be publicly available.

There are two ways in which research findings are shared with others. The researcher may talk to others about them or may write about them. The primary spoken route involves oral presentations at professional meetings, conferences or conventions. Written accounts of the research may appear in a book or book chapter, but more commonly they appear as articles in technical and professional journals. Recently they have also begun to appear in electronic form on the internet or World-WideWeb rather than by more traditional means such as the publication of printed material. Which method of dissemination is chosen depends on the nature and extent of the research findings and on the audience the researcher hopes to reach.

Methods of Dissemination

Presentations at Professional Meetings

In addition to informal descriptions of their research to immediate colleagues, many researchers make formal presentations of their work at meetings of professional or-ganizations. Most researchers belong to some regional or national organizations that hold annual conventions (e.g., American Psychological Society, Psychonomic Soci-ety, Eastern Psychological Association, Society for Research in Child Development, American Psychological Association, Gerontological Society of America). The core activity at these conventions is the presentation of recently completed research, either in the form of a paper that is read to an audience of those interested in the research topic or as a "poster."

One advantage of presenting a paper or poster as a means of making research findings available to others is that it is generally much quicker than getting a written version published. Furthermore, the standards or criteria for getting a convention paper or poster accepted are less stringent than for publication of research in a journal (about 90% of proposed papers are accepted at many meetings compared to an acceptance rate of only about 20% for many of the more prestigious journals). This lower criteria means that one can present the results of pilot studies or single, exploratory studies at meetings whereas journals have increasingly favored manuscripts that report a series of related studies. Being able to present an initial study as a paper allows researchers to try out their ideas on the topic and get critical and constructive feedback from other researchers on both methodological issues and the theoretical/conceptual framework.[1]

Researchers who wish to present a paper or poster at these conventions are typically required to submit, for evaluation, an abstract plus a short form of their paper several months prior to the convention. A committee reviews these and notifies the researcher whether or not their work has been accepted for presentation.

The number of papers being read at these meetings is typically so great that there are several concurrent sessions, focused on different topics, going on in different rooms of the convention center. Even so, the presenter is usually restricted to a fixed time, somewhere between 10 and 20 minutes, to present their paper. This time limitation results in a weakness; the presentation is lacking the "full particulars" that would allow exact replication. Those with strongly related research interests need to contact the presenter later for more details. Another shortcoming of papers is the limited audience (those who chose both to attend this convention and this particular session), although most organizations circulate programs for the conventions that include the abstract so those not in attendance may write to request a printed copy of the paper.

Compared to reading papers at such meetings, which has a long history, the presentation of posters is a more recent development. By the late 1980s most organizations shifted to having a substantial portion of presentations take the form of a written description of the research being posted on one of many boards in a large room for some specified interval of time, for example, Friday, 8:30 to 10:30. The presenter of the poster stands nearby to answer questions and to converse with those interested in the research topic. The poster itself is actually a set of pages that the

---

[1]What is described here is the optimal, cooperative model for progress in science. Unfortunately, sometimes researchers are reluctant to present their ideas and findings until after they have completed a series of studies and have submitted that research for publication. Their concern is that someone else may "steal their good ideas" and get those ideas, or the empirical phenomenon the data show, into print before they do. Attitudes that place personal glory ahead of cooperative efforts to contribute "pieces of the puzzle" slow the rate of progress in the field. This sort of competition is a real influence for many researchers, and understandably it is exacerbated when the research seems to hold great promise of presenting something really new or revolutionary in the field, or when publication of the findings may secure one's employment.

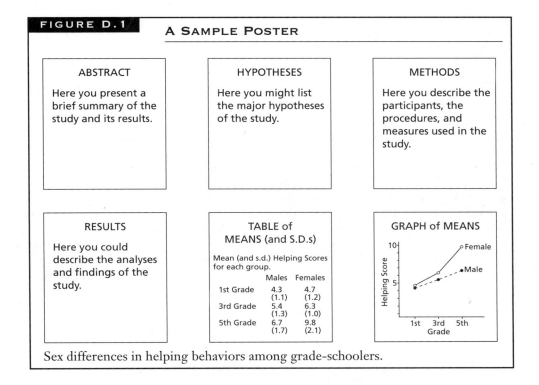

FIGURE D.1

A SAMPLE POSTER

ABSTRACT

Here you present a brief summary of the study and its results.

HYPOTHESES

Here you might list the major hypotheses of the study.

METHODS

Here you describe the participants, the procedures, and measures used in the study.

RESULTS

Here you could describe the analyses and findings of the study.

TABLE of MEANS (and S.D.s)

Mean (and s.d.) Helping Scores for each group.

	Males	Females
1st Grade	4.3 (1.1)	4.7 (1.2)
3rd Grade	5.4 (1.3)	6.3 (1.0)
5th Grade	6.7 (1.7)	9.8 (2.1)

GRAPH of MEANS

Sex differences in helping behaviors among grade-schoolers.

presenter brings and tacks up on a roughly 4 by 6 foot vertical surface. Figure D-1 shows a typical layout for a poster.

For this poster form of presentation to be effective, the researcher should balance the need to provide sufficient information with the need to minimize the amount of material to be read. Ideally, the poster provides the key aspects of procedures, measures, data analyses, and interpretation in a very concise manner. One needs to be able to digest the information with a minimum of reading. Because many people may be reading a given poster at the same time, the print needs to be large enough to be easily read from several feet away; doing this while keeping the total number of pages to ten or fewer dictates presentation of only the key aspects of the study. Most researchers have copies available of at least the abstract, and often of a more detailed description of the study, or they will take names and addresses and send more information to those who request it.

There are major advantages of posters for both the presenter and those who come to the poster session. Because the posters are up for some period of time a viewer and the presenter can have an extended discussion of the research in a one-on-one manner that is not possible during a paper session. For this reason many researchers feel that they receive more valuable feedback during poster sessions than when they present in paper sessions.

Written Reports

Research findings published in a journal article have the potential to reach the widest possible audience because journal articles become part of the continuing "archival record" for work in the field which remains available to future researchers. Furthermore, these archival records are readily accessible because a number of abstracting services allow one to systematically search vast stores of printed materials, for example, *Psychological Abstracts*, and the computerized versions known as *PsycLIT* and *PsycINFO*, which contain abstracts of articles from more than 1,400 journals carrying psychological research plus books and book chapters.

There is a formal procedure for getting research published in scholarly journals. To begin with, a manuscript must be prepared describing the work in detail. Most researchers will spend weeks or months drafting versions of the manuscript, revising these drafts of the manuscript, and seeking critical feedback from colleagues about ways in which the manuscript can be improved. For nearly all journals publishing psychological research, the manuscript must adhere to a format known as **APA style**. (A detailed description of that style, along with a sample paper prepared in that style, are given later in this appendix.) The researcher must select a journal that publishes work in this topic area and submit multiple copies of the manuscript to the editor of that journal. The manuscript, or any description of that work, may only be submitted to one journal at a time.

For most journals the decision about whether or not to publish the work depends on a process known as peer review. The manuscript is sent out by the editor to be evaluated by several other individuals who have expertise in the topic area of the research. For many journals this is done as a "blind review" meaning that the name and institutional affiliation of authors are not provided to the reviewers; this procedure is an attempt to have the publication decision hinge on the quality of the research rather than the reputation of the researcher. Each of the reviewers provides the editor with a detailed critique of the study's theoretical conceptualization, methodology, data analyses, and conclusions. Each reviewer is also asked to indicate whether the manuscript should be published.

Having received these reviews, the editor will then read the manuscript and prepare a summary letter containing the reviewers' main points and the editor's own concerns about the study. It is extremely rare, but on occasion the editor may decide to accept the paper essentially "as is" and require few or no revisions. Even very good manuscripts almost always elicit some suggestions for improvements from the reviewers, and in these cases the editor will conditionally accept the paper pending a revision which addresses the concerns raised by the reviewers. In cases where the work is judged to have merit, but where there are more serious problems, the editor may "reject without prejudice" and invite the author(s) to re-submit after giving careful attention to comments of the reviewers. In such cases the comments often call for gathering additional data, for performing additional data analyses, or for re-framing the study in a different theoretical or conceptual manner, perhaps relating it to other literatures the reviewers felt relevant. If the reviewers or editor have grave doubts about the merit of the study, the manuscript may be simply rejected without opportunity for re-submission. The author(s) may then submit the work to another journal, usually after addressing the issues raised in the critiques received from the prior journal. The acceptance rate is variable across journals, so the author(s) may now choose to send the manuscript to a somewhat less prestigious journal where the chances of publication are higher.

At best, the process takes many months and the feedback, although helpful in making for better published work, is hard on the ego of the author(s) as a rule. Revised articles that a journal editor agrees to publish will often be returned with requests for still further revisions. It commonly takes ten months to two years from initial submission until the published article appears, even when the initial journal agrees to publish the work. This publication lag is one of the reasons that researchers like to attend conventions and discuss the current work in their field. In this age of instant information, this publication lag is also one of the forces contributing to rising interest in having research quickly and widely available by placing it on the WorldWideWeb.

Electronic Dissemination

The future of print journals is unclear. Sale of those journals is a major source of income for some organizations, such as the American Psychological Association (APA), and so the prospect of individuals posting their research findings on their web site, making them readily available at no cost, poses a threat to the future of print journals and a loss of income to organizations publishing the journals. For the authors there are some risks of posting their article on the internet. Since that material can be readily downloaded, another person might incorporate some of this into a work which they then copyright, making the proper attribution of scholarly ideas problematic. In posting an article that has been accepted for publication in a print journal, the author may be violating the copyright transfer agreement with the publisher of the print copy.

In response to this threat of open and free dissemination of research work, some journals have adopted the stance that articles posted on the internet will be considered to have already been published and will not be considered for print publication by these journals (e.g., *New England Journal of Medicine* and the journal *Neuroscience*). The APA adopted an "interim policy" in 1997 that allows the editors of APA journals discretion to treat a posting on the web as prior publication. Thus, any research that has been posted on a web site, even on the researcher's own web site, may be treated as having been previously published and so will not be considered by the journal. Because authors wish their work to appear in the more prestigious journals, this has had a very chilling effect on the rapid sharing of one's research findings via the internet.

A major problem with research reports found posted on the internet is that there is no quality control. Someone who is an incompetent researcher can place his study on a web site as easily as a very competent researcher. For most of what is on the web, there is no peer review. It is possible, of course, to have quality journals that are subject to peer review, but that appear only in an electronic form. *Psycoloquy* is an example of one such journal. Articles can be submitted electronically, and the entire peer review process is conducted electronically. When a version of the manuscript is accepted for publication, it is sent out on an electronic mailing list to all those who have added their e-mail address to that list server. *Psycoloquy* allows individuals to submit commentary on articles, but these commentaries must also pass a peer review screening. Articles remain available in a directory so that anyone can request copies of an earlier article by a file transfer procedure (FTP) at ftp://ftp.princeton.edu/pub/harnad/psycoloquy.

The publication of research will almost surely move more and more toward such electronic forms as the proportion of people in the intended audience who have ready access to the internet increases. The issues of how these are to be funded and who has rights to access the journals, and how, remain to be worked out, but the convenience of being able to call up the journals on one's computer and then print out only selected articles, or selected pages of an article, has an appeal that cannot be denied. At the present time a number of journals exist both in paper print form and in electronic form. However, often a university library cannot subscribe only to the electronic form, but must purchase the printed material in order to receive access to an electronic version.

There are currently two methods available for conducting electronic searches of the research literature. In one case, the database from an abstracting source (such as *PsycINFO*) is available on CD ROMs which libraries can purchase and load onto dedicated computers. An increasingly more common way is for the library to purchase such abstracting services from an on-line vendor so that the search takes place on the internet. For example, at some universities, SilverPlatter is used to access the *PsycINFO* abstracts.

A library also may purchase services such as *Proquest* which allow electronic access to the *full text* of articles in selected journals, as well as abstracts of articles for many more journals. (*Proquest* must purchase the right to carry the articles in electronic form from the journals.) Users are able to electronically search the database of journals carried by *Proquest* and then print out selected pages from articles of interest. Unfortunately, for researchers in the field of psychology, at the present time relatively few psychology-related journals are available for full-text access in databases such as *Proquest*.

These electronic abstracting services are not really the same as having the journal published in electronic form. The copies of abstracts or articles available here are delayed by the usual events that are entailed in production of the hard print copy which must exist before these articles are available electronically.

General Writing Style

Two guiding principles in scientific or technical writing are clarity and brevity. While allusions and metaphoric expressions may be prized as an indication of creativity in much of the writing that students do for literature or humanities classes, these techniques are not appropriate in scientific writing. You need to state the ideas as precisely and as concisely as you can.

Clarity is achieved by using the proper words and simple sentence structure. You should consider whether each word conveys the precise meaning you intend, and whenever possible, write in simple, active declarative sentences. In an effort to make it easier for researchers to follow this advice, the APA has recently changed its stance on "self-references" in research reports. In the past, writers were told to use "the present author" or "the researchers" but not "I" or "we." Furthermore, most scientific works were written with many passive sentence constructions, perhaps because it seemed to lend greater objectivity to the research. For example, one might have written "All students received a pencil without an eraser and were instructed to wait for further instructions." But now authors are allowed—if not encouraged—to use self-references, and so this same idea might be expressed as "I gave each student a pencil without an eraser and asked them to wait for further instructions."

The clarity of the article is also highly dependent upon the organization of the paper. The global structure of most articles is imposed by the journal editors who require authors to follow particular formats, such as the "APA format" which is described in detail later. These formats are designed to maximize the logical flow of ideas across the paper, but authors must still decide how the ideas should unfold within each section of the manuscript. And how one conveys the information in a given paragraph should be sensitive to what the reader already knows. Most writers find it helps considerably to create an outline of the major ideas, and consider the optimal order of these ideas before beginning to write the detailed sentences of individual paragraphs.[2]

The principle of brevity in scientific writing is partly a matter of a no-nonsense style, of saying exactly what one needs to say and nothing superfluous. Brevity is also dictated by the constraints of the space the published article will require. The editor of any journal can accommodate more articles per issue if the articles it contains are written more "tightly," and so the journal is more valuable since it conveys more information. Many authors have come to understand that, from the perspective of the journal editor, "conciseness is next to Godliness."

It may have already occurred to you that these two goals of clarity and brevity may conflict. As one achieves greater and greater brevity there is a danger that what remains cannot clearly convey the full information. One of the authors of this book had an article accepted for publication in a very good journal but was then told to "cut the manuscript's length by half." Consequently, the revised manuscript did not thoroughly explain how the four experiments in that report related to each other. In dealing with this conflict, clarity must be the foremost principle; brevity without clarity is unacceptable whereas clarity without brevity is only unfortunate.

---

[2]The development of word processors has been both helpful and detrimental to effective writing. It is easy to "cut and paste" and to move paragraphs from place to place. While this makes it seem easier to re-organize a paper, it may cause problems when the logical structure of a particular paragraph does not fit in its new location. Therefore, once paragraphs have been re-ordered, the authors must carefully revise their work—re-writing it as necessary in order to make sure that ideas flow in a logical manner.

Some Specific Issues and Common Errors

The importance of precision in word choice is also at the heart of the issue of avoiding "sexist" language. Nearly everyone who is a native speaker of English understands that "man" can convey either a narrower meaning of male *homo sapien* or a broader meaning where it serves to distinguish *homo sapiens* from other species, for example, "Only man among all animals is so concerned about events beyond the here and now." Since the contrast of man to animals is explicit in that example, it is unlikely that it will be taken to mean man as opposed to woman. However, in many uses it may not be so obvious, and the reader may understand the narrow sense when the writer intended the broader sense. For example, which interpretation will the reader take from "If man is to develop better social skills, certain early life experiences are crucial." Here it behooves the writer to use a non-sexist form if the broader meaning is intended, for example, "If people are to develop better social skills, . . .". When the narrower meaning (of man versus woman) is intended, ambiguity can be avoided by using the term "male;" for example, "If males are to develop better social skills, the nature of early life experiences is crucial."

Some of the difficulties of writing in a way that is inclusive of men and women derive from the obligatory requirement in English to indicate the sex of the individual when using singular pronouns (he, she). One may make clear that both sexes are intended, or that the sex of the individual is unknown, by use of "he or she"; for example, "When each participant finished his or her task, he or she chose another." Such a sentence structure is cumbersome, however, and the writer may use a variety of techniques to avoid it. Since the plural pronoun "they" conveys no information about sex of the individuals, it may be possible to use a plural form such as "When participants finished their tasks, they chose another." In casual, conversational language today, the use of "they" as a singular as well as a plural pronoun is now fairly widespread (e.g., "When each participant finished the task they were working on, they chose another"). It remains to be seen whether, and how soon, this solution may become acceptable in scholarly journals.

The last example raises the broader issue of **agreement**. In addition to watching out for gender agreement, one needs to be sensitive to agreement of number and of mass versus count nouns. A common error with regard to number is for writers to treat the word "data," which is plural, as a singular noun. For example, many of us tend to say, "The data is clear on this point" when we should say, "The data are clear on this point." Another error is to use wording that is appropriate for mass nouns with count nouns. A mass noun is the name for something that exists in varying amounts but is not countable as discrete items, for example, snow, milk, or sand. Count nouns, as the name implies, are names for things that occur as separate countable items such as words, people, or tasks. Some common examples of this error include: (1) "The amount of participants was too small" should say "The number of participants . . ." and (2) "the amount of times he threw the ball" should be "the number of times. . . ." In contrast, if you are measuring duration of events (instead of counting them), the proper phrase is "amount of time." Misuse of terms such as "number of" and "amount of" is distracting to readers and detracts from the overall quality of your research report.

Clarity, then, depends upon appropriate vocabulary usage. Three other pairs of terms that students commonly misuse or confuse in psychology papers include: (1) affect versus effect, (2) i.e. versus e.g., and (3) infer versus imply. For the vast majority of uses, the proper word is "effect" when it is being used as a noun, and "affect" when being used as a verb. If X affects Y, then X will have *an* effect on Y. The Latin term *id est* (i.e.) means "that is" while the Latin term *exempli gratis* (e.g.) means "for example," and if, when you encounter these abbreviations, you think of their English translations, it will help you use them properly. The difference between "imply" and "infer" depends on whether we are referring to the speaker or the listener. Speakers or writers can imply something which they do not explicitly state, and listeners or readers can infer what was meant but not spoken.

The clarity of your report will also be negatively affected if it contains factual or logical inconsistencies. One subtle form of this occurs when we attribute human characteristics to inanimate things. Therefore, rather than write "The experiment concluded the program had no effect," we should make it clear that humans have actually reached that conclusion, saying, "The experiment led us to conclude the program had no effect."

Obviously, too, the clarity of the report depends upon readers' familiarity with the terms you use. Abbreviations can cause confusion if they are unfamiliar to the readers. In general, abbreviations should be used only when the abbreviation is already in widespread use, such as MMPI, or when the term will be used repeatedly throughout the manuscript, such as RT for reaction time. Except for a few abbreviations that have essentially reached the status of functioning like words (e.g., IQ, AIDS), all abbreviations must be introduced using a full written version, for example, ". . . were given the Minnesota Multiphasic Personality Inventory (MMPI)." Common units of time measure, such as hr for hour, min for minute, s for second and ms for millisecond can be used without introduction, as can some measures of distance such as cm for centimeter and some measures of speed such as mph for miles per hour. Do not begin a sentence with an abbreviation if you can avoid it.

One last specific writing rule that is directly relevant to research reports has to do with writing numbers. The general rule is to use numerals for numbers with two or more digits, but use words to express numbers below 10. There are, however, several exceptions to this rule. Use numerals if the number denotes the place in a series, e.g., "Trial 3", or "page 2". Also, numbers that give time, dates, ages are typically given in numerals, even if less than 10. For example, "7 years old," "4 hours later," "on June 3, 1999," or "2 hr and 8 min." However, if a sentence begins with a number, it is always written out as a word, for example, "Sixteen participants failed to return for the second session."

Re-writing

Very few writers can produce a passable paper in the initial draft. Most papers presented at conferences or submitted for publication have been through many revisions, perhaps with constructive input from one or more colleagues. You need to get in the habit of re-reading, re-thinking, and re-writing your papers. For students this implies the need to have the paper written before the very last moment, although real world constraints may preclude this some of the time. Nevertheless, you should expect to spend time re-writing the paper. By re-writing we do not simply mean checking for verb tense agreement and considering whether a different word would convey the meaning better. Those are necessary steps, but the re-thinking and re-writing also should be at the higher level of whether the paper is well-organized and easy to comprehend, and whether there are things the reader needs to know but are never explicitly stated. It is often difficult to see "what's missing" from a paper we are writing because we are so close to the study that we forget certain aspects of procedure or analyses need to be made explicit to our readers. In re-reading your paper you should try to adopt the perspective of a naive reader who has no prior knowledge of what you have done or found. It has been said that, "If scientists were fish, the last thing they'd discover is water." Some assumptions are so central to our thinking that we are not really aware of the assumptions, and it often takes a "fresh look" to remind us that we need to be more explicit.

Plagiarism

When researchers submit a manuscript, it is expected that they have followed the same ethical principles that students face when they submit a paper for a grade in a course. Under the principles of Academic (or Professional) Honesty, it is assumed that the writing is all the author's own work. Often, of course, you are not describing your own, wholly original ideas. To the extent that the ideas are someone else's, you must take care to see that this is acknowledged; that is, you must cite a reference to the source of those ideas. Failure to cite your sources is a form of intellectual dishonesty known as **plagiarism**. Your instructors assume intellectual honesty on your part, and your reputation is on the line. If you submit work that you have plagiarized, the instructor will probably refuse to accept the paper and most likely will award a grade of F for the assignment, or possibly even an F for the course. At most institutions that also becomes a part of your permanent record. Similarly, plagiarism by researchers can permanently damage a person's career. Scientists rely on one another to help build the knowledge base within their disciplines, and once an individual has shown intellectual dishonesty, through plagiarism or fabrication of data, that person's reputation has been soiled and may never be recovered.

How do you protect yourself and provide the proper acknowledgment of others' ideas? There are two ways to give credit to your sources, and the one you choose should depend on whether you are using the exact expressions or words of another person or simply describing another's ideas in your own words. If you think that the original wording is perfect for what you want to say—that is, it conveys exactly the essence of the idea and it fits perfectly into the logical flow of your paragraph—then you should quote that author's wording exactly, and indicate that you have done so. For example:

```
This phenomenon has been described as "the failure to
be able to distinguish memories for real events from
memories for events which the person only imagined,
```

```
i.e., thought about, perhaps with the intention to
perform the act" (Smith, 1997, p. 75).
```

[Note that the exact words taken from Smith's paper are enclosed in quote marks, and that the page on which those words appear in the original article is also provided. Also note that there is no period before the closing quotation marks; the sentence is not completed until after the citation.]

On the other hand, if you are simply using the author's ideas, but expressing them in your own words, you need *not* give any page reference, but you do still need to credit the author for the ideas. For example:

```
An important distinction has recently been made be-
tween the sorts of memories we have that are based on
our experience of actual events and the memories for
our thoughts about actions we intended to perform.
Under some circumstances people are not certain about
the source of a particular memory (Smith, 1997).
```

[Note that this gives the same information as the quote in the preceding example, but the logical structure within the paragraph is different.]

The greatest potential for charges of plagiarism arises when you choose to paraphrase the wording of another author. A *very close paraphrase*, especially for more than a few words, can be seen as an effort to take credit for writing which is really derived extensively from the work of another. For example, consider this close paraphrase of the above-quoted sentence from Smith:

```
The phenomenon can be described as the inability to
be able to separate memories for actual events from
one's memories for events which the person only
thought about (e.g., imagined, perhaps with the in-
tention to carry out the action).
```

In this case, even if you were to finish the sentence with the citation "(Smith, 1997)," this may still be considered a form of plagiarism since the paraphrase is so very close to Smith's wording and grammar. Simply inserting synonyms into someone else's sentences is not what we mean when we say "put it into your own words." In a case like this, it would be best to use a direct quote and acknowledge it as such. The point, then, is that you should either use the author's actual words (give a quote) or take the idea and say it in your own words while still giving the author credit for the idea. "Close paraphrasing" may be viewed as plagiarism.

APA Format and Manuscript Preparation

Nearly all journals that publish psychological research require that manuscripts conform to a format for research papers set forth in the *Publication Manual of the American Psychological Association*. This manual is revised from time to time; the 4th edition

TABLE D.1	Sections of an APA-Style Research Report

Title page. Contains a title that indicates the variables studied, the name(s) and institutional affiliation(s) of the author(s), a short title known as the running head, and a page header that appears on all pages of the manuscript.

Abstract. Provides a brief summary of the research question, methods and results; typically not more than 120 words.

Introduction. A statement of the research question and review of related studies that give the empirical context; provides the rationale or theoretical basis for the hypothesized results.

Method. Details of how the research study was conducted, including descriptions of participants, the apparatus or materials employed, and procedures for gathering the data.

Results. Summary descriptions of the data collected, followed by statistical analyses of the data to test research hypotheses. Often this includes reference to tables or figures, which are located at the back of the manuscript sent to a journal. (See below.)

Discussion. Relates the obtained results to the hypotheses, evaluates outcomes and considers implications of the outcomes; contains suggestions for improvements or extensions in future research.

References. An alphabetical listing by author of all sources cited throughout the paper; this allows readers to go back to original sources cited.

Appendices. Included only when there are materials a reader might want to see but which are not necessary in the body of the paper itself, for example, the exact wording of items on a questionnaire.

Author notes. Contains acknowledgment of any financial support or assistance of others in the conduct of the study; also indicates where requests for reprints should be directed.

Footnotes. These should be used sparingly; they provide additional information that serves to supplement or amplify a point but may disrupt the flow of comprehension of the central ideas.

Tables. Most commonly used to present a large amount of numerical data in a compact form; can be used to provide purely verbal information; a heading should make the table intelligible on its own.

Figure captions. An explanation of what is depicted in a figure, including the measures on both the X and Y axes and the groups or conditions being contrasted.

Figures. Graphic displays of data, typically as bar graphs or line graphs. Also sometimes used to show the pattern of visual stimuli, or a representation of the apparatus.

was published in 1994. This standardized format facilitates clear and complete presentation by the author and simplifies comprehension of these reports since the majority of readers are familiar with this structure. Readers know what aspects of the research work are to be found in each section of the article.

The sections of a report, in their proper order, along with brief indications of the contents of that section are provided in Table D-1. The remainder of this appendix presents a detailed description of each section of the APA format, and illustrates them with sample manuscripts ready to be submitted to a journal, and a reprint of a resulting published paper.

Sections of an APA-Format Research Report

Before we describe each of the sections of a research report, we want to make an important point about the report as a whole: It should be written in the past tense. Keep in mind that, at the time you are writing the report, the study has been completed. It is in the past and your description of what was done and what was found should be written in the past tense. The exception is when you are stating a continuing truism. For example, in reporting the results of our statistical analysis, we might say "The data revealed a striking relationship between age and memory span," but in our conclusion we might say "It appears that memory span and age are related." The first sentence is about the specifics of the study whereas the second sentence is about a continuing condition of events in the world.

We also recommend that you follow the common practice of referring to the research being reported as "the present study." This may help you avoid potential confusion between a study from the existing literature that you have just cited and the study being reported in the manuscript. A common error is to refer to "this study" near the end of the introduction where readers will be unable to determine whether it refers to the study just described in the literature review or the study to be described in the method section. Such ambiguity is detrimental to the overall clarity of the report.

Title Page   This page contains five things: the title of the article, the name(s) of the author(s), institutional affiliation of the author(s), a "running head," and a page header. The title should be brief but understood on its own. The variables involved in the study must be indicated, and perhaps the relationship between them, for example, "Speed of Naming Pictured Objects as a Function of the Picture Size" or "The Effect of Type of Background Music on Amount of Time Shoppers Stay in Stores." The title should not contain abbreviations.

The author's first name, middle initial, and last name should be used; an individual should use the same form consistently on all publications. The institutional affiliation shows where the research was conducted; if there is none, the city and state of the author's residence are given. The running head is a shortened version of the title that will appear at the top of pages of the published article. For the titles suggested in the prior paragraph, the running heads might be: "PICTURE SIZE AND NAMING SPEED" and "MUSIC TYPE AND SHOPPING DURATION." (On the manuscript, the running head is given, as shown here, all in capital letters.) The page header is the first few words of the title and it appears at the top of every page of the manuscript.

Abstract   The abstract, presented alone on the second page of the manuscript, is a concise description of the study. It provides the working hypothesis, characteristics of the participants, variables that were manipulated or measured, a summary of the results, and the major conclusions. The abstract should be prepared carefully since it will appear in collections of abstracts of published work (e.g., in PsycINFO) and is all that many potential readers have as a basis for deciding whether or not they want to read your article. The abstract must be self-contained, so it is necessary to define any abbreviations. The length should not exceed about 120 words. Note: no title or author(s) appears at the top of this page.

Introduction   At the top of the third page, the title of the article is repeated, followed by the introduction. The author(s)' names do *not* appear on this page, and no heading is used to label the introduction. This section provides the background for the study. It must make clear the purpose of the research, and provide the question of interest and the working hypothesis. Since these typically derive from other, prior work, the introduction needs to review the related studies in the existing literature and provide the theoretical framework or the rationale that supports the working hypothesis. It is not appropriate to attempt an exhaustive review of the literature; if a recent review article exists, direct readers to this by citing that review. An effective introduction provides the key ideas from prior research in a brief manner, without giving unnecessary detail and at the same time not writing something so cryptic that it can only be understood by those already familiar with the research area.

An important part of a research report is the use of proper citations of your sources. As we discussed earlier in this Appendix, the APA format for citations requires us to present the last name of the author(s) and the year of publication in the body of the text. Here we would like to point out two specific rules for citations for sources with two or more authors. First, in citing a source with two or more authors, the word "and" is written out prior to the last author's name when the list of authors is part of a sentence within the text, but the ampersand sign (&) is used if the list of authors is within a parenthetical citation. For example: one would write " . . . as found by Ellis, Clifford, and Lancaster (1988)" or " . . . as others have found (Ellis, Clifford, & Lancaster, 1988)." (The ampersand sign is always used rather than the written word on the Reference page.)

Second, if a source has two authors, you must provide both names every time the work is cited. When there are three or more authors, the names of all authors are given the first time the work is cited, but subsequent citations of that source should provide the first author's name followed by "et al." (an abbreviation for the Latin phrase *et alii*, which means "and others"). For example, the initial citation of "Meissner, Lichtman, and Walker (1996)" becomes, for subsequent citations, "Meissner et al. (1996)."

Method   This section provides a detailed description of just how the study was carried out. The replicability of your study depends on others knowing what you did, how you measured variables, and how you analyzed the data. If some aspects of your procedures or materials are the same as those described elsewhere in the literature, you may simply refer the reader to that description, for example, "The pictures were the same as those used in my earlier work (Smith, 1996; Jones & Smith, 1997)."

The method section is typically broken into several labeled subsections. A center heading of "Method" is commonly used, followed by side headings at the beginning of each of the following sections: **participants**, **materials** or **apparatus**, and **procedure**. (The participants and procedure sub-sections are required, while materials or apparatus sub-sections are included only when they are relevant to the study.) In the participants section you need to provide details of the sample, such as the sex, age, and other characteristics that were recorded or used as criteria for selection of participants. The total number of participants should be reported, as well as the number of participants in each condition in the study. For example, "The participants were 84 young and 73 older adults who volunteered to be in the study. The young adults, 54 women and 30 men, were students enrolled in psychology classes at Hercules College; their ages ranged from 18 to 31 ($\overline{X}$ = 23.6 years). The older adults, 44 women and 29 men, were community residents of Altair, New York who used facilities of a public 'Senior Center.' All of these older adults were, by self-report, in 'good' or 'very good' health, and had at least some college education. Their ages ranged from 59 to 82 ($\overline{X}$ = 64.5 years). All participants were unfamiliar with the task and materials of this study."

(As a relevant historical note, we should point out the practice of referring to the people who participate in research as "participants" is relatively new. For decades, the term "subjects" was applied to both human and non-human research participants, so you will still encounter the term as you read the existing literature, and of course, the terminology of research design includes expressions such as "within-subject versus between-subject designs." In that context the term subjects is appropriate and still in use, but it is no longer acceptable to refer to people as "research subjects.")

If appropriate, the next sub-section will be the "materials" or "apparatus" section, depending on the nature of the study. If a piece of equipment was developed for the measures taken in this study, a description of this apparatus should be given, perhaps with a figure to facilitate communication of the appearance or function of that equipment. If stimuli were chosen from tests or from an appendix of materials provided in an earlier published report, then a materials section will identify those materials and provide the source, for example, "The category instances used here were the same items shown in Appendix B of Wilson's (1997) recent work." (Not all studies involve "materials" or an "apparatus" requiring description, so this section may be omitted from some reports. For example, a field study that measures whether or not shoppers return the extra change a check-out clerk "accidentally" gives to them does not require any materials or equipment.)

The procedure section provides a step by step description of how the study was carried out. This includes how variables were manipulated and measured, the specific conditions run, how participants were assigned to conditions, instructions the participants received, and any counterbalancing or other control features employed. What was done, and how it was done, need to be presented in sufficient detail to allow a replication of your study.

Results This section presents descriptive statistics and describes the types of inferential analyses employed, as well as the outcomes of these analyses. First you should summarize the performance of the participants in each of the experimental conditions—typically by reporting some measure of central tendency, such as the arithmetic mean or the median, and some measure of dispersion or variability, such as the standard deviation or the median absolute deviation. If additional comparisons are made between subgroups of scores within a condition (e.g., of males' versus females' performances), then the descriptive statistics might be given for the subgroups as well as the condition as a whole. Means and standard deviations should be

| TABLE D.2 | A Sample Table from a Research Report |

Mean reaction times for males and females in the visual and auditory presentation conditions across trials.

| | | | | | TRIAL | | | |
| | 1 | | 2 | | 3 | | 4 | |
Presentation	Vis	Aud	Vis	Aud	Vis	Aud	Vis	Aud
Males	2.3	1.8	2.1	1.7	1.9	1.7	1.7	1.6
Females	2.5	2.0	2.5	1.7	2.3	1.9	2.0	1.8
Combined	2.4	1.9	2.3	1.7	2.1	1.8	1.8	1.7

reported to one significant decimal place beyond the scores themselves. That is, if the scores are whole numbers (e.g., 3, 5, 6, 9, 10), the mean and standard deviation should be reported with one decimal place (e.g., $\overline{X} = 6.6$; $s = 2.9$); if the scores have one decimal place (e.g., 3.2, 5.1, 6.6, 9.7, 10.2), the mean and standard deviation should be reported with two decimal places (e.g., $\overline{X} = 6.96$; $s = 2.99$). (Note that throughout this text we have carried the computations out to six or seven decimal places in order to minimize the rounding error. Once the computation is completed, the value of the statistic would be reported with only one significant decimal place.)

When there are many experimental conditions, it may be simpler to present the performance summaries in the form of a table or a graph rather than to expect the reader to remember a lot of statistics presented verbally. Tables, where one can look back and forth across the cells that represent the conditions of the study, often make it easier to understand the comparisons. You must direct the reader to the table at the appropriate time, and provide an indication of what is notable in that table. For example, for the sample table presented in Table D-2, you might write, "From the mean reaction times seen in Table 2, it is apparent that the visual condition was slower than the auditory on every trial for both males and females."

Tables should *not* be used whenever the results can be clearly presented in a few sentences. For example, it is unnecessary to present tabled results in a simple experiment comparing average performance in just two conditions; presentation of the means (and the standard deviations) of the two groups can be effectively accomplished in one sentence: "The average reaction time for the six-year-olds was 6.8 seconds ($s = 1.3$), while the average reaction time for the eight-year-olds was only 4.5 seconds ($s = 1.1$)."

For at least some readers, graphic representations of performance levels will make it even easier to see the differences in performance between conditions. Graphs are particularly well suited to the presentation of certain outcomes, most notably the interaction of independent variables in determining the measured performance level. As with tables, whenever a graph is used to summarize data, there must be reference to that graph in the body of the text, including a description of what will be found

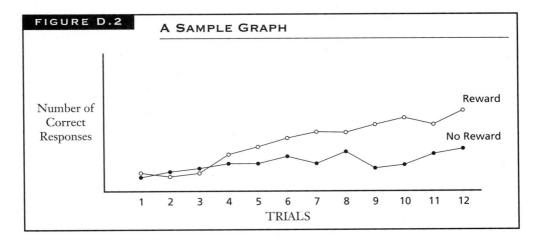

FIGURE D.2 A SAMPLE GRAPH

there. The author signals when they wish the reader to look at the figure in this way, for example, "As can be seen in Figure 2, performance in the rewarded condition was clearly superior from trial 4 on." (A sample graph is presented in Figure D-2.)

Once summary descriptions of the data have been presented, the results of inferential statistical analyses should be described. Be sure to present the name of the statistic, the obtained value (typically reported to two decimal places), the degrees of freedom, and an indication of whether the direction of the effect was as hypothesized. Some statement about the probability of obtaining such an effect by chance should also be reported. Probability information is commonly given in one of two ways: 1) you may simply tell the reader that the alpha level (probability of Type I error) was set at .05 for all analyses and then indicate for each outcome that it was or was not "statistically significant", or 2) if your statistic software provides them, you may choose to present the exact probability of each obtained outcome. The present authors lean toward the latter in most situations. We find it more convincing that something systematic is occurring (i.e., that these results are not simply due to chance variation) when the associated probability of a Type I error is $p = .001$ than when it is $p = .048$, although both are equally well described by saying "with an alpha level of .05 the results were statistically significant." (See our discussion of related material in the section on threats to the validity of null hypothesis testing in Chapter 6.)

In preparation of the manuscript the symbol for the name of the statistical test (e.g., t or F) and the symbol for the associated probability, p, are underscored; they will then be italicized in the printed article. The degrees of freedom are presented in parentheses. An example is "The difference between the means was found to be in the predicted direction and statistically significant, $\underline{t}$ (27) = 3.46, $\underline{p} < .002$."

Discussion This section presents an interpretation of the results along with conclusions about the implications of these data. The structure should parallel the introduction in that the hypotheses of this study should be revisited in light of the evidence from the data. Start with the main hypothesis and progress to other hypotheses in decreasing order of importance or centrality to the purposes of this study. Is there support or lack of support for each hypothesis?

It is appropriate to develop implications, even if these amount to speculations on the part of the author, provided they are clearly labeled as such and fit with known empirical findings in the literature and with relevant theoretical considerations. The author should also point out any shortcomings of the present study, providing suggestions for improvements in future studies and directions for further research.

You do not need to repeat the actual results here, and you should never introduce new results in this section. Sometimes the nature of certain results lead to conclusions that give rise to other hypotheses that are testable with this same data set. Under these conditions it is difficult not to discuss the original analyses prior to describing the second set of analyses. In such cases it may be desirable to structure the manuscript to have a combined Results and Discussion section.

If the manuscript reports the results of several studies, the structure for each experiment would be as described above, with a center head for each study, "Experiment 1", "Experiment 2". Note that Arabic numbers are used to label the individual experiments, and when one of the studies is referred to in the body of the text it is identified this way, with experiment capitalized, for example, "As was seen in Experiment 2, the females were more sensitive than the males." While there is often a short discussion at the end of each experiment, there is generally a discussion of the whole set of experiments following the last experiment in a section labeled General Discussion or Conclusions. An example of a two-experiment study is presented later in this Appendix.

References This section begins on a new page. You must provide a reference for each of the studies or sources cited in the body of the paper, and you give as references *only* those sources that were cited in the text. (To provide a longer list of sources for related reading would be to create a "bibliography" rather than a set of references.) Each reference should be to the source you actually read. If it was only the abstract of an article, then reference the source of that abstract rather than the original article. Similarly, if you have read about the results of a study in another ("secondary") source, such as a textbook or a review article, then your reference should make clear that your knowledge comes from the secondary source. In a case where that secondary source has *mis*represented the results of the original study it is then clear that the faulty scholarship was not your responsibility. The proper formats for the reference citations in the body of the text and for entries on the reference page are given below for a number of different types of sources.

By convention, citations in psychological writings use the surname of the author, along with the date of the publication, in the body of the text. For example, "As noted by Smith (1991), this finding has not been replicated" or "As recently noted

(Smith, 1991), this finding has not been replicated." At the end of the paper, on a separate page with the heading "References," all works cited in the text are listed, alphabetically by surname of the first (or only) author, as shown below. The general formats for various types of sources are provided below; note that the capitalization, punctuation, and underscoring, are critical. Finally, the references, like every other part of the manuscript, are double spaced, and no "extra" blank lines are inserted between the references or sections of the manuscript.

Examples of References Using the APA Format

1. Research Reports:

a. Printed Journals:

Give author(s), date, title of article, name of journal, volume number, and pages. The name of the journal and the volume number are underscored (continuously). For the title of the article, only the first word, the first word of subtitles, and proper names are capitalized. For the name of the journal, every keyword is capitalized.

> Roediger, H. L., & McDermott, K. B. (1995). Creating false memories: Remembering words not presented in lists. Journal of Experimental Psychology: Learning, Memory, and Cognition, 21, 803–814.

b. On-line Journal:

> Green, C. D. (1998, April). Are connectionist models theories of cognition? [23 paragraphs]. Psycoloquy [On-line serial], 9(04). Available FTP: Hostname: princeton.edu   Directory: pub/harnad/psycoloquy/1998.volume.9   File: psyc.98.9.04.connectionist-explanation.1.green

2. Books:

Give author(s), date, title, edition (if applicable), city, publisher. (Give the state or country only if the city is not widely known.) The name of the book is underscored and only the first word, the first word of subtitles, and proper names are capitalized.

a. One or more authors:

> Benjafield, J. G. (1997). Cognition (2nd ed.). Upper Saddle River, NJ: Prentice Hall.
> Seligman, M., and Darling, R. B. (1997). Ordinary families, special children: A systems approach to childhood disability (2nd ed.). New York: The Guilford Press.

b. No author or editor:

Give title, edition (if applicable), year, city, and publisher. Title is underlined and only the first word, the first word of subtitles, and proper names are capitalized. These sources are listed alphabetically by the first key word in the title. The citations in the text of the manuscript should use the first few words of the title (underlined) in place of an author name in the citation. For example:

Citations in the text:

"Dissociation is defined as a process in which certain mental processes split off from the main body of consciousness (<u>Random House dictionary</u>, 1967). The mental processes that separate from the rest of the normally functioning personality are typically portions of the personality that are causing undue emotional stress (<u>The encyclopedic dictionary</u>, 1986)."

References:

<u>The encyclopedic dictionary of psychology</u> (3rd ed.). (1986). Guilford, CT: The Dushkin Publishing Group, Inc.

<u>The Random House dictionary of the English language.</u> (1967). New York: Random House.

c. Edited book:

Lovelace, E. A. (Ed.). (1990). <u>Aging and cognition.</u> Amsterdam: North-Holland.

d. Chapter in an Edited Book:

Give author(s) of the chapter, date, chapter title, editor(s) (initials then last name), book title, edition (if applicable), page numbers of chapter, city, publisher. (Give the state or country only if the city is not widely known.) For the titles of the chapter and the book, only the first word, first word of a subtitle, and proper names are capitalized. The title of the book is underscored.

Yuill, N. (1997). Children's understanding of traits. In S. Hala (Ed.), <u>The development of social cognition</u> (pp. 273–295). East Sussex, UK: Psychology Press.

3. Unpublished Paper:

Williams, J. D. (1998). <u>Childhood memories: Lost or missing?.</u> Unpublished manuscript.

4. Secondary Source:

If you read *about* Smith's work in Browne, include *only the secondary source* (i.e., Browne) on your reference page. In the body of the text, use the format for a "secondary citation." For example:

Citation in text:

" . . . In recent work by Smith (1996, as cited by Browne, 1998), it has been noted that . . ."

Reference:

Browne, V. K. (1998). <u>Models in contemporary memory research.</u> New York: Allegany Publishers.

5. Abstracts (when you have read an abstract but not the original article):

a. From Printed Abstracts, such as *Psychological Abstracts* or *Child Development Abstracts and Bibliography*:

Rose, A. J., & Asher, S. R. (1999). Children's goals and strategies in response to conflicts within a friendship. <u>Developmental Psychology, 35,</u> 69–79. (From <u>Child Development Abstracts and Bibliography,</u> 1999, <u>73,</u> Abstract No. 557).

b. From an On-line Abstract:

Gathercole, S. G. (1998). The development of memory [On-line]. <u>Journal of Child Psychology and Psychiatry and Allied Disciplines, 39,</u> 3–27. Abstract from: SilverPlatter File: PsycINFO: Accession number 1998-00453-001

c. From a CD-ROM:

Darlington, Y. (1996). Escape as a response to childhood sexual abuse [CD-ROM]. <u>Journal of Child Sexual Abuse, 5,</u> 77–94. Abstract from: PsycLIT/EBSCO: PsycLIT Item: 34-80782

6. World Wide Web Sources:

Pausch, R., Proffitt, D., & Williams, G. (1997). Quantifying immersion in virtual reality. <http://www.cs.virginia.edu/ ~ uigroup/publications/97/conferences/siggraph/immersion> (1998, August 29).

7. E-mail Messages:

E-mail citations should appear in the body of the text as a personal communication. They do not appear on the list of references. For example:

Citation in Text:

> "Such individuals have been found to show lower sensitivity to criticism (G. D. Atlas, personal communication, September 2, 1998)."

Appendix   Most research reports do not include an appendix. Sometimes, however, there is detailed information that the reader might want or need, but which would distract the reader from the flow of ideas if it was included in the body of the text. For example, an appendix may present a new testing instrument or a set of stimulus materials that were designed with specific desired properties. Other researchers are then able to use these materials to replicate or expand upon your study. (If they must develop their own instruments or materials, there may be significant differences that preclude a direct replication, even if you believe you have provided a thorough description of the materials in your method section.) If there is more than one appendix, each is given a letter designation (e.g., Appendix A, Appendix B, etc.), and each begins on a new page in the manuscript.

Author Notes   Presented on a separate page, these notes provide information about: a) the institutional affiliation of each author (which may have changed since the research was conducted and so differ from that which appears on the title page), b) the source(s) of financial support for, or assistance in the conduct of, this research, and c) information about how the reader may obtain a reprint of the article. If portions of this report have appeared elsewhere, for example, as one's master's thesis or as a paper read at a convention, that information belongs here. The following is a partially fictitious example of such notes:

> This research was supported by Allegany Foundation Grant AF-30309 and the Alfred University Honors program. A poster based on these data was presented at the 10th annual convention of the American Psychological Society in Washington, D.C., May 1998. We thank Dr. Jana Atlas for helpful comments on an earlier version of this paper and the Canisteo, New York public school system for their cooperation. Kathryn Guiney is now at the Psychology Department, Syracuse University. Correspondence should be addressed to Nancy E. Furlong, Psychology Division, Saxon Drive, Alfred University, 14802-1205 (e-mail: ffurlong@bigvax.alfred.edu).

Footnotes   The footnote section begins on a new page. Footnotes are used sparingly in research reports, and typically provide further explication of a point that is tangential to the main flow of ideas. The location of footnotes is indicated in the body of the text with a superscripted Arabic number. On the footnotes page, each begins with the corresponding Arabic numeral as an indication of where that footnote belongs in the text. For example:

in the body of the text:

" . . . were assumed to have interval-level properties[2] for purposes of these analyses."

on the footnotes page:

[2]Others have argued that these really are only ordinal-level measures if the numbers of measures are less than 10 per cell, but most agree with our assumption under the present conditions.

Tables   Tables are most commonly employed to summarize a great deal of data in a form that facilitates comprehension and comparison across conditions. Each table begins on a new page of the manuscript; the heading of each table should provide enough information so the table can be comprehended on its own. The variables, and their levels, and the units of measurement for numbers presented in the table must be clear. For example, a table heading might read "Times to complete reading of the passages, to the nearest half minute, for the abstract and the concrete passages shown separately for the third and sixth grade students." The author should refer to the table in the body of the text at the point where it is appropriate for the reader to consult the table, referring to the table by number. For example, "As can be seen in Table 2, there were no appreciable differences in error rates for these four conditions."

The table heading should be underscored in the manuscript. As for the numbers appearing in the table, all cells of the table should present data to the same number of decimal places. Notes regarding the table are presented at the bottom of the table; those pertaining to a specific label or cell of the table are indicated by use of a letter-label superscript in the table. For tables giving the results of statistical tests, such as a correlation matrix, the significance of any values in the table may be indicated by a probability note at the bottom of the table. A common procedure in such cases is to place an asterisk beside any value that is significant at the .05 level, a double asterisk beside those that reach the .01 level, and a triple asterisk for .001. For example, a matrix showing Pearson correlation coefficients for the variables of age, socioeconomic status (SES), and reported number of intrusive thought while doing the task (INTH), might look like this:

	AGE	**SES**[a]	**INTH**
AGE	—	.42**	.64***
SES		—	.29*

NOTE: These analyses exclude all participants who lived in nursing homes.
[a]Based on occupational histories plus current income.
*$p < .05$; **$p < .01$; ***$p < .001$.

Figure Captions   Figures are identified by Arabic numerals: Figure 1, Figure 2, and so on. The captions for all figures in the report are provided on this page of the manuscript. Similar to table headings, figure captions need to mention the variables and measurements in graphs. For example, "Figure 1. Numbers of correct responses for students in the Time-stress and in the Control conditions on each of the four learning trials."

Figures   Each figure is presented on a separate page at the end of the manuscript. In the manuscript, the figure's number should be lightly penciled on the back of each figure. Regardless of type of figure (e.g., line graphs, bar graphs, or pie charts) the central issue is whether the figure can be clearly understood and interpreted. To this end it is important to consider the nature of the legend that identifies conditions and the font size. What will the figure look like when reduced to the size it will appear in the journal, perhaps occupying only one column? Make sure the legend, letters and symbols used are readily discriminated and understood. Are the axes clearly labeled and the units of the scale given? Try making a photocopy at a reduction level that renders the figure the size it is likely to be in the journal and see if all elements remain clear.

Manuscript Headings

Most APA-style articles use two or three levels of headings (see the APA Publication Manual for cases requiring more than three levels). The first level of heading is centered and typed in uppercase and lowercase letters. For example:

Method

If only a second level is needed, then that added level should be a side heading that is flush with the left margin, typed in uppercase and lowercase letters, and underscored. Text begins, indented, on the next line of the manuscript. For example:

Procedure
    The participants were randomly assigned to the
three treatments.

If a third level is also needed, the headings are indented, underscored, and end with a period. Only the first word of these headers is capitalized. Text continues on that same line of the manuscript. For example:

    Baseline measures. Reaction times to the pictures
were measured before any treatment.

Sample Manuscripts

To illustrate the APA-format, we present two sample manuscripts prepared according to this format. The first manuscript (Figure D-3) is an example of a simple one-experiment study intended to illustrate the placement of the headings. The second example (Figures D-4 and D-5) shows the format for a two-experiment study. (The first example is completely fictitious while the second example was derived from an actual article that appeared in *Perceptual and Motor Skills*, volume 77, in 1993. The report was shortened from its original three-experiment design and modified for the purpose of illustrating the APA format.)

FIGURE D.3 A SAMPLE RESEARCH REPORT FOR A SINGLE-EXPERIMENT STUDY

Frustration and Helping   1

Running Head: FRUSTRATING EXPERIENCE AND HELPING

Frustration and Helping Among Seven-Year-old Children

Nancy E. Furlong

Alfred University

Frustration and Helping   2

Abstract

Seven-year-old males and females played a game against an adult confederate. It was arranged so that half of the children of each sex won a desirable prize and the other children saw the adult receive the prize. Ten minutes later, the children saw another adult confederate drop a box of crayons and their willingness to help was recorded. A chi-square analysis indicated a non-significant interaction between Sex and Frustration such that the frustrating experience had the same impact on boys and girls.

Frustration and Helping   3

Frustration and Helping Among
Seven-Year-old Children

A number of studies have suggested that frustration increases aggressiveness (e.g.,
Jones, 1962; Martin & Martin, 1974). It could be argued that failure to help another person is
a form of aggression, which would lead to the prediction that frustration will decrease helping.
Previous research has indicated that girls tend to display more helping behavior than boys (e.g.,
Smith, 1968) which may mean that girls are more vulnerable to frustrating experiences. The
purpose of the present study was to test the hypothesis that frustration has a negative impact
on helping behavior, particularly of girls.

Method

Participants

Thirty girls and 30 boys, ranging in age from 7-1 to 7-11 (mean age = 7-7), participated
in the study. Each child was tested individually in the school library.

Materials

A commericially-available deck of "Old Maid" cards was used in the study. The card
depicting the Old Maid was specially marked so that the adult confederate could identify it
from the back side. Before the game began, the deck was arranged so that the Old Maid card
would be dealt to the child and that it would only take an average of 7 turns to complete the
hand.

Frustration and Helping   4

Procedure

The child was invited to play a game of cards with an adult who was introduced as a
new library aide. Each child was dealt the Old Maid card in the initial deal. For half of the
children, the adult deliberately selected the marked Old Maid card during the 5th or 6th round
of play and conspiculously placed it at the end of their row of cards so that the child would be
unlikely to select it before the end of the game. For the other half of the participants, the adult
confederate deliberately avoided selecting the Old Maid so that the child lost the game.

After the game ended, the researcher presented a prize to the winner. In the No-
Frustration condition, the child was given a new pencil as the prize. In the Frustration
condition, the adult confederate was given a new Barbie (for girls) or a new GI Joe (for boys)
and the confederate then left the room, saying "I'm going to go play with this right now."

After the confederate left the room, the researcher read a story about horses to the
child. Ten minutes after the end of the card game, the child was told it was time to return to
class. As the librarian walked past the child's seat on the way to the door, she dropped a box of
crayons, spilling approximately 30 crayons onto the floor. Children who picked up any of the
crayons were scored as "helpful" while children who did not pick up any crayons were scored
as "unhelpful."

Results

In the No-Frustration condition, 14 girls and 11 boys helped pick up some crayons,
while in the Frustrating condition, 12 girls and 5 boys helped. A 2 (Sex) x 2 (Condition) chi-

Frustration and Helping 5

square analysis indicated that the interaction between Sex and Condition was not significant ($\chi^2 = 0.94$, $p > .05$).

Discussion

The results of the study did not support the hypothesis that a frustrating experience would lead to less helping, particularly among girls. Although it did not reach statistical significance, the pattern of scores was in the opposite direction, such that the difference in helping between the two conditions was larger among boys than girls. These results suggest that girls are more helpful than boys, but they are not more susceptible to frustration. Future research is needed to explore the relationship between frustration and helping behavior.

Frustration and Helping 6

References

Jones, D. (1962). Frustration and aggression in a naturalistic setting. Journal of Social Psychology, 12, 34 - 37.

Martin, A. W., & Martin, F. G. (1974). The frustration - aggression connection: Implications for social policy. New York: Applebee Publishing Group.

Smith, L. M. (1968). Sex differences in social behaviors in the elementary classroom. In R. T. Greene (Ed.), Children's social development (pp. 432 - 446). London: Royal Press.

Frustration and Helping 7

Author Note

This research was partially supported by grants from Alfred University and the National Society for Research in Social Development (M5-S673 SD 42). Requests for reprints should be sent to Dr. Nancy E. Furlong, Psychology Division, Alfred University, Alfred, NY 14802.

FIGURE D.4 SAMPLE MANUSCRIPT ILLUSTRATING THE APA FORMAT FOR A TWO-EXPERIMENT STUDY

The Role of Vision   1

Running head: VISION IN SOUND LOCALIZATION

The Role of Vision in Sound Localization

Eugene A. Lovelace and Donna M. Anderson

Alfred University

FIGURE D.4 CONT.

The Role of Vision   2

Abstract

Two experiments examined the role of vision in locating a brief sound (2 s speech noise) from an unseen source in the horizontal left, front quadrant. The head could be freely moved. The first study found the accuracy of pointing a finger was poorer than for aiming one's eyes at the sound, indicating that visual aiming was a more sensitive dependent measure. In the second study no differences were found in the accuracy of aiming one's eyes at a sound when eyes were open versus closed during sound presentation. The prior finding of Shelton, Rodger, and Searle (1982) of more accurate auditory localization with eyes open than closed was not supported.

FIGURE D.4   CONT.

The Role of Vision in Sound Localization

Does visual stimulation alter the apparent source of a sound? Clearly in the case of visual movement which is synchronized with the sound one often observes the phenomenon of "visual capture" whereby the sound appears to originate from the point in space at which the visible movement occurred (e.g., Bertelson & Radeau, 1981). This occurs in ventriloquism and sounds at the movies.

It was reported by Shelton, Rodger and Searle (1982) that, under normal conditions of free head movement, student participants with visual input made less error in localizing a sound source than did those who had their vision occluded by goggles, even though there was no movement visible at the sound source. Shelton et al. employed a stimulus of a very narrow bandwidth (to increase error rates) and asked participants to report the location of the sound by pressing one of several buttons held out of sight in the lap. The present studies explored the purported benefit of visual input during the localization of a sound source when no visual information was associated with the source.[1] In the present studies, more natural stimuli and responses were employed than those used by Shelton et al. (For a recent review of the effects of various stimulus characteristics on sound localization by humans, see Middlebrooks & Green, 1991).

Experiment 1

In order to maximize the likelihood of detecting any benefits of the addition of vision during auditory localization it is desirable to employ the most sensitive index of localization. The present study compared accuracy of pointing one's finger at the sound location with aiming one's

The Role of Vision   4

eyes at the sound source. When attempting to aim the eyes at a sound source, the person kept

their eyes closed during the sound but tried to point closed eyes toward the spot from which the

sound came. When the sound ceased, the person opened his or her eyes and reported a visual

code at the spot to which the eyes pointed. In this fashion it was deemed possible to see whether

people can more accurately aim their eyes toward the origin of a sound than they can point a

finger at that sound.

The stimulus used here (speech noise) has characteristics that occur more commonly than

Shelton et al.'s very restricted bandwidth stimuli.   The response in Shelton et al.'s study was a

finger press of one of eight switches arranged in an arc and corresponding to the positions of the

speakers. The switches were held in the participant's lap; a black cloth covered the box and the

person's hand. In the present study we tested the relative accuracy of two more naturalistic tasks:

(a) having the person point an index finger at the perceived origin of the sound, and (b) aiming

one's eyes at the sound source.

Method

Participants. Participants were 36 student volunteers from Introductory Psychology

courses at Alfred University (all young adults) who received additional course credit for partici-

pation. All participants reported normal hearing and normal or corrected-to-normal vision.

Apparatus. The study was conducted in a room which was sound-deadened by heavy

cloth over fiberglass insulation on the walls and carpeting on the floor and table top. The sound

was a 2-s burst of speech noise (Grason-Stadler Noise generator, Model 9013). The intensity

was adjusted to approximately 70 db SPL as measured at the position of the person's head.

FIGURE D.4 | CONT.

The Role of Vision   5

When initially seated, the student was asked to face a visual marker (short vertical dowel)

and to consider that to be "straight ahead." A single speaker could be moved between trials to any

one of 19 locations in the front, left quadrant (namely, at 7°, 10°, 14°, 18°, 21°, 29°, 32°, 37°, 41°,

44°, 50°, 53°, 58°, 62°, 65°, 71°, 73°, 78°, and 85° to the left of the dowel) arranged in a horizontal

arc at a distance of about 48 inches from the listener's head, as illustrated in Figure 1. A dark

patterned screening curtain hung in front of the speakers so they were not visible. The ears of the

seated participant were in the plane of the speakers. An elasticized cloth blindfold assured that the

person's eyes remained closed on half the trials (the Point Finger condition described below).

(It should be noted that the speaker's position in the present studies is expressed relative to the

forward-facing position the participant adopts between trials but not relative to the participant's

head since the person was free to move the head during stimulus presentation to orient toward the

sound.)

Background music was played between trials to prevent hearing the speaker being moved

to a new location. Locations along the arc, through which the speaker was moved, were marked

on the face of the screening curtain with codes (single letter + digit, e.g., H5) so locations could

be verbally reported (see Point Eyes condition below). One of these codes appeared at each 1°

interval from -18° (18° to the right of the marker pole) to 97°. The letters and digits were used in

random combinations which were nonsystematic with respect to location.

Procedure. Each student served in both the Point Finger and Point Eyes conditions, the

order being counterbalanced across participants. A participant was free to move the head while

FIGURE D.4 CONT.

The Role of Vision   6

locating the sound source in both conditions. Participants were instructed to turn the head forward, toward the marker post, before each trial.

For the entire block of trials in the Point Finger condition the participant wore a blindfold. A trial began with the experimenter saying "ready"; after about a 1-s delay the sound came on and the participant was instructed to "point your finger directly at the place you believe the sound came from. Hold that point until I can record it." The experimenter said "O.K." when the response was recorded. The person then put down the arm, faced forward again, and waited for the next trial.

The experimenter was behind the screening curtain, remaining at the same center location of the arc on all trials. Her head was above the arc of cloth covering the speakers. When the participant pointed, the experimenter moved to be able to sight along the participant's finger to judge the place at which the participant pointed. A paper tape on the back side of the cloth screen specified the degrees from the vertical marker and allowed recording the response to the nearest degree.

In the Point Eyes condition, the participants did not wear a blindfold, but kept their eyes closed during sound presentation, and turned the head during the sound to point closed eyes at the location from which the sound was judged to be coming. When the sound stopped, they opened their eyes and verbally reported the letter/digit code (visible on the front of the screening curtain) that was closest to the point at which their eyes were aimed.

All participants responded to the sound once at each of the 19 locations in each of the two conditions, order of the locations being randomly determined.

FIGURE D.4   CONT.

The Role of Vision   7

Results

The mean error of each pointing response for the Point Finger condition was 5.51° (SD = 3.02°), a value quite similar to the 6.18° obtained in a prior study in this lab using this same condition.[2] In contrast, in the Point Eyes condition the mean error was 3.04° (SD = 1.41°). The matched samples t ratio for testing the difference of these two means was significant, $t(35) = 4.57$, $p < .001$. Further, when tested separately for each order of the conditions, this difference was significant in each order, $ns = 18$, $ts(17) > 2.9$, $ps < .01$. The means (& SDs) for the two conditions for both orders can be seen in Table 1.

Discussion

Clearly, when one's eyes are closed during the presentation of the sound, one can point one's eyes toward a sound source more accurately than one can point a finger at the sound source. This indicates an apparent advantage of using the Point Eyes procedure to measure auditory localization, since it has a smaller error associated with the response. This is assumed to be due to the highly practiced nature of aiming one's eyes as a well-developed skill, compared to the relatively unpracticed task of pointing to a sound. It is possible, of course, that manual pointing is inherently more variable or less accurate due to limitations of motor control (errors in the writing of, or in the execution of, the motor program, cf. Schmidt, 1982) or due to less kinesthetic sensitivity for muscles involved in pointing the finger versus those involved in aiming the eyes. Such hypotheses cannot be assessed without giving individuals extensive practice on such a manual pointing task.

FIGURE D.4 CONT.

The Role of Vision   8

Experiment 2

In order to assess any direct benefits of visual input <u>during</u> sound localization, a second

experiment was conducted to contrast two conditions using the Point Eyes condition and the

verbal report procedure as described in Experiment 1. In this second experiment, on some trials

participants' eyes were open during presentation of the sound and on others they were closed.

Method

Participants. Fifteen students from the same source as those of Experiment 1

participated.

Apparatus and Procedure. The apparatus and general procedure were the same as those in

Experiment 1. The two conditions run were the Point Eyes condition of Experiment 1 and a simi-

lar condition (Look condition) wherein the participants were instructed to open their eyes as soon

as the sound came on. In the Look condition, then, the person's eyes were open while

engaged in the localization of the sound whereas in the Point Eyes condition the eyes were closed

until the sound ceased. In both conditions the mode of response was verbal report of the

letter/digit code closest to the judged origin of the sound.

Results and Discussion

The magnitudes of the localization errors were very similar whether the eyes were closed

during sound presentation (Point Eyes condition) or open (Look condition). Mean absolute

errors for eyes closed was 3.2° (SD = .9°) and for eyes open 3.4° (SD = 1.2°). This small

difference did not approach statistical significance ($\underline{t}(14) = .56, \underline{p} > .50$). Note that these results

provide a total lack of support for the conclusion of Shelton et al. since even the direction of the

FIGURE D.4   CONT.

difference is contrary to the hypothesized benefit of visual information during localization of a sound source.

General Conclusions

Data from the Shelton et al. (1982) study have been cited as support for the notion that vision can improve auditory localization (e.g., Matlin & Foley, 1992). Findings from the present experiments do not provide support for the hypothesis that the presence of visual input during auditory localization will increase the accuracy of locating a stationary sound source. While the conditions of the present studies did not provide an exact replication of Shelton et al. (and thus their findings may be replicable under some conditions), the stimulus and response characteristics of the present research come closer to those involved during localization of sounds in our natural environment. While there is other evidence for benefit from visual input under some conditions (e.g., Warren, 1970) it can be concluded that the presence of vision will not reliably improve the accuracy of localization of a sound source which provides no visual cues such as motion. We conclude, as did Platt and Warren (1972), that any benefits of vision may derive from the precision of the movement of the eyes to point at the sound source, not from having the eyes open by itself.

FIGURE D.4 CONT.

The Role of Vision   10

References

Bertelson, P., & Radeau, M. (1981). Cross-modal bias and perceptual fusion with auditory-visual spatial discordance. Perception & Psychophysics, 29, 578-584.

Matlin, M. W., & Foley, H. J. (1992). Sensation and perception. Boston: Allyn Bacon.

Middlebrooks, J. C., & Green, D. M. (1991). Sound localization by human listeners. Annual Review of Psychology, 42, 135-159.

Platt, B. B., & Warren, D. H. (1972). Auditory localization: The importance of eye movements and a textured visual environment. Perception & Psychophysics, 12, 245-248.

Schmidt, R. A. (1982). Motor control and learning: A behavioral emphasis. Champaign, IL: Human Kinetics.

Shelton, B. R., Rodger, J. C., & Searle, C. L. (1982). The relationship between vision, head motion and accuracy of free-field auditory localization. Journal of Auditory Research, 22, 1-7.

Warren, D. H. (1970). Intermodality interactions in spatial localization. Cognitive Psychology, 1, 114-133.

FIGURE D.4   CONT.

The Role of Vision   11

Author Notes

This research was partially supported by a Faculty Research Award from Alfred

University. We thank David Thomson for his assistance in the collection of data for Experiment

1. A preliminary report of these data was presented at meetings of the Eastern Psychological

Association, April 1992, Boston. Donna Anderson is now School Psychologist with the Wake

County Public Schools, Raleigh, NC. Correspondence concerning this article should be addressed

to E. A. Lovelace, Psychology Division, Alfred University, Saxon Drive, Alfred, NY, 14802-1232

(e-mail: flovelace@bigvax.alfred.edu).

FIGURE D.4   CONT.

The Role of Vision   12

Footnotes

[1]Since visual influences can introduce interference that would increase the magnitude of error in sound localization (as occurs in visual capture), one might even hypothesize that closing one's eyes might result in improved accuracy of sound localization. (The first author had noted he often closed his eyes when trying to localize faint sounds when no visual information existed, e.g., a mouse gnawing in a wall.)

[2]Analyses of absolute (unsigned) errors are reported here for the two experiments. Similar analyses of constant (signed) errors, also performed on these data, did not reflect, with the following exception, any systematic and interpretable findings (and so are not reported in detail). There was a tendency for the error on speakers in the more lateral positions to be judged as located further to the side than they actually were while those closer to the "straight ahead" dowel were judged closer to that dowel's location than they actually were.

FIGURE D.4   CONT.

The Role of Vision   13

Table 1

Means (& SDs) of Errors in Degrees for Point Finger and Point Eyes Conditions by Order of

Condition

Order	Treatment Condition	
	Point Finger	Point Eyes
First	5.68	3.11
	(3.21)	(1.49)
Second	5.34	2.97
	(2.94)	(1.39)
Overall	5.51	3.04
	(3.02)	(1.41)

FIGURE D.4   CONT.

The Role of Vision   14

Figure Caption

<u>Figure 1</u>. Overhead view of the experimental setting, showing the locations of the speakers

relative to the position of the participants.

FIGURE D.4 CONT.

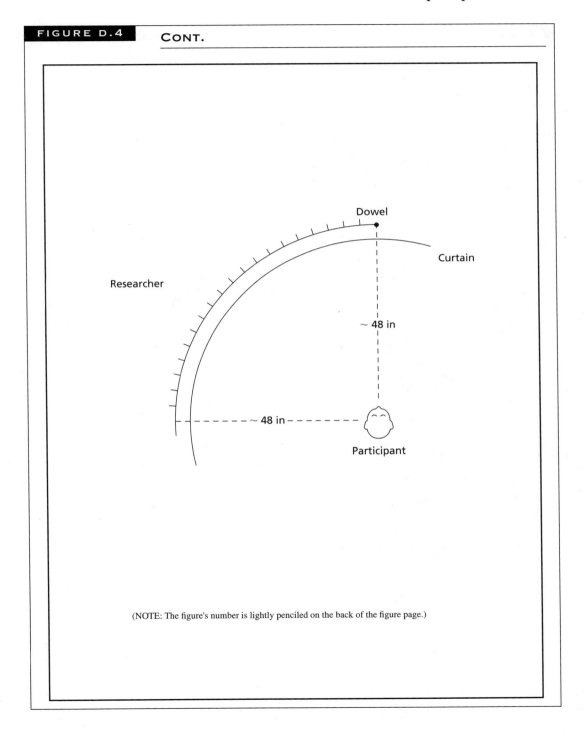

Dowel

Curtain

Researcher

~ 48 in

~ 48 in

Participant

(NOTE: The figure's number is lightly penciled on the back of the figure page.)

FIGURE D.5	THE PUBLISHED MANUSCRIPT (REPRODUCED WITH PERMISSION OF THE PUBLISHER. © PERCEPTUAL AND MOTOR SKILLS 1993.)

Perceptual and Motor Skills, 1993, 77, 843-848.

THE ROLE OF VISION IN SOUND LOCALIZATION

EUGENE A. LOVELACE AND DONNA M. ANDERSON

Alfred University

Two experiments examined the role of vision in locating a brief sound (2 s speech noise) from an unseen source in the horizontal left, front quadrant. The head could be freely moved. The first study found the accuracy of pointing a finger was poorer than for aiming one's eyes at the sound, indicating that visual aiming was a more sensitive dependent measure. In the second study no differences were found in the accuracy of aiming one's eyes at a sound when eyes were open versus closed during sound presentation. The prior finding of Shelton, Rodger, and Searle (1982) of more accurate auditory localization with eyes open than closed was not supported.

Does visual stimulation alter the apparent source of a sound? Clearly in the case of visual movement which is synchronized with the sound one often observes the phenomenon of "visual capture" whereby the sound appears to originate from the point in space at which the visible movement occurred (e.g., Bertelson & Radeau, 1981). This occurs in ventriloquism and sounds at the movies.

It was reported by Shelton, Rodger and Searle (1982) that, under normal conditions of free head movement, student participants with visual input made less error in localizing a sound source than did those who had their vision occluded by goggles, even though there was no movement visible at the sound source. Shelton et al. employed a stimulus of a very narrow bandwidth (to increase error rates) and asked participants to report the location of the sound by pressing one of several buttons held out of sight in the lap. The present studies explored the purported benefit of visual input during the localization of a sound source when no visual information was associated with the source.[1] In the present studies, more natural stimuli and responses were employed than those used by Shelton et al. (For a recent review of the effects of various stimulus characteristics on sound localization by humans, see Middelbrooks & Green, 1991.)

EXPERIMENT 1

In order to maximize the likelihood of detecting any benefits of the addition of vision during auditory localization it is desirable to employ the most sensitive index

This research was partially supported by a Faculty Research Award from Alfred University. We thank David Thomson for his assistance in the collection of data for Experiment 1. A preliminary report of these data was presented at meetings of the Eastern Psychological Association, April 1992, Boston. Donna Anderson is now School Psychologist with the Wake County Public Schools, Raleigh, NC. Correspondence concerning this article should be addressed to E. A. Lovelace, Psychology Division, Alfred University, Saxon Drive, Alfred, NY, 14802-1232 (e-mail: flovelace@bigvax.alfred.edu).

[1] Since visual influences can introduce interference that would increase the magnitude of error in sound localization (as occurs in visual capture), one might even hypothesize that closing one's eyes might result in improved accuracy of sound localization. (The first author had noted he often closed his eyes when trying to localize faint sounds when no visual information existed, e.g., a mouse gnawing in a wall.)

FIGURE D.5   **CONT.**

844   E. A. LOVELACE & D. M. ANDERSON

of localization. The present study compared accuracy of pointing one's finger at the sound location with aiming one's eyes at the sound source. When attempting to aim the eyes at a sound source, the person kept their eyes closed during the sound but tried to point closed eyes toward the spot from which the sound came. When the sound ceased, the person opened his or her eyes and reported a visual code at the spot to which the eyes pointed. In this fashion it was deemed possible to see whether people can more accurately aim their eyes toward the origin of a sound than they can point a finger at that sound.

The stimulus used here (speech noise) has characteristics that occur more commonly than Shelton et al.'s very restricted bandwidth stimuli. The response in Shelton et al.'s study was a finger press of one of eight switches arranged in an arc and corresponding to the positions of the speakers. The switches were held in the participant's lap; a black cloth covered the box and the person's hand. In the present study we tested the relative accuracy of two more naturalistic tasks: (a) having the person point an index finger at the perceived origin of the sound, and (b) aiming one's eyes at the sound source.

Method

    Participants.   Participants were 36 student volunteers from Introductory Psychology courses at Alfred University (all young adults) who received additional course credit for participation. All participants reported normal hearing and normal or corrected-to-normal vision.

    Apparatus.   The study was conducted in a room which was sound-deadened by heavy cloth over fiberglass insulation on the walls and carpeting on the floor and table top. The sound was a 2-s burst of speech noise (Grason-Stadler Noise generator, Model 9013). The intensity was adjusted to approximately 70 db SPL as measured at the position of the person's head.

When initially seated, the student was asked to face a visual marker (short vertical dowel) and to consider that to be "straight ahead." A single speaker could be moved between trials to any one of 19 locations in the front, left quadrant (namely, at 7°, 10°, 14°, 18°, 21°, 29°, 32°, 37°, 41°, 44°, 50°, 53°, 58°, 62°, 65°, 71°, 73°, 78°, and 85° to the left of the dowel) arranged in a horizontal arc at a distance of about 48 inches from the listener's head, as illustrated in Figure 1. A dark patterned screening curtain hung in front of the speakers so they were not visible. The ears of the seated participant were in the plane of the speakers. An elasticized cloth blind-fold assured that the person's eyes remained closed on half the trials (the Point Finger condition described below). (It should be noted that the speaker's position in the present studies is expressed relative to the forward-facing position the participant adopts between trials but not relative to the participant's head since the person was free to move the head during stimulus presentation to orient toward the sound.)

Background music was played between trials to prevent hearing the speaker being moved to a new location. Locations along the arc, through which the speaker

FIGURE D.5   CONT.

VISION IN SOUND LOCALIZATION   845

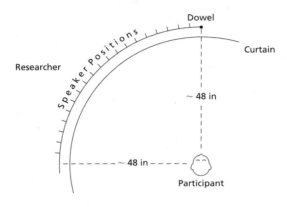

Figure 1. Overhead view of the experimental setting, showing the locations of the speakers relative to the position of the participant.

was moved, were marked on the face of the screening curtain with codes (single letter + digit, e.g., H5) so locations could be verbally reported (see Point Eyes condition below). One of these codes appeared at each 1° interval from -18° (18° to the right of the marker pole) to 97°. The letters and digits were used in random combinations which were nonsystematic with respect to location.

    Procedure. Each student served in both the Point Finger and Point Eyes conditions, the order being counterbalanced across participants. A participant was free to move the head while locating the sound source in both conditions. Participants were instructed to turn the head forward, toward the marker post, before each trial.

    For the entire block of trials in the Point Finger condition the participant wore a blindfold.   A trial began with the experimenter saying "ready"; after about a 1-s delay the sound came on and the participant was instructed to "point your finger directly at the place you believe the sound came from. Hold that point until I can record it." The experimenter said "O.K." when the response was recorded. The person then put down the arm, faced forward again, and waited for the next trial.

    The experimenter was behind the screening curtain, remaining at the same center location of the arc on all trials. Her head was above the arc of cloth covering

FIGURE D.5 CONT.

846   E. A. LOVELACE & D. M. ANDERSON

the speakers. When the participant pointed, the experimenter moved to be able to sight along the participant's finger to judge the place at which the participant pointed. A paper tape on the back side of the cloth screen specified the degrees from the vertical marker and allowed recording the response to the nearest degree.

     In the Point Eyes condition, the participants did not wear a blindfold, but kept their eyes closed during sound presentation, and turned the head during the sound to point closed eyes at the location from which the sound was judged to be coming. When the sound stopped, they opened their eyes and verbally reported the letter/digit code (visible on the front of the screening curtain) that was closest to the point at which their eyes were aimed.

     All participants responded to the sound once at each of the 19 locations in each of the two conditions, order of the locations being randomly determined.

Results

     The mean error of each pointing response for the Point Finger condition was $5.51°$ (SD = $3.02°$), a value quite similar to the $6.18°$ obtained in a prior study in this lab using this same condition.[2] In contrast, in the Point Eyes condition the mean error was $3.04°$ (SD = $1.41°$). The matched samples t ratio for testing the difference of these two means was significant, $t(35) = 4.57$, $p < .001$. Further, when tested separately for each order of the conditions, this difference was significant in each order, $ns = 18$, $ts(17) > 2.9$, $ps < .01$. The means (& SDs) for the two conditions for both orders can be seen in Table 1.

TABLE 1

MEANS (& SD) OF ERRORS IN DEGREES FOR POINT FINGER AND POINT EYES CONDITIONS BY ORDER OF CONDITION

Order	Treatment Condition	
	Point Finger	Point Eyes
First	5.68	3.11
	(3.21)	(1.49)
Second	5.34	2.97
	(2.94)	(1.39)
Overall	5.51	3.04
	(3.02)	(1.41)

[2]Analyses of absolute (unsigned) errors are reported here for the two experiments. Similar analyses of constant (signed) errors, also performed on these data, did not reflect, with the following exception, any systematic and interpretable findings (and so are not reported in detail). There was a tendency for the error on speakers in the more lateral positions to be judged as located further to the side than they actually were while those closer to the "straight ahead" dowel were judged closer to that dowel's location than they actually were.

VISION IN SOUND LOCALIZATION   847

Discussion

    Clearly, when one's eyes are closed during the presentation of the sound, one can point one's eyes toward a sound source more accurately than one can point a finger at the sound source. This indicates an apparent advantage of using the Point Eyes procedure to measure auditory localization, since it has a smaller error associated with the response. This is assumed to be due to the highly practiced nature of aiming one's eyes as a well-developed skill, compared to the relatively unpracticed task of pointing to a sound. It is possible, of course, that manual pointing is inherently more variable or less accurate due to limitations of motor control (errors in the writing of, or in the execution of, the motor program, cf. Schmidt, 1982) or due to less kinesthetic sensitivity for muscles involved in pointing the finger versus those involved in aiming the eyes. Such hypotheses cannot be assessed without giving individuals extensive practice on such a manual pointing task.

EXPERIMENT 2

    In order to assess any direct benefits of visual input *during* sound localization, a second experiment was conducted to contrast two conditions using the Point Eyes condition and the verbal report procedure as described in Experiment 1. In this second experiment, on some trials participants' eyes were open during presentation of the sound and on others they were closed.

Method

    Participants. Fifteen students from the same source as those of Experiment 1 participated.

    Apparatus and Procedure. The apparatus and general procedure were the same as those in Experiment 1. The two conditions run were the Point Eyes condition of Experiment 1 and a similar condition (Look condition) wherein the participants were instructed to open their eyes as soon as the sound came on. In the Look condition, then, the person's eyes were open while engaged in the localization of the sound whereas in the Point Eyes condition the eyes were closed until the sound ceased. In both conditions the mode of response was verbal report of the letter/digit code closest to the judged origin of the sound.

Results and Discussion

    The magnitudes of the localization errors were very similar whether the eyes were closed during sound presentation (Point Eyes condition) or open (Look condition). Mean absolute errors for eyes closed was 3.2° (SD = .9°) and for eyes open 3.4° (SD = 1.2°). This small difference did not approach statistical significance ($t(14) = .56$, $p > .50$). Note that these results provide a total lack of support for the conclusion of Shelton et al. since even the direction of the difference is contrary to the hypothesized benefit of visual information during localization of a sound source.

FIGURE D.5   CONT.

848   E. A. LOVELACE & D. M. ANDERSON

General Conclusions

Data from the Shelton et al. (1982) study have been cited as support for the notion that vision can improve auditory localization (e.g., Matlin & Foley, 1992). Findings from the present experiments do not provide support for the hypothesis that the presence of visual input during auditory localization will increase the accuracy of locating a stationary sound source. While the conditions of the present studies did not provide an exact replication of Shelton et al. (and thus their findings may be replicable under some conditions), the stimulus and response characteristics of the present research come closer to those involved during localization of sounds in our natural environment. While there is other evidence for benefit from visual input under some conditions (e.g., Warren, 1970) it can be concluded that the presence of vision will not reliably improve the accuracy of localization of a sound source which provides no visual cues such as motion. We conclude, as did Platt and Warren (1972), that any benefits of vision may derive from the precision of the movement of the eyes to point at the sound source, not from having the eyes open by itself.

REFERENCES

BERTELSON, P., & RADEAU, M. (1981). Cross-modal bias and perceptual fusion with auditory-visual spatial discordance. *Perception & Psychophysics, 29,* 578-584.

MATLIN, M. W., & FOLEY, H. J. (1992). *Sensation and perception.* Boston: Allyn Bacon.

MIDDLEBROOKS, J. C., & GREEN, D. M. (1991). Sound localization by human listeners. *Annual Review of Psychology,* **42,** 135-159.

PLATT, B. B., & WARREN, D. H. (1972). Auditory localization: The importance of eye movements and a textured visual environment. *Perception & Psychophysics,* **12,** 245-248.

SCHMIDT, R. A. (1982). *Motor control and learning: A behavioral emphasis.* Champaign, IL: Human Kinetics.

SHELTON, B. R., RODER, J. C., & SEARLE, C. L. (1982). The relationship between vision, head motion and accuracy of free-field auditory localization. *Journal of Auditory Research, 22,* 1-7.

WARREN, D. H. (1970). Intermodality interactions in spatial localization. *Cognitive Psychology,* **1,** 114-133.

ANSWERS FOR THE
ODD-NUMBERED EXERCISES
■ ■ ■ ■ ■ ■

Chapter 1

1. There are many possible operational definitions that a researcher could use. For example:

   1st Example: Helping = the number of envelopes the teenager stuffs for a local charity preparing for a fund drive.

   2nd Example: Helping = whether or not the teenager stops to help an elderly person who has dropped a bag of groceries.

   3rd Example: Helping = the amount of money the teenager donates to the local volunteer fire department.

   For a study to compare how often teens help their peers versus adults, these definitions would not be suitable because they do not include both peers and adults as recipients of the helping behavior, so another definition needs to be generated. For example:

   4th Example: Helping = whether or not the teenager holds a door open for someone (either an adult or another teenager) approaching the door carrying a large box.

   5th Example: Helping = whether or not the teenager would be willing to give a dollar to a person (either an adult or another teenager) who doesn't have enough money to pay for a simple meal.

3. Yes, because empirical observation is being used. The variables are clearly defined (such as "responsive" = responding within 2 minutes, etc.) and systematic observation is used.

5. Operational Definitions used are:

   Variable #1: Parental Responsiveness to the crying newborn = how long the baby cries before the parent picks him/her up. (Those parents who consistently pick the baby up within 2 minutes are called "responsive" but if the babies always fall asleep before being picked up, the parents are called "unresponsive".)

   Variable #2: Being Spoiled is generally defined as "crying a lot at 12 months of age," and it is actually measured in two separate ways:

   Operational Definition #1 = the frequency of crying (i.e., the number of crying episodes during a 4-hour period at 12 months of age)

Operational Definition #2 = duration of crying (i.e., the number of minutes/seconds of crying during the 4-hour period at 12 months of age)

7. Yes, Dr. Smith's hypothesis is **testable** because each of the variables in the hypothesis (age, height and muscle coordination) can be operationally defined and measured. The hypothesis is also **falsifiable** because the study could show that muscle coordination is not related to a child's height (so children of all heights have the same level of coordination) *or* the study could indicate that tall children have better coordination than children of average height. In either case, we would conclude that Dr. Smith's hypothesis was false.

9. The most **reliable** measurements in this study would probably be the measurements of height and accuracy of dart throws. If you measured a child's height once and then a second time or if you measured the distance between a dart and the bull's eye twice (without removing the dart), the test-retest reliability would be very high.

   The most **unreliable** or inconsistent measurements are likely to be Dr. Smith's judgments about how well the child plays catch. If, later, Dr. Smith were to see a videotape of some of the children's performance playing catch, he may not judge them the same way (so the test-retest reliability may be very low).

   The ratings of the children's smoothness and accuracy in tracing a drawing could have adequate interrater reliability if the raters are thoroughly trained in advance to recognize tracings that should be rated as a 1 or a 3 or a 6, etc. Without this training, the ratings from the different graduate students could be very inconsistent (and unreliable).

Chapter 2

1. One of many possible answers to the exercise:

   In order to find out if crowding in grade school classrooms causes decreased academic performance and increased aggression among children, we could conduct a study comparing crowded classrooms (e.g., 45 students or more with one teacher) to uncrowded classrooms (e.g., no more than 25 students with one teacher). The ethical issue most likely to arise is risk (or freedom from harm), because the children in the crowded classroom are potentially at risk for low grades and aggressive attacks by their peers.

3. Most of the participants in Milgram's study showed great distress during and after the study, so a modern Institutional Review Board would probably be very concerned with the risk or freedom from (psychological) harm principle.

5. One of many possible answers to the exercise:

   Research on what makes some people convincing liars could potentially be used to actually train people to lie convincingly in order to persuade the public to do things (such as buy bridges and swampland). That is, the "product" of the research may be more harmful than beneficial to society. The decision to continue with such research should be based on a cost-benefit analysis weighing the potential dangers against the potential benefits (which might include new techniques for detecting lies.)

7.   The major ethical issue at stake here is the principle of presenting data in non-misleading ways. (While politicians may not be bound by the ethical responsibility to present data in appropriate ways, researchers are!)

    The incumbent president would certainly emphasize the fact that the unemployment rate dropped by eight-tenths of a percent (.8) during his/her first term in office, and may graph the data like this:

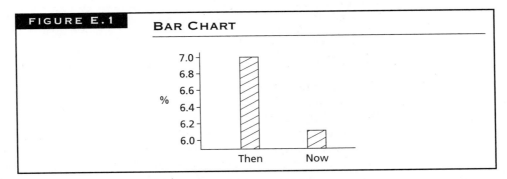

[Note that the Y-axis does not begin at zero, which exaggerates the difference between the bars.]

    In contrast, the challenger would most likely emphasize the fact that the unemployment lines contain more than a half million more people (560,000) than four years before. The graph would probably look like this:

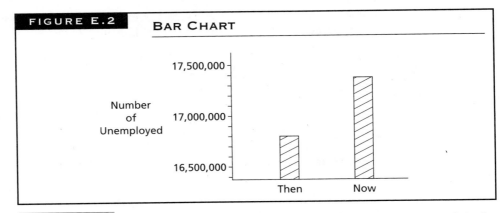

[Note that the graph does not include any reference to the fact that the population increased substantially in size during the four-year period, so an increase in unemployment is to be expected, and a comparison of the "raw" numbers is misleading.]

Chapter 3

1. Type of back pain is qualitative and discrete. Arthritis and ruptured discs are qualitatively different medical conditions. Type of exercise would seem to be qualitative and discrete since the two exercise procedures sound categorically distinct. However, if the new exercise machine involves the same flexibility exercises as the traditional regimen, the difference between them may be quantitative and continuous. Amount of pain is a quantitative variable and the 20-point scale could be considered discrete, since none of the participants are allowed to select a score between 3 and 4 or between 15 and 16.

3. The relationship between rainfall in Liechtenstein and the price of tea in China would most likely be a spurious relationship caused by a third variable: global weather patterns. The weather systems that drop a lot of rain in Liechtenstein may have also resulted in a bumper crop of tea in China, and the over-supply of tea would lower the price.

5. a. Variables of interest = (1) Willingness to try crack cocaine and (2) parental income
    b. Possible values for the variables of interest:
    Let's assume the 4-point rating scale goes from 0 to 3. Chris may circle the number 3 on the "willing to try crack" rating scale while Pat circles the number 1. So Chris' score (or value) is 3 and Pat's is 1. (The only possible values on this variable, then, are 0, 1, 2, and 3.)
    If Chris' parents reported an income of $12,900, and Pat's parents reported an income of $31,275, then Chris' score on the parental income variable is $12,900 and Pat's is $31,275. (There is an almost unlimited number of possible values on the parental income variable.)
    c. The scenario specifies the following constants: **Grade Level and Age Group** (they are all juniors in high school and they are all teenagers), and **Income Year** (parental income reported the "previous April" means that the scores are based on the same year. For example, if the study was conducted in September 1996, then the annual income that is recorded would be from the 1995 tax return.)

7. a. Variables of interest = (1) predicted number of items that will be recalled and (2) actual number of items recalled
    b. Possible values for the variables of interest:
    On a trial where 7 items are in the original array, Chris may predict that she will recall all **7** items while Pat may predict that he will recall **5**.
    Chris may actually recall only **2** items while Pat actually recalls **3**.
    c. The scenario specifies one constant: **Age** (i.e., the subjects are all 4 years old)

9. a. Variables of interest = (1) whether the children watch *Mr. Rogers* frequently or not at all, and (2) helpfulness toward others (as ranked by the teacher)

b.   Possible *values* for the variables of interest:

Pat may get a score of **1** because he watches *Mr. Rogers* frequently, while Chris may get a score of **0** because he never watches the program. (The only possible scores are 0 and 1.)

Pat's teacher may give her a helpfulness rank score of **6** (i.e., she is the 6th most helpful child in the class) while Chris gets a rank of **14**.

c.   The scenario specifies one constant: **Age range** (all are of preschool age)

Chapter 4

1.   The operational definition for the effectiveness of counseling used in the scenario was the client's rating (on the 4-point scale) to the question "How helpful has seeing Dr. Smith been?" An alternative might be to administer a test of depression (like the Beck Depression Inventory) both before and after the six weeks of counseling and measuring how much improvement the client shows. (Thus, the operational definition would be based on how much less depressed the clients are after 6 weeks of counseling using this standardized test.) Another alternative would be to ask family members to rate how much better the client has been since starting counseling. And yet a third alternative would be to ask the client to keep a log indicating the amount of time they spend sleeping each day.

To test the **Predictive (or Criterion) Validity** of any (or all) of these operational definitions we need to start with a clear idea of just what we mean by "effective counseling." One reasonable definition would seem to be that effective counseling leads to a reduction in symptoms (in this case, less depression). Thus, we would want to have a list of symptoms of depression and we would want to be able to measure how many symptoms are present. This would serve as our criterion measure, and we would use our measure of effectiveness (like the one in the scenario) to try to predict the number of symptoms present after the 6 weeks of counseling.

For example, if a client gave a rating of 3, indicating that she felt Dr. Smith was extremely helpful, we would hope to find that she shows fewer symptoms of depression than a client who gave Dr. Smith a rating of 1, etc.

3.   1st var: Child's popularity (number of classmates who think they are one of the nicest)

Level (or scale of measurement) = ratio

Reliability could be tested using test-retest by having the children "vote" again a few weeks later

2nd var: Teacher's rating of the child's popularity (on an 8-point scale)

Level (or scale of measurement) = ordinal

Reliability could be done with test-retest (where the teachers rate each child again a second time) or possibly with interrater reliability by having another teacher who knows this class of children well rate each child, too.

5. 1st var: Teacher's effectiveness ratings

Level (or scale of measurement) = ordinal

Reliability could be tested using test-retest by having the student's evaluate the teacher again a few weeks later or possibly using interrater reliability by having another class evaluate the teacher.

2nd var: Teaching experience

Level (or Scale of Measurement) = Ratio

Reliability should not be an issue since the information will be in the teachers' personnel records (i.e., totally objective).

7. 1st var: Sex of the child

Level (or scale of measurement) = nominal

Reliability should not be an issue since the information will be in the child's school files.

2nd var: Whether or not child shows signs of hyperactivity

Level (or scale of measurement) = nominal

Reliability depends on how hyperactivity is assessed. (If trained observers watch the children and record symptoms, interrater reliability would be appropriate in order to determine who "shows signs" and who does not.)

9. 1st var: Number of times infant initiates an exchange

Level (or scale of measurement) = ratio

Reliability could be tested using interrater reliability by having two or more trained observers watch the videotapes and count the number of positive interactions initiated by the infants

2nd var: Degree of Stranger Anxiety (on 6-point scale)

Level (or scale of measurement) = ordinal

Reliability could be done with interrater reliability by having two or more trained observers watch the infants while the stranger tries to pick them up and rate their anxiety.

Chapter 5

1. Frequency Polygon for data from Table 5-2 is presented in Figure E-3.

3. Descriptive statistics for the sample of Chemistry exam scores:

a. $\overline{X} = \dfrac{330}{10} = 33.0$

b. the Median falls between scores of 30 and 40: Mdn = 35

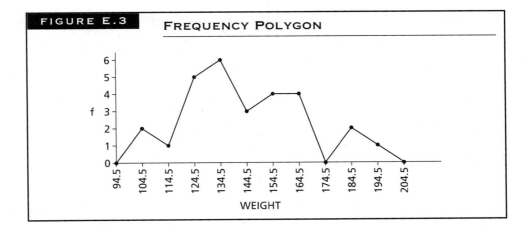

FIGURE E.3   **FREQUENCY POLYGON**

c. Mode = 40

d. Standard Deviation:

$$s = \sqrt{\frac{12500 - \dfrac{330^2}{10}}{10 - 1}}$$

$s = 13.37$ [Note: the Variance is equal to 178.89]

e. the Median Absolute Deviation lies between deviation scores of 5 and 15: MAD = 10

f. Range = 50 − 10

  = 40

g. Number of Categories (or different values of X) = 5

h. Variation Ratio = .70 (or 70%)

5. If John's Chemistry score ($X_{chemistry}$) is 30, his z-score is:

$$z_{chemistry} = \frac{30 - 33}{13.375} = \frac{-3}{13.375} = -0.224$$

If John's Calculus grade ($X_{calculus}$) is 12, his z-score is:

$$z_{calculus} = \frac{12 - 11.5}{3.44} = \frac{0.5}{3.44} = +0.145$$

Therefore, John's "class standing" is higher in Calculus than in Chemistry because he scored slightly above average in Calculus but slightly below average in Chemistry.

7. Regular Diet Group:

$$\overline{X} = \frac{139}{12} = 11.583 \qquad\qquad s = \sqrt{\frac{1633 - \frac{139^2}{12}}{12 - 1}} = 1.44$$

Special Diet Group:

$$\overline{X} = \frac{99}{12} = 8.25 \qquad\qquad s = \sqrt{\frac{833 - \frac{99^2}{12}}{12 - 1}} = 1.22$$

Yes, it appears that the special diet had a positive effect on learning since the mean number of errors for the special diet group (8.25) is quite a bit smaller than the mean number of errors for the regular diet group (11.583), while the variability within the groups is quite similar.

9.

$$p = \frac{\text{\# of rats in entire study making 12 or more errors}}{\text{Total \# of rats in the study}} = \frac{7}{24}$$

$$= 0.2917 \text{ (or 29.17\%)}$$

11. Probability of selecting a freshman:

$$p = \frac{\text{\# of freshmen}}{\text{total \# in class}} = \frac{20 \text{ female} + 5 \text{ male}}{60} = \frac{25}{60} = 0.4167 \text{ (41.67\%)}$$

13. If sex and class status are independent of each other, the probability of selecting a male freshman would be equal to the joint probability of selecting a male and selecting a freshman. That is, if the variables are independent, the probability obtained when we compute the proportion of the class which is made up of freshmen males (i.e., the answer to problem # 12; p = .0833 or 8.33%) should equal the product of the separate probabilities: $p_{\text{Male}} \times p_{\text{Freshman}}$

$$p_{\text{Male}} = \frac{\text{\# of males}}{\text{total \# in class}} = \frac{15}{60} = \qquad p_{\text{Freshman}} = \frac{\text{\# of freshmen}}{\text{total \# in class}}$$

$$= 0.4167 \qquad\qquad = \frac{25}{60} = 0.25$$

therefore, joint probability is:

$$p_{\text{male freshman}} = 0.4167 \times 0.25 = .1042 \text{ (10.42\%)}$$

This joint probability (of 10.42%) is not equal to the probability computed in problem #12 (8.33%), which indicates that the variables are not independent of each other in this class. (The class seems to draw fewer freshmen males than would be expected if the variables were independent.)

15. The area below a score of 92 (with $z = +1.0$) is .84134 (84.134%). This is the probability of randomly selecting a score that is less than 92.

17. The probability that Jill will be in time to get ice cream is 9.175% (since she has only 22 minutes to get there, and the z-score for 22 minutes is -1.33).

19. No, because a score of 85 is not in the top 3% of a normal distribution with a mean of 78 and a standard deviation of 4. (The top 3% has a cut-off point of $X = 85.52$ or a z-score of $+1.88$.)

Chapter 6

1. A **random sample** is one where every member of the population of interest had an equal chance of being selected for the sample. A **representative sample** has the same characteristics (i.e., average, variability, and relative proportions) as the population. **Random samples** tend to be **representative,** especially as the sample size increases.

3. The null hypothesis states that, in the population, there is no relationship between the variables. The research (or alternate) hypothesis is just the opposite, stating that there is a systematic relationship between the variables in the population.

5. Beta (β) is the probability of making a Type II error. Specifically, it is the proportion of random samples that could be drawn from the real population which would result in a Type II error. Power is the ability of the test to avoid Type II errors by correctly rejecting the null hypothesis when it is false. Thus, power and β are in opposition to each other: the higher β, the less power. Anything we do to decrease β, the more we increase our chances of successfully detecting a systematic effect.

7. Type I errors occur when we reject the null hypothesis by mistake and Type II errors occur when we fail to reject the null hypothesis by mistake. The probability of a Type I error is equal to the significance level adopted for the study (i.e., the value of α), and the probability of a Type II error is equal to β, the value of which is unknown.

9. The null hypothesis would say that, in the population, there is no difference (in test performance) among the four different crowding conditions. Any observed difference would be due solely to random sampling error (or chance fluctuations). In notational terms: $H_0 : \mu_1 = \mu_2 = \mu_3 = \mu_4$

   The research hypothesis (H_1) would say that, in the population, test performance under the four different crowding conditions are systematically different. In notational terms: $H_1 : \mu_1 \neq \mu_2 \neq \mu_3 \neq \mu_4$

11. In the following diagrams the null hypothesis predicts that, in the population, the difference between the experimental groups will be 0.00 and that the difference we observed between our two research samples was equal to 8.00. (The solid line represents the sampling distribution and the dashed line represents the real population.)

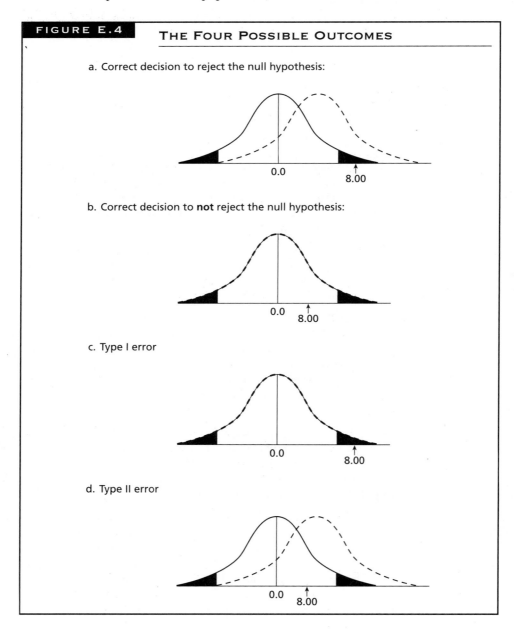

FIGURE E.4   THE FOUR POSSIBLE OUTCOMES

a. Correct decision to reject the null hypothesis:

b. Correct decision to **not** reject the null hypothesis:

c. Type I error

d. Type II error

13. We would reject the null hypothesis (because $88,700 is less than $90,200), and conclude that the cocaine-using engineers earned significantly less than the national average for engineers. There is a 5% chance that we have made a Type I error (since alpha was set at .05).

Chapter 7

1. IV = Public speaking training (taken class vs. not) = a subject variable

   DV = Persuasiveness ratings

   DCVs = (none listed)

   Research method = quasi-experimental

3. IV_1 = Sex of child (male vs. female) = a subject variable

   IV_2 = Mother's occupational status (works outside home vs. does not) = a subject variable

   DV = Number of "sex-inappropriate" occupations named

   DCVs = Age of child

   Research method = quasi-experimental (Both IVs are subject variables)

5. X = Number of absences

   Y = Number of correct answers

   Research method = correlational

7. IV = Level of crowding (alone vs. 1 vs. 10 vs. 30) = a non-subject variable where every participant was tested under every level

   DV = Number of errors on exam

   DCV = all exams were based on SATs and all given in the same room

   Research method = experimental

9. X = Popularity of course

   Y = Number of As given by teachers

   Research method = correlational

11. IV_1 = Sex of child (boys vs. girls) = a subject variable

    IV_2 = Type of model (selfish vs. happily generous vs. neutral/generous) = a non-subject variable where each child saw all three types of models

    DV = Number of M&Ms donated

    DCVs = (none listed)

    Research method = quasi-experimental (If type of model was the only IV, it would be an experiment, but because sex is included, the study is a quasi-experiment)

13. IV_1 = Drug treatment (Clofibrate vs. Placebo) = random assignment to levels of a non-subject variable

IV_2 = Adherence to prescription (85% adherence vs. under 85%) = a subject variable (people either adhered or not on their own)

DV = number of incidents of chest pain experienced over 5 years

DCVs = all participants were middle-aged, all had heart trouble, and all were prescribed the same number of tablets per day.

Research method = quasi-experimental (It started as an experiment, but because at the end it included a comparison of adherers vs. non-adherers, which is a subject variable, it "turned into" a quasi-experiment)

15. IV_1 = Sex (male vs. female) = a subject variable

IV_2 = Age (young vs. elderly) = a subject variable

IV_3 = Film treatment (before vs. after) = a non-subject variable where all participants gave their opinion both before and after seeing the film

DV = Opinion about the law (using the rating scale)

DCVs = (none listed)

Research method = quasi-experimental (because two of the IVs are subject variables)

Chapter 8

1. Appropriate coefficient = Spearman r

$$r_s = 1 - \frac{6\,(16)}{10\,(10^2 - 1)} = 0.903$$

$r_{crit(.05)}$ = .648, and because .903 > .684, we REJECT H_0

There is a significant positive correlation between aggressiveness ratings and prosocial behavior. Generally, children with higher aggressiveness ratings engage in more prosocial behaviors.

3. Appropriate coefficient = Phi (Both X and Y are dichotomous categories)

$$\phi = \frac{(21 \times 25) - (64 \times 30)}{\sqrt{85 \times 55 \times 89 \times 51}} = -.3028331 \approx .30$$

(The negative sign is meaningless, so it is dropped)

$$\chi^2 = 140\,(.3028331^2) = 12.839$$

Degrees of freedom for ϕ = 1, so with α = .05, $\chi^2_{crit(.05)}$ (1) = 3.841

12.839 > 3.841, so REJECT H_0

There is a significant relationship between performance in freshman composition and graduating with a BA degree. Students who pass freshman composition are more likely to graduate than students who fail the course.

5. Appropriate coefficient = Pearson

$$r = \frac{370 - \dfrac{(23)(80)}{6}}{\sqrt{129 - \dfrac{(23)^2}{6}}\ \sqrt{1246 - \dfrac{(80)^2}{6}}} = .7401$$

$r_{crit(.05)} = .8114$, and because $.7401 < .8114$, we cannot reject the H_0

Children's ability to throw darts accurately is not systematically related to their ability to maintain their balance while standing on one foot.

7. Using the r-to-z Table: for $r_1 = +.53$, $z^*_1 = .5901$ and for $r_2 = +.68$, $z^*_2 = .8291$

$$CR = \frac{(.5901 - .8291) - 0}{\sqrt{\dfrac{1}{100 - 3} + \dfrac{1}{100 - 3}}} = -1.66$$

For a Nondirectional (two-tailed) test, $z_{critical} = \pm 1.96$.

Rule: If $-CR$ is less than $-z_{critical}$ or if $+CR$ is greater than $+z_{critical}$, reject the null hypothesis.

-1.66 is not less than -1.96, so we cannot reject the null hypothesis. We would conclude that the correlations are not significantly different.

9. Spearman r (willingness is ordinal and income is ratio)

11. Pearson r (Number of items predicted and number actually recalled are both ratio)

13. Spearman r (Number of times subject is labelest "Nicest" is ratio and Teacher's rating is ordinal)

15. Phi Coefficient (Sex is a true dichotomy and "Winning" is dichotomized from a continuous variable)

Chapter 9

1. The data is presented in Figure E-5. Regression analysis would not be appropriate because the relationship between reaction time and decibel levels is **curvilinear**, not linear.

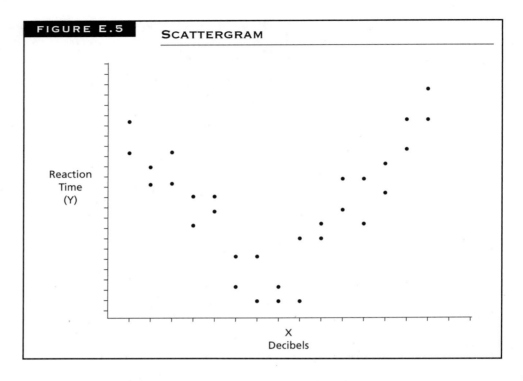

FIGURE E.5   SCATTERGRAM

Reaction Time (Y)

X
Decibels

3. a. From the scatterplot in Figure E-6, we can see the relationship is positive, and it appears to be moderate in magnitude.

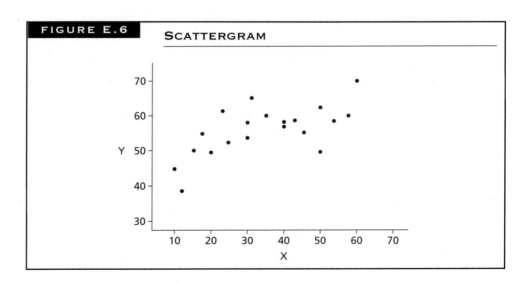

FIGURE E.6   SCATTERGRAM

Y

X

b. The regression analysis requires that we compute the means and standard deviations for X and Y and the correlation coefficient. Following the formulas in Chapters 5 and 8, we find these to be:

$$\overline{X} = \frac{694}{20}, \quad s_x = \sqrt{\frac{28610 - \frac{694^2}{20}}{20 - 1}} \quad \overline{Y} = \frac{1121}{20} \quad s_Y = \sqrt{\frac{63709 - \frac{1121^2}{20}}{20 - 1}}$$

$$= 34.7 \qquad = 15.44 \qquad\qquad = 56.05 \qquad = 6.79$$

Pearson correlation:

$$r = \frac{40182 - \frac{(694)(1121)}{20}}{\sqrt{28610 - \frac{(694)^2}{20}} \; \sqrt{63709 - \frac{(1121)^2}{20}}}$$

$$= +.644$$

Therefore, the Regression Equation is:

$$Y' = .644\left(\frac{6.79}{15.44}\right)X + \left[56.05 - .644\left(\frac{6.79}{15.44}\right)34.7\right]$$

$$\mathbf{Y' = .283\ X + 46.223}$$

The Y' for a woman with X = 24: The Y' for a woman with X = 46

$$Y' = .283\,(24) + 46.223 \qquad\qquad Y' = .283\,(46) + 46.223$$

$$\mathbf{= 53.015} \qquad\qquad\qquad\qquad \mathbf{= 59.241}$$

c. The Y' for a woman with $z_x = +1.3$:

$$z_{y'} = r\,z_x = .644\,(1.3) = 0.8372$$

$$\text{So: } Y' = 6.79\,(0.8372) + 56.05 = \mathbf{61.73}$$

5. The diagram in (c) most closely represents the correlation between Y and X_1 since it appears that about 72% of the Y-circle overlaps with the X-circle. ($r = 0.85$, so the coefficient of determination = $r^2 = .7225$)

7. A Venn diagram of the correlation matrix for the multiple regression (showing multicollinearity) is presented in Figure E-7.

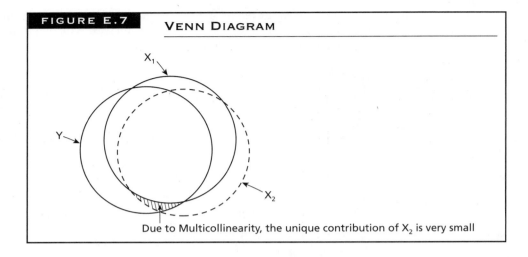

FIGURE E.7   VENN DIAGRAM

Due to Multicollinearity, the unique contribution of X_2 is very small

9. a. $r = -.807$ $Y' = -1.89\,X + 24.981$ $s_{est} = 2.67$

   b. For X = 0, $Y' = 25.0$ For X = 8, $Y' = 9.9$

   For X = 1, $z = -1.45$ therefore, $z_{Y'} = 1.17$ and $Y' = 23.1$

   For X = 6, $z = 1.14$ therefore, $z_{Y'} = -.92$ and $Y' = 13.6$

Chapter 10

1. Identifying designs of problems from Chapter 7:

   7-1.   one-way between-subjects design (IV = public speaking class)

   7-2.   3 (Age) × 2 (Type of memory task) mixed design

   7-3.   2 (Sex) × 2 (Mother's occupational status) between-subjects design

   7-4.   2 (Treatment) × 2 (Type of back pain) between-subjects design

   7-6.   one-way between-subjects design (IV = exposure to *Mr. Rogers*)

   7-7.   one-way within-subjects design (IV = level of crowding)

   7-8.   one-way between-subjects design (IV = commonness of name)

   7-11. 2 (sex) × 3 (type of model) mixed design

   7-12. 2 (sex) × 3 (year in college) mixed design

   7-13. 2 (drug treatment) × 2 (adherence to prescription) between-subjects design

7-14.   2 (responsibility for relative) × 2 (attitude toward euthanasia) between-subjects design [NOTE: Because both variables are categorical, they are each considered IVs; the dependent variable will simply be the frequencies for each of the four categories created by factorially combining the two variables.]

7-15.   2 (sex) × 2 (age) × 2 (before versus after the film) mixed design

3.   Research design = 3 (attractiveness) × 2 (marital status) between-subjects design

5.   Dr. Smith is predicting a **steady increase** in prejudice from age 5 to adulthood. Therefore, he would need to have **a minimum** of three (3) age levels. If he only included 5-year-olds and adults, he would not be able to determine whether or not prejudice actually increases steadily over time.

7.   Potential confound = **maturation:** over a two-month period, 5-year-old children may undergo significant neurological and motoric maturation, regardless of any training.

9.   Potential confound = **instrumentation:** the three graduate students may not have used identical operational definitions when scoring the TAT protocols (and the researcher may have not trained them all the same way because his/her own theories and expectations may have undergone subtle changes over the years).

11.   Potential confound = **regression toward the mean:** the 20 women selected for the study were the ones who had scored the lowest on the sensitivity measure; due to measurement error, we expect many of these low sensitivity scores would have regressed toward the mean (indicating that women were not really that insensitive and that their infants would have developed secure attachments even without the training).

13.   Research method = **quasi-experimental** (because sex and age are subject variables)
Research design = **2 (sex) × 3 (age) × 2 (competence) × 2 (peer presence) between-subjects design.** [We were told in the subjects section that the subjects were "randomly assigned to experimenters and experimental conditions" and the procedures did not say that the children were put through the procedures a second time under new treatment conditions, and therefore, we can infer this was a between-subjects design.]

15.   One of many possible answers for this exercise:
Below is some *hypothetical* data that would reflect an interaction between age and competence training in which training is effective only for the youngest children. That is, more young children who received competence training were helpful compared to their age-mates who did not receive training, but for older children, competence training did not increase help-

fulness: Data in cells represents the percentage of subjects who helped the victim.

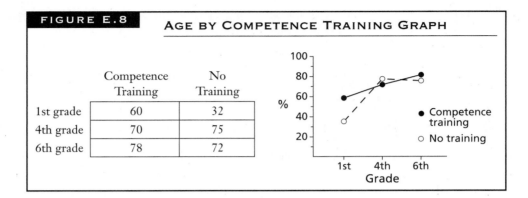

FIGURE E.8

AGE BY COMPETENCE TRAINING GRAPH

	Competence Training	No Training
1st grade	60	32
4th grade	70	75
6th grade	78	72

For Your Information: Peterson's actual results included main effects of age, competence, and peer presence, and a significant three-way interaction among these same variables. This interaction is diagrammed below. There was no effect of sex and no interactions of sex with the other IVs.

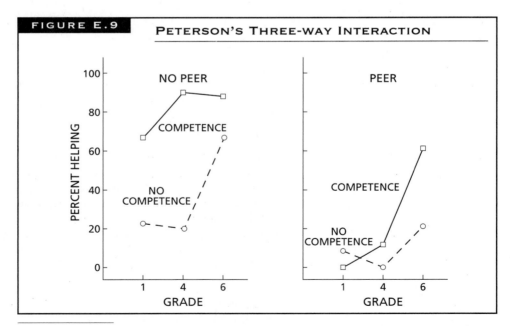

FIGURE E.9

PETERSON'S THREE-WAY INTERACTION

Figure 1. Percentage of first, fourth, and sixth graders helping an unseen victim under conditions of high and low donor competence and peer bystander presence and absence.
Peterson, L. (1983). Role of donor competence, donor age, and peer pressure on helping in an emergency. Developmental Psychology, 19, 873–880. Copyright © 1983 by the American Psychological Association. Reprinted with permission.

Chapter 11

1a. μ and σ are known, so **a z-test is appropriate**

$$H_0: \mu_{\text{Belmore}} = \mu_{\text{national}} \qquad H_1: \mu_{\text{Belmore}} < \mu_{\text{national}}$$

Directional (one-tailed) test: $\alpha = .05$, so $z_{\text{critical}} = -1.64$,

$$z_{\text{obtained}} = \frac{38000 - 40000}{\dfrac{3600}{\sqrt{9}}} = -1.67$$

-1.67 is greater than -1.64, therefore we reject the null hypothesis and conclude that the faculty at Belmore College earn significantly less than the national average.

b. The value of z_{obtained} is the same as above, but z_{critical} is changed to -1.96 because we are now performing a **two-tailed** test with alpha set at .05.
-1.67 is less than -1.96, therefore we cannot reject the null hypothesis and therefore, we conclude that the average salary of faculty at Belmore College is not significantly different than the national average (the \$2,000 difference can be attributed to sampling error).

c. The conclusions from the two z-tests do not agree with each other because the critical value of z for a two-tailed test is larger (or "farther out in the tail") than the critical value of z for a one-tailed test, and the mean for our sample of Belmore faculty happens to fall between the one-tailed critical value and the two-tailed critical value.

3. **Independent Samples *t*-test** $H_0: \mu_1 = \mu_2$ $H_1: \mu_1 \neq \mu_2$ $\alpha = .05$

Summary of Data:	Married Men	Bachelors
Sample Size (n)	$n_1 = 9$	$n_2 = 9$
Mean ($\overline{X}$)	$\overline{X}_1 = 77.333333$	$\overline{X}_2 = 72.888889$
Standard Deviation (s)	$s_1 = 5.5452683$	$s_2 = 5.0110988$

$$s^2_{\text{pooled}} = \frac{(9 - 1)(5.5452683)^2 + (9 - 1)(5.0110988)^2}{(9 - 1) + (9 - 1)} = 27.930556$$

$$s_{\overline{X} - \overline{X}} = \sqrt{\frac{27.930556}{9} + \frac{27.930556}{9}} = 2.491343$$

$$t_{\text{obtained}} = \frac{(77.333333 - 72.888889) - 0.0}{2.491343} = 1.784$$

df $= (9 - 1) + (9 - 1) = 16$; therefore, with $\alpha = .05$ for a two-tailed test,

$$t_{\text{critical}} = \pm 2.120$$

1.784 is less than 2.120, therefore we **fail** to reject the null, and we conclude that married men do not live longer than bachelors (the 4-year difference can be attributed to sampling error).

5. **Related samples *t*-test** $H_0: \mu_{Alcohol} = \mu_{No\ Alcohol}$ $H_1: \mu_{Alcohol} \neq \mu_{No\ Alcohol}$
    $\alpha = .05$

$$\Sigma D = -29 \qquad \Sigma D^2 = 191 \qquad \overline{D} = -2.9$$

$$s_D = \sqrt{\frac{191 - \dfrac{(-29)^2}{10}}{10 - 1}} = 3.4464152$$

$$s_{\overline{D}} = \frac{3.4464152}{\sqrt{10}} = 1.0898522$$

$$t_{obtained} = \frac{-2.9}{1.0898522} = -2.661$$

df $= 10 - 1 = 9$; therefore, with $\alpha = .05$ for a two-tailed test, $t_{critical} = \pm 2.262$

-2.661 is greater than -2.262, therefore we reject the null, and conclude that the percentage of sperm cells with defects is significantly higher after men drink alcohol than when they do not.

7. **One-sample *t*-test** $H_0: \mu_{Diet\ Cola} = \mu_{National}$ $H_1: \mu_{Diet\ Cola} > \mu_{National}$
    $\alpha = .05$

$$t_{obtained} = \frac{3100 - 2800}{\dfrac{600}{\sqrt{25}}} = 2.500$$

df $= 25 - 1 = 24$; therefore, with $\alpha = .05$ for a one-tailed test, $t_{critical} = 1.711$

2.50 is greater than 1.711, therefore we reject the null, and we conclude that the sample of diet cola drinkers consume significantly more calories than the national average.

Chapter 12

1. One-way between-subjects ANOVA

$$SS_{Total} = (1633 + 833) - \frac{(139 + 99)^2}{24} = 105.8333$$

$$SS_{BG} = \frac{139^2 + 99^2}{12} - \frac{(139 + 99)^2}{24} = 66.666633$$

$$SS_{WG} = 105.8333 - 66.666633 = 39.16667$$

Summary Table

Source	SS	df	MS	F	
BG	66.666633	1	66.666633	37.45**	[for $\alpha = .01$, $F_{crit}(1,22) = 7.95$]
WG	39.16667	22	1.7803031		
Total	105.8333	23			

$$**p < .01$$

Post Hoc comparisons are **not** required, therefore we would conclude that there is a significant difference in performance between the two groups. Rats raised on the supplemented diet made significantly fewer errors than rats raised on the regular Rat Chow.

3. A 2×3 (two-way) between subjects ANOVA

$$SS_{Total} = (34 + 90 + 234 + 27 + 91 + 199) -$$

$$\frac{(12 + 20 + 34 + 11 + 21 + 31)^2}{30} = 120.3$$

$$SS_{BG} = \frac{12^2 + 20^2 + 34^2 + 11^2 + 21^2 + 31^2}{5} - \frac{(129)^2}{30} = 89.9$$

$$SS_{WG} = 120.3 - 89.9 = 30.4$$

$$SS_{Sex} = \frac{66^2 + 63^2}{15} - \frac{(129)^2}{30} = 0.3$$

$$SS_{Strategy} = \frac{23^2 + 41^2 + 65^2}{10} - \frac{(129)^2}{30} = 88.8$$

$$SS_{Sex \times Strategy} = 89.9 - 0.3 - 88.8 = 0.8$$

Summary Table

Source	SS	df	MS	F	
Sex	0.30	1	0.3	0.24	[for $\alpha = .05$, $F_{crit}(1,24) = 4.26$]
Strategy	88.8	2	44.4	35.05**	[for $\alpha .01$, $F_{crit}(2,24) = 5.61$]
Sex × Strategy	0.8	2	0.4	0.32	[for $\alpha .05$, $F_{crit}(2,24) = 3.40$]
WG	30.4	24	1.2666666		
Total	120.3	29			

$$**p < .01$$

Dunn Multiple Comparisons for the main effect of strategy

$$c = 3 \text{ and } df_{error} = 24, \text{ so } \mathbf{d_{.05} = 2.58} \text{ and } \mathbf{d_{.01} = 3.26}$$

And therefore:

$$CR_{.05} = 2.58\sqrt{2\,\frac{1.2666666}{10}} = 1.3$$

And:

$$CR_{.01} = 3.26\sqrt{2\,\frac{1.2666666}{10}} = 1.6$$

Comparison	$|$Difference$|$
I vs. II	$2.3 - 4.1 = \mathbf{1.8^{**}}$
I vs. III	$2.3 - 6.5 = \mathbf{4.2^{**}}$
II vs. III	$4.1 - 6.5 = \mathbf{2.4^{**}}$

From this study, we would conclude that there was no overall difference between teenage males and females in the number of times they refused a cigarette, and there was no interaction, indicating that males and females reacted to the different strategies in similar ways. The main effect of Strategy indicated that emphasizing the negative effects of smoking on appearance and attractiveness led to significantly more refusals of cigarettes than either of the other strategies, and emphasizing the financial costs led to significantly more refusals of cigarettes than did emphasizing the health issues.

5. A one-way RM-ANOVA

$$SS_{Total} = (897 + 339 + 1284) - \frac{(83 + 47 + 100)^2}{24}$$

$$= 315.8333$$

$$SS_{Treatment} = \frac{83^2 + 47^2 + 100^2}{8} - \frac{(83 + 47 + 100)^2}{24}$$

$$= 183.0833$$

$$SS_{Subjects} = \frac{6784}{3} - \frac{(230)^2}{24} = 57.1666$$

$$SS_{Treatment \times Subjects} = 315.8333 - 183.0833 - 57.1666 = 75.5834$$

Summary Table

Source	SS	df	MS	F	
Treatment (T)	183.0833	2	91.54165	16.96**	[for $\alpha = .01$, $F_{crit}\,(2,14) = 6.51$]
Subjects (Ss)	57.1666	7	—		
T × Ss	75.5834	14	5.3988142		
Total	315.8333	23			

$$**p < .01$$

Dunn multiple comparisons:

$$c = 3 \text{ and } df_{error} = 14, \text{ so } d_{.05} = 2.78 \text{ and } d_{.01} = 3.65$$

And therefore

$$CR_{.05} = 2.78\sqrt{2 \cdot \frac{5.3988142}{8}} = 3.23$$

And:

$$CR_{.01} = 3.65\sqrt{2 \cdot \frac{5.3988142}{8}} = 4.24$$

Comparison	$|$Difference$|$
S-D vs. C-F	$|10.375 - 5.875| = 4.5^{**}$
S-D vs. N	$|10.375 - 12.5| = 2.125$ n.s.
C-F vs. N	$|5.875 - 12.5| = 6.625^{**}$

From the results of this study, we conclude that when clients received client-focused comments from the counselor, they were significantly less depressed (i.e., they made fewer depressed statements) than when they received self-disclosing or neutral comments. There was no difference between the self-disclosing and neutral comments conditions in the number of depressed statements made by the clients.

7. a. $N = 24$ (the total number of scores)
    b. $k = 8$ (the number of groups in the 2×4 design)
    c. $n = 3$ (the number of scores in each group)
    d. $df_{WG} = N - k = 24 - 8 = 16$
       $df_A = k_A - 1 = 2 - 1 = 1$
       $df_{A \times B} = df_A \times df_B = 1 \times 3 = 3$
    e. three Fs will be computed: main effect of A; main effect of B; A × B interaction
    f. If all Fs are significant, post hocs would be required for the main effect of B (since it compares 4 levels) and the A × B interaction (which compares 8 groups). (No post hocs would be necessary for the main effect of A since it only has 2 levels.)

9.

Source	Sum of Squares	df	Mean Squares	F	
Treatment	60	3	20	6.15^{**}	$[F_{crit(.01)} (3, 27) = 4.64]$
Subjects	70	9	—		
T × S	80	27	3.2510287		
Total	210	39			

$^{**}p < .01$

a. One-way WS or matched-pairs design

b. $k = 4$

c. If it ws a *WS design*, **10 subjects** participated ($df_{Subjects} = 9$, so $n = 10$)

   If it was a *Matching design*, there were 40 subjects ($df_{Total} = 39$, so $N = 40$)

d. If it was a *WS design*, each subject was tested 4 times (once for each treatment)

   If it was a *Matching design*, each subject was assigned to one treatment and tested **once**

e. Yes, post hocs are required for $F_{Treatment}$

11.

Source	SS	df	MS	F	
Outcome	50	2	25.00	10.38**	$[F_{crit(.01)} (2,108) = 4.98]$
Motive	90	3	30.00	12.46**	$[F_{crit(.01)} (3,108) = 4.13]$
O × M	100	6	16.6667	6.92**	$[F_{crit(.01)} (6,108) = 3.12]$
WG	260	108	2.4074074		
Total	500	119			

$$**p < .01$$

a. 3 × 4 BS design

b. $k = 12$

c. $N = 120$

d. Once, since this was a BS design

e. Yes, separate post hocs are required for **each** of the three Fs

13.

Source	SS	df	MS	F	
Grade	75	3	25	4.17*	$[F_{crit(.05)} (3,12) = 3.49]$
Subjects	20	4	—		
G × S	72	12	6		
Total	167	19			

$$*p < .05$$

a. One-way WS or matched-pairs design

b. $k = 4$

c. If it was a *WS design*, 5 subjects participated ($df_{Subjects} = 4$, so $n = 5$)
   If it was a *Matching design*, there were 20 subjects ($df_{Total} = 19$, so $N = 20$)

   d. If it was a *WS design*, each subject was tested 4 times (once for each treatment)

   If it was a *Matching design*, each subject was assigned to one treatment and tested once

   e. Yes, post hocs are required for the F_{Grade}

15.

Source	SS	df	MS	F	
Type of Task	100	4	25	6.25**	$[F_{crit(.01)}\ (4, 76) = 3.65]$
Emotional State	80	2	40	8.00**	$[F_{crit(.01)}\ (2, 38) = 5.39]$
Task × Emotion	48	8	6	1.00 n.s.	$[F_{crit(.05)}\ (8, 152) = 2.02]$
Subjects	380	19	—		
Task × Ss	304	76	4		
Emotion × Ss	190	38	5		
T × E × Ss	912	152	6		
Total	2014	299			

$$**p < .01$$

   a. 5 × 3 WS or matched-pairs design

   b. k = 15

   c. If it was a *WS design*, 20 subjects participated ($df_{Subjects} = 19$, so n = 20) If it was a *Matching design*, there were 300 subjects ($df_{Total} = 299$, so N = 300)

   d. If it was a *WS design*, each subject was tested 15 times (once for each treatment)

   If it was a *Matching design*, each subject was assigned to one treatment and tested once

   e. Yes, post hocs are required for both of the main effects but not for the interaction.

Chapter 13

1. Oneway χ^2

$$\chi^2 = \frac{(24 - 37.3)^2 + (32 - 37.3)^2 + (56 - 37.3)^2}{37.3} = 14.871$$

df = 3 − 1 = 2, so with alpha set at .01, $\chi^2_{critical}$ (df = 2) = 9.210

Because 14.871 is greater than 9.210, we reject the null and conclude that the rate of participation is significantly related to the incentives offered.

Offering incentives of $15 increases participation compared to $5. (This is the largest of the differences in participation; post hoc tests are necessary in order to determine whether a $10 incentive leads to significantly more participation than $5 or significantly less participation than $15.)

3. Cochran's Q

$$Q = \frac{(2 - 1)[2(9^2 + 2^2) - 11^2]}{2(11) - 15} = 7.00$$

[NOTE: To test the null, compare Q to $\chi^2_{critical}$: If $Q \geq \chi^2_{critical}$, reject the null]

df = 2 − 1 = 1, so with α = .01, $\chi^2_{critical}$ (df = 1) = 6.635

Because 7.00 is greater than 6.635, we reject the null and conclude that participants accurately identified the mugger significantly more often if they were sober than if they were drunk when they witnessed the mugging.

5. Kruskal-Wallis H

$$H = \left[\frac{12}{36(36 + 1)} \left(\frac{278.5^2 + 165^2 + 222.5^2}{12} \right) \right] - 3\,(36 + 1)$$
$$= 4.836$$

[NOTE: To test the null, compare H to $\chi^2_{critical}$: If $H \geq \chi^2_{critical}$, reject the null]

df = 3 − 1 = 2, so with α = .05, $\chi^2_{critical}$ (df = 2) = 5.991

Because 4.836 is less than 5.991, we cannot reject the null hypothesis. Therefore, we would conclude there is no significant difference in pain ratings for the three treatment groups. The new exercise machine was not significantly better at reducing pain than the other treatments over a four-week period.

7. Wilcoxon Sum Ranks Test (Wilcoxon-Mann-Whitney T)
   [NOTE: The Kruskal-Wallis H could also be conducted on these data.]

$$\Sigma R_{n1} = 56.5 \text{ and } \Sigma R_{n2} = 114.5$$

$$T' = 8(8 + 10 + 1) - 56.5 = 95.5$$

$$T_{obtained} = \text{the } smaller \text{ value: } \Sigma R_{n1} = 56.5 \text{ or } T' = 95.5$$

$$\text{Therefore, } T_{obtained} = 56.5$$

$$\text{with } \alpha = .05 \text{ for a nondirectional test, } T_{critical} = 53$$

Decision rule: If $T_{obtained}$ is **less than or equal** to $T_{critical}$, reject the null hypothesis

Because 56.5 is not less than 53, we cannot reject the null hypothesis. Therefore, we will conclude there is no significant difference between children who frequently watch *Mr. Rogers* and those who never watch the program in their helpfulness as rated by preschool teachers.
[NOTE: Kruskal-Wallis H = 3.002, which is not significant.]

9. Wilcoxon's Signed Ranks Test (Wilcoxon W)

ΣR for positive ranks = 8.0 and ΣR for negative ranks = 57.5

W = the smaller ΣR, therefore, $W_{Obtained} = 8$

with $\alpha = .05$, $W_{critical}$ (n = 11) = 10

Decision rule: If $W_{Obtained}$ is ***less than or equal to*** $W_{critical}$, reject the null.
Because 8 is less than 10, we reject the null and conclude that ratings of the children's responsiveness during interpersonal interactions were significantly higher on the last day of the program than on the 4th day.
[Note: The results of a single-group pretest-posttest design such as this cannot be interpreted as evidence of causality because of the possibility of time-related confounds.]

11. Twoway χ^2

$$\chi^2 = \frac{(26 - 22)^2}{22} + \frac{(14 - 18)^2}{18} + \frac{(18 - 22)^2}{22} + \frac{(22 - 18)^2}{18} = 3.232$$

df = $(2 - 1)(2 - 1) = 1$, so with alpha set at .05, $\chi^2_{critical}$ (df = 1) = 3.841

Because 3.232 is less than 3.841, we cannot reject the null hypothesis, and we will conclude there is no significant interaction between family history of alcoholism and attitudes toward the proposed legislation.

Chapter 14

1. Data provided: N = 100 and 19%, so p = .19

$$E_{max} = \pm 1.96 \sqrt{\frac{.19 (1 - .19)}{100}} = \pm .07689 \text{ or } \pm 7.7\%$$

95% CI: 19% $\pm$ 7.7% We estimate that between 11.3% and 26.7% of high school sophomores are using marijuana.

3. Data provided: N = 50 and r = .21

for r = .21, $z^* = .2132$ and for a 99% CI, $\alpha = .01$, so $z_{critical} = \pm 2.58$

$$CI_z = .2132 \pm 2.58 \sqrt{\frac{1}{50 - 3}} = .2132 \pm .3763306$$

Therefore, lower $CI_z = .1631306$, so lower $r = .16$

and upper $CI_z = .5895306$, so upper $r = .53$

We can be 99% confident that the population correlation between IQ and creativity lies within the interval of .16 to .53.

5. Data given: $\overline{X}_{masters} = \$8.65 \qquad s_{masters} = 2.03 \qquad n_{masters} = 18$

$\overline{X}_{bachelors} = \$7.80 \qquad s_{bachelors} = 1.98 \qquad n_{bachelors} = 24$

a.

CI for Masters:	CI for Bachelors:
$s_E = \dfrac{2.03}{\sqrt{18}} = 0.4784755$	$s_E = \dfrac{1.98}{\sqrt{24}} = 0.4041658$
for 95% CI ($\alpha = .05$):	for 95% CI ($\alpha = .05$):
$t_{critical}$ (df = 17) = 2.110	$t_{critical}$ (df = 23) = 2.069
$E_{max} = 2.110\,(.4784755) = 1.01$	$E_{max} = 2.069\,(.4041658) = 0.84$
Therefore, 95% CI = $\$8.65 \pm 1.01$	Therefore, 95% CI = $\$7.80 \pm 0.84$
We can be 95% confident that the average hourly wage for counselors with Masters degrees lies within the interval from \$7.64 to \$9.66.	We can be 95% confident that the average hourly wage for counselors with Bachelors degrees lies within the interval from \$6.96 to \$8.64.

b. Minimum difference in hourly wage

df = 40, and for a 95% CI (with $\alpha = .05$): $t_{critical}$ (40) = 2.021

$$s^2_{pooled} = \frac{(18-1)\,2.03^2 + (24-1)\,1.98^2}{(18-1)+(24-1)} = 4.0056125$$

$$s_{\overline{X}-\overline{X}} = \sqrt{\frac{4.0056125}{18} + \frac{4.0056125}{24}} = 0.6240468$$

$E_{max} = 2.021\,(.6240468) = 1.26$

Therefore, the 95% CI = $(8.65 - 7.80) \pm 1.26 = 0.85 \pm 1.26$

The CI is from -0.41 to 2.11. Since a difference score of zero lies within this interval, we can be 95% confident that the minimum difference in hourly wage between counselors with masters and bachelors degrees is zero, so the wages for the two groups may not be different.

7. The average recognition score is higher than the average recall score for all three age groups, and for the young and middle-aged adults, the 95% confidence intervals show no overlap, supporting the conclusion that recognition memory is significantly better than recall at these age levels. However, the overlap of the 95% confidence intervals for the elderly participants, indicates

there is a reasonable possibility that there is no difference between the two forms of memory for this age group.

Chapter 15

1. a. Event sampling: There were a total of 8 episodes during the 6-minute observation period, thus averaging 1.3 episodes per minute.
    b. Partial interval recording: The behavior was observed during 27 (or 75%) of the 10-second intervals.
    c. Whole interval recording: The behavior was continuously present for 12 (or 33.3%) of the 10-second intervals.
    d. Time sampling: The behavior was observed at the start of 19 (or 52.8%) of the 10-second intervals.
    e. Duration: The behavior was performed for a total of 197 seconds during the 6-minute period. That is, the behavior was occurring 54.7% of the time.

    These measures do not seem to "agree" since whole interval recording suggests the behavior occurs only 33% of the time while partial interval recording suggests it occurs 75% of the time. Time sampling and duration both suggest the behavior occurs just over half the time. Thus, the specific measurement procedure adopted can have a large effect on the apparent results, and it is necessary to know exactly what each procedure actually records.

3. Multiple baseline designs demonstrate replication of the treatment effect if the target behaviors all show improvement when the treatment is implemented. The changing criterion design demonstrates replication of the treatment effect if performance shows "sudden" (systematic) changes each time there is an increase in the criterion level.

5. Based on visual inspection of the graph, it appears that, while the conflict resolution training seems to have had an effect on the number of daily conflicts, the addition of the anger management program during the first phase C did not lead to dramatic improvement. During the second phase C, however, conflicts were substantially reduced from previous phases (showing no overlap), suggesting the combination treatment is effective. However, the second baseline (phase A) was characterized by continued ***improvement*** in performance, rather than a return to pre-treatment levels of conflict. This raises the possibility that other things were happening to reduce the conflicts (such as coworkers learning to avoid confrontations with the participants).

7. This graph is from a **multiple baseline design.** Visual inspection of the graph clearly suggests that the social skills training had a systematic impact on the three target behaviors. Number of appropriate requests and percent of eye contact both showed no overlap between baseline and treatment phases. Loudness of speech showed greater variability and 33% overlap, but there is a change in mean from baseline ($\overline{X} = 2.5$) to treatment phase ($\overline{X} = 6.0$). You should also note that the percent of eye contact shows an increasing trend line during baseline, which may suggest that eye contact is

not completely independent of the other target behaviors. That is, as other behaviors showed improvement, eye contact did as well, although when the treatment was directly targeted at eye contact, there was a dramatic increase, indicating that the treatment had functional control over eye contact.

Chapter 16

1. The goal of triangulation in qualitative research is to increase the ***external validity*** of the findings of the study by establishing convergence of evidence. Triangulation involves the use of *mutiple methods*—usually at least three—within the same study (such as direct observations, interviews, and transcription). In contrast, quantitative research relies on the process of *replication* (including both "strict" and "variant" replications) in order to establish the convergence of evidence. Multiple methods, usually across *different* studies, are used to establish the external validity of the findings of quantitative studies.

3. The qualitative methods described in Chapter 16 may be particularly well-suited for exploring new questions about behaviors within complex settings, where the immediate goal is to provide ***descriptions*** of the circumstances under which behaviors occur or fail to occur. (Of course, accurate descriptions of behaviors can lead to accurate predictions of future behaviors as well.) The quantitative methods emphasized earlier in the text are suited for exploring detailed hypotheses about the relationship between specific conditions and behaviors. (The experimental method, for instance, addresses the specific question: "Does X cause Y?") For example, qualitative methods may be useful if a researcher wants to ask the general question: "How has ready access to the World Wide Web changed the daily lives of college students and faculty members?" but quantitative research methods may be better if the question is "Do college students who spend more than two hours per day surfing the net receive lower grades in their courses?"

5. The first step in this exercise is to decide how to define "risk-taking" behavior. There are many different kinds of risk-taking behaviors, each necessitating the use of different archival records. For example, if we decided to study the risk-taking behaviors that result in injury or property damage, some appropriate archival materials may include: police records of complaints, reported crimes, and accident reports; school records; court reports (or transcripts); and hospital records. Alternatively, if we decided to study health-related risk-taking, such as unsafe sexual activity, we could examine records from planned parenthood and abortion clinics, records on pregnancy rates, and the prevalence of sexually-transmitted diseases, and so forth.

7. One of many possible answers to the exercise:
   The following is a sample of interview questions that might be relevant. (The primary question would be followed up, if necessary, with the parenthetical questions.)
   Script: "The goal of my study is to find out which disciplinary techniques work best for children of different ages, so I'm going to ask you some

questions about how you have disciplined your children and how well it seemed to work, OK?"

  a. How many children do you have? (How many boys and how many girls?)

  b. How old are your children now?

  c. Let's start with your oldest child. Tell me about the first time you remember punishing him/her? (What had he/she done and how did you punish him/her?)

  d. Did the punishment work? (How could you tell?)

  e. Now tell me about the most recent incident where you punished your oldest child. (When did it happen, what had he/she done, and how did you punish him/her?)

  f. Did it work?

  g. Have you changed the way you punish your oldest child over the past 5 years? (In what ways?)

  h. Why have you changed the way you discipline your oldest child?

  i. Do you think your new punishment techniques would have worked when the child was younger? (Why or why not?)

  j. Suppose your oldest and youngest children both stole some money from your desk. Would you punish them the same way? (Why or why not?)

Appendix C

1. Region of rejection starts at \$37,768.70; Predicted salary for women (H_1) $\mu = \$38,400$

   For $N = 10$, $z_{critical} = -.55$. Region *beyond* $z = .29115$, therefore power = 29.12%

3. To achieve power at the 80% criterion, the value of $\overline{X}_{critical}$ (from the sampling distribution) must have a z-score equal to $\pm.85$ in the real population (so 30% of the scores lie between it and the predicted mean). To find the minimum sample size, it is necessary to calculate the power for different values of N, until the criterion is reached.

   We started by letting $N = 25$, and found the power equaled 60.26%. Then we let $N = 36$, and found the power equaled 76.12%. Next we let $N = 49$, and found the power equaled 87.49%. This was over the criterion of 80%, so we let $N = 40$, and found the power equaled 80.24%. This meets the criterion, but as a last check, we tried letting $N = 39$, and found the power was only 79.39%. Therefore, we conclude that the minimum sample size (N) is 40.

5. We started by trying $N = 25$, and found the power was equal to only 16.85%. Then we tried increasing values of N until we found that when $N = 197$, power equals 80.24%. Thus, the minimum sample size (N) is 197.

7. We started by trying $N = 25$, and found the power was equal to only 49.6%. We then tried increasing values of N until we found that when $N = 52$, power is equal to 80.24%. Thus, the minimum sample size (N) is 52.

REFERENCES

■ ■ ■ ■ ■

American Psychological Association. (1992). Ethical principles of psychologists and code of conduct. American Psychologist, 47, 1597–1611.

American Psychological Association. (1994). Publication manual of the American Psychological Association (4th ed.). Washington, DC: American Psychological Association.

Asch, S. E. (1955). Opinions and social pressures. Scientific American, 193, 31–35.

Atkinson, J. M., & Heritage, J. C. (1984). Structures of social action. Cambridge: Cambridge University Press.

Atlas, G. D. (1994). Sensitivity to criticism: A new measure of responses to everyday criticisms. Journal of Psychoeducational Assessment, 12, 241–253.

Bavolek, S. J. (1984). Handbook for the adult-adolescent parenting inventory (AAPI). Schaumburg, IL: Family Development Associates, Inc.

Campbell, D. T., & Stanley, J. C. (1963). Experimental and quasi-experimental designs for research. Chicago: Rand McNally College Publishing Company.

Cohen, R. J., Montague, P., Nathanson, L. S., & Swerdlik, M. E. (1988). Psychological testing: An introduction to tests and measurement. Mountain View, CA: Mayfield Publishing Company.

Fielding, N. G., & Fielding, J. L. (1986). Linking data. Qualitative research methods Series No. 4. London: Sage Publications.

Forman, E. A., Minick, N., & Stone, C. A. (Eds.). (1993). Contexts in learning: Sociocultural dynamics in children's development. New York: Oxford University Press.

Franklin, R. D., Allison, D. B., & Gorman, B. S. (Eds.) (1996). Design and analysis of single-case research. Mahwah, NJ: Lawrence Erlbaum Associates.

Gravetter, F. J., & Wallnau, L. B. (1991). Essentials of statistics for the behavioral sciences. St. Paul, MN: West Publishing Company.

Gregory, R. J. (1992). Psychological testing: History, principles, and applications. Boston: Allyn and Bacon.

Haney, C., Banks, W. C., & Zimbardo, P. G. (1973). Interpersonal dynamics in a simulated prison. International Journal of Criminology and Penology, 1, 69–97.

Herrnstein, R. J., & Murray, C. A. (1994). The bell curve: Intelligence and class structure in American life. New York: Free Press.

Howell, D. C. (1997). Statistical methods for psychology (4th ed.). Belmont, CA: Duxbury Press.

Huberman, A. M., & Miles, M. B. (1994). Data management and analysis methods. In N. K. Denzin & Y. S. Lincoln (Eds.), Handbook of qualitative research (pp. 428–444). Thousand Oaks, CA: Sage Publications.

Huck, S. W., & Cormier, W. H. (1996). Reading statistics and research (2nd ed.). New York: HarperCollins College Publishers.

Huff, D. (1954). How to lie with statistics. New York: W. W. Norton & Company, Inc.

Hunter, J. E. (1997). Needed: A ban on the significance test. Psychological Science, 8, 3–7.

Isen, A. M., & Levin, P. F. (1972). The effect of feeling good on helping: Cookies and kindness. Journal of Personality and Social Psychology, 21, 384–388.

Kazdin, A. E. (1982). Single-case research designs: Methods for clinical and applied settings. New York: Oxford University Press.

Keppel, G., & Zedeck, S. (1989). Data analysis for research designs: Analysis of variance and multiple regression/correlation approaches. New York: W. H. Freeman and Company.

Kohn, A. (1992). Defying intuition: Demonstrating the importance of the empirical technique. Teaching of Psychology, 19, 217–219.

Kratochwill, T. R., & Levin, J. R. (Eds.). (1992). Single-case research design and analysis: New directions for psychology and education. Hillsdale, NJ: Lawrence Erlbaum Associates.

Levine, R. V., West, L. J., & Reis, H. T. (1980). Perceptions of time and punctuality in the United States and Brazil. Journal of Personality and Social Psychology, 38, 541–550.

Liebert, R. M., & Baron, R. A. (1972). Some immediate effects of televised violence on children's behavior. Developmental Psychology, 6, 469–475.

Loftus, G. R. (1996). Psychology will be a much better science when we change the way we analyze data. Current Directions in Psychological Science, 5, 161–171.

Middlemist, R. D., Knowles, E. S., & Matter, C. F. (1976). Personal space invasions in the lavatory: Suggestive evidence for arousal. Journal of Personality and Social Psychology, 33, 541–546.

Miles, M. B., & Huberman, A. M. (1994). Qualitative

data analysis: An expanded sourcebook (2nd ed.). Newbury Park, CA: Sage.

Milgram, S. (1963). Behavioral studies of obedience. Journal of Abnormal and Social Psychology, 67, 371–378.

Moll, L. C., & Whitmore, K. F. (1993). Vygotsky in classroom practice: Moving from individual transmission to social transaction. In E. A. Forman, N. Minick, & C. A. Stone (Eds.), Contexts in learning: Sociocultural dynamics in children's development (pp. 19–42). New York: Oxford University Press.

Naglieri, J. A., LeBuffe, P. A., & Pfeiffer, S. I. (1993). Devereux Behavior Rating Scale—School Form. Devon, PA: The Devereux Foundation.

Newman, J., & Krzystofiak, F. (1979). Self-reports versus unobtrusive measures: Balancing method variance and ethical concerns in employment discrimination research. Journal of Applied Psychology, 64, 82–85.

Prather, J., & Fidell, L. S. (1975). Sex differences in the content and style of medical advertisements. Social Science and Medicine, 9, 23–26.

Roscoe, J. T. (1975). Fundamental research statistics for the behavioral sciences (2nd ed.). New York: Holt, Rinehart, and Winston, Inc.

Rosenblith, J. F. (1992). In the beginning: Development from conception to age two (2nd ed.). Newbury Park, CA: Sage Publications.

Rosenhan, D. L. (1973). On being sane in insane places. Science, 179, 250–258.

Schachter, S., & Singer, J. (1962). Cognitive, social, and physiological determinants of emotional state. Psychological Review, 69, 379–399.

Schoggen, P. (1991). Ecological psychology: One approach to development in context. In R. Cohen & A. W. Siegel (Eds.), Context and development (pp. 281–301). Hillsdale, NJ: Lawrence Erlbaum Associates, Publishers.

Shapiro, F. (1995). Eye movement desensitization and reprocessing: Basic principles, protocols, and procedures. New York: Guilford Press.

Shaughnessy, J. J., & Zechmeister, E. B. (1994). Research methods in psychology (3rd ed.). New York: McGraw-Hill, Inc.

Sheskin, D. J. (1997). Handbook of parametric and nonparametric statistical procedures. Boca Raton, FL: CRC Press.

Shrout, P. E. (1997). Should significance tests be banned? Introduction to a special section exploring the pros and cons. Psychological Science, 8, 1–2.

Silverman, D. (1993). Interpreting qualitative data: Methods for analysing talk, text, and interaction. London: Sage Publications.

Tesser, A. (1995). Advanced social psychology. New York: McGraw-Hill, Inc.

Vogt, W. P. (1993). Dictionary of statistics and methodology: A non-technical guide for the social sciences. Newbury Park, CA: Sage Publications.

vos Savant, M. (1996). The power of logical thinking: Easy lessons in the art of reasoning- and hard facts about its absence in our lives. New York: St. Martin's Press.

Winer, B. J., Brown, D. R., & Michaels, K. M. (1991). Statistical principles in experimental design (3rd ed.). New York: McGraw-Hill, Inc.

Yaremko, R. M., Harari, H., Harrison, R. C., & Lynn, E. (1986). Handbook of research and quantitative methods in psychology. Hillsdale, NJ: Lawrence Erlbaum Associates.

GLOSSARY

■ ■ ■ ■ ■ ■

The chapters or appendices where these terms are discussed are indicated in brackets.

AB Design a research design in which a baseline phase (A) is followed by a treatment phase (B). Also see "Pretest-Posttest Design." [15]

ABAB Design a single-subject design in which the baseline phase (A) is followed by a treatment phase (B), and then the treatment is withdrawn, returning to the baseline condition (A), and then the treatment is re-introduced (B). [15]

Accepting the Null Hypothesis the statistical decision made when the results of an analysis do not reach statistical significance. The preferred term is "Failing to Reject the Null Hypothesis." Also see "Non-significant." [6]

Accretion Measure physical traces of behavior in the form of accumulating material (such as the increased amount of litter found in high-traffic areas). [4]

"All Else Equal" Principle phrase referring to the practice of controlling all extraneous variables while manipulating only the level of an independent variable, in order to demonstrate that the experimental manipulation or treatment is the cause of any differences found between groups. If "all else" is indeed equal, the relationship between the independent and dependent variables is unconfounded (or nonspurious). [7]

Alpha (α) Greek letter used to denote level of Type I Error (see Alpha level). [6]

Alpha Level the probability (or percent chance) that the researcher is willing to take of making a Type I Error (rejecting a true null hypothesis). Alpha level is usually set at .05 (5%) or .01 (1%). With smaller alpha levels, it is harder to find statistical significance, but there is less chance that any significant results are due to chance alone. (Also called: probability level, p level, p value, or significance level.) [6]

Alternate Forms Reliability the extent to which performance is consistent on two or more equivalent versions of a test. [4]

Alternate Hypothesis (H_1 or sometimes H_a) in hypothesis testing, any hypothesis which is an alternative to the Null Hypothesis. The Alternative Hypothesis is often also called the Research Hypothesis. [6]

Alternating Treatment Design a single-subject design in which two or more different treatments are presented in an alternating sequence during the treatment phase (B). For instance, Treatment 1 may be administered every morning while Treatment 2 is administered every afternoon, or the two treatments may be administered in random order (one in the morning and one in the afternoon). [15]

American Psychological Association the largest scientific and professional organization representing psychology in the U.S. and the world's largest association of psychologists, the APA works to advance psychology as a science, as a profession, and as a means of promoting human welfare. [2, D]

Analysis of Variance for experiments or quasi-experiments with interval or ratio data, a statistical test of the difference between means from 2 or more groups, on one or more factors. ANOVA is an extension of a t-test, which is used for 2 groups only. The independent variable is categorical (and defines the groups being compared), while the dependent variable(s) are continuous. The ANOVA test statistic is the F ratio, the ratio of the variance between groups to the variance within groups. [12]

Anonymity the practice of keeping no identifying information on the participants from whom data has been gathered. [2]

ANOVA see Analysis of Variance

APA see American Psychological Association

APA Format (or Style) the guidelines for the preparation of a journal manuscript established by the APA, as presented in the *Publication Manual of the American Psychological Association*, currently in its fourth edition (APA, 1994). [D]

Archival Analysis use of archival or textual materials in qualitative or quantitative analyses. (Also called archival research or secondary observation research.) [16]

Archival Materials (or Records) any publicly available information; usually printed or electronically stored, but can include anything available for study (e.g., art, buildings, text, photographs, diaries, credit card receipts). [16]

Association a relationship between two or more variables that can be described statistically. [3]

Authority Approach a way of knowing facts that depends on information provided by others who are believed to have access to the truth. For example, teachers serve as sources of true information for students and, for many people, the Bible is the authority on religious issues. [1]

Available Sample a sample of research participants who were selected because they were conveniently available to the researcher (such as students attending the researcher's own college). [6]

Bar Chart a graph in which vertical bars are centered above each score along the X-axis and the bars are separated from each other by a small space to indicate that scores on variable X represent discrete categories. [5]

Baseline Phase during single-subject designs, the period preceding the introduction of a treatment or following the withdrawal of the treatment. See also "Pretest." [15]

Behavioral Observations a data-gathering technique that involves directly recording ongoing behavioral responses, either in a laboratory or field setting. [4, 7]

Behavioral Ratings a data-gathering technique that involves asking people who are familiar with the participants to describe their behaviors, often using a rating scale. (For example, a teacher may be asked to rate how often a child disrupts the class: never, rarely, sometimes, or frequently.) [4, 15]

Best Estimate the statistic from a research sample provides the best estimate of the population parameter (e.g., $\overline{X}$ is the best estimate of μ, and s is the best estimate of σ). [14]

Beta (β) Greek letter used to denote the probability of a Type II Error, when the researcher fails to reject the null hypothesis when it is false. (Compare with Alpha, and alpha level.) In regression analysis, denotes standardized regression coefficients, which are not discussed in this text. [6]

Between-Subjects ANOVA a statistical procedure (Analysis of Variance) appropriate for analyzing interval or ratio data obtained from Between-Subjects experimental or quasi-experimental designs. [12]

Between-Subjects Designs an experimental or quasi-experimental design in which each participant is tested under only one treatment condition. (All Independent Variables in the design are Between-Subjects Factors.) The mean score for participants in one group is compared with the mean score for participants in the other group(s). (Contrasted with Within-Subjects designs, where the same group of participants is compared at different times or under different treatment conditions.) [10]

Between-Subjects Factor an Independent Variable that has a different group of participants at each level (so that each participant is tested under only one level of that Independent Variable). [10]

Bias for Positive Instances the tendency for people to pay more attention to, and to better recall, events that are consistent with their preconceived beliefs and expectations while they tend to ignore, misperceive or forget "negative instances" or events that contradict their beliefs. (Sometimes referred to as "Confirmatory Bias.") [1]

Biased Sample a sample that is not representative of the population from which it was drawn. [6]

Bimodal A frequency distribution with two modes. In graph form, a bimodal frequency polygon will have two distinct peaks. If the two peaks are not equal in frequency, the score with the higher frequency is referred to as the "major mode" and the peak score with the smaller frequency is referred to as the "minor mode." [5]

Blind Study a research procedure in which the participants and/or the observer does not know which condition the participant is in. When both groups are blind to the treatment conditions, the study is known as a "double blind." In a "single-blind" procedure, either the participants or the observer does not know which condition the participant is in.

Carryover Effects when the effects of one treatment condition influences performance during subsequent conditions in Within-Subjects, Mixed, or Single-Subject designs. [10, 15]

Case Study an in-depth study of a single, representative individual or event. [15]

Categorical Variable see "Qualitative Variable" and "Discrete Variable." [3]

Causal Relationship a relationship between two variables where changes in variable X produce changes in variables Y. True experiments allow researchers to determine that X causes Y, but correlational and quasi-experimental studies do not meet the criteria for establishing causality. (See also "Causality.") [3, 7]

Causality when changes in variable X produce changes in variables Y. The criteria for establishing a causal relationship are: (a) X and Y must be associated or co-vary; (b) the change in X must precede the change in Y; and (c) the relationship must be non-spurious or unconfounded. [3]

Cell a condition or treatment group in a matrix of data.

Central Tendency statistical measures that try to summarize a set of data by describing the typical or average score within the data set. The most common measures of central tendency are the Mean, Median, and Mode. [5]

Chance Fluctuations differences in a variable that are due to random individual or environmental differences rather than the other variables being studied. Also referred to as "random variation," "random error," or "random sampling error." [6]

Changing Conditions Design a variant of an ABAB Single-Subject Design in which two or more treatments are studied by adding phases to the design. For example, in an ABCBAC design, treatment 1 (phase B) follows the baseline phase (A), but then the condition is changed to treatment 2 (phase C). Then the condition is changed back to treatment 1 (phase B) which is followed by a return to baseline (A), and finally, treatment 2 is re-introduced. [15]

Changing Criterion Design a Single-Subject Design used to change an individual's behavior in small, gradual steps by setting a series of intermittent goals that increasingly resemble the final goal. [15]

Chi Square (χ^2) a statistical test for categorical data that measures the differences between observed frequencies and the frequencies that would be expected if chance alone is operating. When there is only one categorical variable, a Goodness-of-Fit Chi Square test is appropriate. For two categorical variables, a twoway Chi Square (also referred to as a Contingency Table test) tests for the presence of an interaction between the variables, such that categorical membership in one variable is associated with membership in a particular category on the other variable. For example, there is an interaction between sex and occupation: women are more likely to be secretaries and men are more likely to be race car drivers. [13]

Cochran's Q a variant of the Chi Square test that is appropriate for dichotomous categorical data from Within-Subjects or Matched-Pairs designs. [13]

Coefficient of Determination a statistic that measures how much of the variance in one variable is accounted for (associated with) the variance in one or more other variables. The coefficient of determination is known as r^2, and is the square of the correlation coefficient. [9]

Coefficient of Non-Determination the proportion of variance in Y that is not accounted for by variance in X; often referred to as error variance or residual variance. It is equal to $1 - r^2$. (Sometimes called the Coefficient of Alienation.) [9]

Common Event a sample statistic whose probability of occurring by chance alone is greater than .05. [6]

Complete Counterbalancing when every possible order of treatments is used in a Within-Subjects Design. [10]

Concurrent Validity the ability of a measure to accurately predict performance on a criterion measure that is obtained at roughly the same point in time. [4]

Condition a treatment group or level of an Independent Variable. [7, 10]

Confederates someone who interacts with the participants in some way (possibly pretending to be another participant) but who is actually helping the researcher by following some pre-planned script.

Confidence Interval a range of values, bounded by the upper and lower confidence limits, that is likely, at a specified level of probability (known as the confidence level), to contain the population parameter. A confidence interval is built around the value of a sample statistic, which serves as our best estimate of the population parameter. For example, from a telephone poll we could say that there is a 95% probability (confidence level) that the percentage of votes candidate A will receive in an upcoming election is between 53% and 59% (the confidence limits), or that s/he will receive 56%, +/− 3%. [14]

Confidentiality a promise of confidentiality to a participant means that they will never be identified individually, and that all information which could identify them is kept by the researcher in a secure location away from the data itself. The performance of any given individual is not revealed to anyone outside the research team. [2]

Confirmatory Bias a bias toward discovering evidence in favor of whatever hypothesis is being tested, which is also called the "Bias For Positive Instances." Researchers often subconsciously see what they want to see, or interpret data in ways which favor their theory, but which may not be warranted given the data or collection methods. [1]

Confound when there are two or more possible explanations for the observed effect, such as when there is uncontrolled variation in an extraneous condition that makes it impossible to isolate the effects of an independent variable. Some common forms of confounding include non-standardization, selection bias (or non-equivalence), maturation, instrumentation, and history. [1, 7, 15]

Confounded Comparison when the difference between two group means has two or more possible explanations, such as when the groups differ on two or more Independent Variables at the same time. For example, the comparison between second-grade boys and fourth-grade girls is confounded because the groups vary in both grade and sex. [12]

Confounded Results results of a study that can be accounted for by two or more possible explanations because all relevant extraneous variables were not controlled. [1, 7]

Constant a value which does not change in different contexts. For example, chromosomal sex (that is, XX for females or XY for males) is a constant within an individual across time. In experimental research, the researcher may control extraneous variables by holding them constant within the study, either by selecting individuals with the same value on the variable (such as selecting only 5-year-olds), or by making sure that all participants receive the same experiences (such as instructions). [3, 7]

Construct Validity the extent to which the measures or variables actually measure the hypothetical construct of interest, or the quality of the operational definitions for the construct. The term "hypothetical construct" refers to psychological traits that are believed to exist although they cannot be directly observed. Intelligence, personality, self-esteem, and need for achievement are examples of constructs that are theoretically important for explaining human behavior, and the process of construct validation involves demonstrating that predictions about relevant behaviors based on the theoretical construct are supported by empirical evidence. [4]

Content Validity when the items on a test or parts of a measurement procedure are representative of the entire range of the construct of interest. For example, a test of biology should cover a wide range of information which experts in biology would agree are representative of the content of the "universe" of biology knowledge, and should not, for example, concentrate only on plant biology. [4]

Contextual Approach research, often using Qualitative methods, that focuses on how specific social and physical environmental factors influence human development and behavior. [16]

Contingency Table a table showing the joint frequencies of two categorical variables (also called cross-tabulation). The relationship (interaction) between the two variables can be tested using a twoway Chi Square (χ^2). [13]

Continuous Variable a variable where the values or scores represent changes in amount or quantity along a continuum of possible values, and where fractional amounts of the variable can be measured. For example, the amount of water in a glass is a continuous quantity. (This in contrast to discrete variables, such as the number of jelly beans in a jar.) [3]

Contributory Cause a relationship between two variables where a change in X makes it more likely (although not certain) that there will be a change in Y. X is neither necessary nor sufficient to cause Y, but the presence of X does contribute to an increase in the probability of Y occurring. A familiar example is smoking (X) and its relationship to cancer (Y). [3]

Control preventing potential confounds by holding extraneous variables constant, either by direct experimenter action (Direct Control) or through randomization (Probabilistic Control). [7, 10]

Control Group a group used in an experimental design which does not receive any of the treatments; the control group is used as a comparison group. [10]

Controlled Variable an extraneous variable that is experimentally controlled or held constant during an experiment in order to prevent confounds. The two types of controlled extraneous variables include directly-controlled variables (DCV) and probabilistically-controlled variables (PCV). [10]

Convenience Sampling the term for a sample of participants who are chosen, not because they are representative of the population, but because they are convenient, such as students in introductory psychology courses. The use of a convenience sample limits the generalizability of results. (Sometimes also called "Available sampling.") [6]

Convergence of Evidence when results from multiple studies lead to the same conclusion. [1]

Correction Factor in ANOVA, the "piece" of the computational Sum of Squares formula that represents the grand mean: $\dfrac{(\Sigma\Sigma X)^2}{N}$ [12]

Correlation the extent to which two variables are related to each other, such that changes in the value of X are accompanied by changes in the value of Y. This relationship is often measured using a correlation coefficient. It is important to remember that a correlation between X and Y may be spuriously caused by an uncontrolled third variable (Z). Thus, correlations between X and Y do not prove that X causes Y. [7, 8]

Correlation Coefficient a statistic that measures the degree to which two variables are related. The magnitude of the relationship is indicated by the value of the coefficient on a scale from 0 to ±1.0, with larger absolute values indicating stronger relationships. A correlation with an absolute value of 1.0 is known as a perfect relationship: every change in X is accompanied by a change in Y. For quantitative variables measured on ordinal, interval, or ratio scales, the Pearson and

Spearman Correlation coefficients also convey information about the *direction* of the relationship. If the values of X and Y are changing in the same direction (i.e., both increasing or both decreasing), it is a positive relationship and the coefficient will be a positive number. If X and Y are changing in opposite directions (i.e., as X increases, Y decreases), it is a negative relationship, and the coefficient will have a negative sign. It is important to remember that the magnitude of a relationship is independent of its direction, and a correlation of −0.5 is equal in magnitude to a correlation of +0.5. [8]

Correlational Method a research design in which the experimenter does not manipulate any of the variables or intervene in an attempt to cause changes in behavior, but rather examines how two or more naturally-occurring variables are related to each other. [7]

Counterbalancing in Within-Subjects and Mixed Designs, a technique used to distribute order and time-related effects equally over all treatment conditions by systematically varying the order of the treatments, so that different participants receive them in different orders. [10]

Co-Variation when two things change systematically together; measured using correlation coefficients. [1, 7, 8]

Criterion Validity the ability of a measure to accurately predict performance on another, independent measure of the same behavior. [4]

Criterion Variable also called a criterion measure, (a) an independent measure of behavior used to establish the criterion validity of a new measurement instrument; or (b) in regression analyses, the variable (Y) that is predicted using one or more predictor variables (X), or (c) sometimes used as another term for a dependent variable in non-experimental studies. (In such studies, the independent variable is often called the predictor variable.) [4, 9]

Critical Range statistic computed in Dunn's Multiple Comparisons post hoc procedure that indicates how different two group means must be in order to be considered significantly different. [12]

Critical Ratio statistic computed to test the difference between two Pearson correlation coefficients. [8]

Critical Value the values in a sampling distribution that define the critical regions of rejection, and separate the significant from non-significant values. These values are used to decide whether or not to reject the null hypothesis. For example, in a normal distribution, the values of z = ±1.96 are the critical values for a non-directional (two-tailed) test with alpha set at .05; if the research outcome has a value of z that is greater than or equal to ±1.96, the Null Hypothesis will be rejected. [6]

Cumulative Frequency in a frequency distribution, the total frequency of all values up to and including the value or category of interest. For example, if, on a test, 3 students received a score of 79%, 10 students received a score of 80%, 5 students received a score of 81%, and 8 students received a score of 82%, the cumulative frequency for a score 81% would be 18 (that is, 3 + 10 + 5). That is, 18 students scored up to and including 81% on the test. [5]

Cumulative Percentage in a frequency distribution, the percentage of scores with values up to and including the value or category of interest; computed by dividing the cumulative frequency by the total number of values in distribution (N). For example, if, on a test, 3 students received a score of 79%, 10 students received a score of 80%, 5 students received a score of 81%, and 8 students received a score of 82%, the cumulative frequency for a score 80% would be 13 (that is, 3 + 10). There are a total of 26 scores, so the cumulative percentage for a score of 80% is 13 divided by 26, which is equal to 50.0%; half of the scores had values of 80 or less. [5]

Curvilinear a relationship in which increases in X are first accompanied by increases (or decreases) in Y, but then there is a change in direction for Y such that, as X continues to increase, Y now decreases (or increases). When these two variables are plotted against each other on a graph, they have a curved shape (either a U or an upside down U shape). Also known as "Non-monotonic." [9]

Cut-Off Point see "Critical Value."

Data the information collected by a researcher, typically coded or transformed into numbers for easier analysis.

Data Transformation changing all the values of a variable by performing some mathematical operation. For example, multiplying proportions by 100 transforms them into percentages. For another example, subtracting the group mean ($\overline{X}$) from a score (X) and then dividing by the group's standard deviation (s) transforms values of X into z-scores. [5]

DCV see "Directly Controlled Variable."

Debriefing a period at the end of an experiment where an explanation is given to participants about the reasons for and nature of the study they have just completed. The debriefing is especially important in studies containing deception. [2]

Deception when participants are intentionally misled or simply not informed about the true goals of the research. [2]

Degrees of Freedom (df) the number of data points in a data set that are free to take on different values under the constraint that the sum of the data points is fixed. For example, if two numbers must add up to 25, the value of the first number can vary from 0 to 25, but the second number will be determined by the constraint that the total must be 25. Thus, the first number has a degree of freedom, but the second number does not. Generally, then, all values in a data set are free to vary except for the last value, which is constrained by the group total, and has no freedom to vary. (Note that in Chi Square contingency tables, the cell frequencies are simultaneously constrained by *both* the row and column totals.) [11, 12, 13]

Demand Characteristics the many cues available to research participants during a study, including cues from the environment, the experimenter, or the materials. These cues often lead the participant to form an idea of the researcher's hypothesis, and sometimes to change their "normal" behavior to conform with these perceived cues. [10]

Dependent Variable the variable which is measured, or the behavior of interest. A participant's value (or score) is presumed to be dependent on changes in one or more other variables (the independent variables). [7, 9]

Descriptive Statistics statistical tests which summarize or organize information about data collected from a sample. (Contrasts with inferential statistics which address research questions about relationships among variables in the population.) [5]

Design see "Research Design."

Deviation Score the difference between a score and the group mean: $(X - \overline{X})$. [5]

Diachronic Reliability the degree to which the same researcher would record (or score) identical events in the same way at two different times, or from one participant to another. (Similar to Test-Retest reliability.) [16]

Difference Score the difference between two scores: $(X_1 - X_2)$. Typically used to measure the amount of change observed in a participant's performance in Within-Subjects or Mixed designs, such as a Pretest-Posttest design. [11]

Dichotomous Variable any variable for which there are only two values. For example, male/female, yes/no, or dead/alive. [8, 13]

Dichotomy see "Dichotomous Variable."

Differential Carryover a form of carryover in which the effects of one treatment condition (A) influences performance during a second treatment condition (B) in a Within-Subjects or Single-Subject design, but where treatment B does *not* have the same influence on treatment A when the order of presentation is reversed. [10, 15]

Direct Observation see "Behavioral Observation."

Directional Test see "One-Tailed Test."

Directly Controlled Variable (DCV) an extraneous variable that is held constant (either across participants or across treatment conditions) through the direct efforts of the researcher. For example, when the researcher gives all participants the same instructions and observes them in the same room, instructions and setting have been directly controlled. Also, if the researcher restricts selection so that only 16-year-olds participate in the study, then age has been directly controlled. [10]

Direction of Correlation whether the values on X and Y change in the same or opposite directions. If a correlation coefficient is positive (between 0 and +1.0), it indicates that as the values on one variable increase, so do the values on the second variable. However, if the correlation coefficient is negative (0 to −1.0), it indicates that as the values on one variable get larger, the values on the second variable get smaller. [8]

Discrete Variables a variable where the values or scores represent changes in amount or quantity measured only in whole-number increments. For example, the number of jelly beans in a jar. (This in contrast to continuous variables, such as the amount of water in a glass.) [3]

Distribution a set of values or scores for a variable. Also referred to as the "data set."

Double Blind when neither the participants nor the observer know which treatment condition the participant is receiving.

Dunn Multiple Comparisons Test a post hoc analysis used for testing the significance of differences between pairs (or combinations) of treatment means after the omnibus ANOVA has resulted in a significant value of *F*. This procedure adjusts the error rate on the basis of the number of comparisons that are of interest to the researcher. (Sometimes referred to as the Bonferroni procedure.) [12]

dv (or D.V.) see "Dependent Variable."

Σ see "Summation Sign." [5]

E_{max} see the "Maximum Error of the Estimate." [14]

Effect the difference among group means that systematically co-varies with change in levels of the Independent Variables. That is, the "effect of the Independent Variable" is the difference between the means for the levels of the IV. [7, 10]

Efficiency (a) the ability of a research design to reach the correct conclusion using the fewest resources (e.g., participants); and (b) the accuracy of a sample statistic in estimating the population parameter. This statistical efficiency is determined by the variability of the statistic's sampling distribution: the less variability, the better the estimate. Similar to the concept of "Power," which also depends upon the variability of the sampling distribution. [6, C]

Empirical data based on direct observation of the phenomenon under study. The basis for the Scientific Approach to the acquisition of knowledge about events and their causes. [1]

Environmental Variable any variable which is a part of the perceived physical environment in which a study is being conducted. For example, the lighting, noise levels, and number of other people present are environmental variables. [1]

Equivalence in Experiments, when groups have a similar "range of variation" on relevant extraneous variables and the differences that inevitably occur are due solely to chance (or random sampling error) and have a probability greater than .05. That is, groups are equivalent if they are not significantly different prior to the manipulation of an Independent Variable. [10]

Equivalent Groups groups that are not significantly different. (See "Equivalence" and "Non-Significant.") [10]

Erosion Measures physical traces of behavior in the form of wear-and-tear. (For example, bare spots on a cemetery lawn may indicate the grave sites that draw the most visitors.) [4]

Error Term in ANOVA, the measure of "Error Variance" used as the denominator of the *F*-ratio. [12]

Error Variance the variability among scores that cannot be attributed to systematic variation in the Independent Variables, but is instead the result of random variation, such as sampling error, measurement error, and individual differences. [12, C]

Estimation using a sample statistic to determine the probable value of the population parameter. If the exact value of the sample statistic is used as the estimate of the parameter, the process is known as "Point Estimation." As an alternative, "Confidence Intervals" may be computed which provide a range of likely values for the population parameter. [14]

Ethics the system of moral principles (of a particular group or individual) by which proper rules of conduct toward others are determined. [2]

Ethics Committee see "Institutional Review Board."

Ethical Principles a set of guidelines adapted by the American Psychological Association, most recently revised in 1992, which provide ethical principles for treatment of human and non-human animals, which researchers should consider and abide by when designing and carrying out research. [2]

Ethological Approach observation and descriptions of behavior in naturally occurring settings, often obtained through naturalistic observation or participant observation. [16]

Event Recording (or Sampling) in Behavioral Observation, a procedure for recording the frequency of a behavior that involves making a note each time the event occurs. The total number of events can then be reported, or the rate of occurrence can be computed by dividing the total number of occurrences by the duration of the observation. [15]

***Ex Post Facto* Design** research that compares groups that were *already different* before the study began, such as a Non-Equivalent Groups Quasi-Experiment, in which the Independent Variable is a Subject Variable (such as sex or race). [7]

Expected Cell Frequency in Chi Square (χ^2) analysis, the number of participants who would be expected to fall into a particular category (or cell) if the Null Hypothesis is true. [13]

Experiment a study in which equivalent groups of participants are treated exactly alike except that they receive different levels of the Independent Variable. Differences in performance on the Dependent Variable can then be attributed to the manipulation of the IV. That is, it can be concluded that the change in the Independent Variable **caused** the difference in the dependent variable. [7]

Experimental Control the control which an experimenter has over the independent variables and some of the extraneous variables in a research setting. For example, there is experimental control over which conditions or treatments a participant is exposed to, and over the exact nature of that treatment. [7, 10]

Experimental Criterion when the purpose of a Single-Subject Design is to determine whether or not a treatment has any effect at all. This is in contrast to a "Therapeutic Criterion." [15]

Experimental Group the participants who receive a non-zero amount of the Independent Variable and whose performance on the dependent variable is compared to a No-Treatment or Placebo Control Group. [10]

Experimental Manipulation the systematic application of different levels of an independent variable (that is, treatments) to different participants or to the same participants at different points in time. [7, 10]

Experimental Method a research method designed to test causal hypotheses by systematically manipulating one or more Independent Variables and measuring performance on a dependent variable. [7]

Explained Variance the amount of variance in Y (the dependent or criterion variable) that can be explained by variance in X (the independent or predictor variable). It is measured by the Coefficient of Determination, which is equal to r^2, and can be contrasted with the Coefficient of Non-Determination (often referred to as error variance or residual variance), which is equal to $1 - r^2$. [9]

External Validity the extent to which the findings of a research study can be generalized to other people and places (i.e., the "real world"). [1]

Extraneous Variable any variable, other than the Independent Variables, that may influence performance on the Dependent Variable. [7]

F-ratio in ANOVA, a statistic that has a measure of the systematic difference among group means in the numerator, and a measure of the error variance (or chance fluctuations) in the denominator. [12]

Face Validity the extent to which a measurement procedure *looks like* it is measuring what it is supposed to measure. For example, do all of the items on the "arithmetic test" ask the person to perform arithmetic? If so, then the test has face validity. [4]

Factor see "Independent Variable."

Factorial Combination each level of each Independent Variable is combined with each level of each other Independent Variable, creating the experimental conditions for the study. For example, if one IV is sex (with two levels: male and female) and the second IV is age (with two levels: 4-years-old and 8-years-old), a factorial combination would include four conditions: 4-year-old boys, 4-year-old girls, 8-year-old boys, and 8-year-old girls. [10]

Factorial Design an experimental or quasi-experimental design with two or more Independent Variables factorially combined. [10]

Failing to Reject the Null Hypothesis the statistical decision made when the results of an analysis do not reach statistical significance. This term is now preferred over the traditional term "Accept the Null Hypothesis." Also see "Non-significant." [6]

Falsifiable Hypothesis a hypothesis is said to be falsifiable if and only if it is stated in a way that can be refuted by empirical means. It is important to note that we can never actually confirm or "prove" a hypothesis is true, but we can find it false by showing that empirical data does not support it. A good hypothesis, then, may be defined as one which has not been falsified after a number of attempts have been made to do so, without success. [1]

Field Experiment experiments or quasi-experiments which are done in naturalistic settings. The independent variable is systematically manipulated, but due to the natural setting, many other environmental factors cannot be controlled and may cause confounds. Field Experiments are part of the larger concept of "Field Studies," which refers to can any kind of research done in a naturalistic setting. [7]

Freedom From Harm the American Psychological Association's guidelines for ethical treatments of research participants state that participating in research should not expose individuals to any situation that has potentially more negative physical or mental effects than "everyday life." Researchers must try to foresee any potential harm that may exist in their procedures, and to try to design experiments that are as harmless for the participants as possible. [2]

Frequency a count of how often an event occurs. Counting the number of times an individual performs a specific behavior (such as how many times a rat presses a lever) is a *measurement* procedure that produces ratio data. Counting the number of individuals who fall into a certain category (such as how many students are from Wisconsin) is usually a *statistical* analysis that is performed after a categorical variable has been measured, producing nominal data. [5]

Frequency Polygon a graph used to represent frequencies for quantitative, continuous variables. The frequency is typically placed on the Y axis, and the values of the variable are placed along the X axis. The frequency of each value of X is represented by a dot above the X axis. The polygon is formed by connecting the dots. (Contrasted with another graph known as a Histogram, where bars are used for each value of X.) [5]

Frequency Table a table which shows the frequency of events or individuals in categories. May include a number of other statistics that describe the data set, including percentages. For example, a frequency table of students of various ages in a swim class, including cumulative frequencies and cumulative percentages:

Age	f	Cumulative Frequency	Cumulative Percentage
10	7	26	100%
9	11	19	73%
8	8	8	31%
N = 26			[5]

Functional Control when a treatment or intervention effectively controls the target behavior. In Single-Subject Designs, functional control is demonstrated when the target behavior changes *appropriately* to changes in treatment. [15]

Generalizability (or Generality) the extent to which the conclusions drawn from a specific sample are applicable to a larger population. (Related to the concepts of "External Validity" and "Inferential Statistics.") [1]

Goodness-of-Fit Test   a Chi Square (χ^2) test applied to a single categorical variable that measures the whether the observed frequencies conform to some theoretical pattern of expected frequencies. (Most often, the Null Hypothesis is the theory that is tested). [13]

Grouped Frequency Table   a frequency table where data is grouped into classes or intervals. Particularly useful when there are a large number of possible values of X. For example, a grouped frequency table of ages of swimmers at the YMCA pool at a given time might look like:

Ages	f
41+	8
31–40	13
21–30	14
11–20	9
0–10	11
	N = 55 [5]

Heteroscedasticity   in regression analysis, a situation where there is a considerable difference in the amount of variance in Y (the criterion variable) across different values of X (the predictor variable). This condition violates the assumption of *homoscedasticity*, and if the violation is severe enough, the results of a Least-Squares Regression Analysis will be invalid. (Nonparametric analyses, which do not require homoscedasticity, would have to be employed.) [9]

Histogram   a graph in which vertical bars are placed above scores along the X-axis and the bars touch each other to indicate that scores on variable X represent continuous quantities. [5]

History   a threat to the internal validity of a study which results from an event which occurs between pre and post-measures. For example, if pretest and posttest measures are to be taken to examine the effects of training about sexual harassment issues in the workplace, and between the two measures, a local court case involving sexual harassment gets a lot of media coverage, it would be hard to tell if the changes in scores on the posttest were due to the training conducted or due to the information gained via the media coverage of the case. [10, 15]

Homoscedasticity   in regression analysis, a situation where the amount of variance in Y (the criterion variable) remains constant across different values of X (the predictor variable). A violation of this assumption is called "Heteroscedasticity." [9]

Hypothesis   a statement about the (potential) relationship between the variables a researcher is studying. They are usually testable statements in the form of predictions about relationships between the variables, and are used to guide the design of studies. [1]

Hypothesis Testing   the standard method used to assess the statistical significance of a study. Empirical observations gathered under standardized conditions are compared with a theoretical Sampling Distribu-

tion. Most frequently, the Null Hypothesis is used to generate the Sampling Distribution, so the procedure is sometimes referred to as "Null Hypothesis Significance Testing." [6]

Hypothetical Construct   a psychological trait that is believed to exist although it cannot be directly observed. Intelligence, personality, self-esteem, and need for achievement are examples of traits that have been constructed because they seem to explain patterns in performance on theoretically related tasks, or patterns of behavior across situations that differ on the surface, but seem to involve the same underlying characteristic or ability. [4]

Idiographic Approach   research focusing on the individual differences among participants and patterns of behavior within individuals. [15]

Implementation Integrity   extent to which an intervention or treatment is appropriately applied to participants. For example, in a Single-Subject Design using positive reinforcement to increase eye-contact in an autistic child, if the positive reinforcements are not administered according to the treatment protocol, the study lacks implementation integrity. [15]

Independence   when the occurrence of one event does not change the probability of another event. That is, when two events are unrelated to each other and the occurrence of one event does not depend upon the other event. [5]

Independent Variable   a variable which is presumed to be the cause of, can be used to predict, or is related to the presence of another variable (the dependent variable). In an experiment, the researcher systematically manipulates the levels of the independent variable in order to see if there is a change in performance on the dependent variable. In quasi-experimental research, when the presumed cause is a "subject variable," the researcher selects participants who already have different values of the independent variable, and compares these groups on the dependent variable. (This is known as a Non-Equivalent Groups design.) The term independent variable is typically used with experimental and quasi-experimental research, while the term "predictor variable" is typically used in correlational research. [7, 10]

Individual Differences   differences among participants on non-manipulable "Subject Variables," such as psychological states or abilities (e.g., mood, intelligence, and personality), physical traits (e.g., eye-hand coordination and upper body strength), and demographic variables (e.g., race, ethnicity, and socioeconomic status). Unless they are directly controlled, individual differences reduce the power of a test by increasing the amount of error variance or chance fluctuations within a data set, and making it more difficult to detect systematic relationships or effects. [6, 7, C]

Inferential Statistics   statistical techniques used to answer research questions by drawing inferences about the relationship between variables within the population. Population parameters are estimated using sample data. [5]

Informed Consent the American Psychological Association's ethical principle which says that every research participant should make the decision to participate in a study only after they have been informed about the study, including what they will be expected to do, and the potential risks they may face. This generally means that a verbal or written description of the study is given to potential participants, after which those who agree to participate are asked to sign a form saying that they are participating willingly. [2]

Institutional Review Board (IRB) a interdisciplinary group, usually of faculty members, which exists at all colleges and universities (sometimes under different names, such as Human Subjects Review Board, etc.) whose function is to review proposals for all research which uses human participants to be sure that the research conforms to reasonable safety and ethical requirements. In their proposals to an IRB, researchers must point out all possible or probable risks, and make a case for their chosen design if risks do exist to the participants. In essence, the IRB performs a cost-benefit analysis when deciding whether to approve each piece of research proposed. [2]

Instrumentation a possible threat to the internal validity of a study which occurs when there is a malfunction of an measurement instrument during a study. Malfunctions of measurement instruments may include failure of mechanical devices (such as a timer with a defective battery), errors in paper-and-pencil recording sheets (such as questionnaires with crucial pages out of order), or a change in the observer (such as a change in expectations about the results of the study, or boredom and fatigue due to the repetitiveness of the observation task). If an instrument does not reliably provide consistent measurements for all participants, throughout the length of the study, it will be unclear whether the resulting data are due to instrument malfunction or actual changes in participant behavior or other measured data. [10, 15]

Interaction when the effect of one independent variable on a dependent variable is not the same at every level of another independent variable. In other words, when the simple effects of an independent variable across levels of another IV are not the same. For example, if a passage typed in a smaller font size (e.g., 8 point) takes longer to read than when it is typed in a larger font size (e.g., 12 point), but only when the light level in the room is low (e.g., 20 watts), not if there is a high light level (e.g., 150 watts), then there is an interaction between font size and light level: the effect of font size on reading speed depends upon the light level in the room. [10]

Intercept the value of Y where a regression line crosses the Y axis (that is, the value of Y when the value of X is zero). This is often called the "Y intercept." [9]

Internal Consistency the degree to which separate items on a test consistently measure the same trait or ability. A form of reliability that includes Split-Half Reliability. [4]

Internal Validity the extent to which a study actually answers the research question it was designed to answer. Internally valid studies are characterized by valid operational definitions, valid measurements, and no confounds. [1]

Inter-Observer Agreement see "Inter-rater Reliability."

Inter-rater Reliability (IRR) the extent of agreement between the scores or ratings which different "raters" give to the same phenomena. One common example is scoring done my multiple judges in sporting events such as ice skating or diving; if the judges all give similar scores, there is said to be high inter-rater reliability. When the raters give scores on a continuous scale, the IRR may computed as a correlation between two raters, or, if there are more than two raters, as the average of correlations between pairs of raters. When the raters are classifying or categorizing behavior (such as "tried to help" or "did not try to help," IRR may be measured as the percentage of classifications where the raters agreed with each other. [4]

Interval Level (or Scale) a scale of measurement where the intervals between numbers are equivalent units, but in which there is no meaningful zero point. Common examples are the Fahrenheit or Celsius temperature scales, where the difference between 50 and 51 degrees is the same as the difference between 31 and 32 degrees, but where 0 degrees does **not** mean the absence of temperature. Because equal intervals in scores always represent an equal difference in the underlying variable, addition and subtraction of interval scores give meaningful results. [4]

Interval Recording an observational procedure where the observation period is broken into smaller intervals, and for each interval a record is kept of whether a target behavior occurred either at some time during that interval (Partial Interval Recording), or throughout the entire interval (Whole Interval Recording). These procedures provide a measure of the frequency of an event. [5]

Interview a verbal interaction between a researcher (interviewer) and an interviewee where a series of questions are asked. The questions may be open-ended or closed (e.g., dichotomous or multiple-choice answers). Interviews can be more flexible than written survey instruments because unexpected answers can be followed up on, or interviewees may indicate that none of the answers are applicable. [4, 16]

Interview Schedule a list of the important issues to be covered during an interview, which may be a list of specific questions (for structured interviews) or of broad topics (for unstructured interviews). The schedule is often used with a "script" that contains a predetermined commentary that is used before and between the questions in an interview, allowing the interview to flow smoothly, and putting the interview questions into context. The schedule and script will usually include pauses to record the answers. [16]

Intuition a way of knowing the truth based on internal feelings about what "must be true." While intuitions are often based upon previous experience and knowledge, they are prone to bias and inaccuracy. (Contrasted with scientific or inferential reasoning processes.) [1]

IV (or I.V.) see "Independent Variable."

Joint Probability the probability of two events occurring together. The joint probability of a combined event is equal to the product of the two events separately. For example, the probability of drawing the ace of spades from a normal deck of cards is equal to the probability of drawing an ace (4 out of 52) times the probability of drawing a spade (13 out of 52). [5]

Kruskal-Wallis *H* a nonparametric statistical procedure used with ordinal data from Between-Subjects designs with two or more samples. [13]

Latin Square a form of partial counterbalancing in which a set of treatment orders are selected such that each treatment occurs in each ordinal position. The number of treatments is equal to the number of different treatment orders needed in the Latin Square. [10]

Least Squares Criterion in regression analysis, the requirement that the regression equation generate the line that comes closer than any other line to passing through all of the points on the scatterplot. That is, the line with the least amount of error (as measured by the sum of the squared deviations between the actual and predicted values of Y). [9]

Least Squares Method of Regression a regression analysis that meets the Least Squares Criterion. [9]

Level of an Independent Variable the values of an independent variable that are selected for comparison, and that define the treatment conditions of the study. For example, in a study to examine the effects of parental reactions on toddlers' play behavior, the researcher may elect to manipulate three types of parental reaction (such as "none," "smiles at toddler," and "frowns at toddler"), and these three conditions are then referred to as the levels of the independent variable. [7, 9]

Level of Measurement the amount of information the measurement procedure can convey about the actual quantity of the variable present and about the actual differences among individuals with different values or scores. There are four levels of measurement. In order, from most to least informative, they are: ratio, interval, ordinal and nominal. The level of measurement determines which statistical analyses are appropriate. (Also referred to as "Scales of Measurement.") [4]

Linear a relationship between two variables in which increases in X are always accompanied by uniform increases (or decreases) in Y. When plotted on a scattergram, the relationship forms a straight line. [9]

Linearity the degree to which a relationship is linear. The Pearson Product-Moment Correlation Coefficient measures linearity. [9]

M a symbol sometimes used for the mean of a sample $(\overline{X})$.

Magnitude of Change in Single-Subject Designs, either (a) the difference between the means of the treatment phases, or (b) the difference in performance at the end of one treatment phase and performance at the beginning of the next phase (indicating how quickly the target behavior reacts to a new treatment condition). [15]

Magnitude of Correlation the degree to which differences in one variable are accompanied by (or associated with) corresponding differences in another variable. Measured using correlation coefficients, the magnitude of a relationship may range from zero (where there is no systematic association at all) to perfect (where, without exception, every change in X is associated with a corresponding change in Y). The magnitude is represented numerically on a scale from 0.0 (zero correlation) to 1.00 (perfect correlation). Also referred to as the "strength of a correlation." [8]

Main Effect in a factorial design, the influence (or effect) of one independent variable on the dependent variable after the data have been collapsed across all other independent variables. [10]

Manipulation see "Experimental Manipulation."

Manipulation Check a procedure that determines whether the Independent Variable is being effectively manipulated. For example, in an experiment comparing frustrated and non-frustrated people, a check may be needed to be sure the frustrating event is truly generating frustration in the participants.

Masking Effect when a causal relationship between X and Y is overlooked because the effect of X was canceled out by another, uncontrolled causal mechanism (Z) which had the opposite effect on Y (thus *masking* X's effect on Y). [3]

Matched-Groups Design a Matching Design that uses random assignment for most of the sample, but assigns the last few participants to the groups in such a way as to equate the means and standard deviations of the groups on some relevant extraneous variable(s) prior to the experimental manipulation of the Independent Variable. [10, C]

Matched-Pairs Designs a Matching Design that identifies pairs of participants with equal or similar scores on some extraneous variable(s) and then assigns one member of each matched-pair to the treatment conditions. [10, C]

Matching Designs research designs in which participants are matched on some relevant subject variable(s) before being assigned to treatment groups in order to make sure that the groups are equivalent on the matching variable(s) prior to the experimental manipulation. Two types of matching designs are Matched-Groups and Matched-Pairs Designs. [10]

Maturation changes that occur in behaviors or characteristics as a result of normal growth and development. A maturation confound (where maturation accounts for the observed changes) may occur in Within-Subjects and Mixed designs that take place over a substantial period of time. Counterbalancing the order of treatments or the inclusion of a No Treatment Control Group may be necessary to rule out maturation confounds. [10, 15]

Maximum Error of the Estimate (E_{max}) a statistic that measures the largest difference between $\overline{X}$ and μ that is likely to occur just by chance. Used in the computation of Confidence Intervals. [14]

Mean a measure of average or Central Tendency that is appropriate for interval or ratio data. It is computed by dividing the sum of the scores by the number of scores. [5]

Mean Square in ANOVA, a measure of variability that equals the average of the squared deviations of X from $\bar{X}$, which is computed by dividing the Sum of Squares by the degrees of freedom. [12]

Measurement the use of rules (or standardized procedures) to assign values to the qualities, attributes, or characteristics of individuals, objects, or events. [4]

Median a measure of average or Central Tendency that is appropriate for ordinal, interval or ratio data. It is the value of X that lies in the middle of the distribution of scores (so half of the scores are above it and half are below it). [5]

Median Absolute Deviation a measure of the spread or dispersion among a set of ordinal, interval or ratio scores. Similar conceptually to the standard deviation, it is the average difference between scores (X) and the group average, only it uses medians as the measures of average rather than the mean, which makes it appropriate for ordinal data. The formulaic expression is: $MAD = Mdn|X - Mdn|$. [5]

Median Split Technique in Single-Subject Designs, a relatively quick method for assessing the rate of change in a behavior during a treatment phase. An informal type of trend analysis. [15]

Method see "Research Method."

Method of Least Squares a regression analysis that meets the Least Squares Criterion. (Also referred to as "Least Squares Method of Regression.") [9,15]

Minimum Difference Between Means the smallest likely difference between two population means, which is determined by finding the Confidence Intervals for the Difference Between Means. If zero falls outside the CI, the smaller CI limit is the minimum difference between the means. [14]

Mixed ANOVA Analysis of Variance for Mixed Designs.

Mixed Design in Experiments or Quasi-Experiments, designs that include at least one Between-Subjects factor and at least one Within-Subjects factor. That is, there are at least two separate groups of participants who are then tested under every level of at least one independent variable. In single-subjects design, studies that include elements from two or more types of single-subjects designs, such as a reversal to baseline and multiple baselines. [10, 15]

Mode the score or category that occurs most often (i.e., has the highest frequency) in a data set. Used as a measure of central tendency, the mode is appropriate for any level of measurement, but is rarely the preferred measure of average for ordinal, interval or ratio scales, where the median or mean are also appropriate. The mode is the *only* measure of central tendency that is appropriate for nominal data. [5]

Moderator Relationship a relationship between X and Y in which X moderates the relationship between a causal variable (Z) and its effect (Y) by suppressing or by strengthening Z's ability to cause Y. [3]

Momentary Recording see "Time Sampling."

Monotonic a relationship between two variables in which increases in X are always accompanied by increases (or decreases) in Y. These changes may or may not be uniform, but there is no change in direction. Linear relationships are a subset of monotonic relationships in which the changes in Y *are* uniform. [9]

Mortality the loss of participants over the course of a study. Can create a confound if participants in one treatment condition drop out at higher rates than participants in other treatment conditions because they do not like something about the study (such as the treatment itself or their performance). [10]

Multicollinearity in Multiple Regression, when two predictor variables are highly correlated with each other, the analysis may misleadingly indicate that only one of those predictor variables significantly contributes to the prediction of the criterion variable. [9]

Multimethod Approach a research strategy in which a variety of different data-gathering techniques are employed to test the same hypothesis. When the results from different methods are consistent with each other, researchers can be more confident about their conclusions. (See also "Convergence of Evidence.") [4, 16]

Multiple-Baseline Design a Single-Subject Design that evaluates the effectiveness of a treatment for two or more target behaviors or in two or more settings. [15]

Multiple Causation when an event has two or more possible causes, any of which may be operating at a given time. For example, an infant may cry for any of a number of different reasons. (Contrasted with "Simple Causation.") [3]

Multiple Regression a statistical procedure that uses two or more predictor variables (X_1, X_2, etc.) to predict a single criterion variable (Y). [9]

N (or n) the number of scores in a data set. For Between-Subjects designs, N represents the total number of participants in the study and n represents the number of participants in one treatment group. For Within-Subjects Designs, N represents the total number of scores in the data set, and n represents the number of participants in the study (and the number of scores in each treatment condition). [5, 12]

Naturalistic Observation a data-gathering technique where behavioral observations are made in the field, so that the behaviors are recorded as they occur in their natural setting. [4, 7]

Necessary Cause if X *must be* present in order for Y to occur, X is a necessary cause of Y. For example, an air temperature below freezing is necessary for snow to fall. [3]

Negative Correlation a systematic relationship between X and Y such that higher values of X tend to be associated with lower values of Y, and lower values of X tend to be associated with higher values of Y. [8]

Negative Skew when an asymmetrical, unimodal distribution peaks near the higher end of the scale, so that the tail points at the smaller values of X. [5]

No Treatment Control Group in an experiment, a group that receives none of the independent variable before the dependent variable is measured. For example, in an experiment on the effects of random bursts of noise on concentration during a learning task, the *experimental group* would be exposed to bursts of noise while the No Treatment Control group would perform the task without noise. [10]

Nominal Level (or Scale) a scale of measurement where the scores or values represent qualitatively distinct categories that have no order. Qualitative variables are always measured on nominal scales, and sometimes, quantitative variables are also measured simply as distinct categories, such as when academic performance is recorded as simply Pass or Fail. [4]

Nomothetic Approach research that focuses on groups for the purpose of identifying the general (i.e., "typical" or "normative") patterns of behavior. [15]

Non-directional Test see "Two-Tailed Test."

Non-equivalence in Experiments, when groups do *not* have a similar "range of variation" on relevant extraneous variables and the difference between the groups (prior to any experimental manipulation) reaches statistical significance because it has a probability of .05 or less. [7]

Non-Equivalent Groups Design Quasi-Experiments where the independent variable(s) is/are subject variables. Subjects are selected for the study on the basis of their value on the independent variable, and random assignment cannot be employed. Consequently, the groups cannot be presumed to be equivalent on every relevant dimension. [7]

Non-linear a relationship between two variables in which increases in X are accompanied by changes in Y that are *not* uniform, so when plotted on a scattergram, the relationship does not follow a straight line. (Contrasted with "Linear.") [9]

Non-monotonic a relationship between two variables in which increases in X are first accompanied by increases (or decreases) in Y, but then there is a change in direction for Y such that, as X continues to increase, Y now decreases (or increases). Also known as "Curvilinear." [9]

Non-parametric Statistics inferential statistics appropriate for ordinal and nominal scales that cannot be assumed to approximate a normal distribution. (Contrasts with parametric statistics.) [13]

Non-reactive Measures measurement procedures that do not allow the participants to know they are being observed, or procedures that do not affect the participants' behaviors. (Contrasted with "Reactive Measures" and "Reactivity.") [4]

Non-significant a common event when chance alone is operating. By convention, when chance alone is operating, events with a probability greater than .05 are considered common and non-significant, while events with a probability of .05 or less are considered rare and significant. [6]

Non-spurious no rival explanation or "third variable" accounts for the relationship between two variables. [3]

Non-standardization a confound that occurs when treatment conditions are not treated exactly alike except for the level of the independent variable. For example, in an experiment comparing two pain medications, if one drug is administered by injection while the other is in pill form, there is a non-standardization confound: any difference in reported pain relief may be due to the difference in administration procedures rather than a difference in the chemical components of the drugs. [7, 0]

Normal Curve see "Normal Distribution."

Normal Distribution a symmetrical, unimodal, bell-shaped frequency distribution. Many human characteristics, such as intelligence, are normally distributed in the population. Important in hypothesis testing because many sample statistics are normally distributed around the population parameter (so Sampling Distributions are often normal curves). Every possible combination of a mean and a standard deviation has its own normal distribution, but they all fit the same mathematical equation. [6]

Null Hypothesis (H_0) the prediction that there is no systematic relationship among the variables in the population, and that any difference or correlation that is observed within the research sample is due solely to chance or random sampling error. [6]

Number of Categories (or Values of X) a measure of variability for categorical data that indicates the number of discrete categories represented within the data set. [5]

Objective Measures measures based on direct use of sensory information from the external world that is publicly available so that different observers are likely to agree on what event has occurred. In contrast with "Subjective Measures," the observer does *not* have to make a judgment about how an event should be interpreted. [1]

Objective Phenomenon behaviors, characteristics, or experiences that are overt (or external), and can be directly observed by another person. Common examples include speech and physical arm or hand movements. [1]

Observation (a) the act of gathering data about the behaviors, attributes, or characteristics of the research participants; (b) the result of the data-gathering process (that is, the score assigned to an individual). [1, 4]

Observed (or Obtained) Cell Frequency in Chi Square (χ^2) analysis, the number of participants who fall into a particular category (or cell). [13]

Observer Drift in Single-Subject Designs, when an observer's definition of the target behavior changes within or across sessions. [15]

One-Tailed Test a procedure for testing the Null Hypothesis in which the entire region of rejection is at one end (i.e., in one tail) of the Sampling Distribution. Also known as "Directional Tests," this procedure is used when the researcher has very strong theoretical or empirical reasons for predicting the direction of the outcome (e.g., that the correlation will be positive rather than negative, or that Group 1 will have higher scores than Group 2 rather than vice versa). [6, 11]

One-way Design an Experiment or Quasi-Experiment with only one Independent Variable. [10]

Operational Definition (a) a precise description of the procedures the researcher followed in order to observe or measure a variable; (b) a precise description of criteria the researcher established for identifying research groups (such as "low IQ" versus "high IQ" groups or "shy" versus "outgoing" groups); and (c) a precise description of the procedures used to manipulate the independent variable to create the experimental conditions. [1]

Order Effects in Within-Subjects or Mixed designs, a general tendency for responses to change systematically from early in a session to later in a session, for instance as a function of practice. This is an example of a Time-Related Effect. [10]

Ordinal Level (or Scale) a level of measurement that has only two of the properties of the real number system: identity and order. Ordinal scales place scores into categories that represent increasing amounts of the attribute, but the precise quantities are not measured, and the difference in amount between adjacent categories is not necessarily the same. For example, the first-place finisher in a race was faster than the second-place finisher, but the actual speeds of these two racers is not known. [4]

Outlier a score that is noticeably discrepant from the other scores in the data set, either because it is unusually high or unusually low, or it lies outside the trend (or general shape) of the data set. [5, 15]

Overstandardization when strict adherence to the rules of standardization threatens the validity of a study. For example, the language necessary to explain a task to four-year-old children may not be suitable for eight-year-olds, and vice versa. The goal of standardization, in this case, is not to use identical language, but to be sure all participants understand the instructions equally well. [10]

Pairwise Comparisons comparisons between pairs of means, typically performed during post hoc analysis, but sometimes performed as part of a set of planned comparisons. [12]

Parameter see "Population Parameter."

Parametric Statistics inferential statistics appropriate for interval and ratio scales that approximate a normal distribution. (Contrasts with nonparametric statistics.) [13]

Partial Counterbalancing a technique for preventing order confounds in Within-Subjects and Mixed designs that involves presenting the treatments in different orders to different participants, but not all possible orders are included. A common form of partial counterbalancing is a Latin Square. [10]

Partial Interval Recording a measure of the frequency of an event; a form of Interval Recording where the observer notes if the target behavior occurs at any point during the time interval. The percentage of intervals is then reported. [15]

Participants the people being observed for the purpose of research.

Participant Observation a qualitative research technique in which the researcher becomes a member of the group being studied and actively participates in the events being recorded. [16]

PCV see "Probabilistically Controlled Variable."

Pearson r a measure of the linear correlation between two variables, both of which are on interval or ratio scales. [8]

Perfect Correlation a systematic relationship between X and Y such that *every* change in X is associated with a proportional change in Y. Perfect correlations are indicated by coefficients of ± 1.00. [8]

Phi Coefficient (ϕ) a nonparametric measure of the correlation between two dichotomous variables. [8]

Physical-Trace Approach studies that measure behavior by recording the physical evidence left behind. Includes Accretion and Erosion measures. [4]

Pilot Studies a dry-run where the procedures and instruments are tested before actual data collection begins.

Placebo Effect originally discovered in medical research, the tendency for participants to show improvements in health or performance when they believed they had received a treatment, even when the treatment involved an inactive substance (such as sugar instead of an analgesic). The effect is attributed to reactivity to demand characteristics present. [10]

Placebo Control Group a group that receives an inactive or ineffective treatment in order to control for reactivity and demand characteristics. [10]

Point Estimation using a sample statistic to estimate the specific value of the population parameter. (Contrasts with Confidence Intervals that identify a *range* of possible values for the population parameter.) [14]

Pooled Variance in t-tests for independent samples, a statistic that averages the random variation of the two groups. The pooled variance is then used to compute an estimate of the standard error. [11]

Population all members of the group of interest to the research hypothesis. That is, the larger group to whom the results are intended to generalize. [5]

Population Parameter a number that summarizes a population of scores, such as the population average and population variability. By convention, Greek letters are used as symbols for population parameters. For example, μ = mean; σ = standard deviation; and ρ = correlation coefficient. [5]

Positive Correlation a systematic relationship between X and Y such that higher values of X tend to be associated with higher values of Y, and lower values of X tend to be associated with lower values of Y. [8]

Positive Skew when an asymmetrical, unimodal distribution peaks near the lower end of the scale, so that the tail points at the larger values of X. [5]

Post Hoc Analysis comparisons among pairs of treatment groups conducted only after the omnibus (or overall) analysis has demonstrated a significant effect. Post hoc tests are required only for independent variables with three or more levels. [12]

Posttest an assessment of performance after the onset of the treatment, typically compared to performance measured prior to the treatment (a pretest). [7, 10]

Power the ability of a test to detect a systematic effect when there is one; that is, the likelihood that the test will correctly reject the Null Hypothesis. [6, C]

Power Analysis a statistical procedure for estimating the probability that a design, with a given sample size, will be able to detect a systematic effect of a given size. [C]

Practical Significance the usefulness of the findings of a study. (Contrasts with Psychological and Statistical Significance.) [6, C]

Practice Effects systematic improvement in performance as a result of repeated exposure to the task or the research setting. [10]

Predicted Y-score (Y′) in regression analysis, the value of Y that is expected for a specific value of X. [9]

Predictive Validity a form of Criterion Validity, the degree to which a test accurately predicts performance on some future criterion variable. [4]

Predictor Variable in regression analyses, the attribute (X) used to estimate (or predict) the value of the criterion variable (Y). [9]

Pretest an assessment of performance prior to the onset of the treatment. [7, 10]

Pretest-Posttest Designs Within-Subjects designs in which the dependent variable is measured twice: before the onset of the treatment, and again after the treatment has been implemented. [7, 10]

Privacy the ethical principle that says participants have the right to expect that their performance on research tasks will not be made public. To protect privacy, researchers must either maintain confidentiality or grant the participants anonymity. [2]

Probabilistic Control in experimental research, holding extraneous variables constant across treatments by using Random Assignment. Random Assignment distributes the extraneous individual differences among participants randomly across the treatments, creating equivalent groups. [7]

Probabilistically Controlled Variables (PCV) in experimental research, extraneous variables that have been controlled (or held constant across treatments) through the process of Random Assignment. [7]

Probability the likelihood that a particular event or outcome will occur, based on the number of ways the outcome can be achieved out of the total number of possible outcomes. [5]

Product (of Behavior) in Physical Trace Research, the physical materials that are purposely *created* during the course of behavior. For example, the notes taken during lectures are "products" of attention behavior. [4]

Proportion the fraction of a total quantity, expressed as a decimal from 0 to 1. [5]

Proportion of Area Under the Curve for any z-score in a normal distribution, the proportion of scores that are either less than or higher than z. The z-Table presents the proportions under the normal curve for two-decimal values of z from 0.00 to 4.00. [5]

Psychological Significance the quality of a researcher's hypotheses or ideas, the internal validity of the research testing the ideas, and the clarity of the results. (Contrasts with Practical and Statistical Significance.)

Q Cochran's Q is a nonparametric test for dichotomous, nominal data from Within-Subjects or Matched-Pairs designs. [15]

Qualitative Research Methods research methods that focus on the contexts in which behavior occurs, and are characterized by a distinct flexibility in data-gathering that allows researchers to redefine their terms or to adopt new measurement procedures as the study progresses. (Contrasts with Quantitative Research Methods.) [16]

Qualitative Variable a categorical variable where each value represents a discrete, mutually exclusive category, so that the differences are in kind rather than amount. For example, the variable "sex" categorizes individuals as male or female. [3]

Quantitative Research Methods research methods that rigorously adhere to the principles of standardized observations and precise operational definitions, and produce numerical scores that are analyzed statistically. (Contrasts with Qualitative Research Methods.)

Quantitative Variable a variable where the values or scores represent changes in amount or quantity. For example, some people are taller (i.e., have more "height") than others. [3]

Quasi-Experimental Method research that compares nonequivalent groups (such as when the independent variable is a subject variable), or observes the same group a number of times. Due to inherent confounds (such as selection bias and time-related effects), quasi-experiments do not allow researchers to draw causal conclusions. [7]

Questionnaire a self-report technique in which participants answer a set of written questions. [4]

r the generic symbol for the correlation between X and Y in a sample of scores. Typically, r stands for the Pearson correlation while r_S stands for the Spearman correlation. [8]

r^2 in Regression and simple correlation analyses, the proportion of the total variability of the criterion variable (Y) that is accounted for by the predictor variable (X). (See the Coefficient of Determination.) [9]

R^2 in Multiple Regression, the proportion of the total variability of the criterion variable (Y) that is accounted for by the combination of the predictor variables (X_1, X_2, etc.). (See the Coefficient of Determination.) [9]

Random Assignment in experiments, the process of assigning participants to treatment conditions using random procedures (such as flipping a coin), so that every participant has an equal chance of being assigned to any of the treatments. [7]

Random Groups Design a between-subjects design in which participants have an equal chance of being assigned at random to any experimental condition. All IVS must be non-subject variables. [7]

Random Sample a sample that has been created through Random Sampling. [6]

Random Sampling a procedure for selecting participants where every member of the population has an equal chance of being selected for the sample, and where every sample has an equal chance of being selected. [6]

Random Sampling Error difference between a sample statistic and the population parameter that is due solely to random chance. (Also called "Sampling Error.") [6, C]

Random Selection see "Random Sampling."

Range the difference between the highest and lowest scores in a data set, the range is a measure of variability for continuous variables on ordinal, interval, and ratio scales. [5]

Rank Sum Test (Wilcoxon-Mann-Whitney *T*) a nonparametric statistical procedure used with ordinal data from a two-sample Between-Subjects design. [13]

Rare Event a sample statistic whose probability of occurring by chance alone is less than or equal to .05. [6]

Ratio Level (or Scale) the highest level of measurement, ratio scores have all of the properties of the real number system: identity, order, equal intervals, and an absolute zero point (where a score of zero means that none of the attribute is present). Multiplication and division of ratio scores give meaningful results. [4]

Rational-Inductive Approach an approach to the acquisition of knowledge or the discovery of facts that is based on logical reasoning processes. [1]

Rationale in establishing causality, the proposed mechanism by which changes in X cause changes in Y. [3]

Reactive Measures measurement procedures that allow the participants to know they are being observed, which may result in "Reactivity." [4, 16]

Reactivity a change in behavior caused by participants' knowledge that they are being observed. [4]

Reasoning the use of logical processes, such as induction, to acquire knowledge or discover facts. [1]

Regions of Rejection that portion of the Sampling Distribution that represents the values that have a low probability of occurring by chance alone, and are considered to be rare events. When a statistic from a research sample falls in the region of rejection, the Null Hypothesis is rejected. [16]

Regression a statistical procedure that uses the correlation between X and Y to predict the value of Y for any value of X. [9]

Regression Equation the mathematical equation for the regression line. The equation is used to compute a predicted value of Y' for any value of X. [9]

Regression Line on a scatterplot, the line (representing the values of Y') that comes closest to passing through all of the points. [9]

Regression to the Mean the tendency for extreme scores to become less extreme over time. [10]

Rejecting the Null Hypothesis the statistical decision made when the results of an analysis reach statistical significance. That is, when the probability of the event occurring by chance alone is .05 or less, we decide that more than chance is operating. [6]

Reliability the consistency of a measurement procedure. The typical procedures for determining reliability include comparing the scores from repeated testing of the same participants, comparing scores from alternate forms of the test, comparing scores from different parts of the test, or comparing scores assigned by different researchers who have observed the same event. [1, 4]

Repeated Measure an independent variable that is set up as a Within-Subjects factor so that participants' behavior is measured (repeatedly) under every level of that independent variable. [10]

Repeated Measures ANOVA Analysis of Variance for Within-Subjects Designs. [12]

Repeated Measures Design see Within-Subjects Design [7]

Replication process of repeating a study (either exactly or in a variant replication) in order to determine whether the results can be reproduced. (See "Convergence of Evidence.") [1]

Representative Cases in single-subject designs or qualitative research, individual participants who are selected for the study because they are comparable to the population on a few relevant dimensions. [16]

Representative Sample a sample that has characteristics that closely resemble the characteristics of the population so that the sample statistics provide accurate estimates of the population parameters. [6]

Research the systematic investigation of a topic intended to discover new information or interpret relationships among existing data on the topic.

Research Design the specific procedures used to gather data in a scientific study. Designs may involve groups of participants or just a single subject, and the participants may be observed just once or repeatedly.

Research Hypothesis (H₁) see "Alternate Hypothesis."

Research Method general approach to gathering data that determines the whether causal conclusions can be drawn. The Experimental Method allows causal conclusions (if the experiment has internal validity), but the Quasi-Experimental and Correlational Methods are inherently confounded, so causal conclusions are not warranted. [7]

Risk the ethical principle that says researchers must protect their participants from any physical or psychological harm that may result from the study. (See also "Freedom From Harm.") [2]

Rival Explanations (or Hypotheses) alternative accounts for observed results. For example, biological differences and sex-role stereotyping are rival explanations for differences between boys and girls. [1]

s symbol for the standard deviation of a sample of scores. [5]

s^2 symbol for the variance of a sample of scores. [5]

Sample a relatively small subset of participants selected from a population. [5]

Sample Statistic a number that summarizes a sample of scores, such as the sample average and sample variability. Sample statistics are used as estimates of the "population parameters." For example, $\overline{X}$ (the mean of a sample of scores) is used as an estimate of μ (the mean for the population). [5]

Sampling selecting participants for the study. Common types of sampling include random sampling, stratified random sampling, and convenience or availability sampling. [6]

Sampling Distribution frequency distribution of sample statistics from all possible random samples, of a particular size, drawn at random from the population. The variation in a sampling distribution is a measure of the fluctuations among samples that occur when chance alone is operating. (Each statistic that can be computed on sample data, including means, correlation coefficients, t, or F, has it own sampling distribution.) [6]

Sampling Error difference between a sample statistic and the population parameter that is due solely to random chance. [6]

Scales of Measurement see "Levels of Measurement."

Scattergram see "Scatterplot."

Scatterplot a graphical representation of the relationship between two variables, where a dot is placed at the point that corresponds to an individual's score along the X- and Y-axes. Visual inspection of scatterplots can provide estimates of the magnitude and direction of the correlation between X and Y. [8]

Scientific Approach (or Empirical Approach) see "Scientific Method."

Scientific Method an approach to gathering information based upon direct and systematic observation and recording of the phenomenon of interest. [1]

Score (or Value) see "Value (or Score)." [3]

Script for Interview a predetermined commentary that is used before and between questions in an interview that allows the interview to flow smoothly, and puts the interview questions into context. [16]

Selection Bias when the treatment groups are not equivalent at the outset of the study. Quasi-Experiments with subject variables as independent variables are confounded due to selection bias. (Also known as nonequivalence.) [7]

Self-Reports data-gathering techniques that rely on participants' descriptions of their own behaviors, feelings, attitudes, and so forth. Most common types of self-report techniques include interviews, questionnaires, and surveys. [4, 16]

Sensitivity of Measurement the ability of the measurement instrument to detect small changes in behavior. [4, 15]

Sensitization when the measurement process itself influences participants' responses by making them more aware of the issues or behaviors under study. (A form of Reactivity.) [10]

Signed Ranks Test (Wilcoxon's W) a nonparametric statistical procedure used with ordinal data from a two-sample Within-Subjects or Matched-Pairs design. [13]

Significance *statistical* significance refers to whether the research outcome is a common event or a rare event when chance alone is operating. (By convention, events with a probability greater than .05 are considered common and non-significant, while events with a probability of .05 or less are considered rare and significant.) *Practical* significance refers to the usefulness of the findings, and *psychological* significance refers to the quality of the idea, the adequacy of the test of the idea, and the clarity of the results. [6]

Significance Level the probability used to define events as rare or common when chance alone is operating. The symbol for the significance level is α (alpha). [6]

Simple Causation when there is one and only one cause of an event. [3]

Simple Effects in the analysis of a factorial design, the effect of an independent variable examined at the levels of another independent variable separately. When the simple effect of an independent variable is not the same at every level of the other independent variable, there is an interaction between the variables. [10]

Single-Blind Procedure a research procedure in which either the participants or the observer does not know the treatment condition to which the participant has been assigned.

Single-Subject Research Design research designs in which one (or a very few) participants are observed under at least two treatment conditions (typically a baseline phase followed by a treatment phase). See also "ABAB Designs," "Changing Conditions Designs," "Changing Criterion Designs," "Alternating Treatment Designs," and "Multiple Baseline Designs." [15]

Skewed Distribution a nonsymmetrical unimodal distribution. When the mode (or peak) is at the lower end of the score scale, the distribution has a positive skew (and its tail points at the larger values of X). When the mode (or peak) is at the higher end of the score scale, the distribution has negative skew (and its tail points at the smaller values of X). [5]

Slope in geometry, the rate at which a line rises or lowers (along the Y axis) as it crosses a given distance along the X axis. In terms of the linear relationship between two variables, it is how much the value of Y changes for every change in X. [9]

Social Desirability Response the tendency for participants to answer questions as they think a "good" person should, even if these answers are not true. For example, if people are asked: "Are you bigoted?" most people will probably say no because few people think it is socially acceptable to be bigoted. [4]

Spearman r a correlation coefficient that measures the degree of monotonic relationship between two variables that are arranged in rank order. [8]

Split-Half Reliability a form of internal consistency that compares the score for one half of an instrument to the score for the other half of the instrument. High levels of similarity in scores across the two halves of the instrument indicate internal consistency. [4]

Spurious Relationship a correlation between X and Y that is due to a third variable (Z) that causes both X and Y independently. [3]

Standard Deviation a measure of the spread or dispersion among a set of interval or ratio scores, it is the average difference between scores (X) and the group mean ($\overline{X}$). [5]

Standard Error (σ_E or s_E) a measure of the average difference between sample statistics and the population parameter. It is the variability of the sampling distribution for the statistic. [6]

Standard Error of the Estimate (s_{est}) in regression analysis, a measure of the average difference between actual values of Y and the estimates of Y (that is, Y') based on the value of X and computed using the regression equation. As the magnitude of the linear relationship between X and Y increases, the error in the estimates will be reduced. [9]

Standard Score a measure of relative standing within a group; the most common standard score is the *z*-score. [5]

Standardization the process of transforming raw data into standard scores such as *z*-scores. [5]

Standardized Scores any common measure that allows comparisons between variables measured on different score scales. The best known standardized scale is *percentage; z*-scores are another standard score that are important to the hypothesis testing process. [5]

Statistic a number that summarizes a body of information. [5]

Statistical Significance whether the research outcome is a common event or a rare event when chance alone is operating. By convention, events with a probability greater than .05 are considered common and nonsignificant, while events with a probability of .05 or less are considered rare and significant. [6]

Stem-and-Leaf Plot a grouped-frequency graph that presents the values of raw scores in a sideways histogram-like format. Unlike standard group-frequency tables and polygons, a stem-and-leaf plot preserves information about each individual score in the data set. [5]

Stratified Random Sampling randomly selecting participants from specified sub-populations based on known proportions within the population in order to create a sample with the same relative proportions, For example, if 23% of the population is Catholic and 3% is Jewish, a stratified random sample with 100 participants would include 23 randomly selected Catholics and 3 randomly selected Jews. [6]

Strength of a Relationship see "Magnitude of a Correlation"

Structured Interview an interview in which every participant are asked a predetermined set of questions in the same order. [16]

Subjects the object or organism being observed for the purpose of research. The preferred term for human subjects is "participants," but it is still acceptable to refer to non-human organisms as "subjects."

Subject Variable an attribute or characteristic of an individual that cannot be experimentally manipulated by the researcher; to study these variables, researchers must select participants because they *already have* the attributes of interest. Sex, race, intelligence, personality, and parental education levels are just a few of the many subject variables that may influence behavior. [7]

Sub-population a subset of the entire population that may be studied because the member of the sub-population differ systematically from other segments of the population. For example, *children* are a sub-population that may be studied separately from adolescents and adults (which are other sub-populations).

Subjective Measures measures based on the personal, internal reactions of the observer. That is, if the observer has to make a judgment about how an event should be interpreted. [1]

Subjective Phenomenon behaviors, characteristics, or experiences that are covert (or internal), and cannot be directly observed by another person. Common examples include thinking and feeling. [1]

Sufficient Cause when X, by itself, is enough to produce the effect (Y). [3]

Sum of Squares a measure of variability that equals the sum of the squared deviations of X from $\overline{X}$: $SS = \Sigma(X = \overline{X})^2$. It is the numerator of the formulas for variance and standard deviation, and it is the measure of variability used in Analysis of Variance. [12]

Summation Sign (Σ) an algebraic symbol instructing us to add (i.e., "get the sum of") a set of numbers. For example, ΣX refers to the sum of the X scores. The rules of algebra say that summation is performed last, unless it is in parentheses. Therefore, ΣX^2 refers to the sum of the squared X scores (i.e., each X is squared and then these squared Xs are added together) while $(\Sigma X)^2$ tells us to add up the X scores and then square that total. [5]

Synchronic Reliability in qualitative research, the degree to which multiple researchers record (or score) an event in the same way at the same point in time. (Similar to inter-rater reliability.) [16]

Systematic Observation a characteristic of scientific research that involves gathering data from each participant under the same conditions. [1]

t-**Distribution** the sampling distribution of *t* created by drawing all possible random pairs of samples of a given size, treating them alike (so the Null Hypothesis is true), and computing *t* for each pair. The shape of this distribution is not normal, but it *is* predictable so that critical values of *t* for different values of N are always the same (and presented in the *t*-Table). [11]

t-**Test** a test of the Null Hypothesis for a one- or two-sample experiment or quasi-experiment. A one-sample *t*-test tests the Null Hypothesis that the sample mean ($\overline{X}$) is equivalent to the population mean, and it is used when the mean (μ) of the population is known, but the standard deviation (σ) of the population is unknown. A two-sample *t*-test tests the Null Hypothesis that two samples means are equivalent to one another; the population mean and standard deviation are unknown. [11]

Temporal Ordering see "Time Priority"

Test-Retest Reliability the degree to which an instrument assigns consistent scores when it is used to measure the same object or event on two separate occasions. [4]

Testable Hypotheses research hypotheses in which all of the terms can be operationally defined and measured. [1]

Textual Analysis examination of the written records of a culture. [16]

Textual Materials written materials that are produced by participants during the course of a research study. For example, participants may be asked to keep a journal or diary in which they record their daily activities. [16]

Therapeutic Criterion when the goal of an intervention in a Single-Subject Design is to improve the participant's behavior until it reaches some acceptable standard. This is in contrast to an "Experimental Criterion" that is used to determine whether the intervention has any effect at all. For example, an intervention may reduce a child's tantrum behavior from eight to four per day, meeting an Experimental Criterion, but a therapist may want to eliminate the tantrums completely, so the Therapeutic Criterion would be zero tantrums per day. [15]

Three-way Design an Experiment or Quasi-Experiment with three independent variables, usually arranged in a factorial combination. [10]

Three-way Interaction when the pattern of interaction between two independent variables depends upon the level of a third independent variable. [10]

Tied Ranking when the scores on an ordinal scale are being rank ordered, and raw scores of equal value are all assigned a rank score that is the mid-point of the ordinal positions occupied by the tied raw scores. This mid-point is known as a *tied rank score*. [8]

Time Priority the principle that says a cause must precede its effect. [3]

Time-Related Effects potential confounds that are due to the passage of time or to the process of repeated measurements in Within-Subjects and Mixed Designs. Some of the most common time-related confounds are practice effects, order effects, maturation, and history. [10, 15]

Time Sampling a measure of the frequency of an event; a form of Interval Recording where the observers notes if the behavior is present or absent at the moment the time interval begins or ends. The percentage of intervals is then reported. (Also called Momentary Recording.) [15]

Time-Series Design a Within-Subjects Quasi-experimental Design where the same participants are observed on multiple occasions, often in the form of a pretest-posttest (or baseline-treatment) design. [7]

Topographical Drift in Single-Subject Designs, when the definition of the target behavior begins to change across time. [15]

Transcript the record of verbal data generated by the process of transcription. Transcripts may also include information about non-verbal elements of the event, such as movements that occur during the event, and so forth. [16]

Transcription organizing verbal data, often by making a verbatim record of participants' verbalizations. [16]

Treatments what the researchers do to the participants as part of the experimental manipulation of the independent variable. Each level of the independent variable (or each factorial combination of levels of two or more independent variables) is a different treatment condition. [7, 9, 15]

Treatment Groups in Between-Subjects and Mixed designs, the groups of participants who are exposed to different levels of the independent variable (or treatments). [7, 9]

Treatment Phase in Single-Subject Designs, the period following the introduction of a treatment. See also "Posttest." [15]

Trend Analysis in Single-Subject Designs, techniques for measuring the rate of change during treatment phases, including the Median-Split Technique and the Least-Squares Method of Regression. [15]

Triangulation in qualitative research, using multiple research methods (such as observation, interviews, and transcription) to examine the same research question. [16]

Two-tailed Test a procedure for testing the Null Hypothesis in which the region of rejection is split into two equal parts, one at each end (i.e., in the two tails) of the Sampling Distribution. Also known as a "Non-Directional Test," this procedure does not predict the specific direction of the outcome. [6, 11]

Two-way Design an Experiment or Quasi-Experiment with two Independent Variables, usually arranged in a factorial combination. [10]

Two-way Interaction when the effect of one independent variable depends on the level of a second independent variable. For example, how much more quickly a person falls asleep after taking a sedative compared to no sedative depends on the amount of alcohol they have consumed in the past 2 hours; thus, the sedative interacts with the alcohol. [10]

Type I Error rejecting the Null Hypothesis when it is true. [6]

Type II Error failing to reject the Null Hypothesis when it is false. [6, C]

Unconfounded Comparison in factorial designs, a post hoc comparison between means from treatment groups that differ on only one independent variable. [12]

Unconfounded Results experimental findings that can be attributed to the independent variable because there are no alternative explanations for the results. [7]

Unequal *n* when the experimental groups do not have the same number of participants.

Unobtrusive Observation measuring participants' behavior when they are unaware that they are being observed. [7, 16]

Unstructured Interview interviews in which the interviewer is free to discuss the participant's answers and ask new questions to follow up interesting responses. No two unstructured interviews will be exactly alike. This is in contrast to *structured interviews*. [16]

Validity the extent to which an instrument or a research design does what it is *supposed to do*. A valid instrument measures the variable it purports to measure, and a valid research study answers the research question it was designed to address. [1, 4]

Value (or Score) an individual's specific attribute or characteristic on a variable. For instance, for the variable of weight, one individual's weight may be equal to 140 pounds; that is, her value (or score) on the variable is 140. [3]

Variability the amount of spread or dispersion among a set of scores; that is, how different the scores in the group differ from one another or from the group average. [5]

Variables attributes or characteristics of people, places or events that can change in value across time, across individuals, or both. The opposite of a variable is a constant. [3]

Variance (σ^2 or s^2) a measure of variability or spread within a set of scores that is equal to the average of the squared deviations of individual scores from the mean. [5]

Variant Replication a study that tries to reproduce the findings of earlier research while simultaneously testing a new, closely related hypothesis. For example, if Smith reported that 8-year-olds outperform 4-year-olds on a memory test, Jones may design a study that also compares 4- and 8-year-olds, but *additionally*, Jones may make a comparison between Smith's memory task and some other type of memory task to see if there is an age difference for both types of memory.

Variation Ratio (v) a statistic that measures the variability in categorical data by measuring the percentage of scores that do not fall into the modal category. [5]

Venn Diagram a type of graph that visually represents the correlation between two variables; greater overlap between the circles representing the variables indicates a stronger relationship. Also, the Coefficient of Determination (r^2) is represented by the overlap between the circles in the diagram. [9]

Verbatim Transcript a word-for-word record of the verbal behavior of participants. [16]

Whole Interval Recording a measure of the frequency of an event; a form of Interval Recording where the observers notes if the target behavior occurs continuously throughout the entire time interval. The percentage of intervals is then reported. [15]

Wilcoxon W (Signed Ranks Test) a nonparametric statistical procedure used with ordinal data from a two-sample Within-Subjects or Matched-Pairs design. [13]

Wilcoxon-Mann-Whitney T (Rank Sum Test) a nonparametric statistical procedure used with ordinal data from a two-sample Between-Subjects design. [13]

Within-Subjects Designs a research design in which every participant is tested under *every* experimental condition. (All independent variables in a Within-Subjects design are Within-Subjects factors.) Comparisons are made between the mean scores of the same group of participants as they are observed at different times or under different treatment conditions. [10]

Within-Subjects Factor an independent variable in which every participant is tested under every level of the independent variable. (Also called a "repeated measure"). [10]

Working Hypothesis a researcher's belief about the relationships among variables that will be discovered during a study; sometimes referred to as the "research question," because studies are designed to test these beliefs. [1]

X generic label for any unspecified variable. Also used to represent the raw score on some variable. [3]

χ^2 see Chi Square

Y generic label for any unspecified variable, it is usually the label for the second of two variables. Also used to represent the raw score on the variable. [3]

Y′ read "Y-prime" or "Y-predict," in regression analysis, the value of Y that is expected for a specific value of X. [9]

z-Score standard scores that indicate the location of raw scores (X) in relation to the mean ($\bar{X}$) in standard deviation units; scores above the mean have positive values of z and scores below the mean have negative values of z. Because they are standard scores, z-scores can be used to make comparisons between different variables. [5]

z-Table also known as the "Areas Under the Normal Curve," this table gives the proportion of the total area of the normal distribution that lies between a specified value of z and the mean of the distribution, and the proportion of the total area that lies beyond z. This table, for example, allows us to determine what proportion of scores in a normal distribution are greater than (or less than) any specified value of z. [5]

z-Test a test of the Null Hypothesis for a single-sample experiment or quasi-experiment when the mean (μ) and standard deviation (σ) of the population of X scores are known. (Also see "t-test.") [11]

Zero Correlation when there is no association or correlation between two variables, and the value of the correlation coefficient is equal to 0. [8]

INDEX

■■■■■■

Note: f *and* t *behind page numbers stand for figures and tables, respectively.*